The Team From The Railway Town

A History of Horwich RMI Football Club

By Michael Latham

2010

The Team From The Railway Town
A History of Horwich RMI Football Club

Published by Rel8 Media
PO Box 29145, Dunfermline, Fife, KY12 7WJ

British Library in Publication Data.
A catalogue record for this volume is available from the British Library.

ISBN 978-0-9555307-2-2

Contents

Introduction and Acknowledgements

The Crown Hotel in Horwich is a real sporting pub and provides a source of information and entertainment for many, as well as consistently fine Joseph Holt's ales.

There are people in here with vast knowledge of football, some less so but the conversation is invariably interesting and stimulating. Many have played the game locally and follow the professional, semi-professional and amateur game with a passion. Between them they support many different clubs but they have one thing in common: an interest and fond memories of the local football club, Horwich Railway Mechanics' Institute FC.

While sipping at a pint of Holt's Mild one evening I was drawn into conversation with Ken Chaisty, a local businessman and long-time supporter of the RMI. Ken was heavily involved in various ways with the club, as founder and organiser of the successful youth side, in fund-raising and as a supporter.

As we chatted we agreed that it was about time someone wrote a book about Horwich RMI before memories dimmed. After all it is 15 years since they left Grundy Hill and moved to Leigh. As there was no rush of volunteers, that someone turned out to be me.

Over the past 18 months the book has become almost an obsession, a fascinating trawl back through Memory Lane and never a drag. I met many people with a deep love and knowledge not only of the football club but of the town of Horwich itself. Ken pointed me in the right direction and accompanied me on several visits to former players, officials and supporters and was a source of encouragement and advice throughout this project.

Quickly I assembled an archive of material, programmes, photographs, faded newspaper cuttings and the like that made the club come alive again. Fortunately there are many hoarders in Horwich and people who realise the importance of historical documents.

In the early months of the book I met up George Bateson, one of RMI's most famous players, long-serving committee men Albert Dickinson and Bert Taylor and Brian Smith, who covered the club's fortunes so expertly for many years in the Horwich Journal. All gave freely of their time and lent me several fine photographs. Brian's reports were a joy to read especially as some of his predecessors sometimes managed not only to write one thousand word reports without mentioning the final score or scorers but frustratingly failed to provide Christian names of prominent players. One player named O'Rourke once scored six goals for RMI but I never managed to discover his Christian name.

Inevitably a book of this nature relies upon the writer spending long hours poring over microfilms of old newspapers, looking back on old matches and putting together a historical record from a number of sources. I must thank the staff of the libraries at Horwich, Westhoughton and Chorley Libraries and Bolton Central Library in particular for their help and encouragement while I took root for many an afternoon or evening session hunched over a machine and also the staff at Horwich Heritage Centre.

I had several huge strokes of luck, notably in finding out that one of RMI's most fervent supporters Chris Foley was a near neighbour of mine in Adlington. Chris's father Terry was a draughtsman and training officer at the Loco Works and also an unofficial historian of the Loco Works. Until his death in 1998 he assembled a wonderful archive of photographs and written material on the RMI. Terry had kept his season members' books from just after the war up until his death and he meticulously recorded the scores and most scorers. He was a brilliant photographer who recorded many RMI games and events for posterity as well as preserving a photographic record of the Works itself. He also wrote a long and detailed history of the football club in manuscript form covering the period from 1946 to 1970 which helped form the basis of my initial researches. With so many personal recollections it helped bring back to life the history of a proud club with deep roots in the community. Thanks to his son Chris the fruits of his labours will finally see the light of day. Chris was also a source of great knowledge on the RMI and retains an avid interest in football though I'm not sure what his dad would think of him now following RMI's arch rivals Chorley.

I also met up with Harold Taylor, who had long family links with the RMI and who acted as secretary and trainer for many years. Harold became involved with football again when he took on the match day secretarial role at Leigh. There are few people with as deep knowledge of non-league football as Harold and he provided a fascinating source of information. By his own admission Harold is not a historian as such but in a remarkable twist of fate he decided to record a match-by-match record of RMI's 1978-79 season in a diary. The newspapers were interrupted by a national strike during the season and so coverage of RMI was patchy to say the least so Harold's diary proved invaluable especially as RMI won the Cheshire County League championship that season. He must have sensed that something was in the air as he has never kept such a diary before or since.

Several long-standing supporters kindly lent me old programmes notably Geoff Downes who was one of the few RMI supporters to carry on following the club when they moved to Leigh and Steve Foy. John Holland remains a well-known figure in the town and is remembered by many for his 30 years' service as referee in the Horwich Sunday League and other local football circles. John was also an avid RMI supporter from childhood and maintained a detailed record of RMI games from 1960 up until 1995 which provided a rich historical record. John remains a huge interest in grass roots football and acts as a refereeing mentor as well as pursuing his love of groundhopping.

I met up with several other former players including John Pallett, perhaps RMI's best-loved goalkeeper who kindly let me borrow several detailed scrapbooks of his career. In talking with former players such as John, Neil McLachlan, Paul Moss and Les Brown their pride and affection for the club was easily apparent. Joan Southworth, sister of the late Jack Bruton, an RMI player who went on to forge a great football career and earn England honours was a delight to meet.

There were coincidences to be found everywhere. For instance while chatting to a fellow ground-hopper, Lee West at Knighton Town of all places he casually mentioned that he attended what proved to be the final football game at Hilton Park and kindly provided me with photographs that appear in the book.

Mentioning photographs I was indebted to Maurice Jones for his expert help in transferring old photographs into a computerised form. Maurice also attended the Leigh Genesis-Wakefield game, the final one of the 2009-10 season to take some of the photographs for this book.

One of the delights of visiting Grundy Hill was to sample the Lancashire hotpot made by Ken Whittaker, one of RMI's longest-serving supporters. People used to say that Ken's hotpot was more consistent than the team. I met up again with Ken to re-live some memories of his days watching RMI and he kindly lent me his son Stephen's meticulously maintained records of RMI's Northern Premier League seasons which proved invaluable. It was good to see old supporters like Ken and John Holland still following Leigh Genesis.

Long-serving club official Gary Culshaw has been a friend for many years and he kindly lent me several photographs plus some programmes he was bequeathed by the late RMI treasurer Dave Swaby. Gary and his son Steven produced an excellent programme for the club for many years through their business Standish Print. I can still remember the delight and pride on Gary's face after RMI defeated Weymouth in the GMAC Cup Final at Grundy Hill. It was good to see him and Alan Leach still involved with the club during the time at Leigh.

Many others have provided valuable help in the writing of this book including Dave Swanton, Andy Sneddon, Graham Lovett, Simon Clegg, Dave Woods and Chris Harte and my thanks go them all. There are many more people too numerous to mention who have contributed in one way or another to what I hope is a comprehensive record of the club.

I thought long and hard about including extra chapters on the club since its move to Leigh in 1995 and decided that to have a complete record was better than an incomplete one. Accordingly this book traces the club's fortunes up until the end of the 2009-2010 season when Leigh Genesis played some sparkling football at times and many of the players stayed loyal to the club despite playing for next to nothing in the second half of the season. The management team of Garry Flitcroft, Matt Jansen and Mike Quigley achieved a lot in difficult circumstances and watching the outstanding Jansen in action on the field was one of the highlights of the season.

Since moving to Leigh the club has earned the support of a diehard group of fans who showed great loyalty in the face of adversity in recent seasons. Matt Lawton has maintained an outstanding unofficial club website with his match reports providing a valuable historical resource.

Finally I am grateful to the knowledge and expertise of Andy McGregor in his work on the design and publishing of the book. Andy travelled down from Fife to visit Horwich for the first time and the site of the old Grundy Hill ground. His advice and encouragement was invaluable.

I can't claim to be Horwich RMI's greatest supporter but I maintained an interest in their fortunes ever since first visiting Grundy Hill for the first time in the early 1980s. Up until the move to Leigh in 1995 I would visit Grundy Hill maybe a dozen times per season, often tempted by Ken's hotpot even on the coldest and wettest of Monday evenings. While they have been at Leigh I have usually managed to watch the side several times a season but like my good friend John Holland the lure of groundhopping has stopped me following a side on a regular basis. I thought it was important to document the history of the club and try to do justice to the hard work and dedication of so many players, officials and supporters and I sincerely hope to have done so. It was thanks to Ken Chaisty that I started on the journey and doubtless when the book is published we shall share a pint of Joseph Holt's finest bitter and reflect on the project. Thanks also to Jennifer Turner for the loan of some oustanding photographs from the archive of her late father, Arthur Riley, a former RMI Secretary

There were many surprises along the way, not least when I found out that RMI were formed in 1902 and not 1896 as was widely accepted. During the course of researching this history I unearthed many events and personalities involving the football club and inevitably it has not been possible to include them all. Some great deeds, some stirring games and great memories come flooding back and I hope the reader gets as much pleasure from the book as I did in its research and compilation.

About The Author

Michael Latham was born in Leigh and brought up in Bolton and has been a lifelong supporter of Bolton Wanderers and Leigh RLFC. A graduate of Bristol University, where he gained an honours degree in Economic and Social History he now has his own accountancy business based in Adlington near Chorley. For much of the past thirty years he has researched the history of rugby league and football and written for a considerable number of local and national newspapers, magazines and sporting publications. He was appointed Chairman of the Association of Sports Historians upon its formation in 1993. For 12 years until 2008 he hosted a weekly hour-long rugby league programme on BBC Radio Lancashire and also reported on local cricket for the station. A self-confessed 'groundhopper' he completed visits to all the current English, Welsh and Scottish Football League and Rugby League grounds during 2005 but these days prefers watching non-league football and local cricket. Currently he is the Vice-Chairman and webmaster of the Northern Premier Cricket League.

Previous books by the author:

Leigh RLFC, An Illustrated History (with Mike Hulme), (Mike RL Publications 1990)
They Played for Leigh (Mike RL Publications, 1991)
They Played for Wigan (with Robert Gate), (Mike RL Publications, 1992)
The Rugby League Myth (with Tom Mather), (Mike RL Publications, 1993)
Leigh RLFC, A Comprehensive Record 1895-1994 (Mike RL Publications, 1994)
Buff Berry and the Mighty Bongers (Mike RL Publications, 1995)
British Rugby League, A Groundhopper's Guide (League Publications Ltd, 2005)
Northern Premier Cricket League Yearbook 2010 (editor), (Scratching Shed Publishing, 2010)
Wigan Warriors Rugby League Club Yearbooks 2006-2010 (joint editor with Graham Emmerson) (Wigan RLFC)

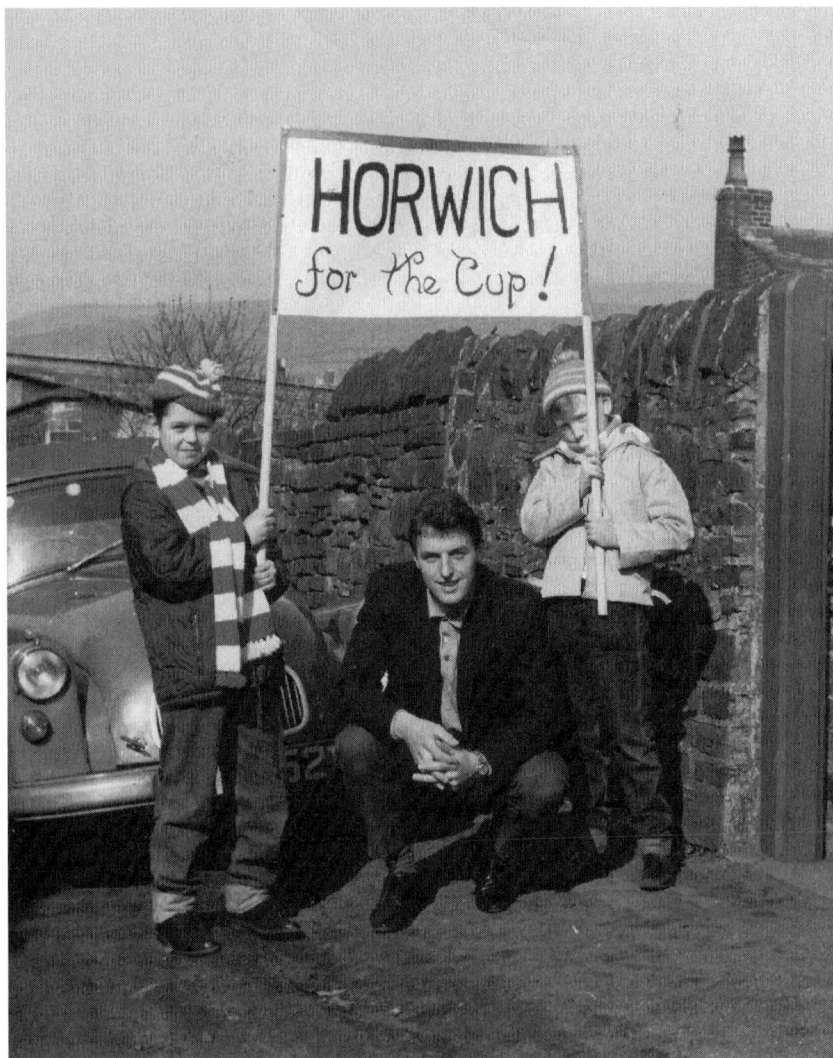

1966 may have been World Cup year but Horwich RMI had equally pressing matters. Two young fans, Ian Gilbert (Left) and Chris Foley (Right) are pictured with striker Brian Robinson, before the Lancashire Combination Cup Final. RMI did not need extra time to win their Cup—defeating Droylsden 5-0 at Chorley.

Foreword

The very name Horwich RMI conjures up an image of all that is good in football. It brings to mind an artisan club, founded on the earnest endeavours of dedicated players, officials and supporters. The concept of the 'works club' links sport to the heart of the community and is an idea well worth re-visiting in an age when commercial interest seems to permeate sport at all levels.

Reading drafts of Michael Latham's text emphasised the romance of a fine football club. The ups and downs in over one hundred years of history make compelling reading. There are periods where survival was the main aim of the club. Those difficult days and years make the infrequent Cup wins and League Championships all the more special for the loyal hard core of supporters.

In recent years the history of Horwich RMI reflects wider changes in football and in society. Re-location, unrealistic ambitions and re-branding . . . . the original club went the way of the Railway Works itself, finding no role in modern Britain.

But memories linger and sometimes affections grow stronger with the passage of time. Michael's detailed research and fluent style will rekindle memories for older fans and will bring the Horwich RMI story to a new generation of local football followers. He was able to track down many people associated with the club over the years and their reminiscences add colour to the story.

The book is one of the most comprehensive ever produced about a football club from outside the top ranks. Michael does justice to the pioneers who started the club and the stalwarts who kept it going down the years. He brings the story right up to date with the move to Hilton Park and the rise and fall of Leigh RMI.

This is a story that will delight and fascinate all true football fans.

Andy McGregor

Early Days

Horwich grew from what was little more than a small village to a small town in a matter of years as a result of the building of the locomotive works. The population of the town rose from 3,761 in 1881 to 12,850 in 1891 and 15,084 in 1901. One of the by-products of the works was the construction of recreational facilities for its employees and the Recreation Ground, situated off Ramsbottom Road provided the focal point for sport and recreation in the town.

In October 1886 the 35-year-old Mr JAF (John) Aspinall was appointed the Chief Mechanical Engineer (CME) of the Lancashire & Yorkshire Railway Company and located at the new locomotive works under construction at Horwich. Mr Aspinall urged the company to introduce a premium-apprentice scheme, the money from which should go into a fund for the building of a Mechanics' Institute. The roots of Horwich Railway Mechanics' Institute Football Club were in place.

Football was long established in Horwich and several fine exponents of the code had been produced by the town. Various football teams using the name Horwich had been playing for many years. The first editions of the Bolton Evening News' football newspaper, the Football Field (which later became known as the Buff) in 1884 gave results each week during the season of matches involving Horwich.

Throughout the 1880s Horwich's games were friendly encounters, often against local, neighbouring teams and usually arranged at short notice. But as football grew in popularity there was a move to establish leagues so that clubs could measure themselves against rival teams and also play competitive, meaningful matches on a regular basis.

In February 1887 the L&Y Railway Company followed Aspinall's advice and voted a sum of £2,500 towards the creation of a Mechanics' Institute. Drawings were later submitted and approved and construction commenced. On 15 December 1888 the new Mechanics' Institute was opened by the Chairman of the L&Y Railway Company, George J Armytage, Esq. Ninety students per week were soon attending classes. The most successful student of those first evening classes was an 18-year-old premium apprentice Henry Fowler, who later in life became Sir Henry Fowler. By 1891 the Loco Works had almost four thousand employees.

Horwich (L&Y) FC representing the Horwich Lancashire & Yorkshire Railway Company was formed in 1888 and in their first season, 1888-89, played 21 games with ten wins and 11 defeats, scoring 49 goals against 46. For an early season game against Bolton Albany the Horwich team lined-up as follows: R Dickinson; T Isherwood, E Green; T Lambert, R Isherwood, C Lambert; P Brierley (capt), J Hampson, J Parkinson, J Yates, T Manson. Their ground was described as being on Chorley New Road.

Another local team was Horwich Olympic otherwise known as Horwich Association. The reporter in the Horwich Journal commented: 'I have heard many express a desire to see Horwich L&Y meet the Association. If a match could be arranged between the two clubs it would no doubt bring a big gate, prove exciting and strengthen both clubs.

'People want rousing out of their slumber. Before they can be got to a football field in Horwich in any great numbers there will have to be more spirited playing and greater rivalry and enthusiasm displayed between opposing forces than has previously been the case.'

The teams did meet at L&Y's ground on 13 April 1889 when the home team won 4-0 before a crowd of 400. But it was to be the last meeting as at the end of this season Horwich Olympic, who played on the Lord Street ground folded after accruing debts of over £50. 'The club officials were left with a small stock, some inflated bladders, goal-posts and several balls,' reported the Horwich Journal.

The teams for that game were as follows. L&Y: Tudor; Thompson, Challen; Caunce, H Smith, McEctrane; T Smith, Attwood, Jones, Slater, Mulloch. Olympic: Nicholls; Green, Isherwood; Settle, Brierley, Dickenson; Bath, Coop, Yates, Manson, Hesketh.

In 1889-90 the L&Y club again played friendly matches and there were two other teams in the town by the end of the year, Horwich Albion and a re-formed Horwich Olympic side, with both clubs sharing the Moorgate ground.

But at the time rugby was the dominant football code in the town as demonstrated by the following report from the Horwich Journal in September 1889. 'Horwich rugby club have 'kicked off' their season,' the newspaper reported. 'The rugby code has initiated itself as a favourite out Horwich-way. The large section from the railway works must have something to pass the time on Saturday afternoons and most of these have come from a district where the rugby code flourishes.'

The famous Wigan player Billy Atkinson helped the club by bringing a team of prominent players for an exhibition game staged on the Horwich ground on 28 August 1889. But there was a note of caution for the rugby club as they were reported to be on the look-out for a new ground as their Crown Lane ground might be required for building purposes.

There was frustration for officials attempting to popularise the football code in Horwich that many sides failed to fulfil their engagements or did not turn up with their full complement of players.

L&Y competed in league football for the first time in the 1890-91 season, playing in the West Lancashire Alliance. Home games were staged on the Recreation Ground and the team was run on strictly amateur lines. The Horwich Journal reported: 'An effort is to be made to obtain for the Horwich club its former good name. We are sure all lovers of football will be pleased to know that this is the case and do all in their power to help its popularity and success.'

But the report added: 'I hope the committee will launch out a little more in making known their matches. That would help bring in more spectators and increase the popularity of the club. Big gates mean something more than mere monetary gain.'

The season began on 6 September 1890 with a 5-3 victory over Crewe Swifts. One week later Horwich journeyed to Barrow, losing 5-2. The Horwich team in these early season engagements was as follows: RT Alsop; F Pearce, J Woodsworth (captain); W Parkinson, T Lambert, G Caunce; JF Hampson, J Attwood, J Clarke, H Deakin, J Golding.

Sport in Horwich appeared on the increase, with the town's rugby club, playing at the Crown Lane ground securing a prestigious early season friendly game against Wigan and two cricket teams, Horwich and Horwich (L&Y) both functioning in the summer months. Wigan played at Crown Lane on Wednesday 10 September 1890 and included several guest players in their ranks including internationals Jim Valentine and Jim Marsh (both Swinton) and Tom Kent (Salford). A crowd of 2,000 witnessed the game and afterwards both teams and officials enjoyed a repast at the Crown Hotel. The lay-out of the pitch lay north-south and had a pronounced slope. At the start of the game Atkinson was described as 'sending the oval downhill in the direction of Crown Lane.'

At the end of the season Horwich played a testimonial game against Bolton Wanderers Reserves as a benefit for two long-serving Horwich footballers, the Parkinson brothers who were both said to have given yeoman service. Horwich forced a creditable 0-0 draw against a team containing several first-team players and one thousand spectators attended the game. The Horwich team was: Nicholls; Hanson, Hampson; J Parkinson, W Parkinson, H Deakin; Toole, Turner, Walsh, Yates and an un-named player.

The first annual dinner of the club was held at the Bee Hive Hotel on 3 July 1891. The club secretary, Mr J Dawson, addressed the gathering and said that the young team had done well considering the 'salary' they were paid, a remark that produced much laughter.

Mr Dawson pointed out that thirty to forty men who were employed on the works played for other neighbouring teams for a few shillings. But with more support and help from the works, Mr Dawson felt that there was the prospect of improvement in the future. He hoped to get the ground covered and protected to a better standard. The team had played 39 games with 22 wins, 14 defeats and three draws.

At the end of September 1891 the Horwich Journal had some sad news to report, with the closure of the Horwich Cricket Club, the oldest sporting organisation in the town. Formed in 1863 they had played on the footprint of the Grundy Hill ground later used by the RMI football club. The ground had also been used for the annual town sports which included exhibitions from Grasmere wrestlers. The two Horwich clubs had both been founder members of the Bolton & District Cricket Association in 1888.

'Next year will see a great change for the old cricket ground is to be abandoned as the (Horwich) club is to be amalgamated with the L&Y,' the Journal reported. 'The present ground has afforded many a gallant struggle for supremacy but its days are numbered and before many years are over it will no doubt be covered with buildings. Many of the old players seem to be falling away and take little practical interest in matches.'

The amalgamated club retained its old title of Horwich CC for a few years until adopting the title Horwich RMI when membership was confined to employees of the railway company. The first game played by the 'merged' club was on Saturday 23 April 1892 against Little Lever at the Recreation Ground. Formerly grazing land, the area was turned into a miniature park through the generosity of L&Y directors William Hinmers and Henry Yates Thompson who personally financed the scheme. The new Recreation Ground, comprising the cricket ground and a bowling green with pavilion was opened to the public for the first time as Little Lever, bowled out for 75 then defeated the home side by 24 runs after dismissing Horwich for 51.

Over 700 spectators attended the game with the admission charges as follows: 'Gentlemen 3d; Ladies free; Children (under 14) 1d.' During the tea interval the L&Y Band played a popular music programme.

Termed the 'Mechanics' Institute Recreation Grounds,' Terry Foley described the eleven-acre-site as follows:

'The grounds were situated in front of the entrance to the L&Y Works on Chorley New Road, or south side (then a road half cobbled and half dirt) being bounded on the east by

Ramsbottom Road (named after Mr John Ramsbottom, an L&Y director who planned the whole of the works and street lay-out). The west side was bounded by the railway while the north side by the old cricket ground (Grundy Hill).

'The boundaries of the park-like grounds were formed of neat iron railings along Chorley New Road and Ramsbottom Road and wooden fences for other portions. In order to hide the view of the cricket ground and bowling green it was necessary to raise earth embankments on the Chorley New Road and Ramsbottom Road sides of the ground. These embankments were finished in a very neat and artistic manner and were profusely planted with shrubs. There were two entrance gates on the Ramsbottom Road side of the grounds.

'The cricket field occupied a central part of flat area of land and a very commodious pavilion was erected for the accommodation of the players, on top of which was a small balcony which was reserved for ladies and privileged spectators. At the west corner of the cricket field was a bowling-green which was 50-yards square and allowed several games to be played at once. A neat tent was built for the bowls and seats were placed around the green for spectators. A mound was raised and planted in-between the green and cricket field.

'When the cricket ground was opened the lawn tennis and other recreational portions of the ground were not yet finished but labourers were employed on every fine day doing what was necessary. The grounds commanded a very fine view of Rivington Pike and the neighbouring hills of Blackrod.

'On all occasions, except gala days the grounds were open free to the public every week-day from 6am to sunset from 1 April to 30 September and from sunrise to sunset between October and March and on Sundays from 9am to sunset. A management committee was appointed to administer the grounds with Mr Tatlow appointed secretary. The miniature park was a source of pride and pleasure for generations to follow.

'The second bowling-green was opened in 1895 and the grass tennis-courts in May 1905. Prior to the opening of the tennis courts the football club played on the site.

'In June 1907 a bandstand was erected (where the BRSA club was later constructed) provided by Mr Thompson. The L&Y band gave concerts twice a week during the summer months. The bandstand was later re-sited to the north-east corner of the grounds in the 1920s due to the noise of increasing road traffic on Chorley New Road. It was finally demolished and put to scrap on 6 August 1941.

'At the turn of the century a children's playground was constructed at the west-end of the grounds. This included swings, slides and see-saws. The playground was dismantled and removed in July 1934.

'Mr Thompson also erected and staffed the Cottage Hospital (1894) as a gift in memory of his late father. He also donated the first book to the Institute library.'

In the 1891-92 season Horwich (L&Y) played in the Lancashire Football Alliance, finishing twelfth out of thirteen clubs, winning only four and losing 20 of 24 league games. The Alliance comprised Adlington, Ashton-in-Makerfield, Cheetham Hill, Chorley, Farnworth Standard, Golborne, Haydock, Kearsley, Leigh, Little Lever, Lytham, Park Lane Wanderers and Horwich (L&Y). Horwich scored 30 goals and conceded 86.

The Horwich Journal was concerned, reporting in January 1892 as follows: 'The Horwich (L&Y) FC are not making the progress anticipated when they commenced. They are the only club in the Lancashire Alliance not to pay a penny to players. The Railway Works employs upwards of four thousand men and boys, among them several noted football men, but no inducement is made by the local club to these players. Instead many accept offers from rival clubs who pay between five to ten shillings per week plus railway fares.'

Mr CE Butterworth, an active member of the Horwich Tradesman's' Association, gave notice to a meeting of that organisation that he wanted to form a town's football club so that men could be paid for playing matches. This, said Mr Butterworth, would benefit the town and prevent what he termed the 'drain' of supporters leaving town on Saturdays to watch rival clubs.

However, Mr Butterworth withdrew the motion when he learnt that the Recreation Grounds Committee had the intention to take up the matter. The great objection to having a club connected with the Railway Institute was the gate question. The gates from cricket matches played on the Recreation Ground were taken by the Railway Institute. How then, he asked, could the teams pay their players when the gate was taken by the Institute?

A New Club Is Formed

To help solve the problem several adherents of the L&Y Club took over the old Crown Lane Rugby football ground. Though they were later to re-form, the Horwich Rugby team had ceased playing after the 1890-91 season and their Crown Lane ground was vacant. It was their intention to board round the field, charge for admission and pay players handsomely for their services. The Crown Lane ground, though, was not as popular as the Recreation Ground as it did not enjoy such a central location in the town.

The Crown Lane ground had been used by the town's rugby team for several seasons. In 1889 the Horwich Journal reported that members of the rugby club had made great efforts to level the playing field, such that it would make an excellent bowling green. But the correspondent was perplexed as to why the rugby enthusiasts 'did not make the effort to raise funds towards boarding around the ground so they can charge a gate.'

At the annual meeting in 1892 at the Toll Bar Inn Mr CE Butterworth, who had been elected the football club chairman said the members had to pull together or else the football club would close down its operations. When they had played at the Recreation Ground the gates from home games were taken from them by the Horwich Mechanics' Institute and this was a major factor in stopping the club making progress. A club connected with the institute, Mr Butterworth continued, could not exist as they proposed keeping the gate money and not paying players and no club could exist without professionals.

If Horwich had a good team playing on a good, enclosed field they could have a future and be able to compete, Mr Butterworth continued, but this season they had lost three players who had been tempted by the money offered by rival clubs. Two months earlier, back in March 1892 the football committee had appealed to the Horwich Tradesman's' association for financial support in helping to form a new club and they had voted them the sum of two guineas to help secure the Crown Lane ground.

At the meeting it was moved that a new club 'Horwich Football Club' be formed. It was felt that there was no benefit from being linked to the railway works and hence there should be no reason why the Horwich club should have 'L&Y' attached to its name. There was a move to join the Lancashire Alliance. Mr Butterworth said that the new club 'meant business.' In their first season after being re-formed Horwich were reported to pay total wages of £8 per week to players.

The AGM of the Football Alliance was held at the Raven Hotel, Wigan on 28 May 1892. It was reported that Horwich (L&Y) had retired and that Horwich FC had applied to be registered in their place. The new club was duly elected alongside another newcomer in Hindley FC.

The following years saw some gradual improvement and Horwich finished tenth in the Alliance in the 1892-93 season. 'With united action and a far seeing and experienced committee one of the best association clubs in Lancashire ought to be established in a few years,' reported the Horwich Journal.

These optimistic notes initially seemed justified as Horwich finished seventh, eighth, sixth and sixth again in successive seasons. One of their best players was a Scottish forward, Jonny Duffus, who had secured employment at the Loco Works. Another Scot, Jimmy Weir, was another prominent forward and he later moved on to play for Bolton

Wanderers, without breaking into their first team.

At the start of the 1892-93 season pen pictures of the signed-on Horwich players included: D Edwards (goalkeeper)- ex Horwich Swifts, has a good, long kick; R (Dick) Hanson (left-back)- a former professional with Hindley, formerly with Horwich Olympic, captain of the side; W Mawdesley (right-back)- from a Blackburn junior team; W Stevenson (right half-back)- ex Farnworth Alliance; Harry Dakin (centre-half)- a splendid, young player; W Farnworth (left half-back)- a tall, young player; L Walker (left-wing)- from the Parish Church side, he also played for the L&Y; R Turner (right wing)- a smart player; JJ Toole (inside-forward)- Only 5ft and aged 17; A Woodruff (centre-forward)- Ex Adlington; J Walsh (left wing) last year's centre-forward for L&Y. The club's head-quarters were at the Toll Bar Inn.

In September 1892 Horwich began the season in style by defeating Adlington 10-0 after leading 4-0 at half-time. Walsh scored four of the goals, Toole three and Woodruff, Turner and Walker were also on target. They then entertained Bolton Wanderers Reserves in a midweek friendly at the Crown Lane ground. Even though it was early season the condition of the playing area left a lot to be desired. The pitch was described as being 'heavy and sloppy' with parts of the ground heavily water-logged. An early season Horwich team read: D Edwards; W Mawdesley, R Hanson (capt); W Stevenson, Harry Dakin, W Farnworth; R Turner, A Woodruff, L Walker, JJ Toole, J Walsh.

Horwich then visited local rivals Adlington in the first round of the Lancashire Junior Cup. Wagonettes were run from Horwich and the attendance was swelled to around the 600-mark with the railway town being well represented. Adlington's ground was then situated behind the Elephant & Castle public house in the highest part of the village. Horwich's earlier 10-0 victory counted for nothing as Adlington turned the tables, winning 5-3 after extra-time. In early October Horwich were thrashed 9-3 at Kearsley and continued to be plagued by inconsistency.

Gradually the Horwich team improved its organisation. For one away game at Skerton near Lancaster in January 1893 the team travelled by saloon carriage thanks to an arrangement made by Mr Horsefield, the Horwich station-master. This civilised arrangement was credited for helping prepare the players for the game, Duffus scoring the only goal in a 1-0 victory.

Betting among spectators was also a common feature of the time. After Horwich lost 2-0 at home to Hindley in February 1893 the Horwich Chronicle reported: 'Those who laid 12 to 8 made a mistake and pounds were lost.'

But the Crown Lane ground was far from popular and gates fell away, especially towards the end of the season. One contributing factor was that without proper boarding around the ground it was possible to secure a good vantage point from a neighbouring field and many spectators chose to watch games in this way without paying an admission charge. The team was reported to be looking for a new ground and eventually took up residence at the Old Racecourse ground in time for the start of the 1893-94 season. Situated where the current Old Lord's housing estate stands, the Old Racecourse ground was a vast expanse and with icy winds blowing down from the Pike was an exposed place in the winter months but was seen as an improvement on Crown Lane.

Meanwhile in July 1893 the Samuel Fielden Wing of the Mechanics' Institute was opened by George Armytage, Esq. The extension comprised a large public hall to seat over 900 people, a new library, reading-rooms and class-rooms. A fully-equipped gymnasium was also being built. The original Institute building was now going to be devoted exclusively for educational classes. It was said that the new Mechanics' Institute would give provision equal to any town in the United Kingdom for its size, for literacy and recreational pursuits. In 1894 a cottage hospital was opened on the site, erected and staffed by L&Y Director Henry Yates Thompson as a gift in memory of his father. On the works the building of the 300th new locomotive was celebrated in that year.

The Old Racecourse ground was christened with an athletics festival organised by the club with profits going into club funds. The festival was held annually in July for several years and was a popular feature of the town's sporting scene. To bring in extra income the ground also began to stage cycling competitions after a track was laid around the edge of the playing area.

The Racecourse had lain dormant since staging its last Horwich Races in 1847. Thomas Hampson's 'History of Horwich' published in 1883 confirms that the Races were first held on 22 August 1837, the ground being that immediately under the 'Manor House' on a spot later covered by Blackrod waterworks. The second Horwich races took place on 2 August 1838 in a field adjoining Anderton Hall. The races were then transferred to an expansive field which became known as the 'Racecourse.'

Despite fixtures often coinciding with periods of inclement weather the races grew in popularity. The Bolton Chronicle carried an account of the races held on 30 July 1840 which gave a flavour of the event: 'Merry throngs were soon seen approaching the field of action from all parts, over hedge and ditch they came as well as by road and highway. The sound of the clamorous drum was now heard, contesting with the loud-lunged trumpet the dominance of noise. At a distance was seen the Union Jack floating on the grand stand, which by half-past one was well filling with visitors. The course was not all that could be desired; to improve it funds will not be found wanting to support a national pastime, the gentlemen of Horwich and district who have so spiritedly supported in the past will not be wanting in the future. The site of the course was excellently chosen, being situate and surrounded with the sweet scenes at the foot of Rivington Pike. At two the grand stand was well filled, and the course crowded with throngs of various descriptions.'

In 1841 the races became a two-day fixture and attracted visitors from all over Lancashire. Under the grandstand Mr Mascall of the Lever Arms Hotel, Bolton had set up a refreshment booth and around the course were huts, stalls and booths selling everything from roast beef and ham to toffee. 'The magnificent view on and adjoining the course cannot be excelled, if equalled, on any other turf in the kingdom,' one observer wrote. 'The Pike, Winter Hill and the beautiful outline of hills give it a most romantic effect which cannot be easily described. The band of the 60th Rifles stood on the grandstand and played during the day, the races lasting two days.' By 1844 the attendance was described as 'extraordinarily large.' On the first day the Willoughby stakes, the tradesmen's gold cup, the hunters' stakes and the sweepstakes were run-off. On the second day the ladies' purse and hurdle sweepstakes took place. By 1845 over fifty stalls had been taken for the races and in 1846 the races extended to three days. One report stated: 'The weather being fine, the trains from Bolton and Manchester were crowded, and every horse that could be spared was yoked to some sort of conveyance, to convey the teeming multitudes to the races, every vehicle from a carriage to a sand cart being brought into requisition. The respectable families of the district were well represented and the Blackrod Band in full uniform played a number of delightful airs.'

The last Horwich races were run on Thursday 5 August 1847 when what was described as 'the usual Horwich race weather- rain with thunder-prevailed, and the damping influence of the atmosphere gave a damping effect to the result.' The final race to be run was for the Bolton Purse, Mr Ridgway's Otterburn defeating Mr Scott's Mrs Candle. There is no explanation as to why this was the last race meeting to be held at Horwich other than for the remark: 'Their short existence- a period of 10 years- may suggest a want of the sympathy and aid so necessary for such institutions, but in glancing over the records such aids will be found to be many and powerful, and their decline must be ascribed to a cause inspired more by the moralist than the sportsman.'

The Horwich Journal was optimistic that the Horwich football club would thrive in its new surroundings. 'Towards the end of last season crowds began to increase and though not large were higher than anything seen previously.' the report stated. 'The club are hoping for crowds of 2,000 and if the grandstand will become a reality it is hoped this will attract a larger attendance of the fair sex.'

The football club enjoyed a good relationship with the senior club of the district, Bolton Wanderers who had become inaugural members of the Football League in 1888. Wanderers often sent a side along for a money-raising friendly at the start of the season. It was appropriate therefore that for Horwich's first match at the Old Racecourse on Wednesday 6 September 1893 a Wanderers' XI containing six regular first-team players provided the opposition. Of the Bolton side on duty that day four players- Bentley, Paton, Somerville and Wilson went on to play for the club in the FA Cup Final at the end of the season when they lost 4-1 to Notts County at Goodison Park.

Horwich, playing in white jerseys lined up as follows: Williams; Grey, Isherwood; Ainsworth, Hanson, McLellan; Walker, Turner, Crompton, Worsley, Walker. The Bolton Wanderers side was: Shuttleworth; Somerville, Bullough; Paton, Weir, Chorlton; Wilson, Willcocks, Bentley, Coghlan, Matthews.

Wanderers won 3-1 and after the game the teams were entertained to tea at the Crown Hotel. The Horwich Chairman Mr Butterworth proposed the toast of the Horwich club. He stated that the club had not done as well as was first expected but the committee had worked hard and ungrudgingly when all had seemed against them. Now, he felt, the dark days were behind them and gates should improve on the new ground. This had been Bolton Wanderers' fourth annual visit and they had much for which to thank them. Sadly for Horwich their 'star' forward Duffus was now back at home in Arbroath.

Horwich's first league game on their new ground was on Saturday 9 September 1893 when they entertained Kearsley. The 'record' attendance of 700 included over one hundred out-of-work colliers and forge-men who were allowed in free of charge. The following Saturday Adlington were the visitors for a local derby in the Lancashire Junior Cup. The tie proved to be a great attraction and Horwich delighted their supporters in a crowd of 1,500 by recording a 5-1 victory. Meanwhile, Horwich also fielded a reserve team in the Wigan & District League.

Interest in the club was on the increase and it was reported that one of the town's tradesmen, Mr Newton, displayed the half-time and full-time scores in his shop window on Saturday afternoons. Mr Newton must have been over-worked on the afternoon of Saturday 2 December 1893 when Leigh visited the Old Racecourse. Horwich recorded a remarkable 17-0 victory after leading 8-0 at half-time. Leigh were bottom of the table having lost all their games but even so Horwich's display was described as outstanding. In the first-half Lee (2), Weir (2), Worsley, Turner (2) and Toole were on the mark. In the second half Toole (2), Worsley (2), Ainsworth, Weir (2), Turner and an own-goal added to the mounting score before the referee, perhaps feeling pity for the visitors, called time with twenty minutes still remaining. It was no great surprise when Leigh folded during the season and their results, including Horwich's famous victory were expunged from the table.

Given that kind of form the Lancashire Junior Cup-tie against Clitheroe early in the New Year was eagerly awaited, following on as it did from a 2-1 win at Chorley (Weir and Doogill scoring) and a crowd of 1,500 was attracted to the Old Racecourse. Horwich put up a good fight and took the game into extra-time before going down 2-1. The Horwich side was: Edwards; McLennan, Isherwood; Crompton, Hanson, Ainsworth; Lee, Turner, Weir, Walker, Worsley.

On 14 February 1894 the Horwich Football Club staged a 'St Valentine's Day Ball' at the Mechanics' Institute. Dancing to the Horwich Old Brass Band continued until 2am. The institute was also granted a license to hold stage-plays and also held several successful art exhibitions. In 1895 a second bowling-green was opened at the Recreation Ground and over 2,000 spectators attended the Horwich Athletics Festival while the Horwich Cycling Club held its first organised sports on the Recreation Ground.

Horwich finished the 1893-94 season in a respectable seventh place in the Lancashire Alliance. They won 11, lost ten and drew five games, scoring 73 goals and conceding 57. Champions were Haydock, who gained 42 points from 26 games with Chorley three points adrift in runners-up position. The other sides in the Alliance were largely based around Wigan (Hindley, Park-Lane Wanderers, Ashton-in-Makerfield, Adlington and Golborne) and Bolton (Farnworth Standard, Little Lever and Kearsley). More far-flung opponents were North Meols, Skerton and Lytham. On New Year's Day Horwich also hosted Scottish opposition for the first time, entertaining Glasgow team Rosslyn Park, holders of the Glasgow West End & District Cup.

The following season, 1894-95, there were several changes to the constitution of the Alliance. Earlestown, Middleton, Lostock Hall and Tonge replaced Chorley, Park Lane, Farnworth Standard and Lytham. Horwich finished eighth with 11 wins, 14 defeats and only one draw from 26 games, with 59 goals for and 70 against, bald statistics that do not do justice to the turmoil of the campaign which is outlined below.

Haydock were champions again, securing 40 points to edge above Hindley by a single point. Several clubs failed to complete their league engagements owing to what was described as the 'inclemency of the weather.' Skerton were worst-affected, failing to complete three games. For the first time Horwich entered the FA Cup but soon bowed out of the competition after losing 3-1 at Rossendale in the first qualifying round on 13 October 1894.

In the summer of 1894 the athletics festival attracted a record crowd of 1,800 which helped boost the club's coffers and Mr JH Moss, the club secretary reported that subscription cards priced at five shillings were selling well. The main players were: Edwards (goal-keeper); McLennan, Clarke (captain), Lewis, Dakin, Walker, Toole, Bridge, Critchley and Dagger, who hailed from Blackpool. Toole was described as a good dribbler but it was regretted that Jimmy Weir, described as the best forward Horwich ever had, was still not around to play alongside him. Worsley, one of Horwich's best players, had signed for Blackpool, but Horwich signed another Scottish player, Thomas Lonie from Dundee Harp.

Horwich began the season with a 3-2 defeat at Bryn against Park Lane Wanderers and then lost 3-1 at home to Bolton Wanderers on Monday 3 September 1894 before a crowd of 800. And after their FA Cup defeat at Rossendale there was a poor attendance for the following home game against Skerton when the reporter from the Horwich Journal hinted that all was not well.

'It was a bitter, cold day and no afternoon to stand on a bleak exposed field,' the report began. 'But that said the poor attendance was the only way the people of Horwich could show their approval or disapproval at an autocratic committee.'

Horwich won that game 5-4 before going down to defeats against Golborne and Adlington, the latter game attracting what was described as a 'record gate' to the villagers' Elephant & Castle ground which was described as being 'in desperate need of levelling.' After a 5-1 defeat at Skerton at the end of November the committee served all the professional players with notice in writing that their professional services could no longer be retained. With the exception of three players, who intimated their willingness to continue to play for the club as amateurs, many players left the club and a new-look side was hastily assembled.

Despite the changes Horwich's fortunes improved, demonstrating that there was a significant pool of football talent in the town. In the first game under what was described as the 'new order' Horwich defeated North Meols with a goal by Bellis and then beat Golborne 4-2 and Ashton 3-0. On Christmas Day 1894 they won 1-0 at Farnworth St James's. The new-look Horwich side was as follows: Hamer; Hardman, Calderbank; Crompton, Dakin, Fielding; Dawson, Beddows, Preston, Dagger, Doogill. Though the run of victories could not be maintained Horwich did remarkably well to keep up standards while reverting to an amateur basis and ended the season in style, defeating Little Lever 6-0 at home.

WJ Whiteley replaced SH Moss as secretary at the AGM of 1895. His address was given as 6 Crown Lane, Horwich. Mr Whiteley reported that Horwich had lost several players from the previous season including Ainsworth, Dagger, Preston and Dallas. Whether they were tempted away to play for money is not recorded.

The traditional friendly with Bolton Wanderers was played on Wednesday 4 September 1895 when Horwich put up a good performance before going down to a 2-1 defeat. They then lost at Prescot in the Lancashire Junior Cup but recovered to win 4-1 at Adlington before another large derby crowd. 'The meeting of these two rivals always attracts a great deal of interest,' reported the Horwich Journal.

Horwich opened their home league programme with a 5-0 home win against Golborne but the Horwich Journal reporter was far from happy, however. He reported: 'I have been asked to call attention to the stentorian lung power of some of the Horwich spectators more part those who occupied the grandstand, who were very demonstrative. Their remarks became at times decidedly objectionable and it must have been unpleasant for the ladies to hear them, uttered as they were in a gruff and tempestuous tone, especially when the language is so clothed as to be unfit for public consumption.'

Horwich competed in the FA Cup for the second time and were represented by the following team for a preliminary round tie against South Shore (Blackpool) on 5 October 1895: Hamer; Hardman, Calderbank; Hibbert, Dakin, Crompton; Smith, Beddows, Bellis, Dawson, Clarke. However, South Shore recorded a 3-0 victory. 'The Loco boys were sadly short of height,' concluded the Horwich Chronicle. Worse was to follow the following week as Horwich crashed 6-0 at Hindley.

But Horwich re-grouped well and a string of victories lifted morale while the committee worked hard to reduce the debts. Until the wintry weather came crowds on the Old Racecourse held up well, with one thousand in attendance for the visit of Skerton in early November. But despite some good results less than 300 turned-up for the visit of Skelmersdale United in 'wintry weather' one month later. At least the faithful supporters were rewarded for their bravery as Horwich romped to a 6-1 victory.

The Alliance was now reduced to 12 clubs, Prescot, Skelmersdale United and Park Lane having joined the competition but Little Lever, Lostock Hall, Tonge, North Meols and Kearsley having left. Earlestown were champions, losing only once in 22 games and recording 36 points, seven clear of runners-up Ashton-in-Makerfield. Horwich won 12, lost eight and drew two games, scoring 43 goals against 34. They finished in sixth position in the table, having been in second place at the turn of the year.

In the home game against Park Lane on 25 January 1896 Horwich forward Beddows scored four goals in 6-0 victory when the home team read as follows: Morgan; Hanson, Brindle; Crompton, Dakin, Walker; Smith, Beddows, Bellis, Clarke, Laurie. Brindle was a particular crowd favourite and was described as the 'champion back of the Pike-ites.'

But despite the generally consistent performances the response from the sporting public of the town was disappointing. As a consequence a public meeting was held on Monday 10 February 1896 at the Co-Operative Hall in the town when the club secretary, Mr WJ Whiteley outlined a precarious financial position. The club was stated to be £132 in debt and the average gate for home games was under £5. Mr Whiteley felt that the only way the club could hope to boost its finances was by attempting to join a higher profile league such as the Lancashire League or Combination.

At the AGM in August 1896 the financial position was slightly improved and liabilities had been reduced by £18 during the year. Receipts totalled £204 including gate money of £97 and subscriptions of £27. Subscriptions had fallen from £51 in the 1894-95 season. The rest of the income came from prize draws, a medal competition and receipts from the annual athletics festival. Players' wages amounted to £89.

In 1896-97 Horwich played in the Lancashire Alliance for the last time, finishing sixth with ten wins, three draws and nine defeats and scoring 52 goals against 42. The season closed on a disappointing note, however, when Horwich lost 8-0 at Bamfurlong.

In this season Horwich changed their colours and played in amber and black quarters. Skerton were champions with 18 wins and four defeats from their 22 games with Prescot runners-up. Bamfurlong Rovers and Whiston replaced Middleton and Golborne. Great rivals Chorley, meanwhile, were champions of the Lancashire League, winning 21 and drawing three of their 28 league games. The two local rivals met in the FA Cup when Chorley rubbed home their superiority with a 5-1 victory. Horwich also fielded a reserve team that played in the Chorley & District League.

Club officials worked hard on the ground during the summer and in the early months of the season. They made improvements to the roadway near the entrance and ensured the grandstand was covered with felting and pitched so that spectators would be sheltered from the wind and rain. The ground was shared with the local cycling club and the Northern Cyclists' Union made a request for the cycle track around the playing area to be widened at the corner to cut down on accidents. As a result thirty loads of cinders were put down and football spectators were then able to stand on the raised cinder banks and get a better view of play.

Several members of the club had all helped with the ground improvements and the following gentlemen were all mentioned in this regard: J Kay, P Carroll, WJ Whiteley, R Hanson, E Harrison, W Houghton, J Critchley, J Worthington and W Jolley. There was also a refreshment tent which was under the control of W Houghton.

Admission to Horwich games was three-pence with an additional two-pence charged for entrance to the grandstand. A season subscription for the grandstand cost five shillings with a ground membership costing three shillings.

The club chairman was Mr James Kay while Mr J Worthington was vice-chairman. The trainers of the team were Messrs F Bailey and A Walsh. Horwich began the campaign with the following side: Hamer; Hanson, Bateman; G Jones, Dakin, Lol Walker; R Turner, W Jones, Clark, R Smith, Laurie.

Lol Walker was stated to be in 'rare form' while Walter Jones was a good acquisition from the Blackpool area. Two Horwich players, Calderbank and Morgan had trials with Bury Reserves while Hardman had a spell with Manchester City, though none of the trio broke into league football.

On 2 January 1897 Adlington visited the Old Racecourse and started the New Year in style with a 3-0 victory. But the Horwich Journal reporter was impressed with the spirit between the two rivals. 'The friendly manner of the players towards one another was a noteworthy feature,' he wrote. 'If other local teams would follow the example of the Adlington and Horwich clubs there would be less ill-feeling between football teams.'

The Football Club Goes Limited

Several clubs in the Alliance were reported to be in financial difficulties and in the summer of 1897 Horwich FC officials opted to make what was a momentous move and successfully applied for membership of the prestigious Lancashire League. To facilitate the move a fund-raising initiative was introduced and it was decided to form a limited company.

The Horwich Journal of Saturday 7 August 1897 reported as follows: 'At last the Horwich Football Club Limited is an accomplished fact. The committee met at the Crown Hotel on Monday evening (2 August) and it was decided to issue 1,000 shares of ten shillings each. This will give everyone the chance of becoming a shareholder and I hope many will respond.'

Among the local businessmen promoting the scheme, it was reported, were Councillor WJ Slater, Mr George Atherton, Mr J Worthington and Mr CE Warburton. The latter two gentlemen were described as football enthusiasts and provisional directors. In addition Mr E Yates and Mr James Kay had both done much to keep the club 'above board' for many years.

But the Journal sounded a cautionary note: 'To survive in the Lancashire League the club will need good players and a fairly large weekly income.'

Looking ahead to the season the Journal felt that clubs in the Lancashire League should be of a far different class than some of those Horwich met in the Alliance. 'There will be more prompt and regular matches at home, which was a big drawback last season and which wearied even the most enthusiastic followers.'

Club secretary WJ Whiteley had been active in securing a squad of players for the forthcoming season which included the following: Goalkeeper was W Park, ex-Bury where he was reserve to Lowe with G Hamer and J Laurie in reserve. Among the backs were Dick Hanson, a player who had rendered yeoman service to Horwich, Wolstenholme, T Eaton, J Crompton, A Valentine (ex-Halliwell Rovers), Lol Walker (a 'good servant who can also play in the forwards') and Harry Dakin, last season's captain, 'who will train the players and also play centre-half when required.'

The forwards included Beddows, back after a spell at Adlington, Jack Tyldesley (ex-Hindley), Bob Turner (an 'outstanding wing'), John Bennett (ex-West Manchester, a 'splendid dribbler') together with Clarke, W Yates, A Laurie, J Aldred and W Fearnhead.

The share capital was fixed at £500 and after what was described as much deliberation Horwich changed from their white jerseys and 'will don the old Everton colours of salmon coloured jerseys and white trousers.'

Subscriptions were fixed at four shillings for the ground, six shillings for the grandstand with admission four-pence to the ground on match-days with an extra charge for admission to the grandstand.

Many ground improvements had been made. 'During the season spectators will be allowed to stand on the cycling track behind each goal. The banking at the top end will accommodate 800 and the lower end one hundred.

'On the east and west stand sides spectators will take up their positions behind railings. These sides have provision for a capacity of 6,000 with a total ground capacity of 7,000.

'It is intended to get a new refreshment bar running the full length of the field from south to north and make an extra entrance on the pavilion side. It is also intended to move the grandstand nearer the hoardings to then enable the cycling track to be enlarged, removing the sharp corners and to improve the entrance to the stand, dressing test and refreshment bar.'

'New dressing rooms have been built at the ground for visiting teams while the home players will change at their head-quarters, Mr J Briggs's Crown Hotel.'

Eight shares were registered in the new company, all of them to Horwich residents. The initial subscribers were: TB Greenhalgh, FM Palmer, WJ Slater, W Hibbert, James Briggs, George Atherton, James Kay and Handel Fletcher.

Horwich were among five new clubs in the Lancashire League for the season 1897-98 alongside New Brighton, Wigan County, Middleton and Rochdale. From the previous season West Manchester, Fleetwood Rangers and Rossendale left and three other clubs, Bacup, Fairfield and Oldham County later withdrew after failing to complete their engagements.

Horwich made their debut in the Lancashire League on Saturday 4 September 1897 when they lost 3-0 at Stockport County. The following players represented Horwich: Park; Hanson, Briscoe; Wolstenholme, Heaton, Walker; Kelly, Beddows, Chadwick, Clarke, Turner. 'It cannot be said that the Horwich XI played to a standard that will be required of them,' reported the Horwich Journal. Horwich's first home league game was against Stalybridge Rovers the following Saturday when they lost 3-2 before 1,000 spectators and they then went down by a single goal at Clitheroe.

At the end of September Horwich played hosts to Accrington Stanley for the first time in the FA Cup and after drawing 1-1 at full-time added three unopposed goals in extra-time. Their first league win was 3-1 against Clitheroe on 2 October before a crowd of 500, but the visitors played with only nine men after two players missed their train. But the following Saturday Horwich lost 3-1 at Wigan County before a crowd of 1,500, the new Springfield Park ground being described as a 'splendid arena.'

October's fortunes improved as Horwich made further progress in the FA Cup, exhibiting 'splendid shooting' to win a Wednesday afternoon replay at Rochdale 6-2 following a 1-1 draw at Horwich. On the last Saturday of the month the eagerly-awaited home derby match with Chorley in the FA Cup third qualifying round was played, Horwich fighting back from 3-0 down at half-time to gallantly lose 3-2, Tyldesley and Leigh scoring second half goals amidst what was described as 'great excitement with hats and caps flying in all directions.' The game attracted a then record 'gate' for a Horwich home game, with the official attendance being recorded as 3,000 and the report described the home team as the 'Loco-ites.'

Horwich signed a new goalkeeper, William Fisher from Blackpool and a new centre-forward, Hugh Lightbown from Little Lever, but results now began to deteriorate although a fighting 1-1 draw was made at Ashton North End towards the end of November. When Rochdale avenged their FA Cup exit with a 3-0 victory at the Old Racecourse just before Christmas the attendance was described as 'poor.'

Meanwhile the town's oldest sporting organisation, Horwich Cricket Club, celebrated their Silver Jubilee with a concert at the Mechanics' Institute on 17 November 1897. Another cricket club briefly flourished in Horwich, playing at what was known as Bobbley Fields, where the Police Station and Victoria Road Methodist Church were later built.

The football club's early season optimism was now fading and the financial position looked far from rosy given the lack of funds for share capital. During November 1897 the directors of the company were elected but club chairman James Kay said the take-up in shares was disappointing due to a crisis in the engineering industry. 'I had expected the working men to come forward in far greater numbers,' he commented after revealing that only 370 shares had been subscribed thus far, insufficient to discharge the previous liabilities. Mr Kay stated there was an urgent need for at least another 200 shares to be taken up for the club to progress.

The eagerly awaited derby game was played on Chorley's Dole Lane ground on Christmas Day and Horwich went down to a 6-0 defeat before a crowd of 6,000. 'It was the first league meeting between the teams, but there was only one team in it,' reported the Horwich Journal.

In mid-January Chorley visited Horwich again this time for the return league engagement. Horwich battled hard and earned a creditable 1-1 draw and they followed that up with a 2-1 win at Rochdale the following Saturday. But the season then closed with a string of defeats. To help bring in funds Lightbown was transferred to Fleetwood for an undisclosed fee.

Horwich's first season in the Lancashire League proved to be a disastrous one in playing terms and they won two and drew two of 26 league games, finishing at the bottom of the table. They scored only 22 goals and conceded 78. Fellow newcomers New Brighton Tower fared much better, finishing champions ahead of Nelson and Stockport County. Wigan County, based at the newly-constructed Springfield Park, a vastly ambitious multi-sports stadium that catered for athletics, cycling, trotting, tennis and bowling as well as football were eighth in their debut season in the league. New Brighton fielded 'many famous players' when they visited Horwich in March, attracting one of the better gates of the season.

At the time New Brighton was a flourishing seaside destination and the New Brighton Tower and Recreation Company constructed a huge complex which included the tower itself, a four-legged structure said to rival the Eiffel Tower in Paris and fairground amusements and walks. They also built an athletics ground beneath the shadow of the tower and created a football team with the aim of providing a winter attraction to the town. Their acquisitions created a sensation at the time, including Jack Robinson, a current England international player and John Goodall both from Derby County.

Horwich put up a brave battle, losing only 2-0 and were later praised for their fighting spirit as they lost by a single goal at New Brighton in the return. But in terms of the finances available for players clubs such as New Brighton, who were duly elected to the Football League for the 1898-99 season and Wigan could dwarf the funds available to Horwich. New Brighton, though, lasted only three seasons in the Football League before folding in the summer of 1901. Wigan County, whose ambitious team-building also included the acquisition of several well-known Football League players, failed in their ambitions to achieve Football League status and folded in the summer of 1900.

At the Horwich club's first AGM since forming a limited company, held on 16 July 1898 Mr

Elias Hall was appointed chairman and it was decided to form a reserve team. It was revealed that a loss of £85 had been made on the first season and there was a further appeal 'for the gentlemen of the town to become shareholders and patrons.'

Horwich's old adversaries Haydock, reigning champions of the Lancashire Alliance, and Crewe Alexandra joined the Lancashire League in 1898-99 with New Brighton, who went on to finish fifth in the Football League Second Division, Nelson and Clitheroe departing.

Prospects were described as 'brighter' in the lead-up to the season but then it was not unusual for local newspapers to act as propaganda sheets for football teams in these days. Horwich had a number of new players including several recruited from the Lancashire Combination outfit Berry's. The team for the opening game at Rochdale was as follows: Briscoe; Birtwistle, Fletcher; Barker, Dakin, Foster; Evan Jones, Langton, Hopkins, Leach and Leigh.

The season began disappointingly as Horwich went down to a 3-1 defeat at Spotland, but there were extenuating circumstances. 'There was a long distance to travel after arrival at Rochdale station and some of the players perspired freely on their way to the field of play,' the Horwich Journal reported.

But goals by Langton and Leigh enabled Horwich to defeat Crewe Alexandra 2-0 at the Old Racecourse in their first home game. In the first qualifying round of the FA Cup Horwich defeated South Shore 2-1. But the visitors appealed against the result on the grounds that the Horwich ground was too narrow, an appeal which was ultimately upheld and Horwich lost the replayed tie by a single goal to nil.

Despite that disappointment and a string of defeats in the autumn, including a 2-0 reverse against Chorley before 2,000 spectators on 5 November Horwich recovered well. They went on to win eight games and record 17 points in 1898-99 with Rochdale and South Shore below them in the final table. They beat Wigan County 1-0 in early December when Birtwistle's goal with what was described as an 'overhead shot' divided the teams before a good attendance at the Old Racecourse.

On Christmas Eve it was 'derby day' once more and Chorley had to fight hard to confirm their superiority with a 1-0 victory before a 3,000 crowd at Dole Lane. Horwich's other 'derby' rivals were Bolton-based Halliwell Rovers but they left the league at the season's end. Horwich closed the season with a fine run of form, defeating Haydock, Rochdale and South Shore in successive home fixtures but despite that finished as the league's lowest goals-scorers with 27 while conceding 47. Chorley were champions for the second time in three seasons with Southport Central runners-up.

In what proved to be their final season in the Lancashire League, 1899-1900, Horwich finished next-to-bottom with five wins, 17 defeats and six draws from 28 games, scoring 27 goals against 70. Only two clubs scored fewer goals than Horwich's meagre tally while only bottom-club Middleton conceded more goals. Stockport County were the champions with Stalybridge Rovers runners-up. Newcomers to the League were future Football League clubs Blackpool and Darwen together with White Star Wanderers (Bootle), Earlestown and South Liverpool. They replaced Ashton North End, Halliwell Rovers and South Shore, the latter club having amalgamated with Blackpool to form a new club.

Horwich retained most of their old players for the season but lost Harry Pennington who was transferred to Chorley. As an incentive to increase support the committee reduced the ground admission by six-pence to three shillings and six and reduced admission to the grandstand by one shilling to five shillings. With Bolton Wanderers having been relegated to the Second Division they hoped to attract better support from the locals who might be less inclined to visit Burnden Park. There was also satisfaction that a junior league for the Horwich district was formed in October 1899.

Meanwhile the Loco Works were going from strength to strength and since opening had constructed a total of 677 engines. The long-serving Mr Aspinall was appointed General Manager of the Lancashire & Yorkshire Railway Company.

But Horwich made a dreadful start and by mid-December had won only one out of 15 league games with four draws. They then crashed 8-0 at Blackpool only two days before Christmas and their season of misfortune was typified by a trip to Stalybridge early in January. The visitors arrived late and the referee reduced the game to one of 35-minutes each-way but Horwich still went down to an 8-0 defeat.

The South African war was raging and the local newspapers carried graphic reports of Horwich men at the front. In the circumstances the battle for two league points on a Saturday seemed hardly to rank in importance. But using the in-vogue military parlance in what was termed as 'the battle of the railway towns' Horwich defeated Earlestown 2-0 before a poor crowd with Tinsley scoring both goals. They also defeated Haydock 3-2 with Tinsley again grabbing a brace. Meanwhile another Horwich player, a finely-built local centre J Calderbank was transferred to Bolton Wanderers for whom he went on to make three league appearances.

Horwich's final league game of a difficult season saw them earn a 2-2 draw at South Liverpool on 21 April 1900. The following Saturday the final of the Adlington Cup took place with Adlington Springfield defeating the newly-formed local works side Horwich (L&Y) 3-2 in front of what was described as a large crowd at the Old Racecourse.

In the summer of 1900 the Horwich Football Club ceased to operate. There was no news of the club's demise in the local newspapers but the preview for the 1900-01 season carried the following comment: 'The old Horwich club has failure writ largely over its portals so Bolton Wanderers have practically a monopoly in the way of football entertainment. The L&Y Company will be running special trains.

'As the Horwich FC passes out of existence many a working man who eagerly invested his savings in a concern which at first bid fair to give a substantial return mourns the loss of his money.'

In its place a new club was formed by the name of Horwich United FC, playing in the Bolton & District Football League. They played on the enclosure of the old Horwich club. 'Horwich stood alone in the district as a town without a club of its own,' the Horwich Journal reported. 'It is hoped that devotees support this club instead of trooping off to watch the teams from other towns. Horwich is a town of 16,000 inhabitants (sic) and could surely support a football club. There is enough football talent in the town.'

Horwich United FC, whose club president was Councillor Fletcher, JP, opened their season on 29 September 1900 when they defeated Turton Reserves 8-1. But the club soon folded and for the next few years many local football followers concentrated their attention on spending their Saturdays on the terraces of Burnden Park watching Bolton Wanderers.

On 21 May 1901 over three thousand people gathered on the Recreation Ground to attend a Thanksgiving Service conducted by the Vicar of Horwich, REV GS St.Patrick Garrett BD for the safe return of ten Horwich soldiers from active service in the South Africa (Boer) War. A procession with bands met the soldiers at Horwich station and paraded them through the flag-bedecked streets of the town.

In 1903 Mr Aspinall moved on to become Associate Professor in Railway Engineering at Liverpool University. He later (in 1917) received a knighthood. In June 1903 Mr HE O'Brien was appointed resident Electrical Engineer at the Loco Works at a salary of £200 per annum. The following year Mr George Hughes was appointed General Manager of the Lancashire & Yorkshire Railway Company with his headquarters at Horwich.

Possibly the earliest photo of an Horwich RMI team, mascot and all. The caption indicates that this was a 'Second Team', playing in the Bolton and District League.

THE BIRTH OF HORWICH RAILWAY MECHANICS' INSTITUTE FOOTBALL CLUB

The first mention of a football club bearing the name Horwich Railway Mechanics' Institute appeared in the Horwich Chronicle of 13 September 1902. The report stated: 'A football club in connection with the Horwich Mechanics' Institute is in the course of formation. The club is to consist wholly of members of the Institute who are employees of the L&Y Railway Company. Although the affairs of the club will be conducted by a committee appointed by the playing members that committee will be subject to the control of the General Institute Committee. No payment is to be made for admission to the matches, which will be played on the Recreation Ground. It is hoped that the playing members will roll up in large numbers and endeavour to make the club a prosperous one.'

Unfortunately many of the early matches went unreported and the club did not feel it necessary to publish details of forthcoming fixtures in the local newspaper. But there was undoubtedly a considerable interest in football in the town. In October 1902 a junior football league was formed in Horwich comprising 12 teams for players not over 16 years of age. Mr F Higson was the driving force behind its formation.

In its extensive review of the year 1902 in the Horwich Chronicle the reporter made the following remarks: 'Senior football in the town is extinct but there are junior clubs in abundance which tends to prove that the love of football amongst the younger portion of the inhabitants, at any rate, did not die with the languishing of the old Horwich Football Club. A club has been formed in connection with the Mechanics' Institute and a good number of members have identified themselves with it.'

The Horwich Journal of 5 September 1903 carried the following preview of the forthcoming football season.

'Horwich RMI Football Club, which sprang into existence towards the close of last season, will again operate on the Recreation Ground.

'The futility of endeavouring to run a professional team in Horwich, no matter on how economical a scale, has in the past been conclusively proved, the easy access to Bolton and other rendezvous of first-class football having been too strong an attraction for local football followers.

'Consequently the collapse of the last Horwich club in the Lancashire League has not been without its lessons, though it has to be regretted that a town which provided several capable exponents of the game who have long ago made reputations in some of the crack clubs of Lancashire and other counties should have been deprived for so long of an institution which, if carefully and judiciously managed, ought to flourish.

'The RMI club was to be run on strictly amateur lines. Mr T Dawson has been the prime mover in its formation and up to date 40 players have been signed. RMI will compete in the Central Lancashire League and the 'C' Division of the Bolton & District League. Officials are confident that two successful teams can be run. There are 150 members on the books and the club is in a sound financial position.'

The Central Lancashire League comprised seven clubs with the others being located around the Rochdale and Bury area. RMI's opponents included Springfield, Haslingden,

Freetown, Edenfield, Ramsbottom and Shuttleworth, each side being played twice at home and away to extend the season to 24 league games.

RMI's opening game, at Heywood based Springfield on Saturday 12 September 1903 went un-reported other than it is known RMI lost, but their first home game was the following Saturday when they entertained Haslingden. RMI won 4-1 and were represented by the following team: Dickenson; Dawson, Hilditch; Russell, Titley, Rigby; Pickles, Jones, Sinclair, Stevenson, Tector. The pitch dimensions at the Recreation Ground were deemed too small for the league and so Horwich's first-team matches were played at the Old Racecourse.

After beating Freetown (Bury) 4-3 and Springfield 5-3 in their next two home games, RMI had made a good start to their league campaign. They then recovered from a five-match losing sequence to record a 5-2 win at Edenfield in the lead-up to Christmas. Results were inconsistent with an 8-4 home win over Springfield followed by a 7-2 defeat at the hands of Freetown when it was reported that 'the covering of snow made good football impossible. The decisions of the referee did not meet with the satisfaction of the spectators and at the close of the match the junior portion showed their disapproval by attacking him with snowballs.'

Nevertheless RMI had completed a satisfactory first season in the league and helped re-establish football in the town and two of the RMI players, H Gittens and Slade, were invited for trials with Bolton Wanderers. At the season's end, however, RMI's officials decided to resign from the Central Lancashire League and concentrate all their efforts on more local football. Both first and reserve teams would compete in the Bolton & District League from 1904-05 onwards. Neighbours Adlington, meanwhile, celebrated lifting the Lancashire Alliance championship. They had moved grounds to a field off Railway Road while their head-quarters were at the Ridgway Arms. Their colours were red and blue.

RMI's first team were placed in the 'A' Division of the league and commenced with a 4-1 victory at defending champions Little Hulton United on 3 September 1904. 'Horwich played a splendid game,' reported the Journal. Mawdesley was credited with three goals and Sutton with the other.

By playing more locally based sides the interest in the team's fortunes grew as every game was a 'derby' match. Left-winger Tector scored the season's second hat-trick in a 3-1 win at Farnworth Alliance when future long-serving RMI chairman Sam Heath went in goal. In the middle of October RMI's match at Blackrod attracted a crowd of 2,500 for a hard-fought goalless draw. 'No small amount of rivalry exists between these two teams,' explained the Horwich Journal.

The league was not without its problems, RMI's scheduled home game against Westhoughton Juniors being postponed at the last minute as the visitors 'could not get a wagonnette' despite the RMI players having changed and the spectators having been admitted to the ground.

The return home game against Blackrod in January attracted a crowd of 2,000, the largest seen at a football match in the town for many years, and RMI wound up a highly satisfactory campaign with a 4-2 win at another Blackrod-based club, Scot Lane in mid-March.

In April 1905 RMI played friendlies home and away against the Great Southern and Western Railway Company of Dublin, a fellow railway works team. The construction of rolling stock had commenced at the company's base in Inchicore in 1852, many years before the Horwich Loco Works. The first match was on Saturday 15 April 1905 when the RMI party of players and officials journeyed to Dublin on the ferry from Holyhead. They drew 1-1 before what was described as a 'big gate.'

The return game was played at Horwich the following Saturday when the visitors were given a conducted tour of the Loco Works and after the match entertained to tea at the Bridge Hotel. RMI held a 2-0 lead at half-time but went down to a 4-2 defeat. The RMI team was: Crossley; Ellis, Rigby; Toole, Aldred, Sale; Tector, Grey, Jackson, Stevenson, Edwards.

RMI played two more seasons in the Bolton & District League, building up the playing strength of the club and attracting new players. When they opened the 1905-06 season with a 5-2 home win over Westhoughton the Horwich team was as follows: L Crossley; T Hulse; T Hilditch; H Rigby; J Smith, J Toole; W Smith, F Grey, I Jackson, J Pickles, E Edwards. Horwich also entered the Lancashire Junior Cup, defeating Farnworth and Farnworth Alliance before losing to Scot Lane in the third round. When Horwich entertained Blackrod in the Bolton Charity Cup a crowd of over one thousand was attracted but the visitors were victorious by a single goal.

RMI's league opponents included Westhoughton, Bolton Temperance, Eagley Institute, Egerton, Little Hulton Albion, Turton, Aspull, Kearsley Athletic, Westhoughton Sacred Heart, Scot Lane and Blackrod.

Terry Foley collected the annual season ticket and membership booklets issued by RMI from their formation until they left the town in 1985. The earliest surviving one in his collection was from 1905-06. A smartly produced, brown backed small booklet it was printed by H Fletcher, New Brunswick Street, Horwich and its contents page made interesting reading:

Season 1905-06

Horwich Railway Mechanics' Institute Football Club

(Members of the Lancashire Football Association)

List of Matches, Officers &c.

The club President was George Hughes, Esq and the following were listed as Vice-Presidents: O Winder, JH Crompton, D Gibson, AD Jones, H Jackson, Dr Jackson, Dr Coates, Mr Attock.

The committee comprised: W Peters (Chairman), OB Street, W Brown, J Birrell, C Lloyd, H Crewe, J Smith, T Smith, C Hazelhurst, R Titterington, H Barlow, Harry Stevenson, J Dickinson. The committee met every Monday evening at the Institute at 8pm.

Charles Edward Warburton was the Honorary Secretary, with Harry Stevenson the groundsman and J Ormrod the Honorary Treasurer. The ground was stated as: Old Racecourse, Horwich. The club colours were: First Team: Blue Shirts and Blue Knickers; Second Team: Blue and White Shirts and Blue Knickers.

The annual subscription was two shillings and sixpence and 'any employee of the L&Y Railway Company and a Member of the Institute wishing to join the club could do so by signing his authority for his subscription to be deducted from the pay lists.'

In 1905 the tennis courts opened at the Recreation Ground for the first time and here, clearly, was the basis of a first-class sports venue. Two years later a bandstand was erected on the Recreation Ground, a gift from L&Y director Henry Yates Thompson.

Conscious that their existing ground had many handicaps if the club was hopeful of progressing into higher leagues, the football club committee was on the look-out for a new ground, as the Horwich Journal reported in September 1906. 'The old ground has had to be re-engaged,' the report stated. 'The efforts of the Institute Committee to obtain new pastures proved unsuccessful.'

RMI also developed their links with local clubs and introduced a medal competition with the final staged at the Horwich ground. They also built upon their relationship with the GSW Railway Company of Ireland and at Christmas-time 1906 RMI's players and players again made the journey to Dublin for the challenge match, on this occasion losing 3-1.

In the 1906-07 season RMI won nine and drew three of their 26 league games and finished in eighth position. Three players, Rigby, Peters and Edwards were selected for a 'Rest of the League XI' to play Adlington Amateurs, the champions. The other sides in the league were: Ramsbottom, Morris Green, Blackrod, Chequerbent, Halliwell Unitarians, Breightmet United, Clifton, Turton Reserves, Daisy Hill United and Eagley Institute. Aspull and Westhoughton Central withdrew during the season.

RMI's progress was such that club officials felt they could now attempt to climb the local football ranks and in the summer of 1907 the club was successfully admitted to membership of the Lancashire Football Alliance. The Alliance had lost a number of clubs, including Turton, Hindley Green, Ince Athletic, Newtown St Mark's, Oldham Athletic Reserves and Wigan Town Reserves. RMI were admitted alongside Skelmersdale United, Ashton Town Reserves, Chorley Reserves and Fleetwood Amateurs.

Before the league season commenced RMI's players and officials were treated to another weekend trip to Dublin where they defeated the GWR club Inchicore 3-2. Ernest Jones, a former Bolton Wanderers and Swindon Town player was responsible for two of the RMI goals.

Though RMI's first league game ended in defeat, a 2-0 reverse against eventual champions Ashton Town Reserves, the club soon adapted to the higher standard. Their next home game, against Chorley Reserves, attracted a good crowd in glorious weather who witnessed a 1-1 draw and then RMI drew 2-2 with Leyland before defeating Atherton Reserves 5-3. But after the good start RMI then suffered from a poor string of results. A run of six defeats and one draw left them bottom of the Alliance at Christmas with just one win from eleven games. 'The Loco men want to put more steam into their work,' commented the Horwich Journal.

In December 1907, meanwhile, a notable milestone in the history of the Loco Works was reached with the completion of the 1,000[th] locomotive to be built at Horwich.

RMI then defeated rivals Adlington by a late goal, in a game played in 'extreme cold' and followed up with victories over Skelmersdale United, Little Hulton United and St Helens Recs Reserves in successive matches. In a disastrous game RMI lost 9-2 at home to Fleetwood Amateurs and they closed the season with three defeats in a row. RMI had won seven and drawn three of their 24 league games and could feel satisfied with their first season in the Alliance.

One former RMI player, Alf Gittins, was playing for Luton Town in the Southern Football League. In one game a critic wrote: 'Gittins' cleverness and artistic work were a delight to watch.'

INTO THE WEST LANCASHIRE LEAGUE AND THE OPENING OF GRUNDY HILL

RMI's officials decided to further improve the standing of the club and successfully applied to join the West Lancashire League for the 1908-09 season. The League had originally been formed in 1905 with the competing clubs based around the Preston area, but was now extending its horizons.

With several locally based and established teams to provide the opposition as well as the reserve outfits of Chorley and Southport Central this move was seen as definite progression for RMI. 'Horwich Railway Mechanics' Institute commences their season against Leyland,' the Horwich Journal stated. 'They have become members of the West Lancashire League and some powerful teams will be encountered.'

RMI's first game in the league ended in a 2-1 home defeat at the hands of eventual champions Leyland. The RMI team was: T Meehan; H Hulse, J Hookham; J Walker, P Greeley, J Smith; J Peters, R Sinclair, E Latham, H Mann, W Smith. Their first home game was a 2-2 draw against Southport Central and after a 1-0 win at Standish, RMI defeated Blackpool Athletic 7-0. RMI had clearly adapted well.

RMI's first season in the West Lancashire League was more than satisfactory and they won 12, drew six and lost only eight of their 26 league games. They finished fifth in the league, 11 points behind Leyland. They closed the season with some high-scoring victories and fielded a settled side that read: T Edwards; T Hulse, J Hookham; J Walker, P Greeley, J Smith (captain); E Beech, F Settle, H Mann, E Latham, E Edwards.

Mann, Latham and Edwards became regular goal-scorers and centre-half Pat Greeley developed a growing reputation for his play. Meanwhile neighbours Adlington lifted the Lancashire Alliance title while the RMI cricket team were champions of the South East Lancashire League.

RMI secretary Arthur Riley represented the club at the West Lancashire League meeting during the summer and RMI held a pre-season social evening at the Café at the top of Gooch Street on Wednesday 26 August 1909 that was well attended. Officially called the 'L&Y Arms, Coffee Tavern,' the Café had been built in 1889 and was a regular meeting place. The chairman Mr W Peters explained that the club would again be run on amateur lines.

The 1909-10 season was the last one played by RMI at the Old Racecourse Ground. Their last game at the ground resulted in a 4-1 victory over Blackpool Athletic on Saturday 23 April 1910 when RMI were represented by the following side: J Longworth; W Benson, J Hookham; T Hulse, C Cummins, J Smith; E Beech, P Greeley (captain), H Mann, H Caunce, T Calderbank.

Greeley, having switched to playing at inside-right, opened the scoring with a fast rising shot. Mann extended the lead before half-time and in the second half, as RMI enjoyed the advantage of the slope, went on to complete his hat-trick, Ball replying for the visitors. RMI fell two places to seventh, with 20 points from their 24 league games.

In a late season fixture pile-up RMI played two games in one day, defeating Park Villa at home 2-1 while a weak team was sent to Longridge, losing 6-0. The campaign ended disappointingly when Bamber Bridge wired at 3-15pm to say they were unable to raise a team for the final game and RMI were awarded the points.

At the end of the season H Mann and J Hookham were selected for the Rest of the League against the league champions (Longridge).

In the summer of 1910 RMI officials made preparations to commence the season at their new Grundy Hill ground which had formerly been used by Horwich Wednesday playing in the Bolton Wednesday League. 'The club head-quarters and playing field have been removed to the field belonging to the railway company adjoining the Recreation Ground,' reported the Horwich Journal. 'The Racecourse Ground has been obtained by the Victoria Wesleyans FC.'

The roll-call of RMI players included the following: J Longworth, R Forrester, J Hookham, W Benson, S Ryder, P Greeley, C Cummins, J Smith, W Peters, F Beech, H Rigby, E Beech, E Latham, H Mann, E Vause, T Calderbank, JT Entwistle and H Whalley.

After opening the new season with a 4-1 defeat at Longridge, RMI staged their first match at their new Grundy Hill ground on 17 September 1910, sharing a 2-2 draw with Lytham. The honour of scoring the first goal fell to the visitors, Fisher's goal giving them an interval lead. Beech and Mann then replied for RMI before Ward scored a late equaliser.

Adlington provided the next opposition at Grundy Hill, helping attract what was described as a record gate of 1,200. RMI beat their old rivals 4-1 with Cummins and Mann each scoring twice. The RMI team was: J Longworth; W Benson, J Hookham; T Hulse, P Greeley (captain), J Smith; E Beech, H Mann, C Cummins, E Vause, E Latham. They soon developed a liking for Grundy Hill, avenging Longridge's first-day victory with a 4-1 success and then beating Morecambe 5-2 (with Cummins scoring four goals).

In the second half of the season RMI gathered consistent results and went on to win the league, finishing one point ahead of Southport Central. They won 14 and drew five of their 24 league games. RMI were unbeaten at home in the league, winning all but three games.

RMI also enjoyed a good run in the league cup competition which was known as the Richardson Cup before falling to old rivals Adlington at the final hurdle following a replay. On the way to the final RMI defeated Longridge and Fleetwood Reserves before a semi-final victory was achieved against Southport Park Villa in a tie staged at Fleetwood. This game attracted a crowd of 2,000 including 500 spectators who journeyed from Horwich on a special train. Playing in the borrowed amber and black jerseys of the Fleetwood club, RMI won 3-0 with Beech scoring twice and Baker adding another goal.

The final was staged at St George's Park, Chorley on Saturday 8 April 1911 when a crowd of 6,000 produced receipts of £83. Upwards of two thousand Horwich supporters went to Chorley on special trains, more than 1,500 tickets being booked at the Loco Works and another five hundred at Horwich Station. The teams were as follows: Horwich: Allison; Caunce, Hookham; Hulse, Greeley, Smith; Beech, Baker, Cummins, Mann, Latham. Adlington: Jardine; Green, Waters; Harrison, Dean, Norris; Wilson, Fox, Berry, Hallas, Holt. Both sides seemed over-awed by the huge crowd and a ragged game ensued. Cummins scored just before half-time and his goal looked to have given RMI the cup until Berry grabbed a late equaliser to set-up a replay a fortnight later.

In between the original and replayed cup finals RMI made sure of the championship by defeating Leyland 2-0 before a Grundy Hill crowd of 1,200. Cummins and Baker got the goals in the first-half. Another large contingent from Horwich followed their heroes to St George's Park for the final replay when RMI lined-up with an unchanged team. For Adlington there was one change, Hanson replacing Waters and playing at left-half with Norris reverting to full-back. The crowd was described as being slightly less than for the first game though still numbered around the 5,000-mark. On this occasion Adlington proved to be the better side and they lifted the Richardson Cup by virtue of second half goals by Dean and Banks.

RMI recovered to defeat Bolton Wanderers Reserves 5-3 at Grundy Hill in a friendly game two days later and the following Saturday were due to play a Rest of the League side in a championship celebration game. Sadly, though this was cancelled due to bad weather. However, Mr Oxley of the league committee journeyed to Horwich with the league shield and made a presentation to 'Patty' Greeley the RMI captain. Mr Oxley stated that RMI's form on their new ground had been instrumental in their success, the team having dropped only two points at home.

In a review of the season the Horwich Journal reported: 'With the change of head-quarters from the Old Racecourse to the new ground the club has progressed wonderfully well. The Mechanics' Institute FC has effected a great improvement in having obtained a new ground on Victoria Road on land belonging to the Railway Company. A new pavilion has been erected and is used in summer by members of the Lawn Tennis Club.' In the 1911 census the population of Horwich was 16,000.

In the 1911-12 season RMI fell to fifth, nine points adrift of champions Higher Walton Athletic. The football club suffered due to industrial unrest with many supporters unable to afford to watch the team due to problems at the works. Inevitably this had an effect on the club's finances. In August 1911 there was a large industrial dispute at the works coinciding with a strike on the railways and no sooner had this been resolved than many of the employees of the loco works were put on short time as a consequence of the miners' strike between March and May 1912.

In the circumstances secretary Arthur Riley reported to the AGM that he felt the season had been fairly successful, with several highlights to report. Grundy Hill was also chosen to stage the Richardson Cup Final on Saturday 20 April 1912 when Chorley Reserves defeated Brinscall 2-1 in front of a crowd of over one thousand spectators.

Before the start of the season drainage work was completed on the ground and what was reported to be a 'splendid banking' shortly to be planted with trees was placed on the Victoria Road side of the ground. 'A decided improvement is the wooden platform for standing on a damp ground,' the report continued. 'This has been completed at considerable expense and can accommodate between 600 and 700 spectators. It is shortly to be extended and it is estimated that there will then be dry-standing for 1,200 spectators.'

Hindley Central became the first visiting team to win a league match at Grundy Hill when they recorded a 1-0 victory on 28 October. But they then failed to complete their league programme and were replaced by Kirkham who took over their fixtures.

But there was a tragedy in November 1911 when T Calderbank, a Horwich player for the previous three seasons died suddenly on 1 November 1911. When RMI hosted Hamilton Central on 11 November 1911 the kick-off was delayed due to Calderbank's funeral and his coffin was carried past the ground by his comrades.

Chorley based Hamilton Central won the West Lancashire League in the 1912-13 season with RMI finishing fourth, five points adrift. For the second time in three seasons RMI were undefeated at home in the league but they suffered six away defeats. At home RMI won 11 of 13 games, drawing one with one abandoned. Away from home they won three, lost six and drew three games. In the Richardson Cup they lost to eventual winners Leyland after defeating Fleetwood away from home.

On the Boxing Day 1912 a team made up of committee and players played Horwich hockey club in a friendly which proved to be a success while in January 1913 RMI recorded their record win, 8-2 away at Walton-le-Dale, surpassing the seven goals recorded against Blackpool Athletic in 1908. Latham scored a hat-trick, including a penalty.

At the AGM on Monday 23 June 1913, described as the tenth in the club's history, chairman Mr W Peters reported a deficit of £9 on the season but stated that this had been covered by a grant from the institute committee. Subscriptions amounted to £50 and gate receipts £42 while railways fares of £34 accounted for the largest item in the expenditure total of £125. Nothing had been paid for wages during the year.

Mr Peters had presided over all the AGMs since the club's formation and he reflected that a great deal had been achieved. The club had started, he said, on a section of the Recreation Ground when they had a portion of the cricket field now occupied by tennis players. But the pitch was not large enough and he was glad that the institute found them a larger field in the end. In between times they had played on the Old Racecourse where they spent a number of years and 'did fairly well considering the position of the ground.'

Mr Peters then announced his retirement from the committee with the secretary Mr Riley following suit while RMI lost two of their most influential players, Beech and Latham who both emigrated to Canada.

A new secretary was appointed with Mr Overton taking over and Mr Bennett as chairman. There was considerable optimism about the prospects as new signings included Jimmy Garside, a former Exeter City player previously with Liverpool and Accrington Stanley. A fitter by trade, he had secured employment at the loco works. Another former Southern League footballer who joined RMI was right-winger Watson from Romford Town while George Porter, an England amateur international who had recently toured the Continent with Lancashire Wanderers would be inside-right. Porter was also prominent in local cricket circles. Burgess, a former Swindon Town reserve born in Birkenhead was another new recruit and right back H Caunce returned to the club.

In the following season, 1913-14, RMI virtually swept all before them. In 30 league games they won 25 and drew two, losing only three times, scoring 96 goals against 34. RMI finished ten points clear of runners-up Leyland. An opening day 4-0 home win over Bamber Bridge, which featured a hat-trick by Settle, was the start of the successful season, when the RMI team read: Anderton; Caunce, Kempster; Toole, Davenport, Hanson; Watson, Davies, Settle, Burgess, Garside. RMI went on to win all 15 league home games during the season, scoring 62 goals against 14. Their only defeats were suffered at Longridge on 15 November (5-2), Freckleton on 11 April (4-1) and Barrow Reserves on 25 April (1-0).

RMI went close to a notable double success, only to lose to Barrow in the final of the Richardson Cup on 28 March 1914. On their way to the final RMI defeated Croston,

Fleetwood Reserves and then Longridge in the semi-final which was staged at Preston North End's Deepdale enclosure when Porter's hat-trick helped them to a 4-0 victory. The final tie was again staged at Deepdale before a crowd of 3,000 with the following players representing RMI: Anderton; Kempster, Stamford; Burgess, Davenport, Hanson; Ashcroft, Porter, Southworth, Parker, Garside. The Barrow side was: Errington; Reardon, Robinson; Sherwin, Arthur, Atkinson; Woods, Dodds, Wardle, Hewitt, Lightfoot. The referee was Mr RT Wilson (Preston).

Barrow took an early lead through Hewitt whereupon Hanson missed a penalty for RMI, his weak shot failing to trouble Errington in the Barrow goal. Dodds then added a second on 20 minutes, but RMI fought back to equalise before half-time through Southworth and Garside. Wardle was carried from the field after being injured and Barrow briefly played with ten men. But the Barrow centre-forward then returned and went on to score an 82nd minute winner that denied RMI.

There was a representative game staged at Grundy Hill on 21 March 1914 when a West Lancashire League XI, including RMI players Garside, McCarthy and Hanson played a Bolton & District League Select XI.

Towards the end of the season RMI forward Southworth struck a rich scoring vein, notching four goals in a 6-1 win over Walton-le-Dale and repeating the feat the following Saturday with four goals in a 9-0 home win over Lytham. On Good Friday, 17 April RMI played two league games at home on the same day. In the morning they defeated Longridge 6-4 and in the afternoon beat Walton-le-Dale 4-0. The following day they beat Southport Central at home 7-0.

THE WAR YEARS

The 1914-15 season was disrupted by the outbreak of war and the league limped along before closing down, with many of the teams struggling for numbers due to players enlisting in the forces. Longridge and Walton-le-Dale both resigned without playing a match and Blackburn St Philip's, Fleetwood Reserves and Lytham all resigned in mid-season. Though it seemed hardly to matter in the overall context of what was happening in the world, RMI finished in third position behind Leyland and Adlington with 25 points from 20 games.

Several hundred men from the Loco Works answered the country's call and joined the army and there was a scarcity of labour in the engineering trades. Though the RMI first team was largely unaffected the reserve team suffered from a shortage of players and as a result decided to sever their connection with the Bolton & District League.

With many teams in the West Lancashire League struggling due to players enlisting in the army and the local newspapers carrying increasingly harrowing reports of casualties from the front line the battle for two points on a Saturday seemed completely meaningless by comparison. When RMI visited Fleetwood Reserves just before Christmas Lieutenant Baxter of the Eighth Liverpool Irish Regiment went around the field recruiting men before the game.

It was an unreal situation in which to be playing football and RMI's seasonal start was delayed until 12 September when they defeated Southport Central 5-1, following up with a 5-0 thumping of Coppull. But after entering the FA Cup for the first time RMI went down to Haslingden in the first qualifying round, losing 3-1.

There was some trouble in the latter stages of the derby at Hamilton Central at Highfield Park in late November. Near the finish two players got at loggerheads and the members of crowd became involved, invading the playing pitch, a free fight ensuing before order was restored. RMI's opponents had a Belgian refugee in goal by the name of D'Plauck, who had represented his country in an unofficial international against an England team.

Some return to pre-war rivalry returned when RMI visited Adlington in the Richardson Cup, securing victory with second half goals by Parker and Ashcroft. RMI played in blue and white shirts instead of their usual red to avoid clashing with the home team, a sign of things to come. Any hopes of a cup success disappeared when RMI lost at home to Southport Central in the second round. 'The conditions were wretched,' the Horwich Journal reported. 'The ground was a quagmire and the wind was strong, carrying with it rain and sleet. It was no surprise that the attendance was only around one hundred spectators.'

What proved to be RMI's final league game in the West Lancashire League was on Friday 30 April 1915 when they defeated Hamilton Central at home 9-2. To help supplement the fixtures, four teams formed a competition known as the Davis Cup at the end of the season with RMI's season ending in a 2-0 defeat at Lancaster on 1 May. The season had been disappointing playing wise and financially and gates were poor, not helped by the fact that many home games clashed with Bolton Wanderers fixtures.

RMI used only 17 players during the campaign, two goalkeepers, three backs, five half-backs and seven forwards. At the AGM the committee praised the players, 'who had stuck loyally to the task' and reported a small surplus on the season with income of £127 and expenditure of £117.

But the worsening international situation ensured that RMI did not play for the next two seasons, the club remaining in abeyance. Neighbours Adlington decided to carry on and joined the Lancashire Combination for the 1915-16 season but after attracting little support for home games elected to transfer all their remaining home games to their opponents' grounds before closing down at the end of the season.

INTO THE LANCASHIRE COMBINATION

In 1917 RMI elected to resume playing and applied for membership of the war-time Lancashire Combination Emergency League. As a result of this move RMI were well placed to apply for membership of the Combination proper when normal peace-time football resumed.

Their first game upon re-forming was a 3-1 defeat at Bryn on 15 September 1917. An attendance of 500 saw football resume at Grundy Hill the following Saturday when Bryn were the visitors but a dour game ended without a goal. The RMI team was: J Anderton; W Benson, H Stamford; T Whittaker, W Norris, J Hookham; J Ashcroft, W Miller, W Taylor, G Burgess, J Garside. It was not until 17 November that RMI managed their first win of the season, goals by Garside (2), Taylor and Stamford accounting for visitors St Helens Alexandra by 4-1.

RMI's game at South Liverpool on 12 January 1918 was marred by controversy, the referee calling a halt to proceedings after a home player refused to leave the field after being sent-off. South Liverpool visited Grundy Hill the following Saturday and were roundly defeated 9-0 with Ashcroft scoring four goals and Taylor a further three.

Fixtures were spasmodic and the league table inevitably disjointed but at least football was being played at Grundy Hill as some semblance of normality returned to daily life. RMI also resumed their long-standing friendship with Bolton Wanderers and played their reserve team in friendly games. RMI won 2-0 at Burnden Park in late November 1917 and repeated the feat by the same score-line in the return game just before Christmas.

The start of the 1918-19 campaign heralded the resumption of regular football and RMI played over thirty games in all. They opened the campaign with a 3-3 draw at Bryn when they were represented by the following team: Anderton; Benson, Kempster; Norris, Taylor, Stamford; Burgess, Ashcroft, Appleton, Tomlinson, Turner. The competition was augmented by the inclusion of the reserve teams of both Everton and Liverpool and that gave RMI players the opportunity to play at both Anfield and Goodison Park.

RMI actually earned their first win of the season when they defeated Liverpool Reserves 2-1 at Grundy Hill before a crowd of 500 in mid-October. They had the services of the Bolton Wanderers goalkeeper Ellison and Smith scored both goals. The return game was played the following Saturday at Anfield as RMI went down to a 4-1 defeat. The two games against Everton Reserves were played in January 1919, RMI going down to a 3-2 defeat at Goodison but then exacting revenge with a thumping 7-1 victory before a crowd of 800 at Grundy Hill. On that occasion Ashurst (3), Smith (2), Taylor (penalty) and Garside were on target for RMI.

There were some new opponents for RMI during the season with Blackpool RAMC, Ashton Hospital, Garswood Hall, Ashton Camp and Rylands Recs among the teams played. At the end of the season an auxiliary competition was added to the schedule to extend the number of games and also enable re-formed teams the chance to play some games in readiness for the resumption of peace-time football in 1919-20.

RMI's old rivals Chorley were one of the teams referred to in the press as 'Armistice Revivalists' and crashed to a 5-1 defeat at Grundy Hill on a snow-covered pitch in March. The prolific centre-forward Smith added three goals to his tally, including two from the penalty mark, in RMI's thumping win. The Chorley side included Tom Rodway, a former

Preston North End stalwart. RMI closed their season with a 3-2 home win over Runcorn and seemed well placed to compete in the Lancashire Combination. The major disappointment of the season was a 4-2 defeat at Ashton Hospital in the first round of the re-formed Lancashire Junior Cup.

After the horrors of the First World War, life returned to a semblance of normality during 1919 and the first post war football season commenced at the end of August.

RMI took part in the Lancashire Combination which featured 18 clubs, including the reserve teams of Tranmere Rovers and Rochdale. Other new clubs to the Combination included the Preston based works team Dick, Kerr's, a company that during the war produced locomotives, cable drums, pontoon bridges, cartridge boxes and munitions. The company was also well known for fielding a well-known ladies' football team comprising women who worked at the factory. On Christmas Day 1917 the women had staged an exhibition match in aid of the local hospital at Deepdale and attracted a crowd of over 10,000. They played on a new ground at Ashton Park.

Plank Lane (Leigh), Prescot and Stalybridge Celtic Reserves also took their place in the Combination and Eccles Borough changed their name to Eccles United. The Eccles United club was run by the local branch of the National Association of Discharged Soldiers and Sailors and all the Eccles team comprised discharged servicemen. Glossop fielded their first-team instead of their reserves in the Combination having failed to earn re-election to the Football League.

In the first match of the season RMI went down 2-1 at Eccles United when they were represented by the following players: Heyes; Benson, Helmsley; McCarthy, Taylor, Burgess; Leach, Ashcroft, Brindle, Barry, Cooper. Ashcroft scored the RMI goal.

RMI's first home game was against Dick, Kerr's when goals by Ashurst, Bleakley and Leach helped them record their first win of the season, 3-2. The following Saturday, however, rivals Chorley came to Grundy Hill and won 4-1. The Magpies went on the become champions with an impressive record of 25 wins and two draws from 34 games with Lancaster Town in runners-up position.

RMI did regain local pride, however, earning a memorable FA Cup third qualifying round victory over Chorley in November. In the first tie, RMI drew 1-1 at St George's Park, before a crowd of 1,500. The replay the following Wednesday afternoon attracted a crowd of 1,000 to Grundy Hill when Cooper, Ashcroft, Barry and Hesmondhalgh all scored in RMI's resounding 4-0 victory. The tie went ahead despite a heavy snowfall. But RMI gallantly failed to reach the first round proper, losing 4-2 at Stalybridge Celtic before a crowd of 2,500 in the next round.

Tom Hesmondhalgh's early season scoring feats attracted the attention of Rochdale and the tall forward, formerly with Bolton Wanderers and Eccles moved to Spotland during December while Tom McCarthy, who had served in the Royal Garrison Artillery in France for four years during the war, left to join Chorley. Hesmondhalgh had netted in perhaps the outstanding result of RMI's season, a 1-0 win at future Football League side Nelson in the first qualifying round of the FA Cup. In the Lancashire Junior Cup, RMI fell at the first hurdle losing 3-2 at Plank Lane.

After Christmas RMI began to field a more settled side and their league position improved considerably. After a run of four successive defeats in late February and early March the team then enjoyed a fine run of success, recording ten victories in their final eleven league games to finish a highly creditable sixth. Remarkably RMI did not feature in one drawn game during the league campaign, winning 20 and losing 14 of their 34 league games. 'The indications are that the public is taking an encouraging interest in RMI,' reported the Horwich Journal. 'They did very well in the latter half of last season.'

When Barry's goal gave RMI victory at Lancaster Town in April a demonstration against the visiting players was made by the home crowd. 'Mud and sods were thrown at them and a large crowd molested them on the way back to the station,' the Horwich Journal reported. 'The match referee was fortunate to escape without serious injury. There was no protection offered from the home officials.'

Joe Winsper, a recruit from local football in the Bolton area became a regular goal-scorer while fullback Dick Lilley, who was also a fine cricketer with Heaton in the Bolton League, was a redoubtable fullback. At the end of the season he moved to Nelson and soon realised his ambition of playing in the Football League. Jimmy Garside, the former RMI, Exeter City, Accrington Stanley and Liverpool outside-left resigned from the league's list of referees to devote more time to his position as assistant secretary of RMI. He had made five appearances for Liverpool in the Football League. Centre-half W Taylor missed only one game and John Ashcroft and James Burgess each played over 30 times. The RMI side for the final game of the season included only four players who had started the campaign. The line-up was: Heyes; Benson, Kempster; Gradwell, Taylor, Burgess; Jones, Moss, Winsper, Gray, Ashcroft.

There was some sad news during the summer months when the death was announced of the former RMI Chairman William Peters. He died on 5 June 1920 at the age of 57.

The composition of the Lancashire Combination for the 1920-21 season was considerably different to that of the previous campaign. Glossop, Stalybridge Celtic, Plank Lane, Prescot and the reserve sides of Tranmere Rovers and Rochdale all left the league being replaced by Atherton, Bacup Borough, Darwen, Leyland, Morecambe and Wigan United. The latter club folded in November 1920 but their fixtures were taken over by a newly-formed club, Wigan Borough who also played at Springfield Park. Leyland moved from Sandy Lane and took over Chorley's old ground at St George's Park after the Magpies took up residence at the site of a former ash tip which was re-named Victory Park.

Goalkeeper Harry Heyes had pre-season trials with Bolton Wanderers which proved unsuccessful though he later fulfilled his dreams of playing League football with Nelson. His deputy Charlie Allison described as 'an old veteran' was on stand-by. But John Ashcroft had moved to Winsford United. The ground was described as being 'in splendid condition' and RMI hoped to erect a stand on the Victoria Road side.

RMI began the new campaign with a 2-1 home defeat at the hands of Atherton and then drew 0-0 at Lancaster Town, the kick-off being put back to 5pm due to a local agricultural show. It took until RMI's sixth match to record their first league win, a 2-1 home success against Hurst. On the following Saturday RMI defeated Accrington Stanley 2-1 before what was stated to be a record crowd for a match at Grundy Hill. The RMI team on that occasion was: Heyes; Nelson, Gradwell; Benson, Pointon, Burgess; Tomlinson, Moss, Winsper, Waller, Barton. Lilley had departed for Nelson, who were to achieve Football League status in 1921 and RMI forward Bill Waller later joined him at Seedhill.

The enthusiasm for football was considerable and when RMI paid their first visit to Chorley's new Victory Park ground on 30 October 1920 the local derby attracted a crowd of 6,000 including at least one thousand supporters from Horwich. After earning a hard-earned point from a goalless draw, RMI suffered a single goal defeat when the Magpies visited Grundy Hill the following Saturday though had some consolation from the proceeds of a 2,000 gate.

Remarkably RMI gave a first-team debut to a young un-named Japanese player who was given the name of Alf Vernon. He was a resident of the Queen Street Mission. Vernon gave RMI good service and earned plaudits for many of what were described as 'capital displays' before being transferred to Eccles United in April 1922.

By the turn of the year RMI had won only two of 12 league games and suffered early round defeats at Nelson in the FA Cup and at home to South Liverpool in the Lancashire Junior Cup. In December Lancaster Town won 8-0 at Grundy Hill, their centre forward Proctor scoring four goals and in January RMI suffered a 9-2 defeat at Rossendale United.

After Christmas RMI won only two games before the end of what became a disastrous season, as they finished bottom of the Lancashire Combination table with just 17 points from 34 games. They failed to record a single away victory and conceded 91 goals while scoring only 34. But fortunately RMI had made many friends in the league and the club was comfortably re-elected at the annual general meeting held at the Pack Horse Hotel in Bolton in June, though could clearly not afford to suffer another bad season.

At the end of the season Barrow, the champions, Accrington Stanley and Wigan Borough (despite finishing second bottom to RMI) all left the Combination to become inaugural members of the newly formed Football League Third Division North. South Liverpool folded and the four newcomers for the 1921-22 season included New Brighton (who had taken over the liabilities of South Liverpool), Skelmersdale United and the reserve teams of Rochdale and Stockport County.

In 1921 the Horwich Loco Works War Memorial was unveiled in remembrance of the 120 employees killed in the First World War.

RMI began the new (1921-22) campaign with a 2-1 defeat at Chorley, Walkden scoring their only goal before a crowd of 3,000. The team was: Horridge; Goodier, Kempster; Burgess, Nicholson, Walkden; Boardman, Burns, Seddon, Lovett, Ashcroft.

In what was described as a 'clean-sweep' of the playing staff, John Ashcroft re-signed from Chorley while Nicholson came from Darwen. E Burns and John Boardman were former Bolton Wanderers reserve players. Bolton born Billy Lovett was a former Exeter City and Blackpool player while several prominent local players joined the club. Smith was a goalkeeper from Horwich Central, while Leach and Schofield came from Breightmet United. Kempster and Burgess were described as veterans.

In October 1921 RMI gave debuts to brothers Tom and Syd Embrey from Westhoughton. Smith had displaced Horridge in goal but he too was soon replaced by the veteran Joe Anderton, a former RMI and Adlington custodian. J Gregory, the Horwich Central goalkeeper, later played for the first-team while inside-left Harry Lovett joined his brother Billy in the RMI team during January 1922.

Though clearly a much more competitive and solid side, RMI's first league victory was not gained until the eighth match of the season when Phythian's goal earned a 1-0 success over Morecambe. The disastrous away form was finally over-turned in March 1922 when RMI's 2-1 victory at Hurst was their first on their travels for nearly two years.

They followed up with wins at Atherton and Rochdale before the season closed as RMI clawed their way to a respectable 12th-placed finish with 30 points gained from 34 games. The defence was much tighter, a total of 59 goals conceded being a big improvement on the previous campaign though only three teams managed fewer than RMI's tally of 45 goals. Lancaster Town, though, ended RMI's hopes of an FA Cup run with a resounding 5-1 victory at Grundy Hill.

In January 1922 the L&Y Railway Company was amalgamated with the LNW Railway Company and Mr George Hughes, CME (chief mechanical engineer) at Horwich was made CME and EE (electrical engineer) of the combined company. Sir Henry Fowler (one of the first pupils when the Institute first opened) was made deputy CME. In this year the RMI Athletic and Harriers Club was formed and later that year the Horwich RMI Brass Band won a prestigious national competition at Crystal Palace, lifting the famous 1,000 Guineas Cup. The Institute Band later gave a concert on behalf of football club funds on 5 February 1923.

However, hopes that RMI were rebuilding solidly after the disastrous 1920-21 season proved premature as the following season proved to be another disastrous campaign. In 1922-23 RMI finished next-to-bottom of the Lancashire Combination with only Great Harwood below them. To make matters worse local rivals Chorley were champions, finishing three points ahead of Lancaster Town. Horwich Central, meanwhile, played in the West Lancashire League and operated from RMI's old ground on the Old Racecourse. Their side included several former RMI players including Hookham, Tomlinson and Burgess.

Chorley made sure of the championship after securing a 1-1 draw at Grundy Hill on Wednesday 2 May 1923 when the visitors were indebted to a late equaliser by Kelly, ten minutes from time after Darlington had given RMI the lead. After the game the Chorley captain George Gray was presented with the cup by Mr R Watson, the Lancashire Combination treasurer and the Lostock Industrial School Band played a selection of music. On that occasion the RMI team was: Davies; Blinkhorn, Gradwell; Mather, Goodlad, Walkden; Embrey, Darlington, Sullivan, Kennedy, Downs.

RMI gained only 24 points from 34 games and their away record was again poor with just six points to show for their travels. Their only away win of the season was on New Year's Day 1923, with a single goal success at Atherton. Again, RMI had to go cap in hand to the Combination's Annual general meeting when they were again successful in being re-elected.

In the FA Cup RMI earned a creditable 1-1 home draw with Chorley before a crowd of 4,000 but went down to a single goal in the replay at Victory Park four days later. The RMI team was: Mather; Gradwell, Blinkhorn; Embrey, Lovett, Walkden; Ryder, Hesmondhalgh, Sowerbutts, Jackson, French.

The Lancashire Combination also inaugurated a league cup competition but RMI's interest ended early after a defeat at the hands of New Brighton. RMI also suffered a first round exit in the Lancashire Junior Cup against Bolton based Breightmet United.

RMI also briefly had a change of strip, marking the occasion of playing in 'newly adopted red shirts' by defeating Rochdale Reserves 4-0 on 30 December 1922.

Hesmondhalgh returned to the club from Rochdale and was a regular goal-scorer throughout the season. Late in the season RMI secured the services of Dan Sullivan, who had been on the books of Bolton Wanderers. Sullivan scored four goals in the last match of the season, a 7-1 demolition of Bacup Borough that hinted at better things to come. The half-back line of Mather, Lovett and Walkden was also becoming established and all three players would serve RMI well in the future.

GROUND IMPROVEMENTS

In October 1922 it was reported that the committee of the Railway Mechanics' Institute had acceded to the request of the football committee to consider a scheme to improve the ground. The club membership now topped the 800-mark. There were plans to build a covered stand, improve the training facilities and ensure that the dressing rooms had showers and hot water baths.

There was an unusual occurrence in December 1922 when the home game against Eccles United was abandoned due to fog after an hour with the visitors leading 2-1. When the game was replayed later in the season the spoils were shared in a 1-1 draw. Generally, RMI's home form was reasonably good though they did suffer a 6-1 defeat at the hands of visitors Fleetwood in March.

The closing weeks of the season were overshadowed by Bolton Wanderers' FA Cup exploits as the Wanderers made it through to the first FA Cup Final to be held at Wembley Stadium. Whenever RMI's home games clashed with those of the Wanderers it was RMI's gates that inevitably suffered. While an official Wembley crowd of 126,047 saw Wanderers beat West Ham United 2-0 on 28 April 1923 in what became one of the most famous football matches of all-time, a meagre attendance saw RMI draw 1-1 at home to league newcomers New Cross.

Meanwhile, there was a big surprise in the final of the Lancashire Junior Cup when West Lancashire League side Croston, old adversaries of RMI from before the war, defeated Bacup Borough. Chorley drew 2-2 at Lancaster to secure the Lancashire Combination title and then hosted Bolton Wanderers soon after their Wembley triumph in a friendly at Victory Park that attracted a gate of 5,759. Bolton won the game emphatically, 8-0.

At RMI's 1923 AGM Vice-Chairman Mr A Emsall presided and stated that the membership of the football club was 700. But there had been a deficit of £230 on the season which had not been satisfactory in either a financial or playing sense. Club secretary Mr W Carter stated that the support from the town was very poor and the committee had their work cut out if the club was to remain in the Combination. In endeavouring to find a winning combination they had tried 35 players during the season. They were still waiting for estimates for the building of a new stand.

President of the club was Mr George Hughes and Mr D Gibson was the chairman. In what was regarded as a very positive development an RMI Supporters' Club was formed in May 1923 with Mr F Rose as the inaugural chairman. At the initial meeting over one hundred were in attendance.

Blackley-based New Cross changed their name to Manchester North End for the following season and New Brighton departed to join the Football League while Hurst moved to the Cheshire League. Four reserve teams were admitted to the Combination for the 1923-24 campaign, those of Accrington Stanley, Southport, Nelson and Wigan Borough. Another reserve side, Stockport County, had left the league after the 1921-22 season.

There was a remarkable change in RMI's fortunes in the 1923-24 season when they rose to a final league placing of fourth with 20 wins and four draws from 38 games. Though Fleetwood were the Combination's outstanding team and finished a resounding 14 points clear of second placed Southport Reserves RMI were only four points short of runners-up spot.

Sullivan continued where he left-off in the previous season and was a regular marksman throughout the campaign. His two goals paved the way for a 3-0 home victory against Bacup Borough on the opening day of the campaign, the kick-off being put back to 6pm as the RMI cricket club had an important league engagement. But RMI started this game with only nine players after AJ Down and Tom Moon were late arriving due to problems on the trains. They had to walk from the station at Blackrod and were understandably below their best when they did join the game during the first-half. RMI then drew 2-2 at home to a Lancaster Town side that had two former England internationals in its ranks, the former Preston North End, Bradford City and Blackburn Rovers outside-right Dicky Bond and the former Glossop and Blackburn Rovers outside-left Joe Hodkinson.

Sullivan found a good partner in another former league player, the former Bury and Blackpool inside forward Harry Hird who enjoyed an excellent first peace-time season at Grundy Hill. Bolton born Hird had figured in some of RMI's war-time teams, in-between war service in the Army. Another good signing was the Bolton born left-winger Harry Croft, who had played league football for Preston North End and Portsmouth after the war. Croft was signed from Atherton.

The trio was seen to their best advantage in an 11-0 demolition of Skelmersdale United in November when Sullivan notched five goals and Hird another three, RMI adapting well to the hard ground. Croft (2) and Walkden were also on the score-sheet. That result helped turn around RMI's season after they had slumped to the bottom of the table with a meagre points-tally of four from their opening ten games.

Hird then scored a hat-trick, including a penalty, in a 3-2 win at Chorley and was also on the mark as RMI recorded a quick-fire double over the Magpies with a 2-1 success at Grundy Hill the following Saturday.

When RMI entertained Rochdale Reserves at the end of October 1923 the occasion was marked by the opening of the new grandstand at Grundy Hill. Described as a 'fine structure' and costing over £800 its erection was sponsored by the committee of the Mechanics' Institute who then took their share of the proceeds from each gate until the costs were met. Underneath the stand were separate rooms for the referee and club secretary and a bar for officials. It could seat 400 spectators though the Horwich Journal struck a pessimistic note. 'It is not anticipated that sufficient support will be forthcoming to fill it,' the report concluded.

Meanwhile several former RMI players were making their mark elsewhere. Goalkeeper Harry Heyes and Bill Waller were both with Chorley and Syd Embrey, brother of Tom, was transferred to Halifax Town in March 1924, but played in only three league games for the Shaymen and later returned to Grundy Hill. Goalkeeper Jack Davies had signed professional forms with Bury and left his employment at the Loco Works.

RMI were leading 2-0 in the return game at Skelmersdale United in April when weather conditions forced the game to be abandoned after 82 minutes. The Combination committee ruled the result should stand. After finishing bottom, Skelmersdale left the Combination at the end of the season and were replaced by Barnoldswick Town while Manchester North End moved to the Cheshire League.

RMI's home form was outstanding and an early season reverse against Fleetwood proved to be their only league defeat at Grundy Hill. The team also recorded six away wins, a considerable improvement on previous seasons. RMI finished the season with an outstanding run of form, recording ten wins and one draw in their final 12 games.

RMI's good run in the Lancashire Junior Cup also added excitement to the season. They defeated Atherton and Bacup Borough, both ties following replays, in the competition before bowing out to Great Harwood but Atherton ended RMI's FA Cup hopes with a 2-1 victory at Flapper Fold, a last-minute goal proving decisive.

Club officials were praised at the AGM for revolutionising the forward line by bringing together Sullivan, Hird and Croft. But it came at a price as the chairman, Sam Heath, reported that there was an adverse balance of £300 and a loss on the season of £175. Gates receipts totalled £382 and subscriptions brought in a further £128 but expenditure of £870 included a wages bill of £422.

It was gratifying, though, to see so many local players establishing themselves at first-team level. Billy Lovett, from Lostock, George 'Tiny' Yates, a towering inside-right who had trials with Wigan Borough, and Sydney Gradwell were all making their mark. Gradwell, a product of Bolton amateur football went on to play for RMI until 1929 before joining Morecambe. His brothers Billy and Alf also played for the club. The oldest player in the team was Francis Walkden, the stalwart left-half.

LANCASHIRE JUNIOR CUP WINNERS

Though the following season, 1924-25, represented something of a disappointment league-wise RMI more than atoned by lifting the Lancashire Junior Cup for the first time in the club's history. RMI finished ninth in the Combination with 14 wins and eight draws from their 36 league games. Morecambe claimed their first title, finishing one point ahead of runners-up Rochdale Reserves. RMI went out of the FA Cup at the first qualifying round stage, losing 4-2 at home Darwen before a crowd of 3,000 after beating Portsmouth Rovers (Todmorden) in the preliminary round.

Despite signing former England international winger Alf Quantrill Chorley finished fourth-bottom and RMI supporters revelled in an early season 3-1 success at Victory Park over a Chorley side including the former Derby County and Preston North End player. After a short stay Quantrill left Chorley and returned to the League with Bradford Park Avenue. The RMI team on that occasion was: Crook; Blinkhorn, Gradwell; T Embrey, Goodlad, Walkden; S Embrey, Yates, Sullivan, Croft, Shaw.

RMI defeated Black Lane, Croston, Morecambe and Eccles United on their way to the Lancashire Junior Cup Final which was staged at Victory Park, Chorley on Saturday 21 February 1925. The side had shown great fight to overcome Eccles in the semi-final, coming from behind to reach the final with goals by Syd Embrey and a Francis Walkden penalty. In the final, RMI defeated Atherton 1-0 with Walkden scored the game's only goal from the penalty spot in the second half. The first-half had been goal-less though Tom Embrey's shot hit the underside of the bar and rebounded to safety while Atherton winger Walsh hit the post.

Horwich were felt to be the stronger and cleverer team with Atherton, despite the efforts of former Bolton Wanderers inside-forward Tom Buchan looking disjointed. The penalty followed a melee in the Atherton goalmouth and Walkden stepped up to shoot hard and low into the corner from the spot. Later Croft, who had briefly left the field, injured after a foul hit the bar with a stinging shot.

The pen-pictures of the RMI players referred to goal-keeper J Crook as having impressed tremendously during the season. He had a 'good nerve and a big kick.' Right-back Fred Blinkhorn was described as the 'best player in the team, a cool, young player' while left-back Stan Gradwell was a 'sound defender.' Right-half Tom Embrey was a 'stout hearted defender who never knows when he is beaten' and captain and centre-half Billy Lovett was described as the 'best man in his position in the Combination.' Left-half Francis Walkden was the 'oldest and most consistent player in the team and a sound penalty-taker,' which proved to be prophetic words.

Outside-right Syd Embrey was 'a smart little player who centres well' and inside-right George Yates 'a hard worker who would run through a brick wall.' Centre-forward Dan Sullivan was a 'popular footballer and the top-scorer in the Combination.' Inside-left Harry Croft was a 'clever forward' and outside-left George Shaw had 'an accurate centre from his left-foot.'

The teams lined up as follows:
RMI: Crook; Blinkhorn, Gradwell; T Embrey, Lovett, Walkden; S Embrey, Yates, Sullivan, Croft, G Shaw.
Atherton: Bury; Bibby, Barrington; W Shaw, Harrison, Sedgwick; Unsworth, Haydock, Rigby, Buchan, SH Walsh.

The referee was N Bromley (Bolton)

The official attendance was 6,409 with receipts of £171. After the game Mr T Watson from the Lancashire Football Association presented the cup to the RMI captain, Billy Lovett and Walkden was chaired from the field by jubilant Horwich supporters. The Horwich team travelled home by a saloon attached to a special train and finished up with high tea and an informal concert at the Greenwood Hotel. An ambition had been realised and it was felt that RMI were firmly on the football map.

The prominent club officials were: D Carter (secretary), D Gibson (chairman), W Darcy (vice-chairman), J Edwards (treasurer) and Eddie Edwards (trainer).

Though Hird had moved on to pastures new, returning to the Football League with New Brighton, Sullivan continued to prove a reliable goal-scorer. And when Sullivan missed some games through injury towards the end of the season RMI unearthed a most satisfactory replacement in Fairhurst who scored five goals in an 8-1 home win over Leyland on only his second appearance for the club. Sadly, Fairhurst was unable to repeat his feat and faded from the scene.

Another newcomer was a promising right-winger John (Jack) Bruton, a coal-miner from Hart Common. The 21-years-old Bruton had trials with Bolton Wanderers but was not considered good enough. Undaunted, he played for a number of local clubs including Wigan Borough but it was with RMI that his skills flourished. Bruton made his RMI debut in a 5-0 home victory over Wigan Borough Reserves on 18 October 1924 and scored his first goal for the club in the 5-3 home win against Accrington Stanley Reserves in January 1925.

After playing only a handful of senior games for RMI Bruton attracted the attention of league scouts and in March 1925 was transferred to Burnley, reportedly signing for the club on an overturned tub at the pit head after completing a shift. RMI received a transfer fee of £125. Bruton almost immediately established himself in Burnley's first division side and scored on his league debut against Newcastle United on 14 March 1925, just days after leaving RMI. Left-back Fred Blinkhorn also joined Burnley and went on to make 15 appearances for the club.

Sullivan scored 32 goals in league and cup games during the season with Yates and Croft each scoring 13. Walkden was credited with nine goals and Fairhurst with seven.

There were several changes once again in the Lancashire Combination for the 1925-26 season. Eccles United joined the Cheshire League and Rochdale Reserves and Leyland, who had finished bottom, also left. Preston North End 'A' joined to maintain the compliment of Football League reserve or 'A' teams at five and also admitted were Hindley Green Athletic, Colne Town and Clitheroe.

As a result RMI once more completed 38 league games and finished seventh with a points-tally of 41 from 19 wins and three draws. No less than six teams scored over one hundred goals during the campaign, champions Nelson Reserves leading the way with 123 goals. RMI's tally was 87, though they also conceded 84 during the season.

To general disappointment from RMI supporters the popular Sullivan was transferred during the closed season to Ashton National and George 'Tiny' Yates tried his luck in league football with Wigan Borough, going on to score ten goals in 35 league games before moving on to Darwen. With the popular winger Harry Croft joining Chorley and the long-serving Walkden moving to Atherton, after surprisingly been given a free-transfer there were several significant changes in the RMI ranks. RMI also transferred a trio of fringe players, Jim Waterhouse, Billy Wilkinson and William Bruton (brother of Jack) to Hindley Green.

RMI gave trials to many players during what became a transitional season and suspended their long-serving goalkeeper Harry Heyes *sine die* during November for an unspecified disciplinary offence. The most notable newcomers were Stanley Mather, an outside left from Horwich Central and Billy Bibby, the former Bolton Wanderers and Atherton full-back. A trio of former Wigan Borough players, Harry Smith, Peter Hopkins and Dick Hampson joined RMI and goalkeeper Horace Brooks stepped up from local football.

RMI started the season with a 5-0 defeat at Southport Reserves when their side was: Heyes; Caldwell, Tinsley; Hopkins, Gore, Sedgwick; Shaw, Beazley, Robinson, Crompton, Boardman. They then lost 5-1 at home to Accrington Stanley Reserves when a new goalkeeper, Taylor from Smithills, was tried.

In the early part of the season S Beazley, a new forward signed from Burscough Rangers, emerged as a regular goal-scorer. Beazley scored three goals in the 5-1 home win over Barnoldswick Town that represented one of RMI's only two league successes in their first dozen games- a troubled start to the season. Another newcomer, J Prescott from Aspull Amateurs, scored four goals on his debut in a 5-1 home win over Fleetwood but very little was heard of him after that. There was another significant debutant in January when Walton, from Horwich Central scored three goals in a 4-0 home win over Great Harwood.

RMI were in bottom place in the Combination table after 12 games and also had suffered heavy cup defeats at the hands of Morecambe (5-0 in the Combination Cup) and Lancaster Town (8-2 in the FA Cup) as well as an 8-0 thrashing in the league at Darwen. But a successful run of nine wins and one draw in a ten-game spell early in the New Year saw RMI climb the table. Wilkinson returned from Hindley Green and trials were given to the former Bury players Regan and Jack Lythgoe. The latter had started his professional career at Gigg Lane before the war and also played for Nottingham Forest, Newport County and Norwich City, making a total of 148 league appearances. Mather scored his first goals for the club with a brace in the 4-2 win over Hindley Green Athletic during that sequence. When RMI defeated Wigan Borough Reserves 6-0 at Grundy Hill on Good Friday 1926 all five members of the forward line were on the score-sheet.

As RMI closed the season with a 4-1 win at Colne Town, their seventh away success of the campaign the make-up of their side showed nine changes from that which started back in August and was as follows: Smith; T Embrey, Bibby; Wilkinson, Goodlad, Sedgwick; Thompson, Beazley, S Embrey, Gradwell, Mather. Beazley finished as top scorer with 18 goals.

Bolton Wanderers, meanwhile, lifted the FA Cup for the second time in four seasons, defeating Manchester City 1-0 at Wembley Stadium before a crowd of 91,447. Wanderers were also a consistent force in the top-flight of English football, having finished fourth, third and eighth in consecutive seasons and it little wonder that RMI's home gates inevitably suffered if their games clashed with attractive fixtures down the road at Burnden.

Horwich RMI, 1908-09

Horwich RMI, circa 1912

Irish opponents at Grundy Hill in the early 1900s—RMI line up for a pre-match photograph with Inchicore FC

No big squads back in Edwardian times– just the basic eleven players and officials pose for this team photograph

Following pages—more RMI team groups from the early 20th Century. Blue and white stripes were usually the chosen team colours although some seasons saw the club wear plain blue jerseys . The impressive Shield in some of the pictures is thought to be the West Lancashire League Championship trophy.

1924-25 team, winners of the Lancashire Junior Cup.
Back (L-R) E Edwards (Trainer), T Embrey, F. Blinkhorn, T Crook, S Gradwell, F Walkden.
Front S Embrey, G Yates, D Sullivan, W Lovett (Captain), H Croft, G Shaw.

Joe Keetley

Jack Bruton, in England kit

C E Sutcliffe Merit Medal awarded to
Stanley Mather, 1928-29

Frank Roberts

JOE KEETLEY THE GOAL MACHINE

The 1926-27 season was noteworthy for RMI achieving the distinction of scoring one hundred league goals during a league campaign for the first time, due in large part to the acquisition of a new centre forward, 29-year-old Joe Keetley who was to become a Horwich legend.

Derby born Keetley was one of a family of 12, eleven boys and one girl, and was the oldest of a remarkable quintet of brothers to play league football, the others being Charlie, Frank, Harold and Tom. Between them the five Keetley brothers made a total of 902 league appearances and scored 514 goals. Joe learned his early football with the Victoria Ironworks team in Derby which on one occasion included seven of the brothers, including an all-Keetley forward line.

When he signed for Liverpool from Accrington Stanley Joe had attracted a transfer fee of £1,200, but after spells with Bolton Wanderers, Accrington Stanley, Liverpool, Wolves, Wrexham and Doncaster Rovers he opted for non league football and a job in the Loco Works. Though his league record of 42 appearances (19 goals) pales into insignificance compared to Charlie, who scored 108 goals in 160 games for Leeds United and Tom who scored 180 goals in 231 appearances for Doncaster Rovers and then 94 in 103 games for Notts County the Football League's loss was most definitely RMI's gain.

With Harry Hird returning to RMI for a third spell and the skilful Mather emerging as a top class player who soon attracted league scouts RMI had few problems scoring goals. In 38 league games they scored 106 goals, conceding 76 as a mid-table position of tenth was achieved. Overall 1,814 goals were scored in the Lancashire Combination season, an average of nearly 4.8 per match. Seven other clubs also scored one hundred or more goals, champions Rossendale United leading the way with 129 while five clubs conceded one hundred or more.

Keetley scored on his RMI debut, in the opening day 6-0 victory over Hindley Green Athletic who went on to concede 146 goals during the season. But he was overshadowed on that occasion by another new signing, the Hindley Green forward Greenough who scored a hat-trick against his old club. Despite his fine start, though, Greenough failed to settle at Grundy Hill and was soon on his way to Atherton. The RMI side was the opening game was: Smith; Bibby, S Gradwell; T Embrey, Goodlad, Sedgwick; Jones, Hird, Greenough, Keetley, J Gradwell.

Keetley showed his versatility by deputising in goal after regular custodian Smith was injured against Barnoldswick on Boxing Day but was unable to prevent a 2-1 defeat. Soon he was back to playing up front and banging in the goals, his fierce shooting with either foot a common feature. Goal-hungry RMI closed their home programme with a thumping 10-0 win over Atherton which followed a 6-2 win at Darwen, in which Keetley scored a hat-trick Mather scored four goals in the Atherton game with Keetley, Yates and Hird each scoring twice.

The highest away win of the season was 7-1 at Great Harwood, who finished bottom of the table but perhaps their best win was a 5-0 thumping of eventual champions Rossendale United at Grundy Hill in November. Keetley and Mather each scored two goals for RMI and outside-left Tom Yates, a Bolton amateur, made the first of many RMI appearances. Full-back Dick Wright proved a fine acquisition from Fleetwood.

Keetley scored 40 goals, 34 of them in the league, and Hird (21) and Mather (15) helped form a potent attack in which Syd Embrey, back from a stint at Halifax Town scored ten goals. But RMI displayed poor form in the cups, losing at home to St Helens Town at the first hurdle of the FA Cup and suffering a surprise defeat at West Lancashire League side Lytham in the Lancashire Junior Cup.

Horwich Central, meanwhile, were now playing at the Longworth Road ground and their goalkeeper, Laithwaite, played several first-team games for RMI in the second half of the season. One of them was at Fleetwood in mid-January when a Hird hat-trick helped RMI to a 3-2 win. The Horwich Journal reported: 'Sections of the home support took the defeat very badly and shortly before the final whistle blew a partisan section of the crowd began to throw sods at the Horwich players and linesman. The police were called and the players escorted from the field.'

Laithwaite lost his place after being injured at Great Harwood, Bibby deputising in goal. In his place came the experienced Jock Goodwin, a Scot who had played for Wigan Borough and Barnsley and he became the regular RMI custodian. RMI also secured the services of the former Bury centre-half John Callagher who was appointed player-coach. After leaving Gigg Lane the Glaswegian, who commenced his career with the famous Renton club had played for Wolves, Wigan Borough and Norwich City.

RMI also signed Holden, a centre-forward from Westhoughton Collieries, inside-right Royle from Blackburn Rovers and James Kenyon, an outside-right who had just been released by Bolton Wanderers.

When RMI beat Atherton 10-0 to close their home programme in style they reached the milestone of one hundred league goals for the first time in the club's history. The RMI team was: Goodwin; Bibby, Wright; Embrey, Sedgwick, Gradwell; Kenyon, Royle, Keetley, Mather, Yates.

Vice-chairman Sam Heath presided over what was described as the club's 25th AGM at the end of May 1927. He stated that it had been a fairly successful season considering a heavy injury-list with as many as five senior players unavailable at any one time. But he already had eleven players signed-on for next season which was unheard of for so early in the summer. Harry Hird, though, was placed on the transfer list but ultimately stayed on for another season.

Mr Heath said he was aiming for a membership of 1,500. Gate receipts had brought in £300 and memberships £386 but the wages bill was £533 and a loss of £195 had been made on the season. The average home 'gate' during the campaign was 1,221. Mr GN Shawcross was the Club President, Mr D Gibson the chairman and Mr W Carter the secretary.

Colne Town left the Combination at the end of the season and Burscough Rangers replaced them for the 1927-28 campaign. It was another season noteworthy for goals, 1,826 being scored at an average over just over 4.8 per game. Runners-up the previous season, Chorley emerged from the pack to become the champions with a four points-margin over Lancaster Town and RMI with fourth-placed Accrington Stanley Reserves also in contention for the title until the last week of the campaign. Fleetwood resigned on 6 February due to financial difficulties and Prescot of the Liverpool County Combination took over their fixtures.

RMI, who lost out on runners-up spot on goals difference, scored 111 goals and conceded 61 as they recorded their best statistics to date in the Combination. RMI won 23 games and drew a further nine, losing just six times. They began the season with a 2-2 draw at Southport Reserves when the side was: Goodwin; Wright, Bibby; Embrey, Sedgwick, Gradwell; Kenyon, Hird, Pemberton, Mather, Yates. Pemberton, a former Heywood and Bury 'A' player was actually preferred to Keetley for the opening game but Keetley soon regained his place in the side. The popular Billy Goodlad was transferred to Rossendale United after failing to agree terms but John Young was signed from Wigan Borough.

At Grundy Hill RMI were virtually invincible with 16 wins and two draws in 19 games. Their sole home league defeat was reserved for the penultimate league game of the season when Chorley won 1-0 before a new Grundy Hill record crowd of 6,500 (£132) on 28 April 1928. For the second time in seven years the RMI supporters had to endure the sight of their closest rivals being presented with the Combination trophy on the Grundy Hill pitch.

Mather, Hird and Keetley formed a lethal combination up front for RMI as the goals flowed. Mather scored five as an under-strength Chorley side was vanquished 8-1 in a Combination Cup-tie and Keetley followed suit with a nap hand in the 6-1 demolition of Barnoldswick Town in the Lancashire Junior Cup.

RMI looked set for a title bid after a fine run of form at the turn of the year as they won eleven and drew five league games during an unbeaten 16-match run. At this stage, with eleven games to play they were second in the table, one point behind Chorley. During this sequence they drew 3-3 at Rossendale United in February but Keetley missed most of the first-half as he was suffering from cold and exposure and RMI had to play with ten men. When Lyons was injured RMI signed Joe Walmsley, the former Darwen centre-half as cover.

But then the wheels came off as RMI unaccountably suffered a shattering 7-1 defeat at Lancaster Town. Though they recovered to beat the reserve sides of Southport and Preston North End in successive games, 4-0 and 5-0 respectively they then lost by a single goal at Chorley in their next away game before a crowd of 7,000 that included an estimated two thousand RMI supporters. A run of two wins and two draws then set up the virtual title decider against Chorley. In what was described as a gruelling but one of the most thrilling games ever staged at Grundy Hill Chorley snatched a late victory when Ball's header was misjudged by Goodwin in the RMI goal with just ten minutes remaining. The RMI side was: Goodwin; Bibby, Gradwell; Embrey, Walmsley, Lyons; Howarth, Hird, Keetley, Mather, Yates.

The season ended disappointingly, however, as a weary RMI side, playing their fifth game in eight days went down 2-0 at Barnoldswick Town and so missed out on the runners-up spot to Lancaster Town. Lancaster had scored 148 league goals, a new Combination record but one which was soon under threat from Keetley and Co.

There was some consolation for missing out on league honours as RMI lifted the Combination Cup for the first time. After victories over Clitheroe, Chorley, Darwen and Morecambe RMI entertained Rossendale United at Grundy Hill in the final on Thursday 3 May 1928 before a crowd of 3,000. The visitors kicked uphill during the first half and the teams turned around with the score-line still blank. But the prolific Keetley then took centre-stage, converting a penalty after Mather had been fouled in the area and firing home a second with a fast and well directed shot late in the game.

The teams were: Horwich RMI: Goodwin; Bibby, Gradwell; Embrey, Sedgwick, Lyons; Parkinson, Hird, Keetley, Mather, Yates. Rossendale United: Bury; Davies, Kirkbright; Bell, Walkden, Lyons; Hall, Hurst, Williams, Toman, Kellett. The referee was L Rudd from Wigan.

After RMI's 2-0 victory TP Campbell, the President of the Lancashire Combination, presided over the presentation ceremony. Before Councillor Knowles of Darwen, the Combination treasurer, presented the cup to Harry Hird, the RMI captain, Mr Campbell remarked, amidst laughter, that 'Horwich produced good engines and also good footballers.'

The RMI officials were as follows: Chairman: D Gibson; Vice-chairman: S Heath; Hon Secretary: W Carter. Eddie Edwards, the popular trainer, was credited for introducing excellent new training methods during the season.

Brief pen pictures of the RMI players accompanied the match report. Scottish goalkeeper John (Jock) Goodwin, who played League football for Wigan Borough and Barnsley was described as 'cool', right-back Billy Bibby as a 'stout-hearted defender' and left-back Stan Gradwell as 'clever but erratic.' In the halves, Tom Embrey was 'a spoiler, afraid of nothing,' centre-half Pat Sedgwick, another former Wigan Borough player, was 'strong and a good feeder' and left-half Alf Lyons was 'young and sturdy.'

Right-winger E Parkinson was a 'strong and forceful player' and inside-right Harry Hird 'an ingenious, clever player who can dribble like Steve Bloomer and beat the best defence' while centre-forward Joe Keetley,' one of the famous goal-scoring Keetley brothers has a shot like a gun.' Inside-left Stanley Mather, described as being on the small side despite reportedly being 5ft7 was 'the hardest worker in the team' and outside-left Tom Yates 'an attractive footballer with brains not brawn.'

RMI also had a good run in the Lancashire Junior Cup reaching the semi-final before losing 3-2 at home to Rossendale United. Along the way they defeated Clitheroe, Little Lever, Breightmet United and Barnoldswick Town. They beat Little Lever 10-1 at Grundy Hill in October, Keetley and Mather each scoring hat-tricks. But RMI bowed out of the FA Cup at Lancaster Town in the second qualifying round.

Four players, Keetley (48), Mather (41), Hird (25) and Yates (23), contributed 137 of the 157 goals that RMI that scored in all games during the season.

At the AGM a bright and optimistic note was struck when it was stated that the fact RMI only used 20 players during the season spoke volumes for trainer Eddie Edwards with his attention to fitness and ability of players and the way he built-up a good team spirit. 'There was a great enthusiasm for Combination football in Horwich,' the report continued and the accounts were the best in the history of the club. At the AGM Sam Heath replaced D Gibson as chairman.

Surprisingly, especially given the glowing terms by which he was described, a free-transfer was granted to captain Harry Hird at the end of the campaign and Walmsley also left the club. William Fisher, a right-half who had played four League games for Wigan Borough was a new recruit alongside H Monks from Atherton. Tom Embrey had been awarded a benefit game and an RMI Select XI played a Combination Select XI at Grundy Hill on Boxing Day, 1927.

INTERNATIONALS AND GOAL RECORDS

There was a proud moment for RMI supporters during May 1928 when Jack Bruton made his England debut, appearing in the 5-1 win over France at the Stade Olympique, Colombes and 3-1 win over Belgium two days later at the Olympic Stadium, Brussels. The following year Bruton made his third and final England appearance against Scotland at Hampden Park when the home side won by the only goal.

During the summer of 1928 ground improvements continued at Grundy Hill. Terracing behind the goal at the Grundy Hill end was completed and the grandstand re-painted. 'The ground looks a picture and will comfortably hold 10,000 spectators should the occasion arise,' was the view of the Horwich Journal. Though that capacity was not tested big crowds did flock to the ground as an eventful and memorable season unfolded. There was another newcomer for the 1928-29 campaign with Manchester Central, based at Belle Vue greyhound stadium, replacing Hindley Green Athletic.

Again RMI were locked in a championship challenge with Chorley and again the Magpies came out on top. Chorley's winning margin was an impressive eleven points but this time RMI secured second place and set a new Combination record by scoring 152 league goals during the season in 38 games. The previous record was set by Lancaster Town who scored 148 in the 1927-28 season. RMI did, though, concede 87 goals. Preston North End 'A', who had played their home games at Leyland left the Combination after this season and were replaced by Lytham.

Keetley and Mather staged their own battle to be RMI's top goal-scorer in a remarkable campaign. Eventually the honour fell to Keetley, but it was a close-run thing; he notched 48 league goals to Mather's 44. In cup games Keetley scored 11 to take his seasonal tally to 59 while Mather added four to make it 48 for the campaign. But Fred Marquis, who scored 55 league goals in 34 games for Lancaster in their record-breaking season at least saw his individual Combination record remain intact under the double challenge from the RMI duo. Keetley reached 50 goals for the season during the 7-0 home win over Dick, Kerr's at Grundy Hill in March. 'He is sometimes criticised but is the most prolific goal scorer RMI have ever had,' the Horwich Journal stated. Yates (16), Monks (15) and Dewsnap (12) also were among the goals.

Looking back on the season and the results the high-scoring was remarkable and the Grundy Hill devotees have never seen anything like it, before or since. In early season Keetley scored four goals against Southport Reserves but still finished on the losing side as RMI went down 5-4. He scored five in a 6-2 home win over Clitheroe and followed that up with a hat-trick in the next match, an 8-2 victory at Atherton. Just before Christmas, RMI hammered Barnoldswick 12-1 at Grundy Hill, Mather scoring six of the goals and Keetley contenting himself to a hat-trick.

The pair continued their scoring feats to the end of the season, combining for seven of the goals in a 10-0 home win over Preston North End 'A' on Good Friday when Mather scored four goals and Keetley three. But other players were also on the mark, a newcomer by the name of Govan, a Chorley youngster who had been playing for Adlington scoring four times in a 5-3 win over Bacup Borough before disappearing from the scene. Late in the season Monks made his mark scoring a hat-trick in the 9-2 home win over Great Harwood.

But RMI were almost as capable of conceding goals as scoring them as evidenced by a late season 9-0 humiliation at Dick, Kerr's. They also lost 6-1 at Rossendale United and 7-3 at Prescot Cables. In the final game of a long season Keetley and Mather were eclipsed by Milner, who helped himself to three goals in the 4-2 home win over Burscough. For the last game of the season the RMI team was: Stanley; Cuerden, Gradwell; Sedgwick, Broadhead, Newton; Greenhalgh, Milner, Keetley, Mather, Yates.

The season was also noteworthy for RMI reaching the first round proper of the FA Cup for the first time, a feat they subsequently achieved on only one more occasion whilst based at Horwich. Their FA Cup campaign began with a stirring win over Chorley, Keetley scoring the only goal before a 4,000 crowd at Grundy Hill. RMI then defeated Dick, Kerr's after a replay and beat Morecambe 3-1 before a crowd of 2,500 at Grundy Hill. In the fourth qualifying round RMI played Workington for the first time, earning a 2-2 draw away from home before winning the replay the following Wednesday afternoon in front of a 2,000 crowd by 3-0.

RMI's first round FA Cup opponents were Scarborough, a professional outfit playing in the Midland League and the tie was played at Grundy Hill on Saturday 24 November 1928. The RMI side was: Goodwin; Bibby, Gradwell; Embrey, Broadhead, Lyons; Dewsnap, Newton, Keetley, Mather, Yates. The visitors were represented by: Hopkins; Armitage, Wallis; Marskill, Ridge, Gilsthorpe; Wainwright, Greatorex, Clayson, Jukes, Harron.

The game was marred by a strong cross-wind and Scarborough appeared to have adopted the better tactics in a typically hard-fought cup-tie. They took the lead on the half-hour when Wainwright converted a penalty after Gradwell brought down Clayson. But five minutes before half-time Keetley equalised to send in the teams at the interval on level terms. Clayson, however, notched what proved to be the winning goal three minutes after the resumption.

Scarborough suffered a scare midway through the second half when their goalkeeper, Hopkins, was injured and had to leave the field. Wainwright deputised and Scarborough packed their defence to close out the game as for once RMI seldom looked like scoring.

On the down side RMI were thrown out of the Lancashire Junior Cup for fielding an ineligible player, R Halliwell, in the victory over Lancaster Town, a decision that was described as affecting the morale of the side.

There sad news with the death announced of former chairman Mr D Gibson in December 1928 and the players wore black armbands as a sign of respect in the home game against Clitheroe.

In February 1929 Billy Bibby, a good servant for RMI over five seasons decided to hang up his boots. He signed off in style as RMI defeated Great Harwood 9-2 in his final match. Bibby had decided to get married and take over the running of a public house in Bury. Goalkeeper 'Jock' Goodwin also requested a free transfer after losing his place in the first-team, initially to Duckworth then to Stanley, an acquisition from the Bolton & District League. One newcomer was centre-half Tom Nuttall from Westhoughton Central, who also played cricket for Little Lever in the Bolton League. It was a disadvantage that, due to cost-cutting measures, RMI did not operate with a reserve team and so any newcomers had to be thrown straight into first-team action.

Reflecting upon the season the Horwich Journal quite rightly stated that 'Grundy Hill has never seen so many goals before.' As well as being a powerful centre-forward equally good with both feet Keetley was also commended for his scheming play. Though on the small side Mather was a remarkably gifted player and his combination with Yates was a feature of RMI's attacking play at this time. The acquisition of Ted Broadhead was also considered important. The tall, fair-haired half-back had previously been a key figure in the Nelson side that lifted the Third Division North championship in 1923. At the end of the season free transfers were given to Goodwin, Lyons, Monks and Dewsnap.

Bolton Wanderers, meanwhile, lifted the FA Cup at Wembley Stadium for the third time in the decade after a 2-0 victory over Portsmouth before a crowd of 92,576.

In 1929-30 RMI fell away and trailed in seventh as Lancaster Town beat Manchester Central to the title by a single point. Lancaster scored 138 goals during the season with RMI again topping the century mark for a fourth successive season with 112. The RMI team for the opening game of the season had several newcomers and lined-up as follows: Stanley; Cuerden, Smith; Sedgwick, Broadhead, Newton; Greenhalgh, Milner, Keetley, Mather, Yates. Later, Jack Davies, described as a class goalkeeper, returned to the club. He had played league football for Bury and Swansea Town. Right-back Frank Thompson, formerly with Manchester City, Swindon Town and Halifax Town, was another new recruit. Cuerden was a signing from local football who soon settled into the first-team.

Keetley showed he had spent the summer sharpening his skills by scoring seven times in the club's annual pre-season trial match for the 'Stripes' against the 'Reds.' And in the early season games Keetley and Mather were among the goals in a series of high-scoring encounters. Mather scored successive hat-tricks against Atherton and Morecambe before eclipsing those feats with five goals in a 12-0 home win over Nelson on 14 September 1929. Keetley also scored five times in this game with Milner accounting for the other two goals.

It was no surprise that Mather's consistent goal-scoring feats should attract attention from Football League clubs. Several approaches were made, notably one by Bolton Wanderers during October 1929. RMI actually agreed terms for Mather's transfer to Burnden Park, but the player then turned down the move, stating he preferred to remain at Grundy Hill. Then aged 23 and a product of junior football he was described as the idol of the Horwich supporters who received the news with delight. Meanwhile, in December 1929 former RMI winger Jack Bruton was transferred from Burnley to Blackburn Rovers for £6,500, then the highest sum Rovers had paid for a player.

Despite suffering a disappointing FA Cup exit, RMI going down 5-3 at Lancaster in a second qualifying round replay after at one stage leading 3-0, the team's league form was good until after Christmas. RMI also enjoyed a successful run in the Lancashire Junior Cup and accounted for Breightmet United, Lancaster and Ashton National on their way to the final.

The final was staged at Deepdale on Saturday 11 January 1930 when RMI defeated Darwen 2-0. Keetley was again the hero, scoring both goals. The game had stirred up what was described as 'cup fever' in the workshops and factories of Horwich and special trains were laid on for the short journey to Preston, but wintry weather reduced the attendance below expectations and a gate of 2,500 was recorded.

The game was married by a snow-covered pitch described as treacherous in parts but RMI adapted far better to the conditions. The teams lined-up as follows: RMI: Davies; Cuerden, Gradwell; Sedgwick, Broadhead (capt), Newton; Blackburn, Milner, Keetley,

Mather, Yates. Darwen: Mulkeen; Dawson, Jenkinson; Slater, Williamson, Quigley; Robinson, Prest, Brogden, Clemmett, Wilson. Mr AR Atkinson of Blackpool was the referee.

There was a fierce snow-storm just before kick-off and the lines were swept to enable the game to proceed. With many players slipping on the treacherous ground chances were at a premium and Prest went closest for Darwen, hitting the bar just before half-time. Davies made several fine saves in the RMI goal to keep the score-sheet blank.

RMI took the lead seven minutes after the resumption when Mather and Yates schemed an opening for Keetley to stab the ball past Mulkeen. Keetley's second goal came twelve minutes from time after he diverted a Yates cross into the net. It had been a hard-fought game in difficult conditions but RMI's victory was well-deserved. The final was especially memorable for RMI winger Sid Blackburn, a product of the Horwich Sunday School League. He had been called-up for his first-team debut on the morning of the game after Tommy Embrey was indisposed. As well as the usual praise bestowed upon the remarkable Keetley the contributions of captain Broadhead and popular trainer Eddie Edwards were highlighted. 'Horwich cannot afford to splash money about,' the Journal reported. 'They have to rely on local lads and Eddie Edwards has done a fine job.' The RMI mascot was seven-years-old Tommy Sedgwick.

At the final whistle, the Horwich Journal reported that there was a 'rousing cheer, rattles and hooters buzzed and Horwich supporters threw their caps in delight. Spectators rushed to the entrance to the dressing rooms and slapped the players heartily on the back as, weary and mud-stained they made their way back off the field.'

Mr CE Sutcliffe, President of the Lancashire FA presented the cup to Ted Broadhead, the RMI captain. The Horwich players travelled back home by road and received a heroes' welcome as they passed through the streets on their way to the Bridge Hotel, where high tea was served followed by a concert.

RMI continued their winning ways by defeating Wigan Borough Reserves 4-3 at Springfield Park the following Saturday and at this stage had won 13 and drawn three of their 18 league games and looked set for another title challenge.

But RMI's form then unaccountably dipped and in a disastrous run they won just one and lost eight of their next nine league games. Several newcomers were introduced into what had been a settled team with Spencer, Topping, Abbott, Cox and Skiffington (described as a Glasgow youth) all getting their chances. RMI also signed Cunliffe, the cousin of the Blackburn Rovers player Arthur Cunliffe, a native of Blackrod who had played for Chorley. Arthur Cunliffe, who won two England caps, was the first player from Blackrod to represent his country and later played for Aston Villa, Middlesbrough, Burnley, Hull City and Rochdale. The outside-left made 299 league appearances and scored 88 goals. Much later another Blackrod resident, Frank Wignall would be making his name with RMI before going on to play for England.

Though RMI regained their form late in the season, embarking on a nine-match unbeaten run that included some high-scoring wins, seventh place was considered to be disappointing after a season that had promised so much.

During the season RMI scored 131 goals in league and cup games, Keetley leading the way with a total of 38, which included 29 in the Combination. Mather was the leading league scorer with 32 and added two goals in cup football. H Milner hit 17 goals, Yates

13 and young Blackburn eight in only 12 appearances.

On 19 April 1930 there was the official opening of the new RMI tennis courts, RMI marking the occasion with a 2-1 home win over Chorley. Meanwhile the season ended with what was becoming a familiar sight at Grundy Hill, a championship-winning team celebrating their success. Lancaster Town secured the Lancashire Combination championship by virtue of their 2-0 victory over RMI in the final game of the campaign, two first half goals steadying the nerves of the visitors.

Reviewing the season the Horwich Journal stated that injuries to key players and an unfortunate alignment of fixtures had accounted for the downturn in form. During February and March seven out of eight league fixtures were away from home and RMI had lost them all. They also bade farewell to the popular Broadhead who joined Morecambe. 'He will be difficult to replace,' the Horwich Journal predicted.

Aside from Keetley and Mather several other players had made their mark. Sedgwick had played in every match at either full-back or half-back while Yates and 'keeper Davies had each missed just one game apiece. In all 31 players had been used and Thompson, Spencer, Moss and Jackson left the club at the season's end.

Atherton left the Combination during the following season, 1930-31 and Rochdale Reserves took over their fixtures. RMI finished fifth, six points behind Darwen, the champions, scoring 119 goals but conceding 73. The season proved to be the last one for many years where RMI really challenged for the title.

Once again RMI's form during the first half of the season was excellent with Keetley and Mather showing no signs of losing their goal-scoring options. To further boost the club's enviable striking powers, 37-year-old Frank Roberts was recruited from Manchester Central. An England international who won four caps Sandbach born Roberts had enjoyed a long and successful career with Bolton Wanderers and Manchester City. He joined Bolton from Crewe in 1914 and went on to score 80 goals in 168 league and cup games despite missing four seasons because of the war where he served in the North Lancashire Regiment.

In the 1920-21 season Roberts formed a fruitful partnership with Joe Smith, the pair accounting for 62 goals as Wanderers finished third in the first division, equalling the club's highest-ever position. Roberts hit 24 league goals and Smith 38 but he left the club under something of a cloud, after insisting on taking over the management of licensed premises, which was against club rules. City paid £3,400 for his services in October 1922 and Roberts went on to reward the outlay by scoring 130 goals in 237 league and cup games including an FA Cup Final appearance against his former club in 1926 when his successor at Burnden Park, David Jack, scored the only goal.

The season began well with RMI 2-1 victors at Roberts' old club Manchester Central to record their first win at Belle Vue. Keetley retained his centre forward spot and with Roberts (the new club captain) and Mather at inside-forward and the experienced Yates at outside-left, RMI boasted an embarrassment of riches indeed. The RMI team was: Davies; Shorrocks, Gradwell; Sedgwick, Crompton, Howarth; Bunyan, Roberts, Keetley, Mather, Yates. Harry Howarth was signed from Accrington Stanley and Farnworth born Norman Crompton was a former Oldham Athletic and Queen's Park Rangers centre-half who was signed from Dartford.

Roberts scored a hat-trick on his home debut, Keetley following suit as Atherton were hammered 6-2 and three days later Nelson were beaten 8-1 at Grundy Hill, Keetley plundering four goals and Roberts and Mather each finding the net twice. Before September was over further high-scoring wins were achieved against Barnoldswick (5-0), Lytham (6-3) and Atherton (10-0), the latter being RMI's record away victory. In that game Mather scored four, Roberts three, Keetley two with Sedgwick also on the mark.

Though old foes Lancaster Town accounted for RMI at the third qualifying round stage of the FA Cup, the club enjoyed another good run in the Lancashire Junior Cup. They beat both Darwen and Prescot before losing 3-0 at Clitheroe in the semi-final just before Christmas. The quarter-final tie against Prescot was one of the most remarkable games ever played at Grundy Hill. After a 1-1 draw at Hope Street on the Saturday the teams replayed at Horwich the following Monday afternoon. With 75 minutes played Prescot were leading 6-2 but RMI fought back to level at 6-6 and then added two further goals in extra-time to record a memorable 8-6 victory, Keetley leading the way with a hat-trick and Mather and Roberts inevitably also on the mark.

But despite the regular marksmanship from their deadly trio RMI were unable to string together a consistent run in the league with their away form a cause for concern. Given the talent at their disposal their final placing was something of a disappointment with ten of their 12 league defeats coming on their travels.

In the league Keetley again led the way with 33 goals in 35 games. Roberts finished just one behind with 32 in 37 and Mather bagged 19 in 32. Keetley added 12 cup-tie goals to take his tally for the season to 45, Roberts scored five to make it 37 in his debut season while a further three from Mather saw him end the season on 22. In all RMI scored 148 goals in league cup, 104 of them contributed by the trio. It was no wonder that RMI were the highest-scoring team in the Combination.

THE END OF THE GOLDEN AGE

But there was a huge shock for the RMI faithful when the club's retained list was announced. Remarkably after five seasons during which he scored a total of 230 goals in league and cup Keetley was among those released. Sweeping changes were made and among the other players released were several who had contributed hugely to what, in retrospect, was a golden age of football at Grundy Hill. Yates, Davies, Crompton and Marston were also on the wait out of the club.

Earlier in the season Keetley had turned down a move to Chorley to remain at Grundy Hill but as the industrial recession continued to bite he lost his job at the Loco Works and this was a contributory factor in him moving on. He returned to haunt RMI in the future, as many suspected he would and was remembered as the most consistent and prolific goalscorer ever to play for the club.

The recession was such that locomotive building was suspended at the Loco Works and work was confined to locomotive repairs. But the Works also diversified and completed a batch of tank engines. In 1932 the Newton Heath Carriage Sheds were closed down and all stock from the Lancashire area now came to Horwich for repair.

Yates played some sparkling games and the former schoolboy international was regarded as one of the cleverest and fastest wing-men in the Lancashire Combination. Goalkeeper Davies had been kept out of the side by the consistent form of Horace Brooks while Tommy Embrey was a staunch and consistent player who rendered the club yeoman service. During the season RMI tried nine different players at left-back, six at right-back and six at outside-right.

Chairman Sam Heath presided at the club AGM and revealed that the club's financial position was such they could still not operate with a reserve team. He thanked the institute committee for their help with the ground but stated that from now on the football club would have to find their own expenses in this regard. The finish to the season, when RMI lost five of their last ten games had been disappointing especially as extra expense on players had been made in an attempt to win the league. The club had started the year with a balance of £219 and ended it with just £69 in hand as players' wages increased by £180 to £639 during the season. On top of that RMI had paid out £117 for a new grandstand.

Before the 1931-32 season got underway Manchester Central moved to the Cheshire County League and Rochdale Reserves also resigned. They were replaced by Barrow Reserves and Fleetwood. Having failed to gain re-election to the Football League, Nelson's first team played in the Combination in place of their reserve side. In a dramatic reversal of fortunes, RMI slipped from fifth to seventeen, with just Morecambe and Accrington Stanley Reserves below them in the table. Wigan Borough Reserves resigned in October 1931 after the senior team also folded and ended their short-lived stay in the Football League. A new club, Wigan Athletic, was formed in 1932 and soon were to renew the town's rivalry with Horwich. Darwen, champions for a second season in a row, reached the third round of the FA Cup but lost 11-1 at Football League champions Arsenal.

Though RMI's season had begun with a 2-0 defeat at Nelson, former Horwich player Milner being among the scorers, normal service seemed to have been resumed as Accrington Stanley Reserves and Fleetwood were routed 10-1 and 6-2 respectively at

Grundy Hill. Briefly, O'Rourke, an inside-right recruited from Farnworth promised to fill Keetley's boots, scoring six goals on his home debut against Stanley and following up with another goal against Fleetwood.

With so many changes to the side after the financial pruning instigated by chairman Heath the side for the opening match contained several new faces and read as follows: Brooks; Abbott, Sedgwick; Shuttleworth, Fisher, Jones; Roberts, O'Rourke, Whitfield, Mather, Taylor.

Among the newcomers were Jimmy Shuttleworth, a former Wigan Borough and Atherton player, Little Lever cricketer Harry Taylor from Nelson, former Preston North End centre-half Ellis Fisher from Lancaster Town (who replaced Crompton who had signed for Darwen), H Crawshaw from Newton Heath LMS, centre-forward H Greenwood from Horwich St Matthews' and left-back Cordingley from Newton-le-Willows. Howarth later re-signed for the club after retiring due to business reasons. Goalkeeper Brooks distinguished himself by saving two penalties in the game at Barnoldswick in September but RMI still lost 3-1.

The much changed side struggled for form and early exits were made from the cup competitions as Chorley won by a single goal in the FA Cup at Grundy Hill and Darwen handed out a demoralising 9-0 thrashing in the Lancashire Junior Cup, Reg Preedy scoring six goals. When Morecambe visited Grundy Hill in September former RMI favourite Stan Gradwell received a warm welcome as he appeared in the visitors' ranks. But one familiar face did return with the popular Harry Hird re-signing for the club after spells with Rossendale and Burscough. Hird was seen as a replacement for the long-serving Stanley Mather who finally achieved his ambition of playing league football when he ended a long association with RMI by signing for Crewe Alexandra.

Despite Hird's return RMI slipped away badly from the standards they had set in previous campaigns. Their away form was dismal and they had just two draws to show for their travels with 20 goals scored and 71 conceded. They suffered heavy defeats at Dick, Kerr's (when Molloy scored seven goals in a 9-3 victory for the Preston based works team in the game at Ashton Park, remarkably Crawshaw scoring a hat-trick for RMI) and 8-1 at Darwen. Fisher left RMI after the Dick, Kerr's game and joined Morecambe. He later became Lancaster's groundsman for over 30 years.

The financial position worsened, a long sequence of away games in February and March adding to the problems and only RMI's reasonable home form kept them out of the re-election positions. Of the 23 points gained during the season, 21 were earned at Grundy Hill. Many new players were tried out, including the chairman's son, A Heath, who made his debut against Burscough alongside a new goalkeeper (Boardman from Skelmersdale United) on Good Friday. Remarkably this was RMI's first home game for nearly eight weeks. Crawshaw helped recruit several players from his old club including left-back Hutton and centre-half Hulme. One bright spot was the award of a benefit to the long-serving Sedgwick who had completed eight seasons with RMI.

It seemed strange to see RMI in such a lowly league position but the reasons were well-known around the town. The committee had released many old players in the hope that new blood would re-invigorate the side but the strategy had been far from a success. As if to ram home the point old favourite Keetley, now with Lancaster, showed that his scoring prowess was far from diminished. He scored twice against his former club in a 3-0 victory at the end of March and added a hat-trick as Lancaster closed a miserable Grundy Hill season with a 4-1 win at the end of April. 'It was one of the blackest seasons in RMI's history,' commented the Buff, the popular Saturday evening sports newspaper produced by the Bolton Evening News.

RMI scored 73 goals in all games during the season compared to 149 in the previous season. Crawshaw was top-scorer with 21 goals, a fine effort in his debut season, and Roberts scored 14. O'Rourke scored eight goals early in the season and Greenwood five (including four in his first two games) before both players faded from the scene.

The club's AGM revealed that gates declined from £450 to £374 and that despite cutting costs a loss of £40 was made on the season. The balance in hand was a precarious £27. Gates had suffered due to loss of membership, the rising toll of unemployment in the town and the general downturn in trade. Mr Heath stated that RMI were far from being the only club in the Combination to suffer in this way but worryingly membership was down to between 300 and 400, when RMI needed 800 members to compete at this level of football.

Rochdale Reserves were re-admitted for the following season, 1932-33 and RMI recovered to finish seventh, again topping a century of goals for the sixth time in seven seasons. Chorley ended Darwen's stranglehold on the title, finishing nine points ahead of runners-up Prescot Cables.

It was a remarkable revival, especially as RMI twice suffered 5-1 defeats in the opening week of the season, at Fleetwood and at home to Chorley. In between those games they did, however, break a long away 'duck' by winning 3-0 at Dick, Kerr's with goals by Masters, Yates and Hurst. It was RMI's first away win in the league since a 7-0 win at Rossendale United in April 1931.

Roberts continued to find the net with regularity and Dick Iddon, a well-travelled centre-forward and Hurst, an inside-left, both became regular marksmen while old crowd favourite Tom Yates made a welcome return. Several players were recruited from Manchester Central including Readett and Casey while the Makinson brothers made their mark, one in goal, the other as a versatile outfield player who scored a hat-trick in the 6-3 win at Lytham in mid-September. The side for the opening game was: N Makinson; Topping, Readett; Shuttleworth, Thornborough, J Makinson; Masters, Hodgkiss, Iddon, Hurst, Yates.

Iddon, who had played two games for Manchester United earlier in his career and later turned out in the league for New Brighton, scored ten goals in October alone, though had the misfortune to see his hat-trick against Barnoldswick expunged from the records. RMI were leading 4-1 after 56 minutes when the game was abandoned due to water-logging. Hurst scored four goals in a 6-1 home win over Burscough and Iddon followed suit in a 6-2 win at Great Harwood.

One prominent recruit was the experienced Bolton-born Eli Thornborough who had twice been twelfth man for Bolton Wanderers in their FA Cup triumphs of 1926 and 1929 and had also played League football for Preston North End. But the centre-half was not a lucky cup omen, certainly as far as RMI were concerned. Despite a battling display RMI were knocked out of the competition when old foes Chorley won what was described as a 'fierce match' by a single goal before a 4,000 crowd at Grundy Hill in mid-October. Despite that RMI's league form was pleasing and in early November, after a 1-0 home win over Fleetwood they were second in the Combination.

Such heady form could not be maintained but RMI seemed back to where they had recently been as an entertaining side with the ability to score goals. Among the newcomers right-back Topping was creating a good impression and he was invited for trials with Manchester United. A new goalkeeper, Turner from Coppull was tried out but a sequence of six defeats in eight games either side of Christmas saw RMI fall off the pace.

Despite the improved results 'gates' were far from satisfactory and in January 1933 chairman Sam Heath stated that a decision would shortly be taken by the committee over whether to continue playing in the Combination next season. The attendances over the next few games would largely determine the decision and as a financial necessity every professional was placed on the transfer list. No sooner had that move been made than Thornborough left for Chorley and Iddon was transferred to Altrincham. Despite their departures treasurer Jack Edwards stated that the financial position was still serious and an appeal was made to Horwich Town Council for financial assistance.

Crawshaw, who had unluckily lost his place at the start of the season, came back into the side after Iddon left and regularly found the net while several of what was by necessity and young and inexperienced team were making the most of their opportunities at first-team level. Coppull born right-winger Arthur Masters, described as 'fast and clever if on the small side' was transferred to Nottingham Forest. He went to make 109 league appearances for Forest, scoring 24 goals and then scored 13 goals in 66 league starts for Port Vale.

In March 1933 Frank Roberts decided to retire from the game after a serious illness. He had played what was described as the 'sunset' of his illustrious career at Horwich and was popular among players and supporters alike. 'Upon his arrival from Manchester Central he put his heart and soul into the game,' the Horwich Journal added.

Grundy Hill staged the final of the LMS Railway Cup on 18 March 1933 when Carlisle played Broad Street, London.

In the closing weeks of the season RMI's young side played some enterprising football and finished in some style, enjoying one run of seven wins in eight games and then ending with three successive league wins. Crawshaw scored a hat-trick as RMI beat Bacup Borough 6-0 in the final game of the season. Cookson, a St Catherine's Horwich Sunday School League player, was drafted in for his first-team debut for the trip to Barrow on Easter Monday. At the age of 15 he was thought to be the youngest player ever to represent RMI.

RMI also played Chorley at Victory Park in the Rawcliffe Hospital Cup, a fund-raising initiative for worthy local causes. The game ended score-less and so the Rawcliffe Cup, a handsome silver trophy was shared six months apiece by the two rivals.

TRYING TIMES

Though the season ended with RMI left with a balance of just £9 chairman Sam Heath said the season had gone far better than many imagined and after due consideration it had been decided to carry on playing in the Combination. It had been a trying season in many regards but the club had emerged stronger and many young players had been introduced into the team to good effect. RMI's away form had also improved markedly with nine wins on their travels, compared to 12 at home. Mr Heath had pleasure in retaining all 23 players who finished the campaign. Westhoughton born Harold Cowburn had shown his commitment to the club, playing in the away game at Lancaster on the afternoon of 8 April despite getting married in the morning.

Despite his transfer Iddon finished the season as top scorer with 22 goals, Billy Hurst scored 18 and Yates and Crawshaw 14 apiece. Roberts contributed nine before his retirement.

In the summer of 1933 Prescot left to join the Cheshire County League and Barnoldswick Town were not re-elected. Leyland Motors and Northern Nomads (who were then based at Patricroft, near Eccles) replaced them. RMI slipped to 16th place in 1933-34, gaining 30 points from their 38 league games. They finished ahead of only Leyland Motors, Morecambe, Northern Nomads and Barnoldswick Town (who came back into the league, taking over the fixtures of Burscough Rangers, who resigned after four matches). Chorley again finished champions.

During the summer months unemployed members of the committee worked on the ground and a recruiting drive was launched in an attempt to increase membership of the club. RMI opened their campaign with a 5-2 home win over Darwen when the following side was on duty: Turner; Pendlebury, Kane; Shuttleworth, Hulme, Phythian; Brindle, Cowburn, Cookson, Hurst, Yates. Old-timer Yates showed he was still a force at this level, scoring a hat-trick and then netting the only goal as RMI won at Lytham.

But early season optimism faded as RMI lost eleven games in succession in the autumn, scoring 17 goals and conceding 45. The sequence included an FA Cup exit at the hands of newly-formed Wigan Athletic. Some consolation from the 3-0 home defeat was RMI's share of a bumper 4,000 'gate' proving that despite several failed ventures Wigan remained a popular attraction and that the town had a support base that would ultimately help them rise back up through the ranks again.

The RMI committee reacted to the long losing run with sweeping changes and the gloom was finally lifted in convincing style with a 5-1 home win over Barrow Reserves in mid November, newcomer Frank Shepherd scoring twice. Harry Tordoff, a former Nelson and Sheffield United centre-half proved a useful recruit. Tordoff had joined the Bramall Lane outfit as the makeweight in a deal also involving the Nelson full-back Harry Hooper. Meanwhile, Blackrod born Jimmy Cunliffe was now playing regular first division football for Everton, playing alongside the legendary Dixie Dean. The inside-right went on to score 73 goals in 174 appearances for the Toffees after signing from Adlington and giving up his job as a plater. He won one England cap against Belgium. Cunliffe's career was seriously curtailed by the outbreak of war though he did briefly re-appear in league football with Rochdale afterwards.

Results gradually improved though there were setbacks along the way, notably a 5-0 home defeat at the hands of Chorley just before Christmas and three heavy defeats at

Darwen (5-1 in the league, 6-0 in the Combination Cup and 5-0 in the Lancashire Junior Cup).

But Yates scored his second hat-trick of the season, including two penalties in a 3-0 win over Southport Reserves on Boxing Day to end a run of poor away form and the New Year saw RMI's forward line regularly among the goals. Shepherd followed suit in a 6-3 win over Lytham. RMI handed out a 6-2 thrashing to Morecambe a week later and then defeated Nelson 7-0 in the Lancashire Junior Cup to make it 19 goals in three games. Bibby, described as a 'centre-forward of bustle and energy' scored five goals. Meanwhile at the other end of the age scale former RMI favourite Jimmy Higham was reported to still be playing regularly for Horwich Co-Op in the local leagues at the age of 40. Yates finished the season with 23 goals while Bibby scored 17 and Frank Shepherd 13. Skiffington, signed from Lytham, scored seven.

The RMI side that closed the season was: Monton; Sharratt, Stubbs; Shuttleworth, Phythian, Ince; Waters, Shepherd, Bibby, Yates, Sleaford.

Despite the entertaining football on offer the response from the Horwich public was disappointing. When RMI resumed their high-scoring vein with a 6-2 home win over Great Harwood in March the 'gate' was only £6. 'All that is needed is for increased support from the town and the club's financial worries would be reduced,' the Horwich Journal stated.

Accounts discussed at the 1934 AGM revealed that total income had fallen from £1,046 in the previous season to £782 with gate receipts down £107 to £261. But the wage bill had been cut by half and at £166 was thought to be the lowest in the Combination. The heavy falling-off in gates, though, remained a huge concern for the committee.

There was sad news during the summer when the hugely popular Stanley Mather announced his retirement from playing due to a long-standing knee injury. Mather tried his luck in league football with Crewe perhaps too late and a total of 13 league appearances represented a scant return for someone of his talent. He must have thought that things may have turned out differently had he accepted the overtures of Bolton Wanderers all those years ago. The Horwich Journal reporter paid Mather a fulsome tribute: 'A smart, wholehearted player with good ball control, his Grundy Hill exploits with Joe Keetley and Tom Yates will never be forgotten.'

In 1934-35 a mid-table position of tenth was attained when Lancaster Town were champions ahead of Fleetwood, Chorley and Clitheroe. Barnoldswick Town had again failed in their re-election bid, being replaced by the reserve team of New Brighton.

RMI began well with a 4-0 home win over New Brighton Reserves, Bibby scoring twice and defeated the New Brighton First XI as RMI made their debut in the Lancashire Senior Cup. Their team for the opening match was as follows: Turner; Johnson, Stubbs; Shuttleworth, Gore, Phythian; Waters, Young, Bibby, Hitchen, Yates.

Among the newcomers was Tom Gore, an experienced centre-half from Margate. He had previously played for Bolton Wanderers, Barrow and Connah's Quay after commencing his career with Horwich. Forward Jerry Young, who played cricket for Farnworth in the Bolton League joined RMI from Morecambe.

Yates again continued his scoring form and in one glorious sequence around Christmas-time scored a total of ten goals in five consecutive games. Though RMI's away form reverted back to being dismal, with only five points gained on their travels (including wins at Clitheroe and Accrington Stanley Reserves) they were a match for most sides at Grundy Hill. Among the best performances were convincing wins over Great Harwood (5-0), Southport Reserves (9-2) and Lytham (6-1).

In the cups RMI enjoyed little fortune, being thrashed 8-1 by Preston North End in the Lancashire Senior Cup at Deepdale, bowing out of the FA Cup at Morecambe and out of the Lancashire Junior Cup at Lancaster. They also crashed 8-2 at Darwen in the league just before Christmas when Reg Preedy, who always seemed to enjoy playing against RMI, scored six goals.

Yates finished the season with 26 goals and was lent valuable support by Atherton born Herbert Butler, who joined RMI in November. The younger brother of the famous Bolton Wanderers and England outside-right Billy Butler, Herbert had been an accomplished Football League player in his own right, predominantly with Blackpool and Crystal Palace. Yates, regarded as the epitome of a sportsmanlike player, blotted his copybook by being sent-off for dissent at Lancaster and with Gregory suffering a broken leg in the cup-tie RMI finished the game with nine men.

At the 1935 AGM a now familiar battle-cry was uttered by Chairman Sam Heath, who again re-iterated that unless RMI received better support they would have to play in a lower league. An average home attendance of 500 and average home 'gates' of £10 per match were insufficient to maintain the side in the Combination. Gates for league games were £268 and for cup-ties £152 against £261 and £144 in the previous season but wages and players' expenses had risen by £91.

There was a surprise in store during the summer of 1935 when a familiar face departed RMI. Eddie Edwards, a former RMI player before the First World War, had also played for Atherton, Bacup, Haslingden, Bury, Chorley, Preston North End, Hurst and Darwen. He lived in Pioneer Street and had been RMI's trainer for the previous 12 years, reputedly never having missed a training session or a match during that period. During his time in charge RMI had won two Lancashire Junior Cups and the Combination Cup.

But Edwards was summarily replaced by another former RMI player, Charles Allison who had been the club's vice-chairman for the previous four years. Allison, who was a goalkeeper during his playing days also played for Crewe and turned out for the RMI cricket team for 15 years. The RMI cricket team, by the way, were celebrating winning the championship of the Bolton & District Association for the first and only time.

A STRUGGLE FOR SURVIVAL

The second half of the 1930s proved to be a disappointing period for RMI and one in which financial pressures and poor results were never far from the forefront. Compared to many of their rivals in the Combination RMI had slender financial resources and, inevitably, struggled to compete against the richer clubs. It was to the huge credit of the committee and the efforts of the small but loyal band of members and supporters that the club remained competitive and that Combination football was maintained at Grundy Hill up until the outbreak of war.

In 1935-36, Lancaster Town again finished as champions, one point ahead of Barrow Reserves. RMI finished 15th out of 21 clubs in the Combination, the Preston based works team Dick, Kerr's having resigned in mid-season. Two new clubs had joined the Combination, Marine from the Liverpool County Combination and a newly-founded and highly ambitious club in South Liverpool.

Alf Thompson, the former Chorley centre-forward, was recruited over the summer alongside James Wagstaffe following his release from Bolton Wanderers but Butler was surprisingly not retained. When RMI lost their opening game, 2-1 at Southport Reserves, only two members of the side, Shepherd and Richards came from outside the area.

Thompson soon made his mark, scoring four goals against Dick, Kerr's in his third game and repeating the feat in a 7-1 thrashing of Breightmet United in the FA Cup. But the highlight of the early season games was a remarkable 8-1 defeat of Chorley at Grundy Hill in late October when Thompson, Hitchen and Yates each scored twice in RMI's highest-ever score against their old rivals. The RMI team on that memorable afternoon was: Davies; Wagstaffe, Richards; Shuttleworth, Gore, Ince; Cowper, Shepherd, Thompson, Hitchen, Yates.

Though there was disappointment as RMI lost 2-1 at home to Stalybridge Celtic in the final qualifying round of the FA Cup after defeating Southport & District League side Crossens, Breightmet United, Leyland Motors and Dick, Kerr's along the way.

RMI suffered some heavy defeats, losing 8-3 at home to Fleetwood in November and 7-3 at Northern Nomads' Patricroft ground in April. They also conceded six goals in each of the away games at New Brighton Reserves, Fleetwood and Clitheroe. In the latter game, played on Easter Saturday, the Clitheroe centre-forward Chatburn scored all six of his side's goals in a 6-3 win. Chorley exacted some revenge for their thrashing at Grundy Hill by winning the return fixture 5-0 at Victory Park.

But with Thompson leading the way RMI's battling side of largely locally-based players produced some remarkable results, the highlight (apart from the win over Chorley) being a 7-1 win over then league leaders Barrow Reserves at Holker Street in mid February. Thompson scored four goals for RMI in that game. RMI also beat New Brighton Reserves 7-1 at Grundy Hill on New Year's Day.

In a review of the season the Horwich Journal reporter thought that RMI's best players were dependable goalkeeper Jack Davies, defenders Wagstaffe, Jackson and Richards, half-backs Aldred and Phythian and the forwards Thompson and Hitchen. Despite battling injuries Thompson scored 39 goals, while Joe Hitchen scored 25. The veteran Yates was credited with 17 goals before deciding to hang up his boots at the end of the season after a long and distinguished career with RMI. Shuttleworth, another long serving player also retired.

A number of local players were tried, with Schofield, Hulbert, Guest, Gerrard, Norris, Aldred, McAweeney, G Davies and Cookson thought to be the most successful. Tommy McAweeney was a former England schoolboy international who hailed from Adlington. But it was disappointing that RMI lost one of their most dependable players when Tommy Gore moved back down south having secured alternative employment. The season closed with a crushing four-goal defeat at Chorley in the Hospital Cup. Benny Jones, the former Bolton Wanderers, Swindon Town, Rochdale, Oldham Athletic and Southend United forward figured briefly in the RMI side.

The traditional venue of the LMS Works Café was used for the AGM of the football club. Concern was again expressed at the lack of public support, with gates for many home games now down to a few hundred but this was hardly considered a new phenomenon. Sam Heath, the long-serving and some would say long-suffering chairman, said that he only decided to keep the club going on the forlorn hope that one day the support might improve.

The accounts showed a deficit of £19 on the season with main sources of income being league gates (£296), cup gates (£147) and members' subscriptions (£239). The major items of expenditure were players' wages (£416) and expenses (£151). Mr Heath stated that he felt the latter two amounts were as low as possible and that the club could hardly make any further economies.

In the circumstances the team had performed creditably and Secretary Frank Mather praised the way the side fought their way through a late season back-log of fixtures, at one stage during April playing five games in seven days. Mr Heath pointed out that only six clubs had scored more goals than RMI but only three clubs had conceded more goals. An injury to Thompson during the season had been a big blow but he had still become a regular goal-scorer. Meanwhile Mr SH Whitelegg was succeeded as Club President by Mr D Williamson, the superintendent of Horwich Loco Works. Sir John Aspinall was awarded the highest honour in engineering, the James Watt Gold Medal in 1936 and on 19 January 1937 died peacefully in his sleep in his 86th year.

In 1936-37 Lytham were not re-elected and the Combination lost another club, former Football League team Nelson resigning just before the start of the campaign. Droylsden joined the Combination from the Manchester League and Prescot Cables returned from the Cheshire County League. RMI finished 15th, losing 21 of their 40 league games. In their second season in the Combination South Liverpool were champions, finishing one point ahead of Accrington Stanley Reserves but then failed in their application to join the Football League.

RMI signed Darwen's George Rowson who was the son of the Farnworth MP Guy Rowson. He went on to become a key player for several seasons. Two schoolmasters from Rivington & Blackrod Grammar school, TH Leek, a former England amateur international and Holroyd played for the club on amateur forms.

RMI gave trials to many players from the Horwich Amateur League with the best prospects reckoned to be right-half Harry Cleworth, centre-half Calderbank and Lane, an outside-left. McGuire, an inside-left said to have once played for Glasgow Celtic's 'A' team also featured. The proven players who performed consistently were Jimmy Clarke, Rowson, Bennett, Wagstaffe, Hitchen, Bullough, Richards, Marsh and Davies.

RMI had opened the season with a 2-2 home draw against Accrington Stanley Reserves when the following side was on duty: Collier; Wagstaffe, Richards; Bennett, Watson, Phythian; Bullough, Rowson, Thompson, Hitchen, Marsh. Norman Watson was a former Wigan Athletic centre-half who had played 173 league games for Leicester City.

League form was inconsistent and after wins over Rossendale United and another tie against Crossens RMI went out of the FA Cup in the third qualifying round against Morecambe. But Thompson was again amongst the goals, hitting five in a 7-1 home win over Clitheroe. He had scored 20 by the end of November after a hat-trick in a 7-4 home defeat by Marine when, to the disappointment of supporters, he was transferred to Bacup Borough. The consistent Sydney Phythian was also transferred to Tranmere Rovers, though he failed to make the first-team at Prenton Park and soon moved to Clitheroe. Bearing in mind the club's financial position RMI's officials simply could not afford to turn down the offers.

James Smith, a local league goalkeeper from Crankshaw's, came into the side before Jack Davies resumed in goal in January after recovering from a lengthy illness. Towards the end of the season Obersby, a locally produced centre-forward, and Frank Ramsbottom, recruited from a Manchester League side began to show promise. At least RMI ended the season in some style, defeating Chorley 2-0 with goals by Ramsbottom and Obersby. The kick-off had been delayed until early evening to avoid a counter-attraction with the FA Cup Final being broadcast 'live' on the radio.

RMI's only away win of the season came during a traditional end-of-season fixture pile-up. They won 3-1 at bottom-of-the-table Northern Nomads with goals by Hitchen (2) and Bullough. Problems with fitting in games before the season's close on the first Saturday in May were exasperated when successive games in mid April against Fleetwood and Rossendale United were abandoned. RMI were leading 3-1 against Fleetwood at Grundy Hill when heavy rain forced abandonment after 78 minutes. The Combination committee decided later that the result should stand. RMI were losing 3-1 at half-time in the game at Dark Lane two days later when another downpour saw the game called-off. RMI lost the replayed game 4-2 as they fitted in four games in six days.

Left-winger Marsh scored 14 goals during the season and Hitchen and Frank Schofield (a former Bolton Sunday School League player) eight apiece with Rowson marking his debut season with seven but despite his mid-season departure Thompson remained as the club's top scorer.

At the AGM on 30 June 1937 long-serving Chairman Sam Heath resigned on health grounds. He had been involved with the club for over 30 years, the last nine as chairman and was regarded as a wonderful worker for RMI. The football club had been his sole hobby and he had stood by the club throughout many difficult times.

Mr Heath said it had been a very trying year. The club had lost several of its better players due to a lack of funds and had lost £13 on the season, ending the campaign with £85 in hand. Gate receipts for league games had fallen £70 to £226 and cup receipts were down £17 to £130. But a great effort had been made to reduce expenses with wages down by £138 from £416 to £278.

RMI dropped further in 1937-38 and though never in danger of having to apply for re-election their return of 33 points from 42 league games was enough to finish only above Barrow Reserves, Great Harwood, Rochdale Reserves and Northern Nomads. Oldham Athletic Reserves had joined the Combination, taking the number of reserve sides up to six. South Liverpool scored 177 goals during a second successive championship-winning campaign, finishing ten points clear of runners-up Clitheroe. South Liverpool established a new Combination record, surpassing the 152 goals by Keetley and Co for RMI during the 1928-29 season and their new record stood until the Combination ceased after the 1981-82 season.

The RMI team for the opening game at Darwen on 28 August 1937 was: Davies; Clarke, Mort; Cleworth, Calderbank, Rowson; McDonald, Hitchen, Schofield, Ramsbottom, Adamson.

RMI had begun the season with successive 5-0 away defeats at the hands of Darwen and Great Harwood but recovered to put in some good performances at home with Ramsbottom, a scheming inside-forward with a goal-scoring ability, a key player. Ramsbottom went on to become top-scorer netting 24 goals in league and cup games during the season. Thompson also made a brief return from Bacup Borough but was troubled by injury and soon left the club again.

RMI raised hopes of an FA Cup run by giving one of their best performances in many years to defeat Morecambe 5-1 in a replayed tie at Grundy Hill following a 2-2 draw at Christie Park. But they then went down by a single goal at Leyland Motors' St George's Park ground in Chorley in the next round despite the backing of 300 supporters from Horwich.

As an indication of the problems RMI faced in competing at this level when they played South Liverpool in October at Grundy Hill the visitors' wage bill was said to be in excess of £60 per week while they were attracting an average attendance of 5,000. RMI put up a game fight but lost 6-3 and several weeks later lost 6-5 at home to Accrington Stanley Reserves. There was another remarkable game against Chorley at Grundy Hill just before Christmas when, on a pitch covered in three inches of snow the two old rivals played out a thrilling 5-5 draw.

At times RMI's defence, particularly away from home was stretched to breaking point and two days after Christmas RMI went down 11-1 at Fleetwood. Davies, the RMI goalkeeper, had to go off injured early in the game with a badly cut knee and Hitchen deputised in goal. Fleetwood took full advantage, Chadwick scoring a double hat-trick.

Among the many new players given their chance Reg Turley, a centre-forward from the Manchester area and Kelly, a winger from Newton Heath Loco impressed. The latter briefly drew comparisons with Jack Bruton while Turley bagged all four goals as RMI defeated Northern Nomads 4-3 at the end of January and a hat-trick in the 6-1 defeat of Southport Reserves a few weeks later. Veteran centre-half Joe Rodway, son of former Preston North End stalwart Tommy also featured briefly in the RMI line-up after joining from Leyland Motors while Porter, a full-back from Hollinwood United and ex-Witton Albion right-half Taylor were also recruited. Joe Rodway had been a member of Chorley's Combination-winning side of 1919-20.

But an up-and-down season ended with typical inconsistency- a fine 2-1 win at Chorley and a 7-0 midweek thrashing of New Brighton Reserves followed by a 5-0 defeat at Clitheroe. Turley hit 17 goals, Chadwick 12 and Guest and Schofield ten apiece and in all games RMI scored 114 goals. But their defence was a concern and only two clubs (Rochdale Reserves and Northern Nomads) conceded more than the 123 that RMI leaked in 42 Combination fixtures. Only seven of their 33 league points were gathered away from home.

Reviewing the season the Horwich Journal reported that the team had played 'some bright and enterprising football at times.' The committee had been striving hard to recapture former glories and gave more trials to prospective new players than ever before. Of those players Whitehead, another newcomer from the Manchester area had impressed in a position which had been a problem position for RMI since Yates's retirement. Turley was a speedy centre-forward while goalkeeper Jack Davies was solid despite a tendency to leave his line too often for the reporter's liking.

Captain Jimmy Clarke, who had played at half-back or full-back had enjoyed an outstanding campaign, while Hitchen, Rowson, Brockbank and Porter were also worthy of note in the end-of-season review.

RMI's good run in the Lancashire Junior Cup had been a highlight of the campaign. They reached the semi-final of the competition after wins over Breightmet United, Great Harwood and Bacup Borough and drew 2-2 against Lancaster City before a £50 gate at Grundy Hill before going down 5-2 in the replay the following Wednesday. Lancaster had been designated city status and the football team became Lancaster City.

An appeal was made at the AGM, held at the LMS Café at the end of June 1938, for more members to join the football club. Gates for league games mustered £263 and for cup-ties £116 but wages and travelling expenses to players had increased. H Leach had succeeded Sam Heath as the RMI chairman, the secretary was Frank Mather while D Williamson, the Loco Works superintendent was club president.

But as the Horwich Journal reported: 'Many of the club's strongest supporters, men between the ages of 20 and 30, have left the town in search of employment and no-one has taken their place. The club has limited resources and it is inadvisable of the committee to outlay money until it is seen to what extent the public are willing to support the club.'

Meanwhile, Grundy Hill had remained for several years the only ground in the Combination where neutral linesmen were not supplied. From its earliest days the RMI club had a designated club linesman who officiated at games. But following an agreement in December 1938 with the Horwich Referees' Society this practice ended and neutral linesmen were then supplied by the local society.

WAR CLOUDS LOOM

As the international situation deteriorated and war clouds loomed the 1938-39 season proved to be the last peace-time season for many years. In September 1938 the construction of air-raid shelters began in earnest around the town and gas masks were distributed among the population. RMI's players reported for training as usual during the summer months and while they were preparing for the season the committee got on with the job of making ground improvements and a refreshment hut was constructed on the popular side of the ground.

Trials were given to many local youngsters and the RMI team that began the season with a 2-1 defeat at Leyland Motors showed several changes including a new goalkeeper in Horwich-born Stanley Valentine. The team read as follows: Valentine; Clarke, Atherton; Hampton, Rooney; Rowson; Brockbank, Kay, Turley, Ramsbottom, Whitehead.

Though results often went against RMI's largely inexperienced side they did win plaudits for battling away throughout the season and producing the occasional shock result. In early September they defeated old rivals Chorley 3-0 at Grundy Hill, Brockbank, Whitehead and Turley on target but they did not win again until they beat Great Harwood 4-1 at home in late November. Ramsbottom scored a hat-trick for RMI that day. In the FA Cup RMI lost 5-4 at home to Skelmersdale United in the first qualifying round.

Not for the first time RMI's away form was poor though a sequence of reversals was briefly ended when, on Boxing Day, RMI won 6-2 at Lancaster with Dickinson (2), Ramsbottom (2), Thompson and Blackburn on the score-sheet. But Lancaster earned a speedy revenge, journeying to Grundy Hill the following day and winning by four goals to two. In the first match of the New Year RMI crashed 6-1 at Chorley, beginning the game with only ten men after Ashworth missed his train connection and worse was to follow. On 21 January 1939 RMI lost 10-3 at Clitheroe, one of their heaviest-ever defeats. On Easter Monday RMI crashed 10-2 at Bangor City with the goal-happy Welshmen having already won 5-2 at Grundy Hill on Good Friday. And late in the season RMI leaked an 8-2 defeat at Rossendale United.

South Liverpool won the Combination again, finishing one point ahead of newcomers Bangor City, who had replaced Northern Nomads. RMI endured a disastrous season, winning seven and drawing seven of 42 league games and finishing second bottom to Droylsden with a meagre points-return of 21. They conceded 143 goals during the campaign- a new club record of an unwelcome kind.

South Liverpool's fixture pile-up in the last few weeks of the season left them sending a reserve team to Grundy Hill to fulfil a league fixture on 3 May 1939. Two days previously South Liverpool had defeated Prescot Cables to win the Combination Cup, followed by a league win over Bacup Borough to make sure of the title the day afterwards. Without the benefit of this information RMI's subsequent 4-0 victory looks highly impressive in the record books especially as South Liverpool defeated Cardiff City to lift the Welsh Cup the following evening. For RMI Ramsbottom, Berry, Hitchen and Hurst scored the goals. Berry was described as being RMI's fifth different centre-forward in the space of as many games. Meanwhile the former RMI centre-forward Clifford Chatburn scored hat-tricks both home and away for Darwen against his old club.

In their last match of the season Great Harwood defeated Morecambe and so moved out of the bottom two places, condemning RMI to make a re-election appeal to the

Lancashire Combination membership. Frank Ramsbottom, whose younger brother Ernest was introduced into the team towards the end of the season enjoyed another excellent campaign and scored 23 goals in league and cup with Thompson netting 12 and Turley and Whitehead seven apiece.

Meanwhile, in May 1939 the Horwich Journal interviewed Jack Bruton at length. He had just retired from playing and had been appointed coach at Blackburn Rovers. 'Bruton brought wing-play to a fine art,' the Journal reported.

Bruton outlined that he had a long association with Hart Common Mission Church and Sunday school and after learning his football in the village went to Hindley Green (Lancashire Alliance) and then had one season as an amateur with Wigan Borough. He then signed amateur forms with Bolton Wanderers and made two appearances in their 'A' (third) team but did not form part of their plans. Upon his release from Burnden Bruton joined Horwich RMI where his displays soon pulled in the scouts. In March 1925 he was transferred to Burnley and so began a highly successful professional career.

By the autumn of 1925 Bruton was a regular in Burnley's first division side and he established himself as a consistent and skilful player who was a huge crowd favourite. He went on to make 167 league appearances at Turf Moor and scored 42 goals. Bruton also represented the Football Association, the Football League representative team and won three caps for England, in 1928 against France and Belgium and in 1929 against Scotland.

There was a shock in store for the Turf Moor faithful when Bruton was sensationally transferred to their arch-rivals Blackburn Rovers in December 1929 for a fee of £6,500. Bruton more than repaid Rovers for their investment, making 324 league appearances and scoring 108 goals   An immensely fast and skilful player and a provider as well as scorer of goals, Bruton was arguably the finest player ever to represent RMI.

Bruton enjoyed a benefit game against Celtic in 1935 and such was his fitness bounced back from a broken leg in January 1938 to be playing again three months later. Bruton was also a successful local cricketer and had trials at Old Trafford for Lancashire. In the Bolton League he played with distinction as an opening batsman and superb cover-point fielder for Westhoughton between 1921 and 1931 and for Tonge between 1932 and 1938 and later played for East Lancashire CC in the Lancashire League.

After retirement as a player just before the Second World War, Bruton joined the Blackburn Rovers backroom staff and became Rovers manager in 1947. He was later manager at Bournemouth.

Though the re-election appeal was successful, and the 1939-40 season began as usual just three league games had been played when war was declared. The Combination immediately suspended operations on 4 September 1939. After a break of one month an emergency war-time competition began.

RMI had lost their opening two Combination fixtures, 9-0 at Rossendale United and 2-0 at home to Accrington Stanley Reserves. The game at Dark Lane had seen RMI field what was described as a completely new team at short notice and it was no great surprise they had been so heavily defeated. But it was to the committee's credit that within a week, especially considering the political turmoil that RMI defeated Lancaster City 4-0 at Grundy Hill on Saturday 2 September 1939 in what became their last peace-time fixture for seven years. Schofield crowned his return to the team with a hat-trick and Turley was also on the mark with a typically opportunist goal in a 4-0 victory.

The game was overshadowed by the imminence of war and O'Connor, the Lancaster centre forward, was delayed travelling to the game from his home in Barrow so the visitors started the game with ten men.

The teams were as follows: RMI: McIntosh; Thornley, Dawson; Baxter, Tate, Holt; Dewsnap, Gates, Thompson, Turley, Schofield. Lancaster: Swan; Stanley, Sant; Wilson, Williamson, Jones; MacArthur, Lane, Ennis, McSorley. The referee was M Horan of Rawtenstall.

War with Germany was declared the following day and the Horwich Journal reported: 'Horwich said a successful good-bye to sport, temporarily at least on Saturday. But sport is now amongst the many things that will have to be pushed into the background to make way for the grim business of war.'

Within a few weeks several clubs that were members of the Lancashire Combination met and decided to participate in a war-time competition. RMI were among the 12 clubs that decided to carry on playing, if only to bring some temporary relief from the war effort.

The RMI committee soldiered on throughout the 1939-40 war-time season before suspending playing after the end of the campaign. Their opening war-time fixture ended in a 5-1 away defeat against Southport Reserves on Saturday 7 October 1939. But the return game the following Saturday ended in a 5-5 draw. The format was to play the same opponents alternatively home and away in successive weeks and given that sides were usually only selected at short notice and were dependent upon availability of players the results were quite often topsy-turvy.

RMI lost 4-1 at home to Darwen in the Lancashire Junior Cup and then began to struggle for regularity of league fixtures. When they went down 6-2 at home to South Liverpool three days before Christmas it was RMI's first game for a month and they did not play at Grundy Hill between 13 January (when they lost 1-0 to Chorley, ex-RMI player McAweeney scoring the only goal) and 9 March when they entertained Rossendale United. That latter game was watched by what was described as a 'wretched attendance' with the Horwich Journal explaining that due to mandatory overtime shifts on the Loco Works many supporters were still at work.

RMI battled through a difficult season, using a vast number of players and often drafting in former players on a Saturday morning when it was discovered they were home on leave for the weekend. RMI's final fixture of the season- and their last for over six years- was on Saturday 11 May 1940 when a goal by Sleaford was sufficient to defeat Rochdale Reserves and partly avenge a 5-0 defeat against the same opponents the week previously. The RMI team was: McIntosh; Thornley, Duckworth; Hartley, Holt, Kirkman; Young, Orton, Hickson, Hardy, Sleaford.

Just before the Rochdale game the Horwich Journal reported: 'The RMI play their last match of the season tomorrow when they entertain Rochdale on the Grundy Hill ground. The RMI have played only three matches at home this year and the absence of the team for long intervals has undoubtedly caused many supporters to lose interest.'

In September 1940 the Horwich Journal reported: 'It does not seem likely that there will be any football at Grundy Hill during the winter season. The Lancashire Football Combination have been unable to get a sufficient number of clubs together to arrange a fixture list and for Horwich RMI, therefore, it looks like being a close season.

'Whether the RMI may be able to arrange a few friendly games remains to be seen, the prospects being so uncertain.' Only six clubs, Chorley, Rossendale United, Accrington Stanley, Bacup Borough, Leyland Motors and Morecambe had intimated a definite wish to carry on with RMI unable to come to a firm decision in the matter.

At the start of the war the Loco Works employees were compelled to work a six-day week including a full day on Saturday. Inevitably this had a drastic effect on gates at the football club. This was later slightly relaxed with shifts ending at Saturday lunch-time but football seemed hardly to rank in importance compared to events elsewhere.

The Combination ceased to play again in 1940-41 before a war-time competition, excluding RMI, was held in seasons 1941-42, 1942-43 and 1943-44. After being suspended again in 1944-45 twelve teams took part in the 1945-46 season. Droylsden and South Liverpool joined the Cheshire County League and nine clubs (RMI, Bangor City, Clitheroe, Fleetwood, Great Harwood, Marine, New Brighton Reserves, Oldham Athletic Reserves and Southport Reserves) did not compete although Netherfield were newcomers. Chorley finished as champions, three points ahead of Netherfield. But it was not until the following season, 1946-47, that a degree of normality returned.

POST WAR REVIVAL

On Thursday 1 August 1946 a special general meeting of the football club was called after which it was announced that RMI were to recommence activities in the Lancashire Combination after a lapse of six years. Mr Frank Mather, the retiring secretary, explained to the meeting the difficulties experienced after the 1939-40 season, not only as a result of the war but also the considerable financial debit balance on the club at that time. It was found to be very difficult to raise money to run the club and as it was thought that the war could only last a couple of years, it was decided to suspend all activities until hostilities were over.

During the war years the ground and its amenities deteriorated badly. The playing pitch more or less reverted into a meadow where sheep grazed and the popular 'scratching shed' had lost most of its roof and the main stand and other structures had been vandalised and left unsafe.

One of the major problems at the time was the scarcity and unavailability of materials with the country still suffering from the effects of the war. Permits were required for the purchase of materials. But by the middle of August 1946 the renovation work had begun and railings were erected around the site, though it was some time before the main stand and 'scratching shed' were able to be used.

The retiring treasurer, Mr J Edwards presented a statement of the club's activities and explained that members' subscriptions had continued during the war years. Due to this fact he was in a happy position to announce that not only had the debt of over £70 been wiped out, but there was now a considerable sum in hand with which to make a fresh start.

Mr Edwards also stated that under the terms of an agreement the railway company was responsible for the restoration of the ground and that they had allocated a significant fund at the club's disposal to this effect.

New officials were appointed to the RMI committee. Mr George Fisher was appointed chairman, Mr Walter Rutter secretary and Mr H Wood treasurer. The other members of the committee were: Messrs J Stubbs, R Fairclough, FW Hart, W Sutton, J Mulhearn, C Grice, H Rutherford, S Walmsley, J Armour, T Embrey, J Rudd, A Harrison, R Marsland, J Smith, R Thomas, E Mackay and R Farnworth.

Trial games were hastily arranged and interest in the revived club was heartening. The first trial was held on Wednesday 14 August 1946 when over thirty players went through their paces. The first professional to be signed was Frank Ramsbottom, the prominent pre-war RMI player who had played with Rossendale United during the war years.

RMI regained their place in a 22-team Combination which included the nine clubs that sat out the previous season together with Nelson and played their first post-war fixture at Dark Lane on Saturday 31 August 1946 when they lost 4-0 to Rossendale United. The RMI team was: Banks; A Haslam, Stubbs; Huddy, Hanna, Arrowsmith; C Brown, J Brown, Westhead, Ramsbottom, Taylor. The following Wednesday, however, two goals by Ramsbottom, one of only a handful of RMI players to return to the club, helped secure a 4-3 victory over Accrington Stanley Reserves with Hamer and Taylor also on the score-sheet.

There were many changes to the side during the early months of the season in an attempt to find the right blend with Eric Spencer, Bert Airey and Jack Tait being three good acquisitions. The team went five successive away games without defeat but suffered a disappointing FA Cup reverse at home to old rivals Darwen.

By November 1946 home gates had averaged only £30 and RMI were struggling to compete against many of the better supported Combination clubs. When RMI played at Nelson's Seedhill ground, for instance, the receipts were £350 while clubs such as Bangor City were averaging £250 gates, Netherfield £200 and Leyland Motors £150. Appeals were made in the local press for better support from the town, but despite the disparity in receipts RMI more than held their own. They won 1-0 at Nelson with outside-right Hamer scoring the only goal. Hamer and RMI's new goalkeeper, Cheadle began to attract the attention of Football League scouts.

Compensation for some erratic form in the league came in a good run in the Lancashire Junior Cup. RMI defeated Astley Bridge, Netherfield and Morecambe on their way to a semi-final date against Rochdale Reserves. The first scheduled tie at Spotland was postponed due to snow but around 600 Horwich spectators travelled over to cheer on their side for the re-arranged game the following week. Despite having the better of the play RMI were handicapped by an injury to centre-forward Crompton and played most of the game with ten men, going down to a 2-0 defeat. The RMI side was: Cheadle; Haslam, Abel; Brewster, Woods, Tait; Hamer, Spencer, Crompton, Ramsbottom, Airey.

After such a long lay-off RMI's first post-war season could be said to be a success especially when considering the difficulties that affected the club. Officials had to build a team from scratch, renovate and improve the ground and attempt to re-awaken public interest while competing with teams with far greater financial resources.

By winning 17 and drawing six of their 42 league fixtures RMI finished a respectable fourteenth. Their best players were said to be Ramsbottom, Hamer, Spencer, Airey, Haslam and Cheadle. The biggest problem was found in securing a reliable strike force and no less than five centre-forwards were given trials in the early months of the season. Injuries were a recurring theme and in the last 15 games of the season RMI were able to field the same side on only one occasion.

Financially RMI lost £217 on the season. Gate receipts realised £766 while players' wages and expenses (£849) were by far the biggest expense. It was announced that for the following season, 1947-48, admission prices would be raised from nine pence to one shilling and that a reserve team would be run on an entirely separate financial basis to the first team, playing in the second division of the Lancashire Combination. As a reminder of the prevailing post war-time restrictions appeals were made for clothing coupons to obtain the badly-needed playing strips and boots. Bacup Borough ended the season as Combination champions, finishing five points ahead of Marine with Netherfield in third position.

Injuries to key players continued to haunt RMI in their second post-war season and even with the backing of a reserve team the results proved disappointing. Many players were given trials and one local player to make his mark was a local youth, John Walton, who was becoming established when he called away to do his National Service. Whilst in the forces Walton was selected for the England amateur team and he went on to win many caps for his country. After his army service Walton went on to represent Burnley, Manchester United, Bury and Coventry City.

Walton's place at RMI was taken by Cliff Meadows who was another promising local youngster. But despite individual successes a feeling of gloom settled over Grundy Hill as the team struggled and faced relegation from the first division of the Lancashire Combination. In their 42 league games RMI won on ten occasions, drawing a further seven times but they lost 25 league games, scoring 58 goals but conceding 104. Southport Reserves were the only team below them in the final table. Only three sides conceded more goals and only two sides scored fewer goals. Wigan Athletic finished as champions with Nelson runners-up. Nelson knocked-out RMI in the FA Cup at the second qualifying round stage, 4-1 at Seedhill.

Robinson top scored with 14 goals during the season, Spencer and Ridings scoring nine apiece. RMI had started the season promisingly, with three wins and two draws in their opening seven games but then endured a run of eight defeats in nine games at the turn of the year. They were prone to inconsistency, losing 5-1 at Leyland Motors in the derby game on Christmas Day but then winning the return on Boxing Day 7-2, Howard scoring a hat-trick. But the defence, particularly away from home, was poor and in one five-match sequence RMI conceded 26 goals, including a 6-4 defeat at Earlestown in the Lancashire Junior Cup and successive defeats of 7-2 at Rossendale United and 6-1 at Prescot Cables. Late in the season they crashed 7-0 at Rochdale Reserves and 6-1 at Barrow Reserves and they won only one of their last eleven league games. It was the first time the club had ever been relegated.

The committee were undaunted and began the following season with a steely determination to recover RMI's place in the top division. At that time the second division of the Lancashire Combination comprised only 13 clubs and so RMI had only a dozen home league games to play over the course of the campaign. There was another Horwich-based team played in this league at the time. 'Pickups' or ACI Horwich as they were then known had risen through the ranks of the Bolton Combination and played at Lord Street on the other side of the town. This 1948-49 season was to be ACI's first at this level of football and there was much interest in the town as to their prospects as well as looking forward to the two local derby games with RMI.

RMI adapted well to the lower level of football and at the halfway stage of the season had only lost one league game and looked a certainty for promotion. Two stalwarts of the team were full-back Alan Haslam and inside-forward Eric Spencer despite the many comings and goings. Other important players included Jim Arrowsmith, Bert Benson, Archie Lennox and goal-keeper Jack Smith.

Towards the end of the season RMI acquired the services of John Brocklehurst on loan from Oldham Athletic. He made an immediate impact on his debut, inspiring RMI's attack and helping them to a 3-2 victory over Lytham that made sure of promotion. Another promising recruit was the centre-forward, Peter Baines.

The RMI team towards the end of the season read as follows: Smith; Haslam, Arrowsmith; Benson, Curless, Lea; Cronshaw, Spencer, Baines, Brocklehurst, H Seddon. In addition Lennox and Longworth were also regular players.

RMI finished one point behind champions Bootle and, as runners-up, winning 19 and drawing one of their 24 league games regained their place in the first division at the first attempt. ACI performed creditably, finishing in mid-table with nine wins and two draws. In Division One Netherfield were champions and Chorley runners-up. The derby matches ended in RMI's favour, RMI winning 5-2 against ACI at Grundy Hill on 13 November 1948 and 4-1 in the return on 18 December.

RMI had several players who could find the net with some regularity and Spencer was top scorer with 14 goals. Thomas scored 12 goals, Seddon 11 and Lennox and Cronkshaw ten apiece. They closed the campaign with a praiseworthy effort against Chorley in the Combination Cup. RMI forced a 2-2 draw at Victory Park but extra-time was not played. The replay was staged at Chorley two days later and this time the home side prevailed 3-1.

Mr Arthur Riley, the secretary of RMI, appealed once again for the support of the townsfolk at the (1949) annual general meeting and reminded members of the continuing need for hard work to maintain a semi-professional football team at Grundy Hill. He referred to the task of re-draining the playing pitch and after a tender of £260 had been received for work on approximately half the pitch it was decided to tackle the job with voluntary labour under expert supervision.

In the course of one month over the summer the members of the committee, assisted by a handful of supporters dug 450 yards of trenches and laid over 1,300 pipes. Despite their relegation the club's balance sheet showed a profit of £81 on the last season, this after £152 had been spent on the ground.

With the pitch drainage and surface levelling complete RMI embarked on another attempt to consolidate their place in the first division, but this again proved a difficult task. Despite the acquisition of Bill Edwards as player-coach RMI drew one and lost five of their opening six games and had earned only three league wins by the turn of the year. Edwards was a respected centre-half who had spent the previous three seasons at Macclesfield Town. The only glimmer of light was provided by the form of a newcomer to the team, former Belle Vue forward Barney Ford and the promise shown by a late season acquisition, Jimmy Mather.

Mather, signed from Newton Heath Loco who acted as something of a nursery team for RMI in the immediate post war years, scored two goals on his debut in a 4-0 defeat of Fleetwood in the final game of the campaign. Over the next few years he would become a Grundy Hill favourite and would invite comparisons with the immortal Joe Keetley.

But RMI again had to apply for re-election with only eight wins and six draws from their 42 league games. Nelson finished as champions, eight points clear of runners-up Wigan Athletic and Prescot Cables. RMI were the lowest scorers in the Combination with 52 goals and also conceded most goals (114). After failing to attract sufficient support they were again relegated to the second division. This was another blow to the committee but at the annual general meeting they again re-iterated their determination to make RMI a strong team in Combination circles. There was a major boost in this long-term aim when a supporters' club was formed in the town under the guidance of energetic secretary Mr Norman Rimmell.

The usual trial matches were held before the 1950-51 season commenced and two promising local players who stood out were full-back Johnny Horrocks and centre-half Harry Grainger. Bert Airey returned to the club after a short spell at Fleetwood as RMI approached the new campaign in good heart despite the disappointment of relegation.

But RMI's start to their second season in division two was a slow one. Their form away from home was excellent and included a 7-2 win at ACI in the second game of the campaign, Coates scoring four goals. But at Grundy Hill they often struggled and to make matters worse RMI lost 3-2 at home to rivals ACI, the derby match attracting a season's best gate of £61. The teams for the game played on 30 August 1950 were as follows: RMI: Mason; Haslam, Horrocks; Ainsworth, Grainger, Walkden; Ford, Coates, Mather, Spencer, Airey. ACI: Hurst; W Seddon, Leather; Benson, Miller, Hill; Hartley, Holt, Wane, Wilson, Morgan. The ACI full-back Leather caused something of a sensation in local football circles with a sensational winning goal, a 40-yard drop-shot fifteen minutes from the end.

Tommy Woodcock, who had briefly appeared for RMI as a winger in 1947 before moving on to become a professional with Blackburn Rovers, returned to the club. He was immediately re-introduced at left-half.

Gradually confidence returned and the team began to perform with more consistency. They won 8-0 at Great Harwood and by the turn of the year RMI topped the table with ACI in a creditable fifth position. This was a fine achievement for both clubs because the Combination Second Division was now much stronger and comprised 22 clubs.

In the background the Supporters' Club was going from strength to strength and various money-making events were being staged. The RMI Supporters' Club was the first organisation to use the large hall of the Mechanics' Institute since 1939 when they held a dance at the venue on 15 December 1950. The building had been taken over by the military during the war years.

In February RMI chalked up their one hundredth league goal of the season in a 3-3 draw against Morecambe Reserves. Jimmy Mather was the player who scored it with an effort described as coming from 'a neat flick off the foot.' 'Flick' was to become Jimmy's nickname.

RMI finished the season as runners-up to St Helens Town on goal-average and were duly elected to return to division one. Both sides earned 64 points with RMI winning 30 games and drawing four. They scored 154 goals- easily the highest total in the league- but conceded 60. St Helens Town scored 132 but conceded only 49. In the hectic end to the season RMI could have lost out on the championship due to their cup commitments. RMI took on the mighty Wigan Athletic in the semi-final of the Combination Cup and were accompanied by fifteen coach-loads of supporters for the game at Springfield Park where a highly creditable 2-2 draw was achieved against the team that lifted the Division One title on goal-average ahead of Nelson. However, the Latics won the replay 3-0 at Grundy Hill.

Over the season RMI's star striker Jimmy 'Flick' Mather went close to breaking the club's individual goal-scoring record with 56 goals, just short of Joe Keetley's long-established tally of 59 in the 1928-29 campaign. Mather and Alan Haslam gained recognition for their individual performances by earning call-ups for a Lancashire Combination Select XI that played the Dutch club NEC Nijmegen at Springfield Park, Wigan as part of the Festival of Britain celebrations. Haslam was described as 'one of the safest defenders in the Combination' whilst Mather scored one of his 'specials' in a 3-3 draw.

The finances of the club showed that £112 had been lost on the season despite a significant donation of £800 from the Supporters' Club. Without this source of income it is doubtful that RMI could have continued in the Combination as gate receipts by comparison amounted to £658. It was decided that the club would issue season tickets for the first time in its history.

The Supporters' Club held its first annual general meeting where it was reported they had won their fight at the annual conference of the National Federation of Supporters' Clubs and that Bolton Wanderers Supporters' Club would not be able to open a branch in Horwich. It was also stated that membership stood at 354.

BACK IN THE TOP FLIGHT

The 1951-52 season commenced with RMI back in division one and this time everyone connected with the club hoped they would stay there. But RMI made a poor start to the season and at one stage Mather was dropped for a run of five first-team matches. But with 16 matches played RMI had gained 16 points and looked well on the way to securing safety.

Injuries again hit RMI hard, the loss of left-half Cunliffe with a broken ankle being a sad blow. Cunliffe had earned some golden write-ups for his displays but when he was fit to resume seemed only a shadow of his former self. Walter Fearnley was injured during October and did not play again all season.

When RMI's regular goal-keeper Mason broke a bone in his hand a young local player, Jack McNulty, was called into the team. He made an immediate impression and played a big part as RMI defeated local rivals Chorley twice in three days, once in the league and also in the FA Cup preliminary round. Another successful signing was Jimmy Hankinson, recruited from third division side Chester.

Horwich ACI, meanwhile, struggled in division two of the Combination and played RMI for what proved to be the final time in the Combination Cup at Grundy Hill. RMI romped to a 9-0 victory with their long-serving inside-forward Eric Spencer in outstanding form despite the efforts of ACI captain Bill Seddon and his colleagues. Spencer was considered to be RMI's most consistent player since the club was re-formed.

One notable innovation during the season was the introduction of a white ball instead of the old dark brown one used previously. This was first used during the match against Clitheroe at Grundy Hill on Saturday 24 November 1951. Spectators reportedly wondered why it hadn't been introduced years before. It was something of a novelty being able to pick out the ball in the November gloom rather than guess its position by the reaction of spectators on the other side of the ground. Spencer and Mather certainly thought so, the pair bagging five of RMI's goals between them in a 7-1 victory.

After five seasons of dour struggle RMI at last established themselves back in division one. Mather, swiftly recalled to the side responded with a glut of goals to prove he could make the transition to the higher grade of football. He went on to notch a total of 42 league and cup goals during the campaign, with Eric Spencer scoring 28. Horrocks missed only one game and Parker and Grainger two apiece.

The team finished 12th in the league with 41 points from their 42 league games, scoring 99 goals whilst conceding 97. Nelson won the championship and finished eight points clear of Lancaster City. RMI's best 'gate' of the season was £94 for the visit of Wigan Athletic. One notable achievement was the win at Rossendale United, RMI's first at Dark Lane for 20 years.

At the end of the season Eric Spencer was awarded a benefit game in recognition of his services to the club. The attendance was hampered by a violent thunderstorm that erupted just before kick-off but over 600 spectators still braved the elements to pay tribute to the popular player. Spencer's XI, including Bolton Wanderers players Stan Hanson, Tommy Banks, Eric Bell and Harry Webster defeated RMI 4-2.

While RMI's officials could celebrate achieving their ambition of staying in the top flight there was sad news from Lord Street where ACI decided to resign from the Combination. The ability of a town the size of Horwich to maintain two teams in the Combination had always been in doubt but ACI made a sterling effort over their four seasons of membership.

ACI's last season, though, had proved disastrous both in financial terms and from a playing point of view. They gained 27 points from 42 league games and finished third from bottom. It had been estimated that an average 'gate' of £15 per home match had been required to keep the team going; but the average was barely £5 per game with just three shillings taken for a game against Great Harwood that was played in a thunderstorm.

RMI immediately recruited ACI's club captain and strong-man defender Bill Seddon on amateur forms and also signed-on the club's promising young winger Sammy Bailey.

At the annual general meeting of the Lancashire Combination a motion was put forward to allowed retired persons to attend Division One games at a reduced price but was heavily defeated. RMI and Ashton United informed the meeting that they had always allowed this concession and intended to continue.

Meanwhile, the RMI Supporters' Club was going from strength to strength. They launched a new money-making initiative and reported that membership had now risen to 1,800 with a target of 4,000 members.

But there was a double blow for RMI's supporters during the summer. The popular duo of Eric Spencer and Alan Haslam both left the club, Spencer joining Cheshire County League outfit Stalybridge Celtic and Haslam moving to St Helens Town.

The loss of Spencer and Haslam was felt almost immediately as RMI crashed 8-1 at Darwen in the opening fixture of the 1952-53 season. But RMI recovered quickly for the visit of Wigan Athletic the following Wednesday. This game set a new Grundy Hill record 'gate' of £122 and the spectators were richly entertained. RMI, leading 3-1 at one stage, had to settle for a 4-4 draw after a thrilling encounter. Newcomers Roy Hatsell and Sammy Bailey added to RMI goals by Jimmy Mather and Jimmy Taylor. Hatsell was a clever inside-forward signed from Clitheroe after previously being on the books of Blackburn Rovers. Kenneth Peel, a former Altrincham player also joined RMI. He was a holder of the Distinguished Service Medal gained whilst serving in the Royal Navy during the war.

Two other new players to create immediately good impressions were the fair-haired midfield player Ernie Roby and local school-teacher Eddie Rudd. RMI looked set to reap the rewards for the hard work and determination by their chairman George Fisher and his committee. The team was getting stronger on the field and some excellent new players had been signed while gate receipts were improving. A large share of the credit for the upturn in fortunes was attributed to the efforts of the Supporters' Club with regular and substantial financial contributions being made to boost the club's coffers.

While RMI looked capable of scoring plenty of goals their defence was porous at times. 'There was some heart-in-the-mouth defending on occasions,' wrote Terry Foley. 'Though the defenders couldn't be criticised for not giving one hundred percent effort many matches could be drawn or lost in the last ten minutes of games with give-away goals, only for the team to put in a storming finish usually grabbing both points in the last few minutes.'

There was disappointment that RMI went out of the major cup competitions early, losing 2-1 at Ashton United in the FA Cup after raising hopes with a 3-0 win at Leyland Motors and 5-3 home win over Chorley (at one stage RMI were 5-0 up) in previous rounds. They also lost 2-1 at Lancaster City in the Lancashire Junior Cup.

On Christmas Day 1952 RMI's goalkeeper Bill Foulkes was rested after injury and a young college student named Horace Lea got his chance in the first-team. Lea made an immediately good impression and played five successive games before returning to college. For the second time in his RMI career Mather was dropped from the side but responded in the only manner he knew- by scoring goals. After six matches on the sidelines Mather returned against Clitheroe and scored four goals. Two weeks later he went one better, scoring five in RMI's 6-2 victory over Rossendale United. Sammy Bailey's displays attracted the attention of League scouts and interest was expressed by Doncaster Rovers and Bradford Park Avenue.

Gradually the defence of the team was re-shaped. A new goalkeeper, Robertson, was recruited and Alan Haslam returned to the club after being released by St Helens Town. Jimmy Taylor moved from outside-right to fill the other full-back position. The RMI team line-up now read: Robertson; Haslam, Taylor; Rudd, Grainger, Hankinson; Bailey, Roby, Mather, Hatsell, Ainscough.

Towards the end of the season RMI's small first-team squad comprising 15 part-time professionals, faced an exhausting schedule. They were still involved in the Combination Cup and in with an outside chance of runners-up spot to Wigan Athletic in the league. It was no surprise that several new players had to be introduced as injuries began to hit hard. RMI lost by a single goal at Springfield Park in the Combination Cup semi-final and finished seventh in the league with 47 points, scoring 109 but conceding 105. Only champions Wigan Athletic (124) scored more goals but only Clitheroe (115) conceded more goals than RMI.

There were some memorable high-scoring encounters with RMI starting the New Year with a 4-2 win at Clitheroe, followed by successive 6-3 defeats at the hands of Ashton United and Netherfield respectively. They then won 6-2 at Rossendale United and won the return game 4-3 at Grundy Hill the following week. Of the five games played in January RMI scored 20 goals and conceded 19.

Spectators at Grundy Hill could hardly complain about lack of entertainment, or goals as high-scoring draws against Marine (5-5) and Ashton United (4-4) followed. And with Mather rediscovering his scoring touch RMI had the ability to punish the best defences. They won 8-0 at home to Fleetwood, Mather scoring four times and 11-0 against Clitheroe, Mather scoring another four to make it 11 goals in his three games against the East Lancashire side. He brought up 50 goals for the season with a brace in a 4-3 home win over Chorley and finished the campaign with 52 goals in league and cup. Roby scored 34, a fine achievement that almost went unnoticed while Hatsell contributed 18 goals. In a shade over three full seasons at Grundy Hill Jimmy Mather had found the net 152 times.

Bolton Wanderers, meanwhile, lost 4-3 to Blackpool in the FA Cup Final at Wembley in one of the most dramatic finals ever staged at the famous stadium, known as the 'Matthews Final' after Stanley Matthews inspired his team to an unlikely comeback from 3-1 down with 20 minutes remaining.

The 1953 RMI annual general meeting was said to be the happiest for many years. 'George Fisher remarked on the fulfilment of many of the club's objectives and stated that if the finances had allowed the playing staff could have been strengthened,' wrote Terry Foley. 'The valuable points might not have been lost in the final weeks and the team could have finished in one of the top-three positions.'

Mr Fisher reported to the meeting that a profit of £113 had been made on the season's activities. Receipts of £4,126 included the hugely significant donation of £1,646 from the Supporters' Club, which was greater than receipts from league games (£1,388). The biggest expenditure item was players' wages and expenses, totalling £2,131. The first-team coach, Bill Hannah, was given praise for having an eye for talent. It was upon his recommendation that RMI had recruited Rudd, Roby and Lea. There was also praise for centre-half Harry Grainger who played in every game during the season, a total of 51 league and cup games, and scored 12 goals- all from the penalty mark

But the problems of competing at Combination level were highlighted when it was revealed the late-season game at Barrow, which had been re-arranged for a Thursday evening, had cost the club £60 for travel, time lost at work and meals- more than the average home gate during the season. In a ground-sharing move that boosted the RMI coffers Bolton Wanderers 'B' side played their home games at Grundy Hill starting in this season.

RMI strengthened their side for the 1953-54 season and signed goalkeeper Lea on a permanent basis as a professional, also recruiting Jack Bickerstaffe straight out of League football. A former Bury, Lincoln City and Halifax Town defender, he sadly missed most of the season due to a broken toe. But RMI lost the services of Jimmy Hankinson to Fleetwood.

The RMI Supporters' Club donated a new flag which was flying proudly at Grundy Hill as a 3-1 opening day victory over Lancaster City was secured. There were several new faces in the RMI ranks including the return of old favourite Barney Ford. A tall full-back, John Popland, went on to give some good performances before being called upon to do his National Service while Tommy Kenny and Colin Evans, both signed on 7 November 1953, were to contribute much to the team's future successes.

Supporters were now able to watch Lancashire Combination division one football at Horwich every Saturday as Bolton Wanderers 'B' team had gained promotion to the top division and continued to use Grundy Hill as their home ground. With the revenue received from this arrangement the RMI committee wisely purchased a small tractor and various attachments for use on the upkeep of the ground. The entire pitch cutting, rolling, pricking, scraping, slitting and brushing could now be done without hiring outside help. Meanwhile Horwich RMI Cricket Club celebrated winning the Bolton Cricket League in 1953 for the first time since the league was formed in 1930 (Horwich joining in 1934). They repeated the feat in 1955, 1978 and 1983.

During the season Jimmy Mather was chosen to play for the Lancashire County team and a young Blackrod-based player, Jimmy Flatters, was called upon to fill the not inconsiderable gap. Flatters rose to the challenge of being the deputy to 'Jimmy Flick' and scored five goals in his first two games.

THE MAGIC OF THE CUP

Wigan Athletic dominated the Combination again and ended up winning the league by a clear 15 points from Netherfield. At one stage, despite a slow start to the season, RMI looked to be in contention for runners-up position but they eventually had to be satisfied with fourth spot, with 47 points from 40 games. When Wigan visited Grundy Hill on 12 February 1954 the match attracted a crowd of 2,135. RMI led up until the 80th minute but Wigan scored three goals in the last ten minutes to emerge as clear victors. There was consolation though that RMI had reached the latter stages of both the Lancashire Junior Cup and the Combination Cup.

In the semi-final of the Lancashire Junior Cup RMI were drawn away at Chorley. In front of a crowd of 4,095 spectators Chorley looked like winning the game after Hatsell, their former RMI forward scored the game's only goal. But with seven minutes remaining RMI were awarded a hotly-disputed penalty which was coolly converted by Harry Grainger. With seconds to go Mather popped up with the winner and he was immediately mobbed by scores of RMI fans who invaded the pitch.

The final was staged at Ewood Park, Blackburn on Wednesday 21 April 1954 and pitted RMI against Wigan Athletic. The game is still described to this day by old-timers as one of the greatest matches ever played involving RMI. Wigan took a 14th minute lead through Harry Penk and increased their advantage through Jackie Lyon's 25th minute shot. But RMI were undaunted and fought their way back into the contest, encouraged by their supporters in a crowd of 8,863 (receipts: £772).

With twenty minutes left Fred Butler pulled back a goal and just four minutes remained when Sammy Bailey raced down the wing and cut inside, flashing a shot that rebounded back off the crossbar. As the ball dropped down Jimmy Mather was first to react and he levelled the scores. Both teams left the field to a standing ovation. 'Even the most diehard Wigan fans said Horwich were well worthy of a win, let alone a draw,' wrote Foley.

The teams were as follows: RMI: Lea; Horrocks, Downes; Kenny, Grainger, Evans; Bailey, Roby, Mather, Butler, Taylor. Wigan Athletic: Lomas; Lindsay, Parkinson; Lynn, Mycock, Banks; Penk, Butler, Lomax, Lyon, Hindle.

Five days later RMI travelled to Springfield Park for the semi-final of the Combination Cup. Though something less than the footballing classic served up at Ewood the game was again fiercely fought and finished as a 1-1 draw, Mather scoring RMI's goal. The attendance at Springfield Park was 9,000 (£402). The replay at Grundy Hill two days later turned into a bruising battle, perhaps as a consequence of players from both sides feeling the strain of the fixture pile-up. But RMI had the last laugh, Mather outwitting three defenders and calmly dribbling the ball past Lomas in the Latics' goal for a trademark effort. Roy Flatters scored another two goals and RMI earned a famous 3-2 victory. The tie produced record receipts for an RMI home game of £228.

On Friday 30 April 1954 RMI faced Chorley at Grundy Hill in the final of the Combination Cup. Much to the delight of the home fans in a crowd of 3,377 (£172) Butler's goal gave RMI the spoils. The goal came two minutes after half-time when the RMI inside-left cleverly placed his shot past Wilson following good approach play by Mather. The teams were: RMI: Lea; Seddon, Downes; Rudd, Grainger, Evans; Bailey, Roby, Mather, Butler, Taylor. Chorley: Wilson; Rigby, Coar; Brierley, Cunliffe, Howard; Dickinson, Gill, Parkes,

Hatsell, Irving. The referee was Mr A Jobling (Morecambe). The cup presentation was made by Councillor WF Raynor from the League Management Committee.

The fixture pile-up was such that while the Cup Final was taking place RMI also fielded a side across town in the Lancashire Combination, playing Netherfield at the De Havilland FC ground. This remarkable chain of events was the only way they could fit in their outstanding fixtures before the end of the season.

Club secretary Arthur Riley solved the problem of having only 16 players on the books by accepting offers of help from amateur footballers from Bolton and Horwich and in doing so RMI sacrificed any hope of the runners-up spot. In Mr Riley's mind was a pre-season agreement with the players that the club would not arrange a fixture on FA Cup Final day, which was Saturday 1 May. Not surprisingly RMI's scratch side went down to a 6-1 defeat. It was RMI's third league game in four days and followed a 2-0 defeat at Darwen on the Tuesday and a 4-0 reverse at Barrow on the Thursday. No wonder club coach Billy Hannah said: 'It is not fair on the players to go on like this, especially when they have to work all day.'

The final match of the crowded season was the Lancashire Junior Cup Final replay, played on Wednesday 5 May 1954 at Chorley. With thirty coach-loads of supporters setting off in convoy from the Crown Hotel and many more travelling on a special train from Horwich station RMI received tremendous backing. A crowd of 8,863 paid £772 but Wigan gained revenge for their Combination Cup semi-final defeat by winning 2-1 in a game not short of controversy or incident.

'Everything went against RMI in the replay of the Lancashire Junior Cup Final,' the Horwich Journal reported. 'Referee JA Rushton of Blackpool awarded Wigan two penalties, both of which were strongly disputed. He also failed to see Lyon using his hand to control the ball in scoring the first goal and he refused RMI's claim for a penalty for a handling offence five minutes from the end.

'Even the weather was against RMI as before the interval RMI faced the wind and then found it had changed direction in the second half to blow even harder against them.'

RMI opened the scoring in the 16th minute when Taylor headed in a Bailey centre. Goalkeeper Harold Lea then saved the first penalty, ironically the first awarded against RMI all season, which was taken by Jack Lindsay. But one minute before half-time Jackie Lyon scored a controversial equaliser for Wigan. The winning goal came from the spot in the 59th minute when Tommy Hindle succeeded in beating Lea, who had a fine game in the Horwich goal.

During April 1954 RMI played a total of 16 games and, giving priority to the cup-ties often played weakened sides in the league games, enlisting the services of local players. In total RMI played 56 games, of which 31 were won, 16 lost and nine drawn. Mather was again top scorer with 37 goals. Roby scored 19 goals and defender Grainger was third in the list with 13, all but one scored from the penalty spot while Flatters netted 11 times.

Strangely, despite all the success gate receipts were down on the previous season by £300 but receipts from cup competitions brought in £900 and the Supporters' Club contributed the remarkable figure of £2,500. RMI's full-strength side was: Lea; Horrocks, Taylor; Seddon, Grainger, Evans; Bailey, Kenny, Mather, Butler, Roby. The reserves were Flatters, Bickerstaffe, Downes, Ford and Popland.

There was a surprise for the fans before the start of the 1954-55 season when the popular Grainger was replaced as captain by Eric Downes. Two new signings, Gordon Atherton and winger Wilson (signed from Skelmersdale United) made good impressions but RMI made their customary slow start to the campaign and were bottom of the table after the first five matches. The first win came by way of a 7-1 thrashing of South Liverpool when Mather scored a hat-trick but an early exit from the FA Cup at the hands of Darwen and an 8-3 defeat at the hands of Chorley in the Combination Cup soon followed.

RMI turned down an approach from Wigan Athletic for Downes and after five seasons Mather relinquished his amateur status and signed professional forms. In November 1954 many supporters were shocked to learn that Grainger had been transferred to Wigan, the pros and cons of his departure being a much-debated topic around town for weeks to come. 'In his five seasons with the club he had missed only one match, due to injury, and he was a great centre-half,' wrote Terry Foley. 'He was much respected by spectator and player alike and was a gentleman on and off the field.'

Grainger's position in the team was filled by Downes who did not let the arguments affect his play and the team then went on an eight-match unbeaten run, moving up the table with new full-back Derek Corcoran, signed from Stalybridge Celtic settling in well. On New Year's Day Wigan Athletic visited Grundy Hill with Grainger made captain for the day and went down to a 3-0 defeat, with Taylor, Butler and Downes (penalty) on the mark for RMI. Before the kick-off the RMI Supporters' Club made a presentation to Grainger to mark his long service to the club.

Downes was then injured and out for a long period and was replaced by Bill Seddon while Ernie Roby was dropped for the first time. 'One felt that the winds of change were blowing across Grundy Hill and in its wake long serving players went and new faces appeared,' Foley wrote.

Jimmy Mather played his last game for RMI in April 1955 and though given a free-transfer his reputation remained firmly intact. He scored 202 goals for RMI and the name 'Jimmy Flick' still brings back happy memories for veteran supporters who were captivated by his skills. Mather was rewarded by a Benefit Match, staged at Grundy Hill on 4 May 1955, becoming only the second player since the war (Eric Spencer being the first) to earn such an accolade.

After seven years' service RMI secretary Mr Arthur Riley resigned in April 1955 and was replaced by his assistant, Mr Bert Lucas. It was said of Mr Riley that his efficient and shrewd handling of the administration side of the club had always played a big part in the success and he was one of the best-known and most popular secretaries in the Combination.

RMI finished eighth in the table with 48 points, scoring 81 goals and conceding 62. Accrington Stanley Reserves were the outstanding team, and finished champions, 14 points ahead of runners-up Rossendale United. Atherton born Fred Butler was top-scorer with 29 goals during the season, Roby hit 21 and Mather 13.

Estimates had been obtained for reducing the Grundy Hill slope by 50 per cent but, not including materials the lowest tender was £1,800 and so the plan was shelved. The RMI committee also decided to stay loyal to the Combination despite several clubs being tempted by a move to the fast-emerging Cheshire County League.

During the summer of 1955 it was announced that Gordon Atherton had been signed by Bury with the promise that if he failed to make the grade in the Football League he would return to RMI. There was no such concern for Atherton soon established himself at Gigg Lane and went on to make over 300 league appearances in two spells with the Shakers, interrupted by a short stint at Swindon Town. Meanwhile, Bill Seddon was transferred to Chorley in November 1955.

As one character went a new one arrived. Billy Lomax of Wigan Athletic fame, who worked at the Loco Works came to RMI via Nelson and scored a hat-trick on his debut on 5 November 1955, ironically against Nelson. By the end of the 1955-56 season, Lomax had 28 goals to his credit. Other newcomers included Dennis Coop, a goal-scoring winger or centre-forward, Frank Layland, a full-back from Blackpool who was a local school-teacher, and local product Arthur Berry. Sammy Bailey was transferred to Wigan Athletic while Francis, signed as Mather's replacement, did not play many games before he received a serious injury. Mather, meanwhile, was now playing for Ashton United alongside his former RMI colleagues Grainger and Corcoran.

The changes did not affect RMI who moved up from eighth the previous season to runners-up position, just two points behind champions Burscough. RMI won 24, drew nine and lost only five of their 38 league games, scoring 104 goals and conceding just 49 equalling their best defensive record in a full season in the top flight of the Combination. Old rivals Wigan Athletic and Chorley were defeated during the course of the season. As well as Lomax's contributions, Butler scored 17 goals, Coop 16 and Roby 15.

RMI began the season with the following side: Lea; Horrocks, Layland; Evans, Downes, Rudd; Kenny, Roby, Francis, Butler, Coop, winning 2-1 at home to Darwen. Wigan Athletic, with an almost completely new side, then played their first home match of the season against RMI and attracted a crowd of over 10,000 spectators, producing receipts of £474. But RMI deservedly gained a share of the spoils in a goal-less draw and then humiliated Latics 4-1 in return game at Grundy Hill nine days later. The game produced a record home league 'gate' for RMI, and a crowd of over 3,500 (receipts: £144) saw RMI goals by Coop (2), Francis and Kenny.

There was a huge disappointment for RMI followers, however, when their favourites were knocked-out of the FA Cup by Leyland Motors. In the Lancashire Junior Cup RMI were drawing 1-1 at Springfield Park when the first round tie was abandoned due to rain after 75 minutes. In the replayed tie Latics won 4-0 before a crowd of 5,461. In the Combination Cup RMI lost 2-1 at Crompton's Recs, a works team based at Ashton-in-Makerfield. Despite those setbacks though RMI's league form was consistent and Lomax made an immediate impression, scoring in each of his first ten games for the club and amassing 20 goals by the end of December.

One of the season's highlights came with a 3-1 derby day win at Victory Park during March when Ernie Roby scored with a tremendous volley from just inside the Chorley half- considered by Foley as one of the finest goals ever scored by an RMI player. 'It could have been a fluke shot but I'd like to think it wasn't,' wrote Foley. 'I always remembered Ernie Roby for that terrific shot.'

Veteran Jimmy Taylor scored his first hat-trick for the club against Fleetwood in late February 1956 in a game that marked the debut of a promising left-back, David Holland. However, Holland's RMI career was hampered when one month later he was called up for his National Service in the RAF. RMI beat Fleetwood 7-1 and also recorded successive 7-2 victories over Prescot Cables and South Liverpool respectively.

Before the start of the 1956-57 season RMI lost a stalwart and loyal servant of the club with the death of Mr Harry Rutherford on 3 June 1956. 'Harry had served the club for some 30 years as committee man and official and had barely missed a match home or away during that time,' wrote Foley. 'He was known to be always on hand at Grundy Hill to greet the visiting team and officials and added much to the good name of the club by his concern and cheerful personality.'

One feature of the season was the club's fine run in the FA Cup as RMI enjoyed their best form in the competition for many years. Lomax scored four goals in a 7-1 win at Lytham in the preliminary round and RMI then defeated Skelmersdale United and Chorley before knocking-out Cheshire County League outfit Mossley at Grundy Hill thanks to Coop's late winner. The final hurdle before the first round proper was at Morecambe. Despite taking several hundred supporters along with the team on a special train RMI went down to a 3-2 defeat at Christie Park.

The FA Cup run, though, had created a great deal of interest in the town and several players were being noticed by Football League clubs. First division Charlton Athletic came in with a bid for two players, Kenny and Holland, but this was eventually turned down by the players themselves. Holland received an RAF posting nearer home that enabled him to play more regularly for the side, but there was the departure of the popular Ernie Roby to Netherfield. Roby, a former Reading player had scored 92 goals during his time at Grundy Hill after joining RMI in September 1952 and was considered to be the fastest forward ever seen at Horwich and a match-winner on his day. However, he had received a bad injury in January 1954 and it was felt his confidence had suffered as a result.

RMI had lost their opening game of the season against Droylsden but when the return match was played at Grundy Hill just before Christmas revenge was exacted with interest. RMI romped to a 10-0 victory with Coop and Butler both registering hat-tricks.

There was another change in the club's off-field structure late in 1956 when long-serving and popular coach Bill Hannah left the club to return to his native Ireland, Eric Downes taking over on a trial period. At the turn of the year RMI topped the table with 29 points from 20 games having strung together a winning run of nine games. The good run helped increase attendances with most Saturday home league games attracting gates of over one thousand, being considerably more when Wigan or Chorley were in town. Over the Christmas period RMI stretched their winning run to nine after successive home wins over Chorley, Fleetwood and Accrington Stanley Reserves. But an unbeaten league run that extended to 14 games (including only one draw) was ended by a 2-1 home defeat at the hands of South Liverpool and RMI then lost 7-2 at Prescot Cables.

Injuries hit hard early in the New Year and on several occasions RMI were down to a bare eleven players available for selection. But a welcome new addition to the playing staff was John Brocklehurst who returned for a second spell from Wigan Athletic. He made an immediate impact helping RMI gain a 7-1 Lancashire Junior Cup win at Nelson but RMI surprisingly bowed out of the competition in the third round at Darwen, who had ex-RMI player Sammy Bailey on their left-wing. Another former Wigan player to move over to Grundy Hill was Jackie Lyon.

In the Combination Cup RMI defeated Ashton United, Southport Reserves, Darwen and then Rossendale United 7-2 on aggregate in the two-legged semi-final to qualify for the final against Morecambe, also played on a home and away basis. In the first leg at

Grundy Hill on 26 April 1957 RMI had the advantage of the slope and strong wind in the first-half but the Morecambe defence played superbly and goalkeeper Udall made several fine saves. Morecambe took the lead just before half-time through Horton. But Billy Lomax scored twice in the space of five minutes in the second half after good approach play by Brocklehurst and Holland to give RMI a 2-1 win. A solid defensive rearguard action then helped RMI draw 0-0 at Morecambe in the return leg four days later to being the cup back to Horwich. Despite being decisively beaten at Christie Park earlier in the season the RMI defence stood firm and captain Eric Downes was presented with the cup by management committee representative Councillor G Brown.

The cup commitments and small squad strength combined to take their toll on RMI's league form. RMI finished fourth in 1956-57 ten points adrift of champions Prescot Cables. They won 22 but drew only three of their 38 league games scoring 93 goals but conceding 70. The only other signing of any note was Sammy Makin, a left-winger from Fleetwood. Leading goal scorers were Coop (33), Lomax (30), Butler (21), Evans and Makin (14 each) and Kenny (11). RMI played seven games in the final ten days of the season, suffering some heavy defeats. They lost 7-1 at Chorley and 9-1 at Wigan Athletic after fielding weakened sides on both occasions, signing on several local Sunday league players to help them through the fixture backlog.

The 1957 annual general meeting revealed that RMI's turnover had risen to almost £6,000, the highest in the club's history and a profit of £141 had been realised on the previous season. An application to run a reserve team in the Lancashire Combination was accepted.

The Supporters' Club members had worked hard to erect a new stand behind the Grundy Hill goal. Consisting of a tubular steel construction with a roof, back and sides, of asbestos, the total cost was over £1,500. Upon completion, however, it was found that the wind gap left between the back and the roof was over the specified nine inches so the whole of the asbestos sheeting had to be replaced.

At the AGM of the Supporters' Club it was revealed that the organisation had realised £4,742 from running their private lottery, out of which sum £2,775 had been donated to the football club and another £126 spent on smoothing out the Grundy Hill embankment and providing track-suits for the players. Supporters' Club official Norman Rimmell closed the meeting with his usual comment: 'I say it again and I will always say it, the football club does not get the support it deserves from a town of this size.'

Changes were also made to the back wall of the 'scratching-shed' opposite the main stand. A sliding wooden panel was built into the back wall. This was opened during periods of high winds to allow the air to pass through and prevent the roof being blown off its base. As ground improvements continued apace the lower pitch was completely resurfaced for training purposes and for the use of junior teams.

Despite scoring 63 goals between them both Coop and Lomax were given free transfers during the summer and Jackie Lyon was also released. The news was all the more surprising considering that Fred Butler had been given promotion at work and there was a doubt over his availability. Colin Evans had also been given his release but he had generously stayed on to help out when the team was handicapped by injuries.

After disappointments and difficulties in 1953-54, *HIC's* hope was that 1954-55 would be a new dawn for the club

The 1950s saw bumper crowds flock to Grundy Hill as this atmospheric photograph and those on the following pages illustrate

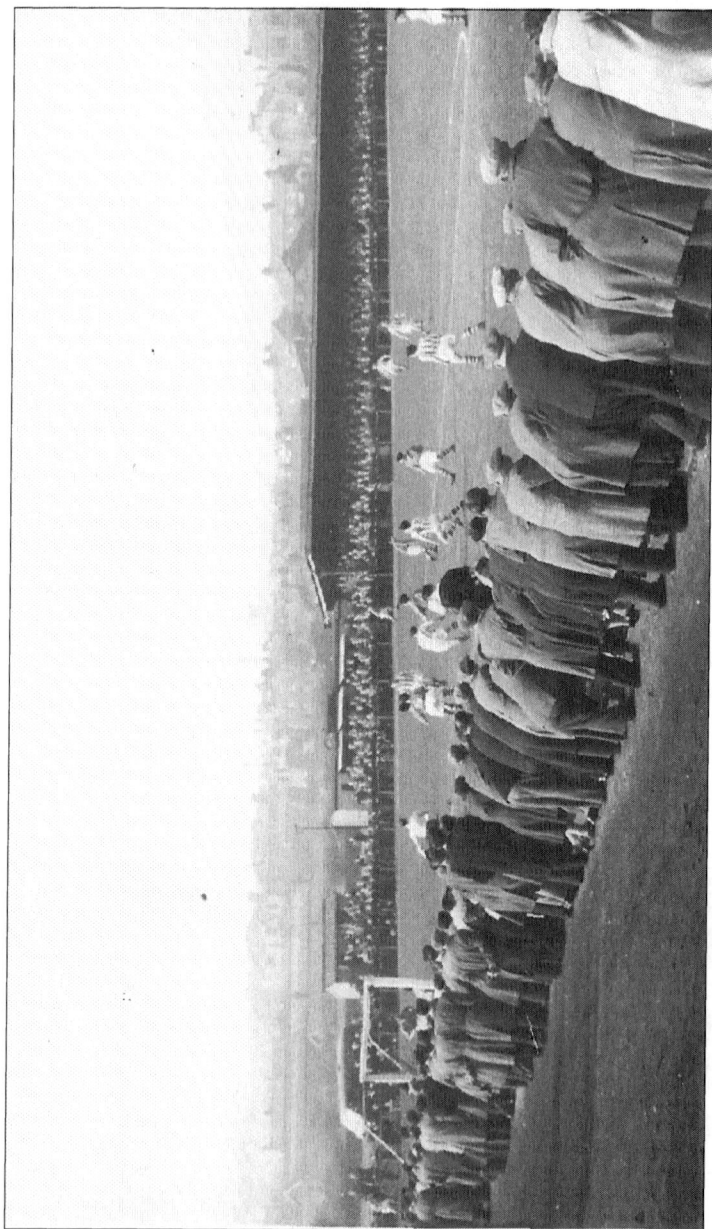

What every well-dressed man in Horwich was wearing, circa 1954

Local landmarks captured in photographs that evoke a golden age for football

Rivington Pike looms over Grundy Hill as RMI attack the Cricket Field end goal

More action pictures before packed crowds at Grundy Hill

Victory over St Helens recorded in inimitable style in the local newspaper

How a local newspaper cartoonist saw the abandoned match against Wigan
Athletic at Springfield Park in 1955-56

SOUTHPORT R. 1
HORWICH RMI. 1

IN WINTRY WEATHER

Miss Sugden might have been a little jealous could she have seen some of the figures' cut in this match

Coop hit the bar and the upright but without luck

Taylor drove high from a Butler gift but R.M.I played good football considering the conditions.

Taylor placed a peach of a pass to BUTLER who made no mistake

Southports No.3 ought to be fitted with a Hacking jacket for he certainly 'hacked' in this game. Their inside right scored with a centre that deceived Lea, floating over his head into the net.

"Even the Ref. wont know you"

Southport winger handled and a wag complained

"But REF — it was only ONE HAND"

TAYLOR seemed to master the conditions better than most and gave the Southport defence a lot of worry

Hig 2.56.

The cartoonist gives his slant on a 1-1 draw away to Southport Reserves during the 1955-56 season

Horwch RMI 10 Droylsden 0, December 1956, as seen by the newspaper cartoonist

Several RMI stalwarts feature in this cartoon following a 2-0 win over
South Liverpool at Holly Park in January 1957

R.M.I. footballer is Singapore "international"

A NAME which is well-known to Horwich R.M.I. supporters is now earning fame in football on the other side of the world. Arthur Berry, who played in several games for R.M.I. as an amateur before he was called up for National Service in 1957, was posted to a R.E.M.E. unit in Singapore and has played in turn for his unit, for the Corps team, for Singapore Army and for All-

ARTHUR BERRY

Singapore. In January he was honoured by the award of R.E.M.E. Corps colours, granted to him by the War Office in London for his "outstanding contribution to sport in the Corps." He also holds Corps theatre colours and the Singapore blazer which is worn by those who have played three times for the colony team.

In January Arthur made an "international" appearance at left-half in a match when All-Singapore beat Japan 3-2. All-Singapore is itself an international team, with Malayans and British Servicemen playing side by side.

Now Craftsman Berry, of 10 Infantry Workshops, R.E.M.E., Arthur is looking forward to sailing home this summer for his demobilization in August.

National Service often deprived clubs like Horwich RMI of key players—but it also afforded some wonderful opportunities. This cutting describes how Arthur Berry was 'capped' for Singapore.

Officials, committee members and playing staff of Horwich R.M.I. F.C. with the Combination Cup. Sharing the trophy with team captain and coach Eric Downes is the mascot, Stephen Walkden. Mr. G. H. Fisher (chairman) is to the left and Mr. H. Lucas (secretary) to the right.

RMI finished fourth in the League in 1956-57, lacking the consistency to challenge Prescot Cables for the title. However, they had a great season in Cup competitions, culminating in winning the Combination Cup. Morecambe were defeated over two legs in the Final to set the club up for their title-winning campaign in 1957-58.

A CHAMPION SEASON

As plans were made for the new season a host of new players were signed, including Roy Cozens from Accrington Stanley, Rex Adams from Northwich Victoria and the former Wigan Athletic trio of Sammy Speakman, Joe Hopwood and Ken Parkin. Eric Downes was appointed captain and coach to the first-team and a newcomer to Grundy Hill, Jimmy Jackson, became trainer-coach to the reserve team.

The pre-season signs from the trial games were promising for RMI supporters than another good season could be achieved. 'It was evident that as well as the new signings RMI had attracted some unknown amateurs of well-above-average ability and their showing against the established players was going to make first-team selection a difficult job,' Foley wrote.

The first-team selected for the opening game against Skelmersdale United was as follows: Lea; Hopwood, Taylor; Brocklehurst, Downes, Parkin; Kenny, Adams, Speakman, Wignall, Makin. Teenager Frank Wignall had been brought in for his debut after Cozens was injured in training.

The second-team for the opening game at Padiham was as follows: Woods; Horrocks, Layland; Holland, Smith, Rudd; Molyneux, Robinson, Jones, Longworth, Bateson.

It was commonplace at that time for Grundy Hill devotees to watch the reserves at home rather than follow the first-team on their travels. Those that turned up for the first reserve team home game against Darwen were full of praise for some of the newcomers. Centre-forward Alan Jones, an aggressive, flying spearhead and Wignall both gave outstanding displays while left-winger Dicky Bateson and centre-half Tom Smith also caught the eye. All four players came from Blackrod.

The season was only a few weeks old before the league scouts began to make their appearance and the Preston newspapers announced that Wignall was to be signed by North End. It was immediately evident that the player was destined for a career in league football but thankfully for RMI no moves were made until the season's close.

RMI's early season plans were disrupted by an influenza outbreak that affected most of the 22-man squad and trainer Tommy Embrey became a victim. It was ironic that after previous seasons, when RMI often struggled to field a bare eleven due to injuries they should still be struggling despite now having the luxury of a reserve team as back-up. There was then the surprising announcement that Rex Adams, signed during the closed season, had decided to retire from football.

Team selection must have proved a difficult task for the committee but a combination of injuries and illness made the job easier when RMI visited Burscough on Saturday 14 September 1957. For that game they included their four 18-year-olds from Blackrod in the team together for the first time, two goals by Wignall deciding the game 2-1 in RMI's favour.

The first big test of RMI's credentials was provided by the visit of Wigan Athletic when RMI fielded the following line-up which had changed considerably since the season's opening game: Lea; Hopwood, Taylor; Smith, Downes, Kenny; Makin, Wignall, Jones, Speakman, Bateman. A crowd of just over 2,500 saw Latics lose their unbeaten record thanks to Wignall's 25th-minute goal, a well-judged lob over the goalkeeper. Joe Hopwood had married on that Saturday but was still keen to play against his former club. After the ceremony he dashed along to Grundy Hill and took up his usual place in the defence.

In the return game at Springfield Park one week later RMI went down 3-2 but could still take heart that they had put together a side that could challenge the best. 'It was unusual to feel the tension of the Athletic players and supporters during the game,' wrote Foley, 'relief coming only at the final whistle.'

A major landmark was recorded on 27 November 1957 when the last steam locomotive to be built at Horwich Loco Works left the premises. It was a BR Standard Class 4, 2-6-0, No. 76099. In 1958 the Horwich Railway Mechanics' Institute was officially handed over to the British Rail Staff Association.

As Christmas approached the team selection was becoming more automatic and the first-choice selection usually read as follows: Lea; Hopwood, Layland; Brocklehurst, Parkin, Rudd; Cozens, Wignall, Jones, Speakman, Bateson. Players of the calibre of Kenny, Smith, Holland, Makin, Taylor, Robinson, Downes and Horrocks all turned out with the reserves and ably filled first-team places when called upon.

One the reasons for the success of the season was the club policy, Foley explained. 'To play in the reserves didn't mean obscurity or just a face to make up the numbers,' he wrote. 'All players were made to feel they were equally important no matter which team they played for. As a consequence RMI had perhaps the biggest squad at their disposal they had ever had, and all the players seemed contented.'

At Christmas-time RMI reached the summit of the Combination following a 3-0 victory over Fleetwood and a 7-1 demolition of Morecambe when every member of the forward line was on the score-sheet. These victories avenged some early season games when RMI lost at Fleetwood, were held to a goal-less draw at Morecambe and also knocked-out of the FA Cup by Mossley. At this stage of the season RMI had won 15 and drawn six of their 24 league games, scoring 60 goals against 27.

The first-team enjoyed a run of 15 games without defeat, having won all their home games, but they then suffered a shock home defeat early in the New Year when Nether-field won 1-0 at Grundy Hill. However, this was swiftly put to one side as RMI won their next game 4-2 at Darwen, Wignall scoring a hat-trick.

On a snow-covered Grundy Hill pitch on Saturday 8 February 1958 the players of RMI and Accrington Stanley Reserves lined-up in the centre circle to observe two minutes' silence in respect of the Munich air disaster involving Manchester United. Black arm bands were worn and this expression of sorrow was shown at all football grounds throughout Europe.

The match turned out to be one of the best of the season, despite the treacherous condi-tions. RMI won 5-1 with Wignall and Jones bagging two goals apiece and Bateson also on the score-sheet. Bateson had now earned himself a regular starting spot, replacing the injury-hampered Sammy Makin in the side. After the popular Makin had a recurrence of ankle trouble he decided to announce his retirement.

Away from league matters, RMI only progressed far in the Lancashire Junior Cup, moving into the semi-finals after defeating in turn St Helens Town, Marine and Lancaster City (who included ex-RMI forward Billy Lomax in their line-up). In the semi-final RMI faced

Burscough at Grundy Hill, a team they had already beaten twice in the league but faced a tough struggle on a bone-hard pitch before emerging victorious thanks to a solitary strike by Wignall. In the other semi-final Chorley defeated Morecambe 2-1 to set up an intriguing final at Ewood Park, Blackburn. To add interest to the cup final the two sides had still also to face one another twice in the league.

In the first league game at Chorley goals by Wignall and Jones earned RMI an impressive 2-1 win before 2,000 spectators, former RMI player Eric Spencer replying for the Magpies. But two days later in the return fixture at Grundy Hill Chorley earned revenge with a 1-0 victory, veteran player-coach Harry McShane scoring the only goal. On the same evening, Prescot Cables, RMI's main rivals for the title lost at home to Wigan Athletic.

With honours even RMI and Chorley met for a third time in the Lancashire Junior Cup Final on Wednesday, 30 April 1958 when 7,139 spectators paid £661 to watch the game at Ewood Park. On the night Horwich never really got going and Chorley dominated the play, growing in confidence. Two former RMI players, Spencer and Colin Evans were prominent in the Chorley side and it was left to the former, as mobile and deadly as ever to decide the issue with a 78th-minute strike after Worthington's header from a Hartley corner was only half-cleared. This was RMI's first away defeat for seven months.

The teams were as follows: RMI: Lea; Hopwood, Taylor; Brocklehurst, Parkin, Rudd; Kenny, Wignall, Jones, Speakman, Bateson. Chorley: Woods; Dunn, Bell; Evans, Cross, Smith; Hartley, Worthington, Littler, Spencer, McShane. The referee was Mr WH Darlington (Bolton).

But RMI quickly got over their disappointment and continued their push for the title. RMI's final league game of the season was at Prescot Cables who were four points adrift with a game in hand and a similar goal average. It looked as though everything would depend on RMI's trip to Prescot until their rivals lost unexpectedly at home to Marine to hand over the title. It was just as well that everything had not depended on the final game as RMI went down to a 4-1 defeat on the Friday evening before the FA Cup Final, though the players had perhaps relaxed with the title already decided.

The final table saw RMI top with 63 points from 42 games, two ahead of Prescot Cables. They won 28, drew seven and lost seven games, scoring 109 goals and conceding 47. Prescot won 26 games drew nine and lost seven, scoring 117 goals against 49. New Brighton came in third with 54 points, one ahead of fourth-placed Wigan Athletic. At long last RMI had achieved their cherished aim of becoming champions of the Lancashire Combination.

During the season RMI played a total of 53 league and cup games scoring 134 goals. Frank Wignall was top-scorer with 42 goals. Alan Jones and Sammy Speakman both scored 23 and George Bateson 15. RMI's other scorers were: Tommy Kenny 7, Eddie Rudd 5, John Brocklehurst 3, Roy Cozens 3, Derek Robinson 3, Jimmy Taylor 3, Sammy Makin 2, Rex Adams 1 and there were four own-goals.

In league games Hopwood made 40 appearances, missing only two games. Lea (39), Parkin (39), Speakman (39), Jones (38), Bateson (38), Wignall (37), Brocklehurst (34), Kenny (32), Layland (26), Rudd (25), Taylor (18) and Cozens (14) were the mainstays.

A souvenir booklet was produced to celebrate RMI's success and the editorial commented: 'Formed in 1896 (sic) the Club owed its birth to the old L&Y Railway Company. This link with the town's major industry has continued and today the Club, though independent in management maintains through its President, Mr ER Brown, the Works Manager, Horwich's close association with the Railway Mechanics' Institute and British Railways, who own the ground.

'The early days were spent in the West Lancashire League but ambition to play in a higher sphere resulted in applications to join the Lancashire Combination. These succeeded in 1915 (sic) and the Club have been members of the Combination ever since.

'The first playing pitch was on the Recreation Ground, on a site now occupied by the tennis courts and a season or two was spent on the old racecourse before the move to the present ground in the 1910-11 season.

'Although the Club had to wait 43 years for the first championship it was awarded the CE Sutcliffe Special Merit Medal in the 1928-29 season after finishing runners-up with 152 goals scored in only 38 games. No other club holds the medal for the donor, envisaging what might arise, discontinued the award.

'The club was unable to recapture the successes of the 1920s in the remaining pre-war years and during the war its activities were suspended. Football re-started in 1946 and although the early years presented difficulties, resulting in relegation to Division 2 twice in three years, the 1950s have seen RMI rise to its greatest heights.'

Pen pictures of the players were included in the booklet and the occupations of the players were described as follows: 'G Bateson- apprentice fitter; J Brocklehurst- a master painter and decorator; R Cozens- electrician; E Downes- textile management; J Hopwood- upholsterer; A Jones- apprentice electrician; T Kenny- master bricklayer; F Layland- schoolmaster; H Lea- schoolmaster; K Parkin- student public health inspector; E Rudd- schoolmaster; S Speakman- accountant's clerk; J Taylor- tool fitter; F Wignall- apprentice fitter.'

The editorial continued as follows: 'The stuff that championship teams are made of is difficult to define. Club officials and players will have their own ideas but to one on the outside of the Grundy Hill organisation three factors have seemed to be responsible. The first is the emphasis placed in recent seasons on the skills of the game as opposed to the vigour, the second is the careful recruitment of playing staff to fit in with preconceived ideas of what qualities are required and the third is level-headed administration ready to profit from errors and to impart confidence in the players that the club is run efficiently.

'Given these factors a championship is bound to be won sooner or later. RMI are the perfect example. No Combination club has a similar record of consistency over the last four seasons at least and it has been obvious that the honour, which has proved so elusive since 1915, was just around the corner.

'At the start of the season the foundation of a championship team was already prepared. All that was needed was the little bit of extra luck vital to success in football. Luck is rarely undeserved and the club has certainly invited its co-operation.

'The result was that new players and old merged into an effective blend, team spirit was of the highest order with every player pulling his weight and the ability inherent in the side blossomed into full fruit.

'The team selectors, whose normal lot is abuse, made their contribution on September 14th. That was the date of the Burscough game when the forward line was re-shuffled into the formation that helped win the championship. That was when the correct building was erected on the foundation ready to receive it.'

The club officials during the championship-winning season were as follows: Mr GH Fisher (Chairman), Mr F Rose (Vice-Chairman); Mr H Lucas (Secretary); Mr J Benthom (Treasurer); Mr H Taylor (Assistant Secretary). The following were also members of the committee: Mr A Dickinson, Mr J Hope, Mr W Holt, Mr J Lee, Mr A Ryder and Mr E Valentine.

Club secretary Mr H Lucas said: 'We're particularly happy to be champions. We feel that the honour has been well earned by a team that has tried all along to play good football and has given a lot of pleasure to the town's football enthusiasts in the process.'

The long-serving Tommy Embrey was trainer with Jimmy Jackson, a former Bolton Wanderers and Carlisle United player the assistant coach. The Supporters' Club officials were: Mr A Oxley (President); Mr H Ashcroft (Chairman); Mr W Humphreys (Vice-Chairman); Mr R Latham (Treasurer); Mr N Rimmell (Secretary). Other members of the committee were Mr C Barcroft, Mr J Crossen, Mr W Ellis, Mr J Gregory, Mr J Hollinshead, Mr T Howarth, Mr W Longworth and Mr T Mason.

In their first season in Division Two of the Lancashire Combination RMI Reserves finished a respectable 11th out of 20 clubs. They won 17 and drew six out of 38 games, scoring 80 goals and conceding 87.

Bolton Wanderers, meanwhile, lifted the FA Cup for the fourth time in their history after Nat Lofthouse's two goals saw them defeat Manchester United 2-0 at Wembley Stadium.

A profit of £71 was shown on the season and RMI's coffers were soon to be boosted further with the sale of star forward Frank Wignall. But first there was a celebration dinner dance to organise. This was held in the Mechanics' Institute on Saturday 7 June 1958 when Mr Thornton, secretary of the Combination made the championship trophy presentation. The chairman of Horwich Council was amongst the invited guests and he added congratulations on behalf of the town. Amidst the celebrations the club remembered two missing faces who would have taken great delight in the achievements, namely the former vice-chairman, the late Mr Harry Pennington and the veteran administrator the late Mr Harry Downes.

Also missing was a third face as trainer Tommy Embrey was ill in hospital. As a mark of appreciation for the man who had given 30 years' service to the club the players presented Mrs Embrey with a miniature cup and wished Tommy a speedy return to health.

It had never been doubted from the first moments when Frank Wignall stepped on the field for RMI that here was a young player destined for higher things. No sooner had the celebrations died down than he was transferred to Everton for a four-figure fee. Envious eyes had been cast at some of RMI's other players and goalkeeper Harold Lea also made the move into league football when he signed for Stockport County who at the time were managed by the former Bolton Wanderers player Willie Moir. To complete the list of high profile departures team captain Johnny Brocklehurst signed for Morecambe and amateurs Derek Robinson and Alan Jones both turned professional, Robinson with Netherfield and Jones with Morecambe. Former coach and centre-half Eric Downes signed for Darwen.

To counteract the departures the RMI committee had to recruit some new players quickly as the new season was dawning. The first to arrive was Bolton born centre-forward Vince Marren, secured for a small fee from Ashton United. Marren had scored over 40 goals in each of his two seasons at Ashton after previously playing in the Bolton Combination and then with Bury (on amateur forms) and Nelson. Bernard Cunningham, a highly regarded goalkeeper who had attracted league scouts in the past soon followed Marren from Hurst Cross. After the club decided to advertise for amateur players to have trials the response was heartening and no less than 65 players wrote in asking to be considered.

Sadly Tommy Embrey severed his long association with RMI due to his continuing ill-health and after initially accepting the appointment as his successor Jimmy Jackson re-signed the post. Second-team coach Jimmy Taylor stepped up to fill the vacancy and Fred Butler made a welcome return after a season out of the game.

Horwich R.M.I. Football Club

Playing Members of the Lancashire Combination

GROUND - GRUNDY HILL, HORWICH
COLOURS - BLUE AND WHITE STRIPES

Championship

SOUVENIR PROGRAMME

SEASON 1957-58

Official Celebration

SATURDAY, 7th JUNE, 1958. MECHANICS' INSTITUTE, HORWICH

RMI's Championship winning team of 1957-58
Standing (Left to Right) J Jackson, J Hopwood, F Layland, E Rudd, H Lea, K Parkin, F Wignall, J Taylor.
Seated (Left to Right) T Kenny, A Jones, J Brocklehurst, S Speakman, R Cozens, G Bateson.

Johnny Brocklehurst, RMI captain, with the Lancashire Combination Championship Trophy

A REBUILDING JOB

The 1958-59 season commenced with Ken Parkin appointed captain and Joe Hopwood vice-captain. For the opening game away to Lancaster City RMI's team showed several changes from the championship-winning season and was as follows: Cunningham; Hopwood, Layland; Holland, Parkin, Rudd; Kenny, Speakman, Marren, Butler, Bateson. Speakman and Bateson scored RMI's goals in a 2-2 draw.

The highlight of the early part of the season was a 3-2 win at Wigan Athletic when Marren, fast becoming a crowd favourite, netted a hat-trick. He followed up with another three goals as Morris Green (Bolton)-based works side Lomax, from the second division of the Combination, were hammered 7-1 in the Combination Cup. At that rate it looked as though RMI had secured another goal-scorer in the mould of Joe Keetley and Jimmy 'Flick' Mather.

Though RMI went out of the FA Cup 2-1 at the hands of Chorley (Spencer scoring the winning goal) there was still some lingering interest in the competition as Brocklehurst's new club, Morecambe, reached the first round proper. Brocklehurst also returned to Grundy Hill to play a significant role as Morecambe recovered from being 3-0 down to draw 3-3, his prompting and passing skills in midfield helping turn the game around. Lea, meanwhile, had firmly established himself in Stockport County's first team and his displays were attracting favourable comment in the national press. He went on to make 117 league appearances for County displaying an instinctive positional sense, a safe pair of hands and good judgement in the air.

Towards the end of the year two RMI players were honoured when they were selected to represent the Lancashire Combination in a game against a South African touring team. Tommy Kenny and Fred Butler's selections were well deserved as both players had contributed much to non-league football.

RMI survived a scare in the Lancashire Junior Cup against Padiham, winning the replay at the Arbories after their Division Two opponents had forced a 3-3 draw at Grundy Hill. To boost the squad three new players were signed at the turn of the year with Norman Hayes and Archie Wright joining the club from Darwen and winger David Jones from Fleetwood. Wright was approaching the veteran stage and was brought to Grundy Hill with the initial intention of helping the young players in the reserve team, but was to take on a more important role in the future.

RMI were in contention for the title until the closing weeks of the season and eventually finished in third position, five points adrift of champions New Brighton and one point behind Prescot Cables, the runners-up. They won 25 and drew nine of their 42 league games.

RMI again reached the final of the Combination Cup but went down 2-0 to Chorley on Monday, 7 May 1959 when the architects of the Magpies' success were again the former RMI players Spencer and Evans. The teams lined-up as follows: Chorley: Ashcroft; Dunn, Fairclough; Evans, Cross, Smith; Hartley, Spencer, Watson, Pearson, Littler. RMI: Cunningham; Hopwood, Layland; Rudd, Seddon, Parkin; Kenny, Speakman, Marren, Holland, Bateson. The referee was H Eccles (St Annes-on-Sea).

Before an attendance of 4,338 at Victory Park (receipts: £250) Chorley captain and player-coach Cyril Fairclough opened the scoring with a spectacular 40-yard free-kick after 20 minutes and Eric Littler's header just before half-time effectively decided the issue. Chorley successfully maintained a close watch on Marren as RMI failed to mount a second half response.

Despite that disappointment, however, the highlight of the season was undoubtedly the scoring feat of Vince Marren who found the net 51 times in as many games.

In the end of season retained list several regular faces were omitted and Cozens, Layland, Speakman and Gradwell were amongst those players to leave the club. The popular wing-half David Holland followed in Horace Lea's footsteps and signed for Stockport County while sadly work commitments forced Fred Butler to finally call time on his football career. Holland went on to make 25 appearances for County, scoring four goals.

RMI Reserves, meanwhile, again finished 11th in Division Two of the Combination, with 13 wins and four draws from 34 games. They scored 71 goals and conceded 73.

The 1959-60 season proved to be one of the most disappointing for many years as RMI slipped to tenth in the Combination securing a point-a-game from their 42 fixtures, their lowest finishing position for eight years. Initially things had appeared to be going well with new faces Bill Murray, a full-back from Netherfield, half-back Bernard Banks from Wigan Athletic and former Chorley inside-forward Dave Pearson all settling in well. Tommy Smith had now completed his army service and was available for selection every week while Archie Wright was appointed player-coach.

RMI started the season with a bang, defeating defending champions New Brighton 2-1 at the Tower Ground and then earning a 5-1 home win over Fleetwood when Pearson scored a hat-trick in the space of five minutes. RMI's team at the start of the season read as follows: Cunningham; Hopwood, Murray; Banks, Smith, Parkin; Kenny, Pearson, Marren, Bateson, D Jones. Early in the season Eric Evans, a former England rugby union international hooker acted as an advisor on training. Evans, who had won 30 caps for his country, captaining England between 1956 and 1958 was still playing club rugby for Sale and was highly respected as a sports coach, having trained at Loughborough College.

After an eight-match unbeaten run RMI's form slipped as injuries and loss of form combined to hamper any hopes of regaining the championship. They also suffered early exits in the cup competitions including a 2-1 defeat at Bacup Borough in the FA Cup first qualifying round. Several new players were brought in including Prescott from Wigan Athletic while Alan Jones returned. Prescott's stay at Grundy Hill was to be a brief one, however. RMI then had to sign a new goalkeeper after Cunningham broke his arm playing at Lancaster. Ironically, Cunningham's replacement was Edgar Bennett, from Lancaster. But as the 1960s dawned RMI began the decade in the worst possible way, losing 5-0 at home to Darwen. 'As a result Wright played his entire first-team in a reserve team game against Northern Nomads, and though a 5-2 win was achieved the performance did not give supporters any great hopes for the rest of the season,' Foley wrote.

While RMI struggled compared to recent seasons one of their former players, Gordon Atherton was receiving rave notices for his performances with Bury. He was declared man-of-the-match after Bury went down to an extra-time defeat in the FA Cup in the derby with Bolton Wanderers. Another local man in the headlines was referee Les Hamer who was appointed to take charge of the FA Cup fourth-round tie between Luton Town and Huddersfield Town.

The chopping and changing of the first-team continued with reserve players Kevin Jones and Bill Smith getting extended run-outs while Eddie Birchall was brought in to replace Prescott at inside forward. In April 1960 a young Adlington based player, 16-year-old Frank Lee was introduced into the reserve team at outside-right. Lee, an apprentice at the Loco Works training school scored two goals in the 3-0 defeat of Glossop and was immediately promoted to the first-team. Another newcomer was a red-haired forward Mick Connelly who made his debut in the final game of the season. Connelly made such an impression that Blackburn Rovers secured his services during the summer.

During the season RMI fielded no less than 56 players in the first and second-team fixtures, 28 of them in the first-team. But failure to achieve a settled blend had contributed to a disappointing season which was reflected in declining gate receipts. Disturbingly, membership of the Supporters' Club was also on the wane with a resultant dip in the income generated from the weekly pool.

On a happier note members present at the club's annual general meeting rose to honour Mr Cecil Tapscott who had given sixty years' support and service to the club. He was made a life-member in recognition of this achievement.

After a disappointing second season which saw him relegated to the reserves on occasion, RMI's record-breaking centre-forward Vince Marren was released by the club and joined Rossendale United. Marren's departure followed a trend and showed that RMI committees had little regard for sentiment or past achievements as previous record goal-scorers Keetley and Mather had also been summarily dismissed when their scoring rates dipped.

Marren had, however, still scored 25 goals and only Pearson (12) managed to emulate him in reaching a double-figure tally. Former captains Ken Parkin and Bill Murray and the long-serving Eddie Rudd were also not retained alongside Norman Hayes, David Jones, Dave Pearson, Edgar Bennett and Alan Hart.

Meanwhile, Horwich Council bought the old ACI ground at Lord Street for use as playing-field with the help of a substantial donation (£310) from Mr WE Ainscow, the managing director of a local towel-weaving firm.

At the 1960 AGM it was revealed that gate receipts now comprised only one-sixth of RMI's income and, compared to some previous seasons the club was operating on a shoestring budget. The Supporters' Club had raised £4,800 during the year and without their efforts the football club would not have been able to sustain Combination football. The Reserves had dropped to 12th in Division Two of the Combination with 30 points from their 34 league games.

Archie Wright was given the title of team manager and was now assisted by a former RMI player, Archie Lennox whose task was to concentrate on building up a strong squad of local players through the second team. Lennox, a member of RMI's immediate post war team, had been secretary of the Horwich Youth League and resigned that position to take up his new duties at Grundy Hill. Bill Seddon was also appointed to the coaching staff. Wright brought in two new Scottish born fullbacks, Armour Ashe from Southport and Fred Pirie from Accrington Stanley after losing Joe Hopwood, who rejected RMI's terms and signed for Wigan Rovers. Ashe and Pirie had played alongside Wright at Stanley.

Other newcomers included the former Manchester City, Chester and Southport player Gordon Davies, signed from Bacup Borough, and Jimmy Birkett, signed on trial from Chorley while amateurs Jim Cunliffe and Frank Lee, both Adlington youngsters, were given their opportunities. In the first match of the season, with Cunningham back in goal after returning from injury, RMI were represented by: Cunningham; Pirie, Ashe; Banks, P Seddon, Berry; Birkett, Birchall, Cunliffe, Davies, Bateson. The second team was as follows: Hudson; Halliwell, Barcroft; W Smith, Bennett, Gaskell; Lee, Kevin Jones, Alan Jones, Whittle, Flanagan.

Old campaigners Tommy Kenny and Tommy Smith were kept on the sidelines at the start of the 1960-61 season to allow the new signings and trial players to show their worth. Of the newcomers Cunliffe and Lee impressed the most. The 17-year-old Cunliffe led the line with dash and fire and soon demonstrated his goal-scoring ability while Lee was quickly picked up on professional terms by Preston North End, though he was later to return to RMI on loan. Lee went on to make 153 league appearances for North End, scoring 22 goals and later played for Southport and Stockport County. Derek Robinson returned after stints at Netherfield and Burscough and scored an early goal in RMI's 4-1 defeat of Darwen to mark his second debut for the club.

The season had barely got underway before the unfortunate Cunningham was injured again and his deputy Ken Hudson took over between the posts. Although Cunningham did make a brief comeback, Hudson's outstanding displays earned him a permanent place in the side. Despite a bright start, however, RMI's slide down the table continued and Wright appeared to change the side nearly every week. Three new forwards were signed in November 1960, namely Bill Lea, who had been on Blackburn Rovers' books and two former Accrington Stanley players, Bobby Entwistle and Jimmy O'Donnell. After their almost customary early exit from the FA Cup, losing 2-0 at Marine, RMI won only seven and drew two of their opening 18 league games.

Off the field it was announced that the Supporters' Club sweep, which had provided thousands of pounds for the parent club, was to be terminated and replaced by a daily draw which would be run under the auspices of the football club itself. The background to this change was the lifting of the ban by the Football Association on clubs taking part in lotteries themselves. A new organisation, known as the Horwich RMI Auxiliary Association was formed to operate the new venture.

At the outset over 10,000 leaflets were printed and distributed around the town explaining the new draw and a target membership of 12,000 was the aim to make a daily draw of £50 possible. The new draw started in March 1961 and by the end of April over 5,000 members had been recruited. The future of the Supporters' Club at that time was undecided. Its other activities had included the running of a canteen on the ground and the arranging of coaches to away matches.

As neighbours Chorley celebrated the championship for a second successive season, RMI fell to 13th in the Combination with 35 points from 42 games, using 38 players during the season. The Reserves finished 14th in Division Two having used 56 players but despite so many changes a profit of £200 was recorded on the year and the wages bill was slashed by £850. As RMI lost exactly half of their games and conceded 94 goals it came as no great surprise when it was announced that six of the twelve professionals were to be released after the end of the campaign. The six retained were old favourites Kenny, Bateson and Tommy Smith alongside Pirie, Livesey and goalkeeper Hudson, who was perhaps the most consistent player during the season. Tommy Kenny was due to commence his tenth season with the club and it was hoped that Smith would encounter much better fortune with injuries. Evergreen George Bateson remained an outstanding player, still showing the speed and skills he first displayed during RMI's championship-winning season and scored ten goals.

Of the departures perhaps the most surprising was that of tall centre-half Peter Seddon, who was still looked upon as a good future prospect. With the income flow from the new pool helping to stem the effect of falling gates RMI sought new and experienced players for the 1961-62 season. But they suffered an unexpected loss when centre-forward Jimmy Cunliffe, who had played for RMI on amateur forms, signed professional forms for Chorley. He had been RMI's leading scorer with 22 goals although turning out for Stockport County for a large part of the campaign before returning to Grundy Hill as a guest player.

RMI immediately signed two experienced former Wigan Athletic players, Fred Taberner and Ken Twidle. Centre-half Alan Herron soon followed in their footsteps while 18-years-old full-back Ken France and wing-half Keith Robinson were other recruits. After his spell with Blackburn Rovers Mick Connelly returned to RMI and full-back Alan Jones, forward Ron Waller, wing-half Terry Webster (ex-Barrow) and the former Southport player Barry Crookhall were other new signings.

Changes in the Lancashire Combination set-up were also announced. The second division was extended to 20 clubs and these would compete in future for the Combination Cup with the first division clubs entering a new Inter-League Challenge Cup with the Cheshire County League. It was felt this innovation might go some way to answering long-standing arguments over which of the two leagues produced the better football.

A BODY BLOW TO THE COMBINATION

The Combination suffered a body blow during the summer when Wigan Athletic resigned their membership and were accepted into the Cheshire County League. Not only did the Combination lose arguably its most influential club but RMI also lost out on the gate money from one of the most eagerly-awaited of derby matches. Ashton United decided to also follow Wigan's route but their application was turned down. As a result they had to re-apply for their old Combination place which was accepted but only by way of them playing in the second division. They went on to win the title at a canter to regain their first division place at the first attempt.

Just before the start of the season it was announced that the RMI Supporters' Club had disbanded. One of their last acts had been to help with the roof extension to the main stand so that this now also covered the paddock area. At the RMI AGM vice-chairman Fred Rose paid tribute to the work of the Supporters' Club over the years.

The new-look RMI team made a good start, winning at 2-0 Padiham and going on a run of six successive victories, including a 3-2 success at Runcorn in the new Inter-League competition. RMI's visit to Runcorn, incidentally, was their first since 1918 when the Linnets were members of the Combination before joining the Cheshire County League upon its formation. 'Big enough and good enough' was the Horwich Journal's reaction to the new recruits. The new first-team line-up read as follows: Hudson; France, Jones; Robinson, Herron, Smith; Connelly, Taberner, Twidle, Waller, Bateson.

But the inevitable disappointment followed as RMI were knocked-out of the FA Cup, 2-0 at the hands of second division Ashton United. By the start of October 1961, though, RMI were the Combination's only undefeated team and the run continued. On 18 November 1961 a new club record was established when RMI extended their unbeaten league run to 16 consecutive matches. The game was a hard-fought affair with Fleetwood fielding three former RMI players in David Jones, John Brocklehurst and Bill Murray. RMI's first league defeat of the season was suffered at Burscough on 2 December 1961 when they went down by the odd goal in five. Prior to that reverse RMI had won 12 and drawn five of 17 league games.

RMI recovered quickly, demolishing Chorley 6-2 at Grundy Hill with Twidle scoring three of the goals. A new centre-forward, Sweeney from Lytham was introduced and at first sight looked a real find, scoring two against the Magpies and another brace the following week in an 8-2 win over Padiham. He went on to score ten goals in his first six games for the club.

By mid-January 1962 RMI had scored 75 league goals, as many as they managed in the whole of the previous season with Twidle, Taberner and the evergreen Bateson frequently on the score-sheet. But strangely, after making such a fine start to his RMI career Sweeney's form suddenly deserted him. The change in fortune appeared to coincide with a complaint made by Northwich Victoria after the sides drew 0-0 in an Inter-League cup-tie at the Drill Field. Vics pointed out that Sweeney had already played against them in the same competition for Lytham earlier in the season. The match was eventually replayed at Northwich and RMI went down to a 2-0 defeat. In that first match at Northwich RMI gave a first-team debut to local boy David Chester, first spotted playing in the Horwich Youth League, after he had produced some consistently good performances in the reserves.

But RMI's fortunes declined during February 1962 due largely to a combination of injuries and sickness. Taberner sustained a bad injury and Twidle was dropped as RMI drew three and lost five in an eight-match sequence. It was during this bad run that Tommy Kenny, offered the post of player-manager at Darwen, severed his long connection with RMI. 'Tommy Kenny was always the model of the perfect club-man,' wrote Terry Foley in tribute. 'Highly skilful and completely dedicated to RMI he always gave of his best and was popular with the supporters. If ever the club compiled a roll of honour for the most prominent players Kenny's name would rank high-up among the best.'

After the set-backs RMI fought back to finish the season strongly, recording five successive victories and rising to a final position of third, nine points behind champions Morecambe and three adrift of runners-up Netherfield. Bacup Borough lost 9-1 at Grundy Hill late in the campaign when Chester scored five of the goals to mark himself down as a terrific prospect. RMI won 26 and drew nine of their 42 league games, scoring 110 goals and conceding only 48. Their defensive record was the best in the Combination and compared especially favourably to bottom-placed Padiham who conceded 154 goals. RMI Reserves, meanwhile, were 14th in Division Two.

George Bateson played in all 49 league and cup games during the season and full-back Kenny France missed just one game which coincided with his wedding day. 'Many RMI supporters thought that the season's football had been the best seen at Grundy Hill since the championship year,' Terry Foley wrote. 'Indeed, many said that the all-out attacking style had even surpassed that shown by the title-winning team.' Taberner scored 27 goals, Twidle 21 and Bateson 15. Sweeney (11), Connelly (11) and Chester (10) also reached double-figures during the campaign.

The Horwich public responded to the new attacking style and gate receipts increased by £400 on the previous season. The new draw had realised almost £12,000 and the club's balance sheet showed that the club had £4,250 in hand compared with £630 at the same time the previous year.

The retained list showed 17 professional players, namely Bades, Bateson, Connelly, France, Gordon, Hall, Herron, Hogg, Hudson, Jarvis, Jones, Livesey, Robinson, Smith, Taberner, Twidle and Waller. Sweeney was transferred to Fleetwood in a direct swap for Bobby Baldwin and David Chester signed professional forms. New signings included Johnny Calver and two Netherfield forwards Charlie Denehy and Geoff Slack. Twidle refused to accept RMI's terms and left the club to sign for Earlestown.

CHANGING TIMES

In 1962 the 169th and last diesel electric shunting locomotive to be built at Horwich (No.4157) left the Works on 28 December. Times were indeed changing and in 1963 a proposal to close Horwich Station was announced. Horwich Works was now part of British Railways Workshops Division and wagons were introduced into the Erecting Shop for repair. In May 1964 the last steam locomotive was repaired at the works as a transition was made from work on locomotives to other railway stock. The RMI committee managed to extend their agreement on the Grundy Hill enclosure but for an increased rent.

While many in the town mourned the passing of an era when Horwich was one of the foremost railway towns in the country, the club looked ahead to the new season with some optimism. Finances were much healthier and an all-time record number of professional players had been signed-up. RMI played a pre-season friendly against Tommy Kenny's Darwen who fielded no less than seven former RMI players in their ranks: Bennett, Longworth, Dunning, Holland, Marren, Sharratt and Jones.

RMI lined up as follows for the first game of the season when a 1-0 victory was achieved against Nelson: Hudson; France, Jones; Robinson, Herron, Smith; Bades, Taberner, Chester, Connelly, Bateson. Mick Connelly scored the only goal and soon found his early season form, scoring a hat-trick in a 4-0 win at Skelmersdale United in the next match but RMI then went down to a 3-0 defeat against Chorley.

Regarded as a big match at the time, RMI's Inter-League cup-tie against a Tranmere Rovers Reserves side that included the former Everton player Dave Hickson attracted a good crowd to Grundy Hill. They saw RMI completely over-run their Cheshire League opponents and Slack (3), Denehy (2) and Taberner (2) were on the mark in a resounding 7-0 victory. RMI bowed out of the FA Cup at the first qualifying round stage, however, losing 3-2 at Netherfield in a replay after a 2-2 draw at Grundy Hill.

Despite that setback the forward line began to click and after 13 league games RMI not only had scored 49 goals but also topped the table. One of the players making his mark was wing-half Keith Robinson who scored with some cracking long-range efforts. Manager Archie Wright maintained his promise of aiming to play attractive, attacking football. Another new player was Eric Shepherd, signed from New Brighton who made his debut in place of the injured Tom Smith as RMI defeated Chorley 3-1 at an almost fog-bound Grundy Hill. At the turn of the year RMI still topped the table with 34 points from 23 games.

At this stage of the season the biggest problem facing RMI was the weather. A mini-ice-age had gripped the north-west resulting in a lay-off from football for some six weeks and there was a considerable back-log of games before the thaw set in at the end of January.

The change in the weather coincided with an administrative change at Grundy Hill as it was announced that after three seasons with the club Archie Wright had accepted the full-time post as manager of Scottish Division One outfit Airdrieonians. Wright, who had originally joined RMI as player-coach to the reserve team before taking over as first-team manager from Jimmy Taylor, was the first RMI manager to have overall responsibility for team selection, a duty previously attended to by the club's committee.

The RMI committee acted quickly to appoint a replacement for Wright and on Monday 11

February 40-year-old Ken Horton took up his duties at Grundy Hill. A former inside-forward with Preston North End, Hull City and Barrow, scoring 56 goals in a total of 264 league appearances, Horton had later moved into non-league football. He was player-manager at Morecambe for three seasons before retiring to concentrate on his business commitments.

Just when it looked as though the long-lying snows were on their way out, a severe frost came down which was followed by fresh snow falls. The Grundy Hill pitch became a solid sheet of thick ice and club officials toured the district in an effort to find a suitable field for training purposes but were unsuccessful in their venture. The quest for new players continued unabated, however, and Peter Blease arrived from Runcorn. It was hoped that Blease would solve the club's centre-forward problem, a position that had held four occupants that season. Mr Horton's first signing of the club was the 26-year-old former Stafford Rangers forward Ray Calderbank.

RMI finally resumed their league programme on Saturday 2 March 1963 on a half-frozen and half-muddy Grundy Hill against a Darwen side that had gained only four points from 19 games. But the visitors, including six Grundy Hill cast-offs sprang a surprise. Centre-forward Jimmy Cunliffe scored twice inside the opening five minutes and inside-forward Bennett added two more to give Darwen a 4-2 victory. Former RMI captain Brocklehurst masterminded the whole affair, slowing the game down to his own pace and even managing pin-point passes on the treacherous surface. While this was RMI's first game since 5 January Darwen had last been in action on 15 December and so not even the long lay-off could be attributed for RMI's shock defeat. The following week, however, RMI recovered from the setback, scoring seven goals without reply at Lytham.

At the beginning of May RMI lost their battle for third place when rivals Ashton United won at Grundy Hill by the only goal of the game. RMI finished fourth with 55 points, three behind the Hurst Cross outfit and 13 points adrift of champions Morecambe, who ousted Chorley for the title on goal-average.

Disappointment in the league was countered by a good run in the Lancashire Junior Cup as RMI again reached the final. Their semi-final victory at Great Harwood was an exciting game, RMI prevailing 5-2 in extra-time with Taberner (2), Bateson, Chester and Calderbank on target. The final was against Morecambe at Deepdale, Preston, coincidentally directly after one of North End's best-known players, full-back Joe Walton, joined RMI from Accrington Stanley to assist Mr Horton and take on the role as player-manager of the reserves team. Left-back Walton had made 401 league appearances for North End in a 15-year career, after beginning his career at Manchester United. Prior to the final RMI also announced their retained list, placing nine of the 24 players on the transfer list including Herron, the centre-half and captain for each of the last two seasons. Keith Robinson, the regular wing-half was another who did not figure in Mr Horton's plans for the future.

The final, played on Wednesday 8 May 1963 was remembered for a last-minute incident that ended RMI's hopes of lifting silverware. With the game locked at 1-1 after Chester's goal for RMI on the hour-mark had cancelled out Roy Fawcett's 26th-minute opener RMI were looking the stronger side. As extra-time loomed the ball appeared to go out of play on RMI's left flank, but with RMI appealing play continued and Morecambe's unmarked left-winger Derek Armstrong secured possession before blasting home the winning goal from 25 yards. Amid the uproar from the jubilant Morecambe fans and the howls of protest from RMI supporters the referee awarded the goal without consulting his linesman. Seconds later the final whistle was sounded.

The teams lined up as follows: RMI: Hudson; France, Jones; Slack, Smith, Shepherd; Taberner, Connelly, Chester, Calderbank, Bateson. Morecambe: Thompson; Cubbage, Mitchell; Dunn, Scot, Keen; Fawcett, Morley, Borrowdale, Whitehead, Armstrong. Referee: H Tonge.

In all games RMI scored 131 goals, Taberner leading the way with 35, followed by Bateson (15), Baldwin (10) and Chester, Blease and Connelly (nine apiece). Taberner, though, refused RMI's terms for the following season and Mr Horton signed Tony Lyden from Morecambe as his replacement. Meanwhile George Bateson enjoyed a well-earned benefit season.

RMI Reserves enjoyed their best season to date in the Combination Division Two and finished in sixth position with 48 points from 38 games. They scored 100 goals and conceded 58. Including cup games the reserves scored 107 goals and their leading scorers were: Pimlott (21), Chester and Blease (18 apiece) and Baldwin (11).

Johnny Pimlott had the distinction of scoring an unusually quick goal, though it came at the start of the second-half rather than the first. Promoted to first-team action on Good Friday against Leyland Motors he collected a pass from Fred Taberner from the re-start after half-time, slipped past three defenders and shot the ball into the net with just 12 seconds on the clock. Incidentally, Pimlott went on to play for Radcliffe Borough, later serving that club as manager and chairman.

During the closed season Archie Lennox relinquished his post at RMI having been appointed manager of Radcliffe Borough, who had applied for division two of the Combination. His place as second team coach was taken by Johnny Ainscough, a former RMI player and subsequently player and trainer at Netherfield.

Mr Horton revealed his football philosophy at the club's annual general meeting in 1963 and laid out his vision for the future. He said that far more important than winning a championship was to have a club that players were anxious to join, one that was respected for its standards of behaviour and play, one that could win and lose games in the right spirit and one that believed that the entertainment on the field should be as high as the players were capable of producing.

The old chestnut of levelling the Grundy Hill playing surface also reared its head again. Chairman George Fisher reported that this had again been seriously considered and that advice from the Turf Research Institute had been obtained. The project would be a large one and the cost would be in the region of £8,000 and would also mean that the pitch could not be used for one complete season. The decision was again taken to defer this matter.

The club's balance sheet showed an increase of £1,100 on the previous year and there was a retained balance of £5,354 though concern was again expressed about declining gate receipts.

New players signed for the forthcoming season included Leo Gornall from Lancaster, Arthur Schofield from Wigan Athletic, Barry Dilworth from Preston North End and Tommy Willighan from Rossendale United.

RMI began the 1963-64 season with a 4-1 home win over Lancaster City when the following team was on duty: Hudson; France, Jones; Slack, Smith, Willighan; Gornall,

Lyden, Chester, Calderbank, Bateson. Chester (2), Bateson and Lyden scored for RMI with Lancaster's goal coming from the former RMI player Keith Robinson, who had been a big crowd favourite at Grundy Hill.

Burscough ended RMI's FA Cup hopes for another season, winning 3-0 at Grundy Hill before 691 spectators. But the following week RMI gained revenge, winning by the same score-line at Burscough in the league. It was almost as if RMI were jinxed in the FA Cup because season after season they made early exits from the competition after giving displays that did not match their usual league form.

There was an amusing incident concerning one RMI player, Ray Calderbank that Terry Foley related. 'Being without much of a 'crowning glory' Calderbank took to wearing a hair-piece, a pretty uncommon practice in those days,' Foley wrote. 'Much confusion was created among the Grundy Hill crowd one day when in one match he started the game wearing his full head of hair and then came out for the second half without it. Even the referee showed doubt as to his identity and took some time to be convinced that RMI hadn't slipped in another player during the interval.'

Concerned about a decline in scoring power, Mr Horton brought in striker Ian Whitehead from Morecambe just before Christmas. Whitehead, a well-known player in non league circles, had scored around one hundred goals in the previous two seasons. In the reserve team the performances of a young former Daisy Hill player Freddy Herring were also attracting rave reviews.

Around the turn of the year RMI strung together a nine-match unbeaten run that lifted the team to fourth place in the table. The reserve team was also producing some good performances, one highlight being a 12-2 thrashing of Vulcan Institute when Dennis Miller, a 17-year-old local product marked his debut with a six-goal haul.

The season was to end with RMI again in fourth place in the Combination with 56 points from 42 games. They finished just five points adrift of champions Chorley (61 points) with Netherfield (60) and New Brighton (58) also ahead of them. The Reserves finished seventh in Division Two with 40 points from their 34 games. A newly-formed Accrington side were allowed to take over Accrington Stanley's fixtures after the Football League club was wound-up in December 1963. They continued to play at Peel Park and won promotion to division one as champions.

Herring's displays in the second team had earned him a call up to the senior side and he made his debut alongside another reserve colleague, centre-half George Denton in a Lancashire Junior Cup-tie against Ormskirk-based Guinness Export at Grundy Hill which RMI won 8-0. RMI went out of the competition at the semi-final stage, losing 1-0 at Nelson, who went on lose to Chorley in the final. They also reached the last four of the Combination Cup before bowing out by a single goal at Marine.

Chester finished as top-scorer with 23 goals, the evergreen Bateson 17, Whitehead 16 and Calderbank 13. Meanwhile Crompton's Recs disbanded after finishing bottom of the division one table. RMI beat Recs 6-0 at Grundy Hill and won the return 2-0 on Easter Saturday.

At the season's end both Herring and Denton signed professional forms for the club. On the outgoing side Calderbank, Lyden and Willighan were among the eight professionals released. The reserve goalkeeper Hogg was also given a free transfer due largely to the club signing a new goalkeeper, initially on amateur forms from the Preston area. John

Pallett went on to become one of RMI's greatest-ever players. Other newcomers included centre-forward Bob Scott, wing-half Eric Atherton from Chorley and the experienced John Valentine from Stalybridge Celtic. The latter took over Ken France's full-back role after he declined to re-sign for RMI.

THE END OF AN ERA

On Wednesday 8 May 1964 there was a ceremonial send-off for the last steam locomotive to be repaired at Horwich Loco Works, a 2-8-0, 8F No. 48756. It was the last of some 50,000 locomotives to have been repaired over the course of 76 years. Later that year, on 25 September 1964, the last passenger train left Horwich Station and in 1966 goods traffic into Horwich Station ended. The Horwich Fork Line was closed on 30 January 1967.

Pallett, meanwhile, had not long to wait for his first-team debut which arrived in the opening game of the 1964-65 season against Bacup Borough. He was given his chance after the regular 'keeper, Hudson, became involved in a dispute with the club. Pallett soon signed semi-professional forms and won over the Grundy Hill crowd with his agility and style. At one time he had looked set to pursue a full-time football career with Preston North End but a broken leg put paid to that ambition.

RMI's team for the opening game was as follows: Pallett; Shepherd, Jones; Slack, Calver, Denton; Gornall, Herring, Scott, Whitehead, Bateson. Herring, Bateson and Whitehead scored the goals in a 3-0 victory.

The new-look RMI team 'clicked' straight away, scoring 20 goals in their first five games including a 5-2 win at Accrington in the FA Cup. But hopes of a long run in the competition were dashed as RMI went out to Lancaster City, after a replay, at the next stage. The most satisfying win was a 6-1 drubbing of Morecambe who were regarded as RMI's 'bogey' side around that time. Former RMI striker Fred Taberner was in the Morecambe ranks.

On Thursday 1 October 1964 one of the most remarkable games ever staged at Grundy Hill took place. RMI defeated visitors Nelson by the amazing score-line of 19-1. Not surprisingly there was some background for RMI's record score and a record defeat for the former Football League side. Nelson turned up for the game with only nine men of whom only one was a regular first-team player. They were due to play an FA Cup-tie two days later and so chose a scratch side to represent the club at Horwich.

'Much was made of the events of the game and the debate even reached the national press,' wrote Terry Foley. 'Was it unfair for RMI to slam 19 goals against such a weak outfit or was it unfair of Nelson to send such a depleted side? The whole affair was a farce and brought the good name of the Lancashire Combination into disrepute'.

George Bateson began the rout with a third-minute goal and the final tally of goal-scorers, with minutes read: Herring (16, 42, 69, 74), Gornall (55, 60, 71), Chester (35, 44, 85), Whitehead (14, 24, 52), Jones (68, 71, 75) Bateson (3, 17) and Smith (88). McKavett scored for Nelson after 58 minutes to make the score 10-1. 'But the biggest cheer of the day was reserved for Tommy Smith,' Foley added. 'He finally succeeded in scoring after his previously hitting the woodwork on two separate occasions.

'What little dignity was left in the game vanished in the closing minutes of the game when goalkeeper Pallett dribbled up-field in an attempt to get his name on the score-sheet.' The RMI side on that record-breaking occasion was: Pallett; Shepherd, Jones; Slack, Smith, Denton; Gornall, Herring, Chester, Whitehead, Bateson.

The following week RMI came back swiftly to earth when they suffered their first league defeat of the season at Lancaster, RMI cast-off Willighan scoring the winning goal.

On Wednesday 18 November 1964 the attention of the club and football fans from Horwich, Blackrod and surrounding areas was drawn to Wembley Stadium where the former RMI player Frank Wignall was to make his debut as England's centre-forward against Wales. After his move from RMI to Everton, Wignall had been transferred to Nottingham Forest and it was with his new club that Wignall began to attract the attention of the national selectors. The RMI club officials sent Wignall a congratulatory telegram before the game. 'One critic wrote that Wignall as the best centre-forward to wear the England shirt since Nat Lofthouse,' Foley noted. 'It was a very proud moment in RMI's history.'

Wignall marked his international debut with a 17th minute goal and added a second on the hour-mark. Despite a late replay from Cliff Jones England won 2-1 before a crowd of 40,000. The England team, managed by Alf Ramsey (later Sir Alf Ramsey) was: Waiters; Cohen, Thomson; Bailey, Flowers, Young; Thompson, Hunt, Wignall, Byrne, Hinton. Of that side George Cohen and Roger Hunt went on to become members of England's World Cup-winning side two years later.

But despite his fine debut Wignall played only one more time for England, in a 1-1 draw against Holland in Amsterdam just before Christmas 1964 when Jimmy Greaves scored England's goal. Wignall did go on to score 107 goals in 323 league appearances and played for Everton, Nottingham Forest, Wolves, Derby County and Mansfield Town before becoming player-manager of King's Lynn in 1973. He later had a successful managerial stint at Shepshed and also owned a garage and showroom in Nottingham.

By the turn of the year, meanwhile, RMI had won 15 and drawn three of their 20 league games and looked set for a title challenge. Chorley led the table but had played six more games. To strengthen the side Mr Horton brought in Westhoughton-born Brian Durkin, a speedy and tricky player who soon gained a first-team spot.

After a good run in the Combination Cup with victories over Blackpool Mechanics, Lytham and New Brighton RMI were well beaten by Chorley in the semi-final, the Magpies winning 3-0. And as the season reached its climax RMI's title hopes faded as they started to draw matches that on the balance of play many felt they should have won. In their last ten league games RMI won two, lost one and drew seven and they had to settle for fourth place for the third season in succession. The Reserves again finished seventh in division two, with 38 points from 32 games.

Netherfield (66pts) were champions with Chorley (63) and Morecambe (62) also surpassing RMI's tally of 61. RMI won 24 and lost only five league games but their final total of 13 draws eventually proved costly. Manager Ken Horton commented that the team's lack of a 'killer instinct' had cost them the championship together with the loss of form of top scorer Ian Whitehead and an injury to team captain Tommy Smith that kept him out of the vital closing matches. They scored 128 goals and conceded 53. In all games Whitehead and Herring each scored 25 goals, Scott 23, Connelly 20 and Bateson 17.

At the season's end the three players that shared the centre-forward position, Scott, Chester and Slack, were all released together with Whitehead. Mr Horton was clearly taking something of a gamble in releasing players with such proven goal-scoring ability and to help replace them he pinned his faith in Leyland Motors' centre-forward Brian Robinson and Billy Runciman, a young amateur who had played for Blackpool's junior sides.

At the 1965 annual general meeting steps were revealed to improve the club's finances after it was reported that over £1,000 had been lost on the season. It was thought that a major contributor to this loss was the redundancies that had occurred on the Loco Works. These were estimated to have cost the club £40 per week through the detrimental effect on the daily draw run by the Auxiliary Association.

The club announced that admission charges would be raised for first-team games to two shillings for adults, one shilling for boys and nine-pence for pensioners. There would be an extra shilling charged for transfer to the stand. Team expenses would be cut by an all-round pruning of wages and by operating with a smaller professional playing staff. All the retained players had signed for the coming season on reduced terms.

On the eve of the 1965-66 season manager Ken Horton was searching frantically to raise two full teams for the kick-off. Injuries, illness and administrative delays in the registration of new players had all added to his problems. But RMI shrugged off fears of a decline by winning their first three games, newcomer Robinson scoring two goals in the opening day win at his old club Leyland Motors and Brian Durkin and newcomer Ray Tong also impressing.

Mick Connelly returned from a bout of sickness to score four goals in RMI's 4-1 defeat of St Helens Town, coincidentally almost 12 months to the day when he last achieved the feat against Rossendale United. But newcomer Denis Bannister, signed from Bolton Wanderers appeared to be struggling with the transition to non-league football. In the reserve side a number of new players were catching the eye, particularly young centre-half Kenny Wright, half-back Coop and inside-forward Runciman.

Despite the promising start, RMI's customary misfortune in the FA Cup continued as they lost to Fleetwood in the early stages of the competition following a replay. Former RMI players Chester, Dilworth and Baldwin all played important roles in Fleetwood's 2-1 victory, Dilworth scoring an extra-time winner as John Pallett's brilliant performance in goal went unrewarded. Another ex-RMI player came back to haunt the club as Ian Whitehead scored the winner for Morecambe to inflict RMI's first league defeat of the season in early October.

The derby game at home to Chorley on 30 October 1965 was considered by old-timers to be one of the best games ever played at Grundy Hill. Before the season's biggest crowd RMI looked to be cruising to victory as they went in at half-time holding a three-goal lead. But the Magpies fought back to tie the scores 3-3. Brian Durkin then put his side back in front before Chorley's centre-half Bob Woods popped up to level the scores again. With just five minutes remaining of an incident-packed game Durkin raced through to settle the issue and give RMI a 5-4 victory that was the talk of the town for weeks afterwards.

Another memorable game was against Burscough in the first match of the New Year. The visitors' aggressive approach resulted in RMI goalkeeper Pallett being the target for several bad fouls in a physical encounter. RMI fought back from two goals down to level through Robinson and Tong before Bateson put them ahead. The game then boiled over as Pallett, always regarded as a gentleman player was sent-off for the first and only time in his career for retaliation after one of the many provocations he had suffered. Burscough levelled matters in the 89th minute and a match featuring frequent clenched fists, scuffles in the crowd and indignant supporters running on to the pitch was referred to by Terry Foley as the 'Battle of Grundy Hill.'

In the Lancashire Junior Cup RMI were matched against their old rivals Wigan Athletic at Springfield Park. Though Mick Connelly gave RMI the lead goals by Derek Houghton and Bert Llewellyn put Latics in front. The visitors were then reduced to ten men when Tommy Smith had to be assisted from the field with damaged ribs. Just before the final whistle Ray Tong scored a dramatic equaliser for RMI to force a replay at Grundy Hill.

The following Saturday, 19 March 1966, no less than 3,300 spectators poured into Grundy Hill producing record club receipts of over £300. It was RMI's biggest crowd for over ten years since Wigan's visit for the Combination Cup semi-final replay in April 1954. Alas for RMI it was Wigan all the way, the full-time professional outfit steamrollering their way to a 5-0 victory. Lyon (2), Brown, Houghton and Llewellyn scored the goals for the visitors. The RMI team was: Pallett; Shepherd, Jones; Valentine, Calver, Denton; Tong, Connelly, Herring, Durkin, Bateson.

Still smarting from this defeat RMI lost their next match 4-0 at Marine the following Wednesday before embarking on a winning streak that saw them finish fifth in the Combination table. They won 26 but drew only three of their 42 games scoring exactly 100 goals and conceding 58. RMI finished nine points shy of champions South Liverpool with Chorley, Skelmersdale United and Marine also occupying the top four places. In the last five seasons RMI's league form had been remarkably consistent with successive finishes of third, fourth, fourth, fourth and fifth respectively. The Reserves finished eighth in a second division reduced to 14 teams after the mid-season resignation of Accrington.

RMI also reached the final of the Combination Cup where they played Droylsden at Victory Park, Chorley on Friday 6 May 1966. To reach the final RMI had defeated Darwen, Nelson, St Helens Town and Clitheroe. Terry Foley wrote that RMI gave their best display of the season in that game as they earned a clear-cut 5-0 victory. Ahead at half-time through Mick Connelly's 21st-minute goal after his cross-cum-shot was mishandled by the Bloods' goal-keeper, RMI's attacking policy was further rewarded with four second half goals. Connelly scored his second eight minutes after the re-start after being set-up by Robinson. Robinson headed in the third goal on 64 minutes, Tong slotted home the fourth and Robinson completed the rout after converting Herring's centre as RMI earned their first honour for eight years. At the conclusion of the game the RMI captain John Calver was presented with the cup by Mr Sam Pilkington, President of the Lancashire Combination. The RMI team was: Pallett; Valentine, Jones; Smith, Calver, Denton; Tong, Connelly, Robinson, Herring, Bateson. The Droylsden team was: Quigley; Stott, Logan; Boyle, J Smith, Walker; Tonge, Plant, Blease, Brown, Campbell. Referee: R Ditchfield (Morecambe).

The club retained all its professionals at the end of the season with the exception of Dennis Bannister, who was released. During the season Brian Robinson scored a total of 50 goals in league and cup. The other leading scorers were: Mick Connelly (21), Ray Tong (14), Fred Herring (14), George Bateson (12) and Brian Durkin (10).

RMI team group, circa 1962

RMI team group, 1963-64

RMI team group, 1967-68

CHORLEY   Black and White

SALISBURY

HOWARTH   EDISBURY

ECCLES   WOODS   SMITH

SHAW   ROWLEY   WROTH   TOMLINSON   ARMSTRONG

Referee:
Mr. I. T. Smith,
Clayton-le-Moors

BATESON   BANNISTER   ROBINSON   HERRING   TONG

COOP   CALVER   CONNELLY

JONES   SHEPHERD

PALLETT

Horwich R.M.I.   Blue and White

3d.   OFFICIAL PROGRAMME   №   310

CHORLEY A.F.C.

Members of the Lancashire
Combination Divisions One
and Two

LANCS. COMBINATION
DIVISION 1.

CHORLEY
v.
HORWICH R.M.I.

SATURDAY,
JANUARY 8th, 1966
Kick-off 3-0 p.m.

Programme for a 'Derby' game at Chorley, January 1966

Goalkeeper John Pallett was a magnificent servant to RMI in the 1960s and early 1970s. He was also an accomplished cricketer, primarily for Leyland in the Northern League, playing in four separate decades. In 1991 he set a new club record in Division Two, scoring 793 runs at an average of 56.64.

Terry Foley, unofficial Historian for the Railway Mechanics' Institute and a great authority on the RMI Football Club, pictured at his desk in the Loco Works.

Supporters always enjoyed their trips to the seaside, especially for early and late season matches.

This programme is for a visit to New Brighton in September 1968.

STALWARTS DEPART AS A NEW HERO EMERGES

The lead-up to the new season (1966-67) brought with it the usual crop of surprises, none more so than when the trio of Bateson, Calver and full-back Jones all signed for the Cheshire League side Runcorn, where they teamed up again with the former RMI full-back Ken France. Left-winger George 'Dicky' Bateson had been a virtual fixture in the RMI side for nine seasons and only missed the occasional match due to injury. Terry Foley wrote: 'He was perhaps the most consistent winger ever to play for RMI and along with Tommy Kenny would long be remembered for the way he could exploit the Grundy Hill slope. Bateson was to return to help the club in its greatest crisis a decade later, an act that summed up the character of the player.' Though known primarily as a goal-provider rather than scorer he had nevertheless scored 116 goals for RMI and added a further three to his tally upon his brief return.

At the club's annual general meeting it was revealed that a profit of £160 had been made on the season. With regret the departure of first-team trainer Bill Seddon was announced after long and loyal service to the club. Seddon's retirement was not to last long, however, and his vast experience would again be utilised in the not too distant future. John Ainscough filled Seddon's place as trainer and Johnny Brocklehurst returned to the club as reserve-team trainer.

Before the start of the 1966-67 season RMI's officials worked hard to bolster the squad and their recruits included centre-half Fred Hitchin, formerly with Chorley and Fleetwood, full-back Keith Smith from Netherfield and young Westhoughton-born centre-forward Gordon Morris who had previously been on Darwen's books. Other new faces were strong-man Cyril Wallwork from Nelson and two more Westhoughton youths, full-back John Ramsdale and half-back Fred Hutchinson.

'It was thought at the time, with all the team changes taking place, that the coming season would be something of a challenge,' wrote Foley. 'But everybody breathed a sigh of relief when the season began with two good home wins over Great Harwood and Clitheroe. RMI's team for the opening game read: Pallett; Hitchen, K Smith; T Smith, Wallwork, Denton; Durkin, Connelly, B Robinson, Herring, Tong. After the initial flourish RMI found goals hard to come by and so recruited a big, hard-shooting forward when Tom Pinder signed from Nelson for a small transfer fee. They also exited the FA Cup at an early stage, losing 1-0 at Chorley.

This particular season also saw the substitutes allowed for the first time and it was on Saturday 29 October 1966 that RMI first took advantage of the new ruling. In the match against Netherfield at Grundy Hill Freddy Herring, scorer of the game's only goal was later injured and substituted by Brian Durkin.

Many of those who had seen Frank Wignall make his debut and were rightfully convinced that there was a star in the making now had another fine prospect to watch. A handful of RMI stalwarts present for the reserve game against Nelson just before Christmas saw Tony Webber, a young college student from Aspull make an immediate impression with his powerful shooting. Incidentally, this was the same Nelson team that had once played in the Football League and were RMI's Combination rivals for many years; sadly they were now struggling in the lower reaches of division two.

One of the best results of the season was achieved at the start of January 1967 when RMI defeated the defending champions South Liverpool at Holly Park, with Fred Herring scoring twice. South Liverpool had the former RMI favourite Sammy Speakman in their line-up.

Webber's displays in the reserves eventually were rewarded by a first-team call-up and he made his debut at home to Chorley on 25 February 1967. Though named at outside-left he was given the freedom to roam the forward-line at will. Webber scored RMI's goal in a 1-1 draw and, according to Terry Foley 'his display of enthusiasm and dash, together with his thunderbolt shot was the highlight of an otherwise dull match.'

The two derby rivals met again in the Lancashire Junior Cup when RMI forced a 1-1 draw at Victory Park, despite being without George Denton who had over-slept after working a night-shift. But Chorley won the replay emphatically by 4-0 and in doing so inflicted RMI's first home defeat of the season.

The season ended with RMI finishing runners-up to Morecambe in the Combination with 63 points from 42 games, a points-tally exactly the same as during the championship-winning season of 1957-58. Morecambe led the table with 69 points from 41 games. Skelmersdale United had become the first Combination club to reach the FA Amateur Cup Final and their scheduled home fixture against Morecambe was not played. Netherfield were third with 62 points and Chorley fourth on 55 points. In Division Two RMI's reserves side finished eighth out of 16 clubs with 31 points from 30 games.

At Grundy Hill the RMI first-team's record was outstanding: played 21, won 18, drawn 3, lost 0, for 53, against 13. Away from home RMI won nine, drew six and lost six, scoring 35 goals against 24. The success was achieved despite not having a prolific scorer in their ranks, the season being very much a team-effort. In all games Pinder was top-scorer with 16 goals, Herring scored 15 and Robinson 14. Denton (12) and Tong (10) also reached double-figures.

The retained list included all the professionals with the exception of centre-forward Brian Robinson and wing-half Eric Eccles but there was a shock for the supporters when left-half and team captain George Denton together with popular forward Freddy Herring rejected terms and signed for Cheshire League Runcorn. The Linnets now had no less than six former RMI players in their ranks. Connelly enjoyed a benefit match in May 1967 in recognition of his service to the club.

IMPORTANT DECISIONS ARE MADE

There were some important decisions for club officials during the summer of 1967. A new Northern Premier League was set to come into operation for the 1968-69 season and applications were underway for membership. RMI easily qualified for inclusion on the strength of their past seasons' records but after careful consideration the RMI committee decided to reject plans to join the new league on the grounds of finance. They pointed to the long journeys that would be involved with hotel bills, time off-work for the playing staff and the additional and rising costs of travel. Club chairman George Fisher stated that if the club had the financial resources they would have jumped at the opportunity but for safety's sake it would be best for the club to decline membership.

'Mr Fisher's statement did provoke mild controversy,' wrote Terry Foley. 'Some supporters thought that the right thing had been done while others contended that the possible higher level of football and new teams in the league would draw in the crowds to Grundy Hill. But over the years the football fans of the town had required some coaxing, even with a championship-winning team.' But in retrospect the decision not to participate in the NPL opened the way for other local sides to establish themselves at a higher level, leaving RMI down the 'hierarchy.'

Comment was made at the annual general meeting on the loss of players to other clubs and the new legislation that ended the practice of retained lists. The new agreement would enable clubs to sign-on players for a specific period of time with an option to extend. First-team trainer Johnny Ainscough resigned his post and this resulted in the return of Bill Seddon to Grundy Hill as his replacement. This move was followed quickly by the appointment of Tom Pinder as reserve-team trainer. The list of new signings included Johnny Robinson, a winger from Chorley who had played previously for Bury and as quite a novelty, the Errington twins, Brian and Allan, from Oswestry Town. Popular forward Mick Connelly moved on to sign for Chorley and the released Robinson was picked up by Lancaster City.

Turning briefly away from playing affairs the club had received many compliments over the past few seasons over the playing surface, despite the slope. 'The surface was lush and green, fit enough to accommodate a game of bowls,' wrote Terry Foley. 'Credit went deservedly to one man, groundsman Bob Turner. Pride of achievement shone in Bob's face and during match days his voice could be heard, warning off anyone apart from those involved in the game that ventured on to his 'holy ground."

It was also at this time that the officials had been considering erecting a social club at the Grundy Hill end of the ground. The venture was looked upon as providing financial aid to the club's future but after snags and opposition from some quarters, coupled with an estimated cost of £40,000 the scheme was finally abandoned.

In the summer ambitious clubs such as Morecambe, Netherfield, Chorley and Fleetwood had been busy all going to considerable lengths to strengthen their teams with an eye on the Northern Premier League, and it looked as though the competition for points was going to be fiercer than ever in the coming season.

RMI's team for the opening game was: Pallett; Hitchen, K Smith; T Smith, Wallwork, Wright; J Robinson, Wallbank, Webber, Runciman, Tong. Substitute: Ashworth. But there was a shock for the supporters as St Helens Town recorded a 2-0 victory at Grundy Hill.

One early season highlight was a 6-4 victory over Guinness Export, when Webber and Runciman each scored hat-tricks. 'Runciman, on his day, showed amazing ability,' wrote Terry Foley. 'He could be brilliant with his passing and his knack of scoring goals from seemingly impossible angles. On the other hand he could be just as bad and frustrating. If he could have found consistency in his good play he would surely have starred in the Football League.'

Runciman soon lost his place as the 1967-68 season unfolded with Brian Durkin returning to the club after initially refusing to re-sign due to other commitments. Phil Parry made his debut with the first-team against Great Harwood on 23 September 1967 after good form in the reserves and went on to become a stalwart RMI player for many seasons. A few weeks later another young reserve team player, midfielder Vernon Lang, also made his first team bow as he started out on what would be a long association with the club.

The Lancashire Combination Cup second round tie with Wigan Rovers developed into a long drawn-out saga. The first game at Grundy Hill finished in a 1-1 draw and the replay at Poolstock was abandoned after nine minutes due to a waterlogged pitch. RMI then lost the replayed game 2-1 but this tie was later declared null and void as Rovers' goalkeeper was found to be ineligible. At the fourth attempt RMI progressed to the next round with a 2-1 win.

But after the usual early FA Cup defeat, this time at hands of Cheshire County League outfit Hyde United, attention switched to the form of Tony Webber whose displays were attracting Football League scouts. Webber gave a brilliant individual display as RMI won 2-1 at Skelmersdale United, scoring both his side's goals. His winning effort, eight minutes from time, was from a seemingly impossible angle and demonstrated his talent and never-say-die attitude to the full.

In December 1967 the teams that would constitute the Northern Premier League for the following season were announced. The Lancashire Combination would lose five of its member sides to the new set-up, namely Chorley, Morecambe, Netherfield, South Liverpool and Fleetwood. It was feared in Combination circles that the prestige of winning the title would disappear with these teams but there were more shocks to follow before the season's end.

Meanwhile, some former RMI players were enjoying success in the FA Cup. Fred Taberner, now with Macclesfield Town, was looking forward to a visit to Fulham after helping his side defeat Stockport County and Spennymoor United. The 'RMI old boys' team, Runcorn, with George Bateson, Freddy Herring, George Denton and Alan Jones in their ranks had caused quite a stir by defeating Notts County before going down at Southport. Local referee Les Hamer, now in his last season on the League list before being forced to take compulsory retirement was honoured by being appointed to officiate at the League Cup Final at Wembley. Leeds United beat Arsenal 1-0 with Terry Cooper scoring the game's only goal on 2 March 1968.

The question mark over Tony Webber's future was finally settled in January 1968 when Bolton Wanderers paid RMI £3,000 for his services. Webber turned out for his debut in the reserves the following day against Stoke City at Burnden Park, cheered on by a large contingent of RMI supporters. Webber's departure left a big gap to plug and after Phil Parry, Runciman and Wallbank filled the position the signing was announced of the ex-Chorley star Peter Watson. After being so often a thorn in RMI's side in the past it took some time for supporters to adjust to the fact that the prolific Chorley striker was now on their side.

The Combination was thrown into further turmoil in March 1968 when three clubs, Skelmersdale United, Droylsden and Ashton United resigned and applied for membership of the Cheshire County League while Southport were also considering moving their reserve team to the Lancashire League. At this moment the Combination would be left with 14 clubs in its first division and 12 in its second and it was felt the standard of football would inevitably deteriorate. George Fisher and his committee acted swiftly and it was decided that RMI would apply for membership of the Cheshire County League. The club was accepted, only hours before the deadline closed for new applications and, with regret a long association with the Lancashire Combination was severed. The Combination carried on in a weakened form until the formation of the North West Counties League in 1982.

Goalkeeper John Pallett completed his 200th consecutive game for RMI in the home game against Rossendale United on 20 April 1968, a remarkable level of consistency from the popular club-man. He celebrated by keeping a clean-sheet in a 5-0 victory.

With RMI heading for a mid-table position in the Combination most interest in the closing weeks of the season centred on the Combination Cup. After their saga with Wigan Rovers, RMI had battled through at the third attempt at the expense of Guinness Export to secure a semi-final tie at Southport Reserves where Ray Tong's re-taken penalty decided the issue. At least RMI would mark their departure from the Combination in some style, with a home final against Morecambe. Meanwhile, RMI's final league game in the Combination ended in a drab 0-0 home draw against Lancaster City. The RMI team was: Pallett; Chadwick, Smith (sub: Ashworth); Westwell, Goodlad, Wright; Bradshaw, Lang, Watson, Runciman, Pilkington.

But the Combination Cup Final, staged four days later on Wednesday 15 May 1968, attracted the biggest crowd of the season to Grundy Hill as Morecambe completed a league and cup double by winning a tightly-contested game 2-1. Left-winger Charlie Lea shot Morecambe into a 55th-minute lead after Pallett parried a Stuart Holding shot and Arnold Timmins added a hotly-disputed penalty five minutes later after he was adjudged to have been fouled by Goodlad. Vernon Lang scored RMI's goal with a 20-yard shot almost immediately but though RMI had marked their last game in Combination football with a wholehearted display Morecambe deserved their victory. The RMI side lined-up as follows: Pallett; Hitchen, K Smith; T Smith, Goodlad, Wright; Bradshaw, Lang, Wallbank, Durkin, Tong.

In the league RMI finished ninth, their lowest placing since the 1959-60 season. They won 19, drew nine and lost 14 games. Despite his departure Webber finished as top-scorer with 20 goals. Wallbank hit 19 goals and Watson nine. The RMI reserve team had a miserable time and finished next to bottom in their last season in the Combination with only 19 points from 32 matches. The Combination committee then turned down RMI's application to continue fielding their reserves in the competition.

After a season of upheaval there was one more shock to come when team manager Ken Horton tendered his resignation, due to a combination of medical advice and business commitments. Horton had proved a successful and popular manager at Grundy Hill and RMI acted hastily to secure his replacement, appointing the Darwen player-manager Mr Paddy Sowden as his successor.

To a certain extent RMI supporters regarded the 1968-69 season as a leap into the unknown with a new manager, a new league and several new players. Mr Sowden brought in a number of new faces, securing the services of Tony Moulden, formerly with Bury and Peterborough United and ex-Chorley striker Barry Tomlinson. George Denton also returned from Runcorn.

These three signings meant that RMI started the season with ten professionals and nine amateurs, their smallest first-team squad for many years. There was a certain amount of trepidation as to how RMI could cope with the new league with such thin resources. The reserve team, meanwhile, had also to adapt to new surroundings. After finishing in the re-election places they had been voted out of the Combination and applied to join the Manchester League. Tom Pinder was appointed trainer to the reserve team and continued to play in times of emergency.

Commenting on the reserve side's re-election failure RMI secretary Bert Lucas said: 'There appeared to be a feeling that we have let the Combination down, which is of course nonsense. Nobody tried to maintain the status of the Combination more than we did and we only resigned our first team when it became apparent there was no hope left. Then we had to think of our spectators.'

INTO THE CHESHIRE COUNTY LEAGUE

RMI's first taste of the Cheshire County League came with the visit of Chester Reserves to Grundy Hill on 10 August 1968. RMI made a good start, winning 3-1 with goals by Tomlinson, Moulden and Durkin. The RMI team was: Pallett; Hitchen, K Smith; Denton, Wallwork, Wright; Moulden, Durkin, Watson, Tomlinson, Parry.

But Skelmersdale United then won 3-1 at Grundy Hill with their outside-left Mickey Burns in outstanding form. Burns, who went on to forge a successful career with Blackpool and Newcastle United, was again a thorn in the RMI side as his side won the return game 4-0 one week later.

RMI brought in several new players to boost the squad, signing Alf Jones from Wigan Athletic, Graham Ashworth from Stockport County, Barry Tomlinson from Chorley and Dave Parkinson from Southport. They were followed by Bill Edisbury, a former Bolton Wanderers player, and Johnny Dalton from Morecambe as Mr Sowden rang the changes. He later added several more players, including Tom Aspinall, Gary O'Loughlin and Frank Armstrong.

But injuries to Peter Watson and Cyril Wallwork cast doubts over their futures with RMI while Brian Durkin cancelled his contract with the club and was eventually to sign for Runcorn. Both Edisbury and Tomlinson were released after extended trial periods. Tommy Smith and Alf Jones, however, recovered from long injury lay-offs to reclaim their first-team spots.

The visit of one of the expected 'big guns' of the league, Stafford Rangers, created much excitement to Grundy Hill. Stafford brought along a large following of supporters and players from both sides responded to the atmosphere as a thrilling 1-1 draw was played out. After eleven league games RMI averaged a point-a-game and had made a satisfactory start.

But despite the new manager and new-look side the familiar failings in the FA Cup continued. After defeating Wigan Rovers following a replay RMI were handed out a thrashing as Mossley recorded a 5-1 win at Grundy Hill.

There was sad news of an old RMI favourite when the death was announced of Eddie Rudd at the age of 39 on 28 November 1968. Signed from Accrington in 1952 Rudd, a school-teacher by profession had played for RMI until retiring at the end of the 1959-60 season and was a strong tackling half-back and a fine club man.

When RMI met Oswestry Town at Grundy Hill on Saturday 19 October 1968 there was a surprise name in the RMI line-up. Rumours had been circulating in the town that Tony Webber had far from enjoyed his time at Bolton Wanderers and that a return to RMI was on the cards. When Webber's return was confirmed he received a hero's welcome from the Grundy Hill faithful.

RMI avenged their FA Cup exit by defeating Mossley 3-1 in the league at Grundy Hill with goals from Tommy Smith, Webber and newcomer Jim Mitchinson but the joy over this fine victory was tempered with the news that centre-half and club captain Wallwork was forced to retire from the game on medical advice. One consolation was that Kenny Wright had proved a most able successor and was turning in some consistently good performances. Webber was also on the mark with a last-minute winning goal at Sandbach to show he had lost none of his opportunism and he went on to finish as top-scorer with 14 goals.

The team had now changed considerably from the start of the season and Mr Sowden continued to bring in new faces, including John McKay, a versatile forward from Wigan Athletic, outside-right Arthur Shaw from Wigan Rovers and outside-left Walt Stanley from St Helens Town. All three players were in the squad for the game at Stafford Rangers when RMI went down to an unlucky 2-1 defeat before 1,912 spectators. The RMI side was as follows: Pallett; Jones, Davies; Denton, Wright, Parry; Shaw, Mitchinson, Webber, Armstrong, Stanley. Substitute: McKay. But this proved to be Stanley's only game for RMI as he was released owing to travelling difficulties.

One of the most significant RMI signings for the future was that of Morecambe's Malcolm Woodward, son of the former Bolton Wanderers player, Tommy Woodward, and like Webber and Mitchinson a Physical Education teacher. But as Terry Foley wrote: 'Grundy Hill had never seen so many players coming and going during a season and the hard core of supporters, the senior citizens were finding it difficult to put a name to a face. 'Who's yon mon, Joe?' 'Dern't know; must be a new 'un,' was typical of the remarks made under the Scratching Shed at every home game.'

Although now in different leagues old rivals RMI and Chorley met again in the quarter-final of the Lancashire Junior Cup. Fred Taberner, now player-manager of the Magpies, did the damage with two goals in his side's 3-0 home victory. As the season drew to a close it was announced that Peter Watson, who had played mainly in the reserves since Webber's return and Tom Aspinall had left the club. Watson subsequently signed for Radcliffe Borough.

RMI finished tenth in their first season in the Cheshire County League, winning 13 and drawing 13 of their 38 games and scoring 54 goals whilst conceding 63. Skelmersdale United, at that stage an all-amateur club, were champions but it was runners-up Stafford Rangers who moved up into the Northern Premier League at the end of the season. Chorley, meanwhile, finished next-to-bottom in the first season of the Northern Premier League and re-joined the Lancashire Combination. But after just one season back in the Combination the Magpies were re-elected to the Northern Premier League for the 1970-71 season when the league was extended from 20 to 22 clubs.

The Combination was now in steep decline and had only 16 clubs in membership for the 1970-71 season, soldiering on until closing down in 1982 when the North West Counties League was formed. For those football followers that remembered the heyday of the Combination its sad and lingering decline brought only sorrow.

Chester Reserves left the Cheshire County League at the end of the season and Marine and Port Vale Reserves were admitted for the 1969-70 campaign. RMI's opponents included far-flung clubs such as Rhyl, Oswestry Town and Frickley Colliery.

After making so many changes to the club's playing personnel during his short time with the club, manager Paddy Sowden did not stay to see the results of his labours bear fruit. Instead he took up a full-time appointment as youth team coach at Blackpool. Despite his departure, Mr Sowden attended the club's annual general meeting in July 1969 and predicted that the club should achieve a top five finish in the following season.

The general feeling was that the club had made a wise move in joining the Cheshire County League. 'The decision to break with the Combination was a good one,' said the chairman, George Fisher. 'I think the league was the weakest it had been in its history and it was like watching a lot of Sunday school teams.'

The club was in a healthy financial position with retained funds of £13,508. The Auxiliary Association draw had been a huge success, generating revenue of £7,161, a figure that dwarfed the total gate receipts of £636. The wage bill amounted to £4,861 so without the draw RMI would clearly have never sustained that level of football on money coming in through the turnstiles. They did lose the services of committee member John Banks, who left to join the board of directors of Bolton Wanderers.

Mr Willie Millar, a 44-years-old Scot was appointed to replace Sowden. A friend of the ex-manager he was a former Partick Thistle, Aberdeen, Stirling Albion, Swindon Town, Gillingham and Accrington Stanley winger and had been acting as trainer-coach at Grundy Hill and so the transition was expected to be seamless, especially as Tom Pinder stepped up from the reserves to fulfil a similar role with the first-team. Greenock-born Bill Calder, a former Leicester City, Bury, Oxford United and Rochdale forward who had scored 96 Football League goals in 252 games, was the major closed season signing from Nantwich while Harry Beech signed after a trial. Beech, a Kearsley-born wing-half had league experience with Bolton Wanderers and Southport and was another former Nantwich player. Pallett signed a new two-year contract after interest from many clubs in his services while Kenny Wright was appointed club captain.

In 1969 the new BRSA Club was opened on Chorley New Road and soon built up a membership of 700. But changes on the works were continuing apace. In 1970 Horwich Loco Works became part of British Rail Engineering Limited and two years later the L&Y Café, a major landmark for nearly a century, was demolished.

RMI began the 1969-70 season with a 4-0 win at Ashton United, Webber and Calder sharing the goals and beginning what was to prove a fruitful striking partnership. The RMI side was: Pallett; Jones, Atkinson; Smith, Wright, Denton; Lang, Beech, Webber, Calder, Woodward. Substitute: Williams.

RMI won six of their opening seven league games in which Calder scored ten goals and Webber a further six, but there was disappointment in the FA Cup as RMI lost to Mossley in the third qualifying round while their first venture in the newly-constituted FA Trophy ended in a 2-1 defeat at Rossendale United in the first qualifying round. The Football Association Challenge Trophy, to give it its full title was introduced by the Football Association in 1969 as a nationwide competition for semi-professional teams who were thus ineligible to enter the FA Amateur Cup. The latter competition was replaced by the FA Vase in 1974 as the FA abolished the distinction between professional and amateur players.

David Donaldson, a Scot from Dunfermline Athletic and David Glasgow, an 18-year-old inside-forward who had been playing for Bolton Wanderers 'A' team were added to the squad, but there was a surprise in March 1970 when Pallett was dropped for the first time in six seasons and replaced in goal by Gerry McEvoy.

In their second season in the Cheshire County League RMI improved considerably and finished fourth with 21 wins and six draws from 38 games. Webber scored 37 goals in all games, Calder 30 and Woodward 15. Skelmersdale United were champions again, finishing 14 points clear of runners-up Mossley (52pts) with Stalybridge Celtic (49) edging RMI (48) for third place.

RMI suffered three defeats at the hands of Skelmersdale United during the season, including a quarter-final knock-out in the Lancashire Junior Cup when future Liverpool star Steve Heighway scored an 87th-minute winner, and endured a run of six consecutive defeats during March. However, they recovered to finish the season strongly with high-scoring wins over Ashton United (6-3 at home) and away at Stalybridge Celtic (7-1) and Marine (5-1). Tranmere Rovers Reserves and Frickley Colliery left the league at the end of the season and Hyde United, Burscough, Rossendale United and Oldham Athletic Reserves joined to extend the competition from 20 to 22 clubs. Guinness Export changed their name to Ormskirk.

At the end of the season the RMI committee made the decision to retain the professional players en bloc, namely Pallett, Jones, Donaldson, Wright, Denton, Lang, Beech, Webber, Calder and Woodward.

George Denton was granted a benefit game in May 1970 when RMI lost a light-hearted game 11-7 to an All Star XI that included Terry Wharton (Bolton Wanderers) and Bryan Douglas (Blackburn Rovers).

At the season's end Tom Smith called it a day after 13 years' excellent service with RMI. One of the most committed players ever to play for the club he had been one of the first names on the team-sheet apart from a two-year stint in the forces while doing his National Service. A sheet metal worker he had joined RMI at the same time as Alan Jones, George Bateson and Frank Wignall and had rejected several offers to move to other clubs, preferring to stay with Horwich. An unselfish player of great ability noted for his sportsmanship Smith ranks as one of the RMI legends.

RMI manager Willie Millar spoke of the club's potential at the 1970 annual general meeting. Gate receipts had increased by £421 on the previous season but their contribution to the club's coffers was small compared to the impact of the Auxiliary Association which had raised the sum of £6,659.

Mr Millar had recommended that the club's reserve side play in the West Lancashire League for the following season, reviving a link with that organisation going back to before the First World War. Bill Seddon and Gordon Stones were the club trainers.

MR CHAIRMAN STEPS DOWN

But it was the end of an era with the long-serving and highly-respected George Fisher stepping down as Chairman having served in that role since 1946. Mr Fisher was granted life membership of the club in recognition of his long and valued service and happily retained his association with RMI for many more years up until his death in April 2006, having attained his century. Mr Harry Jones was appointed chairman but knew Mr Fisher would be a tough act to follow.

RMI began the 1970-71 season with a 0-0 draw at New Brighton when they fielded the following side: Pallett; Wilcox, Parry; Williams, Wright, Denton; Lang, Beech, Webber, Calder, Woodward. Substitute: Donaldson.

The club's secretary Bert Lucas resigned his post in August 1970 due to work commitments and was replaced by Mr Bert Taylor. At the annual general meeting the following summer Mr Lucas was made a life member of the club in recognition of his long and distinguished service. Bill Calder, who had become a firm favourite, left the club in October 1970 to take up a role as player-manager at his former club, Nantwich Town.

And after several seasons of relative prosperity on the financial side there were some worrying signs. Average attendances for home games dipped from around 600 to 400 and the draw was showing declining takings. A new fund-raising scheme was introduced as RMI linked up with Blackpool FC's commercial department to run bingo tickets.

RMI also went out of the FA Cup at the hands of Rossendale United after hopes had been raised by a fine 2-0 win over Northwich Victoria in the first qualifying round, Webber scoring both goals. Rossendale United enjoyed an outstanding season and ended up as champions, seven points clear of Burscough with Skelmersdale United third. RMI bowed out of the FA Trophy after a replay defeat at Fleetwood and old rivals Chorley ended their interest in the Lancashire Junior Cup with a 4-2 victory at Grundy Hill before a crowd of 1,500.

Pallett again lost his place in the side, being replaced by the former Barrow goalkeeper Dick Ellis during January 1971 and at the end of the season both Webber and Woodward rejected terms and looked elsewhere.   They both eventually signed for ambitious Skelmersdale United, who moved up to the Northern Premier League alongside Ellesmere Port Town. Free-transfers were granted to Alf Jones and Noel Nicklin.

Secretary Bert Taylor revealed a few worrying trends in the finances at the annual general meeting and warned club members that RMI would have to scrap the reserve team unless there was improved support through the gates. He said that for some reserve games there had been just half-a-dozen spectators on the terraces. Team manager Willie Millar said he was disappointed at the finish of seventh and hoped for better fortunes in the season to come. RMI had won 16 league games, drawn 12 and lost 14. Woodward was top-scorer with 17 goals, Webber scoring 14 and Wright 12.

Treasurer Jack Bentham resigned after many years in the post leaving a balance of £490 on the accounts, boosted by several good social functions. As had become the custom Mr Cyril Staley, the new manager of British Rail Engineering Limited, Horwich Works, was appointed club president.

The loss of Calder and Webber had been significant and to help solve the goal-scoring problem Mr Miller switched Kenny Wright from defence to centre-forward. He made three significant signings, the Droylsden pair of Terry Smith and Alan Rodgers joining Stuart Holding who was recruited from Morecambe. Two Horwich youngsters, Steve Skitt and Billy Eckersley, both 17-years-old were invited for trials with Leicester City. Skitt returned and broke into the RMI first-team before being snapped up by Preston North End but he failed to break into their League side.

In the 1971-72 season, when Prestwich Heys, Radcliffe Borough and Formby joined the league (Port Vale Reserves having resigned) RMI started brightly with seven wins in their opening ten games. But they then endured inconsistent form and eventually slipped to finish a disappointing thirteenth in a league won comfortably by Rhyl. Worryingly, RMI ended the season losing 12 of their last 16 games and it was clear that a slump both on and off the field had to be arrested.

In the circumstances David Glasgow did remarkably well to finish as top scorer with 19 goals with Ray Nesbitt contributing a further eleven. John Pallett, who had missed the start of the season after a disagreement over terms, returned to the side in mid October and kept a clean sheet in the 0-0 draw at Hyde United and then played as well as ever. But RMI made an early exit in the FA Cup at the hands of Hyde United, bowed out of the FA Trophy at Rossendale United and made most progress in the Lancashire Junior Cup before losing 3-0 at Chorley in the quarter-final.

The end of season AGM was not a happy occasion. On behalf of the RMI committee secretary Bert Taylor stated that drastic measures had to be made to safeguard the club's future which included scrapping the reserve team and reducing the number of professional players. The trainer-coach was to be sacked and replaced with a player-coach. Mr Taylor added: 'We depend on people coming through the gates. If they do not come to watch we may find it difficult to continue.' Manager Mr Millar said he was disappointed with the final league position and he felt injuries and poor performances from some players had contributed to the decline. He said he had used 30 players over the season and the team had struggled for consistency. Millar was particularly disappointed by the decision to scrap the reserve side. 'That decision means our youth policy has gone by the board,' he said. Trainers Bill Seddon and Gordon Stones were both released and Terry McDonald was appointed player-coach. On the committee Mr Bill Joyce, an assistant production manager at British Rail Engineering Workshops became the new club chairman.

The downward trend continued in the following season, 1972-73 when Chorley joined the league after resigning their place in the Northern Premier League, being replaced by Mossley. RMI finished 21st, their lowest league placing since the 1949-50 season. RMI won only six league games but drew a further 16. Their only away league victory came early in the campaign, 3-1 at Prestwich Heys. The derby matches against Chorley were played over the Christmas period, RMI losing by a single goal at home but forcing a 1-1 draw at Victory Park. RMI suffered early knock-outs in both the FA Cup and FA Trophy, losing to Hyde United and Sandbach Ramblers respectively, both following replays while Fleetwood ended RMI's interest in the Lancashire Junior Cup.

At the start of the season RMI had paraded a host of new players including centre-half Tom Singleton from Runcorn, a player with experience of a total of over 200 league games at Peterborough United, Chester and Bradford Park Avenue. Other newcomers included Ron Pickering and Brian Blackledge, both from Chorley and Kennie Millar, son of the manager. The line-up for the opening game at Sandbach Ramblers was as follows: Pallett; Wright, Melling; Millar, Singleton, Lang; Holding, Shaw, Pickering, Skitt, Eckersley. Substitute: Glasgow. Trainer McDonald was then sacked for a breach of club

BRINK OF COLLAPSE

On Friday 19 January 1973 RMI went public over the deteriorating state of club finances. 'RMI on brink of collapse' read the headline in the Bolton Evening News. 'The desperate financial plight of a once-thriving little club was stressed by club secretary Bert Taylor,' the report continued. Mr Taylor described the situation as 'very serious.'

Mr Taylor outlined that in 1968 RMI had elected not to join the newly-formed Northern Premier League due to prohibitive costs and had instead joined the Cheshire County League due to what they felt were declining standards in the Lancashire Combination. 'Since joining the Cheshire League the gates have gone from bad to worse,' Mr Taylor said. 'When added to a decline in the daily draw income and reduced subscriptions the effect on the club's finances has been very serious.' At the same time a similar plea for support was being made by the town's cricket club.

Club chairman Harry Jones resigned his position in February 1973, citing pressure of work and Bill Joyce, assistant production manager at the Loco Works took over the role temporarily.

By February 1973 Mr Millar had only fifteen players from which to select as the playing squad had been cut to its bare bones. These numbers were further reduced when Geoff Shaw and David Glasgow were given free transfers. Glasgow subsequently moved to live in South Africa. Eventually Mr Millar had enough and he decided to quit 'by mutual agreement' after the home game against Droylsden on 25 February 1973. As a result Nesbitt, who finished top scorer with 15 goals, said he would not play for the club again and Billy Eckersley was also released.

Club captain and player-coach Tommy Thompson was promoted to player-manager to replace Millar. The Droylsden game was re-arranged for a Sunday morning with an 11-30 am kick-off so as not to clash with Bolton Wanderers' FA Cup sixth-round tie with Luton Town. At least Mr Millar finished on a high note, goals by Pickering and Gregory giving RMI their first win for eleven games. Ken Patterson, the Eagley Mills goal-keeper was drafted in to replace Pallett who had undergone a knee operation.

Former RMI legend Vince Marren returned to Grundy Hill to help Thompson with training but the season could not end soon enough for the club diehards. RMI drew six and lost nine of their last 15 games after Millar's departure and so finished in the re-election positions. Their last home game of the season, against New Brighton was described in the Horwich Journal as a 'cheerless end to a sad season'. A crowd of less than one hundred saw RMI lost 2-1 with only Pallett, now back again between the posts, Vernon Lang and new signing Harry Seaton, recruited from Nantwich Town described as being above average. Kenny Wright had earned his testimonial match, and it was a pity that was staged at a time when interest in RMI's affairs had fallen. Great Harwood provided the opposition on 2 May 1973.

But Wright was one of several senior players to be released at the season's end alongside Dick Ellis, Harry Beech, George Denton, Phil Parry, Ian Wilcox and Terry McDonald.

RMI proved successful in their re-election bid at the Cheshire County League annual general meeting when champions Buxton moved into the Northern Premier League and Leek Town were admitted to the league. They appointed a new manager in the summer of 1973 as they attempted to re-build. The new incumbent was 33-year-old Bill Urmston, a former chief coach at Bury FC who came strongly recommended. Thompson had decided not to apply for the post.

The only bright spot in what was described as one of RMI's worst ever seasons was Pallett being chosen as Cheshire County League Player of the Year for his performances in goal for the club. Pallett played for the Cheshire County League in an end-of-season representative game against the champions, Buxton. He had now played a total of 430 league and cup games for RMI but the new manager had his own ideas and sadly those did not include one the club's most popular players.

Despite being one of only three professionals to be retained Pallett was shown the door by Urmston who brought in Tony McMahon from Little Lever as his new goalkeeper. Pallett's departure left Ron Pickering and Carlton Wright as the sole remaining players from the previous season at the club as Urmston's side operated on a virtually all-amateur basis. There were only three semi-professional players: Pickering and new signings Peter Gilmore, who had been Lancaster City's manager in the previous season and full-back Mick Saile from Bury. Gary Cooper, one of RMI's most promising players departed for a professional career with Rochdale and later moved on to Southport.

At the club's annual general meeting the financial situation was described as 'precarious' but the committee hoped that progress could be made under a young, go-ahead manager. Chairman Billy Jones, who had taken over from Mr Joyce, re-iterated the point that unless more support was forthcoming through the gates and for the fund-raising events the club remained in danger of folding. But financial prudence had helped produce a profit of £270 on the previous season even though gates and the income from the daily draw had fallen. RMI had saved over £1,000 on wages due to severe cut-backs.

Other new players included John McGlynn, a central defender from Little Lever, former Bury player Jimmy Cassell, a fully qualified FA coach, Jimmy Delaney from Hyde United, Stan Kendall from Bolton Wyresdale, Captain Jeff Gardner from Lancaster City, Bob Hutchinson from Blackburn Rovers and two other ex-Bury players in Nello Olivero and David Smith. David Banks, son of former Bolton Wanderers' legendary full-back Tommy Banks, Dave Brooks, Jimmy Casey and Alex Elliott were other new names.

Urmston's first match in charge was at home to Sandbach Ramblers when a much-changed RMI side earned a 0-0 draw in the season's opener. The first win came in the fifth match as goals by Wright, Elliott and Gardner accounted for visitors Nantwich Town 3-2.

There was a 'blast from the past' in the away game at Hyde United on 29 September 1973 when Vince Marren, who had stayed on at Grundy Hill to help with training was pressed into service as a substitute, 13 years after he last played for RMI. Marren played the last five minutes but RMI went down to a 4-1 defeat.

RMI even got past the first two rounds of the FA Cup after wins over Skelmersdale United and Congleton Town, but lost 4-0 at Altrincham in the third qualifying round when the following side was on duty: McMahon; Pickering, McGlynn; Casey, Banks, Saile; Middleton, Madeley, Elliott, Gardner, Ripley. Substitute: Gorman. They lost 3-0 at home to Skelmersdale United in the FA Trophy and after defeating Atherton Collieries and Darwen bowed out of the Lancashire Junior Cup at the quarter-final stage, 2-0 at Wigan Athletic despite a fighting performance. It was the first meeting between the two old rivals since 1966.

But the financial problems were never far from the surface and as a consequence the management committee considered replacing the blue and white striped jerseys for next season as a cost-cutting measure. An all-white playing strip or one with blue jerseys and white shorts would, they decided be a cheaper option.

Jimmy Cassell finished top scorer with ten goals with Gardner and Gordon Morris, an amateur from Daisy Hill, each scoring nine. At the season's end Urmston was still operating with just three paid players, Mick Saile, Jimmy Delaney and Cassell as Alex Elliott had been sacked for a breach of contract. Urmston continued to ring the changes and well over fifty players turned out for RMI during the season. One of the most promising newcomers was Joe Rios but his work as a waiter meant that his availability was restricted. In the away game at Formby towards the end of the season Urmston was forced to play as a substitute due to a shortage of players.

With a ban on floodlighting due to power cuts and the three-day week, RMI played one more Sunday game, against Radcliffe Borough just before Christmas but this time the experiment was far from successful, less than one hundred spectators lining the Grundy Hill terraces for the 11-30am kick-off. RMI gave one of their best displays of the season to win 3-0.

RMI lost two stalwarts with the deaths of long-serving groundsman Bob Turner and Joe Taylor, who had been skip-man for over 20 years. Another stalwart, Albert Ryder later passed away. But there was happier news as former RMI favourite Tony Webber was in the Morecambe side that defeated Dartford in the FA Trophy Final at Wembley.

RMI improved one place to finish 20th in Urmston's first season but actually gained one fewer league point during the campaign. Even so it was an achievement in itself to avoid re-election considering the difficulties faced by the new manager. It was a close-run thing with RMI only edging to safety after a 2-1 home win over Prestwich Heys in the final league game of the campaign. Cassell and Gardner scored after the visitors had led 1-0 to mark RMI's final game, for the time being at least, in the famous blue and white stripes. Urmston had battled hard with limited resources and helped inspire some battling performances that showed the team had plenty of character. In the last month of the season RMI achieved two high-scoring home wins, both 4-1 against Stalybridge Celtic and Hyde United respectively and an outstanding 5-0 victory at Rhyl (when Cassell scored the only hat-trick of RMI's season).

Marine beat Rossendale United to the title on goal average with Chorley finishing third. Ormskirk left the Cheshire County League at the end of the season and were replaced by New Mills.

In March 1974 the Horwich RMI Operatic Society held the last public function to be held at the Institute and in June of that year the Education Authority decided to abandon the Institute as an additional class-room facility. On 1 December 1974 the now empty and shuttered Institute caught fire and the top floor dressing-rooms, staircase and roof were all destroyed.

But as one landmark disappeared, a new one appeared as the town gained a splendid new facility when the Horwich Leisure Centre was opened in September 1974, transforming the appearance of the Chorley Old Road end of Grundy Hill. Times indeed were changing.

The controversial move to change the playing strip did take place and in season 1974-75 RMI played in blue jerseys with white shorts. Mick Saile, who had achieved an ever-present appearances tag in his first season, was the only professional to be retained and Vic Dougherty, Ron Pickering and Tony Shiels were among those players to be released.

Though the 1974-75 season brought a significant improvement on the pitch with RMI finishing in mid-table there were growing signs that football at Grundy Hill appeared unsustainable unless a drastic change was made in the club's organisation.

Memories of a great RMI favourite, Jimmy 'Flick' Mather were rekindled among the older end of supporters when RMI signed his son, Paul Mather. Sadly Mather junior was soon released but he did go on to forge a successful non league career and went on to play against RMI many times. Mr Urmston made a host of new signings including Eric Chadwick, Mike Cairns and Derek Greenwood while Phil Parry returned. Saile continued as club captain after taking over the role during the previous season.

At the club's annual general meeting in July 1974 concern over the financial position was again expressed. Chairman Alex Milner told the meeting: 'It's no use wrapping it up. If Horwich people want Cheshire County League football they are going to have to make up their minds. We are in a serious situation.'

After years of dwindling membership among railway works employees secretary Bert Taylor said it was time to abandon the policy of all committee-men being recruited from the works and to open up positions on the committee to 'outsiders.'

Proceeds from the auxiliary association fell alarmingly by over £2,000 to £2,845 and only by reducing wages from £3,621 to £2,611 had the club managed to stay afloat. Sadly the meeting was attended by only a handful of people which demonstrated that interest in the club was possibly at an all-time low.

On the field RMI were beginning to reap the rewards for the hard work of Urmston but off the field the club's future looked bleak. In October 1974 the situation was spelt out in the starkest of terms by the chairman and treasurer when it was reported that the season would be RMI's last unless there was a quick upsurge in income. There was no money left in club funds to continue much longer. It was costing £100 per week to run the club and income was nowhere near that mark. To cover the deficit the treasurer was having to draw upon a reserve fund of about £1,000. In days gone by the club had raised £300 per week from the daily draw but this income source was now down to around £25 per week.

A special meeting was called to discuss the situation on Sunday 8 December 1974 but only four members of the public turned up to attend. The chairman's verdict was damning. 'The question of whether the people of Horwich want a Cheshire League football club in the town was apparently announced last Sunday,' Mr Milner said. Secretary Bert Taylor added: 'It was a flop.'

A local enthusiast, Ernie Jones, who had once been on Bolton Wanderers' books began to get involved with the club and in February 1975 started 'target golf' at Grundy Hill as a fund-raising initiative. But it seemed a lone cry in the wilderness as RMI struggled financially through the campaign. At the start of April it was reported the committee would decide 'within the next fortnight' whether to continue after the end of the campaign. They needed £2,000 in the kitty to guarantee playing in the 1975-76 season. They did succeed in renting out the ground to Oldham Athletic B team which helped increase income slightly.

Considering the off-field turmoil the results were more than encouraging and RMI won 17 and drew seven of their 42 league games to finish 11th. They had begun the season with six wins in their first eight games and made progress in the FA Cup, defeating Formby and Ashton United before losing 2-0 at home to Accrington Stanley in the second qualifying round. In the FA Trophy RMI lost 1-0 at Hyde United and went of the Lancashire Junior Cup at the hands of Rossendale United. One of the highlights of the season was a 1-0 home win over Chorley on Boxing Day when a trial player Sid Willison scored a 25th-minute winner but the Magpies gained revenge with a 2-0 win on Boxing Day. In all games Eric Chadwick scored 15 goals and Morris 13.

Leek Town were champions, two points ahead of Winsford United but Oswestry Town and Oldham Athletic Reserves left the league at the end of the season. Middlewich Athletic, St Helens Town and Darwen were newly admitted but Sandbach Ramblers, despite finishing third, folded. At one stage it looked as if RMI would follow suit.

But finally, on 9 May 1975 it was announced that RMI would continue in the Cheshire County League. The chairman said he was confident that the £2,000 target could be reached during the summer. One thousand letters appealing for support were to be distributed around the town and Ernie Jones organised a new fund-raising drive. But the club reached a new low when, at the annual general meeting on 30 July 1975, the chairman, the secretary and the team manager all resigned en bloc.

A NEW REGIME

With only eight days to go before the start of the 1975-76 season RMI were struggling to raise a team. The club was now being run by a new regime spearheaded by former RMI player and trainer Bill Seddon who was operating as caretaker-secretary and team manager. An RMI steering group appointed Ernie Jones as chairman and 1950s favourite Alan Jones was put in charge of training. Peter Murphy came in as treasurer and long-serving committee man Albert Dickinson became assistant secretary.

With only five players signed up RMI organised trials for amateur players and a playing staff was hastily recruited. Colin Black, John McGlynn, David Ainscough and Phil Parry were re-signed and former RMI players George Bateson, Brian Kenny and Fred Herring all returned to the club. Parry and Herring were the only two professional players signed-on at this stage and one more professional was needed to meet the criteria for entering the FA Cup competition.

The following team represented RMI as they opened the season with a 1-1 draw against New Mills at Grundy Hill: Wood; Hunt, Parry; Ainscough, Kenny, Wilson; Wignall, Jones, Herring, Black, Bateson. Substitute: Worden. Steve Jones, Alan Wilson, Alan Wignall, John Wood and Roy Hunt were all local players recruited after trials.

In their second league game RMI went down 9-1 at Winsford United but at least the team was still in existence after all the doubts over the summer months. And a positive move was made in September 1975 as Alan Kirkman began what was to be a long association with RMI when he was appointed manager. Aged 39, Kirkman was a former professional player with Manchester City, Rotherham United and Newcastle United and had been player-manager at Netherfield and manager at Rossendale United. Bill Seddon stepped aside to concentrate on his role as secretary.

Mr Kirkman strengthened the side by recruiting Mick Hennessey from Blackrod Villa and Ray Silous who had moved to the area from the south. In conjunction with Preston North End FC a new fund-raising initiative was developed.

In October 1975 came what was to prove a highly significant event as a local businessman, Chris Healey, aged 34 was recruited onto the committee. Mr Healey, who had played for Castleton in the Lancashire Amateur League was a director in the Georgian House hotel and restaurant and also involved in a firm of building contractors. Mr Healey stated that he would be willing to act as a guarantor to the bank and was honoured to be involved in such a historic club. With these developments morale in the club began to rise and at last it looked as though the dark days were lifting.

Work began on sprucing up the Grundy Hill ground which had steadily fallen into a state of some disrepair. A railway carriage was placed on the training pitch side of the ground for use as a canteen and the previous canteen was converted into use as a club room. The new money-raising scheme proved to be a success and achieved 1,300 subscribers by Christmas. In December 1975 Mr Healey took over as chairman.

Gradually Mr Kirkman recruited a competitive side, one key signing being Malcolm Richmond, a teacher at Rivington & Blackrod High School who had scored in Morecambe's FA Trophy win over Dartford at Wembley. Glyn Barker was signed from Rossendale United and Mr Kirkman added two more of his former Dark Lane colleagues in Bob Grimshaw and David O'Neill while successfully converting Silous from a midfield player to centre-half.

During March and April RMI began to push away from the re-election zone and they eventually finished in 18th place, with 29 points from 42 games. Marine were champions with 64 points, one ahead of runners-up Chorley, who won 4-0 at Grundy Hill on Boxing Day and then 6-0 at Victory Park on New Year's Day. RMI also twice conceded seven goals, losing 7-2 at Marine and 7-0 at Leek Town. But Mr Kirkman made RMI a much more solid side and a run of five successive draws during February and early March showed that his charges were now much more difficult to beat. Vital wins over Prestwich Heys, Rhyl and Rossendale United were secured at Grundy Hill and RMI only lost six of their last 18 games, even though nine were draws. In the run-in Richmond and Barker each scored some important goals. Richmond ended as top scorer with eight goals with Barker adding six more. Earlier in the season Black had scored seven goals.

Old rivals Wigan Athletic visited Grundy Hill for a Lancashire Junior Cup first-round tie on Saturday 3 January 1976 and romped into a 4-0 half-time lead. But RMI held firm in the second half and prevented any more goals, also having the consolation of the receipts from their share of a 500-plus 'gate'. With the Latics finally going on to achieve Football League status two years later, this proved to be the final meeting between the two old adversaries.

Meanwhile RMI officials attended a meeting at Leyland on Tuesday 3 February 1976 to investigate a return to the Lancashire Combination but refused to commit and decided to remain in the Cheshire County League.

One other significant development was the formation of a youth team, known as Horwich Mariners which was based at the club. The team was named after Bolton born Paul Mariner who had worked at British Aerospace's Lostock factory and played part-time for Chorley before earning a move into the Football League with Plymouth Argyle in 1973. Mariner went onto earn a big money move to Ipswich Town and later played for Arsenal and Portsmouth, scoring 175 goals in 511 Football League appearances and earning 35 international caps. But he never forgot his roots and was a hugely popular player, not only with his own club's supporters. After living and coaching abroad Mariner returned to English football as coach to Plymouth Argyle in October 2009 and became manager two months later.

In May 1976 the RMI club held its first sporting dinner at the Georgian House raising £330 towards club funds, a sum equivalent to the receipts from five home games. The club had achieved its objective of survival and raised the necessary funds for Mr Kirkman to bring in better quality players after Christmas and move up the table. All the playing staff were retained, something of a novelty in itself and a sign that after so much instability and uncertainty sound building blocks for the future were now firmly in place.

Over the next two seasons, Mr Kirkman built up the RMI team and re-established them as a force. In 1976-77 they moved up from 18th to eighth and improved their position by one place and six more league points in the 1977-78 campaign.

Key to the improvement was in the selection of good quality players from the local non league scene and the fielding of settled sides. In 1976-77 RMI also had three consistent goal scorers with Malcolm Richmond finishing top scorer with 19 goals and Glyn Barker netting 17. Bobby Grimshaw supported the pair with 14 goals. In the second half of the campaign RMI hit a rich vein of form and concluded the season with a string of good results with nine wins, five draws and only three defeats in their last 17 games.

But RMI's all-too familiar disappointing results in the major cup competitions continued with first-hurdle exits in both the FA Cup and FA Trophy at the hands of Worksop Town and New Brighton respectively. In the Lancashire Junior Cup, though, RMI enjoyed a run through to the semi-final, defeating Burscough, Radcliffe Borough and Accrington Stanley before losing 5-2 at Chorley. The Magpies also recorded a league double over RMI as they finished the season runners-up, eight points behind champions Winsford United.

Though Richmond departed in the summer of 1977 RMI maintained their good form the following season and Barker's goal-scoring prowess provided the cutting edge to a team whose growing defensive organisation saw them concede only 50 league goals, their best record since the 1966-67 season. Barker scored 16 goals and Grimshaw (11) and Dennis Kilgannon (10) supported him ably. There was a double blow in the cups at the hands of Chorley, however, to consider. The Magpies knocked out RMI in the FA Cup with a 1-0 victory at Victory Park and followed up with another single goal win at Grundy Hill in the FA Trophy. At least RMI had the better of the Christmas league games, drawing 1-1 at Grundy Hill and then earning a 1-0 win at Victory Park when Kilgannon scored the winning goal; and they finished two places above the Magpies in the table. Marine were champions, four points ahead of Stalybridge Celtic. The Cheshire County League now added a second division for the 1978-79 season with Prestwich Heys relegated and Fleetwood Town newly admitted.

ANOTHER CHAMPIONSHIP SEASON

By the summer of 1978 RMI, under the chairmanship of Chris Healey appeared as well placed to mount a challenge to the top clubs as at any time in their history. Long-serving Harold Taylor had strong family links with RMI that began when his grandmother Catherine washed the team kit for many years. His father, also named Harold and Uncle Joe also gave the club many years of service in various roles of kit men and dressing room attendants carrying out the hundreds of small jobs that often go unnoticed but are vital to the day-to-day running of a football club.

Harold obviously sensed something was in the air as he maintained a diary of games throughout the season, faithfully recording results, teams, scorers and a brief note of the main events. It proved to be a marathon task, as RMI went on to play no less than 62 matches during the season, ending up as champions of the Cheshire County League. To the delight of many traditionalists RMI reverted to playing in their traditional blue and white striped jerseys during the season, a move which brought them good fortune.

The season began well with six successive wins signalling RMI's intentions. The RMI team for the opening game of the season against Burscough at Grundy Hill was as follows: Foster; Parry, Kershaw; Greenan (capt), Silous, Grimshaw; Lang, O'Neill, Walton, Burrows, Kilgannon. Sub: Froggatt. Goals by Walton and Burrows gave RMI a 2-1 win. They remained unbeaten in the league until losing 4-1 at home to Stalybridge Celtic on 14 April 1979. Ironically Paul Mather, son of former RMI favourite Jimmy 'Flick' Mather scored a hat-trick for Stalybridge that day. Despite being turned down by RMI after going for trials he still went on to forge a good non league career. Their final league record was an outstanding one: Played 42, Won 35, Drawn 2, Lost 5, For 89, Against 45 and Points 72.

Nine months after commencing with a 2-1 win over Burscough RMI concluded a momentous campaign with a 2-0 victory over runners-up Witton Albion in the League Shield.

There was plenty of drama along the way notably in a draining FA Trophy tie against Tow Law Town. The original tie in County Durham was abandoned after 51 minutes on an icy and snow-bound pitch and RMI had to make the long journey to the north-east again the following Saturday. A goal by Barker earned a 1-1 draw and the tie was replayed at Grundy Hill the following Monday afternoon, Pearson (2), Barker (2), Greenan and an own goal accounting for the runaway 6-0 victory. Unfortunately RMI went out in the first round proper to another Northern League side, losing 2-1 at Spennymoor United. In the FA Cup RMI were defeated at Morecambe in the third qualifying round but stayed focused and consistent in the league.

In all games John Pearson, who made a goal-scoring debut against Congleton Town in late August, scored 29 goals and Barker and Greenan 21 apiece giving RMI a consistent strike-force. They managed without the services of O'Neill who was transferred to Macclesfield Town in December for £650.

In league games Lang and Kershaw were ever-present with Greenan missing just one game and Pearson two. Foster (38 league appearances); Parry (36), Ainscough (32) and Burrows (30) were other mainstays. In all games seven players made more than fifty appearances for RMI during the campaign: Foster, Parry, Kershaw, Lang, Ainscough, Greenan and Pearson.

RMI clinched the championship with a 2-1 win at Marine on Monday 30 April 1979. Harold Taylor wrote: 'The day dawned wet and windy, the day when RMI could clinch the Cheshire County League championship, a day that three years ago looked impossible when the club was on the verge of disbanding.

'But due to the hard work of a few, the club picked up and now the day had arrived where they could take the championship from the reigning champions Marine, and at their ground.

'All the team reported fit and well and the journey to Liverpool went well. The game got underway with Marine doing all the attacking, in front of a very large crowd with plenty of supporters from Horwich. In the 15th minute the home side went ahead with an own goal from the Horwich 'keeper, the ball bouncing off Foster's knee and over the line.

'RMI started to come more into the game and just before half-time equalised through Allan Froggatt. Four minutes into the second half Glyn Barker slotted the ball home after good work by Lang, Pearson, Burrows and Froggatt. There was no further scoring and RMI had secured the championship. At the end the RMI supporters embraced their heroes on the field and in the dressing room afterwards the champagne flowed.'

The RMI team on duty at Rossett Park was: Foster; Parry, Green; Greenan, Ainscough, Kershaw; Burrows, Pearson, Barker, Lang, Froggatt. Sub: Connaghan.

Victory was especially sweet for the managerial pair of Kirkman and Crompton who had been denied the title on goal difference when at Rossendale United five years previously.

RMI still had seven fixtures to fulfil before a long and eventful season came to a close. Not surprisingly they went down 4-1 at Formby on the following day after the Marine game and also suffered defeats against Hyde United, Winsford United and Witton Albion thereby missing out on setting a new league record for points in a season which stood at 73 (set by Altrincham in season 1965-66).

During the season Grundy Hill staged some big games, none more so than on Boxing Day when a crowd of around 1,500 spectators saw Barker and Kilgannon get the goals in a 2-1 win over Chorley. Over one thousand spectators saw RMI play Morecambe in a Lancashire Junior Cup replay that ended scoreless after extra-time, Greenan's penalty earning RMI a 1-0 win in the second replay at Christie Park. But RMI then went out of the competition in the quarter-final, losing 2-0 in a replay at Chorley.

There was an unusual occurrence in the league game at Burscough with goalkeeper Foster arriving late at the ground. Phil Parry deputised in goal until Foster came on after 25 minutes and kept a clean sheet, Pearson scoring the only goal of the game.

The season closed with a 'Champions versus Runners-Up' match at Grundy Hill when RMI finished in style, defeating Witton Albion 2-0 with goals by Ray Silous and Glyn Barker. At the game Mr Eric Hinchcliffe the Cheshire County League President, presented the championship trophy to Billy Greenan. The RMI captain capped a momentous season by being voted Players' Player of the Year.

Brian Smith reported in the Horwich News: 'Horwich RMI Football Club became Cheshire County League champions within a few years of being on the brink of extinction. It was a glorious achievement, of which all at Grundy Hill are justifiably proud.

'It's been a season of records for Horwich RMI. Their remarkable success in going until 14 April before losing their first league game has prompted them to claim several records-they have 35 league victories this season, they went 27 games without defeat (26 of which were victories) but also had 21 consecutive wins.

'They have secured a club record number of points by the club in any season. Their tally of 72 is 20 points better than their previous best in the Cheshire County League and nine better than their Lancashire Combination championship tally in 1958.'

But as Smith was quick to remind his readers, the club had almost ceased to exist: 'With barely a fortnight left before the start of the 1975-76 season, the club's former regime, reeling under a finance crisis, proposed the disbandment of Horwich RMI.

'That was at the club's annual general meeting. But a faction of those present decided on an attempt to save Horwich RMI. They were committee members Albert Dickinson, who has been with the club for 25 years, Ray Ashton, Bill Seddon, a former player and trainer and Peter Murphy.

'They assembled a team together and despite one or two disastrous defeats finished the season in 18th place out of 22.

'In 1976-77 they were eighth, last year they claimed seventh position and now-CHAMPIONS. It is their first honour since joining the Cheshire County League in 1968-69.

'Club officials are quick to acknowledge the part played by team manager Mr Alan Kirkman and his assistant, Denis Crompton who have patiently built a strong side over the past four years.

'Said club chairman Chris Healey: 'I attribute our success mainly to good management bringing the right players to RMI. Off the field we have been able to maintain the finances to enable Mr Kirkman and Mr Crompton to bring quality players to Horwich.'

Mr Kirkman in turn spoke of the efforts made by the players. 'There is a great team spirit among the players and in the club itself,' he said. 'Everybody works for each other, whether on the committee or in the team. Our work-rate on the field has been a major factor in the championship. We're the best side in the league. You need effort before you can use skill, and everyone has worked hard and done their job. Their skill is a bonus.'

A championship celebration dinner dance was held at the Georgian House on Friday 25 May with cabaret by Mr Ray 'Slim' Randell. Tickets for the event were priced at £8. All the players were retained apart from Burrows who moved to live in Australia and Mr Kirkman was voted Cheshire County League Manager of the Year.

The Horwich RMI youth side also had a fine season. They had been renamed Horwich RMI Youth Team in August 1978 after three highly successful seasons playing as Mariner's XI in local junior football. They had joined the Bolton Boys Federation in 1974 with Ken Chaisty, a local businessman the club's founder. Starting out as Horwich Albion they changed their name after one season when Paul Mariner became club president and they joined the Leyland and District League.

Simon Farnworth, the RMI youth team goalkeeper was selected to play for England in a schoolboy international against Eire in April 1979. On Saturday 9 June 1979 Farnworth, aged 15, was in goal for England Schoolboys against West Germany when a crowd of 92,000 witnessed a 2-2 draw. Farnworth went on to forge a successful league career, playing over 400 league games in total for Bolton Wanderers, Bury, Preston North End and Wigan Athletic before training to be a physiotherapist.

At the end of the season youth team founder Ken Chaisty retired his post having seen the side struggle at first but then go from strength to strength. George Bateson took over as youth team coach. Mr Chaisty played tribute to co-organiser Ernie Williams and other helpers Ernie Morris and Dave Hart and was especially proud that over the five years RMI's youth side had never had a player sent-off.

Witton Albion and Marine, who were second and third behind RMI joined the Northern Premier League for the 1979-80 season and Curzon Ashton and Bootle replaced relegated New Brighton and Middlewich Athletic as the top division reverted to 20 member clubs.

There was a setback for RMI as they began the defence of their title, losing 1-0 to New Mills in the opening match of the season when the following side was on duty: Foster; Parry, Silous; Greenan, Ainscough, Kershaw; Kilgannon, Pearson, Baldwin, Lang, Froggatt. Sub: Barker.

Geoff Foster missed some games when he went on a cricket tour to Barbados with a Central Lancashire League side. Ian Senior, who went on to enjoy a long career in non-league football with a number of clubs deputised in goal. Denis Haslam joined the club from Walker's and began a long association with RMI.

In January 1980 RMI joined the Manchester County FA lottery in a new fund-raising initiative. Club chairman Chris Healey had frequently warned against complacency and said the club would need to carry on raising cash aggressively in order to compete at this level of the non-league scene.

The season proved to be something of a disappointment after the previous one and RMI finished eighth with 39 points from their 38 league games. Pearson was top scorer with 18 goals, followed by Barker (16) and Greenan (10). RMI did not start well, taking until their sixth league game to record their first win and crashed out of the FA Cup and FA Trophy at the hands of Lancaster City and Gainsborough Trinity respectively. A four-match winning run in the autumn, including a 2-1 home derby success over Chorley, promised much but RMI then lost four and drew two of their next six games. The inconsistency continued until the end of a campaign which ended with Stalybridge Celtic as champions, seven points clear of Winsford United with Chorley in third position. Rhyl and Radcliffe Borough were relegated and replaced by Prescot Cables and Kirkby Town. RMI had won 5-4 at Rhyl in January in what was described as a thrilling encounter.

Towards the end of the season RMI played their first team in a Bolton Hospitals Cup-tie at Burnden Park and fielded a scratch team the same evening against Nantwich Town in their final league fixture. Not surprisingly an RMI side containing eight players from the under-18s team went down to a 4-0 home defeat. George Bateson's son Karl was one of the players drafted into the side. The Cheshire County League took a dim view of the affair and fined the club £100 for fielding a weakened side and a further £25 for having several unregistered players.

Cheshire League Champions 1978-79

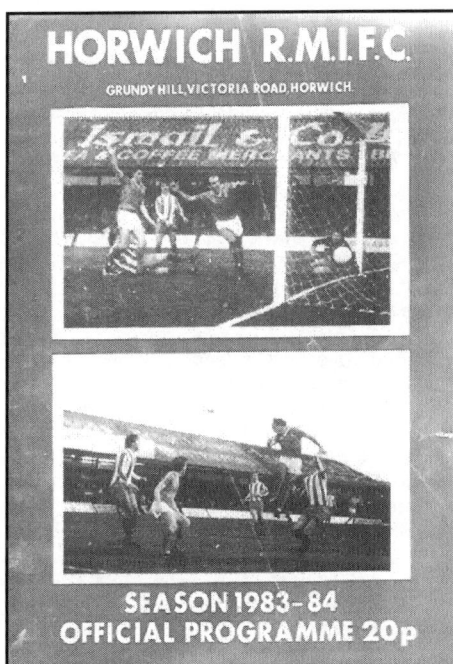

The programme is from 1983-84 but the pictures are from the FA Cup
tie against Blackpool in 1982-83

INTO THE LIGHT

At the club's AGM in June 1980 it was stated that the erection of floodlights at Grundy Hill was now to become a priority. Twelve clubs in the Cheshire County League already had floodlights and those without them were thought to lack ambition.

The Cheshire County League would be changing its name to the North West Counties League shortly, club chairman Mr Healey revealed, and RMI would have to continue to pursue their fund-raising schemes, not only to maintain the playing staff but also to raise the estimated sum of £10,000 to install floodlights at Grundy Hill. Pertinently manager Mr Kirkman revealed at the AGM that he had wanted to build on his league-winning side with three players but the club could not afford them.

In the 1980-81 season RMI fell one place to finish ninth and the following season, their last in the Cheshire County League they slipped to 16th with just 12 wins and seven draws from 38 games.

The 1980-81 season was noteworthy for the installation of floodlights at Grundy Hill. The lights were officially switched on at a specially arranged friendly game against a Manchester United XI on Wednesday 4 March 1981. The official attendance for the game was 1,495 but many gatecrashers gained entry into the ground without paying for admission. Despite that the receipts were around £1,000 and went some way towards recouping the total cost of the lights.

The line-ups were as follows: RMI: Cavanagh; Parry, Green; Silous, Kershaw, O'Neill; Lang, Froggatt, Greenan, Haslam, McLachlan. Subs: Pearson, Ahert, Frost.
Manchester United XI: Roche; Whelan, Keen; Lane, Connell, Sloan; Davies, Lynan, McGarvey, Duxbury, Grimes. Sub: Worrall.

The visitors, who included Paddy Roche, Scott McGarvey, Ashley Grimes and Mike Duxbury in their side, were 4-0 ahead at half-time with goals by Lynan (2), Duxbury and a Ray Silous own-goal. But RMI battled back in the second half, Dennis Haslam and Alan Frost reducing the arrears as the game finished 4-2.

RMI were knocked-out of both the FA Cup and FA Trophy at the first hurdle, losing to North Ferriby United and Penrith respectively and their league form was erratic. They did, however, end the season with silverware, lifting the Westhoughton Charity Cup for the second season in succession after a 3-1 win at Daisy Hill on Saturday 9 May 1981. Their end-of-season form had, however, been poor with only three victories in their last 17 games. RMI did reach the quarter-final of the Lancashire Junior Cup but lost 3-1 to Barrow at Holker Street after extra-time, following a 1-1 draw at Grundy Hill.

Long-serving defender Phil Parry was rewarded for his loyalty with a testimonial match and RMI entertained a Bolton Wanderers XI on 22 April 1981 when a crowd of 360 (receipts: £180) saw the visitors win an entertaining game 3-2. Parry had initially joined RMI as a 17-year-old and had made over 500 appearances for the club.

Neil McLachlan began a long association with the club when he signed for RMI from Morecambe in mid-November. He went on to finish the season as the club's second top scorer with nine goals, one behind Allan Froggatt. But three of RMI's most consistent players left the club. Goalkeeper Martin Bowring retired as a player after joining the police force in January while Steve Green moved to Australia and Barker joined

Stalybridge Celtic.

Nantwich Town were champions, three points ahead of runners-up Hyde United and relegated Kirkby Town and New Mills were replaced by Glossop and Accrington Stanley. Many long-standing RMI supporters remembered what proved to be their last visit to Kirkby Town in October. The official attendance was 58 of which an estimated forty had travelled from Horwich, Barker scoring twice in a 2-1 victory.

In 1981-82 RMI began the season with a 3-0 win at St Helens Town, Barker, Walsh and the returning Webber on target and followed that up with a 3-1 home win over Stalybridge Celtic. But they again struggled for consistency in the league after that and the season tailed off in disappointing fashion. McLachlan made his mark and finished with 25 goals in league and cup with Webber scoring 15 goals and Lang 10. In the major cups RMI defeated Skelmersdale United and Witton Albion in the FA Cup before losing 4-0 at home to Hyde United. In the FA Trophy they defeated Ashton United and Darwen but then lost 1-0 at home to Chorley early in the New Year.

Goalkeeper Tommy Cavanagh lost his place to Ian Senior and joined old team-mates Billy Greenan and Barker at Stalybridge Celtic while Ray Silous and Billy Kershaw were now at Ashton United. Economies were made during the autumn and several more seasoned players left Grundy Hill while late in the campaign Tony Webber left to become player-manager at Glossop.

Alan Kirkman, it was later revealed, had intended quitting his post at the end of the season but after a poor run of results he departed in late January, RMI having won just one of their previous eight league games. Kirkman cited work and home commitments for his decision. He had done a fine job during his time at the club and would be back in due course. There must have been some frustration, however, that the priority of the club committee was focused on building up funds to pay for the floodlights and enabling the ground to meet A-grade standards required for inclusion in the top division of the North West Counties League for the following season rather than on team-building. Bill Seddon stood in on a temporary basis until former RMI defender Ken Wright was appointed manager in late February. Wright, aged 38, had been manager at Daisy Hill and spent five years at Radcliffe Borough, three as player-manager.

The final champions of the Cheshire County League were Hyde United, who finished seven points ahead of runners-up Chorley. Both clubs moved up to the Northern Premier League while the remaining 18 clubs joined the newly-formed North West Counties League. RMI finished 16th with just 31 points from their 38 games, ending the season with seven successive defeats but the hard work from their committee had ensured the club met the necessary ground-grading requirements to play in the top division next season. Rossendale United and Fleetwood Town, despite both finishing above RMI in the league, were not as fortunate and were placed in the second of three divisions.

INTO THE NORTH WEST COUNTIES LEAGUE

In 1982-83 RMI played in the newly-constituted North West Counties League which was formed as a result of a merger between the Cheshire County League and the Lancashire Combination and discovered a new goal-scoring hero. Tony Caldwell was signed in the summer of 1982 from Irlam Town and soon made himself a Grundy Hill legend. Caldwell had scored 33 goals for Irlam in the 1981-82 season and his signing was seen a huge coup. Huge it was, for Caldwell's goals saw RMI not only regain their league form but also reach the first round proper of the FA Cup for only the second time in their history.

RMI fought their way through the early FA Cup rounds, defeating in turn South Liverpool, New Mills, Oswestry Town and Caernarfon Town and then played reigning Alliance League champions Runcorn in the fourth qualifying round. After a 2-2 draw at Grundy Hill, when Allan Froggatt (penalty) and Neil McLachlan scored their goals, RMI won a dramatic replay at Canal Street the following Tuesday before a crowd of 1,100. RMI 'keeper Tony McMahon made a superb penalty save to deny Elfyn Edwards early in the second half and the tie went into extra-time. The game was still dead-locked with two minutes remaining when Kilgannon launched himself at a Les Brown cross and found the net with a diving header.

RMI's reward was a trip to Bloomfield Road to play Blackpool on Saturday, 20 November 1982. RMI took along one thousand fans to the seaside including bell-ringing Bolton town crier Bob Sherrington, a Horwich man, for one of the biggest games in the club's history. In his programme notes Blackpool manager Sam Ellis wrote: 'I take particular pleasure in welcoming Horwich to Bloomfield Road and congratulate them on getting this far- for the first time in 54 years. Horwich's victory over Runcorn in the last round was very hard earned and well deserved, and any non-league team who can come out on top of the Alliance League Champions over two games must be given the greatest respect by any lower Division club.'

The teams lined up as follows: Blackpool: Hesford; Bardsley, Hart; Deary, Hetzke, Serella; Hockaday, Noble, Bamber, Pashley, Downes. Sub: Jeffries. RMI: McMahon; Griffiths, Parry; Waywell, Silous, Kilgannon; Garrett, Haslam, Caldwell, Lang, McLachlan. Sub: Brown.

At half-time RMI went into a heroes' welcome from their supporters after holding the fourth division side to 0-0. But when Ray Silous was injured four minutes into the second half, RMI's hopes faded. Silous had kept Blackpool danger-man Dave Bamber quiet but within two minutes of his departure Bamber won a header in the penalty area and though the ball rebounded off the bar Terry Pashley was on hand to force the ball home from close range. Bamber added a second with ten minutes remaining after a solo run and John Deary's 89th minute penalty wrapped up a 3-0 win for the home side. RMI went closest when Caldwell's free-kick hit the side-netting. But there was consolation from a £3,000 share of the gate from the attendance of 5,280, Blackpool's largest of the season up until that point. The hosts also presented RMI officials with a souvenir plaque to mark the occasion. Highlights of the tie were later shown on BBC's Match of the Day programme.

There was another big game in store for the RMI fans to savour when they played Chorley in the final of the Lancashire Junior Cup at Springfield Park, Wigan. Along the way to the final RMI had defeated Accrington Stanley 8-2, Caldwell and Jimmy Garrett each scoring hat-tricks and then Barrow and Southport. But the final, played on

Wednesday 20 April 1983, was ruined by dreadful weather with the pitch a quagmire following heavy rain, sleet and snow. Thunder rolled and lightning flashed around the ground during the game and after an even first-half RMI slipped to a 3-0 defeat in front of a crowd of 1,323. RMI played in an unfamiliar all-yellow strip after losing the toss for first-choice kit.

Former Bolton Wanderers striker Garry Jones opened the scoring in the 56th minute, slotting the ball home after a cross hit the post, and lobbed McMahon for a well-taken second with twenty minutes remaining. Mather, so often a thorn in RMI's side, added a third with three minutes left.

RMI manager Ken Wright said: 'The lads battled hard but defensive slips cost us the match and the conditions didn't suit our game. It was a lottery.'

The teams lined-up as follows: Chorley: Wood; Lees, Knight; Bingham, Twentyman, Lugg; Mather, Jackson, Clayton, Jones, Cook. Sub: Robinson.
RMI: McMahon; Griffiths (capt), Parry; Waywell, Silous, Kilgannon; Garrett, Haslam, Caldwell, Lang, Lancaster. Sub: Froggatt. Referee: I Hendrick (Preston).

In all RMI scored 120 goals in 59 games, Caldwell accounting for 44 of the total. He played what proved to be his final game for RMI at Leyland Motors in the final league game of the season, scoring his sixth hat-trick of the campaign in a resounding 7-1 victory. During the season Jimmy Garrett scored 17 goals and Neil McLachlan 14. Burscough were the inaugural division one champions with Radcliffe Borough and Colne Dynamoes winning their respective divisions. RMI finished a highly respectable third with 54 points from 38 games. They won 22, drew ten and lost only six, scoring 77 goals and conceding only 35, their best defensive record since 1948-49 (when they let-in 28 goals but in only 24 games in the second division of the Lancashire Combination).

There was one remarkable goal during the season, RMI goalkeeper Tommy Cavanagh taking advantage of a strong wind to beat opposite number Tony McMahon, the former RMI 'keeper during the game at Glossop. But for all Caldwell's scoring feats full-back and captain Dave Griffiths was chosen as Player of the Year. Bolton born Paul Moss, signed from Winsford United, scored his first RMI goal at Nantwich in November 1982 and went on to forge a fine career with the club.

In February 1983 a new development scheme was launched following the purchase of the Grundy Hill ground from British Rail. It was hoped to raise a total of £30,000 in share capital, a target that proved way too ambitious. Two months later a collection for a newly established fund to 'Save Horwich Works' was taken at home games.

One piece of sad news during March 1983 was the death of Clive Carr, a former RMI committee member and reserve team manager at the age of 41.

The work-force at the Loco Works had declined to around the 1,400-mark and on 23 December 1983 despite protests and trade union resistance the works were finally closed, bringing to an end almost a century's rich tradition of craftsmanship and engineering. The foundry and the spring shop continued in use after this date, although the work force was eventually reduced from 1,400 to 300. In this form it was sold by British Rail Engineering Limited to the Parkfield Group in 1988. The rail connection to the works was finally removed in 1989. The site is now an industrial estate, appropriately named 'Horwich Loco', with most of the buildings still continuing in use.

In the late spring of 1983 a floodlit cricket competition was staged at Grundy Hill which proved to be a popular fund raising initiative. Kearsley were the first winners of the competition with Central Lancashire League side Oldham lifting the cup in 1984 and 1985. The format was for 12-over games to be played by teams of seven players per side. Sixteen teams competed for the trophy in 1986 but sadly the competition was eventually washed-out and was scaled down to eight teams the following year before being abandoned. Over the years Test players such as Mudassar Nazar, Ravi Shastri, Mohsin Khan, Mohinder Amarnath, Franklyn Stephenson, Geoff Marsh and Hartley Alleyne played at Grundy Hill under the lights.

During the summer of 1983 RMI broke with tradition in appointing George Fisher as Club President. Traditionally the position had gone to the town's railway works manager but with the factory due to close the honour was bestowed upon the long-serving and highly respected Mr Fisher, who had served as club chairman from 1946 to 1970. Aged 78 he had quit the chairman's role after retiring from his job as production manager at the works but had continued ever since to attend RMI's home games.

RMI left the North West Counties League behind in the summer of 1983 and were promoted into the Northern Premier League, a hugely ambitious step that would add significantly to the club's expenditure on travel costs and wages. Sadly for Grundy Hill devotees Caldwell would not be making the step with them. After much deliberation Bolton Wanderers manager John McGovern signed Caldwell, at the time aged 24 and a very late starter in Football League terms.

'Bolton seemed very reluctant to sign Tony and seemed concerned about his age,' Harold Taylor recalled. 'I told the manager he would have no need to worry and that I was confident Tony would score goals in any company. He was just a natural goal scorer.'

McGovern was quoted as follows: 'Tony is no youngster but I have given him the chance to make the grade in League football after his huge success in non league football with Horwich.'

Caldwell quickly repaid Taylor's faith, earning his place in Wanderers' Third Division side and by playing three games sparked the clause that meant RMI would receive the £2,000 transfer fee under the terms of the agreement. In Caldwell's fourth league game in a Bolton jersey he became a new club hero, scoring an incredible five goals in an 8-1 demolition of Walsall at Burnden Park and went onto score 23 goals in 38 league and cup games for his new club.

The following season Caldwell was again a consistent goal-scorer for Wanderers despite playing in a side struggling in the lower reaches of Division Three. Despite injury problems he scored 18 goals in the league and a further four in cup games, a total of 22 in 40 games. He scored a hat-trick as Wanderers enjoyed another high-scoring home victory, 7-2 over Plymouth Argyle in September 1984, a rare highlight in a generally difficult season.

In 1985-86 Caldwell's goals took Wanderers to Wembley in the Freight Rover Trophy. He scored five goals in the competition including home and away strikes in Wanderers' two-legged Northern Final victory over Wigan Athletic, but Wanderers lost 3-0 to Bristol City in the Final, Caldwell hitting the bar early in the game. Caldwell's last season at Burnden Park was in 1986-87 when they were relegated to the fourth division after losing to Aldershot in the play-offs, one of the bleakest days in the club's history. In his final game Caldwell scored twice against Aldershot at Burnden but despite that the 'Shots' prevailed 3-2 on aggregate. In four seasons Caldwell scored 78 goals in 175 league and cup games for Wanderers and must have represented the best £2,000 the club ever spent.

Manager Ken Wright had been in doubt over Caldwell's ability to make the grade at Burnden Park. After Caldwell's five-goal feat Wright commented: 'It was typical Caldwell goal-scoring and it is a feather in the cap of RMI that we have helped him achieve Football League status.'

INTO THE NORTHERN PREMIER LEAGUE

Even without Caldwell in the ranks RMI made a good job of establishing themselves in the Northern Premier League, which at that time was level two of the non-league pyramid feeding directly into the Alliance Premier League (later re-named the Conference). They finished eighth with 18 league wins and nine draws from 42 league games. They joined the league alongside Rhyl, replacing Netherfield and Tamworth. Barrow went on to become champions with Matlock Town runners-up, trailing in 20 points behind.

Caldwell may have departed but in Ray Redshaw, Paul Moss and Neil McLachlan RMI had three consistent goal-scorers and the trio accounted for a total of 60 goals between themselves in all games. Redshaw, who was signed from Glossop where he had been Cheshire County League Player of the Year in 1981-82 was top scorer with 24, Moss hit 20 and McLachlan 16. Another astute signing proved to be that of Dave Liptrot from Bolton Wyresdale, who soon developed into an accomplished player at that level. He went on to score nine goals in his debut season, Allan Froggatt contributing eight.

Redshaw was a tigerish player in the penalty area and had a keen eye for goal while the wholehearted Moss, who came up through the tough school of Bolton Combination football was direct and uncompromising though blessed with a deft touch. McLachlan, a tall, skilful and experienced player equally effective out wide or down the middle, was another vastly under-rated player.

Vernon Lang proved to be a remarkably durable and consistent player throughout the season, playing in 62 out of a possible 65 games. Goalkeeper Tony McMahon, who re-joined the club, missed only four games and defenders Steve Waywell and Ray Silous both made 60 appearances. Dennis Haslam (55), Moss (54) and Ian Edwards (51) also topped the half-century mark with McLachlan (49), Redshaw (44) and Glyn Stephens (43) not far behind.

RMI's first game in the Northern Premier League ended disappointingly in a 1-0 home defeat at the hands of Matlock Town when RMI lined up as follows: McMahon; Griffiths, Edwards; Waywell, Silous, Stevens; Garrett, Haslam, Moss, Lang, McLachlan. Sub: Nichol. Their first win was in their third game, 3-1 at Worksop Town. They enjoyed a good run in the FA Cup, accounting for Farsley Celtic, Buxton and Southport in successive rounds before bowing out 4-3 at Macclesfield Town in a fourth qualifying round replay following a goal-less draw at Grundy Hill. After defeating Macclesfield in the FA Trophy the previous week the Silkmen thus gained a quick revenge.

RMI played a total of 23 cup-ties during the season, reaching the quarter-finals of the League Cup and Lancashire Junior Cup and fighting their way through to the final of the Dairy Crest Lancashire Floodlit Cup, a new competition that had been introduced to provide midweek fixtures in the second half of the season. The final was staged at Deepdale on 30 April 1984 with Southport running out 4-0 winners. It was a ragged performance by an RMI side badly missing the absent Moss and McLachlan.

Neil Wood opened the scoring for Southport in the sixth minute and Andy Mutch's volley four minutes later put the Sandgrounders firmly in control. RMI had a chance to get back into the game midway through the first-half but captain Vernon Lang saw his penalty saved by Paul Evans after Jay McComb had handled Glyn Stephens' header. There was no way back for RMI after that and Mutch, later to become an accomplished Football League player with Wolverhampton Wanderers drove home his second goal in the 65th minute before completing an impressive hat-trick with a lob over Tony McMahon twelve minutes from time. The RMI side was: McMahon; Nichol, Edwards, Hill, Silous, Stephens, Redshaw, Haslam, Liptrot, Lang, Lancaster. Substitutes: Bell (for Stevens) and Wilson (not used).

To further boost the club's fund-raising efforts RMI appointed their first full-time commercial manager in December 1983 when Jacqueline Platt took over the role. At the same time the first phase of ground improvements began under a 12-month Manpower Services Commission scheme as workers tidied up the terraces and surrounding areas and laid stone paths at Grundy Hill. But there was a sad departure when the long-serving Harold Taylor left after a difference of opinion with Chris Healey. Taylor, who had a family link with the club going back to the 1920s was sacked from his post as trainer and relinquished his role as secretary, David Wood taking over. But happily after a short gap Taylor resumed as trainer.

To the dismay of traditionalists RMI were now playing in an all-blue strip with barely discernable white stripes, but thankfully it proved to be only a temporary measure. The club sponsors, Cambrian Soft Drinks had ordered the new strip for next season and the design reverted to wide stripes.

RMI's second season in the NPL was another successful one and to achieve a final placing of ninth in a very strong league was a noteworthy achievement. Despite losing star striker Ray Redshaw, who moved into the Football League with Wigan Athletic after being watched by Latics manager Harry McNally, RMI started the campaign with a pre-season cup success.

The Cambrian Cup was introduced to make pre-season games more competitive and ten teams entered the competition, arranged in two groups of five. RMI drew at Daisy Hill before beating Leyland Motors, Lancaster City and Burscough to qualify for the final. They played Barrow at Grundy Hill on Wednesday 15 August 1984, three days before the start of the league season. The game remained scoreless despite thirty minutes of extra-time but RMI then lifted the cup after emerging victorious from the ensuing penalty shoot-out.

In mid October 1984 Ken Wright departed to take over as manager of Chorley , replacing Tom Haworth, obviously feeling that the Magpies offered more potential in terms of supporters through the turnstiles. Mr Wright was quoted in the Bolton Evening News: 'I have enjoyed my time at Horwich but one of the biggest factors was the gates.' RMI had abandoned their reserve side on financial grounds, though the team was revived a year later and played in the Bolton Combination.

The loyal Alan Kirkman returned as manager, initially in a caretaker capacity until the end of the season with his position subsequently extended. Club captain Vernon Lang, who earlier in the year had been chosen to represent the Northern Premier League in a representative game against an England Non-League XI at Holker Street, Barrow (the NPL won the game 2-0 on 21 March 1984) was appointed as Kirkman's assistant. Later in the season Lang was awarded a testimonial. Phil Parry left with Wright for Victory Park and there were justifiable fears that others would follow. To the delight of RMI supporters their side beat Chorley 1-0 in a late season game at Grundy Hill, Paul Jones scoring the only goal before a crowd of 600.

RMI began their league programme with an unbeaten run of six games but then their fortunes declined and they suffered early departures from both the FA Cup and FA

Trophy. They lost 2-1 at Winsford United in the second qualifying round of the FA Cup after victory over Lincolnshire side Appelby Frodingham in the first meeting of the two sides. Buxton knocked-out RMI in the FA Trophy at the third attempt after two drawn ties. But in an exhausting final two months of the season when 21 games were played in 57 days, RMI put together a consistent run of form, with 14 wins, three draws and only four defeats.

Stafford Rangers were champions with 86 points, four ahead of runners-up Macclesfield Town. Bangor City had been relegated from the Alliance Premier League so RMI had two Welsh clubs as opponents and the league was a far-flung one with Workington, Grantham and Goole among the competing teams. The Welsh contingent was increased in the following season when Caernarfon Town joined from the North West Counties League.

After losing his job as manager at Burnden Park, John McGovern, a double European Cup-winning captain under Brian Clough at Nottingham Forest, decided to resume his playing career. McGovern had established links with RMI during the Caldwell signing and while he finalised plans to move abroad where he intended setting up a business and severing his ties with the game the club was delighted to have a player of his ability and experience in their ranks. McGovern played 535 Football League games and also won league championships with Derby County and Forest. McGovern made his RMI debut against Matlock Town on 1 March 1985, setting up an equaliser for Andy Stafford in a 1-1 draw.

With McGovern pulling the midfield strings, RMI reached the final of the Floodlit Cup and defeated South Liverpool 2-0 at Deepdale on 30 April 1985, Paul Moss scoring both goals of an exciting game. McGovern helped create the opening goal, sending Allan Froggatt clear on the right for Moss to convert the cross after 31 minutes. With 12 minutes remaining Moss wrapped up the game after fine work by McLachlan. It must have seemed a far cry for McGovern from Forest's European triumphs but he impressed everyone at the club with his willingness to get involved and his easy-going nature.

In total RMI played 61 games, 42 in the league and a further 19 in cup competitions. Allan Froggatt missed only one game, an outstanding run of consistency while Paul Moss (58 appearances), Neil McLachlan (57) and Tony McMahon (56) proved almost as durable. Full-back Joe Nichol (52), Vernon Lang (50) and Ray Silous (49) were other virtual fixtures in the side. Moss led the way in the scoring ranks with 22 goals in league and cup, followed by McLachlan (19) and Froggatt (14).

But the growing costs of competing at this level, coupled with the fact that RMI were one of the poorest supported clubs in the league meant it was always going to be a struggle to survive. Mr Kirkman was invited to continue as manager but Chris Healey resigned as Chairman, Brian Froggatt replacing him. The long-serving Albert Dickinson was appointed vice-chairman and made a life member.

In 1985-86 the Northern Premier League was sponsored for the first time and became known as the Multipart League. While Gateshead won eight of their last nine matches to finish champions. RMI slipped to 16th in the league, losing half of their 42 league games. But with only six draws, the other 15 games being won RMI comfortably finished above the re-election zone despite having one point deducted for a breach of league rules.

In successive weeks in early October RMI suffered exits from the FA Trophy and FA Cup, the former in an ignominious 9-1 defeat at Northern League outfit Brandon United, the latter in a more respectable 2-0 defeat at Rhyl. In between those two ties RMI also went down 7-2 at Macclesfield Town in the league. Manager Alan Kirkman was sacked before the match at the Moss Rose against Macclesfield and chairman Brian Froggatt and secretary David Wood resigned on 2 November after what amounted to a vote of 'no confidence' from a small number of members.

Chris Healey returned as chairman and appointed Allan Froggatt, ironically son of the outgoing chairman as player-manager to replace Kirkman. RMI then enjoyed a fine run of consistent midseason form, embarking on an unbeaten run that stretched to 16 games and included eleven wins and five draws, before a 3-1 defeat at Gateshead in mid January. The run included a 3-1 Boxing Day win at Chorley when Paul Moss (2) and Charlie Cooper were on target. RMI also enjoyed another run of five wins and a draw in six games, including a 2-1 home win over eventual champions Gateshead. But the season ended in disappointment after RMI lost five of their last six games including a Floodlit Trophy Semi-Final reversal at Chorley and five days after the campaign ended Allan Froggatt was sacked as manager.

Paul Moss made 59 appearances during the season with Brian Hart (57), Joe Nichol (55) and goalkeeper Michael Allison (51) also topping the half-century mark. Other regulars were Allan Froggatt (44), Neil Peters (43), Charlie Cooper (42) and Mark Russell (42). Moss enjoyed his most prolific season for the club, scoring 28 goals in league and cup while a newcomer Tony Ellis, signed from Northwich Victoria, scored 13 goals in 31 appearances and his performances soon attracted the scouts.

Though aged 21 and a comparatively late starter in Football League terms, Ellis, an elegant and skilful striker, was snapped up by Joe Royle and moved to Oldham Athletic, later enjoying two spells with Preston North End and a highly productive one at Blackpool. He also played for Stoke City, Bury, Stockport County, Rochdale and Burnley and scored 185 goals in 518 league appearances, commanding combined transfer fees of £750,000. Gateshead were promoted to the Conference, replacing relegated Barrow while Matlock Town and Goole Town were both re-elected after finishing in the bottom two places.

Off the field RMI launched a new fund-raising initiative with the launch of the One Hundred Club while the annual Grand National draw, organised by Ken Chaisty and John Allen provided a valuable source of funds. The AGM revealed that it was costing £28,000 per season to operate at this level of football but despite the increasing costs a healthy profit of £5,000 had been returned. During the spring Grundy Hill also staged five home games for the newly-formed Bolton Braves American football team.

Former RMI favourite Tony Webber was appointed as manager during the summer but in the following season the club's decline continued. RMI won only three league games, drew 12 and earned just 20 points, their lowest tally in a complete season since 1920-21. They finished 68 points behind champions Macclesfield Town who replaced Gateshead in the Conference. Burton Albion joined the Southern League to make way for relegated Frickley Athletic. RMI won just twice at home in the league, against Buxton and Worksop Town and their only success on their travels was in their last away game of the campaign, when they won 1-0 at Burton Albion.

With Moss and Ellis both having departed (Moss joining Chorley) RMI suffered from a lack of scoring power and veteran forward Mick Moore finished top scorer with a highly commendable ten goals in league and cup. Neil McLachlan and Wayne Lancaster each scored seven goals. Goalkeeper Michael Allison topped the appearances chart with 55, one ahead of Brian Hart (54), Chris Walmsley (52), Moore (41) and John Fielding (41).

Webber admitted to the Bolton Evening News that he had underestimated the size of the task. The crisis points came with humiliating defeats at the hands of Chorley (4-0 in the League Cup at home) and Hyde United (5-0 away in the League). To make matters worse Chorley, under Ken Wright's management were flying high and earned national newspaper attention after beating fallen giants Wolverhampton Wanderers 3-0 in an FA Cup first round second replay at Burnden Park, with former RMI players Mark Edwards and Charlie Cooper both on the score sheet. Former RMI favourite Paul Moss had scored in the previous two drawn ties, which both finished 1-1. Chorley then drew 0-0 with Preston North End in a second round tie staged at Ewood Park before losing 5-0 in the replay at Deepdale.

The roots of RMI's problems, many supporters felt stemmed back to the sacking of Froggatt and the majority of the first-team squad. That left RMI with only two signed-on professionals, goalkeeper Michael Allison and Brian Hart. Webber recruited players who would go on to serve RMI well in future years, notably defender Paul Booth who had been on Bolton Wanderers' books and midfielder Chris Walmsley from Daisy Hill, but did not see out the team-building. Webber's resignation followed a Lancashire Junior Cup defeat against Bacup Borough on 5 February and was accepted by the committee. Brian Hart, the club captain and second team manager Geoff Foster were asked to look after first-team affairs in the interim period before a permanent replacement was appointed.

The new man in charge proved to be Les Rigby, a PE lecturer at Wigan College, who had previously been the manager of a number of non-league clubs including Wigan Athletic and at the time of his appointment was assistant manager at Barrow. As a player Rigby had accumulated over 700 appearances primarily with Wigan Athletic, Lancaster City and Netherfield. Widely respected throughout the non league game, Mr Rigby had been in management for 26 years after beginning as player-manager at Lytham, also numbering Fleetwood, Great Harwood, Altrincham, Chorley, Morecambe and Rossendale United among his former clubs. For three seasons between 1972 and 1975 he managed Wigan Athletic and was their last part-time manager before they entered the Football League, taking them to the FA Trophy Final in 1973 when they lost to Scarborough. Rigby took charge for the first time against Witton Albion on 28 February 1987 and swiftly introduced a solid backroom staff, bringing in Alan Kirkman as assistant manager and Malcolm Richmond as trainer.

RMI and Workington, who finished second from bottom, were successfully re-elected as the league set-up was re-organised. A new Premier League and First Division was brought into the NPL and the club went on to finish a respectable 13th in season 1987-88. The change in fortunes was largely down to the arrival of Mr Rigby who galvanised the club and re-invigorated players and supporters alike.

GMAC CUP SUCCESS

The season was especially memorable for RMI's success in the GMAC Cup, a competition in which they had never previously enjoyed much success. Derived from the old inter-league cup competition, the cup was competed for between sides in the Conference, NPL, Southern League and Isthmian Leagues, or levels one and two of the non-league pyramid.

The competition began in early September 1987 when RMI drew 1-1 at South Liverpool before winning the replay 2-1 at Grundy Hill. After bowing out of the early stages of the FA Cup and FA Trophy in successive weeks, with successive home defeats against St Helens Town and South Liverpool respectively, the GMAC Cup assumed greater importance. Faz Page and former Barrow player Shaun Rodgers scored in a 2-1 win at Workington and Duncan Podmore's goal against Marine at Grundy Hill earned RMI a tie against Altrincham at Moss Lane on 1 December 1987 when goals by Page and Phil Power earned RMI a notable 2-1 win.

After a wait of several weeks the quarter-final tie was against Northwich Victoria in February. After Rodgers earned a draw at the Drill Field on a bitterly cold evening, goals by Page, Howarth and Hart earned RMI a 3-2 win in the replay to set up a semi-final tie at home to Enfield. This game was staged at Grundy Hill on Sunday 27 March 1988 the day after RMI had lost 2-0 in the league at Barrow. Two goals by Page and an own goal earned RMI another fine scalp. Many RMI supporters travelled up to Christie Park for the second semi-final in the competition and saw Weymouth defeat Morecambe on Sunday 26 April.

One of the most important games in RMI's history came along when the final was staged at Grundy Hill against Weymouth on Sunday 8 May 1988, a gloriously sunny day with play taking place on the adjoining cricket ground. The game had almost a carnival atmosphere with several hundred Bolton Wanderers fans swelling the attendance to 1,149 still celebrating Wanderers' 1-0 win at Wrexham the day before that earned a last-day promotion from division four and began the club's long haul back up the Football League ladder. Stuart Morgan, the Weymouth manager had been far from happy with the choice of venue and was quoted as saying: 'I thought the final would have been staged on a better pitch.'

The game began in dramatic fashion when RMI goalkeeper Michael Allison was injured inside the first minute after a crunching challenge by Gerry Nardiello. Allison was treated on the pitch for nine minutes before he was taken to hospital, happily later returning in time for the cup presentation.

Brian Hart went in goal and went on to enjoy an inspired game that earned him the Man of the Match award as goals by Neil McLachlan and Faz Page earned RMI the cup.

McLachlan, who had climbed off the treatment table to play in the game, scored the opening goal just before half-time, climbing above John Smeulders in the Weymouth goal to head in Chris Walmsley's cross. Ten minutes after the re-start Page guided an Ian Street corner into the net. Hart made several fine saves while Paul Booth headed a Shaun Teale shot off the line as RMI held on deservedly to their lead.

Afterwards RMI manager Les Rigby said: 'We took both goals very well and it was a magnificent team performance. We beat four Vauxhall Conference clubs and won it on merit to say the least.' The Weymouth manager Morgan said: 'We were never allowed to play and never fully tested the stand-in 'keeper.'

The teams were as follows: RMI: Allison (Schofield); Hart, Mitchell; Booth, Howard, Senior; Walmsley, Street, Power, Page, McLachlan. Weymouth: Smeulders; Pugh, Gibson; Teale, Compson, Conning; Myers, Roberts, Iannone, Nardiello, Lewis.

The season was not over as RMI entertained Rossendale United in the Floodlit Cup quarter-final two days later, winning 3-1. But after reaching the last four the organisers decided to complete the competition the following season. RMI eventually played the semi-final tie away at Hyde United on Halloween and went down to a 2-1 defeat.

In the league RMI finished 13th in the Premier Division with 17 wins and nine draws from 42 games. Only four clubs managed fewer than their 46 goals but they did have an outstanding defensive record, conceding just 42 goals, a record surpassed by only four clubs including champions Chorley.

Managed by former RMI favourite Ken Wright the Magpies, with a host of ex-RMI players in their ranks reached the heady heights of the Vauxhall Conference after an outstanding season in which they lost just six league games and finished three points clear of runners-up Hyde United. Between October and April the Magpies lost just once in 26 league games. Ray Redshaw, Paul Moss, Glyn Stephens, Charlie Pawsey and Mark Edwards were all mainstays of the Magpies side. Edwards and Redshaw each scored 21 league goals during the season.

Shepshed Charterhouse from the Southern League were transferred to the NPL to replace Chorley as the bottom three clubs in the GM Vauxhall Conference were all southern-based. At the end of the season Workington were relegated and Oswestry Town, having sold their ground, resigned.

In total RMI played 66 first-team games during the season, which was a massive commitment for a part-time playing and managerial squad. Glenn Walker was ever-present in the league, including five substitute appearances, and missed only two games in all. Paul Booth played in 60 games, Brian Hart in 59, Faz Page in 57 and Phil Power (despite an absence while he went for trials with a club in Malta) 50. In total 34 players turned out for RMI including Ian Cockbain, the former Lancashire cricketer who was injured in his only game for the club. Page was leading scorer with 20 goals in all competitions, Walker scoring 12 goals and Power 10.

Sadly, Les Rigby was unable to build on the success as he was forced to resign from his post early in the following season due to ill-health after spending time in hospital. Alan Kirkman was appointed as Rigby's replacement in November 1988 and former RMI player Mal Richmond joined him as his assistant. In 1988-89 RMI trailed in a disappointing 20th in a league now re-titled the HFS Loans League, just one point clear of the relegation zone. Barrow earned the championship while Worksop Town finished bottom and were relegated. RMI won only seven league games with 14 draws and while scoring goals remained a problem, with only 42 in total, the defence conceded 70. Their defence of the GMAC Cup ended at the first hurdle. Re-titled the Clubcall Cup, RMI lost 3-0 at Fleetwood Town in early September and crashed out of the FA Cup with a 5-0 defeat at Emley.

An early season 2-0 win at Southport, with Page and Moore on target, was RMI's only success in the league until they beat Rhyl 2-1 at Grundy Hill at the end of September.

Mainstays of the side were Paul Booth (54 appearances in all games), Brian Hart (53), Mark Schofield (47), Michael Allison (45), Chris Walmsley (45), Jon Senior (45) and Neil McLachlan (45). Walmsley, Walker and Page all tied for top-scorer with seven goals each.

Chorley, meanwhile, secured another season in the Conference with a respectable 17th placed finish. Their team was augmented by former RMI favourite Phil Power who finished as the Magpies' top scorer with 16 league goals while Paul Moss contributed nine. Chorley's average attendance was 891.

In 1989-90 RMI's league form improved and they rose to 14th in the Premier Division despite having three points deducted for a registration issue. They scored 66 goals, the best for several seasons but conceded 69. The season was dominated by Colne Dynamoes who were climbing the pyramid at a seemingly unassailable rate of knots and operated with a full-time playing squad. But after becoming champions with a record points-tally of 102 they were refused entry to the GM Vauxhall Conference as their Holt House ground did not meet the required standards. Gateshead, as runners-up, took their place and during the summer Colne owner Graham White disbanded the club. The two Welsh clubs, Caernarfon Town and Rhyl finished in the relegation places.

Midfielder Jon Senior made 49 out of a possible 54 appearances with Ian Mullineux (48 appearances), Mark Schofield (48), Dave Liptrot (47), Chris Walmsley (47), Glenn Walker (47), Paul Booth (44), goalkeeper Steve Davies (42) and Ollie Parillon (41) other mainstays. Liptrot, a quick and skilful forward who had been playing at Chorley made a welcome return and gave RMI a scoring presence they had missed for several seasons. He scored 16 goals, all in the league, with midfielder Walmsley weighing in with 13 and striker Daryl McCarty 11. The consistent Walker hit nine.

Derby games against the Magpies were back on the agenda in 1990-91 after Chorley's stint in the Conference ended in relegation after two-seasons in the top echelon of the non-league game. Chorley had finished one point adrift of safety with Power again top scorer with 11 league goals. Former RMI favourite Tony Caldwell joined Chorley and hit five goals in 19 appearances after finishing his Football League career with spells at Bristol City, Grimsby Town and Stockport County following his departure from Burnden Park.

The season was played with only 21 clubs due to Colne's late withdrawal on the eve of the season. Chorley finished 14th in the Premier Division, two places and one point better off than RMI. Witton Albion, who bolstered their side with several former Colne players, finished runaway champions, 16 points clear of runners-up Stalybridge Celtic. South Liverpool, forced to play their home matches at Bootle following an arson attack on their Holly Park ground resigned at the end of the season and Whitley Bay, Emley and Accrington Stanley were all promoted to the Premier Division.

RMI beat Chorley 2-1 at Victory Park in September, Chris Walmsley (penalty) and Marvin Baldwin on target while Jon Senior's goal earned a point from a 1-1 draw in the return game the following March.

RMI had begun the season with a 2-1 win at Shepshed Charterhouse when their side was: Almond; Hart, Mullineux; Booth, Parillon, Walmsley; Senior, McLachlan, Walker, Liptrot, McCarthy. Subs: Madrick, Baldwin.

Paul O'Berg, an experienced former Football League forward primarily with Scunthorpe

United and who had also played in New Zealand and Malta had taken over as RMI chairman during the summer of 1990 after becoming involved with a travel agency in Bolton. He was actually RMI's first player-chairman, appearing regularly in the side.

After a run of five successive defeats Alan Kirkman was sacked as manager and Malcolm Richmond, his assistant, and scout Lyndon Hesketh also departed. Mr O'Berg took over as caretaker manager and presided over a 2-1 win over Gainsborough Trinity before a new manager was appointed. That new man was Kenny Wright, who returned to Grundy Hill for a second stint in charge during November 1990, taking charge for the first time on 1 December 1990.   Since leaving Chorley Wright had been manager at Radcliffe Borough. He was given a mandate to get the club back into the top half of the table and one of his first acts was to bring in goalkeeper John Henry formerly with Irlam and Leek, to replace Andrew Almond. He also switched striker Walker, formerly with Crewe, Marine and Warrington to left-back and brought in Neil Rowbottom from Rossendale United.

RMI had hopes of a good FA Cup run after disposing of Morecambe after a replay and then Irlam Town but disappointingly bowed out of the competition at the third qualifying round stage losing 3-1 at home to Colwyn Bay.

But RMI embarked on a good run in the FA Trophy, accounting for Alfreton Town, Rhyl, Sutton Coldfield Town, Bedworth United, Gretna and Redbridge Forest in successive rounds and reaching the last eight for the first time. Brian Hart scored the only goal of a dour home tie against Alfreton in front of 136 at Grundy Hill before Glenn Walker, Neil McLachlan and Chris Walmsley got the goals in a 3-2 home win over Rhyl when 138 were in attendance. In their first ever game with Sutton Coldfield RMI won 3-1 at Coles Lane (attendance: 145) with Daryl McCarty, McLachlan and Jon Senior on target.

In the first round proper RMI played another new opponent Bedworth United, from near Coventry, at Grundy Hill and Walker and former Rossendale United and Accrington Stanley player Marvin Baldwin scored in a 2-1 win before 168 spectators. Their next opponents were Gretna, the first time RMI had ever played a Scottish side in a competitive fixture. The tie was postponed on its original date and re-staged at Grundy Hill on Monday 18 February 1991 when Alan Ainscow and Daryl McCarty scored RMI's goals in a 2-1 win before a crowd of 313. Five days later they beat eventual Isthmian League champions Redbridge Forest 2-1 at Grundy Hill with Dave Liptrot and Ollie Parillon getting the goals in front of 411 spectators.

But RMI's best-ever run in the competition ended when they played Conference side Altrincham away in the quarter-finals on 16 March 1991 going down to a 5-0 defeat before a crowd of 1,486. Altrincham went on to lose a two-legged semi-final against Wycombe Wanderers.

RMI did not suffer any negative reaction from that crushing disappointment, however, and enjoyed a run of six successive league victories before losing their final game of the season at home to Witton Albion.

Parillon and McCarty both played in 55 games in league and cup with Glenn Walker (52), Dave Liptrot (52) and Jon Senior (47) also regular players. Liptrot again finished as top scorer with 15 goals in all competitions with McCarty (14) and Walker (13) also reaching double figures during the season.

Bolton born Alan Ainscow, who had enjoyed a distinguished league career, making a combined total of 473 league appearances with Blackpool, Birmingham City, Everton,

Wolves and Blackburn Rovers played in 36 RMI games and though now in his late 30s still looked a class performer.

Striker Tony McDonald had made his RMI bow towards the end of the 1990-91 season, following his former manager Ken Wright from Stainton Park, scoring a hat-trick in one game against Bangor City. His move from Radcliffe Borough had initially been on loan but RMI hurriedly made the transfer a permanent one and in 1991-92 McDonald hit ten goals, with the returning Ray Redshaw top-scorer with 15.

RMI improved to finish 13th with Chorley's slide continuing as they finished in the relegation places only to earn a reprieve when Bangor City were forced to resign to join the newly formed League of Wales. Stalybridge Celtic earned promoted as champions, 14 points ahead of runners-up Marine. Colwyn Bay elected to defy the Wales FA and stay in the English pyramid, playing their home games at Northwich Victoria's Drill Field ground in the following season.

Fullback Ian Lloyd, signed from Mossley, made 49 appearances and the consistent Paul Booth and midfielder Paul Griffin each made 47. Redshaw (43), goalkeeper John Henry (41) and former Chorley centre-half Craig Wardle (41) were other mainstays.

RMI suffered disappointment in the cups, losing 4-2 at Emley in the second qualifying round of the FA Cup and going down at the first hurdle in the FA Trophy at home to Marine. But they achieved a consistent run of form between December and early February when they enjoyed an unbeaten run of 13 games, including six wins.

In 1992-93 RMI again finished 13th but the goals-for tally improved markedly with 72 against 44 in the previous season though they did concede 79 as opposed to only 52. The rise in scoring power was down to the exciting partnership between strikers Redshaw and McDonald who between them hit 43 goals during the season, McDonald top-scoring with 23. Back from Chorley, the popular Paul Moss contributed nine goals. Champions Southport moved upwards to be replaced by relegated Boston United. Founder members Goole Town were relegated alongside Mossley with Bridlington Town and Knowsley United being promoted. Bridlington played their 'home' games 70 miles away at Doncaster Rovers' Belle Vue as their own ground was deemed not up to standard while Knowsley occupied the Alt Park ground that was formerly home to Huyton rugby league club.

RMI had a string of consistent players with defender Andy Westwell (49 appearances), Griffin (46), Redshaw (44), McDonald (44), Lloyd (44) and Moss (39) forming the backbone of the side. But RMI suffered disappointment, bowing out of the FA Cup by a single goal defeat at Macclesfield Town and losing at home to Winsford United in the FA Trophy.

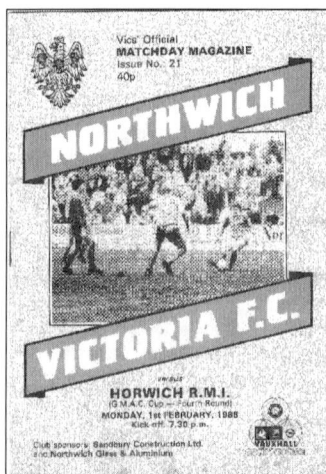

Programmes from the GMAC Cup run—LEFT from the 1-1 drawn match away to GM Vauxhall Conference side Northwich Victoria at the Drill Field. RIGHT—from the dramatic Final against another Conference side, Weymouth, played at Grundy Hill.

BELOW—the teams take to the field at Grundy Hill for the Final, with a cricket match in progress on the Recreation Ground, Horwich playing Egerton in the Bolton Cricket League.

RMI goalkeeper Michael Allison is injured early in the GMAC Cup Final

RMI on the attack during the second half

Neil McLachlan heads in the opening goal in the GMAC Cup Final

'Faz' Page rises high to head the second goal for Horwich against Weymouth

The GMAC Cup is held aloft by RMI's Jon Senior

RMI players with the Cup after the memorable win over Weymouth

Stand-in goalkeeper Brian Hart and the injured Michael Allison celebrate the GMAC Cup win

After the dust had settled—RMI players and staff line up for an official team photograph with the GMAC Cup

RUGBY LEAGUE COMES TO GRUNDY HILL

Meanwhile professional rugby league was staged at Grundy Hill as Chorley Borough moved their base from Victory Park. The club's chairman at the time was Lindsay Hoyle, later to become the town's Member of Parliament. The first game at the ground was a third division league match against Ryedale-York on Sunday 30 August 1992 when the visitors won 23-13 before a crowd of 483. The next home game attracted an attendance of 518 for the 'derby' with Blackpool Gladiators, the visitors winning 28-16.

Though Chorley recorded their first victory of the season in their next game, winning 18-15 at Nottingham City, the team struggled and had to wait until just before Christmas for their next winning pay packet as they defeated Blackpool who played at the Blackpool Mechanics FC ground. The first home victory of the season was not until February when Chorley defeated Barrow 22-20 at Grundy Hill before a crowd of 222, by which time John Taylor had been replaced as coach by long-serving forward Carl Briscoe.

The Rugby Football League abandoned the three division structure following a special meeting of clubs on 10 March 1993 and it was decreed that three clubs would lose their senior status and be demoted to a new National Conference League. After battling hard for survival Chorley were one of three clubs to lose their senior status at the end of the season and were relegated to the National Conference alongside Nottingham City and Blackpool Gladiators. They looked to have secured safety after defeating Nottingham City and Highfield in their last two home games, the latter one attracting a season's best crowd of 767 but as Chorley's players watched Highfield recovered and escaped the relegation places by winning their final two games of the season at Barrow and Nottingham.

Chorley's crowds averaged 434 at Grundy Hill in their first season, an increase of 40 on the previous season at Victory Park. After playing a second season at Grundy Hill in 1993-94 in the relative obscurity of the National Conference Chorley moved back to Victory Park and later regained their senior status in 1995.

Meanwhile at the annual RMI sportsman's dinner held at the Georgian House Hotel on 5 August 1993 another famous name from the football world joined the illustrious roll-call of guest speakers when former Manchester United legend George Best was in attendance.

But the club was rocked by the departure of manager Ken Wright just weeks before the start of the new season. Wright had decided to take up the offer to become Phil Staley's assistant manager at Accrington Stanley. In his place RMI moved swiftly to appoint Mick Holgate as manager.

RMI began the season with a 1-1 draw against Matlock Town at Grundy Hill before a crowd of 207. The RMI team was: Bibby; Edmunds, Curwen; Hill, Thomas, McLachlan; Griffin, Haslam, McDonald, Hallows, Hughes. Subs: Marsden, Peake. They then won 2-0 at Holker Street against Barrow, McDonald and Dobson on the mark to silence the majority of a crowd of 1,268. But a string of six successive defeats, including exits from the FA Cup (1-0 at Chorley) and FA Trophy (2-0 at home against Congleton Town) followed and demonstrated that the season was going to be an uphill struggle.

McDonald, after beginning the following season in scoring form, was transferred to Chorley for a reported fee of £5,000, a record incoming transfer for RMI. In his place RMI recruited the experienced Barry Diamond and largely thanks to Diamond's goals they finished just one place above the relegation zone in 1993-94, the last full season at Grundy Hill.   They won eight, drew 12 and lost 22 games, scoring 50 goals and conceding 75.

Scottish born Diamond began his career with Gillingham and then moved into the Scottish League with Dumbarton before playing in semi-professional football for the first time with Barrow and Workington. After a second spell with Barrow he joined Finnish side Olun Palloseura and began his Football League career with a loan spell at Stockport County before scoring 16 goals in 52 games for Rochdale. He had a short spell on loan at Wrexham and then made 22 appearances, scoring three goals, for Halifax Town. After spells with Gainsborough Trinity, Morecambe, Colne Dynamoes, Mossley and Hyde United he played in South Africa before joining Altrincham. He subsequently played for Chorley, Stalybridge Celtic, Curzon Ashton, Rossendale United and Mossley before joining RMI.

Former Hyde United defender Chris Molloy had a fine debut season at full-back and made 37 appearances.   Centre-half Mark Thomas (36), midfielder Peter Cottom (36), Warren Peake (35), Andrew Leach (35), Richard Bibby (33) and Paul Griffin (31) were the mainstays of a much-changed side with a total of 42 players used during the season. Goalkeeper Michael Allison returned to Grundy Hill after two seasons with Chesterfield in which he made 16 league appearances and later stints at Morecambe and Witton Albion. Diamond scored 19 goals in 27 appearances, a fine effort in a struggling side with McDonald (8) and Leach (6) next in the list.

Marine finished champions, one point ahead of Leek Town but were denied promotion as their ground did not meet Conference standards. Witton Albion's relegation from the Conference led to Leek being transferred to the Southern League. Bridlington folded at the end of the season and Guiseley and Spennymoor United were promoted.   In November 1994 the league was re-named the Unibond League.

Chorley Rugby League playing at Grundy Hill, during the 1992-93 season

GOODBYE TO HORWICH

It was clear that the following season, 1994-95 would be a struggle and so it proved even though RMI began brightly with three wins out of their first four games. They opened the season with a 2-1 home win over Gainsborough Trinity when their side was: Allison; Kent, Molloy; Cuddy, Thomas, Griffin; Fahey, Robinson, Diamond, Nugent, Kilshaw. Subs: Leach, Cottom, Bibby. Barry Diamond scored both RMI goals before a crowd of 147.

The next home game was on Bank Holiday Monday evening in what proved to be the final RMI-Chorley derby game at the ground. A crowd of 327 saw RMI thrash the Magpies 6-0 with Diamond (2), Robinson (2), Gale and Kilshaw on the mark. After that fine start, though, RMI's fortunes declined and they lost their next six games before young Horwich born striker Andrew Leach scored twice in a 4-1 home win over Buxton. Barrow then visited Grundy Hill and handed out a 6-1 drubbing and RMI's fortunes nose-dived again. They had also suffered exits at the first hurdle in both the FA Cup and FA Trophy at the hands of Burscough and Nuneaton Borough respectively.

Off the field came news that football's days at Grundy Hill were numbered as Horwich RMI entered into a deal to buy the Hilton Park ground of Leigh rugby league club and move out of town. The Bolton Evening News had more. 'A dramatic rescue package that guarantees the future of Leigh rugby league club for at least 50 years was today hailed a lifeline,' the report stated.

'The partnership deal also gives a welcome boost to neighbouring Northern Premier League soccer club Horwich RMI which will move from its present Grundy Hill ground to share facilities at Leigh's Hilton Park.

'The innovative deal which will effectively secure the future of the two clubs who are steeped in he North West sporting traditions will mean that Grundy Hill Estates Ltd, owners of the Horwich ground, will sell Grundy Hill to house building company Fairclough Homes North West and buy Hilton Park from the proceeds.'

Gary Culshaw, the chairman of RMI was quoted as follows: 'This is a marvellous opportunity for two clubs who are facing uncertain futures to re-establish themselves as a force in their respective sports,' he said. 'The shareholders of Grundy Hill Estates Limited, who are also the die-hard Horwich supporters were 99 percent in favour of the sale to Fairclough Homes and the move to Hilton Park and we do not doubt that Bolton's councillors will have their interests at the forefront when they come to make their decision about Grundy Hill.'

Leigh, one of the founder members of the Northern Union (which was later renamed the Rugby Football League) had fallen on hard times financially only 13 years on from winning the first division championship. They had been relegated from division one at the end of the 1993-94 season and been in administration for three years. After being forced to sell their best players for pressing financial reasons they were expecting to lose their ground for development.

But Horwich's town mayor warned that the rescue deal could spell the beginning of the end for Horwich RMI. Cllr Mark Perks said: 'This means that there will be no FA football played in Horwich after nearly one hundred years of tradition and I predict that within the next decade Horwich RMI will cease to exist. They are virtually saying that whatever the supporters say it's tough and it is very bad news for the club and for the town.' He added the club should have sold off spare playing land to fund improvements to the Grundy Hill ground to ensure senior football continued in Horwich.

But Mr Culshaw replied: 'In a public meeting we said we could not make a decision without the approval of the Grundy Hill shareholders who are the committed supporters of RMI and they voted 99.5percent in favour of the move.

'With the new ground grading regulations coming into force in 1996 it could mean the end of RMI if we stay at Grundy Hill and to bring our present ground up to GM Vauxhall Conference standards would cost far in excess of any money we would receive from selling part of the ground.

'With the small gates at Grundy Hill we would continue to lose money every season and I am confident the short move to Hilton Park will ensure the long term future and success of Horwich RMI.'

Manager Mick Holgate and his assistant Mark Edwards were sacked just before Christmas 1994. Edwards had only been in the role a matter of months after the early season departure of Ray Silous. Soon later Holgate took up the post as assistant development officer for the Cheshire FA; he had been in at Grundy Hill only 18 months and had been regarded as something of a miracle worker for preserving RMI's Premier League status in his first season given the slender resources with which he had to work.

In Holgate's place RMI appointed Brian Hart as manager and Alan Kirkman as his assistant. Hart, son of the club secretary and a former RMI captain had worked with Kirkman at Atherton Collieries and had been playing for Breightmet United. Chairman Gary Culshaw resigned in protest at Holgate's sacking and was reported as follows: 'Some of the people who voted him out weren't doing a lot for the club, so it was a case of the tail wagging the dog.'

Chris Healey resumed as chairman and RMI at least celebrated Christmas by completing a double success over Chorley, Leach (2) and Gayle on the mark in a 3-2 win at Victory Park on Boxing Day before a crowd of 251. But RMI then lost each of the next four games, including a 1-0 home defeat at the hands of Darwen in the ATS Trophy, the sponsored name for the Lancashire Junior Cup. That cup-tie, played at Grundy Hill on Wednesday 18 January 1995 'attracted' a paying gate of 21, and was thought to be the lowest-ever crowd for a first-team game at the ground.

RMI then drew 4-4 at home to Emley and lost 2-1 at Hyde United before the start of February heralded what proved to be the final ever game at Grundy Hill. Colwyn Bay were the visitors on Saturday 4 February 1995 when the RMI team was: Allison; Kent, Phoenix; Senior, Thomas, Booth; Hatton, Robinson, Diamond, Hallows, Bates. Subs: Fahey, Marsden, Blenkinship.

In the programme notes manager Brian Hart wrote: 'Today possibly sees our last appearance at Grundy Hill with our proposed move to Hilton Park, Leigh nearing reality. Having played at Grundy Hill myself for a number of years today will be a day for fond memories and victory plus the three points would be a great send-off.'

There was no certainty at the time that this would be the last game as the move to Hilton Park had not finally been cleared and many supporters felt that it was a pity that the occasion was not marked in a more fitting way.

The report in the Bolton Evening News summed up the occasion well after visitors Colwyn Bay scored the only goal of a drab game. 'Leigh bound RMI signed off at Grundy Hill without a fanfare or a victory,' the report stated. 'Less than 200 fans witnessed the final home game before the move to Leigh but they had little to cheer. Horwich look far more solid now that Brian Hart has re-organised the side but as before they are short of a marksman.'

The only goal of the game, and the last to be scored at Grundy Hill arrived in the 55th minute when Graham Roberts pounced on a half-clearance to fire the ball home before a crowd of 166.

The ground developers gave RMI just two weeks to clear everything out before the bulldozers arrived and an assembly of committee men and supporters set about dismantling everything that could be moved. The turnstiles, which RMI had originally purchased from Manchester Belle Vue were bought by Spennymoor United while Trafford took the stand seats. Horwich Bowling Club inherited the club house, piece by piece while the floodlights and furniture were retained and stored at Leigh for possible future use and Radcliffe Borough acquired a set of kerbstones.

Three RMI stalwarts, Bill Seddon, Raymond Ashton and Albert Dickinson worked as hard as anyone and earned praise from Chairman Chris Healey. 'It was magnificent to see them helping us, because they are so important to the club,' Mr Healey told the Bolton Evening News. 'When they said they were 100 per cent behind the transfer because they knew the club was going nowhere in Horwich, it was an enormous boost for the move, because all three are Horwich through and through. I can't thank them enough for their contributions.'

Two experienced RMI players were also wholeheartedly behind the move to Hilton Park. Goalkeeper Mike Allison said: 'I started my career at Horwich and it used to be a great advantage playing at home but now the place is a complete disgrace- the worst I have ever seen. Hilton Park in contrast is a great place to play with all the facilities, changing rooms, boardroom and players' bar under one roof.'

Experienced striker Barry Diamond added: 'The set-up at Hilton Park is more professional, it inspires players to become professional in their attitude which will benefit the football club in the long term. In comparison to Grundy Hill Hilton Park is like Buckingham Palace, but having said all of that the surroundings are superficial. It is all about what happens on the pitch, whether that pitch is Grundy Hill or Hilton Park.'

The last season as Horwich RMI ended ingloriously with the club rooted to the foot of the Premier Division table, with nine wins, four draws and no less than 29 defeats. RMI scored 49 but conceded 94 goals.

Their first game at Hilton Park was against Boston United on Saturday 4 March 1995, the visitors winning 4-0 before a crowd of 481. The attendance was the highest in the Unibond League on the day and history was made as a round ball was kicked around the hallowed turf made famous by the oval ball game. With pensioners and children admitted free of charge the crowd was well in excess of five hundred. The RMI team was: Allison; Fagan, Phoenix; Pilling, Thomas, Kent; Hatton, Sheppard, Diamond, Thorpe, Brady. Subs: Leach, Bates, Blenkinship. Further home games followed against Guiseley (lost 2-0), Knowsley United (lost 2-1), Marine (lost 4-1), Matlock Town (lost 3-0) and Accrington Stanley (lost 5-1).

The campaign ended in three successive away games but after a 7-1 thrashing at Morecambe, goals by Jon Senior and Andrew Leach earned RMI a 2-1 win at Guiseley. What proved to be the final game as Horwich RMI was on Saturday 6 May 1995 when the trip to Rossett Park ended in a 2-0 defeat against Marine, the club's 12th defeat in their final 13 games. It was an occasion for deeply contrasting emotions. Marine, in their centenary season had clinched the championship before the game and were understandably in celebratory mood. But for the visitors it was the end of an era- the last game as Horwich RMI and the final game in the Premier Division before relegation.

For many years greengrocer Ken Whittaker and his pals had taken a magical mystery tour of the Unibond League. This group of RMI's most diehard fans travelled to away games the length and breadth of the league. They had clubbed together to buy their own transport, a second-hand Bedford painted in the Horwich team colours and they renewed the upholstery and spruced up the bodywork. 'We got the idea after we had a bad experience after hiring a mini-bus,' Ken explained. 'The bus had several mechanical faults and chugged along at a snail's pace. As a result we missed the first-half of a game at Gainsborough and we said: 'never again.'

'We needed reliable transport to ensure we all got on the terraces in time for kick-off.' Ken was also responsible for the Lancashire Hotpot that made visiting the canteen at Grundy Hill such a pleasure, particularly on cold Monday evenings when supporters had rushed to the game straight from work without any tea. His Hotpot is still remembered vividly today. Ken's son Stephen kept immaculate records of RMI's games and kindly allowed me to borrow them for inclusion in this history. One of the mini-bus-group of supporters was Arthur Chadwick, who penned a small article that Marine kindly reproduced in their programme:

'Dear Programme Editor,
'As you may be aware this is the very last time that a team bearing the name of Horwich RMI AFC (the longest name in English Football) takes to the field.
'Ironically it was on this very ground that Horwich clinched their last championship in 1979, the Cheshire County League Division One. When winning their last trophy, the GMAC Cup in 1988, Marine was the 'scalp' claimed in the third round.
'Long-time supporters will no doubt be able to recall their own memories of Marine v Horwich matches from the Lancashire Combination days through the various leagues to the Premier Division of the Unibond League.
'Today's game has added interest for both teams. Horwich will be aiming to ensure Whitley Bay don't leapfrog above them and leave them with the wooden spoon and certain relegation. Marine will be enjoying retaining their Unibond Premier Division title.
'Regardless of the outcome of today's match I am sure the mini-bus contingent from Horwich will go home with memories of yet another hospitable day at College Road.
'What better place to bring to an end the name of the GREAT little club, Horwich RMI, AFC.'

Marine opened the scoring when Lunden headed home a Murray corner and Camden beat the offside trap to score the second goal five minutes from time. With Chorley losing at Whitley Bay RMI sadly confirmed Arthur's worst fears and finished with the wooden spoon. Marine were champions for a second season in a row, four points ahead of Morecambe. RMI and Whitley Bay were relegated and replaced by Blyth Spartans and Bamber Bridge. The final Horwich RMI team line-up was: Blenkinship; Fagan, Phoenix; Senior, Marsden, Hart; Hatton, Griffin, Diamond, Orrell, Fahey. Subs: Leach, Pilling, Bibby.

At the end of the season Arthur's prediction came true and at the club's AGM the name change to Leigh RMI was confirmed by a vote of members, 40 voting for the name change with eleven against.

'Relegated Horwich RMI will be known as Leigh RMI next season when the club will begin life in the Unibond First Division,' reported the Bolton Evening News. RMI chairman Chris Healey welcomed the decision and said: 'I was surprised at the size of the majority for this change and I'm certain it will secure the future of the club financially by attracting more sponsorship and support from the local community. The club will now be able to concentrate its efforts spending money on building a better team.'

Mr Healey dismissed criticism from some supporters that the decision had been taken too soon after their controversial move from Grundy Hill to Hilton Park and stated the decision would be discussed with members of Horwich Town Council. He added: 'It was much better and fairer for our existing membership to make this decision now rather than waiting until later when there would have been an influx of new members living in the Leigh area.'

So by May 1995 there had been a change of name and Grundy Hill was no more, the victim of the eager bulldozers. Former assistant manager Alan Kirkman became a member of the management committee and helped to co-ordinate the coaching staff. Former RMI player Steve Waywell, a former Curzon Ashton and Ashton United manager came in as joint manager and the coaching staff also included Ray Silous and Barry Diamond.

More chapters in the history of a club with a rich and proud tradition were waiting to be written but for Horwich RMI it was all over.

An aerial view of Grundy Hill showing the cricket field to the right

It could be a scene from an LS Lowry painting . . . A match in progress at
Grundy Hill in the 1950s

Grundy Hill in the 1970s

The Covered Enclosure at Grundy Hill in the early 1990s

The Main Grandstand at Grundy Hill in the early 1990s

Demolition of the Main Grandstand at Grundy Hill in 1995

Demolition of Grundy Hill in progress, 1995

Sport continues at Horwich RMI—a cricket match in progress on a fine evening in June 2010. The houses behind the cricket field are built on the site of the old Grundy Hill football ground

Many of the landmarks are familiar even if the much-loved football ground is gone. Some former players and supporters of the RMI football club still enjoy watching cricket at the adjoining Recreation Ground where they can reminisce about the 'glory days'.

Many great players had graced the field at Grundy Hill down the years.

The three pictured here all went on to have successful careers in the Football League.

Frank Wignall
Tony Caldwell
Tony Ellis

Wignall (right) is probably the only former RMI player to become an international manager—he was in charge of the Qatar national team in 1975/6

HORWICH RMI—STATISTICAL SECTION

Season-by-Season Results and Scorers

Summary Statistics

1907-08   Lancashire Alliance

Date		H/A	Comp	Opponents	Res	F	A	Goalscorers
Sep	7	a	Friendly	Dublin GWR	W	3	2	Unknown 3
	14	h	League	Ashton Town Reserves	L	0	2	
	28	h	League	Chorley Reserves	D	1	1	Humphries
Oct	12	h	League	Leyland	D	2	2	Unknown 2
	26	h	League	Atherton Reserves	W	5	3	Unknown 3
Nov	2	a	League	Chorley Reserves	L	1	6	Unknown
	9	h	League	Southport Central Reserves	D	2	2	Unknown 2
	16	a	League	Walkden Central	L	0	3	
	23	a	League	Tyldesley Albion	L	1	3	Unknown
Dec	7	a	League	Little Hulton United	L	2	3	Unknown 2
	14	a	League	Fleetwood Amateurs	L	2	5	Townend, Riding
	21	a	League	Ashton Town Reserves	L	1	3	Unknown
	28	h	League	Adlington	W	1	0	Unknown
Jan	4	h	League	Skelmersdale United	W	4	0	Jones 2, Edwards, Opponent
	18	h	League	Little Hulton United	W	4	3	E Jones 3, Edwards
	25	h	League	St Helens Recs Reserves	W	2	0	Unknown 2
Feb	1	a	League	Kirkham	L	1	3	Unknown
	22	a	League	Southport Central Reserves	W	3	0	Sharrocks 2, Smith
	29	h	League	Fleetwood Amateurs	L	2	9	E Jones 2
Mar	14	a	League	Adlington	L	1	2	Unknown
	21	h	League	Kirkham	W	3	0	Peters 2, Boulton
	28	a	League	St Helens Recs Reserves	L	1	4	Unknown
Apr	4	a	League	Leyland	L	0	2	
	11	a	League	Skelmersdale United	L	0	5	
	18	h	League	Hindley Central	L	1	2	Unknown
	25	h	League	Tyldesley Albion	L	2	4	Jones, Edwards
						45	69	

1908-09   West Lancashire League

Date		H/A	Comp	Opponents	Res	F	A	Goalscorers
Sep	5	h	League	Leyland	L	1	2	Latham
	12	a	LJC 1	Chequerbent	L	1	3	Unknown
	19	h	League	Southport Central Reserves	D	2	2	Peters, Smith
	26	a	League	Standish North End	W	1	0	Unknown
Oct	3	h	League	Blackpool Athletic	W	7	0	Unknown 7
	17	h	League	Banks St Stephens	W	5	2	Mann 2, Edwards, Sinclair, Unknown
	24	a	League	Chorley Reserves	L	1	2	Latham
	31	h	League	Fleetwood	W	3	1	Edwards 2, Smith
Nov	7	a	League	Kirkham	L	0	2	
	14	h	League	Lostock Hall Loco	L	0	3	
	21	a	League	Fleetwood	D	1	1	Mann
Dec	5	a	League	Southport Central Reserves	D	3	3	Mann 2, Smith
	12	h	League	Bamber Bridge Corinthians	W	2	0	Mann, Rigby
	19	a	League	Blackpool Athletic	L	1	2	Walsert
	26	h	League	Chorley Reserves	D	0	0	
Jan	2	a	League	Leyland	L	1	2	Mann
	9	h	League	Standish North End	D	0	0	
	16	a	LC 1	Standish North End	L	1	2	Edwards
Feb	6	a	League	Coppull Central	L	1	4	Mann
	13	h	League	Southport Park Villa	W	4	1	Mann 2, Edwards, Latham
	20	h	League	Coppull Central	W	3	1	Latham, Greeley, Beech
Mar	13	h	League	Longridge	W	6	0	Mann 3, Hulse, Latham, Edwards
	20	a	League	Longridge	W	2	1	Mann, Edwards
	27	h	League	Kirkham	W	2	1	Mann 2
Apr	24	a	League	Banks St Stephens	D	0	0	
						48	35	

1909-10 West Lancashire League

Date		H/A	Comp	Opponents	Res	F	A	Goalscorers	Notes
Sep	4	h	LJS 1	Worsley Road IM	W	6	1	Mann 2, Beech 2, Gollins 2	
	11	h	League	Southport Central	L	1	3	Beech	
	18	a	League	Banks St Stephens	L	2	5	Unknown 2	
	25	a	LJS 2	Eagley Institute	D	1	1	Mann	
Oct	2	h	LJS 2	Eagley Institute	D	2	2	Settle 2	AET; Won on toss
	9	a	LJS 3	Little Lever	L	1	2	Unknown	
	16	h	League	Banks St Stephens	D	2	2	Unknown 2	Replayed
	23	a	League	Blackpool Athletic	D	1	1	Latham	
	30	h	League	Morecambe	W	5	0	Gollins 2, Latham 2, Grelley (pen)	
Nov	13	h	League	Leyland	L	1	3	Latham	
	20	a	League	Southport Central	W	1	0	Grelley	
Dec	4	a	League	Kirkham	L	0	1		
	18	a	League	Leyland	D	0	0		
Jan	15	a	LC 1	Lytham Athletic	D	1	1	Gollins	
	22	a	LC 1	Lytham Athletic	W	2	0	Vause, Sharrocks	
Feb	5	a	League	Lytham Athletic	L	3	4	Gollins, Vause (pen), Cummings	
	12	a	LC 2	Morecambe	L	2	4	Gollins, Beech	
	19	a	League	Longridge	W	2	0	Vause, Grundy	
	26	a	League	Morecambe	L	3	4	Unknown 3	
Mar	5	h	League	Fleetwood	L	1	4	Benson	
	12	a	League	Southport Park Villa	L	0	1		
	19	h	League	Lostock Hall Loco	W	2	1	Calderbank, Collins	
	25	h	League	Banks St Stephens	W	6	1	Grelley 3, Calderbank, Grundy, Collins	
	28	a	League	Fleetwood	L	1	2	Calderbank	
Apr	2	h	League	Kirkham	D	0	0		
	9	h	League	Lytham Athletic	W	5	1	Mann 3, Calderbank, Beech	
	11	a	League	Lostock Hall Loco	D	0	0		
	16	h	League	Southport Park Villa	W	2	1	Mann, Cummings	
	16	a	League	Longridge	L	0	6		
	18	a	League	Bamber Bridge Corinthians	L	0	3		
	23	h	League	Blackpool Athletic	W	4	1	Mann 3, Grelley	
	30	h	League	Bamber Bridge Corinthians	Cxl				
					57	55			

1910-11   West Lancashire League

Date		H/A	Comp	Opponents	Res	F	A	Goalscorers
Sep	10	a	League	Longbridge	L	1	4	Mann
	17	h	League	Lytham	D	2	2	Beech, Mann
	24	a	League	Lostock Hall Locos	L	2	4	Latham 2 (1pen)
Oct	1	h	League	Adlington	W	4	1	Cummings 2, Mann 2
	8	a	League	Fleetwood Reserves	D	2	2	Cummings 2
	15	h	League	Longridge	W	4	1	Cummings 2, Beech, Mann
	22	a	League	Southport Park Villa	W	4	2	Mann 2, Beech, Vause
	29	h	League	Southport Central	D	2	2	Vause, Opponent
Nov	12	h	League	Morecambe	W	5	2	Cummings 4, Mann
	19	a	League	Coppull Central	W	5	0	Cummings 3, Mann, Beech
Dec	3	a	League	Kirkham	L	1	2	Unknown
	10	a	League	Banks St Stephens	L	0	1	
	17	h	League	Fleetwood Reserves	W	2	1	Cummings, Latham
	24	a	League	Adlington	W	3	2	Mann 2, Latham
Jan	7	h	League	Kirkham	W	5	0	Baker 3, Latham (pen), Cummings
	14	h	LC 1	Longridge	W	2	0	Cummings 2
	28	a	League	Lancaster Town Reserves	W	1	0	Cummings
Feb	4	h	LC 2	Fleetwood Reserves	W	2	1	Latham, Beech
	11	h	League	Lostock Hall Locos	W	4	0	Smith, Latham, Cummings, Mann
	18	a	League	Leyland	D	1	1	Cummings
Mar	4	1	LC SF	Southport Park Villa	W	3	0	Beech 2, Baker
	11	h	League	Banks St Stephens	W	5	2	Latham 4, Cummings
	18	h	League	Coppull Central	W	5	2	Cummings 2, Mann, Baker, Beech
	25	h	League	Southport Park Villa	W	2	0	Mann (pen), Baker
Apr	1	a	League	Lytham	W	3	0	Cummings 3
	8	2	LC Final	Adlington	D	1	1	Cummings
	15	h	League	Leyland	W	2	0	Cummings, Baker
	22	2	LC Final	Adlington	L	0	2	
	24	h	Friendly	Bolton Wanderers Reserves	W	5	3	Cummings 3, Latham, Mann
	29	h	League	Rest of League	Cxl			
		1	at Fleetwood			78	38	
		2	at Chorley					

1911-12 West Lancashire League

Date		H/A	Comp	Opponents	Res	F	A	Goalscorers
Sep	2	a	LJS 1	Westhoughton PC Guild	L	2	3	Walton, Cummings
	9	h	League	Longridge	D	0	0	
	16	a	League	Chorley Reserves	W	3	1	Walton 2, Settle
	23	h	League	Lytham Athletic	W	3	0	Walton, Settle, Unknown
Oct	7	a	League	Hamilton Central	D	0	0	
	14	h	League	Morecambe	D	2	2	Settle (pen), Walton
	21	a	League	Higher Walton Albion	L	2	4	Grattedge, Settle
	28	h	League	Hindley Central	L	0	1	
Nov	4	a	League	Morecambe	D	1	1	Walton
	11	h	League	Hamilton Central	W	6	0	Walton 2, Settle 2, Lane, Mann
	18	a	League	Lytham Athletic	W	3	1	Mann 2, Settle
	25	h	League	Fleetwood Reserves	W	4	1	Walton, Lane, Grelley, Settle
Dec	9	a	League	Coppull Central	L	0	4	
	16	a	League	Longridge	L	0	6	
	23	h	League	Coppull Central	W	5	1	Mann 4, Beech
	30	h	League	Adlington	W	3	2	Cummings 2, Beech
Jan	1	a	League	Fleetwood Reserves	L	0	3	
	6	a	LC 1	Morecambe	L	1	5	Unknown
	27	a	League	Kirkham	W	3	1	Unknown 3
Feb	3	a	League	Adlington	L	1	3	Mann
	24	h	League	Brinscall Rovers	W	2	0	Lane, Walton
Mar	2	a	League	Leyland	L	1	3	Mann
	9	h	League	Walton-le-Dale	W	2	1	Walton, Mann
	16	a	League	Brinscall Rovers	W	3	2	Caunce, Lane, Walton
Apr	6	h	League	Chorley Reserves	W	5	1	Mann, Unknown 4
	13	h	League	Higher Walton Albion	W	2	0	Walton, Wilkinson
	27	h	League	Leyland	D	1	1	Unknown
						55	47	

1912-13 West Lancashire League

Date		H/A	Comp	Opponents	Res	F	A	Goalscorers	Notes
Sep	14	h	League	Walton-le-Dale	W	6	1	Walton 2, Wilkinson, Sackfield, Lane, Unknown	
	28	h	League	Hamilton Central	D	1	1	Latham	
Oct	5	a	League	Longridge	L	0	2		
	12	h	League	Kirkham & Wesham	W	2	0	Johnson, Toole (pen)	
	26	h	League	Lytham	Ab	0	0		
Nov	2	a	League	Fleetwood Reserves	D	2	2	Latham, Birchall	
	9	h	League	Southport Central	W	4	1	Walton 2, Wilkinson, Birchall	
	16	a	League	Freckleton	W	3	0	Latham 2, Wilkinson	
	23	h	League	Higher Walton Albion	W	2	0	Walton, Birchall	
	30	a	League	Leyland	L	1	4	Birchall	
Dec	14	a	League	Adlington	L	2	3	Lane, Birchall	
	21	h	League	Adlington	W	5	1	Birchall 3, Unknown 2	
	28	h	League	Coppull Central	W	1	0	Harrison (pen)	
Jan	4	a	League	Walton-le-Dale	W	8	2	Unknown 8	
	18	h	League	Fleetwood Reserves	W	1	0	Unknown	
	25	a	League	Southport Central	L	0	2		
Feb	1	a	League	Chorley St Peter's	W	4	2	Walton 2, Latham, Smith	
	8	a	LC 1	Fleetwood Reserves	W	2	0	Birchall, Latham	
	15	a	League	Hamilton Central	L	2	5	Latham, Wilkinson	
	22	h	League	Freckleton	W	1	0	Sackfield	
Mar	1	h	LC SF	Leyland	L	2	5	Jones, Birchall	
	8	a	League	Kirkham & Wesham	L	0	1		
	15	a	League	Lytham	D	2	2	Latham (pen), Birchall	
	22	h	League	Chorley St Peter's	Ab	2	0	Unknown 2	Ab 30'
Apr	5	h	League	Longridge	W	1	0	Unknown	
	12	h	League	Leyland	W	3	1	Latham, Unknown 2	
						57	35		

1913-14 West Lancashire League

Date		H/A	Comp	Opponents	Res	F	A	Goalscorers
Sep	13	h	League	Bamber Bridge	W	4	0	Settle 3, Davies
	20	a	League	Southport Central	W	1	0	Settle
	27	h	League	Kirkham & Wesham	W	3	1	Walton 2, Garside
Oct	4	a	League	Coppull Central	W	2	1	Porter, Watson
	11	h	League	Hamilton Central	W	4	0	Porter 3, Settle
	18	a	League	Lytham	W	2	1	Fallon 2
	25	h	League	Leyland	W	1	0	Porter
Nov	1	h	League	Freckleton	W	3	2	Burgess, Taylor, Proctor
	8	h	League	Barrow Reserves	W	2	0	Porter, Fallon
	15	a	League	Longbridge	L	2	5	Burgess, Unknown
	22	h	League	Fleetwood Reserves	W	4	1	Porter, Unknown 3
	29	a	League	Hamilton Central	W	3	0	Taylor 2, Burgess
Dec	6	h	League	Adlington	W	3	1	Taylor 3
	13	a	League	Kirkham & Wesham	W	6	1	Taylor 4, Burgess 2
	20	h	League	Blackburn St Philips	W	3	1	Porter, Taylor, Parker
	26	a	League	Blackburn St Philips	D	1	1	Ashcroft
Jan	3	a	LC 1	Croston	W	3	2	Unknown 3 (1pen)
	17	a	League	Adlington	D	2	2	Parker, Ashcroft
	24	a	League	Croston	W	3	1	Taylor, Unknown 2
	31	a	LC 2	Fleetwood Reserves	D	3	3	Southworth, Devenport, Garside
Feb	7	h	LC 2	Fleetwood Reserves	W	3	1	Garside, Devenport, Taylor
	14	a	League	Fleetwood Reserves	W	2	0	Unknown 2
	21	1	LC SF	Longridge	W	4	0	Porter 3, Ashcroft
	28	a	League	Bamber Bridge	W	2	1	Unknown 2
Mar	7	h	League	Walton-le-Dale	W	6	1	Southworth 4, Porter, Parker
	14	h	League	Lytham	W	9	0	Southworth 4, Porter 3, Ashcroft, Parker
	28	1	LC Final	Barrow Reserves	L	2	3	Southworth, Garside
Apr	4	h	League	Croston	W	4	2	Stamford (pen), Parker, Garside, Taylor
	11	a	League	Freckleton	L	1	4	Taylor
	17	a	League	Walton-le-Dale	W	4	0	Unknown 4
	17	h	League	Longridge	W	6	4	Unknown 6
	18	h	League	Southport Central	W	7	0	Porter, Taylor, Unknown 5
	25	a	League	Barrow Reserves	L	0	1	
May	7	a	League	Leyland	W	3	2	Unknown 3
		1	at Preston North End			108	42	

1914-15 West Lancashire League

Date		H/A	Comp	Opponents	Res	F	A	Goalscorers
Sep	12	h	League	Southport Central	W	5	1	Unknown 5
	19	h	League	Coppull Central	W	5	0	Taylor, Unknown 4
	26	a	FA Cup PR	Haslingden	L	1	3	Unknown
Oct	3	a	League	Adlington	L	0	1	
	10	h	League	Leyland	L	1	2	Ashcroft
	24	a	League	Blackburn St Philips	W	3	1	Settle 2, Stamford (pen)
Nov	7	h	League	Standish	W	4	1	Settle, Parker, Ashcroft, Grelley
	14	a	League	Southport Central	W	2	1	Settle, Parker
	21	h	League	Adlington	D	1	1	Garside
	28	a	League	Hamilton Central	D	1	1	Stamford
Dec	5	h	League	Freckleton	W	6	1	Settle 5, Parker
	12	a	League	Fleetwood Reserves	W	4	1	Parker 2, Ashcroft, Unknown
	19	a	League	Standish	L	1	4	Unknown
	26	h	League	Croston	W	8	0	Garside 3, Parker 3, Settle, Baker
Jan	2	a	League	Coppull Central	L	0	1	
	9	a	League	Lancaster Town Reserves	W	2	0	Garside, Parker
	16	a	League	Tarleton	D	2	2	Unknown 2
	23	a	LC 1	Adlington	W	2	1	Parker, Ashcroft
	30	h	League	Tarleton	W	4	1	Ashcroft 2, Parker, Garside
Feb	6	a	League	Freckleton	W	4	0	Garside, Parker, Settle, Unknown
	13	h	LC 2	Southport Central	L	1	2	Baker
	27	a	League	Croston	L	1	2	Unknown
Mar	6	h	League	Lancaster Town Reserves	W	6	0	Baker 3, Burgess, Ashcroft, Benson
	20	a	Davis Cup	Great Harwood	L	2	3	Unknown 2
	27	h	Davis Cup	Great Harwood	L	1	2	Greeley
Apr	2	h	Davis Cup	Padiham	W	5	3	Unknown 5
	3	a	Davis Cup	Padiham	L	1	2	Baker
	10	a	League	Leyland	L	0	3	
	17	h	Davis Cup	Lancaster Town Reserves	W	6	3	Unknown 6
May	1	a	Davis Cup	Lancaster Town Reserves	L	0	2	
						79	45	

1917-18   Lancashire Combination (Emergency League)

Date		H/A	Comp	Opponents	Res	F	A	Goalscorers
Sep	15	h	League	Brynn	L	1	3	Unknown
	22	h	League	Brynn	D	0	0	
	29	h	League	South Liverpool	L	0	2	
Oct	6	h	League	South Liverpool	L	0	4	
	27	h	League	Tranmere Rovers Reserves	L	1	4	J Ashcroft
Nov	10	h	League	Tranmere Rovers Reserves	L	0	2	
	17	h	League	St Helens Alex	W	4	1	Garside 2, Taylor, Stamford
	24	h	Friendly	Bolton Wanderers Reserves	W	2	0	Ashcroft, Johnson
Dec	1	h	League	St Helens Alex	D	2	2	Unknown 2
	15	h	Friendly	Bolton Wanderers Reserves	W	2	0	Garside, Unknown
Jan	12	h	League	South Liverpool	Ab	1	2	Unknown
	19	h	League	South Liverpool	W	9	0	Ashcroft 4, Taylor 3, Burgess, Johnson
	26	h	League	Tranmere Rovers Reserves	D	0	0	
						22	20	

1918-19   Lancashire Combination (Emergency League)

Date		H/A	Comp	Opponents	Res	F	A	Goalscorers
Sep	14	h	League	Brynn	D	3	3	Tomlinson 2, Appleton
	21	a	League	South Liverpool	L	1	5	Tomlinson
	28	h	League	South Liverpool	D	2	2	Taylor, Tomlinson
Oct	5	a	League	Brynn	L	0	1	
	12	h	League	Plank Lane	L	1	2	Taylor (pen)
	19	h	League	Liverpool Reserves	W	2	1	Smith 2
	26	a	League	Liverpool Reserves	L	1	4	Smith2
Nov	2	a	LJC 1	Ashton Hospital	L	2	4	Smith, Garside
	9	h	League	Blackpool RAMC	L	3	5	Stamford (pen), Smith, Unknown
	23	a	League	Ashton Hospital	W	5	1	Unknown 5
	30	a	League	Rylands Recs	D	3	3	Unknown 3
Dec	7	a	League	Garswood Hall	L	1	4	Tomlinson
	21	a	League	Runcorn	L	0	3	
	28	h	League	Tranmere Rovers Reserves	L	2	3	Smith, Ashurst
Jan	1	a	League	Chorley	D	1	1	Smith
	4	a	League	Tranmere Rovers Reserves	L	0	4	
	11	a	League	Everton Reserves	L	2	3	Burgess, Ashurst
	18	h	League	Everton Reserves	W	7	1	Ashurst 3, Smith 2, Taylor (pen), Garside
	25	h	League	Prescot	L	1	2	Smith
Feb	1	a	League	Ashton Camp	L	0	1	
	8	h	League	Ashton Hospital	L	0	2	
	15	a	League	Prescot	L	0	4	
	22	a	League	Plank Lane	L	1	2	Green
Mar	1	h	League	Garswood Hall	W	4	0	Smith 2, Ashurst, Tomlinson
	8	h	League	Lancaster United	D	1	1	Smith
	15	a	League	Lancaster United	L	2	3	Hird 2
	22	h	League	Chorley	W	5	1	Smith 3, Tomlinson, Leach
Apr	5	h	Friendly	Bury Reserves	W	5	0	Unknown 5
	12	a	Friendly	Bury Reserves	D	3	3	Unknown 3
	19	h	League	Runcorn	W	3	2	Wood, Taylor (pen), Brockbank
						61	71	

1919-20   Lancashire Combination

Date		H/A	Comp	Opponents	Res	F	A	Goalscorers
Aug	30	a	League	Eccles United	L	1	2	Ashcroft
Sep	6	h	League	Dick, Kerr's	W	3	2	Ashurst, Bleakley, Leach
	13	h	League	Chorley	L	1	4	Burgess
	20	a	League	South Liverpool	W	3	0	McCarthy, Hesmondhalgh, Kempster
Oct	4	a	League	Accrington Stanley	L	0	3	
	11	a	FA Cup 1Q	Nelson	W	1	0	Hesmondhalgh
	18	h	LJC 1	Plank Lane	L	2	3	Hesmondhalgh, McCarthy
	25	a	FA Cup 2Q	Hamilton Central	W	1	0	Hesmondhalgh
Nov	1	h	League	Rochdale Reserves	W	7	2	Barry 2, Hesmondhalgh, Cooper, Ashcroft, Jones, Burgess
	8	a	FA Cup 3Q	Chorley	D	1	1	Jones (pen)
	12	h	FA Cup 3Q	Chorley	W	4	0	Cooper, Ashcroft, Barry, Hesmondhalgh
	15	a	League	Dick, Kerr's	L	1	5	Hesmondhalgh
	22	a	FA Cup 4Q	Stalybridge Celtic	L	2	4	Cooper, Hesmondhalgh
	29	h	League	Lancaster Town	W	3	1	Jones, Burgess, McCarthy
Dec	6	h	League	Eccles United	L	2	3	Barry, Hesmondhalgh
	13	a	League	Rochdale Reserves	W	1	0	Unknown
	27	a	League	Barrow	W	1	0	Woodhouse
Jan	1	a	League	Plank Lane	L	2	3	Unknown 2
	3	h	League	Prescot	W	3	1	Cooper, Jones, Woodhouse
	10	a	League	Chorley	L	0	2	
	17	a	League	Tranmere Rovers Reserves	L	3	7	Unknown 3
	24	a	League	Prescot	W	2	1	Jones, Unknown
	31	h	League	Tranmere Rovers Reserves	L	1	2	Jones
Feb	7	h	League	Glossop	W	3	0	Woodhouse, Barry, Jones
	14	h	League	Stalybridge Celtic	W	5	0	Woodhouse, Barton, Ashcroft, Barry, Burgess
	21	a	League	Glossop	L	2	3	Unknown 2
	28	a	League	Hurst	L	0	1	
Mar	6	h	League	Great Harwood	L	0	4	
	13	a	League	Stalybridge Celtic	L	2	3	Wilcox, Woodhouse
	20	h	League	Hurst	W	2	1	Barry, Winsper
	27	h	League	Accrington Stanley	W	3	2	Winsper 2, Barry
Apr	2	h	League	Plank Lane	W	3	1	Unknown 3
	3	a	League	Great Harwood	W	2	0	Brindle, Winsper
	7	a	League	Lancaster Town	W	1	0	Barry
	10	h	League	Fleetwood	L	1	3	Winsper
	14	h	League	South Liverpool	W	4	1	Unknown 4
	17	h	League	Rossendale United	W	1	0	Lilley (pen)
	24	a	League	Rossendale United	W	3	0	Unknown 3
	30	h	League	Barrow	W	2	1	Unknown 2
May	1	a	League	Fleetwood	W	4	1	Gray 2, Winsper, Unknown
						83	67	

1920-21 Lancashire Combination

Date		H/A	Comp	Opponents	Res	F	A	Goalscorers
Aug	28	h	League	Atherton	L	1	2	Unknown
Sep	4	a	League	Lancaster Town	D	0	0	
	11	a	League	Dick, Kerr's	L	1	2	Ashcroft
	18	h	League	Leyland	L	3	4	Lomax, Waller, Tomlinson
	25	a	League	Leyland	D	1	1	Tomlinson
Oct	2	h	League	Hurst	W	2	1	Moss, Winsper
	9	a	FA Cup 1Q	Nelson	L	0	3	
	16	h	LJC 1	Wigan United	W	5	0	Moss, Hutchinson, Benson, Winsper, Pointon
	23	h	League	Accrington Stanley	W	2	1	Winsper, Waller
	30	a	League	Chorley	D	0	0	
Nov	6	h	League	Chorley	L	0	1	
	13	h	LJC 2	South Liverpool	L	2	3	Waller 2
	20	h	League	South Liverpool	L	0	1	
	27	a	League	Accrington Stanley	L	0	3	
Dec	4	h	League	Lancaster Town	L	0	8	
	11	a	League	Great Harwood	D	2	2	Barry, Morris
	18	h	League	Rossendale United	L	1	3	Moss
	25	h	League	Great Harwood	L	1	4	Unknown
	26	a	League	Eccles United	L	0	6	
Jan	8	a	League	Hurst	D	1	1	Smith
	15	a	League	South Liverpool	L	1	5	Carr
	22	a	League	Rossendale United	L	2	9	Barry, Tomlinson
	29	h	League	Dick, Kerr's	D	3	3	Benson, Cameron, Holmes
Feb	5	a	League	Darwen	L	0	4	
	12	h	League	Bacup Borough	W	4	0	Winsper 2, Smith, Taylor
	19	a	League	Bacup Borough	L	0	5	
	26	a	League	Atherton	D	1	1	Burgess
Mar	5	h	League	Darwen	D	1	1	Walkden
	12	h	League	Eccles United	L	0	1	
	25	h	League	Wigan Borough	L	1	4	Unknown
	26	a	League	Fleetwood	L	1	5	Boardman
	28	a	League	Wigan Borough	L	0	2	
Apr	2	h	League	Barrow	D	1	1	Smith
	6	h	League	Fleetwood	W	3	1	Unknown 3
	9	a	League	Barrow	L	0	3	
	16	h	League	Morecambe	L	1	3	Yates
	23	a	League	Morecambe	L	0	3	
						41	97	

1921-22 Lancashire Combination

Date		H/A	Comp	Opponents	Res	F	A	Goalscorers
Aug	27	a	League	Chorley	L	1	2	Walkden
Sep	3	h	League	Leyland	D	0	0	
	10	a	League	Great Harwood	D	1	1	Unknown
	17	h	League	Chorley	D	1	1	Lovett
	24	a	FA Cup PR	Morecambe	D	0	0	
	27	h	FA Cup PR	Morecambe	W	2	1	Unknown 2
Oct	1	h	League	Fleetwood	L	1	2	Lovett
	8	h	FA Cup 1Q	Lancaster Town	L	1	5	Phythian
	15	h	LJC 1	Atherton	L	1	3	Leach
	22	h	League	Bacup Borough	D	1	1	Gradwell (pen)
	29	a	League	Skelmersdale United	L	0	1	
Nov	5	h	League	Morecambe	W	1	0	Phythian
	19	a	League	Rossendale United	L	0	5	
	26	h	League	Rossendale United	L	2	5	Burgess, Embrey
Dec	3	h	League	Skelmersdale United	W	3	2	Burns 3
	17	h	League	Darwen	W	2	1	Burns, Crompton
	24	a	League	Bacup Borough	L	2	3	Gradwell, Phythian
	26	h	League	Great Harwood	W	2	0	Unknown 2
	31	h	League	Hurst	W	2	0	Bleakley 2
Jan	2	a	League	Morecambe	L	0	1	
	7	h	League	Lancaster Town	L	0	3	
	14	a	League	Lancaster Town	L	0	4	
	21	a	League	Leyland	L	2	3	Phythian, Embrey (pen)
	28	h	League	Dick, Kerr's	W	1	0	Burns
Feb	4	a	League	Dick, Kerr's	L	3	4	Thompson 2, Oxley
	11	a	League	Darwen	L	0	4	
	18	a	League	Eccles United	L	0	2	
	25	h	League	Eccles United	W	3	0	Thompson, Burns, H Lovett
Mar	11	a	League	Hurst	W	2	1	Boardman, Own goal
	18	h	League	Stockport County Reserves	W	5	3	Thompson 2, Ashcroft, Boardman, Walkden
	25	a	League	Stockport County Reserves	L	0	2	
Apr	1	a	League	Atherton	W	1	0	W Lovett (pen)
	8	a	League	New Brighton	D	1	1	Oxley
	14	h	League	Rochdale Reserves	W	3	1	Unknown 3
	18	a	League	Rochdale Reserves	W	2	1	Unknown 2
	19	h	League	Atherton	L	2	3	Ashcroft (pen), Unknown
	22	a	League	Fleetwood	D	1	1	Unknown
	29	h	League	New Brighton	L	0	1	
						49	68	

1922-23 Lancashire Combination

Date		H/A	Comp	Opponents	Res	F	A	Goalscorers	Notes
Aug	26	h	League	Dick, Kerr's	D	0	0		
Sep	2	a	League	Morecambe	L	1	5	Hesmondhalgh	
	9	a	League	Hurst	D	2	2	Walkden, French	
	12	a	LCC 1	Leyland	D	2	2	Unknown 2	
	16	h	League	Skelmersdale United	W	3	2	Walkden (pen), Hesmondhalgh, Sowerbutts	
	20	h	LCC1	Leyland	W	2	1	Sowerbutts 2	
	23	a	FAC PR	Leyland Motors	L	1	2	Sowerbutts	Awarded on appeal
	30	h	League	Leyland	W	2	1	Lovett, Walkden (pen)	
Oct	7	h	FAC 1Q	Chorley	D	1	1	Sowerbutts	
	11	a	FAC 1Q	Chorley	L	0	1		
	14	a	LJC 1	Breightmet United	L	1	2	Hesmondhalgh	
	18	a	LCC 2	New Brighton	L	0	1		
	21	h	League	Darwen	D	2	2	Clayton, Thompson	
	28	a	League	New Brighton	L	2	3	Powell, Jackson	
Nov	4	a	League	Skelmersdale United	L	1	2	French	
	11	h	League	Rossendale United	D	1	1	Lovett	
Dec	9	a	League	Rossendale United	L	2	5	Darlingon, Ryder	
	16	h	League	Eccles United	Ab	1	2	Lovett	Ab 60'
	25	a	League	Chorley	L	1	4	Darlington	
	26	a	League	Leyland	D	3	3	Butler, Mather, Ryder	
	30	h	League	Rochdale Reserves	W	4	0	Darlington 2, Walkden, French	
Jan	1	a	League	Atherton	W	1	0	Unknown	
	6	a	League	Darwen	L	2	4	Williams, French	
	13	h	League	Great Harwood	L	1	2	Yates	
	27	h	League	Hurst	L	0	3		
Feb	3	h	League	Lancaster Town	L	1	2	Hesmondhalgh	
	10	a	League	Eccles United	L	2	5	Hesmondhalgh, Opponent	
	17	h	League	Morecambe	W	3	1	Hesmondhalgh, Mather, Clancy	
	24	a	League	Lancaster Town	L	0	4		
Mar	3	h	League	Fleetwood	L	1	6	Hesmondhalgh	
	24	a	League	Bacup Borough	L	0	1		
	30	h	League	Atherton	W	2	1	Unknown 2	
	31	h	League	Eccles United	D	1	1	Darlington	
Apr	2	a	League	Fleetwood	L	1	3	Unknown	
	7	a	League	Great Harwood	D	2	2	Hesmondhalgh, Sullivan	
	18	h	League	New Brighton	D	1	1	Hesmondhalgh	
	21	a	League	Rochdale Reserves	L	1	2	Unknown	
	23	a	League	Dick, Kerr's	L	2	4	Sullivan 2	
	25	a	League	New Cross	L	0	1		
	28	h	League	New Cross	D	1	1	Kennedy	
May	2	h	League	Chorley	D	1	1	Darlington	
	5	h	League	Bacup Borough	W	7	1	Sullivan 4, Blinkhorn, Darlington, Walkden	
						62	88		

1923-24 Lancashire Combination

Date		H/A	Comp	Opponents	Res	F	A	Goalscorers
Aug	25	h	League	Bacup Borough	W	3	0	Sullivan 2, Moon
	29	h	League	Lancaster Town	D	2	2	Downs, Moon
Sep	1	a	League	Southport Reserves	L	0	1	
	5	a	League	Atherton	L	2	5	Taylor, Sullivan
	8	a	League	Fleetwood	L	1	2	Unsworth
	15	h	League	Fleetwood	L	0	1	
	22	a	FA Cup PR	Great Harwood	W	2	1	Sullivan, Unknown
	29	a	LCC 1	Wigan Borough Reserves	W	4	1	Hird 2, Sullivan, Moon
Oct	6	a	FA Cup 1Q	Atherton	L	1	2	Sullivan
	13	a	LJC 1	Atherton	D	0	0	
	20	a	League	Eccles United	L	0	3	
	27	h	League	Rochdale Reserves	L	2	3	Hird, Sullivan
	31	h	LJC 1	Atherton	W	3	0	Hird 2(1pen), Sullivan
Nov	3	h	League	Southport Reserves	L	0	2	
	10	h	LJC 2	Bacup Borough	D	2	2	Hird 2
	17	a	League	Great Harwood	D	1	1	Unknown
	24	h	League	Skelmersdale United	W	11	0	Sullivan 5, Hird 3, Croft 2, Walkden
	27	a	LJC 2	Bacup Borough	W	1	0	Sullivan
Dec	8	a	LJC 3	Great Harwood	L	2	3	Hird 2
	15	a	League	Chorley	W	3	2	Hird 3 (1pen)
	22	h	League	Chorley	W	2	1	Hird, Croft
	25	a	League	Dick, Kerr's	L	1	1	Unknown
	26	a	League	Morecambe	D	2	0	Unknown 2
	29	a	League	Wigan Borough Reserves	L	0	2	
Jan	1	h	League	Rossendale United	W	3	0	Unknown 3
	2	h	LCC 2	Southport Reserves	L	2	3	Unknown 2
	5	h	League	Accrington Stanley Reserves	W	2	1	Sullivan, Hird
	12	a	League	Leyland	W	1	2	Unknown
	19	a	League	Accrington Stanley Reserves	L	3	4	Hird 2 (1pen), Sullivan
	26	h	League	Dick, Kerr's	L	5	1	Hird 3, Sullivan 2
Feb	2	a	League	Darwen	W	0	3	
	9	h	League	Wigan Borough Reserves	L	1	0	Hird (pen)
	16	a	League	Rossendale United	W	1	0	Unknown
	23	h	League	Manchester North End	W	3	1	Hird (pen)
Mar	1	a	League	Lancaster Town	L	1	2	Hart
	8	h	League	Darwen	W	2	1	Croft, Hird
	15	a	League	Rochdale Reserves	W	4	2	Sullivan 2, Perks, Hird
	22	h	League	Eccles United	W	1	0	Walkden
	29	h	League	Leyland	W	3	0	Sullivan 2, Croft
Apr	5	a	League	Manchester North End	W	3	0	Sullivan 2, Lovett
	10	a	League	Skelmersdale United	W	2	0	Unknown 2
	14	h	League	Morecambe	W	1	0	Sullivan
	18	h	League	Nelson Reserves	W	1	0	Sullivan
	19	a	League	Nelson Reserves	D	2	2	Unknown 2
	21	a	League	Bacup Borough	L	1	2	Unknown
	26	h	League	Great Harwood	W	2	0	Lovett, Hart
	30	h	League	Atherton	W	2	0	Sullivan, T Embrey
						89	61	

1924-25   Lancashire Combination

Date		H/A	Comp	Opponents	Res	F	A	Goalscorers
Sep	6	a	League	Chorley	W	3	1	Croft 2, Sullivan
	10	h	League	Atherton	L	0	4	
	13	a	League	Wigan Borough Reserves	W	2	1	Sullivan, S Embrey
	17	h	LCC 1	Southport Reserves	L	1	3	Unknown
	20	h	FA Cup PR	Portsmouth Rovers	W	4	2	Walkden (2pens), Sullivan, Ryan
	27	a	League	Accrington Stanley Reserves	L	0	1	
Oct	4	h	FA Cup 1Q	Darwen	L	2	4	Croft, Sullivan
	11	a	LJC 1	Black Lane (Bolton)	W	2	1	Yates, Sullivan
	18	h	League	Wigan Borough Reserves	W	5	0	Sullivan 3, Unknown 2
	25	h	League	Chorley	D	2	2	Sullivan 2
Nov	1	a	League	Southport Reserves	W	3	1	Yates, Croft, Sullivan
	8	h	LJC 2	Croston	D	2	2	Sullivan 2
	15	a	League	Great Harwood	L	2	3	Gradwell, Opponent
	22	a	LJC 2	Croston	W	3	0	Sullivan 2, Yates
	29	a	League	Morecambe	L	1	2	Sullivan
Dec	6	h	LJC 3	Morecambe	W	3	1	Walkden (pen), Yates, Sullivan
	13	h	League	Nelson Reserves	W	5	1	Yates 2, Sullivan 2, Croft
	20	h	League	Southport Reserves	W	1	0	Yates
	25	a	League	Eccles United	D	3	3	Yates 2, Walkden (pen)
	26	a	League	Lancaster Town	L	0	4	
Jan	1	h	League	Eccles United	D	2	2	Croft, Sullivan
	3	h	League	Accrington Stanley Reserves	W	5	3	Goodlad, Bruton, Walkden (pen), Ryan, Yates
	10	a	League	Dick, Kerr's	D	1	1	Sullivan
	17	h	League	Rossendale United	W	4	0	Sullivan 2, Croft, Blinkhorn
	24	h	LJC SF	Eccles United	W	2	1	S Embrey, Walkden (pen)
Feb	7	a	League	Bacup Borough	L	1	2	Croft
	21	1	LJC Final	Atherton	W	1	0	Walkden (pen)
	28	a	League	Nelson Reserves	W	6	1	Sullivan 4, Croft 2
Mar	3	h	League	Lancaster Town	D	0	0	
	7	h	League	Bacup Borough	D	1	1	Gradwell
	14	a	League	Darwen	D	1	1	T Embrey
	16	a	League	Rochdale Reserves	L	0	3	
	24	a	League	Rossendale United	L	1	3	T Embrey
	28	a	League	Leyland	W	5	3	Fairhurst 2, Walkden, Shaw, Croft
Apr	4	h	League	Rochdale Reserves	L	0	1	
	10	a	League	Fleetwood	L	0	3	
	11	h	League	Morecambe	L	0	3	
	13	h	League	Leyland	W	8	1	Fairhurst 5, Walkden, Croft, S Embrey
	18	h	League	Great Harwood	W	3	0	Sullivan 2, Croft
	22	h	League	Darwen	W	3	0	Yates 3
	24	h	League	Barnoldswick Town	W	3	0	Sullivan 3
	25	h	League	Dick, Kerr's	L	0	3	
	28	a	League	Barnoldswick Town	L	2	3	Unknown 2
	29	a	League	Atherton	L	0	2	
May	2	h	League	Fleetwood	D	1	1	Gradwell
		1	at Chorley FC			94	74	

1925-26 Lancashire Combination

Date		H/A	Comp	Opponents	Res	F	A	Goalscorers
Aug	29	a	League	Southport Reserves	L	0	5	
Sep	2	a	CC 1	Morecambe	L	0	5	
	5	h	League	Accrington Stanley Reserves	L	1	5	Beazley
	12	h	League	Barnoldswick Town	W	5	1	Beazley 3, Thompson 2
	19	h	FA Cup PR	Barnoldswick Park Villa	W	2	1	S Gradwell (pen), J Gradwell
	26	h	League	Chorley	L	1	2	Beazley
Oct	3	a	FA Cup 1Q	Lancaster Town	L	2	8	T Embrey, J Gradwell
	10	h	League	Fleetwood	W	5	1	Prescott 4, Thompson
	17	a	League	Rossendale United	L	3	6	S Embrey 2, Cartwright
	24	h	League	Darwen	L	3	4	S Embrey, Beazley, Cartwright
	31	a	League	Fleetwood	L	0	4	
Nov	14	a	League	Darwen	L	0	8	
	21	a	LJC 1	Bacup Borough	L	1	2	J Gradwell
	28	a	League	Lancaster Town	L	2	4	Lythgoe, Prescott
Dec	5	h	League	Southport Reserves	L	0	1	
	12	a	League	Nelson Reserves	D	2	2	Lythgoe, Beazley
	19	a	League	Accrington Stanley Reserves	W	2	0	Beazley 2
	25	h	League	Clitheroe	W	6	2	Unknown 6
	26	a	League	Bacup Borough	L	1	2	J Gradwell
Jan	1	a	League	Morecambe	L	1	4	J Gradwell
	2	h	League	Lancaster Town	W	2	1	Beazley, Goodlad
	9	h	League	Great Harwood	W	4	0	Walton 3, Thompson
	16	a	League	Barnoldswick Town	D	2	2	Beazley, Lythgoe
	23	h	League	Hindley Green Athletic	W	4	2	Mather 2, Walton, Thompson
	30	h	League	Bacup Borough	W	1	0	Beazley
Feb	6	a	League	Preston North End 'A'	W	3	1	Wilkinson, Lythgoe, Mather
	13	h	League	Dick, Kerr's	W	2	1	Wilkinson, Mather
	20	h	League	Colne Town	W	4	0	Lythgoe 2, Regan, Beazley
	27	a	League	Dick, Kerr's	W	2	1	Beazley, Regan
Mar	6	a	League	Hindley Green Athletic	W	3	1	Regan, Beazley, T Embrey
	13	h	League	Nelson Reserves	L	0	2	
	20	h	League	Rossendale United	L	1	4	Lythgoe
	27	h	League	Preston North End 'A'	L	1	3	Lee
Apr	2	h	League	Wigan Borough Reserves	W	6	0	Thompson, Beazley, Lee, Mather, Goodlad, Unknown
	3	a	League	Great Harwood	W	2	1	Thompson, Wilkinson
	5	a	League	Wigan Borough Reserves	D	4	4	Unknown 4
	14	a	League	Chorley	L	1	2	Little
	17	a	League	Clitheroe	W	4	2	J Embrey 2, Crossley, Beazley
	21	h	League	Atherton	W	3	1	Crossley 2, Holden
	24	h	League	Morecambe	W	1	0	Thompson
	28	a	League	Atherton	L	1	4	S Embrey
May	1	a	League	Colne Town	W	4	1	Gradwell 2, Beazley, Sedgwick
						92	100	

1926-27 Lancashire Combination

Date		H/A	Comp	Opponents	Res	F	A	Goalscorers
Aug	28	h	League	Hindley Green Athletic	W	6	0	Greenough 3, Keetley, Jones, Hird
Sep	1	h	League	Lancaster Town	L	1	5	Unknown
	4	h	FA Cup EPR	St Helens Town	L	2	4	Bibby, Greenough
	8	a	League	Atherton	L	2	4	Unknown 2
	11	h	League	Colne Town	W	5	1	Greenough 3, Hird 2 (1pens)
	13	h	LCC 1	Lancaster Town	D	1	1	Unknown
	25	h	League	Wigan Borough Reserves	D	2	2	Keetley, Hird
	29	a	LCC1	Lancaster Town	L	0	3	
Oct	9	a	League	Nelson Reserves	D	2	2	Keetley 2
	16	a	League	Clitheroe	L	1	2	S Embrey
	23	a	LJC 1	Burscough Rangers	W	4	0	Keetley 3, Opponent
	30	h	League	Great Harwood	W	3	1	Keetley 2, S Embrey
Nov	7	h	League	Accrington Stanley Reserves	W	4	1	Keetley 2, Hird, Gregson
	14	h	League	Bacup Borough	W	4	3	Hird 2, Keetley, S Embrey
	21	a	LJC 2	Lytham	L	0	2	
	28	h	League	Rossendale United	W	5	0	Hird 2, Keetley 2, Mather
Dec	4	a	League	Bacup Borough	D	2	2	Keetley, Hird
	11	a	League	Preston North End 'A'	W	1	0	Mather
	18	h	League	Preston North End 'A'	W	2	1	Sedgwick, Hird
	26	h	League	Barnoldswick Town	L	1	2	Unknown
Jan	1	a	League	Wigan Borough Reserves	L	2	4	Mather 2
	8	h	League	Nelson Reserves	W	2	1	Thompson, Hird
	15	a	League	Fleetwood	W	3	2	Hird 3
	29	a	League	Accrington Stanley Reserves	D	2	2	Keetley, S Embrey
Feb	5	a	League	Southport Reserves	L	1	2	Mather
	12	h	League	Southport Reserves	W	3	2	S Embrey, England, Opponent
	19	a	League	Great Harwood	W	7	1	Keetley 2, S Embrey 2, Hird (pen), Mather, Opponent
	26	h	League	Morecambe	L	2	4	S Embrey, T Embrey
Mar	5	a	League	Hindley Green Athletic	L	3	5	S Embrey 2, Hird
	12	h	League	Darwen	L	0	1	
	19	a	League	Rossendale United	L	3	5	Yates, Mather, Unknown
	26	a	League	Colne Town	W	4	1	Kenyon, Hird, Goodlad, Mather
Apr	2	a	League	Chorley	L	2	4	Keetley 2
	9	h	League	Chorley	L	3	4	Mather, Yates, Keetley
	11	h	League	Clitheroe	W	3	1	Unknown 3
	16	h	League	Lancaster Town	D	2	2	Hird (pen), Kenyon
	18	a	League	Barnoldswick Town	L	0	2	
	20	h	League	Dick, Kerr's	W	2	0	Unknown 2
	23	a	League	Dick, Kerr's	L	1	3	Keetley
	27	h	League	Fleetwood	W	3	0	Unknown 3
	30	a	League	Darwen	W	6	2	Keetley 3, Yates, Mather, Royle
May	4	h	League	Atherton	W	10	0	Mather 4, Yates 2, Hird 2, Keetley 2
	7	a	League	Morecambe	L	1	2	Mather
						113	86	

1927-28 Lancashire Combination

Date		H/A	Comp	Opponents	Res	F	A	Goalscorers	Notes
Aug	27	a	League	Southport Reserves	D	2	2	Mather, Hird	
	31	h	League	Lancaster Town	W	3	1	Mather, Hird, Pemberton	
Sep	3	a	League	Great Harwood	W	2	0	Mather, Hird (pen)	
	7	h	League	Nelson Reserves	W	4	2	Yates 2, Leather, Hird (pen)	
	10	h	League	Clitheroe	W	5	0	Mather 2, Yates, Keetley, Hird	
	14	a	League	Atherton	W	2	1	Keetley 2	
	17	h	League	Bacup Borough	W	3	0	Mather, Yates, Hird (pen)	1
	19	a	LJC 1	Clitheroe	W	2	1	Hird, Mather	
	24	a	League	Morecambe	D	1	1	Keetley	
	28	h	LCC 1	Chorley	W	8	1	Mather 5, Keetley, Wright, Yates	
Oct	1	h	FA Cup 1Q	Skelmersdale United	W	3	0	Yates, S Embrey, Pemberton	
	8	a	League	Accrington Stanley Reserves	L	2	3	Keetley 2	
	15	a	FA Cup 2Q	Lancaster Town	L	1	2	Hird	
	22	h	LJC 2	Little Lever	W	10	1	Keetley 3, Mather 3, Yates 2, Hird (pen), Kenyon (pen)	
	29	h	League	Barnoldswick Town	L	3	5	Keetley 2, Hird	
Nov	5	a	LJC 3	Breightmet United	W	2	1	Kenyon, Keetley	
	12	h	League	Morecambe	W	3	0	Mather 2, Yates	
	19	a	LJC 4	Barnoldswick Town	D	2	2	Hird, Keetley	
	26	h	League	Wigan Borough Reserves	W	2	0	Hird, Keetley	
	30	h	LJC 4	Barnoldswick Town	W	6	1	Keetley 5, Hird	
Dec	3	a	League	Wigan Borough Reserves	W	3	2	Hird, Yates, Keetley	
	10	h	League	Hindley Green Athletic	W	4	3	Keetley 2, Mather, Yates	
	17	h	LJC SF	Rossendale United	L	2	3	Hird, Mather	
	24	a	League	Fleetwood	D	4	4	Mather 3, Yates	
	31	a	League	Darwen	D	1	1	Keetley	
Jan	2	h	LCC 2	Darwen	W	4	2	Keetley 2, Mather, Yates	
	7	h	League	Darwen	D	1	1	Mather	
	14	a	League	Preston North End 'A'	D	2	2	Embrey, Hird	
	21	h	League	Fleetwood	W	5	0	Hird 2, Mather 2, Blackburn	
	28	a	League	Hindley Green Athletic	W	5	2	Keetley 4, Yates	
Feb	3	h	League	Dick, Kerr's	W	4	1	Keetley 3, Parkinson	
	10	a	League	Rossendale United	D	3	3	Mather, Hird, Yates	
	17	h	League	Burscough Rangers	W	6	3	Keetley 2, Yates, Hird, Sedgwick, Mather	
	24	a	League	Burscough Rangers	W	6	3	Mather 3, Hird, Yates, Parkinson	
Mar	3	h	League	Great Harwood	W	4	3	Hird, Keetley, Sedgwick, Yates	
	10	a	League	Dick, Kerr's	W	2	1	Keetley, Hird	
	17	h	League	Accrington Stanley Reserves	W	3	1	Yates 2, Keetley	
	24	a	League	Lancaster Town	L	1	7	Mather	
	31	h	League	Southport Reserves	W	4	0	Mather 2, Sedgwick, Hird	
Apr	6	h	League	Preston North End 'A'	W	5	0	Mather 3, Keetley, Parkinson	
	7	a	League	Chorley	L	0	1		
	14	a	League	Nelson Reserves	W	3	1	Yates, Keetley, Mather	
	16	h	League	Atherton	W	7	0	Keetley 3, Yates 2, Parkinson, Mather	
	18	a	LCC SF	Morecambe	D	0	0		
	21	a	League	Bacup Borough	D	1	1	Mather	
	25	a	League	Clitheroe	D	2	2	S Embrey, Hird	
	28	h	League	Chorley	L	0	1		
	30	h	LCC SF	Morecambe	W	3	1	Parkinson, Embrey, Keetley	
May	2	h	League	Rossendale United	W	3	1	Unknown 3	
	3	h	LCC Final	Rossendale United	W	2	0	Keetley 2 (1pen)	
	5	a	League	Barnoldswick Town	L	0	2		
1 - Some sources give this as an FA Cup tie									
						156	76		

1928-29 Lancashire Combination

Date		H/A	Comp	Opponents	Res	F	A	Goalscorers
Aug	25	a	League	Morecambe	L	2	4	Keetley, Dewsnap
	29	h	League	Lancaster Town	W	3	1	Mather, Yates, Newton
Sep	1	a	League	Southport Reserves	L	4	5	Keetley 4
	5	h	League	Southport Reserves	W	3	2	Mather 2, Keetley
	8	a	League	Burscough Rangers	W	3	1	Mather 2, Keetley
	12	h	League	Prescot Cables	L	1	2	Mather
	15	h	League	Clitheroe	W	6	2	Keetley 5 (1pen), Mather
	19	a	League	Atherton	W	8	2	Keetley 3, Newton 2, Mather 2, Yates
	22	a	League	Clitheroe	W	5	3	Mather 2, Entwistle, Dewsnap, Yates
	25	h	LCC 2	Manchester Central	W	4	2	Keetley 3 (1pen), Yates
	29	h	FA Cup 1Q	Chorley	W	1	0	Keetley
Oct	6	a	League	Great Harwood	W	4	2	Yates, Mather, Keetley, Murphy
	13	a	FA Cup 2Q	Dick, Kerr's	D	1	1	Yates
	17	h	FA Cup 2Q	Dick, Kerr's	W	3	0	Mather 2, Keetley
	20	h	League	Barnoldswick Town	W	12	1	Mather 6, Keetley 3, Yates, Monks, Dewsnap
	27	h	FA Cup 3Q	Morecambe	W	3	1	Dewsnap, Mather, Monks
Nov	3	h	League	Accrington Stanley Reserves	W	5	0	Mather 2, Keetley 2, Monks
	10	a	FA Cup 4Q	Workington	D	2	2	Keetley, Dewsnap
	14	h	FA Cup 4Q	Workington	W	3	0	Monks 2, Keetley
	17	a	LJC 1	Lancaster Town	D	2	2	Keetley, Opponent
	19	h	LJC 1	Lancaster Town	W	2	0	Mather, Newton
	24	h	FA Cup 1	Scarborough	L	1	2	Keetley
Dec	1	a	League	Preston North End 'A'	L	2	3	Mather, Keetley
	8	a	LCC 3	Clitheroe	L	2	3	Keetley, Embrey
	15	h	League	Bacup Borough	W	5	3	Govan 4, Monks
	22	h	League	Wigan Borough Reserves	W	2	1	Keetley, Yates
	26	a	League	Lancaster Town	D	3	3	Unknown 3
	29	h	League	Nelson Reserves	L	3	4	Mather 2, Yates
Jan	1	a	League	Chorley	L	1	2	Embrey
	5	a	League	Nelson Reserves	W	6	0	Mather 3, Keetley 2, Monks
	12	h	League	Rossendale United	D	3	3	Dewsnap 2, Keetley
	19	h	League	Morecambe	W	3	0	Newton 2, Monks
	26	a	League	Rossendale United	L	1	6	Yates (pen)
Feb	2	h	League	Darwen	W	7	0	Keetley 3, Monks 2, Mather, Dewsnap
	9	a	League	Darwen	W	4	1	Keetley 2, Dewsnap, Yates
	23	h	League	Great Harwood	W	9	2	Monks 3, Keetley 2, Mather 2, Dewsnap, Yates
Mar	2	a	League	Prescot Cables	L	3	7	Monks 2, Keetley
	9	h	League	Dick, Kerr's	W	7	0	Keetley 4, Mather, Dewsnap, Opponent
	16	a	League	Manchester Central	L	3	5	Mather 3
	23	h	League	Wigan Borough Reserves	W	2	1	Mather, Yates
	29	h	League	Preston North End 'A'	W	10	0	Mather 4, Keetley 3, Jackson, Yates, Opponent
	30	h	League	Chorley	L	3	5	Mather 2, Broadhead
Apr	1	a	League	Barnoldswick Town	L	3	4	Dewsnap, Mather, Keetley
	6	h	League	Atherton	W	3	0	Mather 2, Greenhalgh
	13	a	League	Accrington Stanley Reserves	W	2	0	Mather, Greenhalgh
	18	a	League	Dick, Kerr's	L	0	9	
	20	a	League	Bacup Borough	W	2	1	Keetley, Yates
	24	h	League	Manchester Central	W	5	0	Mather 3, Yates, Keetley
May	4	h	League	Burscough Rangers	W	4	2	Milner 3, Greenhalgh
Disqualified from LJC for fielding an ineligible player								
						176	100	

1929-30   Lancashire Combination

Date		H/A	Comp	Opponents	Res	F	A	Goalscorers	Notes
Aug	31	h	League	Rossendale United	D	4	4	Milner 2, Keetley (pen), Mather	
Sep	4	h	League	Atherton	W	5	0	Mather 3, Greenhalgh, Keetley	
	7	a	League	Morecambe	D	4	4	Mather 3, Yates	
	14	h	League	Nelson Reserves	W	12	0	Keetley 5, Mather 5, Milner 2	
	18	h	League	Southport Reserves	L	1	2	Milner	
	21	a	League	Southport Reserves	W	2	1	Mather, Milner	
	28	h	League	Bacup Borough	W	2	0	Keetley 2	
Oct	2	h	LCC 2	Manchester Central	W	2	1	Mather 2 (1pen)	
	5	h	FA Cup 1Q	Breightmet United	W	1	0	Keetley	
	12	a	League	Atherton	W	3	1	Mather 2, Milner	
	19	h	FA Cup 2Q	Lancaster Town	D	1	1	Yates	
	23	a	FA Cup 2Q	Lancaster Town	L	3	5	Keetley 2, Yates	
	26	h	League	Wigan Borough Reserves	W	3	1	Milner, Keetley, Yates	
Nov	2	h	LJC 1	Breightmet United	W	3	1	Keetley 3	
	9	h	League	Clitheroe	W	5	0	Milner 2, Mather, Newton, Woods	
	16	a	League	Burscough Rangers	L	1	2	Milner	
	23	h	LJC 2	Lancaster Town	W	3	1	Keetley, Newton, Milner	
	30	a	League	Darwen	W	4	2	Mather 2, Milner, Newton	
Dec	7	a	LJC SF	Ashton United	W	3	0	Yates, Sedgwick, Opponent	
	14	a	League	Clitheroe	W	5	1	Mather 2, Keetley, Milner, Yates	
	21	h	League	Burscough Rangers	W	4	2	Mather 3, Newton	
	26	h	League	Morecambe	W	6	1	Mather, Unknown 5	
	28	a	League	Great Harwood	Ab	5	1	Milner 2, Mather, Keetley, Eckersall	Ab 70'
Jan	1	a	League	Chorley	D	1	1	Mather	
	2	h	LCC 3	Darwen	L	1	2	Milner	
	4	h	League	Accrington Stanley Reserves	W	3	1	Mather, Milner, Newton	
	11	1	LJC Final	Darwen	W	2	0	Keetley 2	
	18	a	League	Wigan Borough Reserves	W	4	3	Woods, Keetley, Broadhead, Milner	
	25	h	League	Darwen	L	3	6	Keetley 2, Mather	
Feb	1	a	League	Prescot Cables	L	1	2	Keetley	
	8	a	League	Dick, Kerr's	L	1	2	Yates	
	12	a	League	Manchester Central	L	1	3	Keetley	
	15	a	League	Nelson Reserves	L	1	6	Keetley	
	22	h	League	Prescot Cables	W	2	1	Milner, Yates	
Mar	1	a	League	Lancaster Town	L	2	5	S Blackburn, Keetley	
	8	a	League	Accrington Stanley Reserves	L	0	3		
	15	a	League	Bacup Borough	L	2	4	Keetley 2	
	22	h	League	Lytham	W	6	1	Keetley 2, Newton 2, Embrey, S Blackburn	
	29	h	League	Barnoldswick Town	W	4	0	S Blackburn 2, Keetley, Broadhead	
Apr	5	h	League	Great Harwood	W	8	0	Keetley 2, Mather 2, Hilton, Yates, S Blackburn, Opponent	
	8	a	League	Great Harwood	W	3	1	S Blackburn 2, Mather	
	12	h	League	Dick, Kerr's	D	2	2	Mather, J Blackburn	
	18	h	League	Manchester Central	D	0	0		
	19	h	League	Chorley	W	2	1	S Blackburn, Yates	
	21	a	League	Barnoldswick Town	W	2	0	Sharrocks, Milner	
	26	a	League	Lytham	D	2	2	S Blackburn, Opponent	
	29	a	League	Rossendale United	L	1	3	Keetley	
May	3	h	League	Lancaster Town	L	0	2		
		1	at Preston NE			136	82		

1930-31 Lancashire Combination

Date		H/A	Comp	Opponents	Res	F	A	Goalscorers
Aug	30	a	League	Manchester Central	W	2	1	Mather, Keetley
Sep	3	h	League	Atherton	W	6	2	Keetley 3, Roberts 3
	6	h	League	Nelson Reserves	W	8	1	Keetley 4, Roberts 2, Mather 2
	8	a	League	Barnoldswick Town	D	3	3	Keetley 2, Roberts
	13	a	League	Clitheroe	L	2	4	Mather, Howarth
	17	h	League	Barnoldswick Town	W	5	0	Keetley 2, Roberts, Powell, Sedgwick
	20	h	League	Lytham	W	6	3	Roberts 2, Blackburn 2, Keetley, Sedgwick
	24	a	League	Atherton	W	10	0	Mather 4, Roberts 3, Keetley 2, Sedgwick
	27	a	League	Bacup Borough	W	2	1	Keetley, Blackburn
Oct	1	h	LCC 1	Clitheroe	L	3	4	Keetley 2, Sedgwick
	4	h	FA Cup 1Q	Burscough Rangers	W	5	1	Keetley 4, Sedgwick
	11	a	League	Darwen	D	1	1	Powell
	18	a	FA Cup 2Q	Lytham	D	2	2	Rimmer, Roberts
	22	h	FA Cup 2Q	Lytham	W	4	1	Keetley, Roberts, Crompton, Opponent
	25	h	League	Great Harwood	D	2	2	Blackburn, Roberts
Nov	1	h	FA Cup 3Q	Chorley	W	3	0	Mather, Roberts, Crompton
	8	h	LJC 1	Darwen	W	3	1	Crompton, Yates, Bunyan
	15	a	FA Cup 4Q	Lancaster Town	L	1	3	Mather
	22	a	LJC 2	Prescot Cables	D	1	1	Keetley
	24	h	LJC 2	Prescot Cables	W	8	6	Keetley 3, Blackburn 2, Mather, Yates, Roberts
	29	a	League	Wigan Borough Reserves	W	4	2	Keetley 2, Yates, Blackburn
Dec	6	a	LJC SF	Clitheroe	L	0	3	
	13	a	League	Burscough Rangers	L	1	2	Kay
	20	a	League	Dick, Kerr's	L	2	6	Keetley 2
	26	a	League	Prescot Cables	L	2	4	Unknown 2
	27	h	League	Manchester Central	W	4	3	Keetley 2, Marston, Sedgwick
Jan	1	h	League	Prescot Cables	W	4	0	Roberts, Keetley, Powell, Marston
	3	a	League	Nelson Reserves	W	4	1	Roberts, Crompton, Powell, Kay
	17	h	League	Clitheroe	W	3	0	Keetley 2, Marston
	24	a	League	Lytham	L	1	4	Keetley
Feb	7	a	League	Morecambe	L	1	2	Roberts
	14	h	League	Darwen	W	3	2	Keetley, Unknown 2
	21	h	League	Rossendale United	D	4	4	Mather 2, Roberts, Keetley
	28	h	League	Morecambe	W	5	2	Keetley 2, Roberts, Mather, Opponent
Mar	14	h	League	Accrington Stanley Reserves	L	4	5	Roberts 2, Keetley, Mather
	21	h	League	Dick, Kerr's	W	2	1	Keetley, Marston
	28	a	League	Great Harwood	W	3	1	Keetley 2, Roberts
	30	a	League	Lancaster Town	L	0	1	
Apr	3	h	League	Bacup Borough	W	5	0	Maybury, Yates, Mather, Roberts, Marston
	4	h	League	Wigan Borough Reserves	W	4	1	Roberts 3, Marston
	6	a	League	Accrington Stanley Reserves	L	1	2	Embrey
	11	a	League	Chorley	L	1	4	Mather
	13	h	League	Lancaster Town	W	2	1	Mather, Opponent
	18	h	League	Burscough Rangers	L	1	3	Roberts
	22	h	League	Chorley	D	0	0	
	25	a	League	Rossendale United	W	7	0	Roberts 4, Worthington 2, Opponent
	30	a	League	Southport Reserves	L	1	3	Unknown
May	2	h	League	Southport Reserves	W	3	1	Worthington, Roberts, Mather
Rochdale Reserves took over the fixtures of Atherton								
						149	95	

227

1931-32   Lancashire Combination

Date		H/A	Comp	Opponents	Res	F	A	Goalscorers
Aug	29	a	League	Nelson	L	0	2	
Sep	5	h	League	Accrington Stanley Reserves	W	10	1	O'Rourke 6, Greenwood 2, Taylor, Roberts
	7	h	League	Fleetwood	W	6	2	Mather 2, Greenwood 2, O'Rourke, Roberts
	12	a	League	Barnoldswick Town	L	1	3	Mather
	15	a	LCC 1	Great Harwood	L	0	4	
	19	a	League	Barrow Reserves	L	0	4	
	26	h	League	Morecambe	W	2	1	Mather, Greenwood
Oct	3	h	FA Cup 1Q	Chorley	L	0	1	
	10	h	League	Darwen	W	3	1	Roberts 2 (1pen), Crawshaw
	17	h	League	Clitheroe	W	2	1	Hart 2
	24	a	League	Lytham	L	0	4	
	31	h	League	Great Harwood	W	2	1	O'Rourke, Roberts
Nov	7	a	LJC 1	Darwen	L	0	9	
	14	h	League	Lytham	L	2	3	Shuttleworth, Sharrock
	21	h	League	Southport Reserves	W	3	0	Hird, Crawshaw, Worthington
	28	h	League	Barrow Reserves	L	2	4	Crawshaw 2
Dec	5	a	League	Chorley	L	3	6	Crawshaw 2, Roberts
	12	h	League	Prescot Cables	L	3	4	Greenhalgh, Roberts, Hird
	19	a	League	Fleetwood	L	0	1	
	26	h	League	Dick, Kerr's	L	2	4	Sedgwick, Lawson
Jan	1	a	League	Dick, Kerr's	L	3	9	Crawshaw 3
	2	h	League	Nelson	W	4	3	Crawshaw 2, Hilton, Greenhalgh
	9	a	League	Southport Reserves	D	1	1	Crawshaw
	16	a	League	Accrington Stanley Reserves	L	2	4	Hulme, Greenhalgh
	23	a	League	Barnoldswick Town	D	2	2	Roberts, Marshall
	30	h	League	Bacup Borough	W	5	1	Roberts 3, Crawshaw 2
Feb	6	a	League	Morecambe	L	2	3	Hilton, Crawshaw
	13	a	League	Burscough Rangers	D	4	4	Crawshaw 2, Roberts, Hilton
	20	a	League	Darwen	L	1	9	Crawshaw
	27	a	League	Clitheroe	L	1	2	Crawshaw
Mar	12	a	League	Great Harwood	L	0	5	
	25	h	League	Burscough Rangers	L	1	2	Crawshaw
	26	a	League	Lancaster Town	L	0	3	
Apr	2	h	League	Rossendale United	W	2	0	Roberts, Hilton
	9	a	League	Bacup Borough	L	1	2	Crawshaw
	16	h	League	Chorley	L	1	3	Hilton
	19	a	League	Rossendale United	L	1	5	Hulme (pen)
	23	a	League	Prescot Cables	L	0	5	
	30	h	League	Lancaster Town	L	1	4	Roberts
Wigan Borough Reserves resigned and their record was expunged								
						73	123	

1932-33   Lancashire Combination

Date		H/A	Comp	Opponents	Res	F	A	Goalscorers	Notes
Aug	27	a	League	Fleetwood	L	1	5	Iddon	
Sep	1	a	League	Dick, Kerr's	W	3	0	Masters, Yates, Hurst	
	3	h	League	Chorley	L	1	5	Thornborough (pen)	
	5	h	League	Dick, Kerr's	D	0	0		
	10	a	League	Lytham	W	6	3	Makinson 3, Iddon 2, Hurst	
	13	a	League	Bacup Borough	W	3	1	Hurst, Iddon, Roberts	
	17	a	LCC 1	Chorley	L	0	5		
	21	h	League	Southport Reserves	D	4	4	Roberts 2, Hurst, Topping	
	24	h	League	Morecambe	W	4	0	Roberts 2, Hurst, Masters	
Oct	1	h	FA Cup 1Q	Burscough Rangers	W	4	1	Iddon 3, Masters	
	8	h	League	Burscough Rangers	W	6	1	Hurst 4, Iddon, Yates	
	15	h	FA Cup 2Q	Chorley	L	0	3		
	22	a	League	Great Harwood	W	6	2	Iddon 4, Roberts, Hurst	
	29	h	League	Barnoldswick Town	Ab	4	1	Iddon 3, Masters	Ab 56'
Nov	5	a	League	Rossendale United	W	3	1	Yates 2, Masters	
	12	h	League	Fleetwood	W	1	0	Iddon	
	19	a	League	Prescot Cables	L	0	2		
	26	h	League	Lancaster Town	W	4	3	Roberts 2 (1pen), Yates, Iddon	
Dec	3	h	League	Nelson	W	5	2	Glynn 2, Iddon, Hurst, Yates	
	10	h	League	Darwen	D	4	4	Pape, Hurst, Roberts, Opponent	
	17	a	League	Clitheroe	L	1	8	Hurst	
	24	a	League	Southport Reserves	L	0	4		
	26	a	League	Nelson	L	1	2	Readett	
	31	h	League	Rossendale United	D	2	2	Iddon, Opponent	
Jan	2	a	League	Rochdale Reserves	W	4	2	Iddon 2, Hurst, Hulme	
	7	a	League	Chorley	L	2	6	Iddon, Opponent	
	14	h	League	Rochdale Reserves	L	1	3	Pape	
	21	h	LJC 1	Breightmet United	L	2	3	Cowburn, Hulme	
	28	h	League	Barnoldswick Town	W	3	2	Crawshaw 2, Yates	
Feb	4	a	League	Morecambe	W	5	2	Crawshaw 2, Cowburn 2, Hurst	
	11	h	League	Lytham	W	4	2	Cowburn 2, Preston, Shuttleworth	
	18	a	League	Burscough Rangers	L	1	2	Crawshaw	
Mar	4	h	League	Great Harwood	W	2	0	Hulme, Hurst	
	11	a	League	Barnoldswick Town	W	5	1	Hurst 2, Yates 2, Cowburn	
	25	h	League	Accrington Stanley Reserves	W	3	1	Gregory, Yates, Crawshaw	
Apr	1	h	League	Prescot Cables	W	5	2	Yates 2, Crawshaw 2, Cowburn	
	8	a	League	Lancaster Town	L	3	4	Crawshaw, Yates, Hulme	
	14	h	League	Barrow Reserves	D	2	2	Hilton, Crawshaw	
	15	a	League	Accrington Stanley Reserves	L	0	1		
	17	a	League	Barrow Reserves	L	0	1		
	22	a	League	Darwen	W	4	1	Hulme 2, Crawshaw, Yates	
	25	a	Hospital Cup	Chorley	D	0	0		
	29	h	League	Clitheroe	W	2	1	Cookson, Hulme	
May	2	h	League	Bacup Borough	W	6	0	Crawshaw 3, Hulme, Shuttleworth, Readett	
						117	95		

1933-34   Lancashire Combination

Date		H/A	Comp	Opponents	Res	F	A	Goalscorers
Aug	26	h	League	Darwen	W	5	2	Yates 3, Hurst, Opponent
	30	a	League	Lytham	W	1	0	Yates
Sep	2	a	League	Rochdale Reserves	L	0	4	
	4	h	League	Nelson	W	4	1	Crawshaw 2, Hulme, Yates
	7	a	League	Dick, Kerr's	L	0	3	
	9	h	League	Rossendale United	L	2	3	Hulme (pen), Yates
	16	a	League	Chorley	L	3	7	Crawshaw 2, Brindle
	23	a	League	Morecambe	L	1	2	Hilton
	30	h	FA Cup 1Q	Wigan Athletic	L	0	3	
Oct	7	a	League	Accrington Stanley Reserves	L	2	6	Hulme (pen), Yates
	14	h	League	Leyland Motors	L	2	4	Hilton, Hulme
	17	a	LCC 2	Darwen	L	0	6	
	21	h	League	Fleetwood	L	1	5	Hulme (pen)
	28	a	League	Lancaster Town	L	2	5	Cowburn, Phythian
Nov	4	h	League	Clitheroe	L	3	5	Yates 2 (1pen), Cowburn
	11	a	League	Great Harwood	L	1	2	Hilton
	18	h	League	Barrow Reserves	W	5	1	Shepherd 2, Phythian (pen), Yates, Skiffington
	25	a	League	Bacup Borough	L	0	1	
Dec	2	h	League	Northern Nomads	W	4	0	Phythian 2, Shepherd, Yates
	9	a	League	Barnoldswick Town	D	1	1	Yates
	16	h	League	Chorley	L	0	5	
	26	a	League	Southport Reserves	W	3	2	Hilton 2, Hulme (pen)
	30	a	League	Darwen	L	1	5	Hilton
Jan	2	h	League	Southport Reserves	W	3	0	Yates 3 (2pens)
	6	h	League	Rochdale Reserves	W	3	2	Bibby (pen), Shepherd, Yates
	13	a	League	Nelson	D	1	1	Skiffington
	20	a	LJC 1	Northern Nomads	W	3	0	Shepherd 2, Bibby (pen)
	27	h	League	Lytham	W	6	3	Shepherd 3, Skeffington 2, Yates
Feb	3	h	League	Morecambe	W	6	2	Skiffington 2, Bibby 2, Yates, Ince
	10	h	LJC 2	Nelson Reserves	W	7	0	Bibby 5, Shepherd, Phythian
	17	h	League	Accrington Stanley Reserves	D	1	1	Skiffington
	24	a	League	Leyland Motors	L	1	2	Bibby (pen)
Mar	3	a	League	Fleetwood	L	0	4	
	10	a	LJC 3	Darwen	L	0	5	
	17	a	League	Clitheroe	L	2	4	Shuttleworth, Bibby
	24	h	League	Great Harwood	W	6	2	Bibby 2, Yates 2, Waters 2
	31	a	League	Barrow Reserves	L	1	2	Bibby
Apr	7	h	League	Bacup Borough	W	3	2	Bibby, Yates, Shuttleworth
	14	a	League	Northern Nomads	L	3	6	Bibby 2, Yates
	21	h	League	Barnoldswick Town	W	3	2	Waters 2, Shepherd
	24	a	League	Rossendale United	D	4	4	Unknown 4
	28	h	League	Dick, Kerr's	L	0	1	
May	5	h	League	Lancaster Town	L	1	5	Shepherd
	12	a	Hosp Cup	Chorley	L	3	4	Shepherd, Yates, Phythian
Barnoldswick Town took over fixtures of Burscough Rangers, who resigned								
						98	125	

1934-35   Lancashire Combination

Date		H/A	Comp	Opponents	Res	F	A	Goalscorers
Aug	25	h	League	New Brighton Reserves	W	4	0	Bibby 2, Hitchen, Opponent
	29	h	League	Chorley	L	1	2	Young
Sep	1	a	League	Lancaster Town	L	3	4	Bibby 3
	3	a	LSC 1	New Brighton	W	4	3	Yates 2, Bibby, Phythian
	5	a	League	Chorley	L	0	4	
	12	a	League	New Brighton Reserves	L	3	4	Unknown 3
	15	a	LSC 2	Preston North End	L	1	8	Unknown
	19	h	LCC 2	Clitheroe	D	1	1	Yates
	22	h	League	Accrington Stanley Reserves	W	5	2	Young 2, Sleaford, Yates, Shonokan
	29	h	FA Cup 1Q	Morecambe	L	1	3	Hitchen
Oct	6	a	League	Barrow Reserves	L	1	3	Phythian
	13	h	League	Rochdale Reserves	W	3	1	Sleaford, Shepherd, Yates
	20	h	League	Great Harwood	W	5	0	Yates 2, Shuttleworth, Hitchen, Cocker
	27	a	League	Fleetwood	L	0	4	
Nov	3	h	League	Rossendale United	L	1	2	Yates
	10	a	League	Lytham	L	0	1	
	17	h	League	Nelson	D	2	2	Young, Shepherd
	24	a	League	Morecambe	L	1	3	Butler
Dec	8	a	League	Darwen	L	2	8	Yates (pen), Hitchen
	15	h	League	Darwen	W	4	3	Young, Yates, Ince, Shepherd
	22	a	League	Clitheroe	W	3	2	Yates 2, Hitchen
	26	h	League	Southport Reserves	W	9	2	Yates 4 (2pens), Butler 2, Shepherd, Young, Hitchen
Jan	1	h	League	Leyland Motors	W	4	0	Yates 2, Shepherd, Butler
	5	h	League	Lancaster Town	W	1	0	Butler
	19	a	League	Dick, Kerr's	L	0	1	
	26	a	League	Southport Reserves	L	2	4	Yates, Affleck
Feb	2	a	League	Accrington Stanley Reserves	W	5	3	Butler 4, Hitchen
	9	h	LJC 1	Morecambe	W	2	0	Butler, Affleck
	16	h	League	Barrow Reserves	W	3	0	Butler, Affleck, Opponent
	23	a	League	Rochdale Reserves	L	2	5	Gore, Yates
Mar	9	a	LJC 2	Lancaster Town	L	0	2	
	16	a	League	Rossendale United	L	2	4	Hitchen, Yates
	23	h	League	Lytham	W	6	1	Butler 3, Yates 2, Shepherd
	30	a	League	Nelson	L	1	5	Yates
Apr	6	h	League	Morecambe	W	2	0	Shepherd, Shuttleworth
	9	a	League	Bacup Borough	L	1	3	Shuttleworth
	13	h	League	Clitheroe	D	1	1	Young
	16	a	League	Great Harwood	W	4	2	Unknown 4
	19	a	League	Northern Nomads	D	3	3	Young, Griffiths, Affleck
	20	h	League	Dick, Kerr's	L	1	2	Shepherd
	22	h	League	Northern Nomads	W	2	1	Yates, Shuttleworth
	23	h	League	Fleetwood	L	2	3	Gore (pen), Yates
	27	a	League	Leyland Motors	L	0	2	
May	4	h	League	Bacup Borough	W	2	1	Guest, Shuttleworth
						100	105	

1935-36   Lancashire Combination

Date		H/A	Comp	Opponents	Res	F	A	Goalscorers
Aug	31	a	League	Southport Reserves	L	1	2	Hitchen
Sep	4	h	League	Bacup Borough	W	5	2	Thompson 2, Yates, Hitchen, Young
	7	h	League	Dick, Kerr's	W	5	1	Thompson 4, Hitchen
	10	a	League	Nelson	L	0	2	
	14	a	League	Bacup Borough	L	0	2	
	18	h	League	Nelson	D	3	3	Thompson, Cowper, Shuttleworth
	21	h	FA Cup PR	Crossens	W	2	0	Thompson, Shepherd
	25	a	League	Lytham	W	4	1	Hitchen 3, Wagstaffe (pen)
	28	h	League	Rochdale Reserves	D	3	3	Cowper 2, Shepherd
Oct	2	h	LCC 2	Great Harwood	W	8	0	Thompson 3, Hitchen 2, Cowper 2, Shepherd
	5	h	FA Cup 1Q	Breightmet United	W	7	1	Thompson 4, Hitchen 3
	12	h	League	Barrow Reserves	D	2	2	Shepherd, Hitchen
	19	h	FA Cup 2Q	Leyland Motors	W	3	2	Thompson 2, Gore
	26	h	League	Chorley	W	8	1	Hitchen 2, Thompson 2, Yates 2, Gore (pen), Shepherd
Nov	2	h	FA Cup 3Q	Dick, Kerr's	W	4	2	Yates, Shepherd, Gore, Cowper
	9	h	League	Morecambe	W	3	2	Yates 2, Hitchen
	16	h	FA Cup 4Q	Stalybridge Celtic	L	1	2	Hitchen
	23	h	League	Fleetwood	L	3	8	Wagstaffe, Cowper, Gregory
	30	a	League	Great Harwood	D	2	2	Yates, Shuttleworth
Dec	7	h	League	Clitheroe	L	1	4	Yates
	14	a	League	Darwen	L	2	4	Shuttleworth, Hitchen
	21	h	League	Rossendale United	W	5	1	Thompson 2, Shuttleworth (pen), Hitchen, Sutton
	26	a	League	New Brighton Reserves	L	2	6	Unknown 2
	28	h	League	Southport Reserves	W	2	1	Thompson, Yates
Jan	1	h	League	New Brighton Reserves	W	7	1	Thompson 2, Yates, Hitchen, Bullough, Ince, Opponent
	11	h	League	Leyland Motors	W	5	1	Yates 3, Thompson 2
	18	h	League	Lancaster Town	L	1	2	Schofield
	25	h	League	Lytham	W	3	1	Hitchen 2, Phythian
Feb	1	a	League	Rochdale Reserves	D	2	2	Hitchen, Yates
	8	a	LJC 2	Clitheroe	L	0	2	
	15	a	League	Barrow Reserves	W	7	1	Thompson 4, Schofield, Shuttleworth, G Davies
	22	h	League	Northern Nomads	W	4	3	Thompson 3, Opponent
	29	a	League	Chorley	L	0	5	
Mar	7	h	League	Marine	D	3	3	Thompson 2, Yates
	14	a	League	Morecambe	L	1	3	Thompson
	21	a	League	Marine	L	2	3	Hitchen, Thompson
	23	a	LCC 3	Darwen	L	0	5	
	28	a	League	Fleetwood	L	0	6	
Apr	1	a	League	Lancaster Town	L	0	5	
	4	h	League	Great Harwood	W	3	2	Cookson, Shuttleworth (pen), Hitchen
	10	a	League	Accrington Stanley Reserves	W	3	1	Hitchen, Sutton, Thompson
	11	a	League	Clitheroe	L	3	6	Yates 2, Jones
	13	h	League	Accrington Stanley Reserves	L	1	2	Schofield
	14	a	League	Northern Nomads	L	3	7	Thompson, Schofield, Opponent
	18	h	League	Darwen	W	4	2	Phythian, Sutton, Schofield, McAweeney
	22	a	League	South Liverpool	L	3	5	McAweeney 3
	25	a	League	Rossendale United	D	0	0	
	30	h	League	South Liverpool	D	1	1	Schofield
May	2	a	League	Leyland Motors	L	1	3	Cookson
Dick, Kerr's resigned and their record was expunged								
						133	126	

1936-37 Lancashire Combination

Date		H/A	Comp	Opponents	Res	F	A	Goalscorers	Notes
Aug	29	h	League	Accrington Stanley Reserves	D	2	2	Thompson, Marsh	
Sep	3	a	League	Leyland Motors	D	1	1	Thompson	
	5	a	League	Southport Reserves	D	1	1	Hitchen	
	9	h	League	Leyland Motors	D	1	1	Thompson	
	12	a	League	New Brighton Reserves	L	1	6	Thompson	
	16	a	League	Clitheroe	W	7	1	Thompson 5, Unknown 2	
	19	h	League	Bacup Borough	W	3	0	Schofield, Thompson, Marsh	
	22	a	League	Bacup Borough	L	1	3	Hitchen	
	26	a	League	Lancaster Town	L	1	3	Thompson	
	29	a	LCC 2	Accrington Stanley Reserves	L	0	4		
Oct	3	h	FA Cup 1Q	Rossendale United	W	3	1	Thompson, Schofield, Bullough	
	10	a	League	Prescot Cables	L	1	2	Marsh	
	17	h	FA Cup 2Q	Crossens	W	5	0	Thompson 2, Marsh, Bullough, Opponent	
	24	a	League	Darwen	L	1	2	Opponent	
	31	h	FA Cup 3Q	Morecambe	L	0	2		
Nov	7	a	League	Barrow Reserves	L	1	3	Thompson (pen)	
	14	h	League	Rochdale Reserves	W	3	2	Thompson 2, Phythian	
	28	h	League	Marine	L	4	7	Thompson 3, Schofield	
Dec	5	a	League	Morecambe	D	1	1	Maguire	
	12	h	League	Rossendale United	W	4	1	Schofield 2, Rowson, Ogden	
	19	a	League	South Liverpool	L	0	2		
	26	a	League	Accrington Stanley Reserves	L	0	2		
Jan	1	h	League	Droylsden	L	1	2	Greenhalgh	
	2	h	League	Southport Reserves	L	2	3	Rowson, Clarke	
	9	h	League	New Brighton Reserves	W	5	0	Rowson 2, Schofield, Marsh, Opponent	
	16	a	League	Chorley	L	0	5		
	23	h	LJC 1	Darwen	L	1	4	Hartley	
	30	h	League	Lancaster Town	D	2	2	Rowson, Hough	
Feb	6	a	League	Clitheroe	D	3	3	Marsh 2, Hough	
	13	h	League	Prescot Cables	W	4	2	Marsh 2, Rowson, Hartley	
	20	a	League	Fleetwood	L	3	4	Schofield 2, Marsh	
	27	h	League	Darwen	L	0	4		
Mar	6	a	League	Great Harwood	L	1	3	Birchall	
	13	h	League	Barrow Reserves	D	1	1	Marsh	
	20	a	League	Rochdale Reserves	L	1	3	Cookson	
	27	h	League	Northern Nomads	W	5	2	Obersby 2, Birchall, Rowson, Opponent	
Apr	3	a	League	Marine	L	1	2	Hitchen	
	10	h	League	Morecambe	L	1	2	Obersby	
	15	h	League	Fleetwood	W	3	1	Bullough 2, Marsh	Ab 78' stands
	17	a	League	Rossendale United	Ab	1	3	Marsh	Ab h/t
	19	a	League	Northern Nomads	W	3	1	Hitchen 2, Bullough	
	26	a	League	Droylsden	L	2	3	Cleworth, Hitchen	
	27	h	League	South Liverpool	L	2	5	Hitchen, Opponent	
	28	h	League	Great Harwood	W	3	1	Marsh, Obersby, Hitchen	
	30	a	League	Rossendale United	L	2	4	Unknown 2	
May	1	h	League	Chorley	W	2	0	Ramsbottom, Obersby	
	8	a	Hospital Cup	Chorley	L	0	4		
						90	111		

1937-38　Lancashire Combination

Date		H/A	Comp	Opponents	Res	F	A	Goalscorers
Aug	28	a	League	Darwen	L	0	5	
	31	a	League	Great Harwood	L	0	5	
Sep	4	h	League	Droylsden	W	2	1	Schofield 2
	6	h	League	Great Harwood	W	3	1	Ramsbottom, Thompson, Bullough
	11	h	League	Prescot Cables	L	2	3	Bullough, Ramsbottom (pen)
	14	a	League	Bacup Borough	L	1	2	Hitchen
	18	a	League	New Brighton Reserves	D	0	0	
	20	a	League	Clitheroe	L	0	5	
	25	h	League	Lancaster City	W	3	1	Hitchen, Ramsbottom, Brockbank
	29	a	LCC 1	Clitheroe	L	3	5	Turner, Cookson, Opponent
Oct	2	a	FA Cup 1Q	Morecambe	D	2	2	Ramsbottom 2
	6	h	FA Cup 1Q	Morecambe	W	5	1	Turner 2, Hitchen, Guest, Cleworth
	9	h	League	Oldham Athletic Reserves	W	3	1	Guest 2, Chadwick
	16	a	FA Cup 2Q	Leyland Motors	L	0	1	
	23	h	League	South Liverpool	L	3	6	Guest, Ramsbottom, Hitchen
	30	a	League	Marine	L	4	5	Thompson 2, Rowson, Opponent
Nov	6	h	League	Morecambe	L	0	2	
	13	a	League	Southport Reserves	L	1	3	Ramsbottom
	20	h	League	Rossendale United	D	1	1	Chadwick
	27	h	League	Rochdale Reserves	W	4	0	Chadwick 3, Guest
Dec	4	h	League	Accrington Stanley Reserves	L	5	6	Chadwick 3, Rodway, Rowson
	11	a	League	Leyland Motors	W	4	2	Chadwick 3, Guest
	18	h	League	Chorley	D	5	5	Guest 2, Schofield 2, Ramsbottom
	27	a	League	Fleetwood	L	1	11	Unknown
Jan	1	h	League	Darwen	L	2	3	Kelly, Chadwick
	8	h	League	Fleetwood	W	4	1	Ramsbottom 2 (2 pens), Kelly, Schofield
	15	h	LJC 1	Breightmet United	D	1	1	Ramsbottom
	19	h	LJC 1	Breightmet United	W	4	0	Schofield 2, Guest, Kelly
	22	a	League	Prescot Cables	L	1	2	Turley
	29	a	LJC 2	Great Harwood	W	1	0	Schofield
Feb	5	a	League	Lancaster City	L	1	4	Schofield
	12	h	League	Bacup Borough	W	2	0	Ramsbottom 2
	19	a	LJC 3	Bacup Borough	W	2	1	Turley, Schofield
	26	h	League	Northern Nomads	W	4	3	Turley 4
Mar	5	a	League	South Liverpool	L	0	5	
	12	h	LJC SF	Lancaster City	D	2	2	Hitchen, Guest
	16	a	LJC SF	Lancaster City	L	2	5	Turley 2
	19	a	League	Morecambe	L	0	2	
	26	h	League	Southport Reserves	W	6	1	Turley 3, Ramsbottom, Clarke, Brockbank
Apr	2	a	League	Rossendale United	L	0	4	
	11	a	League	Oldham Athletic Reserves	D	2	2	Unknown 2
	13	a	League	Droylsden	L	3	7	Unknown 3
	15	a	League	Barrow Reserves	L	1	2	Unknown
	16	a	League	Accrington Stanley Reserves	L	0	4	
	18	h	League	Barrow Reserves	W	6	2	Ramsbottom 3 (1 pen), Whitehead, Brockbank, Turley
	20	h	League	Marine	L	2	3	Turley 2
	23	h	League	Leyland Motors	W	3	2	Ramsbottom 3
	25	a	League	Northern Nomads	L	2	3	McAweeney, Brockbank
	26	a	League	Rochdale Reserves	D	2	2	Ramsbottom, Clarke (pen)
	30	a	League	Chorley	W	2	1	Ramsbottom, Turley
May	4	h	League	New Brighton Reserves	W	7	0	Ramsbottom 2, Turley 2, Bohan, Hitchen, Clarke (pen)
	7	h	League	Clitheroe	L	0	5	
						114	141	

1938-39　Lancashire Combination

Date		H/A	Comp	Opponents	Res	F	A	Goalscorers
Aug	27	a	League	Leyland Motors	L	1	2	Ramsbottom
	31	h	League	Marine	W	4	2	Ramsbottom, Whitehead, Clarke (pen), Turley
Sep	3	h	League	Accrington Stanley Reserves	L	0	4	
	7	h	League	Chorley	W	3	0	Brockbank, Whitehead, Turley
	10	a	League	Oldham Athletic Reserves	L	1	3	Ramsbottom
	14	a	League	Marine	L	3	4	Kay 2, Brockbank
	17	h	League	Clitheroe	L	1	2	Kay
	21	a	League	New Brighton Reserves	L	2	7	Turley, Ramsbottom
	24	h	League	New Brighton Reserves	L	1	2	Turley
	26	a	LCC 1	Droylsden	W	4	3	Turley 3, Ramsbottom
Oct	1	h	FA Cup 1Q	Skelmersdale United	L	4	5	Ramsbottom 2, Hitchen, Opponent
	8	h	League	Barrow Reserves	L	2	3	Brockbank, Ramsbottom
	15	a	League	South Liverpool	L	1	4	Wood
	22	h	League	Prescot Cables	L	0	2	
	29	a	League	Bacup Borough	D	3	3	Ramsbottom 2, Whitehead
Nov	5	h	League	Morecambe	D	2	2	Conlan, Brockbank
	12	a	League	Droylsden	D	2	2	Owen, Brockbank
	19	h	League	Great Harwood	W	4	1	Ramsbottom 3, Thompson
	26	a	League	Southport Reserves	L	1	6	Clarke
Dec	3	h	League	Fleetwood	D	0	0	
	10	a	League	Darwen	L	1	4	Blackburn
	17	h	League	Rochdale Reserves	L	1	2	Clarke (pen)
	26	a	League	Lancaster City	W	6	2	Dickinson 2, Ramsbottom 2, Thompson, Blackburn
	27	h	League	Lancaster City	L	2	4	Thompson 2
	31	a	League	Accrington Stanley Reserves	L	2	5	Dickinson 2
Jan	2	a	League	Chorley	L	1	6	Ramsbottom
	14	h	League	Oldham Athletic Reserves	D	3	3	Hitchen, Ramsbottom, Whitehead
	21	a	League	Clitheroe	L	3	10	Dunn, Whitehead, Ashworth
	28	a	LJC 1	Bacup Borough	L	2	5	Gilligan, Whitehead
Feb	11	a	League	Barrow Reserves	L	2	4	Dickinson 2
	18	h	LCC 2	Darwen	L	3	4	Dickinson, Ramsbottom, Whitehead
	25	a	League	Prescot Cables	L	3	5	Thompson, Jones, Ramsbottom
Mar	4	h	League	Bacup Borough	W	2	0	Thompson, Jones
	11	a	League	Morecambe	L	0	5	
	18	h	League	Droylsden	W	4	2	Ramsbottom 2, Thompson, Opponent
	25	a	League	Great Harwood	L	2	4	Thompson, Wilkinson
Apr	1	h	League	Southport Reserves	D	3	3	Thompson, Gillingham, Ramsbottom
	7	h	League	Bangor City	L	2	5	Thompson 2
	8	a	League	Fleetwood	L	1	4	Opponent
	10	a	League	Bangor City	L	2	10	Unknown 2
	15	a	League	Darwen	L	1	3	Thompson
	17	h	League	Rossendale United	D	2	2	Unknown 2
	22	a	League	Rochdale Reserves	L	0	1	
	25	h	League	Leyland Motors	L	0	1	
	29	a	League	Rossendale United	L	2	8	Unknown 2
May	3	h	League	South Liverpool	W	4	1	Ramsbottom, Berry, Hitchen, Hurst
						93	160	

1939-40   Lancashire Combination

Date		H/A	Comp	Opponents	Res	F	A	Goalscorers
Aug	26	a	League	Rossendale United	L	0	9	
	30	h	League	Accrington Stanley Reserves	L	0	2	
Sep	2	h	League	Lancaster City	W	4	0	Schofield 3, Turley
League suspended due to outbreak of war						4	11	
War Emergency League (Lancashire Combination)								
Oct	7	a	League	Southport Reserves	L	1	5	Hartley
	14	h	League	Southport Reserves	D	5	5	Rimmer, Holt (pen), Unknown 3
	21	h	LJC 1	Darwen	L	1	3	Rimmer
	28	h	League	Leyland Motors	D	1	1	Rimmer
Nov	11	a	League	Leyland Motors	L	3	4	Turley 2, Young
	18	h	League	Great Harwood	W	4	1	Rimmer 2, Smethurst, Hartley (pen)
	25	a	League	Great Harwood	L	3	5	Turley, Young, Hartley
Dec	22	h	League	South Liverpool	L	2	6	Sleaford 2
	30	h	League	Clitheroe	D	3	3	Rimmer, Young, Turley
Jan	1	a	League	Chorley	L	0	1	
	6	a	League	Clitheroe	L	0	3	
	13	h	League	Chorley	L	0	2	
	20	a	LCC 1	Southport Reserves	L	1	3	Hickson
Mar	9	h	League	Rossendale United	L	0	4	
	16	a	League	Rossendale United	L	0	7	
	23	h	League	Bacup Borough	W	4	3	Hickson 2, Hardy, Holt
	30	a	League	Bacup Borough	D	2	2	Sleaford, Turley
Apr	13	a	League	South Liverpool	L	3	5	Unknown 3
May	4	a	League	Rochdale Reserves	L	0	5	
	11	h	League	Rochdale Reserves	W	1	0	Sleaford
						34	68	

1946-47 Lancashire Combination

Date		H/A	Comp	Opponents	Res	F	A	Goalscorers
Aug	31	a	League	Rossendale United	L	0	4	
Sep	4	h	League	Accrington Stanley Reserves	W	4	3	F Ramsbottom 2, Hamer, Taylor
	7	h	League	Lancaster City	L	0	2	
	11	a	League	Morecambe	L	2	7	Unknown 2
	14	a	League	Barrow Reserves	D	1	1	F Ramsbottom
	19	a	League	Leyland Motors	W	1	0	Hamer
	21	a	FA Cup PR	Great Harwood	W	6	2	Hamer 3, F Ramsbottom 2, Spencer
	28	a	League	Netherfield	D	1	1	Bevan
Oct	5	a	FA Cup 1Q	Darwen	D	1	1	Unknown
	9	h	FA Cup 1Q	Darwen	L	0	2	
	12	h	League	Fleetwood	W	4	1	Cronkshaw, Spencer, Tait, Brown
	19	h	League	Great Harwood	D	1	1	Cronkshaw
	26	a	League	Bangor City	D	2	2	Rimmer 2
Nov	2	a	League	Nelson	W	1	0	Hamer
	9	h	League	Prescot Cables	L	1	4	Brown
	16	h	League	Morecambe	W	4	1	Crompton 2, Haslam (pen), Hamer
	23	a	League	Bacup Borough	L	0	3	
	30	h	LJC 1	Astley Bridge	W	3	0	Crompton 2, Brown
Dec	7	a	League	Clitheroe	L	0	3	
	14	h	League	Southport Reserves	W	5	0	Haslam 2 (1pen), Brewster, Miller, Unknown
	21	h	LJC 2	Netherfield	W	2	0	F Ramsbottom, Spencer
	25	a	League	New Brighton Reserves	L	2	3	Crompton 2
	26	h	League	New Brighton Reserves	W	3	2	Crompton, Hamer, Tait
	28	h	League	Rossendale United	W	4	0	Crompton, Hamer, F Ramsbottom, Opponent
Jan	1	a	League	Accrington Stanley Reserves	L	1	5	Airey
	4	h	League	Marine	W	2	0	F Ramsbottom, E Ramsbottom
	11	h	League	Nelson	W	4	2	Spencer 2, Brewster, Crompton
	18	h	LJC QF	Morecambe	W	3	1	Airey 2, E Ramsbottom
	25	a	League	Lancaster City	W	1	0	Spencer
Mar	1	a	LJC SF	Rochdale Reserves	L	0	2	
	8	a	League	Marine	L	0	3	
	15	h	League	Bacup Borough	L	0	3	
	22	h	League	Barrow Reserves	W	4	3	Airey, Spencer, Unknown 2
	29	a	League	Chorley	W	4	1	Arrowsmith 2, Haslam (pen), Hamer
Apr	5	a	League	Southport Reserves	L	1	2	Spencer
	7	a	League	Rochdale Reserves	L	0	1	
	12	h	League	Clitheroe	D	3	3	F Ramsbottom 2, Abel
	19	h	League	Darwen	W	4	1	E Spencer 2, Haslam, Austin
	23	h	LC 1	Chorley	L	1	6	E Spencer
	26	h	League	Leyland Motors	W	3	1	Hamer, E Spencer, F Ramsbottom
	30	h	League	Rochdale Reserves	L	1	4	Opponent
May	3	h	League	Chorley	W	2	1	Case, Haslam (pen)
	6	a	League	Great Harwood	L	2	5	Unknown 2
	10	a	League	Darwen	L	2	5	E Ramsbottom 2
	14	h	League	Netherfield	D	3	3	E Ramsbottom 2, Opponent
	17	h	League	Bangor City	W	6	0	E Ramsbottom 4, Airey 2
	20	a	League	Oldham Athletic Reserves	L	2	4	Hamer, Haslam
	26	a	League	Fleetwood	L	1	3	E Ramsbottom
	28	h	League	Oldham Athletic Reserves	L	1	3	E Ramsbottom
Jun	7	a	League	Prescot Cables	L	0	2	
						99	107	

1947-48 Lancashire Combination Division 1

Date		H/A	Comp	Opponents	Res	F	A	Goalscorers
Aug	23	a	League	Nelson	L	1	3	F Ramsbottom
	27	h	League	Rossendale United	W	2	0	Spencer, Heyes
	30	h	League	Prescot Cables	D	2	2	Spencer, Crompton
Sep	6	h	League	Rochdale Reserves	D	1	1	Hodson
	9	h	League	Barrow Reserves	W	1	0	Crompton
	13	a	League	New Brighton Reserves	L	1	5	Spencer
	20	h	League	Southport Reserves	W	2	0	Spencer, Crompton
	27	a	League	Lancaster City	L	1	4	Kindred
Oct	4	a	FA Cup 1Q	Leyland Motors	W	2	1	Woodcock, Kindred
	11	a	League	Oldham Athletic Reserves	D	0	0	
	18	a	FA Cup 2Q	Nelson	L	1	4	Haslam (pen)
	25	a	League	Marine	L	2	3	Spencer, Crompton
Nov	1	h	League	Morecambe	W	1	0	Hamer
	8	a	League	Chorley	L	0	1	
	15	h	League	Bangor City	D	3	3	Warburton, Hodson, Crompton
	22	h	League	Marine	W	3	1	Crompton, Robinson, Heyes
	29	h	League	Fleetwood	L	0	3	
Dec	6	a	League	Darwen	L	0	2	
	13	h	League	Clitheroe	L	1	2	Ridings
	20	a	LJC 1	Earlestown	L	4	6	Ridings 2, Robinson, Hodson
	25	a	League	Leyland Motors	L	1	5	Robinson
	26	h	League	Leyland Motors	W	7	2	Howard 3, Warburton 2, Crawshaw, Easey
Jan	1	a	League	Rossendale United	L	2	7	Ridings, Easey
	3	a	League	Prescot Cables	L	1	6	Finch
	10	a	League	Netherfield	L	1	3	Spencer
	24	h	League	Accrington Stanley Reserves	W	3	2	Robinson, Young, Finch (pen)
	31	h	League	New Brighton Reserves	D	2	2	Robinson 2
Feb	7	a	League	Southport Reserves	L	0	3	
	14	h	League	Lancaster City	L	1	2	Spencer
	21	a	League	Accrington Stanley Reserves	L	2	4	Abel, Ridings
	28	h	League	Oldham Athletic Reserves	W	1	0	Hodson
Mar	6	h	League	Wigan Athletic	L	0	1	
	17	h	LC 1	Chorley	W	2	1	Ridings 2
	20	a	League	Morecambe	L	2	3	Ridings, Opponent
	26	h	League	Bacup Borough	W	4	3	Spencer 2, Robinson, Young
	27	h	League	Chorley	L	2	3	Robinson, Ridings
	29	a	League	Bacup Borough	L	0	4	
	31	h	LC 2	Astley & Tyldesley Collieries	W	2	1	Robinson 2
Apr	3	a	League	Bangor City	D	2	2	Robinson 2 (1pen)
	7	a	League	Wigan Athletic	L	0	1	
	10	h	League	Netherfield	L	2	3	Tait, Robinson
	12	h	LC 3	Rossendale United	L	1	4	Holden
	14	h	League	Nelson	D	1	1	Young
	17	a	League	Fleetwood	L	0	1	
	20	a	League	Rochdale Reserves	L	0	7	
	24	h	League	Darwen	W	2	1	Haslam (pen), Robinson
	28	a	League	Barrow Reserves	L	1	6	Unknown
May	1	a	League	Clitheroe	L	0	3	
						70	121	

1948-49 Lancashire Combination Division 2

Aug	21	h	League	Bolton Wanderers 'B'	W	2	1	Benson, Seddon
	28	a	League	Oldham Athletic 'A'	W	4	1	Spencer 2, Benson, Opponent
Sep	4	h	League	Stubshaw Cross Rovers	W	3	2	Haslam (pen), Spencer, Benson
	11	h	League	Lancaster City Reserves	W	1	0	Hankin
	18	a	League	Bootle	W	1	0	Lee
	25	h	League	Nelson Reserves	W	5	1	Benson 2, Seddon 2, Spencer
Oct	2	a	FA Cup 1Q	Clitheroe	L	1	3	Haslam (pen)
	9	a	League	Barnoldswick	L	0	3	
	16	h	League	Darwen Reserves	W	4	0	Haslam (pen), Pearson, Lee, Lennox
	23	a	League	Stubshaw Cross Rovers	W	4	1	Thomas 3, Spencer
	30	h	League	Oldham Athletic 'A'	W	11	2	Thomas 3, Lennox 2, Seddon 2, Spencer, Cronkshaw,
								Haslam (pen), Opponent
Nov	6	a	League	Bolton Wanderers 'B'	W	2	0	Lennox, Cronkshaw
	13	h	League	ACI Horwich	W	5	2	Cronkshaw 2, Benson, Thomas, Spencer
	27	a	LJC 1	Lancaster City	L	1	4	Spencer
Dec	4	a	League	Darwen Reserves	W	4	2	Seddon 2, Spencer, Cronkshaw
	18	a	League	ACI Horwich	W	4	1	Thomas 2, Lennox 2
Jan	1	h	League	Barnoldswick	W	3	0	Lennox, Spencer, Seddon
	8	h	League	Great Harwood	W	5	1	Thomas, Lennox, Benson, Seddon, Opponent
	15	a	League	Great Harwood	W	3	0	Cronkshaw, Seddon, Thomas
	29	h	League	Belle Vue	W	6	2	Lennox 2, Spencer, Cronkshaw, Lee, Thomas
Feb	5	h	CC 1	Bolton Wanderers 'B'	W	2	0	Lennox, Opponent
	12	h	League	Bootle	L	2	3	Cronkshaw, Benson
	19	a	League	Belle Vue	L	0	1	
Mar	5	a	League	Lytham	W	2	1	Spencer, Baines
	12	h	League	Lytham	W	3	2	Baines, Spencer, Brocklehurst
Apr	2	a	League	Nelson Reserves	L	0	1	
	9	a	League	Lancaster City Reserves	D	1	1	Spencer
	11	a	CC 2	Chorley*	D	2	2	Cronkshaw, Seddon
	13	a	CC 2	Chorley	L	1	3	Cronkshaw
* Match Abandoned at full time, no extra-time played								
						82	40	

1949-50　Lancashire Combination Division 1

Date		H/A	Comp	Opponents	Res	F	A	Goalscorers
Aug	20	a	League	Chorley	L	1	2	Baines
	24	h	League	Nelson	D	2	2	Spencer, Baines
	27	h	League	Rossendale United	L	1	4	Baines
	30	a	League	Nelson	L	0	6	
Sep	3	a	League	New Brighton	L	1	3	Ford
	7	h	League	Bangor City	L	0	1	
	10	h	League	Bootle	W	2	0	Spencer, Kay
	14	a	League	Bangor City	L	0	7	
	17	a	FA Cup PR	Rossendale United	L	2	5	Thomas, Edwards
	24	a	League	Prescot Cables	L	2	4	Thomas, Spencer
Oct	1	h	League	Lancaster City	W	3	1	Edwards 3
	8	a	League	Oldham Athletic Reserves	L	0	4	
	15	h	League	Barrow Reserves	D	2	2	Dooley 2
	22	a	League	Morecambe	L	2	5	Spencer, Opponent
	29	h	League	Accrington Stanley Reserves	L	2	3	Baines, Lennox
Nov	5	a	League	Ashton United	L	0	3	
	12	h	League	Clitheroe	L	0	1	
	19	a	LJC 1	Skelmersdale United	L	3	6	Bowman 3
	26	h	League	Oldham Athletic Reserves	L	1	3	Spencer
Dec	3	a	League	Barrow Reserves	L	0	5	
	10	h	League	Wigan Athletic	W	3	2	Haslam (pen), Fearnley, Unknown
	17	h	League	Chorley	L	0	3	
	24	a	League	Rossendale United	L	0	3	
	26	a	League	Marine	L	1	4	Whitter
	31	h	League	New Brighton	W	5	2	Ford 2, Bowman 2, Lythgoe
Jan	7	h	League	Rochdale Reserves	D	3	3	Fearnley 2, Bowman
	14	a	League	Bootle	D	0	0	
	21	a	League	Rochdale Reserves	D	2	2	Bowman 2
	28	h	LC 2	Bolton Wanderers 'B'	W	4	0	Spencer 3, Ford
Feb	4	h	League	Prescot Cables	L	0	3	
	11	a	League	Darwen	D	1	1	Fearnley
	18	a	League	Lancaster City	L	1	3	Wild
	25	h	League	Marine	L	2	5	Fearnley, Curless
Mar	4	a	League	Netherfield	L	2	8	Walkden, Ford
	11	h	League	Morecambe	W	3	1	Haslam (pen), Spencer, Fearnley
	18	a	League	Accrington Stanley Reserves	L	1	2	Spencer
	25	h	League	Ashton United	W	2	1	Haslam (pen), Spencer
Apr	1	a	League	Clitheroe	L	0	2	
	7	h	League	Southport Reserves	L	0	2	
	8	h	League	Darwen	W	1	0	Ford
	10	a	League	Southport Reserves	L	2	3	Unknown 2
	12	h	LC 3	De Havilland	W	5	1	Spencer, Fearnley, Haslam (pen), Bowman, Opponent
	15	a	League	Fleetwood	L	0	4	
	22	h	LC 4	Droylsden United	L	1	6	Unknown
	24	h	League	Netherfield	L	0	3	
	29	a	League	Wigan Athletic	L	0	1	
May	6	h	League	Fleetwood	W	4	0	Mather 2, Fearnley, Spencer
						67	132	

1950-51   Lancashire Combination Division 2

Date		H/A	Comp	Opponents	Res	F	A	Goalscorers
Aug	19	h	League	Hindsford	W	4	1	Spencer, Lord, Coates, Airey
	22	a	League	ACI Horwich	W	7	2	Coates 4, Haslam (pen), Spencer, Opponent
	26	a	League	Leyland Motors	D	4	4	Airey 2, Haslam, Ford
	30	h	League	ACI Horwich	L	2	3	Airey, Spencer
Sep	2	h	League	Padiham	L	0	1	
	6	a	League	Droylsden United	W	4	0	Coates 2, Mather 2
	9	a	League	Darwen Reserves	W	4	1	Mather 2, Spencer 2
	11	h	League	Droylsden United	L	4	5	Coates, Haslam (pen), Unknown 2
	16	a	FA Cup PR	Great Harwood	W	4	1	Mather 2, Coates 2
	23	a	League	Bacup Borough	W	3	0	Spencer, Mather, Grainger (pen)
	30	a	FA Cup 1Q	Rossendale United	L	5	6	Spencer 3, Mather, Coates
Oct	7	h	League	Morecambe Reserves	W	4	0	Airey, Mather, Ford, Coates
	14	a	League	Bolton Wanderers 'B'	W	4	2	Spencer 2, Mather, Coates
	21	h	League	Lomax (Bolton)	W	5	0	Mather 3, Ford, Spencer
	28	a	League	St Helens Town	L	1	2	Mather
Nov	4	h	League	Lytham	W	5	1	Mather 3, Airey, Coates
	11	h	League	Great Harwood	W	8	1	Spencer 2, Coates 2, Mather 2, Ford, Airey
	18	a	LJC 1	Fleetwood	L	2	4	Mather, Coates
	25	a	League	Chorley Reserves	W	6	3	Mather 2, Spencer, Ford, Woodcock, Opponent
Dec	2	h	League	Atherton Collieries	W	3	1	Mather 3
	9	a	League	Stubshaw Cross Rovers	L	2	6	Mather 2
	23	h	League	Leyland Motors	W	2	0	Airey, Mather
Jan	6	h	League	Netherfield Reserves	W	9	0	Mather 4, Spencer 4, Airey
	13	h	League	Darwen Reserves	W	5	2	Spencer 2, Haslam 2 (2pens), Airey
	20	a	League	Wigan Athletic Reserves	W	4	3	Airey 2, Mather, Woodcock
	27	h	League	Wigan Athletic Reserves	W	3	1	Mather 2, Coates
Feb	3	h	League	Bacup Borough	W	2	1	Coates 2
	10	a	League	Hindsford	L	2	3	Grainger (pen), Coates
	17	a	League	Barnoldswick	W	3	0	Airey, Coates, Mather
	24	a	League	Morecambe Reserves	D	3	3	Mather, Coates, Airey
Mar	3	h	League	Bolton Wanderers 'B'	W	2	0	Coates, Grainger (pen)
	10	a	League	Lomax (Bolton)	W	4	2	Smith 2, Spencer 2
	17	h	League	St Helens Town	D	1	1	Grainger (pen)
	23	h	League	Lancaster City Reserves	W	7	2	Coates 2, Mather 2, Woodcock, Grainger (pen), Haslam
	24	a	League	Lytham	L	1	2	Mather
	26	a	League	Lancaster City Reserves	W	7	0	Ford 3, Mather 2, Smith, Fearnley
	31	h	League	Great Harwood	W	6	2	Fearnley 2, Mather 2, Blower, Grainger (pen)
Apr	4	h	LC 2	ACI Horwich	W	3	0	Spencer 2, Mather
	7	a	League	Nelson Reserves	L	2	3	Mather, Lee
	14	h	League	Chorley Reserves	W	3	0	Mather 2, Walkden
	17	a	League	Padiham	D	1	1	Unknown
	18	h	LC 3	Bolton Wanderers 'B'	W	2	0	Mather 2
	21	a	League	Atherton Collieries	W	2	0	Ainsworth, Mather
	24	a	LC 4	Southport Reserves	W	3	2	Mather, Spencer, Ford
	28	h	League	Stubshaw Cross Rovers	W	3	1	Mather, Spencer, Airey
	30	h	League	Nelson Reserves	W	2	0	Spencer, Ford
May	4	h	LC SF	Wigan Athletic	D	2	2	Mather, Spencer
	5	a	League	Netherfield Reserves	W	5	0	Airey 2, Coates 2, Spencer
	8	a	LC SF	Wigan Athletic	L	0	3	
	9	h	League	Barnoldswick	W	5	0	Mather 2, Ford, Halliwell, Coates
						175	78	

1951-52   Lancashire Combination Division 1

Date		H/A	Comp	Opponents	Res	F	A	Goalscorers
Aug	18	h	League	Rochdale Reserves	L	1	5	Grainger (pen)
	22	a	League	Bootle	W	3	0	Laing, Greenhalgh, Grainger (pen)
	25	a	League	Morecambe	D	0	0	
	29	h	League	Bootle	W	4	3	Mather 2, Taylor, Laing
Sep	1	h	League	Netherfield	W	3	2	Mather, Coates, Spencer
	8	a	League	St Helens Town	L	1	3	Coates
	12	a	League	Chorley	L	0	2	
	15	a	FA Cup PR	Chorley	W	5	2	Mather 2, Greenhalgh, Spencer, Woodcock
	17	h	League	Chorley	W	2	1	Mather 2
	22	h	League	Rossendale United	W	4	2	Spencer 2, Greenhalgh 2
	29	a	FA Cup 1Q	Rossendale United	L	2	4	Spencer, Mather
Oct	6	a	League	Darwen	D	1	1	Mather
	13	h	League	New Brighton	L	5	2	Taylor, Edgar, Spencer, Greenhalgh, Opponent
	20	a	League	Fleetwood	L	1	5	Wilson
	27	h	League	Lancaster City	L	0	3	
Nov	3	h	League	Wigan Athletic	L	1	2	Spencer
	10	h	League	Marine	L	1	8	Wilson
	17	a	League	Oldham Athletic Reserves	W	3	0	Mather 2, Spencer
	24	h	League	Clitheroe	W	7	1	Spencer 3, Mather 2, Airey, Laing
Dec	1	a	League	Ashton United	L	1	3	Mather
	8	h	League	Earlestown	W	5	0	Spencer 3, Airey 2
	15	a	LJC 2	Wigan Athletic	L	0	2	
	22	h	League	Morecambe	D	2	2	Airey, Unknown
	25	h	League	Blackpool 'B'	W	3	0	Mather 2, Airey
	26	h	League	Blackpool 'B'	W	4	1	Mather 2, Taylor, Laing
	29	a	League	Netherfield	L	0	2	
Jan	5	h	League	St Helens Town	W	6	2	Mather 2, Laing, Taylor, Spencer, Opponent
	12	h	LC 1	Astley Bridge	W	2	1	Spencer, Mather
	19	a	League	Southport Reserves	L	0	2	
	26	a	League	Rossendale United	W	3	1	Mather 2, Spencer
Feb	2	h	LC 2	Horwich ACI	W	9	0	Grainger 2 (2pens), Mather 2, Spencer 2, Taylor 2, Unknown
	9	h	League	Barrow Reserves	L	1	2	Laing
	16	a	League	Rochdale Reserves	D	4	4	Mather 4
	23	h	League	Southport Reserves	W	4	0	Mather 4
Mar	1	a	League	New Brighton	D	2	2	Spencer, Laing
	8	h	League	Fleetwood	L	1	3	Grainger
	15	a	League	Marine	D	2	2	Mather, Grainger
	22	a	League	Wigan Athletic	D	1	1	Spencer
Apr	5	h	League	Oldham Athletic Reserves	W	4	2	Mather 2, Spencer, Laing
	7	a	LC 3	Bolton Wanderers 'B'	W	3	1	Spencer 2, Aspinall
	11	h	League	Nelson	L	2	5	Mather 2
	12	a	League	Clitheroe	L	1	2	Unknown
	14	a	League	Nelson	L	1	5	Unknown
	16	h	League	Darwen	W	9	1	Mather 4, Ford 3, Airey, Spencer
	19	h	League	Ashton United	W	2	1	Spencer, Laing
	21	a	League	Barrow Reserves	L	1	8	Crompton
	22	h	LC 4	Nelson	W	2	1	Ford, Mather
	23	a	League	Lancaster City	L	1	3	Airey
	25	a	LC SF	Fleetwood	L	0	1	
	26	a	League	Earlestown	L	2	3	Cunliffe, Unknown
						122	109	

1952-53   Lancashire Combination Division 1

Date		H/A	Comp	Opponents	Res	F	A	Goalscorers
Aug	23	a	League	Darwen	L	1	8	Hatsell
	27	h	League	Wigan Athletic	D	4	4	Hatsell, Bailey, Mather, Taylor
	30	h	League	Clitheroe	W	4	0	Mather 2, Hatsell, Peel
Sep	1	a	League	Wigan Athletic	L	0	2	
	6	a	League	Netherfield	W	2	1	Mather, Hatsell
	10	h	League	Prescot Cables	W	2	1	Hatsell, Grainger
	13	a	FA Cup PR	Leyland Motors	W	3	0	Grainger (pen), Peel, Hatsell
	16	a	League	Prescot Cables	L	1	2	Newby
	20	h	League	Rochdale Reserves	W	3	2	Roby 2, Laing
	24	h	LC 1	Astley Bridge	W	8	1	Mather 5, Laing, Roby, Rudd
	27	h	FA Cup 1Q	Chorley	W	5	3	Roby 2, Hatsell 2, Mather
Oct	4	a	League	Lancaster City	W	2	1	Mather, Grainger (pen)
	11	a	FA Cup 2Q	Ashton United	L	1	2	Grainger
	18	h	League	Bootle	W	5	4	Roby 3, Mather, Taylor
	25	a	League	Bootle	W	2	0	Mather 2
Nov	1	h	League	Accrington Stanley Reserves	L	1	4	Roby
	8	a	League	Accrington Stanley Reserves	D	4	4	Roby 2, Grainger (pen), Bailey
	15	a	LJC 1	Lancaster City	L	1	3	Mather
	22	a	League	Nelson	L	0	3	
	29	h	League	Blackpool 'B'	W	3	1	Roby, Dickinson, Hatsell
Dec	13	h	League	New Brighton	W	3	1	Ainscough 2, Hatsell
	20	a	League	Darwen	D	3	3	Grainger 2 (2pens), Hatsell
	25	a	League	Southport Reserves	D	1	1	Roby
	27	h	League	Southport Reserves	D	2	2	Grainger (pen), Hatsell
Jan	3	a	League	Clitheroe	W	4	2	Mather 4
	10	a	League	Ashton United	L	3	6	Mather 2, Hatsell
	17	h	League	Netherfield	L	3	6	Roby 2, Mather
	24	a	League	Rossendale United	W	6	2	Mather 5, Roby
	31	h	League	Rossendale United	W	4	3	Roby 3, Hankinson
Feb	7	a	League	Rochdale Reserves	D	3	3	Roby, Mather, Grainger (pen)
	14	h	League	Marine	D	5	5	Mather 3, Roby 2
	21	a	League	Lancaster City	L	3	4	Mather 2, Hatsell
	28	h	League	Oldham Athletic Reserves	W	4	2	Mather 2, Roby 2
Mar	14	h	League	Morecambe	D	2	2	Roby, Hatsell
	21	a	League	New Brighton	W	3	0	Mather, Hatsell, Grainger (pen)
	25	a	LC 2	Bolton Wanderers 'B'	D	3	3	Roby, Hatsell, Mather
	28	h	League	Ashton United	D	4	4	Roby, Hatsell, Mather, Grainger (pen)
	30	h	LC 2	Bolton Wanderers 'B'	W	2	0	Mather, Roby
Apr	3	a	League	Fleetwood	L	0	3	
	4	a	League	Chorley	W	4	0	Mather 2, Taylor 2
	6	h	League	Fleetwood	W	8	0	Mather 4, Hankinson 3, Bailey
	9	h	League	Barrow Reserves	D	1	1	Roby
	11	h	League	Nelson	D	0	0	
	13	h	LC 3	Clitheroe	W	11	0	Mather 4, Roby 3, Hankinson, Rudd, Bailey, Grainger (pen)
	15	h	League	Chorley	W	4	3	Mather 2, Roby, Hankinson
	18	a	League	Blackpool 'B'	D	1	1	Mather
	20	a	LC SF	Wigan Athletic	L	0	1	
	22	a	League	Marine	L	0	4	
	25	h	League	Barrow Reserves	D	2	2	Roby, Mather
	27	a	League	Oldham Athletic Reserves	L	1	4	Taylor
	29	a	League	Morecambe	L	1	4	Ainscough
						143	118	

1953-54   Lancashire Combination Division 1

Date		H/A	Comp	Opponents	Res	F	A	Goalscorers	Notes
Aug	19	h	League	Lancaster City	W	3	1	Hazelton, Foster, Roby	
	22	a	League	Rossendale United	L	1	2	Mather	
	25	a	League	New Brighton	W	2	1	Foster, Hazelton	
	29	h	League	Chorley	W	1	0	Grainger (pen)	
Sep	2	h	League	New Brighton	W	5	1	Mather 2, Taylor, Grainger (pen), Roby	
	5	a	League	Rochdale Reserves	W	3	0	Mather 2, Roby	
	8	h	LC 1	Lomax (Bolton)	W	3	1	Mather, Foster, Hazelton	
	12	h	League	Nelson	W	5	2	Mather 2, Taylor 2, Seddon	
	14	a	League	Nelson	D	2	2	Foster, Taylor	
	19	a	League	Wigan Athletic	L	1	2	Mather	
	23	a	League	Accrington Stanley Reserves	L	1	2	Mather	
	26	h	FA Cup 1Q	Darwen	D	1	1	Grainger (pen)	
	29	h	FA Cup 1Q	Darwen	L	2	3	Roby, Hill	AET
Oct	3	a	League	Ashton United	W	2	0	Roby, Mather	
	10	a	League	Oldham Athletic Reserves	L	1	4	Grainger (pen)	
	17	h	League	Southport Reserves	W	2	0	Ford, Mather	
	24	a	League	South Liverpool	L	2	5	Foster, Ford	
	31	h	League	Darwen	L	2	4	Grainger 2 (2pens)	
Nov	7	a	League	Fleetwood	L	3	4	Ford, Roby, Mather	
	14	h	League	Prescot Cables	L	1	3	Mather	
	21	a	League	Netherfield	W	5	0	Flatters 2, Ford 2, Roby	
	28	h	League	Marine	W	4	1	Flatters 3, Unknown	
Dec	5	a	League	Bolton Wanderers 'B'	L	2	3	Ford, Flatters	
	12	a	League	Lancaster City	L	0	3		
	19	h	League	Rossendale United	W	4	0	Roby 2, Evans, Flatters	
	25	h	League	Bolton Wanderers 'B'	W	2	1	Bailey, Grainger (pen)	
Jan	2	a	League	Chorley	D	1	1	Bailey	
	9	h	LC 2	Darwen	W	1	0	Roby	
	16	h	League	Rochdale Reserves	W	3	1	Roby, Grainger (pen), Kenny	
	23	a	LJC 1	Skelmersdale United	D	4	4	Mather 2, Kenny, Opponent	
	30	h	LJC 1	Skelmersdale United	W	1	0	Roby	
Feb	6	h	League	Wigan Athletic	L	1	3	Roby	
	13	a	LJC 2	Fleetwood	W	2	1	Mather 2	
	20	h	League	Ashton United	W	8	1	Mather 4, Kenny 2, Flatters, Grainger (pen)	
	27	h	League	Oldham Athletic Reserves	D	1	1	Mather	
Mar	6	a	League	Southport Reserves	W	3	1	Grainger (pen), Bailey, Opponent	
	13	h	League	South Liverpool	W	1	0	Grainger (pen)	
	20	a	LJC 3	Burscough	W	2	0	Mather 2	
	27	h	League	Fleetwood	W	4	2	Taylor, Grainger (pen), Mather, Roby	
Apr	3	a	League	Prescot Cables	W	2	0	Mather, Evans	
	4	h	League	Barrow Reserves	W	5	0	Roby 2, Mather, Downes (pen), Bailey	
	10	a	LJC SF	Chorley	W	2	1	Grainger (pen), Mather	
	14	h	LC 3	Fleetwood	W	4	0	Mather 2, Roby, Taylor	
	16	a	League	Morecambe	D	1	1	Mather	
	17	a	League	Marine	D	1	1	Mather	
	19	h	League	Morecambe	W	6	0	Butler 3, Roby 2, Flatters	
	21	1	LJC Final	Wigan Athletic	D	2	2	Butler, Mather	
	23	h	League	Accrington Stanley Reserves	W	3	0	Evans, Mather, Opponent	

Season details continued on next page

1953-54   Lancashire Combination continued

Date		H/A	Comp	Opponents	Res	F	A	Goalscorers
	26	a	LC Semi-Final	Wigan Athletic	D	1	1	Mather
	27	a	League	Darwen	L	0	2	
	28	h	LC Semi-Final	Wigan Athletic	W	3	2	Flatters 2, Mather
	29	a	League	Barrow Reserves	L	0	4	
	30	h	LC Final	Chorley	W	1	0	Butler
	30	2	League	Netherfield	L	1	6	Unknown
May	5	3	LJC Final	Wigan Athletic	L	1	2	Taylor
						125	83	
	1 at Blackburn Rovers							
	2 Home game at De Havilland FC (Two games on one day)							
	3 at Chorley FC							

1954-55 Lancashire Combination Division 1

Date		H/A	Comp	Opponents	Res	F	A	Goalscorers
Aug	21	h	League	Rochdale Reserves	D	2	2	Mather, Downes
	25	h	League	Burscough	L	0	2	
	28	a	League	Wigan Athletic	L	0	2	
Sep	1	a	League	Burscough	L	0	2	
	4	h	League	South Liverpool	W	7	1	Mather 3, Butler 2, Grainger (pen), Opponent
	8	h	League	Bolton Wanderers 'B'	L	1	2	Butler
	11	h	FA Cup PR	Skelmersdale United	W	1	0	Butler
	13	a	LC 1	Chorley	L	3	8	Butler 3
	18	h	League	Lancaster City	L	2	4	Roby, Butler
	25	h	FA Cup 1Q	Darwen	L	0	1	
Oct	2	h	League	Ashton United	D	2	2	Flatters 2
	9	a	League	Oldham Athletic Reserves	D	2	2	Butler 2
	16	h	League	Marine	W	3	2	Roby 3
	23	a	League	New Brighton	W	4	2	Butler 2, Kenny, Mather
	30	h	League	Barrow Reserves	W	5	0	Roby 2, Butler 2, Mather
Nov	6	a	League	Morecambe	D	0	0	
	13	h	League	Southport Reserves	W	2	1	Kenny, Butler
	20	a	League	Chorley	W	2	0	Mather, Evans
	27	h	League	Accrington Stanley Reserves	L	2	3	Mather, Downes
Dec	4	a	League	Blackpool 'B'	L	0	2	
	11	h	League	Nelson	W	2	0	Mather, Butler
	18	a	League	Rochdale Reserves	D	1	1	Mather
	25	a	League	Darwen	L	0	1	
	27	h	League	Darwen	W	4	0	Kenny 2, Mather, Butler
Jan	1	h	League	Wigan Athletic	W	3	0	Downes (pen), Taylor, Butler
	8	a	League	Fleetwood	D	1	1	Mather
	22	h	LJC 1	Netherfield	W	3	2	Roby 2, Kenny
	29	h	League	Fleetwood	W	1	0	Atherton
Feb	5	a	League	Lancaster City	D	0	0	
	12	a	LJC 2	Darwen	W	3	1	Roby 2, Evans
	19	a	League	Ashton United	W	3	0	Roby, Butler, Opponent
Mar	5	a	League	Marine	W	2	1	Taylor, Roby
	12	h	League	New Brighton	W	4	1	Roby 3, Kenny
	19	h	LJC 3	Wigan Athletic	L	1	3	Atherton
	26	h	League	Morecambe	W	7	2	Roby 2, Atherton 2, Butler 2, Evans
	30	h	League	Oldham Athletic Reserves	W	4	3	Butler 2, Roby, Atherton
Apr	2	a	League	Southport Reserves	L	2	3	Rudd, Roby
	8	a	League	Rossendale United	D	2	2	Butler 2
	9	h	League	Chorley	W	1	0	Roby
	11	h	League	Rossendale United	W	2	1	Butler, Roby
	12	a	League	Barrow Reserves	L	1	4	Mather
	16	a	League	Accrington Stanley Reserves	L	0	2	
	20	h	League	Netherfield	W	2	1	Evans (pen), Butler
	23	h	League	Blackpool 'B'	L	1	4	Evans
	25	a	League	South Liverpool	W	2	1	Unknown 2
	28	a	League	Netherfield	L	0	2	
	30	a	League	Nelson	L	0	3	
May	2	a	League	Bolton Wanderers 'B'	W	2	0	Butler 2
						92	77	

1955-56   Lancashire Combination Division 1

Date		H/A	Comp	Opponents	Res	F	A	Goalscorers	Notes
Aug	20	h	League	Darwen	W	2	1	Butler, Francis	
	22	a	League	Wigan Athletic	D	0	0		
	27	a	League	Marine	L	0	1		
	31	h	League	Wigan Athletic	W	4	1	Coop 2, Francis, Kenny	
Sep	3	a	League	Netherfield	L	1	3	Roby	
	7	a	LC 1	Crompton's Recs	L	1	2	Unknown	
	10	h	FA Cup PR	Skelmersdale United	W	3	2	Roby 2, Evans	
	17	a	League	Lancaster City	W	2	0	Butler, Opponent	
	24	a	FA Cup 1Q	Leyland Motors	L	0	1		
Oct	1	a	League	St Helens Town	W	4	2	Berry 2, Butler, Roby	
	8	h	League	Accrington Stanley Reserves	W	3	2	Evans, Roby, Coop	
	15	a	League	Nelson	L	2	3	Coop, Kenny	
	22	h	League	Chorley	D	2	2	Coop, Kenny	
	29	a	League	Bacup Borough	W	2	0	Coop, Butler	
Nov	5	h	League	Nelson	W	5	1	Lomax 3, Butler, Bailey	
	12	a	League	Burscough	L	1	3	Lomax	
	19	h	League	Morecambe	W	3	2	Lomax 2, Butler	
	26	a	League	Prescot Cables	W	7	2	Lomax 4, Coop 2, Butler	
Dec	3	h	League	South Liverpool	W	7	2	Lomax 3, Butler 2, Evans, Coop	
	10	h	League	Ashton United	W	3	0	Lomax 2, Coop	
	17	a	League	Darwen	D	3	3	Evans, Butler, Lomax	
	24	h	League	Marine	W	4	0	Lomax 2, Coop, Evans	
	26	a	League	Accrington Stanley Reserves	W	5	1	Coop 3, Butler, Lomax	
	31	h	League	Netherfield	W	2	0	Coop, Lomax	
Jan	14	a	League	Ashton United	W	2	1	Butler, Coop	
	21	a	LJC 1	Wigan Athletic	Ab	1	1	Lomax	Ab 75'
	28	a	LJC 1	Wigan Athletic	L	0	4		
Feb	4	a	League	Southport Reserves	D	1	1	Butler	
	11	h	League	St Helens Town	W	4	2	Roby 2, Kenny, Evans	
	18	a	League	Rossendale United	D	2	2	Butler 2	
	25	h	League	Fleetwood	W	7	1	Taylor 3, Roby, Butler, Kenny, Lomax	
Mar	3	a	League	Chorley	W	3	1	Roby, Lomax, Kenny	
	10	h	League	Bacup Borough	D	4	4	Kenny, Lomax, Taylor, Roby	
	17	a	League	New Brighton	W	1	0	Lomax	
	24	h	League	Burscough	L	0	1		
	31	a	League	Morecambe	D	1	1	Roby	
Apr	2	a	League	Fleetwood	D	1	1	Roby	
	11	h	League	Prescot Cables	W	4	2	Lomax 2, Holland, Kenny	
	14	h	League	South Liverpool	W	3	0	Lomax, Roby, Taylor	
	21	h	League	Southport Reserves	W	2	0	Roby, Evans	
	25	h	League	New Brighton	D	1	1	Unknown	
	28	h	League	Lancaster City	W	3	2	Roby, Butler, Rudd	
May	2	h	League	Rossendale United	W	3	0	Taylor, Unknown 2	
						109	59		

1956-57 Lancashire Combination Division 1

Date		H/A	Comp	Opponents	Res	F	A	Goalscorers
Aug	18	a	League	Droylsden	L	1	2	Lomax
	25	h	League	Darwen	W	4	0	Lomax, Evans, Holland, Coop
	29	h	LC 1	Ashton United	W	3	2	Lomax 2, Evans
Sep	1	a	League	Fleetwood	L	2	3	Evans, Kenny
	3	h	League	Prescot Cables	W	3	2	Lomax, Rudd, Opponent
	8	a	FA Cup PR	Lytham	W	7	1	Lomax 4, Butler 2, Evans
	15	a	League	Marine	L	1	2	Roby
	19	h	LC 2	Southport Reserves	W	2	1	Evans 2 (1pen)
	22	h	FA Cup 1Q	Skelmersdale United	W	2	1	Evans, Makin
	29	h	League	Ashton United	W	4	1	Coop 3, Evans
Oct	6	h	FA Cup 2Q	Chorley	W	3	0	Kenny, Evans, Coop
	13	a	League	Netherfield	W	3	1	Lomax, Butler, Makin
	20	h	FA Cup 3Q	Mossley	W	1	0	Coop
	27	a	League	Nelson	W	2	1	Evans 2
Nov	3	a	FA Cup 4Q	Morecambe	L	2	3	Makin, Evans
	10	a	League	Bacup Borough	D	3	3	Lomax 2, Butler
	17	h	League	Lancaster City	W	2	1	Coop, Makin
	24	a	League	Southport Reserves	W	1	0	Lomax
Dec	1	h	League	Morecambe	W	4	2	Coop 3, Butler
	8	h	League	Netherfield	W	5	0	Butler 2, Kenny, Lomax, Coop
	15	h	League	Droylsden	W	10	0	Butler 3, Coop 3, Kenny 2, Lomax, Makin
	22	a	League	Darwen	W	3	1	Butler 2, Rudd
	25	h	League	Chorley	W	4	1	Coop 2, Lomax, Evans
	29	h	League	Fleetwood	W	2	0	Coop, Holland
Jan	1	h	League	Accrington Stanley Reserves	W	5	0	Coop 3, Makin, Lomax
	5	h	League	South Liverpool	L	1	2	Evans
	12	a	League	Prescot Cables	L	2	7	Coop 2
	19	a	LJC 1	Nelson	W	7	1	Kenny 3, Lomax 2, Coop, Makin
	26	a	League	South Liverpool	W	2	0	Makin, Coop
Feb	2	h	League	Wigan Athletic	W	3	2	Makin 2, Butler
	9	a	League	Ashton United	L	1	6	Coop
	16	a	League	Skelmersdale United	W	4	1	Coop, Billington, Butler, Brocklehurst
	23	h	LJC 2	Clitheroe	W	2	0	Makin 2 (1pen)
Mar	2	a	League	Accrington Stanley Reserves	W	1	0	Coop
	9	h	League	Nelson	W	3	0	Kenny, Coop, Butler
	16	h	LJC 3	Darwen	D	1	1	Coop
	23	a	LJC 3	Darwen	L	1	3	Butler
	27	h	League	Skelmersdale United	L	0	1	
	30	a	League	Lancaster City	L	0	1	
Apr	3	h	LC 3	Darwen	W	3	1	Makin 2, Coop
	6	h	League	Southport Reserves	W	3	0	Lomax 2, Butler
	8	h	LC SF 1st Leg	Rossendale United	W	4	2	Butler, Lomax, Coop, Kenny
	10	h	League	New Brighton	D	2	2	Kenny, Lomax
	13	a	League	Morecambe	L	0	4	
	16	a	LC SF 2nd Leg	Rossendale United	W	3	0	Coop 2, Taylor
	19	a	League	Burscough	L	0	3	
	20	h	League	Marine	W	5	1	Lomax 3, Butler 2
	22	h	League	Burscough	W	2	0	Brocklehurst, Lomax
	24	a	League	New Brighton	L	0	1	
	26	h	LC Final 1st Leg	Morecambe	W	2	1	Lomax 2
	27	a	League	Chorley	L	1	7	Lyon
	29	a	League	Wigan Athletic	L	1	9	Billington
	30	a	LC Final 2nd Leg	Morecambe	D	0	0	
May	1	h	League	Bacup Borough	D	3	3	Horrocks, Lomax, Butler
						136	87	

1957-58 Lancashire Combination Division 1

Date		H/A	Comp	Opponents	Res	F	A	Goalscorers
Aug	24	h	League	Skelmersdale United	W	3	1	Adams, Makin, Wignall
	31	a	League	Fleetwood	L	0	1	
Sep	4	a	League	Morecambe	D	0	0	
	7	h	FA Cup PR	Mossley	D	1	1	Speakman
	9	h	League	Darwen	W	6	1	Speakman 3, Makin, Wignall, Robinson
	11	a	FA Cup PR	Mossley	L	1	2	Speakman
	14	a	League	Burscough	W	2	1	Wignall 2
	18	h	League	Burscough	W	6	1	Wignall 2, Taylor 2 (2pens), Bateson, Kenny
	21	h	League	Wigan Athletic	W	1	0	Wignall
	25	h	LC 1	Glossop	W	3	1	Speakman, Bateson, Opponent
	28	a	League	Wigan Athletic	L	2	3	Wignall, Taylor (pen)
Oct	5	a	League	Droylsden	W	3	2	Speakman, Wignall, Bateson
	12	h	League	Prescot Cables	W	2	0	Wignall, Bateson
	19	a	League	Nelson	D	2	2	Bateson, Speakman
	26	a	League	Southport Reserves	W	4	1	Jones 2, Speakman, Bateson
Nov	2	a	League	Netherfield	D	2	2	Wignall, Speakman
	9	h	League	Rossendale United	W	2	1	Wignall, Bateson
	16	a	League	Bacup Borough	D	1	1	Wignall
	23	h	League	New Brighton	W	2	1	Speakman, Jones
	30	a	League	Accrington Stanley Reserves	D	2	2	Jones 2
Dec	7	h	League	Lancaster City	W	4	1	Speakman 4
	14	a	League	Ashton United	D	2	2	Wignall 2
	21	a	League	Skelmersdale United	W	2	1	Jones, Bateson
	26	a	League	South Liverpool	W	2	1	Speakman, Wignall
	28	h	League	Fleetwood	W	3	0	Jones 2, Wignall
Jan	1	h	League	Morecambe	W	7	1	Brocklehurst 2, Speakman, Cozens, Wignall, Jones, Bateson
	4	h	League	Netherfield	L	0	1	
	11	a	League	Darwen	W	4	2	Wignall 3, Brocklehurst
	18	h	LJC 1	St Helens Town	W	6	1	Wignall 3, Jones 2, Cozens
Feb	1	a	League	Crompton's Recs	W	2	1	Speakman, Cozens
	8	h	League	Accrington Stanley Reserves	W	5	1	Wignall 2, Jones 2, Bateson
	15	h	League	Droylsden	W	5	1	Rudd 2 (2pens), Speakman, Bateson, Opponent
	22	a	LJC 2	Marine	D	2	2	Rudd, Wignall
Mar	1	h	LJC 2	Marine	W	4	0	Kenny 2, Wignall, Jones
	8	a	League	Southport Reserves	W	2	0	Jones, Robinson
	15	h	LJC 3	Lancaster City	W	4	0	Kenny, Jones, Bateson, Opponent
	22	a	League	Rossendale United	L	2	4	Jones, Robinson
	26	h	League	Crompton's Recs	W	2	0	Jones, Bateson
	29	h	League	Bacup Borough	W	3	1	Kenny, Speakman, Wignall
	31	h	LC 2	Rossendale United	W	3	2	Wignall 2, Kenny
Apr	4	a	League	Marine	W	3	1	Wignall 2, Kenny
	5	a	League	New Brighton	D	0	0	
	7	h	League	Marine	L	0	1	
	9	a	LC 3	Ashton United	L	0	2	
	12	h	LJC SF	Burscough	W	1	0	Wignall
	14	a	League	Chorley	W	2	1	Wignall, Jones
	16	h	League	Chorley	L	0	1	
	19	a	League	Lancaster City	W	3	1	Wignall, Jones, Speakman
	21	h	League	Nelson	W	5	0	Wignall 3, Jones, Bateson
	23	h	League	South Liverpool	W	3	0	Speakman, Rudd (pen), Wignall
	26	h	League	Ashton United	W	7	1	Wignall 2, Jones 2, Rudd, Bateson, Speakman
	30	1	LJC Final	Chorley	L	0	1	
May	2	a	League	Prescot Cables	L	1	4	Opponent
		1	at Blackburn Rovers FC			134	59	

1958-59   Lancashire Combination Division 1

Date		H/A	Comp	Opponents	Res	F	A	Goalscorers
Aug	23	a	League	Lancaster City	D	2	2	Speakman, Bateson
	27	h	League	Skelmersdale United	W	4	3	Rudd 2 (2pens), Butler, Kenny
	30	h	League	Droylsden	W	5	1	Marren 2, Cozens, Butler, Opponent
Sep	2	a	League	Skelmersdale United	L	1	2	Cozens
	6	a	FA Cup PR	Crompton's Recs	W	4	1	Butler, Speakman, Bateson, Rudd (pen)
	8	a	League	Wigan Athletic	W	3	2	Marren 3
	13	h	LC 1	Lomax (Bolton)	W	7	1	Marren 3, Cozens 2, Butler 2
	17	h	League	Southport Reserves	W	3	0	Marren, Butler, Kenny
	20	a	FA Cup 1Q	Chorley	L	1	2	Cozens
	23	a	League	Fleetwood	W	2	0	Kenny, Cozens
	27	a	League	Chorley	L	1	3	Butler
Oct	1	h	LC 2	Crompton's Recs	W	7	1	Marren 3, Speakman 2, Cozens, Rudd
	4	h	League	Oldham Athletic Reserves	W	5	1	Speakman 2, Bateson, Cozens, Marren
	11	h	League	Morecambe	D	3	3	Cozens 2, Speakman
	18	a	League	Prescot Cables	D	2	2	Speakman, Marren
	25	h	League	Marine	W	4	1	Marren, Rudd (pen), Cozens, Dean
Nov	1	a	League	Burscough	D	1	1	Speakman
	8	h	League	Ashton United	W	3	1	Marren 2, Cozens
	15	a	League	New Brighton	L	0	2	
	22	h	League	Darwen	W	2	1	Rudd, Marren
	29	a	League	Clitheroe	W	2	0	Marren, Kenny
Dec	6	h	League	Fleetwood	W	3	1	Marren, Speakman, Butler
	13	a	League	Netherfield	W	2	0	Butler, Marren
	20	h	League	Lancaster City	D	1	1	Marren
	26	h	League	South Liverpool	W	4	0	Marren 2, Kenny, Speakman
	27	a	League	South Liverpool	W	2	1	Marren 2
Jan	1	h	League	Netherfield	L	2	4	Marren, Butler
	3	a	League	Droylsden	W	1	0	Butler
	24	h	LJC 1	Padiham	D	3	3	Marren, Butler, Rudd
	31	a	LJC 1	Padiham	W	1	0	Marren
Feb	7	a	League	Nelson	W	2	0	Marren, Speakman
	14	h	League	Chorley	W	2	1	Marren, Bateson
	28	a	League	Morecambe	L	0	3	
Mar	7	h	League	Prescot Cables	D	1	1	Marren
	14	a	League	Marine	D	1	1	Jones
	21	a	LJC 2	Wigan Athletic	L	1	3	Marren
	27	a	League	Rossendale United	W	2	1	Marren, Jones
	28	a	League	Ashton United	D	3	3	Marren 2, Speakman
	30	h	League	Rossendale United	W	4	1	Marren 3, Speakman
Apr	4	h	League	New Brighton	L	1	2	Bateson
	8	h	LC 3	Netherfield	W	3	1	Speakman, Marren, Cozens
	11	a	League	Darwen	W	2	1	Rudd, Marren
	13	h	League	Wigan Athletic	L	0	1	
	15	h	League	Burscough	W	2	1	Bateson, Marren
	18	h	League	Clitheroe	W	4	0	Marren 2, Kenny, Jones
	20	h	League	Nelson	D	2	2	Bateson, Marren
	21	h	LC SF	Rossendale United	W	3	0	Bateson 2, Marren
	22	h	League	Bacup Borough	L	3	5	Marren 2, Kenny
	25	a	League	Southport Reserves	W	3	0	Marren 2, Jones
	27	a	League	Oldham Athletic Reserves	W	3	1	Marren, Jones, Kenny
	30	a	League	Bacup Borough	W	2	1	Bateson 2
May	7	a	LC Final	Chorley	L	0	2	
						125	71	

1959-60 Lancashire Combination Division 1

Date		H/A	Comp	Opponents	Res	F	A	Goalscorers
Aug	22	h	League	Fleetwood	W	5	1	Pearson 3, Marren, D Jones
	25	a	League	New Brighton	W	2	1	Pearson, Bateson
	29	a	League	Darwen	D	2	2	Marren, Kenny
Sep	2	h	League	New Brighton	D	2	2	D Jones 2
	5	h	League	Southport Reserves	W	3	1	Marren 2, Banks (pen)
	7	a	LC 1	Lomax (Bolton)	W	5	2	Marren 3, Banks (pen), Hayes
	12	a	League	Oldham Athletic Reserves	W	2	1	Marren, Opponent
	16	a	League	South Liverpool	D	1	1	Marren
	19	h	FA Cup 1Q	Bacup Borough	L	1	2	Marren
	26	h	League	Burscough	W	3	1	Marren, Prescott, Hughes
	28	a	LC 2	Chorley	L	1	3	Barcroft
Oct	3	a	League	Wigan Athletic	L	2	3	Marren, Banks
	10	h	League	Wigan Athletic	L	2	3	D Jones, Pearson (pen)
	17	a	League	Bacup Borough	W	6	0	Marren 3, Prescott, D Jones, Hayes
	24	h	League	Nelson	W	2	1	Parkin, Hayes
	31	a	League	Rossendale United	L	2	3	Banks, Prescott
Nov	7	h	League	Chorley	L	0	3	
	14	a	League	Netherfield	W	4	1	Prescott, Pearson, Hayes, Opponent
	21	h	League	Prescot Cables	D	2	2	D Jones, Prescott
	28	a	League	Lancaster City	D	0	0	
Dec	5	h	League	Skelmersdale United	W	5	1	Pearson 2, A Jones 2, D Jones
	12	a	League	Ashton United	L	0	2	
	19	a	League	Fleetwood	L	1	4	Prescott
	26	a	League	Southport Reserves	D	1	1	Marren
Jan	2	h	League	Darwen	L	0	5	
	16	a	LJC 1	Prescot Cables	D	1	1	D Jones
	23	h	LJC 1	Prescot Cables	W	1	0	Prescott
	30	h	League	Marine	L	3	4	Hayes 2, D Jones
Feb	5	h	League	South Liverpool	W	4	2	Kenny, Marren, Prescott, Opponent
	13	a	LJC 2	Rossendale United	D	3	3	Pearson 2, Marren
	20	h	LJC 2	Rossendale United	L	4	5	Pearson 2, Marren, Kenny
Mar	5	h	League	Bacup Borough	D	2	2	K Jones, Marren
	12	a	League	Nelson	L	1	2	K Jones
	19	h	League	Oldham Athletic Reserves	L	2	4	Kenny, D Jones
	26	a	League	Chorley	L	1	4	Marren
Apr	2	h	League	Netherfield	W	3	2	Birchall, Bateson, K Jones
	9	a	League	Prescot Cables	L	0	1	
	11	h	League	Rossendale United	W	3	0	Birchall 2, Marren
	15	h	League	Morecambe	W	1	0	Kenny
	16	h	League	Lancaster City	W	5	2	Marren 2, Birchall, Bateson, Kenny
	18	a	League	Morecambe	L	0	2	
	20	a	League	Marine	W	2	1	Marren, Birchall
	23	a	League	Skelmersdale United	L	0	3	
	25	a	League	Earlestown	L	0	2	
	27	h	League	Lytham	L	1	2	Kenny
	30	h	League	Ashton United	W	3	0	Jones, Birchall, Bateson
May	2	a	League	Lytham	W	1	0	A Jones
	4	h	League	Earlestown	D	1	1	T Smith
	6	a	League	Burscough	L	2	3	Birchall 2
						98	92	

1960-61 Lancashire Combination Division 1

Aug	20	a	League	Skelmersdale United	W	4	2	Cunliffe 2, Birkett, Davies
	22	a	League	Earlestown	D	2	2	Bateson, Cunliffe
	25	h	LC 1	Oldham Athletic Reserves	W	3	2	Cunliffe 2, Birchall
	27	h	League	Marine	W	4	2	Birchall, Bateson, Birkett, Cunliffe
	31	h	League	Earlestown	L	0	3	
Sep	3	a	League	Clitheroe	L	0	1	
	7	h	League	Fleetwood	W	4	1	Birchall, Kenny, Davies, Banks
	10	a	FA Cup 1Q	Marine	L	0	2	
	14	h	League	Clitheroe	W	4	2	Birkett 2, Cunliffe, Smith
	17	a	League	Lytham	L	1	2	Birchall
	21	h	LC 2	Chorley	L	3	4	Cunliffe 2, Birkett
	24	h	League	Darwen	W	4	1	Cunliffe 2, Robinson, Birkett
Oct	1	a	League	Prescot Cables	L	1	2	Birchall
	8	a	League	Droylsden	D	2	2	Birchall 2
	15	h	League	Bacup Borough	W	5	1	Cunliffe 2, Birkett, Kenny, Bateson
	22	a	League	Oldham Athletic Reserves	L	1	4	Cunliffe
	29	h	League	Nelson	L	2	3	Bateson, Cunliffe
Nov	5	a	League	Rossendale United	L	1	6	Cunliffe
	12	h	League	New Brighton	L	1	3	Gregory
	19	a	League	Chorley	L	0	5	
	26	h	League	Droylsden	W	3	2	Entwistle, Lea, Bateson
Dec	3	a	League	Morecambe	D	2	2	Entwistle, O'Donnell
	10	h	League	Burscough	W	2	0	Banks, Entwistle (pen)
	17	h	League	Skelmersdale United	W	4	0	Entwistle 2, Banks, Bateson
	24	a	League	Wigan Athletic	L	1	5	Unknown
	26	h	League	Wigan Athletic	L	0	1	
	31	a	League	Marine	L	0	2	
Jan	7	a	League	Ashton United	W	1	0	Lea
	21	a	LJC 1	Wigan Rovers	W	2	0	Gregory, Entwistle
	28	h	League	Ashton United	L	1	2	O'Donnell
Feb	4	h	League	Lytham	D	3	3	O'Donnell, Lea, Entwistle
	18	h	LJC 2	Morecambe	L	2	3	Lea, Sharrock
	25	h	League	Netherfield	L	1	3	Pritchard
Mar	4	a	League	Bacup Borough	L	1	5	Bromilow
	11	h	League	Oldham Athletic Reserves	L	1	3	Bateson
	18	a	League	Nelson	L	1	2	Robinson
	25	h	League	Rossendale United	W	4	1	Robinson, Livesey, Sharrock, Cunliffe (pen)
	31	a	League	Lancaster City	L	0	2	
Apr	1	a	League	New Brighton	L	0	6	
	3	h	League	Lancaster City	D	2	2	Chester, Hull
	10	h	League	Chorley	L	1	3	Bateson
	12	a	League	Darwen	W	5	3	Cunliffe 3, Connelly, Opponent
	17	h	League	Prescot Cables	W	2	1	Cunliffe 2
	22	h	League	Morecambe	D	1	1	Kenny
	27	a	League	Netherfield	D	2	2	Livesey, Bateson
	29	a	League	Burscough	L	0	1	
May	2	a	League	Fleetwood	W	1	0	Bateson
						85	105	

1961-62   Lancashire Combination Division 1

Date		H/A	Comp	Opponents	Res	F	A	Goalscorers
Aug	19	a	League	Padiham	W	2	0	Robinson, Connelly
	23	h	League	Skelmersdale United	W	1	0	Waller
	26	h	League	Leyland Motors	W	6	2	Taberner 2, Twidle 2, Waller, Opponent
	31	a	League	Skelmersdale United	W	2	1	Twidle, Waller
Sep	2	a	IL Cup 1	Runcorn	W	3	2	Twidle, Taberner, Waller
	6	a	League	Marine	W	3	1	Twidle, Taberner, Waller
	9	h	FA Cup 1Q	Ashton United	L	0	2	
	13	h	League	Marine	W	4	0	Connelly, Bateson, Taberner, Waller
	16	a	League	Rossendale United	W	2	0	Connelly, Twidle
	18	h	IL Cup 2	Mossley	W	1	0	Twidle
	20	a	League	Nelson	D	1	1	Bateson
	23	h	League	Oldham Athletic Reserves	W	1	0	Bateson
	30	h	League	Lancaster City	D	1	1	Bateson
Oct	7	a	League	Morecambe	L	0	4	
	14	h	League	Clitheroe	D	2	2	Connelly, Opponent
	21	a	League	Netherfield	D	4	4	Waller, Taberner, Twidle, Opponent
	28	h	League	Southport Reserves	W	4	0	Twidle, Bateson, Waller, Taberner
Nov	4	a	League	New Brighton	W	2	0	Connelly, Twidle
	11	h	League	Lytham	W	2	1	Bateson, Twidle
	18	a	League	Fleetwood	D	1	1	Robinson
	25	h	League	Darwen	W	4	2	Bateson 2, Taberner, Twidle
Dec	2	a	League	Burscough	L	2	3	Twidle, Taberner
	9	h	League	Chorley	W	6	2	Twidle 3 (1pen), Sweeney 2, Taberner
	16	h	League	Padiham	W	8	2	Twidle 2, Sweeney 2, Taberner 2, Bateson, Opponent
	26	h	League	Earlestown	W	1	0	Twidle
	30	a	League	Earlestown	W	3	1	Taberner 2, Bateson
Jan	6	a	League	Prescot Cables	D	3	3	Sweeney 2, Connelly
	13	h	League	Nelson	W	5	0	Sweeney 4 (2pens), Taberner
	20	h	LJC 1	South Liverpool	W	2	1	Partington, Bateson
	27	h	League	Prescot Cables	W	2	0	Connelly, Bateson
Feb	3	h	League	Rossendale United	D	1	1	Smith
	10	a	LJC 2	Clitheroe	W	4	3	Taberner 3, Smith
	17	a	League	Lancaster City	L	1	2	Sweeney
	21	a	IL Cup 3	Northwich Victoria	D	0	0	
	24	h	League	Morecambe	D	1	1	Bateson
Mar	3	a	League	Clitheroe	L	0	1	
	10	h	League	Netherfield	D	2	2	Connelly, Twidle
	17	a	LJC 3	Fleetwood	L	0	3	
	21	a	League	Oldham Athletic Reserves	L	0	2	
	24	h	League	New Brighton	L	0	1	
	28	h	IL Cup 3	Northwich Victoria	L	0	2	
	31	a	League	Lytham	W	2	0	Connelly, Opponent
Apr	3	a	League	Leyland Motors	W	4	0	Unknown 4
	14	a	League	Darwen	W	3	2	Twidle, Bades, Bateson
	16	a	League	Southport Reserves	L	0	3	
	20	h	League	Bacup Borough	W	9	1	Chester 5, Taberner 3, Bades
	21	h	League	Burscough	W	3	1	Taberner, Chester, Connelly
	23	a	League	Bacup Borough	W	3	0	Chester 2, Taberner
	28	a	League	Chorley	W	3	0	Taberner, Bades, Connelly
May	2	h	League	Fleetwood	W	6	0	Taberner 3, Chester 2, Bateson
						120	61	

1962-63 Lancashire Combination Division 1

Date		H/A	Comp	Opponents	Res	F	A	Goalscorers	Notes
Aug	18	h	League	Nelson	W	1	0	Connelly	
	22	a	League	Skelmersdale United	W	4	0	Connelly 3, Slack	
	25	a	League	Chorley	L	0	3		
	30	h	League	Skelmersdale United	W	2	1	Slack 2	
Sep	1	h	IL Cup 1	Tranmere Rovers Reserves	W	7	0	Slack 3, Denehy 2, Taberner 2	
	6	h	League	Rossendale United	W	8	1	Taberner 3, Bateson 2, Slack, Denehy, Connelly	
	8	h	FA Cup 1Q	Netherfield	D	2	2	Denehy, Taberner	
	10	a	League	South Liverpool	D	1	1	Taberner	
	13	a	FA Cup 1Q	Netherfield	L	2	3	Baldwin, Connelly	AET
	15	a	League	Bacup Borough	W	6	2	Chester 2, Calver, Taberner, Bateson, Opponent	
	22	h	League	Prescot Cables	W	3	2	Bateson (pen), Bades, Chester	
	27	h	League	South Liverpool	W	3	0	Bades, Taberner, Bateson	
	29	a	League	Morecambe	L	0	4		
Oct	6	h	League	Earlestown	W	7	2	Baldwin 2, Taberner 2, Waller 2, Robinson	
	13	a	League	Darwen	W	6	1	Taberner 2, Waller, Bateson, Bades, Robinson	
	20	h	League	Lytham	W	8	2	Taberner 3, Waller 2, Bades, Baldwin, Robinson	
	27	a	League	Fleetwood	W	2	0	K Robinson, Taberner	
Nov	3	h	League	New Brighton	L	1	4	Waller	
	10	a	League	Marine	W	4	2	Taberner 3, Waller	
	17	h	League	Burscough	W	4	0	Taberner 2, Bateson, Bades	
	24	a	League	Lancaster City	L	1	2	Waller	
Dec	1	h	League	Southport Reserves	W	3	0	Bateson 2 (1pen), Taberner	
	8	a	League	Clitheroe	L	0	1		
	22	h	League	Chorley	W	3	1	Baldwin, Bateson (pen), Taberner	
	26	a	League	Ashton United	D	1	1	Baldwin	
Jan	5	h	League	Netherfield	W	2	1	Taberner 2	
Mar	2	h	League	Darwen	L	2	4	Blease, Baldwin	
	9	a	League	Lytham	W	7	0	Blease 3, Connelly, Taberner, Calderbank, Bateson (pen)	
	13	a	League	Nelson	L	0	3		
	16	h	LJC 1	Rossendale United	W	2	1	Taberner, Calderbank	
	19	a	League	Rossendale United	W	5	2	Blease 2, Connelly, Calderbank, Smith	
	23	a	League	New Brighton	W	2	1	Taberner, Blease	
	26	a	League	Earlestown	W	2	1	Bateson, Baldwin	
	28	a	League	Burscough	L	0	1		
	30	h	League	Marine	W	2	1	Calderbank, Opponent	
Apr	1	a	IL Cup 2	Wigan Athletic	L	0	2		
	4	h	League	Bacup Borough	L	2	3	Taberner 2	
	6	h	LJC 2	Northern Nomads	W	3	0	Baldwin 2, Taberner	
	12	h	League	Leyland Motors	W	3	1	Pimlott 2, Taberner	
	13	h	League	Lancaster City	D	0	0		
	15	a	League	Leyland Motors	D	1	1	Chester	
	17	a	League	Southport Reserves	L	1	2	Chester	
	20	h	LJC 3	Clitheroe	W	2	1	Pimlott, Connelly	
	22	a	League	Netherfield	D	2	2	Chester, Bateson	
	25	a	League	Prescot Cables	W	2	1	Unknown 2	
	27	h	League	Clitheroe	W	4	2	Jarvis 2, Blease 2	
	29	a	LJC SF	Great Harwood	W	5	2	Taberner 2, Bateson, Chester, Calderbank	
May	1	h	League	Ashton United	L	0	1		
	4	h	League	Morecambe	L	0	2		
	8	1	LJC Final	Morecambe	L	1	2	Chester	
	9	h	League	Fleetwood	W	2	0	Chester, Bateson	
						131	72		
		1 at Preston North End FC							

254

1963-64 Lancashire Combination Division 1

Date		H/A	Comp	Opponents	Res	F	A	Goalscorers
Aug	24	h	League	Lancaster City	W	4	1	Chester 2, Bateson, Lyden
	26	a	League	Barrow Reserves	L	1	4	Chester
	31	a	LC 1	Accrington Stanley	W	3	0	Calderbank 2, Opponent
Sep	5	h	League	Prescot Cables	W	3	0	Chester, Lyden, Gornall
	7	h	FA Cup 1Q	Burscough	L	0	3	
	12	h	League	Ashton United	D	0	0	
	14	a	League	Burscough	W	3	0	Calderbank, Lyden, Chester
	16	a	League	Ashton United	D	0	0	
	21	a	League	Rossendale United	W	2	1	Calderbank 2
	26	h	League	Skelmersdale United	W	4	1	Lyden 2, Chester, Bateson (pen)
	28	h	League	Rossendale United	W	3	0	Calderbank, Bateson (pen), Chester
Oct	5	a	League	Nelson	L	0	3	
	10	h	LC 2	Chorley	W	2	0	Bateson (pen), Lyden
	12	a	League	Clitheroe	L	0	1	
	19	h	League	Fleetwood	L	1	2	Connelly
	26	a	League	Chorley	L	3	5	Willighan, Chester, Lyden
Nov	2	h	League	Southport Reserves	W	3	1	Calderbank, Lyden, Bateson
	9	a	League	Droylsden	L	2	5	Bateson, Calderbank
	23	a	League	Morecambe	Ab	0	0	
	30	h	League	Netherfield	W	2	1	Bateson 2
Dec	7	a	League	New Brighton	W	1	0	Calderbank
	14	a	League	Lancaster City	D	2	2	Whitehead, Hudson
	21	h	League	Barrow Reserves	W	6	1	Bateson 2, Whitehead, Calderbank, Slack, C Robinson
	26	h	League	Leyland Motors	W	5	1	Bateson 3, Calderbank, Opponent
	28	a	League	Leyland Motors	W	5	0	C Robinson 2, Calderbank, Gornall, Whitehead
Jan	1	a	League	Morecambe	D	1	1	C Robinson
	4	a	League	Marine	D	1	1	Gornall
	18	h	LJC 1	Maghull	W	1	0	C Robinson
	25	h	League	Marine	W	2	1	Whitehead 2
Feb	1	a	League	South Liverpool	L	0	1	
	8	a	LJC 2	Lancaster City	W	1	0	Whitehead
	15	h	League	Nelson	W	2	0	Chester, Bateson
	22	h	League	Clitheroe	W	2	0	Schofield, Opponent
	29	a	League	Fleetwood	D	3	3	Calderbank, Chester, Gornall
Mar	7	h	League	Chorley	L	2	3	Slack, Bateson
	14	h	LJC 3	Guinness Export	W	8	0	Whitehead 4, Chester 3, Herring
	17	a	League	Southport Reserves	W	2	1	Bateson, Whitehead
	21	h	League	Droylsden	W	4	1	Chester 3, Dilworth
	27	h	League	Bacup Borough	W	2	0	Chester, Whitehead
	28	a	League	Crompton's Recs	W	2	0	C Robinson, Connelly
	30	a	League	Bacup Borough	W	1	0	Herring
Apr	1	h	LC 3	Great Harwood	W	5	0	Chester 2, Dilworth 2, Slack
	4	a	LJC SF	Nelson	L	0	1	
	6	h	League	Crompton's Recs	W	6	0	Chester 2, Whitehead 2, Slack, C Robinson
	11	a	League	Netherfield	L	0	2	
	13	h	League	Prescot Cables	L	1	2	Denton
	16	a	LC SF	Marine	L	0	1	
	18	h	League	New Brighton	D	0	0	
	20	h	League	Burscough	W	3	2	Whitehead, Herring, Denton (pen)
	23	h	League	South Liverpool	W	3	1	Dilworth, Chester, Bateson
	25	a	League	Skelmersdale United	W	2	1	C Robinson, Chester
	27	h	League	Morecambe	D	2	2	Whitehead, Herring
						111	56	

1964-65   Lancashire Combination Division 1

Date		H/A	Comp	Opponents	Res	F	A	Goalscorers
Aug	22	h	League	Bacup Borough	W	3	0	Whitehead, Bateson (pen), Herring
	27	h	LC 1	Blackpool Mechanics	W	3	2	Herring, Scott, Whitehead
	29	a	League	Leyland Motors	W	3	1	Battersby, Bateson (pen), Scott
Sep	3	h	League	Morecambe	W	6	1	Whitehead 3, Denton, Herring, Bateson
	5	h	FA Cup 1Q	Accrington Stanley	W	5	2	Scott 3, Whitehead, Herring
	8	h	LC 2	Lytham	W	4	0	Whitehead, Slack, Battersby, Bateson (pen)
	12	a	League	Nelson	W	4	1	Bateson 2 (1pen), Connelly, Scott
	17	h	League	Rossendale United	W	7	4	Connelly 4, Battersby, Bateson, Scott
	19	h	FA Cup 2Q	Lancaster City	D	1	1	Battersby
	23	a	FA Cup 2Q	Lancaster City	L	1	2	Slack
Oct	1	h	League	Nelson	W	19	1	Herring 4, Gornall 3, Chester 3, Whitehead 3, A Jones 3, Bateson 2, T Smith
	3	h	League	Burscough	W	4	1	Bateson, Herring, Chester, Gornall
	10	a	League	Lancaster City	L	1	2	Scott
	17	h	League	Southport Reserves	W	5	1	Whitehead 2, Gornall 2, Scott
	20	a	League	New Brighton	L	0	3	
	24	a	League	Marine	D	1	1	Chester
	26	a	League	Prescot Cables	D	0	0	
	31	h	League	Accrington	W	3	0	Whitehead, Denton, Scott
Nov	7	a	League	Clitheroe	W	2	1	Herring, Scott
	14	h	League	Chorley	D	2	2	Whitehead 2
	21	a	League	Great Harwood	W	3	1	Whitehead 2, Gornall
	28	h	League	Fleetwood	W	5	2	Whitehead 2, Herring 2, Bateson
Dec	5	a	League	South Liverpool	L	0	2	
	12	a	League	Bacup Borough	W	4	1	Whitehead, Denton, Scott, Slack
	19	h	League	Leyland Motors	W	5	4	Scott 3, Herring 2
Jan	9	a	League	Droylsden	D	2	2	Whitehead, Scott
	16	h	LJC 1	Northern Nomads	W	6	1	Whitehead 2, Scott 2, Herring, Bateson
	23	a	League	Barrow Reserves	W	2	0	Scott 2
	30	h	League	Droylsden	D	1	1	Whitehead
Feb	6	a	LJC 2	Skelmersdale United	D	1	1	Bateson
	13	h	LJC 2	Skelmersdale United	L	1	2	Whitehead
	20	h	League	Lancaster City	W	2	0	Connelly, Bateson
	27	a	League	Southport Reserves	W	4	0	Herring 2, Scott, Gornall
Mar	6	h	League	Marine	D	1	1	Scott
	9	a	League	Rossendale United	W	2	1	Connelly 2
	13	a	League	Accrington	D	0	0	
	16	a	LC 3	New Brighton	W	2	1	Bateson, Slack
	18	h	League	Skelmersdale United	W	5	0	Chester 3, Herring 2
	20	h	League	Clitheroe	W	3	1	Herring 2, Connelly
	8	a	League	Morecambe	L	1	4	Connelly
	23	a	League	Skelmersdale United	W	5	1	Connelly 2, Slack, Bateson, Roberts
	27	a	League	Chorley	D	1	1	Connelly
	29	a	League	Burscough	W	2	1	Connelly, Bateson
Apr	3	h	League	Great Harwood	D	1	1	Connelly
	5	h	League	Barrow Reserves	D	3	3	Connelly 2, Durkin
	10	a	League	Fleetwood	D	2	2	Dilworth, Herring
	12	a	LC SF	Chorley	L	0	3	
	16	h	League	Netherfield	D	1	1	Connelly
	17	h	League	South Liverpool	L	1	2	Scott
	19	a	League	Netherfield	W	3	2	Connelly 2, Gornall
	24	h	League	New Brighton	D	0	0	
	29	h	League	Prescot Cables	W	9	0	Herring 3, Shepherd 2, Roberts 2, Durkin, Denton (pen)
						152	68	

1965-66 Lancashire Combination Division 1

Date		H/A	Comp	Opponents	Res	F	A	Goalscorers
Aug	21	a	League	Leyland Motors	W	4	1	B Robinson 2, Herring, Opponent
	28	h	League	Nelson	W	2	1	Denton, Herring
	30	a	League	Southport Reserves	W	3	2	B Robinson 2, Durkin
Sep	4	h	FA Cup 1Q	Burscough	W	2	1	B Robinson, Tong
	9	h	League	Southport Reserves	D	2	2	B Robinson, Tong
	11	h	League	St Helens Town	W	4	1	Connelly 4
	13	a	League	Bacup Borough	W	4	0	B Robinson 3, Connelly
	18	h	FA Cup 2Q	Fleetwood	D	3	3	B Robinson, Durkin, Denton
	23	a	FA Cup 2Q	Fleetwood	L	1	2	B Robinson
	25	a	League	Barrow Reserves	W	2	0	Connelly 2
	28	a	LC 1	Darwen	W	3	0	B Robinson, Connelly, Tong
Oct	2	h	League	Morecambe	L	0	1	
	9	a	League	Burscough	W	5	0	B Robinson 3, Bateson 2
	16	h	LC 2	Nelson	D	4	4	B Robinson 2 (1pen), Herring, Durkin
	19	a	LC 2	Nelson	W	3	1	B Robinson, Connelly, Tong
	23	a	League	Lancaster City	W	2	0	Herring, Connelly
	30	h	League	Chorley	W	5	4	B Robinson 2, Durkin, Bateson, Unknown
Nov	13	a	League	St Helens Town	W	6	1	Bateson 2, B Robinson, Tong, Durkin, Herring
	20	a	League	Great Harwood	W	2	0	Tong, B Robinson
	27	h	League	Fleetwood	L	0	2	
Dec	4	a	League	Clitheroe	L	1	2	B Robinson
	11	h	League	Guinness Export	W	7	1	Connelly 2, Herring 2, Bateson, Durkin, Opponent
	18	a	League	Netherfield	L	1	2	Coop
Jan	1	h	League	Burscough	D	3	3	B Robinson, Bateson, Tong
	8	a	League	Chorley	D	0	0	
	15	a	LJC 1	Guinness Exports	W	2	1	Durkin, Tong
	22	h	League	Lancaster City	W	1	0	Tong
	29	h	League	Leyland Motors	W	3	1	B Robinson 3
Feb	5	h	LJC 2	Radcliffe Borough	W	4	1	B Robinson 2 (1pen), Durkin, Bateson
	19	a	League	Bacup Borough	W	2	0	Connelly, Bateson
Mar	1	a	League	Nelson	W	2	0	B Robinson, Bateson
	5	h	League	Rossendale United	W	5	2	Herring 2, Bateson, Connelly, T Smith
	12	a	LJC 3	Wigan Athletic	D	2	2	Connelly, Tong
	19	h	LJC 3	Wigan Athletic	L	0	5	
	23	a	League	Marine	L	0	4	
	26	a	League	Morecambe	L	2	4	B Robinson, Bateson
	28	a	League	Prescot Cables	W	2	1	B Robinson, Connelly
	31	h	LC 3	St Helens Town	W	3	1	B Robinson 2, Connelly
Apr	4	h	League	South Liverpool	L	1	2	B Robinson
	8	h	League	Droylsden	L	1	2	Opponent
	9	a	League	Guinness Export	L	0	1	
	11	a	League	Droylsden	W	2	1	Herring 2
	14	h	League	Skelmersdale United	L	2	4	B Robinson, Opponent
	16	h	League	Great Harwood	W	3	2	Connelly, Runciman, Durkin
	18	h	League	Prescot Cables	W	2	0	B Robinson, Bannister
	19	h	LC SF	Clitheroe	W	3	1	B Robinson 2, Tong
	21	h	League	Barrow Reserves	W	5	1	B Robinson 3, Tong 2
	23	a	League	Fleetwood	W	1	0	Herring
	25	a	League	Rossendale United	L	2	3	B Robinson, Durkin
	28	h	League	Netherfield	W	1	0	B Robinson
	30	h	League	Clitheroe	W	5	1	B Robinson 3, Runciman, Opponent
May	3	a	League	Skelmersdale United	L	1	3	B Robinson
	4	h	League	Marine	W	4	2	Herring 2, Connelly, Opponent
	6	1	LC Final	Droylsden	W	5	0	Connelly 2, B Robinson 2, Tong
	7	a	League	South Liverpool	L	0	1	
		1	at Chorley			135	80	

257

1966-67   Lancashire Combination Division 1

Date		H/A	Comp	Opponents	Res	F	A	Goalscorers
Aug	20	h	League	Great Harwood	W	5	1	B Robinson 3, Durkin, Herring, Connelly
	23	h	League	Clitheroe	W	2	1	Runciman, Denton (pen)
	27	a	League	Fleetwood	L	0	1	
Sep	3	a	FA Cup 1Q	Chorley	L	0	1	
	6	h	League	South Liverpool	D	0	0	
	10	a	League	Barrow Reserves	L	2	3	Tong, Denton (pen)
	17	a	League	Darwen	W	3	1	B Robinson 2, Durkin
	20	h	LC 1	Great Harwood	W	1	0	Runciman
	24	a	League	Wigan Rovers	L	1	2	Connelly
Oct	1	h	League	Fleetwood	W	2	1	Pinder, Connelly
	8	a	League	Chorley	D	1	1	Ramsdale
	15	h	League	Guinness Export	W	4	0	Ramsdale 2, Pinder, Denton (pen)
	22	a	League	St Helens Town	W	2	1	Pinder 2
	29	h	League	Netherfield	W	1	0	Herring 2, Denton, B Robinson
Nov	5	a	League	Morecambe	L	0	2	
	12	h	League	St Helens Town	W	2	0	Ramsdale, Denton
	19	a	League	Burscough	D	1	1	B Robinson 3, Durkin, Herring, Connelly
	26	h	League	Droylsden	W	2	0	Pinder, Tong
Dec	3	a	League	Leyland Motors	W	4	1	Denton, Pinder, Herring, Tong
	17	a	League	Great Harwood	L	0	1	
	24	h	League	Southport Reserves	W	4	1	B Robinson, Tong, Herring, Pinder
Jan	7	a	League	South Liverpool	W	3	0	Herring 2, Opponent
	14	a	LJC 1	Bacup Borough	W	2	0	B Robinson, Opponent
	21	a	League	Lancaster City	D	1	1	Herring
	28	h	League	Barrow Reserves	W	3	1	B Robinson 2, Tong
Feb	4	h	LJC 2	Marine	W	2	0	Tong, Fleming
	18	a	League	Bacup Borough	W	2	0	Tong, B Robinson
	25	h	League	Chorley	D	1	1	Webber
Mar	4	a	League	Guinness Export	W	2	0	B Robinson, Herring
	11	a	LJC 3	Chorley	D	1	1	Tong
	18	h	LJC 3	Chorley	L	0	4	
	21	a	LC 2	Skelmersdale United	L	1	2	Connelly
	24	h	League	Darwen	W	3	2	Connelly 2, B Robinson
	25	a	League	Netherfield	D	2	2	Webber, Pinder
	29	h	League	Wigan Rovers	W	3	1	Webber, Durkin, Denton (pen)
Apr	1	h	League	Morecambe	D	1	1	Herring
	4	h	League	Lancaster City	W	3	0	Pinder, Connelly, Wright
	10	a	League	Skelmersdale United	W	2	0	Herring, Denton
	11	h	League	Rossendale United	W	3	1	Webber (pen), Denton, Herring
	13	a	League	Marine	L	4	5	Herring 2, Denton, B Robinson
	15	h	League	Burscough	W	4	0	Webber 3, Tong
	18	h	League	Skelmersdale United	W	3	1	Pinder, Herring, Denton
	20	h	League	Marine	W	2	1	Pinder, Tong
	22	a	League	Droylsden	D	1	1	Denton, Pinder, Herring, Tong
	27	a	League	Clitheroe	W	2	0	Pinder 2
	29	h	League	Leyland Motors	W	2	0	Herring, Denton (pen)
May	1	a	League	Southport Reserves	W	1	0	Runciman
	4	h	League	Bacup Borough	W	3	0	Pinder 3
	6	a	League	Rossendale United	D	1	1	Denton (pen)
						95	45	

1967-68   Lancashire Combination Division 1

Date		H/A	Comp	Opponents	Res	F	A	Goalscorers	Notes
Aug	19	h	League	St Helens Town	L	0	2		
	23	a	League	Clitheroe	W	2	0	Wallbank, Opponent	
	26	a	League	Droylsden	D	1	1	Wallbank	
Sep	2	a	League	Kirkby Town	W	1	0	Runciman	
	9	h	League	Prescot Cables	W	5	1	Wallbank 3, Webber, Wright	
	12	h	League	Guinness Export	W	6	4	Runciman 3, Webber 3	
	16	h	FA Cup 1Q	Wigan Rovers	W	3	1	Webber 2, Runciman	
	23	h	League	Great Harwood	W	2	0	Parry, T Smith	
	26	h	LC 2	Wigan Rovers	D	1	1	Parry	
	30	h	FA Cup 2Q	Hyde United	L	0	3		
Oct	3	a	LC 2	Wigan Rovers	Ab	0	1		Ab 9'
	7	h	League	Barrow Reserves	W	6	2	Wallbank 3, Webber 2 (1pen), Pilkington	
	10	a	LC 2	Wigan Rovers	L	1	2	K Smith	Replayed
	14	a	League	Morecambe	L	0	2		
	21	h	League	Netherfield	W	3	1	Webber, T Smith, Tong	
	28	a	League	Skelmersdale United	W	2	1	Webber 2, Runciman	
Nov	4	h	League	Southport Reserves	D	1	1	Wallbank	
	11	a	League	Bacup Borough	L	1	2	Webber	
	18	h	League	Wigan Rovers	W	5	1	Webber 3 (1pen), Wallbank, Tong	
	25	a	League	Rossendale United	W	4	1	Webber 2, Wallbank, Unknown	
Dec	2	h	League	Marine	W	4	1	Webber, Durkin, Bradshaw, Opponent	
	16	a	League	St Helens Town	L	0	1		
	23	h	League	Droylsden	W	4	0	Webber, Wallbank, Durkin, Tong	
	26	a	League	Burscough	L	1	3	Webber	
	30	h	League	Burscough	D	2	2	Tong, Opponent	
Jan	6	h	League	Kirkby Town	L	0	3		
	20	h	LJC 1	Wigan Rovers	W	1	0	T Smith	
	27	a	League	Prescot Cables	L	0	1		
Feb	3	h	LJC 2	Fleetwood	L	1	3	Durkin	
	10	h	League	Fleetwood	W	3	1	Tong 2, Wallbank	
	17	a	League	Lancaster City	D	1	1	T Smith	
	24	a	League	Barrow Reserves	W	1	0	Wallbank	
	27	h	League	Morecambe	L	0	2		
Mar	2	a	LC 2	Wigan Rovers	W	2	1	Watson, Durkin	
	9	a	League	Guinness Export	L	0	1		
	12	a	League	Fleetwood	L	0	3		
	16	a	League	Netherfield	D	0	0		
	23	h	League	Skelmersdale United	D	1	1	Bradshaw	
	30	a	League	Southport Reserves	D	1	1	Durkin	
Apr	6	h	League	Bacup Borough	W	6	0	Wallbank 3, T Smith, Durkin, Watson	
	8	h	LC 3	Guinness Export	D	0	0		
	12	h	League	South Liverpool	W	3	0	Watson 2 (1pen), Wallbank	
	13	a	League	Wigan Rovers	L	0	2		
	15	a	League	South Liverpool	L	2	3	Watson 2 (1pen)	
	20	h	League	Rossendale United	W	5	0	Watson 2, Durkin 2, Lang	
	22	h	League	Clitheroe	D	2	2	Tong, Durkin	
	27	a	LC 3	Guinness Export	D	0	0		
	29	a	League	Marine	W	1	0	Pilkington	
	30	a	League	Chorley	W	1	0	Unknown	
May	1	1	LC 3	Guinness Export	W	2	1	Tong, Lang	
	4	h	League	Chorley	L	1	2	Wallbank	
	6	a	League	Great Harwood	L	1	3	Watson	
	8	a	LC SF	Southport Reserves	W	1	0	Tong (pen)	
	11	h	League	Lancaster City	D	0	0		
	15	1	LC Final	Morecambe	L	1	2	Lang	
						92	67		

1968-69   Cheshire County League

Date		H/A	Comp	Opponents	Res	F	A	Goalscorers
Aug	10	h	League	Chester Reserves	W	3	1	Tomlinson, Moulden, Durkin
	13	h	League	Skelmersdale United	L	1	3	Watson (pen)
	17	a	League	Witton Albion	D	1	1	Durkin
	21	a	League	Skelmersdale United	L	0	4	
	24	h	League	Winsford United	D	1	1	Tomlinson
	27	a	League	Stalybridge Celtic	L	2	3	Tomlinson, Watson
	31	a	LC 1	New Brighton	W	2	0	Watson 2
Sep	3	h	League	Stalybridge Celtic	W	3	2	Watson (pen), Tomlinson, Durkin
	7	h	League	Stafford Rangers	D	1	1	T Smith
	14	a	League	New Brighton	L	0	1	
	21	a	FA Cup 1Q	Wigan Rovers	D	1	1	Watson
	25	h	FA Cup 1Q	Wigan Rovers	W	2	0	Aspinall, Moulden (pen)
	28	h	League	Rhyl	W	3	2	Wright, Moulden (pen), Durkin
Oct	5	h	FA Cup 2Q	Mossley	L	1	5	Durkin
	12	a	League	Chester Reserves	W	3	1	O'Loughlin, Aspinall, Hobson
	19	h	League	Oswestry Town	D	0	0	
	26	a	League	Nantwich Town	L	0	5	
Nov	9	a	League	Mossley	L	0	3	
	16	h	League	Ellesmere Port Town	D	1	1	Hobson
	23	a	League	Buxton	D	2	2	T Smith, Aspinall
	30	h	League	Witton Albion	L	1	2	Webber
Dec	7	a	League	Rhyl	D	3	3	Webber 2, T Smith
	14	a	League	Tranmere Rovers Reserves	D	1	1	O'Loughlin
	21	h	League	Mossley	W	3	1	T Smith, Webber, Mitchinson
Jan	4	a	League	Sandbach Ramblers	W	3	2	Mitchinson, Webber, Opponent
	11	h	LJC 1	Wigan Rovers	W	2	1	Mitchinson, Webber
	18	h	League	Sandbach Ramblers	W	3	2	Mitchinson, Webber, Mackay
	22	1	LC 3	Winsford United	L	1	2	Webber
	25	h	League	Buxton	W	2	1	Mackay, Opponent
Feb	1	a	LJC 2	St Helens Town	W	1	0	Mackay
	15	a	League	Stafford Rangers	L	1	2	Opponent
	22	h	League	Guinness Export	L	0	2	
Mar	1	a	League	Oswestry Town	L	2	3	Webber, Woodward
	3	h	League	New Brighton	D	0	0	
	8	a	LJC 3	Chorley	L	0	3	
	10	h	League	Ashton United	W	3	1	Webber 2, Mackay
	15	a	League	Guinness Export	W	1	0	Webber
	22	h	League	Tranmere Rovers Reserves	W	2	0	Woodward, Armstrong
Apr	1	a	League	Frickley Colliery	D	1	1	Moulden
	4	h	League	Droylsden	W	3	2	Woodward, Moulden, Mackay
	5	a	League	Ellesmere Port Town	D	1	1	Webber
	7	a	League	Droylsden	L	0	2	
	9	h	League	Frickley Colliery	D	1	1	Webber
	12	h	League	Nantwich Town	L	0	4	
	19	a	League	Winsford United	D	1	1	Mackay
	26	a	League	Ashton United	W	1	0	Lang
		1	at Witton Albion FC			64	75	

1969-70 Cheshire County League

Date		H/A	Comp	Opponents	Res	F	A	Goalscorers
Aug	9	a	League	Ashton United	W	4	0	Webber 2 (1pen), Calder 2
	11	a	League	Port Vale Reserves	L	0	1	
	15	a	League	Droylsden	W	2	0	Webber, Calder
	16	h	League	Buxton	W	3	1	Calder 2, Webber
	23	a	League	Frickley Colliery	W	2	1	Webber, Opponent
	26	h	League	Port Vale Reserves	W	3	0	Calder 2, Webber
	30	h	League	Winsford United	W	3	0	Calder 2, Lang
Sep	3	a	League	New Brighton	W	3	0	Calder 2, Webber
	6	a	League	Sandbach Ramblers	D	2	2	Woodward, Lang
	13	h	LC 1	Ellesmere Port Town	W	4	1	Webber 3, Wright
	20	h	FA Cup 1Q	Guinness Export	W	3	1	Woodward, Webber, Calder
	27	h	League	Ellesmere Port Town	L	1	2	Webber
Oct	4	a	FA Cup 2Q	Formby	W	2	1	Webber, T Smith
	11	h	League	Oswestry Town	W	3	1	Webber 3
	18	a	FA Cup 3Q	Mossley	L	1	2	Alf Jones
	25	h	League	New Brighton	W	3	0	Calder 2, Woodward
Nov	1	a	League	Tranmere Rovers Reserves	D	1	1	Opponent
	8	a	FAT 1Q	Rossendale United	L	1	2	Webber
	19	a	League	Witton Albion	L	2	3	Woodward, Wright
	22	h	League	Frickley Colliery	W	3	0	Calder 2, Woodward
	29	a	League	Mossley	W	3	2	Webber 2, Beech
Dec	6	a	League	Ellesmere Port Town	W	1	0	Wright
	13	h	League	Droylsden	W	2	1	Webber, Calder
	26	h	League	Marine	W	3	2	Wright, Calder, Woodward
Jan	3	a	League	Oswestry Town	L	2	4	Daly, Webber
	10	h	League	Rhyl	W	5	0	Woodward 2, Webber, Donaldson, Calder
	17	a	LJC 1	Clitheroe	W	3	1	Calder 2, Webber
	24	h	League	Sandbach Ramblers	W	4	1	Webber, Woodward, Calder, Lang
	31	h	League	Guinness Export	D	0	0	
Feb	7	h	LJC 2	St Helens Town	D	1	1	Lang
	21	a	LJC 2	St Helens Town	W	2	0	Woodward, Webber
	28	h	League	Witton Albion	W	3	1	Woodward 2, Webber
Mar	3	h	League	Stalybridge Celtic	L	3	4	Webber (pen), Calder, Donaldson
	5	a	LJC 3	Skelmersdale United	L	0	1	
	7	a	League	Skelmersdale United	L	1	4	Thompson
	10	a	League	Winsford United	L	1	2	Williams
	14	a	LC 2	Rhyl	L	1	2	Webber
	17	h	League	Nantwich Town	L	2	3	Thomson, Williams
	19	a	League	Buxton	L	1	4	Webber
	21	a	League	Nantwich Town	W	2	1	Webber, Glasgow
	28	h	League	Mossley	L	0	4	
	30	a	League	Guinness Export	D	3	3	Webber 2, Calder
Apr	1	h	League	Ashton United	W	6	3	Calder 3, Woodward, Glasgow, Opponent
	4	h	League	Tranmere Rovers Reserves	D	0	0	
	7	h	League	Skelmersdale United	L	1	3	Opponent
	11	h	Jubilee Cup	Marine	L	0	1	
	14	a	League	Stalybridge Celtic	W	7	1	Webber 3, Calder 2, Woodward, Beech
	18	a	League	Rhyl	D	3	3	Beech 2, Webber
	21	a	League	Marine	W	5	1	Glasgow 2, Calder, Woodward, Webber
						111	72	

1970-71 Cheshire County League

Date		H/A	Comp	Opponents	Res	F	A	Goalscorers
Aug	15	a	League	New Brighton	D	0	0	
	18	a	League	Hyde United	D	1	1	Fitzgerald
	22	h	League	Burscough	L	1	2	Calder
	26	a	LC 1	Oswestry Town	W	6	2	Williams 3, Glasgow, Woodward, Webber
	29	a	League	Sandbach Ramblers	D	1	1	Glasgow
Sep	1	a	League	Buxton	D	1	1	Woodward
	8	h	League	Ormskirk	L	1	2	Calder
	12	a	League	Droylsden	W	2	1	Woodward 2
	15	h	League	Buxton	D	1	1	Nicklin
	19	h	FA Cup 1Q	Northwich Victoria	W	2	0	Webber 2
	23	a	League	Winsford United	D	2	2	Glasgow, Wright
	26	h	League	Nantwich Town	W	2	1	Glasgow, Donaldson
	30	a	League	Oswestry Town	L	1	2	Donaldson
Oct	3	h	League	New Brighton	D	1	1	Woodward
	6	h	League	Ashton United	W	2	1	Woodward, Webber
	10	a	FA Cup 2Q	Rossendale United	L	1	3	Opponent
	17	a	League	Burscough	L	1	3	Webber
	24	a	League	Mossley	D	3	3	Nicklin, Glasgow, Wright
	31	h	FAT 1Q	Fleetwood Town	D	1	1	Woodward
Nov	4	a	FAT 1Q	Fleetwood Town	L	1	3	Opponent
	7	h	League	Hyde United	W	4	1	Nicklin, Webber, Fitzgerald, Beech
	21	a	League	Witton Albion	L	1	2	Woodward
	28	h	LJC 1	Northern Nomads	W	6	1	Beech 2 (1pen), Webber, Lang, Woodward, Williams
Dec	5	h	League	Mossley	W	2	0	Wright, Webber
	12	a	League	Port Vale Reserves	W	2	0	Wright, Beech
	19	h	League	Rossendale United	W	4	0	Wright 2, Williams, Unknown
	26	h	League	Oldham Athletic Reserves	L	2	3	Woodward, Lang
	28	a	League	Oldham Athletic Reserves	L	0	1	
Jan	3	h	LJC 2	Chorley	L	2	4	Woodward, Williams
	23	a	League	Ellesmere Port Town	L	1	5	Wright
	30	h	League	Oswestry Town	W	4	0	Lang 2, Wright, Fitzgerald
Feb	6	h	League	Stalybridge Celtic	L	0	1	
	15	a	League	Skelmersdale United	L	3	4	Wright, Lang, Beech (pen)
	20	h	League	Rhyl	W	1	0	Denton
	27	h	League	Marine	W	1	0	Wright
Mar	6	h	League	Skelmersdale United	W	2	1	Webber, Wright
	13	h	League	Winsford United	W	6	1	Webber 2, Woodward 2, Wright, Wilcox
	15	a	League	Ashton United	L	0	2	
	20	a	League	Marine	W	2	1	Webber, Beech (pen)
	22	a	League	Nantwich Town	D	1	1	Webber
	27	h	League	Ellesmere Port Town	L	1	2	Donaldson (pen)
	31	a	League	Ormskirk	L	1	2	Fitzgerald
Apr	3	h	League	Sandbach Ramblers	D	0	0	
	9	h	League	Port Vale Reserves	W	1	0	Woodward
	10	a	League	Stalybridge Celtic	W	4	2	Nicklin, Woodward, Beech, Denton
	12	a	League	Rossendale United	D	0	0	
	15	h	League	Witton Albion	D	2	2	Woodward 2
	17	h	League	Droylsden	W	1	0	Webber
	24	a	League	Rhyl	L	1	2	Beech
						86	69	

1971-72   Cheshire County League

Date		H/A	Comp	Opponents	Res	F	A	Goalscorers
Aug	14	h	League	Formby	D	2	2	Holding, Fitzgerald
	16	a	League	Radcliffe Borough	L	2	3	Holding, Beech (pen)
	21	a	League	Sandbach Ramblers	W	1	0	Wilcox
	24	h	League	Radcliffe Borough	L	0	4	
	28	h	League	Witton Albion	W	3	2	Wright, Eckersley, Beech (pen)
	30	h	LC 1	Formby	W	2	1	Fitzgerald, Williams
Sep	4	a	League	New Brighton	W	1	0	Lang
	6	h	League	Ormskirk	W	1	0	Holding
	11	h	League	Stalybridge Celtic	W	1	0	Holding
	14	h	League	Burscough	W	4	0	Skitt 2, Glasgow, Wilcox
	18	h	FA Cup 1Q	Hyde United	D	1	1	Glasgow
	20	a	FA Cup 1Q	Hyde United	L	0	2	
	25	h	League	Nantwich Town	W	1	0	Glasgow (pen)
Oct	2	a	League	Nantwich Town	L	1	4	Glasgow
	6	a	LC 2	Oswestry Town	L	3	6	Glasgow 2, Lang
	9	h	League	Buxton	L	1	3	Glasgow
	16	a	League	Hyde United	D	0	0	
	23	a	League	Winsford United	L	1	2	Jones
	30	a	FAT 1Q	Rossendale United	L	0	2	
Nov	6	a	League	Formby	W	3	2	Glasgow 3
	13	a	League	Ormskirk	L	0	2	
	20	a	League	Oswestry Town	D	2	2	Glasgow, Holding
	27	h	LJC 1	Northern Nomads	W	3	0	Lang 2, Eckersley
Dec	4	a	League	Burscough	L	0	4	
	11	h	League	Marine	W	1	0	Glasgow
	18	h	League	Sandbach Ramblers	D	3	3	Skitt, Nesbitt, Glasgow
	27	h	League	Rossendale United	D	3	3	Glasgow 2 (1 pen), Skitt
	28	a	League	Rossendale United	L	1	5	Glasgow
Jan	1	h	League	Prestwich Heys	L	1	2	Nesbitt
	8	a	LJC 2	St Helens Town	W	2	0	Nesbitt, Holding
	15	h	League	New Brighton	W	2	1	Rigby, Beech
	18	a	League	Oldham Athletic Reserves	L	1	2	Glasgow
	22	a	League	Stalybridge Celtic	W	3	2	Holding, Lang, Nesbitt
	29	a	League	Mossley	D	2	2	Williams, Lang
Feb	5	h	League	Droylsden	W	2	1	Nesbitt, Shaw
	6	a	LJC 3	Chorley	L	0	3	
	12	a	League	Ashton United	L	0	3	
	19	a	League	Buxton	L	2	5	Holding, Nesbitt
	26	h	League	Hyde United	L	1	3	Beech
Mar	4	h	League	Winsford United	W	2	0	Denton, Glasgow
	11	a	League	Witton Albion	L	0	1	
	18	a	League	Droylsden	L	0	4	
	25	h	League	Oswestry Town	L	0	1	
	31	h	League	Oldham Athletic Reserves	W	3	1	Beech (pen), Nesbitt, Skitt
Apr	3	a	League	Prestwich Heys	L	0	2	
	8	a	League	Rhyl	L	0	3	
	15	a	League	Mossley	L	1	3	Nesbitt
	22	a	League	Rhyl	L	2	4	Nesbitt, Beech (pen)
	26	a	League	Marine	W	1	0	Nesbitt
	29	h	League	Ashton United	W	6	1	Skitt 2, Glasgow, Nesbitt, McGill, Beech (pen)
						72	97	

1972-73   Cheshire County League

Date		H/A	Comp	Opponents	Res	F	A	Goalscorers
Aug	12	a	League	Sandbach Ramblers	L	0	1	
	17	a	League	Ormskirk	D	0	0	
	19	h	League	Radcliffe Borough	D	2	2	Shaw 2
	21	a	LC 1	Radcliffe Borough	D	1	1	Melling (pen)
	26	a	League	Oldham Athletic Reserves	D	1	1	Miller
	29	h	League	Witton Albion	D	4	4	D Thompson 2, Nesbitt, Pickering
	31	h	LC 1	Radcliffe Borough	L	1	2	Pickering
Sep	2	a	FA Cup PR	Prestwich Heys	D	3	3	Holding, Shaw, Nesbitt
	5	h	FA Cup PR	Prestwich Heys	W	4	1	Eckersley 2, Lang, Nesbitt
	9	a	League	Prestwich Heys	W	3	1	Pickering, Lang, Wright
	13	a	League	Witton Albion	L	0	3	
	16	h	FA Cup 1Q	Hyde United	D	3	3	Shaw 2, Eckersley
	18	a	FA Cup 1Q	Hyde United	L	0	1	
	23	a	League	Formby	L	2	3	Nesbitt 2
	30	h	FAT 1Q	Formby	W	2	1	Eckersley, Holding
Oct	7	a	League	Rhyl	L	2	4	Williams (pen), Glasgow
	14	a	League	Nantwich Town	D	1	1	Nesbitt
	21	a	League	Oswestry Town	L	2	6	Nesbitt, O'Donnell
	28	h	FAT 2Q	Congleton Town	W	1	0	Holding
Nov	4	h	League	Prestwich Heys	W	5	1	Holding 4, Nesbitt
	11	h	FAT 3Q	Sandbach Ramblers	D	1	1	Holding
	13	1	FAT 3Q	Sandbach Ramblers	L	0	4	
	18	h	League	Winsford United	W	3	2	Holding 2, Nesbitt
	25	h	LJC 1	Fleetwood Town	L	0	2	
Dec	2	a	League	Ashton United	L	2	3	Nesbitt, Williams
	9	h	League	Rhyl	W	4	0	T Thompson, Nesbitt, Shaw, Pickering
	16	h	League	Sandbach Ramblers	W	1	0	Lang
	23	a	League	Radcliffe Borough	L	3	6	Pickering, Shaw, Melling (pen)
	26	h	League	Chorley	L	0	1	
	30	h	League	Oldham Athletic Reserves	D	2	2	Nesbitt 2
Jan	2	a	League	Chorley	D	1	1	Nesbitt
	6	a	League	New Brighton	L	0	1	
	13	h	League	Buxton	L	0	4	
	27	a	League	Buxton	D	1	1	Pickering
Feb	3	a	League	Hyde United	D	1	1	Nesbitt
	10	h	League	Nantwich Town	L	0	2	
	17	a	League	Burscough	D	1	1	Lang
	25	h	League	Droylsden	W	2	0	Pickering, Gregory
Mar	3	h	League	Stalybridge Celtic	D	0	0	
	10	h	League	Marine	L	3	4	T Thompson 2, Gregory
	17	a	League	Winsford United	L	1	2	Pickering
	24	h	League	Oswestry Town	D	0	0	
	27	h	League	Ormskirk	L	0	1	
	29	h	League	Hyde United	L	2	3	Cooper, Lang
	31	h	League	Ashton United	L	0	1	
Apr	5	a	League	Marine	L	0	5	
	7	a	League	Stalybridge Celtic	D	1	1	Williams (pen)
	14	h	League	Burscough	D	1	1	Hayes
	16	a	League	Droylsden	L	1	3	Hayes
	20	a	League	Rossendale United	D	1	1	Seaton
	21	h	League	Formby	D	2	2	Pickering, Seaton
	23	h	League	Rossendale United	L	1	5	Pickering
	28	h	League	New Brighton	L	1	2	Pickering
		1 at Witton Albion FC						
						73	102	

1973-74   Cheshire County League

Date		H/A	Comp	Opponents	Res	F	A	Goalscorers
Aug	25	h	League	Sandbach Ramblers	D	0	0	
	28	h	LC 1	Marine	L	0	2	
Sep	1	a	League	Radcliffe Borough	L	1	2	Gardner
	4	a	LC 1	Marine	L	1	2	Wright (pen)
	8	h	League	Nantwich Town	W	3	2	Wright, Elliott, Gardner
	11	h	League	Witton Albion	L	2	3	Gorman 2
	15	h	FA Cup 1Q	Skelmersdale United	W	3	1	Wright 2, Elliott
	19	a	League	Witton Albion	D	1	1	Gardner
	22	a	League	New Brighton	W	1	0	Small
	24	a	League	Droylsden	L	1	2	Saile
	29	a	League	Hyde United	L	1	4	Elliott
Oct	6	h	FA Cup 2Q	Congleton Town	W	2	0	Gardner, Wright
	13	h	FAT 1Q	Skelmersdale United	L	0	3	
	20	a	FA Cup 3Q	Altrincham	L	0	4	
	27	h	League	Marine	L	0	1	
Nov	7	a	League	Oswestry Town	L	0	3	
	10	h	League	Ormskirk	L	1	3	Gardner
	17	a	League	Prestwich Heys	W	1	0	Saile
	24	h	LJC 1	Atherton Collieries	W	3	1	Cassell, Wright, Middleton
Dec	8	h	League	New Brighton	L	1	2	Morris
	15	a	League	Marine	L	1	3	Pickering
	16	h	League	Radcliffe Borough	W	3	0	Morris 2, Hayes
	22	h	League	Ashton United	L	0	1	
	26	h	League	Chorley	W	1	0	Pickering
	29	a	League	Leek Town	L	1	5	Gardner
Jan	1	a	League	Chorley	L	1	2	Hayes
	5	h	League	Oldham Athletic Reserves	L	1	2	Rios
	6	h	LJC 2	Darwen	D	2	2	Morris, Cassell
	12	a	LJC 2	Darwen	W	1	0	Gardner
	19	a	League	Ormskirk	W	2	1	Gardner, Opponent
	26	h	League	Burscough	L	1	2	Hayes
Feb	9	a	League	Nantwich Town	D	2	2	Pickering, Cassell
	23	a	League	Stalybridge Celtic	L	1	3	Pickering
	24	a	LJC 3	Wigan Athletic	L	0	2	
Mar	2	h	League	Rhyl	L	2	3	Morris, Hayes
	9	a	League	Burscough	D	1	1	Morris
	16	h	League	Formby	L	1	2	Pickering
	19	h	League	Droylsden	L	1	2	Cassell
	23	h	League	Leek Town	L	0	2	
	25	a	League	Sandbach Ramblers	L	2	3	Cooke 2
	30	a	League	Oldham Athletic Reserves	L	0	1	
Apr	2	a	League	Formby	L	0	3	
	6	h	League	Stalybridge Celtic	W	4	1	Pickering 2, Cassell, Morris
	9	h	League	Winsford United	D	1	1	Gerrard
	12	a	League	Rossendale United	L	0	5	
	13	h	League	Hyde United	W	4	1	Middleton 2, Cassell, Morris
	15	h	League	Rossendale United	L	1	2	Morris
	20	a	League	Rhyl	W	5	0	Cassell 3, N Olivero, Mansfield
	22	a	League	Ashton United	D	1	1	Cassell
	24	a	League	Winsford United	L	0	1	
	27	h	League	Oswestry Town	D	0	0	
	30	h	League	Prestwich Heys	W	2	1	Cassell, Gardner
						64	91	

1974-75 Cheshire County League

Date		H/A	Comp	Opponents	Res	F	A	Goalscorers
Aug	17	a	League	Ashton United	D	1	1	Chadwick
	20	a	LC 1	Chorley	L	0	1	
	24	h	League	Oswestry Town	W	3	0	Morris 2, Cassell
	31	a	League	Sandbach Ramblers	W	5	1	M Olivero 2, Cairns 2, Morris
Sep	3	h	League	Burscough	W	3	1	M Olivero (pen), Morris, Cairns
	9	a	League	Hyde United	W	4	3	Chadwick 2, Cairns, Cassell
	14	a	FA Cup 1Q	Formby	W	2	0	Greenwood, Cairns
	21	a	FAT 1Q	Hyde United	L	0	2	
	24	a	League	Stalybridge Celtic	D	2	2	Morris, Chadwick
	28	h	League	New Brighton	W	3	0	Chadwick 2, Rios
Oct	2	a	League	New Brighton	L	1	3	Chadwick
	5	a	FA Cup 2Q	Ashton United	W	2	0	Cassell 2
	12	a	League	New Mills	L	1	4	Morris
	16	a	League	Witton Albion	D	0	0	
	19	h	FA Cup 3Q	Accrington Stanley	L	0	2	
	26	h	League	Hyde United	W	3	0	Chadwick 2, Ellison
Nov	2	a	League	Prestwich Heys	D	1	1	Cassell
	9	h	League	Leek Town	L	0	2	
	16	a	LJC 1	Rossendale United	L	0	2	
	23	h	League	Oldham Athletic Reserves	L	0	1	
	30	h	League	Droylsden	L	0	2	
Dec	7	a	League	Nantwich Town	W	2	1	Rios, Morris
	14	h	League	Rhyl	W	2	1	Rios (pen), Morris
	21	h	League	Winsford United	W	2	1	Morris, Chadwick
	28	a	League	Oswestry Town	L	0	1	
Jan	1	a	League	Chorley	L	0	2	
	4	h	League	Sandbach Ramblers	L	0	3	
	11	a	League	Radcliffe Borough	W	2	1	Morris, Delaney
	18	h	League	Witton Albion	D	3	3	Rios, Chadwick, M Olivero
Feb	8	h	League	Marine	W	2	1	Morris, Delaney
	15	a	League	Burscough	D	1	1	Black (pen)
	22	h	League	Prestwich Heys	L	1	2	Delaney
Mar	1	a	League	Leek Town	L	1	2	Chadwick
	8	h	League	Formby	W	1	0	Delaney
	15	a	League	Oldham Athletic Reserves	L	0	1	
	16	h	League	Radcliffe Borough	L	1	2	J Olivero
	22	a	League	Droylsden	L	1	2	Chadwick
	28	h	League	Rossendale United	D	2	2	Saile, Chadwick
	29	h	League	Nantwich Town	L	1	2	Chadwick
	31	a	League	Rossendale United	L	0	1	
Apr	3	a	League	Marine	W	2	1	Morris 2
	5	a	League	Rhyl	L	0	2	
	8	a	League	Formby	W	3	1	Black 2, McGlyn
	12	a	League	Winsford United	L	1	2	Ainscough
	22	h	League	Chorley	W	1	0	Williams
	26	h	League	Stalybridge Celtic	W	2	1	Black, Saile
	28	h	League	Ashton United	W	1	0	Greenwood
May	1	h	League	New Mills	L	1	2	Ainscough
						64	66	

1975-76   Cheshire County League

Date		H/A	Comp	Opponents	Res	F	A	Goalscorers
Aug	16	h	League	New Mills	D	1	1	Black
	19	a	LC 1	St Helens Town	D	1	1	Bateson
	23	a	League	Winsford United	L	1	9	Bateson
	25	a	League	Droylsden	L	0	3	
	27	h	LC 1	St Helens Town	L	1	2	Bateson
	30	h	FA Cup PR	Farsley Celtic	D	1	1	Silous
Sep	2	h	League	Marine	L	0	4	
	6	a	League	Radcliffe Borough	W	4	1	Black 2, Jones, Wignall
	8	1	FA Cup PR	Farsley Celtic	W	2	1	Black, Hunt
	10	a	League	Marine	L	2	7	Black 2
	13	a	FA Cup 1Q	Radcliffe Borough	L	0	4	
	20	h	FAT PR	Middlewich Town	W	2	1	Silous, Taylor
	27	h	League	Leek Town	D	1	1	Hennessey
Oct	4	a	League	St Helens Town	W	1	0	Kirkman
	11	a	FAT 1Q	Nantwich Town	D	1	1	Herring
	15	h	FAT 1Q	Nantwich Town	L	0	3	
	18	a	League	Burscough	D	2	2	Kirkman, Leaf
	25	h	League	Darwen	L	0	1	
Nov	1	a	League	New Brighton	W	1	0	Silous
	8	h	League	Middlewich Town	L	1	2	Herring
	15	h	League	Radcliffe Borough	L	1	3	Whittle
	22	h	League	Nantwich Town	L	2	5	Black (pen), Taylor
	29	a	League	Stalybridge Celtic	L	1	3	Taylor
Dec	6	a	League	Ashton United	L	0	3	
	13	a	League	Witton Albion	L	0	3	
	20	a	League	Formby	W	1	0	Morris
	26	h	League	Chorley	L	0	4	
	27	h	League	Witton Albion	D	1	1	Taylor
Jan	1	a	League	Chorley	L	0	6	
	3	h	LJC 1	Wigan Athletic	L	0	4	
	17	h	League	Ashton United	W	2	0	Herring, Richmond
	24	a	League	Leek Town	L	0	7	
Feb	7	h	League	St Helens Town	L	0	1	
	14	a	League	Rhyl	D	1	1	Richmond
	16	a	League	Hyde United	D	1	1	Barker
	21	h	League	Burscough	D	1	1	Barker
	28	a	League	Darwen	D	1	1	Barker
Mar	6	h	League	New Brighton	D	1	1	Silous
	13	h	League	Winsford United	L	0	1	
	20	h	League	Prestwich Heys	W	4	1	Richmond 3, Barker
	23	h	League	Rhyl	W	2	0	Richmond, O'Neill
	27	a	League	Nantwich Town	L	1	5	Richmond
	29	a	League	Prestwich Heys	D	0	0	
Apr	3	h	League	Stalybridge Celtic	D	2	2	Barker, Roberts
	6	h	League	Droylsden	D	1	1	Richmond
	10	h	League	Hyde United	D	0	0	
	16	a	League	Rossendale United	L	0	1	
	17	a	League	New Mills	L	2	3	O'Neill, Roberts
	19	h	League	Rossendale United	W	2	1	Barker, Kershaw
	24	h	League	Formby	L	1	2	Herring
	27	a	League	Middlewich Town	L	0	1	
		1 at Bacup Borough						
						50	108	

1976-77 Cheshire County League

Date		H/A	Comp	Opponents	Res	F	A	Goalscorers	Notes
Aug	21	a	League	Rhyl	D	0	0		
	24	h	League	Rossendale United	L	0	2		
	28	h	League	New Brighton	W	4	0	Kershaw, Baldwin, Richmond, Opponent	
	31	a	League	Radcliffe Borough	D	1	1	Grimshaw	
Sep	4	a	League	Burscough	L	1	2	Silous	
	8	a	LC 1	Marine	L	0	2		
	11	h	League	Winsford United	W	3	1	Richmond 2, Barker	
	13	a	League	Droylsden	D	2	2	Black, Grimshaw (pen)	
	18	h	FA Cup 1Q	Worksop Town	D	1	1	Opponent	
	22	a	FA Cup 1Q	Worksop Town	L	0	1		
	25	a	League	New Mills	W	2	1	Barker, Kershaw	
Oct	2	h	League	Leek Town	L	1	2	Silous	
	16	h	League	Hyde United	W	3	0	Richmond 2, Davenport	
	23	a	League	Stalybridge Celtic	W	3	0	Davenport 2, Grimshaw (pen)	
	30	a	FAT 1Q	New Brighton	L	0	1		
Nov	6	h	League	Witton Albion	W	1	0	Richmond	
	13	a	LJC 1	Burscough	Ab	0	0		Ab 12'
	17	a	LJC 1	Burscough	D	1	1	Barker	
	20	h	LJC 1	Burscough	W	4	3	Barker 2, Grimshaw, O'Neill	
	27	a	League	Darwen	L	0	1		
Dec	18	h	League	Nantwich Town	W	6	0	Baldwin 3, Richmond 2, O'Neill	
	27	h	League	Chorley	L	1	3	Richmond	
	28	a	League	New Brighton	D	2	2	Richmond, Connaghan	
Jan	1	h	League	Rhyl	W	3	2	Connaghan, Richmond, Grimshaw	
	8	h	LJC 2	Radcliffe Borough	W	4	0	Richmond 2, Grimshaw, Barker	
	22	h	League	Burscough	L	1	2	Barker	
	29	h	League	New Mills	W	3	1	Barker, Grimshaw, Opponent	
	31	a	League	Witton Albion	L	0	2		
Feb	5	a	League	Leek Town	L	0	2		
	19	a	LJC 3	Accrington Stanley	W	3	2	O'Neill 2, Barker	
	26	h	League	Stalybridge Celtic	L	1	3	Richmond	
Mar	5	a	League	Ashton United	L	1	2	Richmond	
	12	a	LJC SF	Chorley	L	2	5	O'Neill, Grimshaw	
	14	a	League	Hyde United	D	1	1	Barker	
	19	a	League	Winsford United	L	1	4	Grimshaw	
	22	h	League	Ashton United	W	3	2	Herring, Richmond, O'Neill	
	26	a	League	Middlewich Town	W	2	1	Richmond, Barker	
Apr	2	h	League	Darwen	W	2	0	Richmond, Kershaw	
	5	h	League	Prestwich Heys	D	2	2	Barker 2	
	8	h	League	St Helens Town	W	2	0	Black, Connaghan	
	9	a	League	Prestwich Heys	W	3	2	Grimshaw, Connaghan, Richmond	
	11	a	League	Rossendale United	W	1	0	Barker	
	14	a	League	Formby	L	0	3		
	16	a	League	Nantwich Town	D	0	0		
	20	h	League	Droylsden	D	2	2	Barker, Herring	
	23	h	League	Radcliffe Borough	W	4	2	Black, Kershaw, O'Neill, Grimshaw	
	26	h	League	Middlewich Town	W	4	2	Kershaw 2, Barker, Grimshaw	
	28	a	League	Marine	L	1	3	Barker	
	30	a	League	St Helens Town	D	0	0		
May	3	h	League	Formby	W	3	0	Grimshaw 2, Silous	
	5	a	League	Chorley	L	1	2	Bowen	
	7	h	League	Marine	D	1	1	Connaghan	
						87	74		

1977-78 Cheshire County League

Date		H/A	Comp	Opponents	Res	F	A	Goalscorers
Aug	20	a	League	Winsford United	D	1	1	Barker
	23	h	League	Burscough	W	5	2	O'Neill 3, Barker, Froggatt
	27	a	League	Droylsden	D	1	1	Barker
	30	h	League	Hyde United	D	1	1	O'Kane
Sep	3	a	League	New Brighton	L	0	1	
	6	a	League	Radcliffe Borough	D	2	2	O'Neill, Kershaw
	10	h	League	Ashton United	L	1	2	Grimshaw (pen)
	13	a	League	Rossendale United	D	0	0	
	17	h	FA Cup 1Q	Barrow	W	1	0	Kilgannon
	20	a	League	Stalybridge Celtic	L	0	2	
	24	h	League	Leek Town	W	1	0	Murphy
Oct	1	a	League	Rhyl	W	2	0	Kilgannon, Grimshaw
	8	a	FA Cup 2Q	Chorley	L	0	1	
	15	a	FAT 1Q	Prestwich Heys	W	3	1	Kilgannon, Barker, O'Kane
	22	h	League	Nantwich Town	W	3	2	Barker, Grimshaw, Connaghan
	29	a	League	Prestwich Heys	W	4	2	Barker, Silous, Connaghan, Lang
Nov	5	a	League	Witton Albion	D	1	1	Barker
	12	h	FAT 2Q	Droylsden	W	2	0	O'Kane, Grimshaw
	19	a	League	Ashton United	W	3	2	O'Kane 2, Grimshaw
	26	h	League	New Brighton	W	1	0	Grimshaw
Dec	3	h	FAT 3Q	Chorley	L	0	1	
	10	a	League	Darwen	L	0	1	
	17	a	League	Hyde United	W	1	0	Silous
	26	a	League	Chorley	W	1	0	Kilgannon
	27	h	League	Formby	D	0	0	
	31	h	League	Droylsden	W	2	1	Barker, Silous
Jan	3	h	League	Chorley	D	1	1	Barker
	7	h	LJC 1	Morecambe	D	1	1	O'Kane
	10	a	LJC 1	Morecambe	L	2	4	Kilgannon, Kershaw
	14	h	League	New Mills	W	2	0	Barker 2
	21	h	League	Stalybridge Celtic	D	0	0	
	28	a	League	Marine	L	0	5	
Feb	11	a	LC 1	Formby	L	0	2	
	25	a	League	Middlewich Town	W	2	0	Kilgannon, Grimshaw
Mar	4	a	League	Nantwich Town	W	1	0	Grimshaw
	11	h	League	Middlewich Town	D	0	0	
	18	h	League	St Helens Town	W	2	1	Barker, Greenan
	24	a	League	St Helens Town	D	0	0	
	25	h	League	Darwen	L	2	3	Kershaw, Kilgannon
	27	h	League	Rossendale United	W	4	0	Greenan 2, Kilgannon, Connaghan
Apr	1	a	League	Burscough	L	0	2	
	2	h	League	Radcliffe Borough	W	1	0	Greenan
	5	a	League	New Mills	D	1	1	Barker
	8	h	League	Marine	D	1	1	O'Kane
	11	a	League	Leek Town	W	4	3	Grimshaw 2, O'Kane, Barker
	15	h	League	Prestwich Heys	W	3	1	Kilgannon, O'Neill, Connaghan
	22	a	League	Formby	L	2	4	Grimshaw, Connaghan
	23	h	League	Winsford United	L	1	3	Greenan (pen)
	29	h	League	Rhyl	W	3	2	Barker 2, Connaghan
May	7	h	League	Witton Albion	D	2	2	Connaghan 2
						71	60	

1978-79   Cheshire County League Division 1

Date		H/A	Comp	Opponents	Res	F	A	Goalscorers	Notes
Aug	18	h	League	Burscough	W	2	1	Walton, Burrows	
	22	h	League	St Helens Town	W	2	0	Burrows, Froggatt	
	26	a	LC 1	Congleton Town	W	2	1	Pearson, Froggatt	
	29	h	League	Darwen	W	1	0	Opponent	
Sep	2	a	League	Stalybridge Celtic	W	2	0	Silous, O'Kane	
	6	a	League	Rhyl	W	3	1	Pearson 2, Greenan	
	9	h	League	New Mills	D	2	2	Silous, Greenan (pen)	
	12	h	LC 2	Kirkby Town	L	1	3	Kershaw	
	16	h	FA Cup 1Q	Leyland Motors	W	2	1	Pearson 2	
	19	a	League	Ashton United	W	4	1	Barker 2, Silous, Connaghan	
	23	h	League	Winsford United	W	1	0	Pearson	
	30	h	League	New Brighton	W	3	1	Barker, Lang, Greenan (pen)	
Oct	7	a	FA Cup 2Q	Curzon Ashton	W	2	1	Connaghan, Greenan (pen)	
	14	a	FAT 1Q	Whitley Bay	W	4	1	Barker, O'Neill, Pearson, Lang	
	21	a	FA Cup 3Q	Formby	D	0	0		
	25	h	FA Cup 3Q	Formby	W	5	1	Pearson 2, Lang, O'Kane, Connaghan	
	28	h	League	Leek Town	W	2	0	Greenan 2 (2pens)	
Nov	4	a	FA Cup 4Q	Morecambe	L	1	3	Pearson	
	11	h	FAT 2Q	Ashington	W	3	0	O'Neill, Pearson, Barker	
	18	a	League	Radcliffe Borough	W	1	0	Barker	
	25	h	League	Formby	W	3	2	Barker 2, O'Neill	
Dec	2	a	FAT 3Q	Tow Law Town	Ab	0	0		Ab 51'
	9	a	FAT 3Q	Tow Law Town	D	1	1	Barker	
	11	h	FAT 3Q	Tow Law Town	W	6	0	Pearson 2, Barker 2, Greenan, Opponent	
	16	a	LJC 1	Bacup Borough	W	3	1	Barker, Pearson, Green	
	17	h	League	Fleetwood Town	W	1	0	Barker	
	26	h	League	Chorley	W	2	1	Barker, Kilgannon	
	30	a	League	St Helens Town	W	2	0	Lang, Barker	
Jan	17	a	FAT 1	Spennymoor United	L	1	2	Burrows	
Feb	20	a	LJC 2	Morecambe	D	3	3	Greenan (pen), Kilgannon, Froggatt	
	24	h	League	Marine	W	2	0	Greenan (pen), Pearson	
	26	a	League	Hyde United	W	1	0	Froggatt	
Mar	3	h	League	Droylsden	W	5	1	Greenan 3 (2pens), Pearson, Kershaw	
	4	h	LJC 2	Morecambe	D	0	0		
	10	a	League	Leek Town	W	2	1	Lang, Burrows	
	14	a	LJC 2	Morecambe	W	1	0	Greenan (pen)	
	17	h	League	Ashton United	W	1	0	Silous	
	18	h	LJC 3	Chorley	D	0	0		
	21	a	LJC 3	Chorley	L	0	2		
	24	h	League	Witton Albion	W	2	0	Silous, Burrows	
	31	a	League	Burscough	W	1	0	Pearson	
Apr	2	a	League	Droylsden	W	5	3	Pearson 3, Burrows, Greenan (pen)	
	4	a	League	Middlewich Town	W	4	1	Greenan (pen), Pearson, Silous, Ainscough	
	7	h	League	Middlewich Town	W	3	1	Pearson 2, Burrows	
	10	h	League	Rhyl	W	1	0	Pearson	
	13	a	League	Chorley	W	2	1	Greenan 2 (1pen)	
	14	h	League	Stalybridge Celtic	L	1	4	Barker	
	16	a	League	Rossendale United	W	3	1	Pearson 2, Connaghan	
	19	a	League	Rossendale United	W	5	1	Kershaw, Greenan, Pearson, Lang, Burrows	
	21	h	League	Nantwich Town	W	2	1	Ainscough, Barker	
	22	a	League	Darwen	D	0	0		
	24	a	League	New Mills	W	2	1	Barker, Froggatt	
	26	a	League	Nantwich Town	W	3	1	Lang 2, Froggatt	
	28	a	League	Fleetwood Town	W	2	1	Burrows 2	
	30	a	League	Marine	W	2	1	Froggatt, Barker	

Season details continued on next page

Date		H/A	Comp	Opponents	Res	F	A	Goalscorers
May	1	a	League	Formby	L	1	4	Pearson
	3	h	League	Radcliffe Borough	W	4	2	Burrows 2, Barker, Opponent
	5	h	League	Hyde United	L	1	3	Greenan
	7	a	League	Winsford United	L	0	3	
	11	a	League	New Brighton	W	2	1	Kershaw, Pearson
	21	a	League	Witton Albion	L	1	4	Greenan (pen)
	24	h	League Shield	Witton Albion	W	2	0	Silous, Barker
						126	65	

1979-80   Cheshire County League Division 1

Date		H/A	Comp	Opponents	Res	F	A	Goalscorers
Aug	18	h	League	New Mills	L	0	1	
	22	h	League	Rossendale United	D	2	2	Parry 2
	25	a	League	Leek Town	L	1	2	Barker
	27	a	League	Droylsden	L	1	2	Greenan
Sep	1	h	League	Fleetwood Town	D	0	0	
	8	a	League	Darwen	W	2	0	Barker, Pearson
	10	a	League	Winsford United	W	3	2	Barker 3
	15	h	FA Cup 1Q	Darwen	W	4	1	Pearson 2, Barker, Greenan (pen)
	22	h	LC 2	St Helens Town	L	2	5	Barker 2
	29	h	League	Leek Town	W	1	0	D Haslam
Oct	1	a	League	Hyde United	L	2	4	Pearson, Greenan
	6	a	FA Cup 2Q	Lancaster City	L	0	4	
	13	a	League	Chorley	D	1	1	Barker
	20	h	League	Bootle	W	1	0	Barker
	27	a	League	Bootle	W	2	0	Pearson, Kershaw
Nov	3	h	League	Chorley	W	2	1	Pearson, Barker
	10	h	League	Darwen	W	4	0	Barker 2, Pearson, Connaghan
	13	a	League	Ashton United	L	3	4	Pearson 2, Barker
	17	a	League	New Mills	D	0	0	
	24	a	League	Nantwich Town	L	0	1	
Dec	1	a	FAT 1Q	Gainsborough Trinity	L	0	1	
	8	h	League	Droylsden	L	2	3	Greenan (pen), Opponent
	26	h	League	St Helens Town	D	0	0	
Jan	5	h	LJC 1	Darwen	W	3	1	Greenan (pen), Kershaw, Pearson
	12	a	League	Rhyl	W	5	4	Pearson, Lang, Connaghan, Greenan (pen), Silous
	22	a	League	Burscough	L	0	2	
	26	a	League	Radcliffe Borough	D	2	2	Pearson, D Haslam
Feb	9	h	LJC 2	South Liverpool	L	0	2	
	16	h	League	Ashton United	W	3	1	G Haslam, Pearson, Froggatt
	23	a	League	Fleetwood Town	D	1	1	Silous
Mar	1	a	League	Formby	L	1	2	Pearson
	8	h	League	Formby	W	2	1	Pearson, Greenan (pen)
	15	a	League	St Helens Town	D	1	1	D Haslam
	22	h	League	Winsford United	D	1	1	Greenan
	29	a	League	Stalybridge Celtic	W	2	1	Greenan (pen), Silous
Apr	4	h	League	Radcliffe Borough	D	0	0	
	5	h	League	Burscough	D	0	0	
	7	a	League	Curzon Ashton	D	1	1	Barker
	12	h	League	Hyde United	L	0	2	
	19	h	League	Stalybridge Celtic	L	0	3	
	22	a	League	Rossendale United	L	0	2	
	26	a	League	Rhyl	W	2	1	Pearson, Lang
	30	h	League	Curzon Ashton	W	5	0	Pearson 2, Greenan (pen), D Haslam, Barker
May	3	h	League	Nantwich Town	L	0	4	
						62	66	

1980-81 Cheshire County League Division 1

Date		H/A	Comp	Opponents	Res	F	A	Goalscorers
Aug	16	h	League	Nantwich Town	D	3	3	Pearson, Haslam, Wilson
	18	a	League	Droylsden	L	2	3	Pearson, Greenan (pen)
	23	a	League	New Mills	W	3	1	Froggatt 2, Barker
	27	h	League	Darwen	W	1	0	Parry
	30	h	League	Bootle	D	0	0	
Sep	3	a	League	Ashton United	D	1	1	Froggatt
	6	a	League	Burscough	W	2	0	Haslam, Pearson
	10	h	League	Formby	D	1	1	Barker
	13	a	FA Cup 1Q	North Ferriby United	L	0	1	
	16	a	League	Rossendale United	L	0	3	
	20	a	LC 1	Curzon Ashton	W	2	1	Haslam, Greenan (pen)
	27	h	League	Hyde United	W	1	0	Pearson
Oct	4	a	League	Kirkby Town	W	2	1	Barker 2
	11	h	FAT 1Q	Penrith	L	0	3	
	18	a	League	Winsford United	L	0	4	
	21	1	Hospital Cup	Leyland Motors	L	0	2	
	25	h	League	Ashton United	W	3	2	O'Neill, Barker, Greenan (pen)
Nov	1	a	League	Hyde United	L	0	2	
	8	h	League	Prescot Cables	D	0	0	
	15	h	League	Curzon Ashton	W	3	0	Froggatt 2, McLachlan
	29	h	League	St Helens Town	W	1	0	McLachlan
Dec	6	h	League	New Mills	W	4	0	Haslam 2, Froggatt, McLachlan
	13	a	League	Leek Town	L	1	2	Silous
	20	h	League	Droylsden	D	1	1	McLachlan
	26	a	League	Chorley	L	0	2	
	27	a	League	Nantwich Town	W	4	2	McLachlan 2, Silous, Haslam
Jan	1	h	League	Fleetwood Town	W	3	0	Green, Lang, Opponent
	3	h	LJC 2	Leyland Motors	W	2	0	McLachlan, Froggatt
	24	a	League	St Helens Town	L	3	4	Greenan 2 (1pen), Silous
	31	h	League	Kirkby Town	W	2	0	Lang, McLachlan
Feb	7	h	LJC 1	Marine	W	2	1	Kilgannon, Greenan (pen)
	14	a	League	Stalybridge Celtic	L	0	1	
	21	a	League	Formby	L	0	1	
	28	a	League	Curzon Ashton	D	0	0	
Mar	12	h	LJC 3	Barrow	D	1	1	Froggatt
	14	a	LJC 3	Barrow	L	1	3	Haslam
	18	h	League	Leek Town	L	1	2	Greenan (pen)
	27	h	LC 2	Hyde United	D	0	0	
	31	h	League	Burscough	W	1	0	McLachlan
Apr	4	h	League	Stalybridge Celtic	L	0	1	
	7	h	League	Chorley	L	1	2	Unknown
	11	a	League	Bootle	L	0	3	
	13	a	LC 2	Hyde United	L	1	3	O'Neill
	18	a	League	Fleetwood Town	L	1	2	Froggatt
	28	h	League	Rossendale United	D	2	2	Unknown 2
	30	a	League	Darwen	W	1	0	Unknown
May	2	h	League	Winsford United	W	3	1	Greenan, Ford, Froggatt
	7	a	League	Prescot Cables	D	2	2	Unknown 2
						62	64	
		1	at Chorley					

1981-82   Cheshire County League Division 1

Date		H/A	Comp	Opponents	Res	F	A	Goalscorers
Aug	15	a	League	St Helens Town	W	3	0	Barker, Welsh, Webber
	17	h	League	Stalybridge Celtic	W	3	1	Webber, Kershaw, Greenan
	22	h	LC1	Lirkby Town	L	1	4	O'Neill
	25	a	League	Darwen	W	2	1	Webber, Greenan
	29	h	League	Prescot Cables	L	0	1	
	31	h	League	Accrington Stanley	L	1	2	McLachlan
Sep	5	h	FA Cup PR	Skelmersdale United	W	4	0	McLachlan, Lang, Webber, Ainscough
	7	a	League	Accrington Stanley	D	2	2	Webber, McLachlan
	12	a	League	Hyde United	L	1	3	Grimshaw
	14	h	League	Nantwich Town	L	0	4	
	19	h	FA Cup 1Q	Witton Albion	W	2	0	McLachlan 2
	21	a	League	Curzon Ashton	L	0	2	
	26	a	League	Glossop	D	2	2	McLachlan, Cavanagh
	28	h	League	Fleetwood Town	W	2	1	O'Neill, Barker
Oct	3	h	FA Cup 2Q	Hyde United	L	0	4	
	10	a	League	Droylsden	W	4	0	McLachlan 2, O'Neill, Walsh
	12	h	League	Curzon Ashton	D	3	3	McLachlan 2, Lang
	17	h	League	St Helens Town	W	3	1	McLachlan 3
	24	h	FAT 1Q	Ashton United	W	3	0	Lang 2, McLachlan
	31	a	League	Stalybridge Celtic	W	3	2	McLachlan 2, Garrett
Nov	3	a	League	Chorley	L	0	1	
	7	h	League	Leek Town	W	2	0	McLachlan, Grimshaw
	9	h	League	Hyde United	L	1	3	Walsh
	14	a	League	Prescot Cables	D	2	2	McLachlan 2
	16	1	Hospital Cup	Burscough	W	1	0	McLachlan (pen)
	21	h	League	Formby	L	0	2	
	23	h	League	Ashton United	W	1	0	Webber
	28	a	FAT 2Q	Darwen	D	2	2	Webber 2 (2pens)
Dec	1	h	FAT 2Q	Darwen	W	3	2	McLachlan, Webber, Lang
	5	a	League	Nantwich Town	D	0	0	
	6	a	Hospital Cup	Chorley	L	1	3	McLachlan
	19	a	League	Ashton United	L	0	1	
Jan	4	h	FAT 3Q	Chorley	L	0	1	
	16	a	LJC 1	Clitheroe	W	6	1	Lang 2, McLachlan, Froggatt, Webber (pen), Opponent
	23	h	League	Darwen	L	1	2	Higgins
	30	h	LJC 2	Accrington Stanley	L	2	3	Webber (pen), Haslam
Feb	1	h	League	Droylsden	W	3	1	Lang, Webber (pen), Grimshaw
	6	a	League	Winsford United	D	2	2	Webber (pen), Walsh
	8	h	League	Rossendale United	L	1	4	McLachlan
	13	a	League	Bootle	W	2	1	Hart, Grimshaw
	15	h	League	Burscough	L	1	3	Walsh
	20	h	League	Bootle	D	3	3	Webber 2, McLachlan
	27	a	League	Formby	W	4	1	Walsh, O'Neill, Grimshaw, Lang (pen)
Mar	16	a	League	Leek Town	L	2	3	Garrett, Edwards
	20	a	League	Burscough	L	0	3	
	22	h	League	Glossop	L	1	3	Garrett
	27	a	League	Fleetwood Town	L	1	2	Lang (pen)
Apr	5	h	League	Winsford United	L	1	2	Rigby
	12	h	League	Chorley	L	0	4	
	20	a	League	Rossendale United	L	1	4	Kilgannon
						83	92	
		1	at Chorley					
		2	The Rossendale United away game was played at Droylsden					

274

1982-83   North West Counties League Division 1

Date		H/A	Comp	Opponents	Res	F	A	Goalscorers
Aug	14	h	League	Prescot Cables	D	2	2	Caldwell, Mannion
	16	a	League	Lancaster City	W	2	1	Caldwell, Silous
	21	a	League	Winsford United	D	1	1	Opponent
	23	h	League	Accrington Stanley	D	1	1	McLachlan
	28	h	League	Leek Town	W	2	0	McLachlan, Kilgannon
	30	a	League	Ashton United	W	2	1	McLachlan, Caldwell (pen)
Sep	4	a	FA Cup PR	South Liverpool	W	4	1	McLachlan 3, Caldwell
	8	a	League	Bootle	L	0	1	
	11	h	League	St Helens Town	W	2	1	Garrett, Caldwell
	13	h	League	Formby	W	4	0	Caldwell 2, Garrett, Silous
	18	a	FA Cup 1Q	New Mills	W	3	0	McLachlan 2, Caldwell
	20	h	League	Glossop	L	0	1	
	27	a	League	Curzon Ashton	W	2	1	Caldwell (pen), McLachlan
Oct	2	h	FA Cup 2Q	Oswestry Town	W	5	1	Caldwell 3, McLachlan, Silous
	9	a	League	Congleton Town	W	3	0	Caldwell 2, Garrett
	16	h	FA Cup 3Q	Caernarfon Town	D	2	2	Lang, Opponent
	20	a	FA Cup 3Q	Caernarfon Town	W	2	0	McLachlan, Froggatt (pen)
	23	a	FAT 1Q	Shildon	D	2	2	Froggatt (pen), McLachlan
	26	h	FAT 1Q	Shildon	L	1	3	Silous
	30	h	FA Cup 4Q	Runcorn	D	2	2	Froggatt (pen), McLachlan
Nov	2	a	FA Cup 4Q	Runcorn	W	1	0	Kilgannon
	6	a	League	Nantwich Town	L	2	4	Moss, Waywell
	13	a	LC 1	Bootle	D	1	1	Moss
	15	h	LC 1	Bootle	W	3	0	Caldwell, Garrett, Opponent
	20	a	FA Cup 1	Blackpool	L	0	3	
	27	h	League	Bootle	W	1	0	Caldwell
Dec	4	a	League	Stalybridge Celtic	D	0	0	
	6	h	League	Ashton United	L	2	3	Caldwell, Kilgannon
	14	h	League	Darwen	D	2	2	Caldwell, Garrett
	18	a	League	Accrington Stanley	W	4	0	Caldwell 2, Moss, Garrett
Jan	8	a	League	Leek Town	D	0	0	
	15	h	League	Curzon Ashton	W	2	0	Murfin, Waywell
	18	a	League	Burscough	W	2	1	Caldwell, McLachlan
	22	h	LJC 1	Accrington Stanley	W	8	2	Caldwell 3, Garrett 3, Kilgannon, Froggatt
	29	h	League	Lancaster City	W	5	1	Caldwell 3, Garrett 2
Feb	5	a	League	Glossop	D	1	1	Parry
	15	h	LJC 2	Barrow	W	3	0	Parry, Garrett, Opponent
	19	h	League	Congleton Town	D	1	1	Silous
	26	a	League	Darwen	L	1	3	Garrett
Mar	5	h	LJC SF	Southport	W	2	1	Caldwell, Opponent
	7	h	League	Winsford United	W	2	1	Caldwell, Waywell
	12	a	LC 2	Leyland Motors	W	3	1	Brown 2, Caldwell
	16	a	League	Penrith	W	5	3	Caldwell 3, Lancaster 2
	19	h	League	Nantwich Town	W	3	0	Froggatt 2, Silous
	21	h	League	Rhyl	L	0	1	
	24	h	League	Stalybridge Celtic	W	4	1	Caldwell, Silous, Lang, Kilgannon
	26	a	League	Formby	D	1	1	Caldwell
	28	h	League	Penrith	W	5	1	Caldwell 3, Lancaster 2

Season details continued on next page

Date		H/A	Comp	Opponents	Res	F	A	Goalscorers
Apr	2	h	League	Leyland Motors	W	1	0	Garrett
	4	a	League	Rhyl	W	1	0	Caldwell
	9	a	LC 3	Darwen	D	0	0	
	14	h	LC 3	Darwen	L	1	2	Garrett
	16	a	League	St Helens Town	W	2	0	Garrett, Caldwell (pen)
	20	1	LJC Final	Chorley	L	0	3	
	23	h	League	Burscough	W	2	0	Caldwell, Haslam
	25	a	League	Prescot Cables	D	0	0	
	30	a	League	Leyland Motors	W	7	1	Caldwell 3, Silous, Lancaster, Garrett, Griffiths (pen)
						14	6	
		1	at Wigan Athletic					

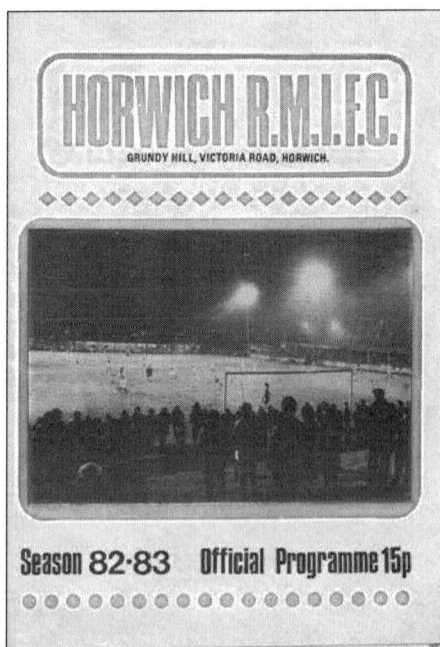

RMI programme cover for 1982-83 showing
off the new floodlights

1983-84 Northern Premier League

Date		H/A	Comp	Opponents	Res	F	A	Goalscorers
Aug	20	h	League	Matlock Town	L	0	1	
	23	a	League	Morecambe	D	1	1	Lang (pen)
	27	a	League	Worksop Town	W	3	1	Moss 2, McLachlan
	29	h	League	Southport	W	2	1	McLachlan, Haslam
Sep	3	h	League	Grantham	L	1	2	Moss
	6	a	League	Rhyl	L	0	3	
	10	h	League	Stafford Rangers	W	2	1	Stevens, Hampson
	13	a	League	Macclesfield Town	D	2	2	McLachlan, Lang
	17	a	FA Cup 1Q	Farsley Celtic	W	4	1	Waywell 2, McLachlan, Lang (pen)
	19	h	League	Workington	W	1	0	Lang (pen)
	24	a	League	Grantham	L	1	2	Liptrot
	27	a	League	Barrow	L	0	2	
Oct	1	a	FA Cup 2Q	Buxton	W	1	0	Liptrot
	3	h	League	Gainsborough Trinity	W	2	1	Moss 2
	8	h	League	Rhyl	L	0	3	
	10	a	League	Mossley	W	2	1	Moss, Haslam
	15	h	FA Cup 3Q	Southport	W	2	1	McLachlan, Liptrot
	17	h	League	Morecambe	W	3	1	Moss 2, Waywell
	22	a	FAT 1Q	Macclesfield Town	W	1	0	Redshaw
	29	h	FA Cup 4Q	Macclesfield Town	D	0	0	
Nov	1	a	FA Cup 4Q	Macclesfield Town	L	3	4	Silous, Froggatt (pen), Stevens
	5	a	League	Witton Albion	L	1	7	Froggatt (pen)
	7	h	Floodlit Cup	Morecambe	W	3	2	McLachlan, Redshaw, Edwards
	12	h	League	Macclesfield Town	D	1	1	Redshaw
	15	a	Floodlit Cup	Great Harwood Town	W	1	0	Liptrot
	19	h	League	Goole Town	W	4	0	Moss 3, Redshaw
	21	h	Floodlit Cup	Lancaster City	L	2	5	Liptrot, Wilson
	26	h	FAT 2Q	Winsford United	W	4	1	McLachlan 2, Redshaw, Moss
Dec	3	a	League	Oswestry Town	W	6	0	Redshaw 2, Haslam, McLachlan, Moss, Opponent
	17	h	FAT 3Q	Marine	L	0	1	
	19	h	League	Burton Albion	D	0	0	
	26	a	League	Chorley	D	2	2	McLachlan, Froggatt (pen)
	31	a	NPL Cup 1 1st Leg	Morecambe	D	0	0	
Jan	2	h	League	Barrow	D	0	0	
	7	a	League	South Liverpool	L	0	1	
	14	a	League	Workington	L	1	3	Redshaw
	17	a	Floodlit Cup	Morecambe	W	3	2	Redshaw, Froggatt, Nicholl
	31	h	LJC 2	Radcliffe Borough	W	5	0	Redshaw, Froggatt, Haslam, McLachlan, Lancaster
Feb	4	a	League	Burton Albion	W	2	1	Redshaw 2
	6	h	LC 1 2nd Leg	Morecambe	W	4	2	Liptrot 2, Froggatt (pen), Redshaw
	11	h	NPL Cup 2	Burton Albion	D	1	1	Stevens
	13	h	LJC 3	Accrington Stanley	D	1	1	Froggatt (pen)
	18	h	League	Witton Albion	D	1	1	Liptrot
	22	a	LC 2	Burton Albion	W	2	1	Redshaw, Opponent
	25	a	LJC 3	Accrington Stanley	L	0	1	

Season details continued on next page

Date		H/A	Comp	Opponents	Res	F	A	Goalscorers
Mar	3	h	NPL Cup 3	Hyde United	L	0	2	
	10	h	League	Oswestry Town	W	4	2	Redshaw 2, Moss 2
	13	a	League	Matlock Town	L	0	1	
	17	h	League	Mossley	W	2	0	Redshaw, McLachlan
	20	a	Floodlit Cup	Lancaster City	W	4	2	Moss 2, Redshaw, Liptrot
	24	a	League	Southport	D	2	2	McLachlan, Waywell
	26	h	Floodlit Cup	Great Harwood Town	W	3	0	McLachlan, Redshaw, Lang (pen)
Apr	4	a	League	Goole Town	L	0	2	
	7	a	League	Gainsborough Trinity	W	2	0	Moss, Lancaster
	8	h	League	Buxton	W	3	0	McLachlan 2, Moss
	10	a	League	Buxton	W	2	0	Haslam, Silous
	14	h	League	South Liverpool	D	1	1	Lancaster
	16	a	League	Marine	W	1	0	Moss
	21	a	League	Stafford Rangers	L	1	3	Haslam
	23	h	League	Chorley	L	3	4	Redshaw, Stevens, Froggatt
	25	h	League	Marine	W	1	0	Redshaw
	28	h	League	Hyde United	W	2	1	Redshaw, Opponent
	30	1	Floodlit Cup Final	Southport	L	0	4	
May	3	a	League	Hyde United	L	0	2	
	5	h	League	Worksop Town	L	2	3	Redshaw 2
		1	At Preston North End FC			33	29	

Ken Wright, a great servant to RMI as player and Manager

1984-85   Northern Premier League

Date		H/A	Comp	Opponents	Res	F	A	Goalscorers
Aug	18	h	League	Grantham	W	2	0	Liptrot, Lang
	22	a	League	Workington	W	4	0	McLachlan 2, Moss, Liptrot
	25	a	League	Witton Albion	D	2	2	McLachlan, Edwards
	27	h	League	Morecambe	W	4	1	Edwards 2, Lancaster, Froggatt
Sep	1	h	League	Worksop Town	D	1	1	Froggatt
	4	a	League	Mossley	W	2	0	McLachlan, Edwards
	8	a	League	Oswestry Town	L	1	2	Opponent
	10	h	League	Burton Albion	L	1	3	Edwards
	15	h	FA Cup 1Q	Appelby Frodingham	W	3	0	McLachlan, Edwards, Stevens
	17	h	League	Workington	W	3	0	McLachlan, McCrory, Lang
	22	h	League	Macclesfield Town	D	0	0	
	25	a	League	Morecambe	D	1	1	Pawsey
	29	a	FA Cup 2Q	Winsford United	L	1	2	Froggatt
Oct	6	a	League	Marine	D	2	2	McCrory, Pawsey
	9	a	League	Rhyl	L	0	3	
	13	h	League	Southport	L	1	2	Froggatt
	20	a	FAT 1Q	Buxton	D	0	0	
	22	h	FAT 1Q	Buxton	D	2	2	McLachlan 2
	27	h	League	Stafford Rangers	D	1	1	Stevens
	29	h	FAT 1Q	Buxton	L	2	4	McLachlan, Stevens
Nov	6	h	League	Matlock Town	D	1	1	P Jones
	10	h	Presidents Cup	Macclesfield Town	W	2	1	McLachlan, Lang
	12	h	Floodlit Cup	Great Harwood Town	L	0	2	
	17	a	League	Gainsborough Trinity	W	3	1	Moss, Lancaster, P Jones
	20	h	League	Witton Albion	L	0	2	
	24	h	League	Oswestry Town	W	1	0	Moss
	27	a	League	Worksop Town	D	4	4	Moss 2, P Jones, N Jones
Dec	1	h	League	Hyde United	L	0	1	
	3	a	LJC 1	Radcliffe Borough	W	2	1	Moss, Froggatt
	10	h	League	Mossley	D	1	1	Moss
	15	a	League	Buxton	W	2	0	Moss, P Jones
	23	a	Presidents Cup	Macclesfield Town	L	1	3	Moss
	26	a	League	Chorley	D	1	1	Silous
	29	h	League	Rhyl	D	3	3	McLachlan 2, Froggatt
Jan	30	h	LJC 2	Great Harwood Town	W	6	1	Moss 3, McLachlan, N Jones, Hart
Feb	2	a	League	Hyde United	L	1	2	Moss
	5	a	League	Macclesfield Town	L	1	2	McLachlan
	25	h	LJC 3	Barrow	L	1	2	Froggatt
Mar	1	h	NPL Cup 1	Matlock Town	D	1	1	Stafford
	4	a	NPL Cup 1	Matlock Town	L	1	2	Froggatt
	9	h	League	Marine	W	2	0	McLachlan, Cooper
	11	h	League	Goole Town	L	1	2	Froggatt
	16	a	League	Matlock Town	W	3	2	Moss, Cooper, Silous
	20	a	Floodlit Cup	Leyland Motors	W	2	0	Moss, Froggatt
	23	h	League	Gainsborough Trinity	W	4	1	Moss, Cooper, Stafford, Haslam
	25	a	Floodlit Cup	Lancaster City	W	1	0	Cooper
	27	a	Floodlit Cup	Great Harwood Town	W	1	0	Froggatt
	30	a	League	Bangor City	L	1	2	Sheridan

Season details continued on next page

Date		H/A	Comp	Opponents	Res	F	A	Goalscorers
Apr	1	h	Floodlit Cup	Leyland Motors	W	4	1	Sheridan 2, McLachlan 2
	3	a	League	Burton Albion	L	0	1	
	6	a	League	Southport	W	2	0	Sheridan, McLachlan
	8	h	League	Chorley	W	1	0	P Jones
	10	h	Floodlit Cup	Lancaster City	W	4	1	Cooper 2, Froggatt, Silous
	13	a	League	Stafford Rangers	D	1	1	McLachlan
	16	a	League	South Liverpool	W	2	0	Moss, Froggatt
	20	a	League	Grantham	L	0	2	
	27	h	League	Buxton	W	1	0	Lang
	29	h	League	South Liverpool	D	2	2	Moss, Froggatt
	30	1	Floodlit Cup Final	South Liverpool	W	2	0	Moss 2
May	2	h	League	Bangor City	W	3	0	Moss 2, Hart
	4	a	League	Goole Town	D	1	1	Fitzharris
		1	at Preston North End FC			103	73	

Grundy Hill in the 1980s

1985-86   Northern Premier League

Date		H/A	Comp	Opponents	Res	F	A	Goalscorers
Aug	24	h	League	Worksop Town	L	1	3	Moss
	26	a	League	Southport	L	0	2	
	31	a	League	South Liverpool	L	0	1	
Sep	2	h	League	Workington	L	0	3	
	7	a	FA Cup 1Q	Skelmersdale United	D	2	2	Moss, Froggatt
	11	h	FA Cup 1Q	Skelmersdale United	W	3	0	Moss 2, Walker
	14	h	League	Oswestry Town	W	2	1	Walker, Froggatt
	17	a	League	Morecambe	D	1	1	G Cooper
	21	a	League	Bangor City	L	1	3	Walker
	23	h	League	Hyde United	L	1	4	Moss
	28	a	FA Cup 2Q	Congleton Town	D	2	2	Moss 2
	30	h	FA Cup 2Q	Congleton Town	W	2	0	Moss, G Cooper
Oct	5	a	FAT 1Q	Brandon United	L	1	9	Froggatt
	8	a	League	Macclesfield Town	L	2	7	Walker, Carney
	12	a	FA Cup 3Q	Rhyl	L	0	2	
	14	h	League	Marine	L	2	3	Moss, Buckley
	19	h	League	Gainsborough Trinity	W	2	1	Gilsenen, Buckley
	23	a	League	Mossley	L	2	3	Walker, Opponent
	26	a	League	Buxton	L	0	1	
	28	h	League	Caernarfon Town	W	1	0	Moss
Nov	2	h	League	South Liverpool	L	0	1	
	6	a	League	Workington	D	0	0	
	9	a	Presidents Cup 1	Witton Albion	W	1	0	Pawsey
	12	h	League	Macclesfield Town	W	2	0	Moss 2
	16	a	League	Matlock Town	W	3	1	Moss 2, Froggatt
	18	h	Floodlit Cup	Ashton United	W	3	0	Moss 2, Opponent
	23	h	League	Burton Albion	W	2	1	Ellis, Pawsey
	28	a	Floodlit Cup	Radcliffe Borough	W	5	1	Moss 2, Peters, Fielding, Buckley
	30	h	League	Goole Town	W	4	0	Ellis 3, Stafford
Dec	4	a	Floodlit Cup	Leyland Motors	D	2	2	Peters, Hart
	7	a	League	Witton Albion	W	4	1	Peters, Ellis, C Cooper, Fielding
	9	h	Floodlit Cup	Leyland Motors	W	4	1	Moss 2, Ellis, Stafford
	14	h	Presidents Cup 1	Witton Albion	D	1	1	C Cooper
	21	a	League	Goole Town	D	1	1	Ellis
	26	a	League	Chorley	W	3	1	Moss 2, C Cooper
Jan	1	h	League	Southport	D	1	1	Moss
	11	a	League	Rhyl	W	1	0	C Cooper
	18	a	League	Gateshead	L	1	3	Ellis
	29	h	LJC 1	Blackpool Mechanics	L	0	2	
Feb	1	h	NPL Cup 1	Workington	L	0	2	
	15	a	League	Marine	L	0	1	
Mar	6	h	League	Mossley	L	0	1	
	8	h	League	Matlock Town	W	3	1	Froggatt 2, C Cooper
	10	h	Presidents Cup 2	Worksop Town	D	2	2	Moss, Haslam
	12	a	Presidents Cup 2	Worksop Town	L	1	2	Haslam
	15	a	League	Hyde United	L	0	1	
	22	h	League	Witton Albion	L	0	1	
	29	a	League	Caernarfon Town	L	0	2	
	31	h	League	Chorley	D	0	0	

Season details continued on next page

1985-86 Northern Premier League Continued

Date		H/A	Comp	Opponents	Res	F	A	Goalscorers
Apr	2	h	Floodlit Cup	Radcliffe Borough	W	3	1	Moss, Owen, Hart
	5	h	League	Rhyl	W	2	1	Moss, Owen
	8	h	League	Buxton	D	2	2	Ellis, Owen
	10	a	Floodlit Cup	Ashton United	W	5	1	Ellis 2, Owen, C Cooper, Haslam
	12	h	League	Gateshead	W	2	1	Moss, McCarthy
	14	a	League	Gainsborough Trinity	W	3	0	Ellis 2, Moss
	19	a	League	Worksop Town	L	1	2	Russell (pen)
	23	h	Floodlit Cup SF	Chorley	L	1	2	Hart
	26	a	League	Oswestry Town	L	0	1	
	30	a	League	Burton Albion	L	0	3	
May	2	h	League	Morecambe	W	2	1	Owen, Kolojeski
	3	h	League	Bangor City	L	1	2	Peters
						91	95	

Long-serving Neil McLachlan, pictured at Grundy Hill in the early 1990s

1986-87   Northern Premier League

Date		H/A	Comp	Opponents	Res	F	A	Goalscorers
Aug	16	h	League	Matlock Town	L	2	4	Thompson 2
	20	a	League	Workington	D	0	0	
	23	h	League	Oswestry Town	L	0	2	
	25	a	League	Southport	D	1	1	Opponent
	30	a	League	Bangor City	L	0	2	
Sep	2	h	League	Morecambe	L	1	2	Blow
	6	h	League	Burton Albion	D	0	0	
	9	a	League	Barrow	L	0	3	
	13	a	FA Cup 1Q	Chorley	L	1	2	Moore
	17	a	League	South Liverpool	L	0	2	
	20	h	League	Hyde United	L	3	4	Moore 2, Lowe
	22	h	League	Buxton	W	2	1	McLachlan 2
	27	a	League	Matlock Town	L	1	2	Hart
	30	a	League	Marine	L	1	5	Podmore
Oct	4	h	FAT 1Q	Ferryhill Athletic	W	3	2	Walmsley, Howlett, Thompson
	6	h	League	Barrow	L	0	1	
	15	a	League	Worksop Town	L	2	4	Blow (pen), Howlett
	18	h	League	Goole Town	L	2	3	Hart, Gummerson
	21	a	League	Buxton	L	0	2	
	25	h	League	Witton Albion	L	1	2	McLachlan
	27	h	Floodlit Cup	Great Harwood Town	W	3	0	Moore 2, Haddon (pen)
Nov	1	h	FAT 2Q	Consett	D	0	0	
	5	a	FAT 2Q	Consett	L	1	2	Thompson
	8	a	League	Mossley	D	0	0	
	10	h	GMAC Cup 1	Runcorn	L	0	2	
	15	h	League	Macclesfield Town	L	0	1	
	22	a	League	Caernarfon Town	L	0	3	
	29	h	NPL Cup 1	Chorley	L	0	4	
Dec	6	a	LJC 1	Skelmersdale United	W	3	1	Moore, Walmsley, Lloyd
	13	a	NPL Cup 1	Chorley	L	0	3	
	15	h	Floodlit Cup	Radcliffe Borough	L	1	2	Lloyd
	26	a	League	Chorley	L	0	3	
	27	h	League	Bangor City	D	0	0	
Jan	1	h	League	Southport	L	2	3	Lancaster, Blow
	3	a	League	Gainsborough Trinity	L	0	2	
	24	a	League	Hyde United	L	0	5	
	28	a	Floodlit Cup	Accrington Stanley	D	1	1	Lancaster
Feb	3	h	LJC 2	Bacup Borough	L	0	2	
	7	h	League	South Liverpool	L	0	1	
	14	h	League	Caernarfon Town	D	1	1	Gay
	16	h	League	Workington	D	1	1	McLachlan
	28	a	League	Witton Albion	D	1	1	Walmsley
Mar	3	a	League	Goole Town	D	0	0	
	14	a	League	Macclesfield Town	D	2	2	Lancaster, Podmore
	18	a	League	Rhyl	L	2	6	Walmsley, Moore
	21	h	League	Worksop Town	W	3	2	Moore 2, McLachlan
	24	a	Floodlit Cup	Irlam Town	W	2	0	Lancaster, Walmsley
	30	h	League	Mossley	L	1	3	Fielding

Season details continued on next page

Date		H/A	Comp	Opponents	Res	F	A	Goalscorers
Apr	4	h	League	Gainsborough Trinity	L	0	1	
	5	a	Floodlit Cup	Radcliffe Borough	D	1	1	Lancaster
	9	h	Floodlit Cup	Irlam Town	L	0	2	
	13	h	League	Rhyl	D	1	1	Podmore
	15	a	League	Oswestry Town	L	2	3	McLachlan, Richmond
	16	h	Floodlit Cup	Accrington Stanley	L	2	3	Lancaster, Walmsley
	18	a	League	Morecambe	L	0	1	
	20	h	League	Chorley	D	2	2	Podmore, Silous
	25	a	League	Burton Albion	W	1	0	Lancaster
	28	a	Floodlit Cup	Great Harwood Town	W	2	0	Moore, McLachlan
May	2	h	League	Marine	L	1	3	Podmore
						56	112	

Mickey Moore pictured at Grundy Hill

Finance was always a problem for small football cubs—Horwich RMI, in common with many other clubs, launched a lottery to raise funds

1987-88   Northern Premier League (Premier Division)

Date		H/A	Comp	Opponents	Res	F	A	Goalscorers	Att
Aug	22	a	League	Matlock Town	W	4	0	Page 3, Haslam	380
	24	h	League	Barrow	D	1	1	Haslam	380
	29	h	League	Frickley Athletic	L	1	2	Schofield	319
	31	a	League	Southport	L	0	1		420
Sep	5	h	League	Worksop Town	W	2	0	Walker, Hulme	241
	9	a	GMAC Cup 1	South Liverpool	D	1	1	Power	135
	12	h	FA Cup 1Q	South Liverpool	D	1	1	Page	192
	16	a	FA Cup 1Q	South Liverpool	W	4	3	Power 2, Walker 2	170
	19	a	League	Gainsborough Trinity	L	0	1		176
	21	h	GMAC Cup 1	South Liverpool	W	2	1	Hulme, Opponent	225
	26	a	FA Cup 2Q	St Helens Town	D	0	0		156
	29	h	FA Cup 2Q	St Helens Town	L	2	3	Page, Haslam	307
Oct	3	h	FAT 1Q	South Liverpool	L	1	2	Walmsley	173
	7	a	GMAC Cup 2	Workington	W	2	1	Page, Rodgers	166
	10	h	League	Workington	W	2	0	McLachlan, Hulme	219
	14	a	League	Workington	D	2	2	Page, Walker	190
	17	h	League	Bangor City	W	3	2	Podmore, Walker, Opponent	273
	19	h	League	Caernarfon Town	L	0	1		319
	24	a	League	Morecambe	L	2	3	Podmore, Page	450
	26	h	League	Goole Town	L	0	2		248
Nov	4	h	GMAC Cup 3	Marine	W	1	0	Podmore	207
	7	a	League	Gateshead	L	0	1		150
	11	a	League	Caernarfon Town	W	4	2	Schofield 2, Power, Rodgers	212
	14	h	League	South Liverpool	L	1	2	Page	202
	16	h	League	Marine	D	0	0		198
	21	a	League	Bangor City	D	0	0		331
	25	a	LJC 1	Burscough	W	1	0	Walmsley	96
	28	h	League	Mossley	W	1	0	Walker	186
Dec	1	a	GMAC Cup 4	Altrincham	W	2	1	Page, Power	674
	5	a	League	Oswestry Town	W	3	2	Walker, Power, Opponent	238
	7	h	League	Rhyl	D	0	0		227
	12	h	League	Gainsborough Trinity	W	1	0	Fielding	187
	26	a	League	Mossley	W	2	0	Page 2	245
	28	h	League	Chorley	L	0	1		826
Jan	9	a	NPL Cup 1	Eastwood Hanley	W	1	0	Walmsley	35
	16	h	League	Matlock Town	W	2	0	Power 2	207
	20	h	Floodlit Cup	Leyland Motors	L	1	3	Howarth	109
	30	h	LJC 2	Lancaster City	L	2	3	Walmsley, Walker	153
Feb	9	a	GMAC Cup 5	Northwich Victoria	D	1	1	Rodgers	220
	13	a	League	Marine	L	0	1		240
	20	a	NPL Cup 2	Bangor City	L	0	3		293
	23	h	GMAC Cup 5	Northwich Victoria	W	3	2	Page, Howarth, Hart	336
	27	h	League	Oswestry Town	W	2	1	Walker, Mitchell	205
Mar	1	a	League	Buxton	L	1	2	Moore	260
	5	a	League	Hyde United	L	0	2		410
	12	a	League	Witton Albion	W	1	0	Street	330
	15	a	League	Goole Town	D	1	1	Walker	215
	17	h	Floodlit Cup	Lancaster City	W	5	0	Page 2, Seddon 2, Senior	112
	21	h	League	Hyde United	L	1	4	McLachlan	339
	26	a	League	Barrow	L	0	2		892
	27	h	GMAC Cup SF	Enfield	W	3	1	Page 2, Opponent	822
	30	a	Floodlit Cup	Leyland Motors	W	1	0	Walmsley	100

Season details continued on next page

1987-88 Northern Premier League Premier Division Ctd

Date		H/A	Comp	Opponents	Res	F	A	Goalscorers	Notes
Apr	2	a	League	Worksop Town	W	2	1	Page, McLachlan	260
	4	a	League	Frickley Athletic	D	0	0		350
	6	h	League	Morecambe	L	0	1		259
	9	h	League	Witton Albion	W	1	0	Senior	206
	11	h	League	Southport	D	1	1	McLachlan	234
	16	h	League	Gateshead	W	2	1	Walmsley, Street	249
	18	a	League	Chorley	L	0	1		780
	20	a	Floodlit Cup	Barrow	W	5	3	Street 2, Power 2, Page	200
	21	a	Floodlit Cup	Lancaster City	W	2	1	McLachlan, Hart	100
	23	a	League	Rhyl	W	1	0	Howarth	250
	26	a	League	South Liverpool	D	1	1	McLachlan	150
	29	h	League	Buxton	W	1	0	Walker	174
May	8	h	GMAC Final	Weymouth	W	2	0	McLachlan, Page	1149
	10	h	Floodlit Cup QF	Rossendale United	W	3	1	Walker, Hart, Henshaw	100
						92	73		

The home Floodlit Cup tie v Barrow was not played

RMI Captain and later Player Manager Brian Hart

1988-89   Northern Premier League Premier Division

Date		H/A	Comp	Opponents	Res	F	A	Goalscorers	Att
Aug	20	a	League	Caernarfon Town	D	2	2	Walmsley, Podmore	304
	22	h	League	Barrow	L	0	3		289
	27	h	League	Worksop Town	D	1	1	Page	244
	29	a	League	Southport	W	2	0	Page, Moore	300
Sep	3	h	League	Buxton	L	0	1		240
	6	a	Clubcall Cup 1	Fleetwood Town	L	0	3		343
	10	a	League	Goole Town	L	1	3	Howarth	242
	12	h	League	Mossley	L	0	1		255
	17	h	FA Cup 1Q	Droylsden	D	3	3	Howarth 2, Page	174
	20	a	FA Cup 1Q	Droylsden	W	2	1	Page, Moore	217
	24	a	FAT 1Q	Goole Town	L	0	3		219
	26	h	League	Rhyl	W	2	1	Senior, McLachlan	209
Oct	1	a	FA Cup 2Q	Emley	L	0	5		406
	3	a	League	Mossley	L	0	1		250
	8	h	League	Frickley Athletic	L	1	4	Seddon	160
	15	a	League	Matlock Town	D	0	0		403
	17	h	League	Caernarfon Town	W	3	0	Page 2, Moore	239
	22	h	League	Southport	L	2	5	Moore, Walmsley	328
	29	a	League	Stalybridge Celtic	D	1	1	Mills	376
	31	h	Floodlit Trophy SF	Hyde United	L	1	2	Page	168
Nov	5	h	League	Matlock Town	D	1	1	Schofield	146
	7	h	League	Hyde United	L	0	2		315
	12	h	League	Marine	L	0	1		215
	15	a	League	Bangor City	L	2	3	Schofield, Moore	325
	26	a	League	Marine	D	2	2	Walmsley, Hart	269
Dec	3	h	League	Stalybridge Celtic	W	1	0	Walmsley	211
	7	a	LJC 1	South Liverpool	L	0	2		56
	10	h	League	Gainsborough Trinity	L	0	4		147
	17	a	NPL Cup 1	Frickley Athletic	L	0	2		199
	26	h	League	Morecambe	L	1	2	Walmsley	335
	31	h	League	Bangor City	L	0	3		219
Jan	2	a	League	Barrow	L	1	2	Booth (pen)	590
	7	a	League	South Liverpool	L	2	4	Walmsley, Walker	105
	11	a	League	Rhyl	L	1	6	Dalgleish	220
	14	a	League	Worksop Town	W	2	0	Cameron, Opponent	177
	21	h	League	Goole Town	D	1	1	Seddon	215
	24	h	League	Fleetwood Town	D	1	1	Walmsley	243
	28	a	League	Fleetwood Town	L	0	2		374
	30	h	Floodlit Cup	Lancaster City	W	3	0	Woodcock 2, McLachlan	131
Feb	4	h	League	Shepshed Charterhouse	L	0	1		265
	7	a	Floodlit Cup	Stalybridge Celtic	L	0	2		160
	11	a	League	Morecambe	L	0	1		206
	18	h	League	Witton Albion	D	2	2	Schofield, Hart	264
	21	a	Floodlit Cup	Lancaster City	L	0	2		150
Mar	7	a	League	Frickley Athletic	D	3	3	Woodcock, Walker, Dalgleish	281
	11	a	League	Shepshed Charterhouse	W	2	1	Walker 2	232
	13	h	Floodlit Cup	Stalybridge Celtic	D	1	1	Walker	85
	18	a	League	Hyde United	D	0	0		465
	27	h	League	South Liverpool	W	2	0	Walker 2	226
Apr	2	a	League	Gateshead	L	0	1		150
	14	a	League	Buxton	D	0	0		336
	22	h	League	Gateshead	D	1	1	Cooper	
	26	a	League	Gainsborough Trinity	D	1	1	Dalgleish	
	29	a	League	Witton Albion	L	1	2	Haslam	
						52	96		

1989-90 Northern Premier League Premier Division

Date		H/A	Comp	Opponents	Res	F	A	Goalscorers
Aug	26	h	League	Shepshed Charterhouse	L	1	2	Liptrot
	28	a	League	Southport	L	1	2	Seddon
Sep	2	h	League	Bishop Auckland	L	1	2	Liptrot
	4	h	League	Frickley Athletic	D	2	2	Liptrot, Walker
	9	a	League	Caernarfon Town	L	0	1	
	12	a	League	Goole Town	D	1	1	Liptrot
	16	a	FA Cup 1Q	Caernarfon Town	L	1	3	Booth (pen)
	23	h	FAT 1Q	Mossley	L	0	4	
	27	a	League	Rhyl	W	2	1	Liptrot, Webster
	30	h	League	Gainsborough Trinity	D	1	1	Walker
Oct	2	h	League	Morecambe	W	1	0	McCarty
	7	a	League	Gainsborough Trinity	D	1	1	McCarty
	12	h	Clubcall Cup 1	Bangor City	L	0	1	
	16	h	League	Goole Town	W	1	0	Walmsley
	21	h	League	Stalybridge Celtic	D	1	1	Walmsley
	25	a	League	Colne Dynamoes	L	2	4	Liptrot, Smith
	28	h	League	Bangor City	D	2	2	Liptrot, Smith
	30	h	Floodlit Cup	Leyland Motors	W	3	1	Walker, Smith, Haslam
Nov	4	a	League	Mossley	W	2	1	Liptrot, Walmsley
	11	h	League	South Liverpool	D	2	2	Walker, Walmsley
	18	h	League	Colne Dynamoes	L	1	3	Dalgleish
	20	h	League	Matlock Town	W	2	0	Liptrot, Smith
	25	a	League	South Liverpool	D	1	1	Booth (pen)
	29	h	Floodlit Cup	South Liverpool	L	1	2	Walmsley
Dec	2	a	League	Stalybridge Celtic	W	1	0	Schofield
	3	a	League	Bishop Auckland	L	0	5	
	7	h	LJC 1	Padiham	W	1	0	McCarty
	9	h	League	Gateshead	W	4	1	McCarty 2, Seddon, Parillon
	16	a	NPL Cup 1	Bangor City	L	1	3	Senior
	18	h	League	Witton Albion	W	1	0	McCarty
	26	a	League	Morecambe	W	2	1	Liptrot, Madrick
	29	a	League	Buxton	L	0	2	
Jan	1	h	League	Southport	W	5	4	Seddon 2, Mullineux, Walker, Parillon
	6	a	League	Gateshead	L	2	3	Walker, McCarty
	13	h	League	Mossley	L	2	3	Walker, McCarty
	20	a	League	Marine	D	1	1	Dalgleish
Feb	10	a	League	Shepshed Charterhouse	W	2	0	Walker, Liptrot
	14	a	LJC 2	Darwen	L	2	3	McCarty, Walmsley
	21	a	Floodlit Cup	South Liverpool	L	0	1	
	24	h	League	Caernarfon Town	W	5	1	Walmsley 2 (1pen), Walker, McCarty, Liptrot
Mar	3	a	League	Matlock Town	D	3	3	Liptrot 2, Opponent
	10	a	League	Frickley Athletic	L	0	2	
	12	h	Floodlit Cup	Chorley	L	1	2	Senior
	17	h	League	Hyde United	L	0	2	
	20	a	League	Bangor City	W	2	1	Senior, Opponent
	24	h	League	Rhyl	D	1	1	Dalgleish
	27	a	League	Witton Albion	L	0	2	
Apr	7	h	League	Marine	L	1	3	McCarty
	9	a	Floodlit Cup	Leyland Motors	D	0	0	
	13	a	League	Hyde United	W	3	2	Liptrot 2, Walmsley
	16	h	League	Fleetwood Town	W	3	2	Walmsley (pen), Dalgleish, McLachlan
	27	h	League	Buxton	D	1	1	Walmsley (pen)
May	5	a	League	Fleetwood Town	D	2	2	Walmsley 2 (1pen)
	7	a	Floodlit Cup	Chorley	W	1	0	Baldwin
						77	89	

1990-91   Northern Premier League Premier Division

Date		H/A	Comp	Opponents	Res	F	A	Goalscorers	Att
Aug	18	a	League	Shepshed Charterhouse	W	2	1	Walmsley (pen), Walker	401
	20	h	League	Morecambe	D	1	1	Hart	324
	25	h	League	Frickley Athletic	D	1	1	Parillon	198
	27	a	League	Southport	L	0	2		415
Sep	1	a	League	Matlock Town	L	1	2	Walker	289
	3	h	League	Leek Town	L	0	3		268
	8	h	League	Bishop Auckland	D	2	2	Parillon, Senior	210
	10	a	League	Chorley	W	2	1	Walmsley (pen), Baldwin	605
	15	a	FA Cup 1Q	Morecambe	D	2	2	Parillon, McCarty	285
	17	h	FA Cup 1Q	Morecambe	W	3	0	McCarty 2, Liptrot	249
	22	h	FAT 1Q	Alfreton Town	W	1	0	Hart	136
	25	a	League	Witton Albion	L	1	4	Liptrot	712
	29	a	FA Cup 2Q	Irlam Town	W	3	1	McCarty 2, Walker	105
Oct	2	a	League	Marine	L	1	2	Baldwin	254
	6	h	League	Goole Town	L	1	3	McCarty	165
	8	h	Inter-League Cup 1	Marine	L	4	5	McLachlan 3, Walmsley	148
	13	h	FA Cup 3Q	Colwyn Bay	L	1	3	Walker	288
	15	h	League	Fleetwood Town	L	0	2		236
	20	h	FAT 2Q	Rhyl	W	3	2	Walker, McLachlan, Walmsley (pen)	138
	23	a	League	Stalybridge Celtic	L	0	3		309
	27	h	League	Gainsborough Trinity	W	2	1	McCarty, Taylor	153
Nov	2	h	League	Buxton	W	4	0	Taylor, Madrick, Senior, Ainscow	327
	5	h	League	South Liverpool	L	2	4	McCarty, Senior	235
	10	a	League	Droylsden	L	1	3	Liptrot	381
	17	a	NPL Cup 1	Harrogate Town	D	2	2	Liptrot 2	215
	24	h	League	Hyde United	W	2	0	Walker, Smith	251
	28	a	League	South Liverpool	L	0	3		148
Dec	1	a	FAT 3Q	Sutton Coldfield Town	W	3	1	McCarty, McLachlan, Senior	145
	3	h	NPL Cup 1	Harrogate Town	W	2	1	McLachlan, Senior	145
	8	a	LJC 1	Westhoughton Town	L	0	1		65
	15	h	NPL Cup 2	Southport	D	3	3	Ainscow 2, Walker	238
	29	a	League	Bangor City	L	1	3	Ainscow	322
Jan	1	h	League	Southport	D	2	2	Liptrot, Schofield	402
	12	h	FAT 1	Bedworth United	W	2	1	Walker, Baldwin	168
	19	h	NPL Cup 2	Southport	L	0	2		264
	22	h	Floodlit Cup	Leyland Motors	L	0	2		66
	26	h	League	Marine	D	0	0		217
	28	h	League	Stalybridge Celtic	L	0	1		251
Feb	18	h	FAT 2	Gretna	W	2	1	Ainscow, McCarty	313
	23	h	FAT 3	Redbridge Forest	W	2	1	Liptrot, Parillon	411
Mar	2	a	League	Mossley	L	3	5	McCarty, McLachlan, Walker	262
	9	h	League	Chorley	D	1	1	Senior	498
	16	a	FAT QF	Altrincham	L	0	5		1486
	19	a	League	Morecambe	L	2	5	McCarty, Liptrot	226
	23	h	League	Matlock Town	W	5	0	Liptrot 2, Schofield, Opponents 2	186
	26	a	League	Fleetwood Town	L	2	3	Walker (pen), Griffin	233
	30	a	League	Goole Town	L	1	4	Baker	245

Season details continued on next page

Date		H/A	Comp	Opponents	Res	F	A	Goalscorers	Notes
Apr	1	h	League	Bangor City	W	4	1	McDonald 3, Liptrot	184
	3	a	League	Buxton	L	1	5	McDonald	326
	6	a	League	Frickley Athletic	W	1	0	Griffin	95
	13	a	League	Bishop Auckland	W	2	1	Walker 2 (1pen)	216
	20	h	League	Shepshed Charterhouse	W	3	0	McCarty, McLachlan, Senior	171
	22	a	League	Hyde United	W	3	0	McLachlan, Liptrot, Schofield	315
	25	h	League	Droylsden	W	2	1	McCarty, Walmsley	203
	27	a	League	Leek Town	W	2	1	Liptrot 2	413
	29	h	League	Witton Albion	L	1	2	Walker (pen)	290
	30	a	League	Gainsborough Trinity	L	1	4	Liptrot	192
May	4	h	League	Mossley	L	2	4	O'Berg 2	

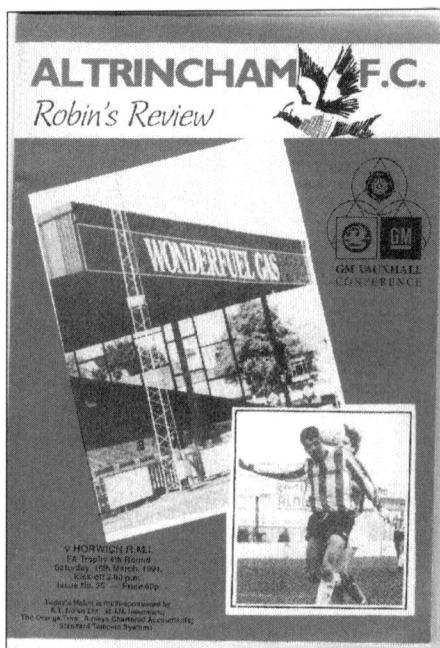

Programme for the FA Trophy Quarter Final at Altrincham -
the first time that RMI had reached the last eight of the
major non-league knock-out competition.

1991-92   Northern Premier League Premier Division

Date		H/A	Comp	Opponents	Res	F	A	Goalscorers	Att
Aug	24	a	League	Shepshed Albion	W	3	1	McDonald 2, McCarty	309
	26	h	League	Frickley Athletic	L	1	3	Walker	249
	31	h	League	Matlock Town	W	2	1	McDonald 2	208
Sep	2	a	League	Emley	D	0	0		542
	7	a	League	Gainsborough Trinity	L	0	4		258
	9	h	League	Bangor City	L	0	1		263
	14	h	FA Cup 1Q	Ilkeston Town	W	1	0	Redshaw	161
	17	a	League	Southport	D	1	1	McLachlan	408
	21	h	League	Bishop Auckland	W	2	0	Redshaw 2	206
	23	a	League	Hyde United	D	1	1	Lloyd (pen)	436
	28	a	FA Cup 2Q	Emley	L	2	4	Lloyd, Haddon	378
Oct	5	h	League	Whitley Bay	L	1	2	Redshaw	214
	9	a	League	Fleetwood Town	W	2	1	Redshaw 2	214
	12	a	League	Buxton	L	0	5		354
	14	h	League	Fleetwood Town	L	0	1		269
	19	a	League	Leek Town	L	1	3	Schofield	411
	26	h	League	Goole Town	W	2	1	Redshaw, McDonald	169
Nov	2	a	League	Frickley Athletic	W	2	0	Schofield, Griffin	151
	5	h	League	Stalybridge Celtic	D	0	0		243
	9	a	League	Morecambe	D	0	0		418
	12	a	League	Marine	L	1	2	Lloyd (pen)	261
	16	h	League	Gainsborough Trinity	W	3	0	Edwards 2, Schofield	237
	23	h	League	Buxton	D	0	0		258
	26	h	NPL Cup 2	Knowsley United	L	1	2	Redshaw	149
	30	h	FAT 1Q	Marine	L	1	3	Griffin	189
Dec	3	a	LJC 1	Bacup Borough	W	2	1	Griffin, Redshaw	150
	6	h	League	Accrington Stanley	D	1	1	Edwards	252
	10	a	League	Bangor City	W	2	1	Redshaw, Gale	151
	14	a	League	Whitley Bay	W	3	1	Edwards, Gale, Schofield	253
	16	h	League	Droylsden	W	1	0	Redshaw	234
	26	a	League	Chorley	D	0	0		539
	28	h	League	Marine	W	1	0	McDonald	283
Jan	1	h	League	Southport	D	1	1	McDonald	410
	4	a	League	Accrington Stanley	D	1	1	McDonald	365
	11	a	League	Mossley	D	1	1	Gale	296
	18	h	League	Shepshed Albion	D	0	0		277
	20	h	LJC 2	Rossendale United	D	0	0		184
Feb	3	a	LJC 2	Rossendale United	W	3	2	McDonald, Gale, Wardle	197
	11	a	LJC 3	Great Harwood Town	L	1	2	Hughes	124
	15	a	League	Matlock Town	L	0	1		234
	22	a	League	Bishop Auckland	W	3	1	McDonald, Gale, Westwell	202
	29	h	League	Hyde United	L	0	2		254
Mar	7	a	League	Droylsden	L	1	5	Redshaw	204
	9	h	League	Mossley	L	1	2	Griffin	198
Apr	4	h	League	Leek Town	D	1	1	Redshaw	227
	6	h	League	Emley	W	3	0	Redshaw, Gale, Griffin	220
	11	a	League	Stalybridge Celtic	L	0	2		628
	20	h	League	Chorley	D	2	2	Redshaw, O'Brien	586
	22	h	League	Morecambe	L	0	2		210
	25	a	League	Goole Town	L	0	1		215
						55	66		

1992-93　Northern Premier League Premier Division

Date		H/A	Comp	Opponents	Res	F	A	Goalscorers	Att
Aug	22	h	League	Gainsborough Trinity	W	2	0	Moss, Hughes (pen)	189
	25	a	League	Marine	L	0	3		344
	29	a	League	Leek Town	D	0	0		346
Sep	2	h	League	Fleetwood Town	W	2	1	McDonald 2	208
	5	h	League	Whitley Bay	D	3	3	McDonald, Redshaw, Wardle	189
	8	a	League	Buxton	D	2	2	Redshaw, Wardle	243
	12	h	FA Cup 1Q	Goole Town	W	1	0	McDonald	165
	19	h	League	Goole Town	W	3	1	Redshaw, Moss, Westwell	173
	22	a	League	Morecambe	L	2	3	McDonald, Griffin	356
	26	h	FA Cup 2Q	Worksop Town	D	1	1	McDonald	147
	28	a	FA Cup 2Q	Worksop Town	W	5	1	Redshaw 2, Griffin, Moss, Lloyd	475
Oct	3	a	League	Matlock Town	L	2	3	McLachlan, Hughes (pen)	288
	7	h	League	Colwyn Bay	L	0	2		173
	10	a	FA Cup 3Q	Macclesfield Town	L	0	1		789
	13	a	League	Droylsden	W	3	1	McDonald, Redshaw, Gale	203
	17	h	League	Droylsden	W	2	1	Moss 2	183
	24	h	League	Hyde United	L	3	5	Moss, Griffin, Westwell	172
	31	a	League	Gainsborough Trinity	D	2	2	Lloyd, Hughes (pen)	338
Nov	7	a	League	Emley	L	3	5	McDonald 2, Redshaw	250
	10	a	League	Southport	L	2	3	Redshaw, Hughes (pen)	883
	14	h	League	Leek Town	D	1	1	Moss	210
	21	a	League	Frickley Athletic	L	1	2	Moss	148
	28	h	FAT 1Q	Winsford United	L	1	2	Hughes (pen)	176
Dec	9	h	League	Winsford United	W	2	0	Griffin, Wardle	207
	12	a	NPL Cup 3	Matlock Town	L	1	3	Wardle	293
	16	h	League	Mossley	W	5	2	Redshaw 3, Westwell, Opponent	156
	19	h	League	Emley	L	1	3	McDonald	225
Jan	6	h	League	Southport	D	1	1	Haslam	339
	9	a	League	Mossley	W	4	1	McDonald 2, Redshaw 2	208
	16	a	League	Hyde United	L	1	4	McDonald	251
	20	a	LJC 2	Accrington Stanley	L	0	4		350
	30	h	League	Barrow	L	0	2		303
Feb	7	a	League	Chorley	D	2	2	McDonald, Curwen	328
	13	a	League	Bishop Auckland	L	0	1		215
	17	h	League	Accrington Stanley	D	2	2	Redshaw, Westwell	255
	27	h	League	Frickley Athletic	W	3	1	McDonald 2, Redshaw	196
Mar	6	h	League	Buxton	W	3	0	Redshaw 2, Wright	174
	13	h	League	Morecambe	L	0	1		265
	16	a	League	Goole Town	W	2	1	Redshaw, Moss	188
	20	a	League	Colwyn Bay	L	2	4	Redshaw, McDonald	131
	24	h	League	Marine	L	0	3		201
	27	a	League	Accrington Stanley	L	1	2	McDonald	508
	30	a	League	Barrow	D	1	1	McDonald	941
Apr	3	h	League	Matlock Town	L	2	4	McDonald, Curwen	186
	5	a	League	Winsford United	L	1	3	McDonald	242
	10	h	League	Chorley	W	2	1	McDonald, Wright	410
	12	a	League	Fleetwood Town	D	1	1	Curwen	146
	14	h	League	Bishop Auckland	W	2	1	McDonald, Curwen	186
	17	a	League	Whitley Bay	W	1	0	Redshaw	156
						81	91		

1993-94 Northern Premier League Premier Division

Date		H/A	Comp	Opponents	Res	F	A	Goalscorers	Notes	Att
Aug	21	h	League	Matlock Town	D	1	1	McDonald		207
	24	a	League	Barrow	W	2	0	McDonald, Dobson		1268
	28	a	League	Buxton	D	4	4	McDonald, McLachlan, Opponents 2		252
	30	h	League	Bridlington Town	L	0	1			258
Sep	4	h	League	Boston United	L	0	5			243
	8	a	League	Accrington Stanley	L	0	1			337
	11	a	FA Cup 1Q	Chorley	L	1	3	McDonald		407
	15	h	League	Morecambe	L	1	3	Wright		213
	18	h	FAT 1Q	Congleton Town	L	0	2			67
	25	h	League	Bishop Auckland	W	2	1	Hill, Hallows		158
	29	h	League	Colwyn Bay	L	2	3	Griffin, Opponent		148
Oct	2	a	League	Frickley Athletic	L	2	5	McDonald (pen), Curwen		199
	6	h	League	Fleetwood Town	L	2	3	McDonald, Thomas		153
	9	a	League	Matlock Town	L	0	1			385
	11	a	League	Winsford United	W	3	1	McDonald 2, Leach		249
	23	h	League	Barrow	L	0	2			323
	26	a	League	Marine	D	1	1	Leach		372
	30	a	League	Whitley Bay	L	1	3	Thomas		202
Nov	6	h	League	Winsford United	L	0	2			185
	9	a	League	Knowsley United	L	0	1			168
	13	a	League	Bishop Auckland	L	0	1			402
	20	h	League	Hyde United	L	0	1			168
	27	a	League	Fleetwood Town	W	3	2	Holman 2, Nugent		181
Dec	1	h	LJC 1	Fleetwood Town	W	3	0	Curwen 2, Hallows		30
	4	a	League	Boston United	L	1	2	Diamond		884
	11	h	NPL Cup 2	Great Harwood Town	D	1	1	Irvine		48
Jan	1	a	League	Leek Town	L	0	2			447
	3	h	League	Leek Town	L	0	1			163
	15	h	League	Whitley Bay	D	1	1	Diamond		151
	18	a	LJC 2	Barrow	W	2	1	Diamond, Thomas		386
	23	h	League	Gainsborough Trinity	L	1	2	Diamond		158
	29	a	League	Hyde United	D	1	1	Redshaw		291
Feb	5	a	League	Droylsden	W	2	1	Diamond, Opponent		227
	8	a	LJC 3	Bamber Bridge	W	3	1	Diamond 2, Nugent	AET	299
	12	h	League	Frickley Athletic	D	1	1	Diamond		352
	19	h	League	Droylsden	D	2	2	Diamond 2		160
Mar	1	a	LJC SF	Southport	L	0	2			521
	3	a	NPL Cup 2	Great Harwood Town	L	1	2	Diamond (pen)		62
	5	a	League	Chorley	D	1	1	Diamond (pen)		294
	12	a	League	Gainsborough Trinity	L	0	4			383
	19	h	League	Buxton	W	1	0	Diamond		159
	26	h	League	Chorley	D	2	2	Leach, Opponent		363
Apr	2	h	League	Marine	L	3	5	Phoenix 2, Leach		264
	4	a	League	Morecambe	D	1	1	Leach		234
	13	h	League	Knowsley United	W	3	0	Diamond 2, Leach		96
	16	a	League	Emley	D	1	1	Diamond		168
	19	a	League	Colwyn Bay	L	0	1			104
	26	h	League	Accrington Stanley	L	2	4	Diamond, McLachlan		185
	26	a	League	Bridlington Town	W	2	0	Diamond, Marsden		32
	30	h	League	Emley	D	1	1	Diamond		151
						61	87			

1994-95   Northern Premier League

Date		H/A	Comp	Opponents	Res	F	A	Goalscorers	Att
Aug	20	h	League	Gainsborough Trinity	W	2	1	Diamond 2	147
	23	a	League	Knowsley United	L	1	2	Kilshaw	80
	27	a	League	Frickley Athletic	W	2	1	Griffin, Nugent	151
	29	h	League	Chorley	W	6	0	Diamond 2, Robinson 2, Gale, Kilshaw	327
Sep	3	h	League	Bishop Auckland	L	0	2		154
	6	a	League	Barrow	L	0	1		789
	10	a	FA Cup 1Q	Burscough	L	0	1		256
	14	h	League	Witton Albion	L	0	1		135
	17	h	FAT 1Q	Nuneaton Borough	L	0	3		95
	20	a	League	Colwyn Bay	L	1	3	Leach	512
	24	h	League	Buxton	W	4	1	Leach 2, Phoenix, Thomas	161
	28	h	League	Barrow	L	1	6	Leach	199
Oct	1	a	NPL Cup 1	Great Harwood Town	L	2	5	Phoenix 2 (2pens)	73
	4	a	League	Spennymoor United	L	1	2	Gale	278
	8	h	League	Droylsden	D	2	2	Edwards, Gale	165
	12	h	League	Morecambe	L	0	2		261
	15	a	League	Whitley Bay	W	3	0	Edwards 2, Nugent	141
	17	a	League	Emley	D	1	1	Edwards	264
	22	a	League	Buxton	L	0	4		223
	29	a	League	Droylsden	L	1	2	Nugent	155
Nov	5	a	League	Winsford United	W	3	2	Edwards 2, Leach	136
	9	h	League	Winsford United	W	1	0	Edwards	161
	19	h	League	Spennymoor United	D	0	0		175
	26	a	League	Matlock Town	L	2	3	Thomas, Griffin	325
Dec	3	a	League	Gainsborough Trinity	L	0	1		358
	10	h	League	Whitley Bay	L	2	3	Thomas, Edwards	164
	17	h	League	Hyde United	L	0	1		209
	26	a	League	Chorley	W	3	2	Leach 2, Gale	251
	31	a	League	Witton Albion	L	1	2	Leach	405
Jan	7	a	League	Accrington Stanley	L	0	3		403
	14	h	League	Frickley Athletic	L	0	3		172
	18	h	LJC 2	Darwen	L	0	1		21
	21	h	League	Emley	D	4	4	Diamond, Phoenix, Bates, Bedson	175
	28	a	League	Hyde United	L	1	2	Diamond	461
Feb	4	h	League	Colwyn Bay	L	0	1		166
	11	a	League	Boston United	L	0	4		572
	18	a	League	Bishop Auckland	L	1	2	Diamond	123
Mar	4	h	League	Boston United	L	0	4		481
	15	h	League	Guiseley	L	0	2		269
	25	h	League	Knowsley United	L	1	2	Fagan	205
	29	h	League	Marine	L	1	4	Diamond	291
Apr	8	h	League	Matlock Town	L	0	3		177
	15	h	League	Accrington Stanley	L	1	5	Fagan	306
	17	a	League	Morecambe	L	1	7	Orrell	605
	22	a	League	Guiseley	W	2	1	Senior, Leach	459
May	6	a	League	Marine	L	0	2		723
Home games from Mach 4 onwards at Hilton Park, Leigh									
						51	104		

The first game at Hilton Park, on 4 March 1995. Still playing under the name of Horwich RMI, the result was a 4-0 defeat. The attendance of 481 was considerably up on later attendances at Grundy Hill. However, they were 'lost' in the wide open spaces of Hilton Park.

HORWICH R.M.I. F.C.

FIRST MATCH AT HILTON PARK

HORWICH R.M.I. F.C.

S
E
A
S
O
N

1
9
9
4
-
9
5

THE UNIBOND LEAGUE PREMIER DIVISION
Saturday 4th March 1995 Kick-Off 3.00 p.m.

HORWICH R.M.I. v BOSTON UNITED

Today's Match Sponsor:
NATIONAL WESTMINSTER BANK
LEE LANE, HORWICH.

OFFICIAL PROGRAMME 60p

THE UniBond LEAGUE

Horwich RMI League Results Summary

Season	Comp	P	W	D	L	F	A	PTS	Posn	Teams
	Horwich (L&Y)									
1891-92	Lancashire Alliance	24	4	0	20	30	86	8	12	13
	Horwich									
1892-93	Lancashire Alliance	26	9	6	11	62	68	24	10	14
1893-94	Lancashire Alliance	26	11	5	10	73	57	27	7	14
1894-95	Lancashire Alliance	26	11	1	14	59	70	23	8	14
1895-96	Lancashire Alliance	22	12	2	8	43	34	26	6	12
1896-97	Lancashire Alliance	22	10	3	9	52	42	23	6	12
1897-98	Lancashire League	26	2	2	22	22	78	6	14	14
1898-99	Lancashire League	24	8	1	15	27	47	17	11	13
1899-1900	Lancashire League	28	5	6	17	27	70	16	14	15
	Horwich RMI									
1902-03	Friendlies									
1903-04	Central Lancashire League									
1904-05	Bolton & District League									
1905-06	Bolton & District League									
1906-07	Bolton & District League									
1907-08	Lancashire Alliance	25	7	3	15	42	67	17	?	15
1908-09	West Lancashire League	26	12	6	8	52	35	30	5	14
1909-10	West Lancashire League	23	8	4	11	40	42	20	7	13
1910-11	West Lancashire League	24	14	5	5	66	35	33	1	13
1911-12	West Lancashire League	26	13	6	7	54	41	32	5	14
1912-13	West Lancashire League	24	14	4	6	55	32	32	4	13
1913-14	West Lancashire League	30	25	2	3	96	34	52	1	16
1914-15	West Lancashire League	20	11	3	6	62	24	25	3	11
1915-16	Did not play									
1916-17	Did not play									
1917-18	Lancashire Combination (WTEL)									
1918-19	Lancashire Combination (WTEL)									
1919-20	Lancashire Combination	34	20	0	14	72	59	40	6	18
1920-21	Lancashire Combination	34	4	9	21	34	91	17	18	18
1921-22	Lancashire Combination	34	12	6	16	45	59	30	12	18
1922-23	Lancashire Combination	34	7	10	17	54	76	24	17	18
1923-24	Lancashire Combination	38	20	4	14	72	49	44	4	20
1924-25	Lancashire Combination	36	14	8	14	74	60	36	9	19
1925-26	Lancashire Combination	38	19	3	16	87	84	41	7	20
1926-27	Lancashire Combination	38	18	5	15	106	76	41	10	20
1927-28	Lancashire Combination	38	23	9	6	111	61	55	3	20
1928-29	Lancashire Combination	38	24	2	12	152	87	50	2	20
1929-30	Lancashire Combination	38	20	6	12	112	70	46	7	20
1930-31	Lancashire Combination	38	21	5	12	119	73	47	5	20
1931-32	Lancashire Combination	36	10	3	23	73	108	23	17	20
1932-33	Lancashire Combination	38	21	5	12	107	82	47	7	20
1933-34	Lancashire Combination	38	13	4	21	85	107	30	16	20
1934-35	Lancashire Combination	38	16	3	19	91	88	35	10	20
1935-36	Lancashire Combination	40	14	8	18	103	111	36	15	21
1936-37	Lancashire Combination	40	11	8	21	82	91	30	15	21
1937-38	Lancashire Combination	42	14	5	23	92	123	33	18	22
1938-39	Lancashire Combination	42	7	7	28	80	143	21	21	22
1939-40	Lancashire Combination (Competition disbanded)	3	1	0	2	4	11	2	n/a	22
1939-40	Lancashire Combination (WTEL)	18	3	4	11	32	62	10	n/a	10
	Did not play 1940-46 due to war									
	WTEL - War Time Emergency League									

Horwich RMI Results Summary

Season	Comp	P	W	D	L	F	A	PTS	Posn	Teams
1946-47	Lancashire Combination	42	17	6	19	83	93	40	14	22
1947-48	Lancashire Combination D1	42	10	7	25	58	104	27	21	22
1948-49	Lancashire Combination D2	24	19	1	4	75	28	39	2	13
1949-50	Lancashire Combination D1	42	8	6	28	52	114	22	22	22
1950-51	Lancashire Combination D2	42	30	4	8	154	60	64	2	22
1951-52	Lancashire Combination D1	42	17	7	18	99	97	41	12	22
1952-53	Lancashire Combination D1	42	17	13	12	109	105	47	7	22
1953-54	Lancashire Combination D1	40	21	5	14	95	65	47	4	21
1954-55	Lancashire Combination D1	42	20	8	14	81	62	48	8	22
1955-56	Lancashire Combination D1	38	24	9	5	104	49	57	2	20
1956-57	Lancashire Combination D1	38	22	3	13	93	70	47	4	20
1957-58	Lancashire Combination D1	42	28	7	7	109	47	63	1	22
1958-59	Lancashire Combination D1	42	25	9	8	95	57	59	3	22
1959-60	Lancashire Combination D1	42	17	8	17	82	76	42	10	22
1960-61	Lancashire Combination D1	42	14	7	21	75	94	35	13	22
1961-62	Lancashire Combination D1	42	26	9	7	110	48	61	3	22
1962-63	Lancashire Combination D1	42	25	5	12	107	59	55	4	22
1963-64	Lancashire Combination D1	42	24	8	10	91	51	56	4	22
1964-65	Lancashire Combination D1	42	24	13	5	128	53	61	4	22
1965-66	Lancashire Combination D1	42	26	3	13	100	58	55	5	22
1966-67	Lancashire Combination D1	42	27	9	6	88	37	63	2	22
1967-68	Lancashire Combination D1	42	19	9	14	79	52	47	9	22
1968-69	Cheshire County League	38	13	13	12	54	63	39	10	22
1969-70	Cheshire County League	38	21	6	11	93	59	48	4	22
1970-71	Cheshire County League	42	16	12	14	67	55	44	7	22
1971-72	Cheshire County League	42	16	6	20	61	82	38	13	22
1972-73	Cheshire County League	42	6	16	20	57	83	28	21	22
1973-74	Cheshire County League	42	10	7	25	52	74	27	20	22
1974-75	Cheshire County League	42	17	7	18	60	59	41	11	22
1975-76	Cheshire County League	42	8	13	21	42	90	29	18	22
1976-77	Cheshire County League	42	19	10	14	72	58	46	8	22
1977-78	Cheshire County League	42	19	14	9	62	50	52	7	22
1978-79	Cheshire County League D1	42	35	2	5	89	45	72	1	22
1979-80	Cheshire County League D1	38	13	12	13	53	52	38	8	22
1980-81	Cheshire County League D1	38	15	9	14	53	49	39	9	22
1981-82	Cheshire County League D1	38	12	7	19	58	72	31	16	22
1982-83	North West Counties League D1	38	22	10	6	77	35	54	3	22
1983-84	Northern Premier League	42	18	9	15	64	59	63	8	22
1984-85	Northern Premier League	42	16	14	12	67	50	62	9	22
1985-86	Northern Premier League	42	15	6	21	53	63	50	16	22
1986-87	Northern Premier League	42	3	12	27	36	85	20	22	22
1987-88	Northern Premier League Prem	42	17	9	16	46	42	60	13	22
1988-89	Northern Premier League Prem	42	7	14	21	42	70	35	20	22
1989-90	Northern Premier League Prem	42	15	13	14	66	69	55	14	22
1990-91	Northern Premier League Prem	40	13	6	21	62	81	45	16	21
1991-92	Northern Premier League Prem	42	13	14	15	44	52	53	13	22
1992-93	Northern Premier League Prem	42	14	10	18	72	79	52	13	22
1993-94	Northern Premier League Prem	42	8	12	22	50	75	35	20	22
1994-95	Northern Premier League Prem	42	9	4	29	49	94	31	22	22

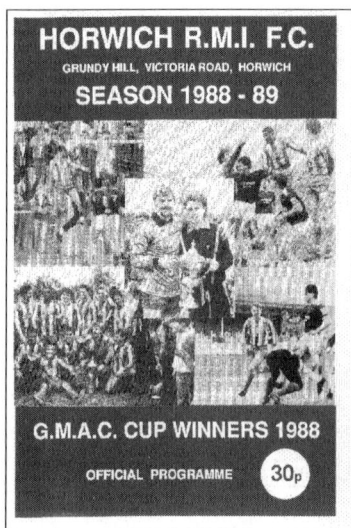

HORWICH R.M.I. F.C.
GRUNDY HILL, VICTORIA ROAD, HORWICH
SEASON 1988 - 89

G.M.A.C. CUP WINNERS 1988

OFFICIAL PROGRAMME 30p

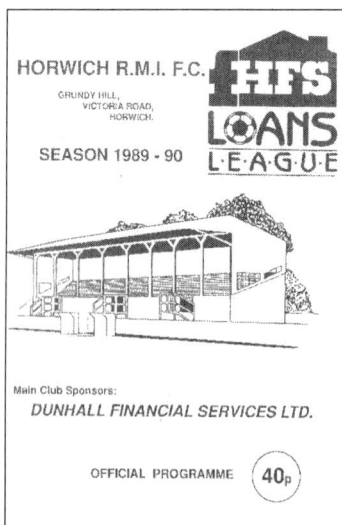

HORWICH R.M.I. F.C.
GRUNDY HILL,
VICTORIA ROAD,
HORWICH.

SEASON 1989 - 90

HFS
LOANS
L·E·A·G·U·E

Main Club Sponsors:
DUNHALL FINANCIAL SERVICES LTD.

OFFICIAL PROGRAMME 40p

Some programme covers from the later seasons. Below (right) is the programme for the very last match under the name Horwich RMI, played at Marine's Rossett Park on 6 May 1995.

HORWICH R.M.I. F.C.
GRUNDY HILL, VICTORIA ROAD, HORWICH.

HORWICH R.M.I. F.C.

S
E
A
S
O
N

1
9
9
2
-
9
3

Main Club Sponsors:
CAUNCE
BROTHERS LTD.

HFS
LOANS
L·E·A·G·U·E

OFFICIAL PROGRAMME 50p

Marine AFC Centenary Year

A Rossy special with delight for this young supporter - One of the many goals that won the championship - Picture courtesy of Crosby Herald

We are the champions......

1. MARINE   41 28 11 2 81 27 95
2. MORECAMBE 42 28 10 4 99 34 94

Saturday, May 6th, 1995
MARINE V
HORWICH RMI
UNIBOND LEAGUE
Kick-off 3.0pm   80p
Match sponsors:
Crosby Herald

Horwich RMI Club Records 1902-1995

HORWICH RMI CLUB RECORDS 1903-1995

Formed:	1902
Changed name to Leigh RMI	1995
Grounds:	
Recreation Ground	1902-03
Old Racecourse Ground	1903-1910
Grundy Hill	1910-1995
Hilton Park, Leigh	1995

Honours:
League:

West Lancashire League	Champions: 1910-11; 1913-14
Lancashire Combination	Champions (Division One): 1957-58
	Runners-up (Division One): 1928-29; 1955-56; 1966-67
	Runners-up (Division Two); 1948-49; 1950-51
Cheshire County League	Champions (Division One): 1978-79

Cup:
West Lancashire League Cup (Richardson Cup)

	Runners-up: 1910-11; 1913-14
Lancashire Combination League Cup	Winners: 1927-28; 1953-54; 1956-57; 1965-66
	Runners-up: 1958-59; 1967-68
Lancashire Junior Cup	Winners: 1924-25; 1929-30
	Runners-up: 1953-54; 1957-58; 1962-63; 1982-83
GMAC Cup	Winners: 1987-88
Lancashire Floodlit Cup	Winners: 1984-85
	Runners-up: 1983-84

HIGHEST SCORING WINS

Date	Venue	Comp	Opponents	Res	F	A
01/10/1964	h	League	Nelson	W	19	1
20/10/1928	h	League	Barnoldswick Town	W	12	1
14/09/1929	h	League	Nelson Reserves	W	12	0
24/11/1923	h	League	Skelmersdale United	W	11	0
30/10/1948	h	League	Oldham Athletic 'A'	W	11	2
13/04/1953	h	LC 3	Clitheroe	W	11	0
04/05/1927	h	League	Atherton	W	10	0
22/10/1927	h	LJC 2	Little Lever	W	10	1
29/03/1929	h	League	Preston North End 'A'	W	10	0
24/09/1930	a	League	Atherton	W	10	0
05/09/1931	h	League	Accrington Stanley Reserves	W	10	1
15/12/1956	h	League	Droylsden	W	10	0

HEAVIEST DEFEATS

Date	Venue	Comp	Opponents	Res	F	A
27/12/1937	a	League	Fleetwood	L	1	11
21/01/1939	a	League	Clitheroe	L	3	10
10/04/1939	a	League	Bangor City	L	2	10
01/01/1932	a	League	Dick, Kerr's	L	3	9
29/02/1908	h	League	Fleetwood Amateurs	L	2	9
22/01/1921	a	League	Rossendale United	L	2	9
20/02/1932	a	League	Darwen	L	1	9
29/04/1957	a	League	Wigan Athletic	L	1	9
23/08/1975	a	League	Winsford United	L	1	9
05/10/1985	a	FAT 1Q	Brandon United	L	1	9
18/04/1929	a	League	Dick, Kerr's	L	0	9
07/11/1931	a	LJC 1	Darwen	L	0	9
26/08/1939	a	League	Rossendale United	L	0	9

LEADING SCORERS IN A SEASON (League and Cup):

Player	Season	Goals
Joe Keetley	1928-29	59
Jimmy Mather	1950-51	56
Jimmy Mather	1952-53	52
Vince Marren	1958-59	51
Brian Robinson	1965-66	50
Joe Keetley	1927-28	48
Stanley Mather	1928-29	48
Joe Keetley	1930-31	45
Tony Caldwell	1982-83	44
Jimmy Mather	1951-52	42
Frank Wignall	1957-58	42
Stanley Mather	1927-28	41
Joe Keetley	1926-27	40

LEADING SCORERS IN AN RMI CAREER (League and Cup):

Player	Seasons	Goals
Joe Keetley	1926-1930	230
Jimmy Mather	1949-1954	202
Stanley Mather	1925-1931	169
Tom Yates	1926-1935	141
George Bateson	1957-1975	119
Neil McLachlan	1980-1993	113
Tony Webber	1966-1981	107
Eric Spencer	1946-1951	105
Harry Hird	1918-1931	101

MOST GOALS IN A MATCH

Player	Seasons	Goals	Opponents
Stanley Mather	1928-29	6	Barnoldswick Town (League)
O'Rourke	1931-32	6	Accrington Stanley Reserves (League)

Horwich RMI League Record By Opponents 1907-1995

	Season								
	First Played	Last Played	P	W	D	L	Ab	F	A
Accrington Stanley	1919	1993	16	3	5	8	0	21	33
Accrington Stanley Reserves	1923	1958	51	21	5	25	0	125	119
Accrington	1964	1964	2	1	1	0	0	3	0
ACI Horwich	1948	1950	4	3	0	1	0	18	8
Adlington	1907	1914	12	6	2	4	0	26	19
Ashton Camp	1918	1918	1	0	0	1	0	0	1
Ashton Hospital	1918	1918	2	1	0	1	0	5	3
Ashton Town Reserves	1907	1907	2	0	0	2	0	1	5
Ashton United	1949	1982	56	28	10	18	0	115	85
Atherton	1920	1930	22	14	1	7	0	72	33
Atherton Collieries	1950	1950	2	2	0	0	0	5	1
Atherton Reserves	1907	1907	1	1	0	0	0	5	3
Bacup Borough	1920	1967	72	41	11	20	0	186	110
Bamber Bridge	1908	1913	4	3	0	1	0	8	4
Bangor City	1938	1991	24	6	6	12	0	39	56
Bank St Stephens	1908	1910	7	3	2	2	0	20	13
Barnoldswick	1948	1950	4	3	0	1	0	11	3
Barnoldswick Town	1924	1933	21	9	4	7	1	64	37
Barrow	1919	1994	18	3	4	11	0	10	31
Barrow Reserves	1913	1967	42	16	8	18	0	95	90
Belle Vue	1948	1948	2	1	0	1	0	6	3
Bishop Auckland	1989	1994	12	5	1	6	0	15	19
Blackburn St Philip's	1913	1914	3	2	1	0	0	7	3
Blackpool Athletic	1908	1909	4	2	1	1	0	13	4
Blackpool B	1951	1954	6	3	1	2	0	12	10
Blackpool RAMC	1918	1918	1	0	0	1	0	3	5
Bolton Wanderers B	1948	1954	8	6	0	2	0	17	9
Bootle	1948	1982	16	10	3	3	0	28	18
Boston United	1993	1994	4	0	0	4	0	1	15
Bridlington Town	1993	1993	2	1	0	1	0	2	1
Brinscall Rovers	1911	1911	2	2	0	0	0	5	2
Brynn	1917	1918	4	0	2	2	0	4	7
Burscough	1954	1983	54	23	11	20	0	93	75
Burscough Rangers	1927	1932	12	6	1	5	0	38	27
Burton Albion	1983	1986	8	3	2	3	0	6	9
Buxton	1968	1994	34	12	10	12	0	48	56
Caernarfon Town	1985	1989	10	4	2	4	0	16	13
Chester Reserves	1968	1968	2	2	0	0	0	6	2
Chorley	1919	1994	124	38	28	58	0	187	251
Chorley Reserves	1907	1951	8	4	2	2	0	20	14
Chorley St Peter's	1912	1912	2	1	0	0	1	6	2
Clitheroe	1925	1967	58	27	7	24	0	140	122
Colne Dynamoes	1989	1989	2	0	0	2	0	3	7
Colne Town	1925	1926	4	4	0	0	0	17	3
Colwyn Bay	1992	1994	6	0	0	6	0	5	14
Congleton Town	1982	1982	2	1	1	0	0	4	1
Coppull Central	1908	1914	10	7	0	3	0	27	14
Crompton's Recs	1957	1963	4	4	0	0	0	12	1
Croston	1913	1914	4	3	0	1	0	16	5

	Season		P	W	D	L	Ab	F	A
	First Played	Last Played							
Curzon Ashton	1979	1982	8	4	3	1	0	16	7
Darwen	1920	1982	86	40	15	31	0	189	187
Darwen Reserves	1948	1950	4	4	0	0	0	17	5
Dick, Kerr's	1919	1935	33	11	5	17	0	62	74
Droylsden	1936	1994	62	29	13	20	0	130	105
Droylsden United	1950	1950	2	1	0	1	0	8	5
Earlestown	1951	1962	10	5	2	3	0	23	15
Eccles United	1919	1924	13	2	3	7	1	16	30
Ellesmere Port Town	1968	1970	6	1	2	3	0	6	11
Emley	1991	1994	8	1	5	2	0	14	15
Everton Reserves	1918	1918	2	1	0	1	0	9	4
Fleetwood	1908	1967	78	31	10	37	0	154	168
Fleetwood Amateurs	1907	1907	2	0	0	2	0	4	14
Fleetwood Reserves	1910	1914	9	6	2	1	0	21	11
Fleetwood Town	1978	1993	20	8	5	7	0	29	28
Formby	1971	1982	24	9	5	10	0	38	39
Freckleton	1912	1914	6	5	0	1	0	18	7
Frickley Athletic	1987	1994	16	4	5	7	0	21	30
Frickley Colliery	1968	1969	4	2	2	0	0	7	3
Gainsborough Trinity	1983	1994	24	11	4	9	0	33	34
Garswood Hall	1918	1918	2	1	0	1	0	5	4
Gateshead	1985	1989	8	3	1	4	0	12	12
Glossop	1919	1982	6	1	2	3	0	9	10
Goole Town	1983	1992	20	6	6	8	0	27	28
Grantham	1983	1984	4	1	0	3	0	4	6
Great Harwood	1919	1967	57	35	8	13	1	168	92
Guinness Export	1965	1969	10	5	2	3	0	23	12
Guiseley	1994	1994	2	1	0	1	0	2	3
Hamilton Central	1911	1914	7	3	3	1	0	17	7
Higher Walton Albion	1911	1912	3	2	0	1	0	6	4
Hindley Central	1908	1911	2	0	0	2	0	1	3
Hindley Green Athletic	1925	1927	6	5	0	1	0	25	13
Hindsford	1950	1950	2	1	0	1	0	6	4
Hurst	1919	1922	8	4	2	2	0	11	10
Hyde United	1970	1994	48	12	10	26	0	58	86
Kirkby Town	1967	1980	4	3	0	1	0	5	4
Kirkham	1907	1911	9	4	1	4	0	15	10
Kirkham & Wesham	1912	1913	4	3	0	1	0	11	3
Knowsley United	1993	1994	4	1	0	3	0	5	5
Lancaster City	1937	1982	47	20	11	16	0	85	72
Lancaster City Reserves	1948	1950	4	3	0	1	0	16	3
Lancaster Town	1919	1936	36	8	6	22	0	48	103
Lancaster Town Reserves	1911	1914	3	3	0	0	0	9	0
Lancaster United	1918	1918	2	0	1	1	0	3	4
Leek Town	1973	1993	28	8	5	15	0	28	48
Leyland	1907	1924	26	9	7	10	0	47	46
Leyland Motors	1933	1982	34	21	5	8	0	98	52
Little Hulton United	1907	1907	2	1	0	1	0	6	6

	Season								
	First Played	Last Played	P	W	D	L	Ab	F	A
Liverpool Reserves	1918	1918	2	1	0	1	0	3	5
Lomax	1950	1950	2	2	0	0	0	9	2
Longridge	1910	1913	12	6	1	5	0	24	29
Lostock Hall Locos	1908	1910	5	2	1	2	0	8	8
Lytham	1910	1962	32	20	4	7	1	101	50
Lytham Athletic	1909	1911	4	3	0	1	0	14	6
Macclesfield Town	1983	1986	8	1	4	3	0	10	15
Manchester Central	1928	1930	6	3	1	2	0	15	12
Manchester North End	1923	1923	2	2	0	0	0	4	3
Marine	1935	1994	92	35	16	41	0	163	193
Matlock Town	1983	1994	24	8	5	11	0	40	36
Middlewich Town	1975	1978	8	5	1	2	0	16	8
Morecambe	1911	1994	108	31	27	49	1	183	205
Morecambe Reserves	1950	1950	2	1	1	0	0	7	3
Mossley	1968	1992	28	11	5	12	0	47	48
Nantwich Town	1968	1982	30	12	6	12	0	48	61
Nelson	1931	1965	46	20	10	16	0	107	84
Nelson Reserves	1924	1950	20	12	3	5	0	70	31
Netherfield	1946	1967	40	16	10	14	0	76	80
Netherfield Reserves	1950	1950	2	2	0	0	0	14	0
New Brighton	1921	1978	56	24	14	18	0	87	68
New Brighton Reserves	1934	1948	14	5	2	7	0	40	38
New Cross	1922	1922	2	0	1	1	0	1	2
New Mills	1974	1980	14	6	4	4	0	24	18
Northern Nomads	1933	1937	10	6	1	3	0	33	29
Oldham Athletic 'A'	1948	1948	2	2	0	0	0	15	3
Oldham Athletic Reserves	1937	1974	36	11	7	18	0	59	72
Ormskirk	1970	1973	8	2	1	5	0	6	11
Oswestry Town	1968	1987	24	9	4	11	0	40	37
Padiham	1950	1961	4	2	1	1	0	11	4
Penrith	1982	1982	2	2	0	0	0	10	4
Plank Lane	1918	1919	4	1	0	3	0	7	8
Port Vale Reserves	1969	1970	4	3	0	1	0	6	1
Prescot	1918	1919	4	2	0	2	0	6	8
Prescot Cables	1928	1982	56	19	11	26	0	109	116
Preston North End 'A'	1926	1928	8	5	1	2	0	26	10
Prestwich Heys	1971	1977	14	8	3	3	0	30	18
Radcliffe Borough	1971	1979	18	7	5	6	0	34	33
Rhyl	1968	1989	40	20	8	12	0	72	68
Rochdale Reserves	1919	1954	40	15	10	15	0	81	88
Rossendale United	1920	1981	106	43	21	41	1	237	250
Runcorn	1918	1918	2	1	0	1	0	3	5
Rylands Recs	1918	1918	1	0	1	0	0	3	3
Sandbach Ramblers	1968	1974	14	6	5	3	0	25	19
Shepshed Albion	1991	1992	2	1	1	0	0	3	1
Shepshed Charterhouse	1988	1990	6	4	0	2	0	10	5
Skelmersdale United	1908	1970	38	24	1	13	0	95	61
South Liverpool	1917	1917	62	21	10	30	1	114	117

	Season First Played	Last Played	P	W	D	L	Ab	F	A
Southport	1983	1992	20	4	8	8	0	29	35
Southport Central	1912	1914	9	6	1	2	0	23	10
Southport Central Reserves	1907	1908	4	1	3	0	0	10	7
Southport Park Villa	1908	1910	5	4	0	1	0	12	5
Southport Reserves	1923	1967	72	36	13	23	0	159	116
Spennymoor United	1994	1994	2	0	1	1	0	1	2
St Helens Alexandra	1917	1917	2	1	1	0	0	6	3
St Helens Recs Reserves	1907	1907	2	1	0	1	0	3	4
St Helens Town	1950	1982	28	17	5	6	0	55	27
Stafford Rangers	1968	1984	6	1	3	2	0	7	9
Stalybridge Celtic	1919	1991	40	16	9	15	0	66	58
Standish	1914	1914	2	1	0	1	0	5	5
Standish North End	1908	1908	2	1	1	0	0	1	0
Stockport County Reserves	1921	1921	2	1	0	1	0	5	5
Stubshaw Cross Rovers	1948	1950	4	3	0	1	0	12	10
Tarleton	1914	1914	2	1	1	0	0	6	3
Tranmere Rovers Reserves	1917	1969	11	1	4	6	0	11	24
Tyldesley Albion	1907	1907	2	0	0	2	0	3	7
Walkden Central	1907	1907	1	0	0	1	0	0	3
Walton-le-Dale	1911	1913	5	5	0	0	0	26	5
Whitley Bay	1991	1994	8	3	2	3	0	15	13
Wigan Athletic	1947	1960	24	6	3	15	0	33	51
Wigan Athletic Reserves	1950	1950	2	2	0	0	0	7	4
Wigan Borough	1920	1920	2	0	0	2	0	1	6
Wigan Borough Reserves	1923	1930	16	11	2	3	0	46	24
Wigan Rovers	1966	1967	4	2	0	2	0	9	6
Winsford United	1968	1994	36	14	8	14	0	56	62
Witton Albion	1968	1994	40	8	13	19	0	50	73
Workington	1983	1987	10	4	4	2	0	14	9
Worksop Town	1983	1988	12	5	3	4	0	24	22

THE WITCH

OFFICIAL MATCH DAY PROGRAMME OF
MIDDLEWICH ATHLETIC F.C.

Season 1977/78

VOL. 2 No. 19

CHESHIRE COUNTY LEAGUE

ATHLETIC

versus

HORWICH R.M.I

SATURDAY, 25th FEBRUARY, 1978. K.O. 3 p.m.

ST. HELENS TOWN A. F. C.
Heighton Rd., Sutton, St. Helens

ST·HELENS TOWN
VERSUS
HORWICH R.M.I

SATURDAY 24th JANUARY 1981

OFFICIAL PROGRAMME, 10p

R.LUNT
for the finest
Diamond
& Gold
Jewellery

Horwich RMI FA Cup Record By Opponents

	P	W	D	L	F	A
Accrington Stanley	2	1	0	1	5	4
Altrincham	1	0	0	1	0	4
Appelby Frodingham	1	1	0	0	3	0
Ashton United	3	1	0	2	3	4
Atherton	1	0	0	1	1	2
Bacup Borough	1	0	0	1	1	2
Barnoldswick Park Villa	1	1	0	0	2	1
Barrow	1	1	0	0	1	0
Blackpool	1	0	0	1	0	3
Breightmet United	2	2	0	0	8	1
Burscough	3	1	0	2	2	5
Burscough Rangers	2	2	0	0	9	2
Buxton	1	1	0	0	1	0
Caernarfon Town	3	1	1	1	5	5
Chorley	16	6	2	8	26	21
Clitheroe	1	0	0	1	1	3
Colwyn Bay	1	0	0	1	1	3
Congleton Town	3	2	1	0	6	2
Crompton's Recs	1	1	0	0	4	1
Crossens	2	2	0	0	7	0
Curzon Ashton	1	1	0	0	2	1
Darwen	7	1	2	4	10	13
Dick, Kerr's	3	2	1	0	8	3
Droylsden	2	1	1	0	5	4
Emley	2	0	0	2	2	9
Farsley Celtic	3	2	1	0	7	3
Fleetwood	2	0	1	1	4	5
Formby	4	3	1	0	9	2
Goole Town	1	1	0	0	1	0
Great Harwood	3	3	0	0	12	4
Guinness Export	1	1	0	0	3	1
Hamilton Central	1	1	0	0	1	0
Haslingden	1	0	0	1	1	3

	P	W	D	L	F	A
Hyde United	6	0	2	4	4	14
Ilkeston Town	1	1	0	0	1	0
Irlam Town	1	1	0	0	3	1
Lancaster City	3	0	1	2	2	7
Lancaster Town	6	0	1	5	9	24
Leyland Motors	7	4	0	3	11	8
Lytham	3	2	1	0	13	4
Macclesfield Town	3	0	1	2	3	5
Marine	1	0	0	1	0	2
Morecambe	11	4	3	4	21	18
Mossley	5	1	1	3	5	10
Nelson	3	1	0	2	2	7
Netherfield	2	0	1	1	4	5
New Mills	1	1	0	0	3	0
North Ferriby United	1	0	0	1	0	1
Northwich Victoria	1	1	0	0	2	0
Oswestry Town	1	1	0	0	5	1
Portsmouth Rangers	1	1	0	0	4	2
Prestwich Heys	2	1	1	0	7	4
Radcliffe Borough	1	0	0	1	0	4
Rhyl	1	0	0	1	0	2
Rossendale United	5	1	0	4	13	19
Runcorn	2	1	1	0	3	2
Scarborough	1	0	0	1	1	2
Skelmersdale United	9	7	1	1	25	11
South Liverpool	3	2	1	0	9	5
Southport	1	1	0	0	2	1
St Helens Town	3	0	1	2	4	7
Stalybridge Celtic	2	0	0	2	3	6
Wigan Athletic	1	0	0	1	0	3
Wigan Rovers	3	2	1	0	6	2
Winsford United	1	0	0	1	1	2
Witton Albion	1	1	0	0	2	0
Workington	2	1	1	0	5	2
Worksop Town	4	1	2	1	7	4

LEIGH RMI / LEIGH GENESIS
History and Statistics

Waywell Takes Charge

In 1995-96 Leigh RMI consolidated in Division One of the Unibond League with a modest 14th place finish. Of 40 matches played they won 14, drew seven and lost 19, scoring 53 goals and conceding 59. Their opening game of the season resulted in a 2-1 win at Harrogate Town when the following side was on duty: Curtis; Brown, Phoenix; Senior, Schofield, McCarty; Griffin, Birch, Monk, Shaw, Walmsley. Subs: Briffa, Hutchinson, Diamond. Monk and Shaw got the goals.

After winning their opening two games RMI then drew two and lost five of their next seven games and a managerial change was made with Steve Waywell appointed in sole charge.

RMI played Scottish opposition for the first time in league football against Gretna, losing 3-1 at both Raydale Park in September and at Hilton Park the following month. They also opposed Atherton Laburnum Rovers for the first time in league football, losing 3-1 at Crilly Park in August before a crowd of 178 and then winning 3-1 at Hilton Park in February before a season's best home crowd of 202. Clearly the Leigh public needed some encouragement to watch football at the ground and it was noticeable that very few of the old fans had followed RMI from Horwich.

In the winter months RMI's form improved and a run of seven wins and one draw from eight games lifted spirits before inconsistent form returned. Lancaster City and Alfreton Town were promoted and sadly Fleetwood folded at the end of the campaign.

RMI suffered early exits in the cup competitions losing 3-0 at Guiseley in the first qualifying round of the FA Cup, 2-0 at home to Matlock Town in the second qualifying round of the FA Trophy (following a 7-0 home victory over Bridgnorth Town in a first qualifying round replay) and 2-0 at Morecambe in the Lancashire Junior Cup, now re-titled the ATS Trophy.

Over the season attendances for league games averaged 154. Chris Shaw led the goal-scoring ranks with 20 in league and cup followed by Tony Briffa (eight), Jimmy Birch (six) and Ian Monk and Chris Walmsley (four apiece). There was a lot of work to be done on and off the field if the club was to establish itself at Hilton Park.

In March 1996 came the sad news that Les Rigby, truly one of non league's great characters had died in his sleep after a long illness. True to form, Les had spent what proved to be his final evening watching Chorley defeat Boreham Wood to reach the quarter-finals of the FA Trophy.

For all he achieved in the game as player and manager it was said he regarded his greatest feat in leading RMI to their victory over Weymouth. Harold Taylor recalled: 'He used to say it was the equivalent of Rochdale winning the FA Cup. He'll be sadly missed in football. He was a great bloke, a good friend and well-respected everywhere. As a manager, he was absolutely fantastic and he had a marvellous rapport with the players.

'When we were going to play that final against Weymouth, he got wind of the fact that their manager, Stuart Morgan, was in the crowd watching us at one of our matches leading up to it. He rooted him out afterwards and said: 'Come on Stuart, this is a good time to toss up for where we play it.' He flicked the coin up in the air but didn't call. He just said: 'We're at home!' That was Les all over - a real character!' Sadly Les's first heart attack saw him forced to relinquish his post at RMI through ill health. RMI Chairman

Chris Healey said: 'We were absolutely devastated at the time when Les had to stand down as our manager. I'm not too sure what his role was at Chorley but I think we may well have been his last club as a full manager. He was an absolutely superb fellow.'

Unibond League Secretary Duncan Bayley, who was sat with Les at what was tragically to be his last game, paid tribute: 'He was one of the great characters of the last 20 or 30 years, making a significant contribution to the management side of non-league football.'

In 1996-97 Stocksbridge Park Steels and Flixton joined the league alongside relegated Droylsden and Matlock Town. RMI enjoyed a highly successful season and clinched runners-up position and promotion by edging out Lincoln United in an exciting finish.

RMI won 24, drew 11 and lost only seven league games, scoring 65 goals and conceding only 33. With 83 points they finished two points behind champions Radcliffe Borough and level on points with Lincoln United. But RMI earned promotion by virtue of a better goal difference, with plus 32 against Lincoln's plus 31 (78 goals against 47). Farsley Celtic finished fourth on 77 points. Radcliffe and RMI shared the league's best defensive record during the season.

The end to the season could hardly have been more dramatic. In the penultimate home game of the season RMI and Radcliffe Borough shared a thrilling 2-2 at Hilton Park before a season's best crowd of 830. All the scoring came in the first half, Keith Evans' fourth-minute opener for the home side being cancelled out by Ian Lunt before Dave Bean gave the visitors the lead. Martin James, one of several former Football League players recruited by Waywell then equalised three minutes before half-time.

That result set up a nerve-wracking final Saturday of the campaign with RMI players, officials and supporters having to endure half an hour of 'extra-time' agony before claiming their promotion place.

After being held to a scoreless draw by Gretna before a crowd of 151 at Hilton Park and Radcliffe Borough confirmed as champions, the final score from Lincoln's game was eagerly awaited. RMI had to hope that third-placed Lincoln would not beat Whitley Bay by two clear goals and pip them to promotion at the death.

The Lincoln game had been held up in the first-half due to a serious injury to a player and to extend the tension, with Lincoln leading 1-0, RMI players and officials had to endure untold mental torture as the second half ran six minutes over.

But Lincoln failed to get that vital second goal and Leigh became the first club in Unibond history to regain a place in the top flight after relegation since the introduction of two divisions.

Manager Steve Waywell reflected: 'It's been a long hard slog and then having to endure the wait at the end made it all the more nerve-wracking.

'The tension and importance of the occasion was evident in our performance and while it would have been nice to have clinched promotion in a more clear-cut way, I'm delighted for the players and the chairman who have worked so hard this season.

'Now we can start to plan for the Premier Division and hopefully give Leigh a football team they can be proud of.'

Chairman Chris Healey said: 'This is probably the most important day for this club in the last ten or 15 years. Better opposition, many local derbies and increased interest should see bigger gates at Hilton Park next season.

'The public of the town have been magnificent in the closing weeks of the season and I know that the players have been delighted by the way Leigh people have responded.'

In the closing weeks of the season RMI had put together a fine run of consistent results, suffering just one defeat (2-1 at home to Bradford Park Avenue) in their 17 games. In that sequence they won 11 and drew five. Average attendances, boosted by the 'bumper' gate against Radcliffe averaged 186 in league games.

RMI also enjoyed a good run in the FA Cup defeating Belper Town, Alfreton Town, Billingham Synthonia and Marine on their way to a fourth qualifying round home tie against Runcorn. But the Linnets earned revenge for RMI's victory over them at the same stage in 1982 with a 4-2 success at Hilton Park. Some consolation was provided by a gate of 820.

In all games Chris Shaw, a former Ashton United, Witton Albion, Oldham Town and Radcliffe Borough forward scored 28 goals with his striking partner Keith Evans (ex-Hyde United, Ashton United, Curzon Ashton and Irlam) netting 21. Dave Ridings, a talented midfield player with League experience at Halifax Town and Lincoln City scored ten goals.

In 1997-98 RMI's fine upsurge continued as they finished third in the Unibond League Premier Division with 76 points from 42 games. They won half (21) of their league games, drew 13 and lost eight, scoring 63 goals against 41. Barrow (84 points) were champions with Boston United (78 points) runners-up. RMI just edged out Runcorn and Gainsborough Trinity (both 75 points) and Emley (74). Having been forced to direct the bulk of their available budget on ground improvements rather than the playing staff Radcliffe Borough by comparison failed to come to terms with the step-up and were relegated alongside Alfreton Town.

After beating Accrington Stanley 1-0 RMI bowed out of the FA Cup at the second qualifying round stage, losing 4-0 at Halifax Town. They went out of the FA Trophy on penalties at the hands of Grantham in the first round after defeating Frickley Athletic, Radcliffe Borough and Bradford Park Avenue in the qualifying rounds. Their League Cup campaign ended in an ignominious 5-2 defeat at Chorley while Marine ended RMI's interest in the Lancashire Junior Cup.

In all games Evans hit 18 goals, Shaw and Lee Cryer (a new signing from Atherton LR) 14 apiece and midfield players Eric Rostron and Ridings nine apiece. League attendances averaged 236 with the visit of Altrincham attracting the season's highest crowd, 449.

Relegated Gateshead and Stalybridge Celtic joined the Premier Division in 1998-99 alongside promoted Whitby Town and Worksop Town. RMI finished in eighth position with 63 points from 42 games, with 16 wins, 15 draws and 11 defeats. Altrincham (80 points) were champions, four points ahead of runners-up Worksop Town (76).

RMI began the season with a 2-1 defeat at Worksop Town when their line-up was as follows: Felgate; Locke, Wallace; Turpin, Schofield, Smyth; Monk, Ridings, Matthews, Brady, McCrae. Subs: Kay, Cryer, Rostron. Neil Matthews, an experienced Football

League striker with a career record of 68 goals in 258 games made a goal-scoring debut after signing from Guiseley and went on top the scoring charts with 16 goals in league and cup. The consistent Evans hit 15 and Ridings contributed ten goals from midfield.

The team's form was better away from home with 28 points gained at Hilton Park and 35 on their travels. 'With the benefit of a few additions we have the backbone of a very good side,' was Steve Waywell's end-of-season assessment. 'Our home form needs addressing and the last few games underlined that.'

The Fulham Cup Ties

But the highlight of the season was RMI's fine run in the FA Cup. After beating Winsford United, Worksop Town and Droylsden they earned a high profile tie that represented only the club's third appearance in the first round of the competition in its history. Goalkeeper and Captain Dave Felgate, a veteran of 612 league games, 238 of them for Bolton Wanderers was outstanding in each tie, all of which were won with 2-1 score-lines.

RMI were drawn away to a Fulham side rejuvenated by the deep pockets of Mohammed al Fayed and the appointment of Kevin Keegan as manager. Though then in the third tier of the league system Fulham went on to reach the Premier League in 2001. Leigh's achievement in reaching that stage attracted the attention of the national media and the club organised a media day to satiate the demand for stories about the David and Goliath tie.

In an outstandingly written piece in the Independent Andrew Longmore commented: *'Lancastrians will identify Leigh RMI as the club formerly known as Horwich. The initials stand for Railway Mechanics' Institute and date back to the days when Horwich was the main locomotive-building works for the Lancashire and Yorkshire Railway. The works were originally at Newton Heath where there were once two clubs. At Leigh, they often wonder what happened to Manchester United.*

'Horwich's traumatic move to Leigh involved a far greater leap than a mere six-mile journey south west. Unsigned boundaries were crossed. Horwich is Bolton Wanderers and football; Leigh is rugby league. As if to emphasise the sense of dispossession, the newly-formed Leigh RMI arrived at Hilton Park, home of Leigh Rugby League Club, in March 1995 and lost their first match 4-0 to Boston United. They lost all their remaining five home matches that season and were relegated. As a welcome, it was rather less than Eccles cakes and hot cocoa. Crowds, initially intrigued by the aliens, slumped to 150, roughly where the interest had left off on the draughty slopes of Grundy Hill, the idiosyncratic ground on the side of Rivington Pike which had been home for almost 100 years.

'Many of the old Horwich fans have yet to be seduced into the new territory. Grundy Hill sloped 16 feet from top diagonal to bottom diagonal and had the contours of corrugated iron, but until the new footballing nanny state prohibited such extreme drops, the ground was Horwich's prime asset. Weymouth once turned up for the final of the Bob Lord Trophy with Shaun Teale, who moved on to Bournemouth and Aston Villa, in their ranks and froze at the prospect of mountaineering.

'They lost the match when they saw the slope,' chuckles Chris Healey, the chairman of Leigh RMI and architect of the move. 'But I always reckoned there were more goals scored up the hill than down it. I was almost tarred and feathered when we left. They draped a coffin with the colours of Horwich and paraded it round the ground, but really we had no option. Crowds were down, we had to level out the slope but had no money and people had no enthusiasm for fundraising. We wouldn't have been in existence if we'd have stayed.' Grundy Hill is a housing estate now. The vice-chairman's daughter lives over the penalty spot. 'Sometimes progress has a price,' says Healey.

Healey admitted that he had underestimated the strength of traditional barriers between soccer and rugby league but then added: 'The local press is starting to take us seriously and the supporters' club now has 150 members. This match against Fulham is beginning to open their eyes.'

Steve Waywell, the manager, was in the side that lost 3-0 at Blackpool in 1982. He was also a member of the Burnley side which won the FA Youth Cup. Nine of the team went on to play in the first-team; he was one of the two who didn't and instead had to settle for a career in non-league football and a job in the building industry. For Waywell, though, the tie brought him face to face with his footballing idol. Whenever he had no game to play Waywell would stand on the Kop at Anfield and watch Keegan play for Liverpool in his prime.

Like Waywell many of his RMI side had never quite got the breaks, such is the thin dividing line between success and failure in football. Full-back Mike Wallace, for instance, once played in the same England Under-18 side as Alan Shearer; Felgate was once the verge of joining Liverpool until Lincoln trebled the asking price and Mike Hooper was bought instead.

Felgate revealed that his time at Leigh had rejuvenated his interest in football having suffered rejection when given a free-transfer by Wigan Athletic two years previously. 'I'd been in the game 19 years, knew all the tricks and suddenly I fell out of love with it,' Felgate said. But he was persuaded to go training again by a friend and then Leigh stepped in with a tempting offer. 'Someone like Dave Beasant is a good yardstick for me. He's still playing in the Premier League and he's nearly 40,' Felgate said. 'The crosses look a bit further away these days and on Sunday mornings I walk like Robocop, but if I ever thought I couldn't play to my best, I'd pack it in.'

RMI took an estimated 1,500 supporters to London, enjoying the £20 'all-in' offer after retail giant Asda sponsored the coaches. The Asda superstore dominated the approach to Hilton Park 'With luck, some might come and watch us every home game,' said Healey.

After heroically drawing 1-1 at Craven Cottage Felgate earned nationwide publicity for his heroics and rich praise from the Fulham manager. The 38-year-old defied Fulham with a string of outstanding stops and Keegan later described Felgate's goal-keeping display as 'just about the best I've ever seen, because of the number of great saves.' RMI manager Steve Waywell said: 'He does it week-in, week-out for us. Kevin Keegan asked how much we want for him and I've told him a million.'

RMI actually took the lead when Tony Whealing curled in a left-foot shot from a free-kick with Dirk Lehmann's header levelling matters ten minutes before half-time. The teams lined-up as follows on Sunday 15 November 1998. Fulham: Taylor; Uhlenbeck, Symons, Coleman, Brevett; Collins, Davis (Trollope), Hayward, Salako (Horsfield); Peschisolido, Lehmann. RMI: Felgate; Hill, Locke, Turpin; Prescott, Smyth, Ridings; Evans, Whealing; Monk (Cryer), Matthews. The referee was Mr P Rejer (West Midlands) and the attendance was 7,965.

The replay was staged at Hilton Park on Tuesday 24 November and attracted a huge degree of local and national interest. An all-ticket crowd of 7,125 saw Fulham win 2-0 in a game screened live on Sky Sports. Fulham's Canadian born forward Paul Peschisolido settled the tie with two first-half goals, the first from the penalty spot on the half-hour, the second ten minutes later. The teams lined-up as follows. RMI: Felgate; Prescott, Hill, Locke, Turpin, Whealing; Smyth, Ridings, Evans; Monk, Matthews (Cryer). Fulham: Taylor; Symons, Morgan, Coleman; Uhlenbeck, Smith (Brazier), Bracewell (Hayward), Trollope, Brevett; Horsfield, Peschisolido (Salako). The referee was again Mr P Rejer.

But RMI later suffered a giant-killing of their own, beaten at home by Droylsden, one division below them in the final of the Unibond League President's Cup final on 15 April 1999. On their way to the final RMI had defeated Ashton United, Altrincham and Runcorn. The Bloods dominated for long periods and deservedly led 2-0 going into the final ten minutes. Wes Kinney scored the opening goal after ten minutes and Mick Jones added a second on the half-hour. Though Tony Black reduced the arrears with nine minutes remaining RMI were unable to force an equaliser in a grandstand finish.

RMI manager Steve Waywell said: 'We lost it in the first half giving silly goals away, didn't compete and were always second best and once again we had individuals who didn't perform.'

A Champion Season

In 1999-2000 RMI enjoyed a marvellous campaign and lifted the Unibond League Premier Division title, earning promotion to the National Conference League. Leigh began the season with a 1-0 win at Blyth Spartans, Neil Matthews scoring the only goal, when their team was: Felgate; Locke, Wallace; P Jones, Turkington, Butler; Monks, Ridings, Ross, Matthews, S Jones. Substitutes: Turpin, Carr, Entwistle.

With 23 teams in the league RMI faced a demanding 44-game schedule but won 26 games, drew ten and lost just eight times, scoring 87 goals (the highest tally in the league) and conceding 44, a defensive record bettered by only four clubs. With 88 points, or exactly two-per-game, they were deserved champions and their playing style earned widespread praise. Hyde United (86 points) finished runners-up with Gateshead (82) in third position and Marine (80) fourth.

The only disappointment came in cup competitions with RMI bowing out of the FA Cup at Northern League Crook Town following a replay after beating Blyth Spartans in an earlier round.

Again Leigh's away form was actually more impressive than that at Hilton Park and manager Waywell had his own theory for the reasons why. 'Our away record is very good and I think we play better away from Hilton Park because when sides come to us they see the superb facilities and they lift their game accordingly,' pointed out Waywell.

Fittingly RMI clinched the title with a 3-1 win at Spennymoor United with two games still to play. Waywell said: 'It was a great journey home from Spennymoor, but what we have achieved hasn't sunk in yet.

'The team have been tremendous. And to win it with two still to play is a bonus. We can go out and relax and enjoy ourselves instead of going down to the wire. The club has come along way in the last five years and it is down to our chairman Chris Healey. He gave me a four-year contract that has still 12 months to run. He has never put me under any pressure and has been totally loyal. I now want to return that loyalty but I won't be thinking about the Conference for a couple of weeks. I would also like to thank the fans who travelled to Spennymoor and made so much noise.'

Victory was RMI's 12th league win of the campaign away from Hilton Park. They took the lead in the 20th minute with a Ged Kielty header and extended their lead on the hour-mark when Mark Ward, a vastly experienced midfield player with 465 league appearances under his belt most at the top level converted a penalty after Steve Jones had been tripped. After Zang pulled a goal back Jones clinched victory with a late goal.

Jones, then aged 22 proved to be a real find and soon attracted a host of admirers from Football League club scouts. After once being on the books at Blackpool and Bury he had returned to Ireland to play for Sligo Rovers before trying his luck again in this country. He led the RMI scoring charts with 23 goals in league and cup, followed by Tony Black (22), the experienced Brian Ross (18) and Dave Ridings (10). But Ward, the former Oldham Athletic, West Ham United, Manchester City, Everton and Birmingham City player then left to take up the role as player-manager at Altrincham.

Into The National Conference

The remarkable climb up the football pyramid continued in 2000-01 as RMI finished fifth in their first season in the Conference. They won 19, drew 11 and lost 12 games, scoring 63 goals against 57. Rushden & Diamonds (86 points) were champions with Yeovil Town (80) runners-up. Dagenham & Redbridge (77) and Southport (69) also bettered RMI's impressive haul of 68 points.

Effectively RMI were the 97th highest placed football club in the country, despite having a part-time playing squad on a relatively modest budget compared to the resources at the disposal of many of the Conference rivals who had full-time playing squads.

RMI had opened the season with silverware after defeating Lancaster City 2-1 in the Peter Swales Challenge Shield, the traditional seasonal opener played between the Unibond's League's reigning champions and league cup holders. Andy Mason and a Farrell Kilbane own goal sandwiched Chris Ward's goal for Lancaster before a crowd of 251 at Hilton Park. Former Manchester United and Wales's midfielder Clayton Blackmore made his RMI debut on trial. Lancaster later earned revenge by knocking out RMI in the Lancashire Junior Cup, now renamed the Lancashire FA Marsden Trophy.

The first Conference game was against Dagenham & Redbridge with the visitors winning 2-1 before a crowd of 451. The Leigh line-up was as follows: Felgate; Monk, Harris; Blackmore, Scott, Jones; Udall, Kielty (Mason), Farrell (Cumiskey), Black, Swan. Blackmore left the club after this game.

But Leigh then recovered to win 2-1 at Southport and 1-0 at Kettering Town before defeating Scarborough 2-0 at Hilton Park. The first ten days of the league season had been hectic but with nine points in the bag RMI were already well on the way towards achieving the first aim of any promoted side, that of survival.

Life in the big league was never easy but RMI were competitive, played some attractive football and for the most part tight in defence. They met several teams for the first time in league football including former Football League outfits Doncaster Rovers, Hereford United and Chester City. The highest home league crowd of the season was 1,405 for the midweek visit of Rushden & Diamonds in October when Jones got the only goal midway through the second half. 'I think we'll have set one or two tongues wagging with that result,' said Leigh boss Steve Waywell. When RMI played the return at Nene Park Black silenced the vast majority of the 3,882 crowd with a second half equaliser meaning that RMI took four points against the eventual champions.

RMI also reached the first round of the FA Cup again after a thrilling 4-3 win at Scarborough in the fourth qualifying round, Tony Black scoring a hat-trick. Their reward was a home draw against Millwall, but the tie was switched to their opponents' ground at the New Den due to the high costs of policing had the game taken place at Hilton Park. Millwall, who scored after only 48 seconds through a Neil Harris penalty won 3-0 with further second half goals by Marc Bircham and Paul Moody.

The teams lined-up as follows on Sunday 19 November 2000. Millwall: Warner; Lawrence, Ryan; Bircham, Nethercott, Dolan; Livermore, Moody (Braniff), Harris, Reid (Kinet), Ifill. RMI: Felgate; Trees, German; Durkin, Farrell, Swan; Monk (Matthews), Ridings, Kielty (Harris), Black, Jones. The referee was Mr SJ Lodge (Barnsley) and the attendance was 6,907.

Leigh went out of the FA Trophy at the hands of Hereford United, losing 2-1 in a fourth round replay at Hilton Park after forcing a creditable 0-0 draw at Edgar Street.

Steve Jones was RMI's leading scorer in the league with 19 goals, followed by Tony Black and Dave Ridings (12 apiece). In all games Jones scored 22 goals, Black 18 and Ridings 13. Jones and the vastly-experienced Andrew Farrell were ever-present in the league. Having clocked-up 534 league appearances with Colchester United, Burnley, Wigan and Rochdale Farrell had joined RMI from Morecambe.

Former Altrincham midfielder Ged Kielty and Ridings both made 40 league appearances followed by ex-Oldham Athletic product Iain Swan (39), Black (37), Dave German (34) and Ian Monk (30). The former Bolton Wanderers fullback Nicky Spooner made 22 league appearances and Dave German, who had joined RMI from Winsford United in 1999 made 34 appearances and established himself as something of a cult hero among the fans. Dave Felgate shared the goalkeeping duties with Craig Dootson after enjoying glorious swansong to his illustrious career playing in 24 Conference games.

At the end of the season the Derry born Jones, who had made his name during two outstanding seasons at Hilton Park was transferred to Crewe Alexandra for £75,000 and went on to embark on a successful Football League career winning 29 Northern Ireland caps.

Despite the success the Leigh public seemed reluctant to come down to Hilton Park on a regular basis and RMI had the lowest average attendance in the league - just 604, well below the break-even figure which was around the 1,000 mark. In contrast Rushden & Diamonds averaged 3,876 and Yeovil Town 3,415 and all but five of the Conference clubs averaged four-figure crowds.

'You can't force people to come through the gate,' reflected Chairman Chris Healey. 'And that's why we are working so hard to raise the profile in the town. My disappointment is not with the size of our crowds but that the people of Leigh are missing a treat.

'It would seem that the higher we go in the league, the lower the crowd we attract. On the whole we are playing good football, scoring goals and have only lost one league game in 2001.'

RMI finished their first season in the Conference with a 2-1 win at Morecambe that not only clinched fifth but ensured they qualified for the following season's LDV Vans Trophy. Dave Ridings and Steve Jones (penalty) scored late goals to end a superb season in style.

Leigh manager Steve Waywell reflected on the campaign. 'Overall, I think our players and supporters have been nothing short of exceptional this year,' he said. 'We have had the odd bad patch like everyone this year, but our commitment has been 110percent and we have played tremendously to surprise a lot of people. As for next season, it will be a new challenge. People will think that they know our game and can beat us but we will have to carry on working hard and hopefully we can prove them wrong again. I'll be meeting the chairman soon to discuss the forthcoming season and I will hopefully be looking to boost the squad yet further. We deserved to win today, and fifth place is deserving of our hard work since August.'

The RMI side which closed the season was: Felgate; Trees, German; Kielty, Farrell,

Swan; Monk, Ridings, Hayder (Morrell), Black, Jones. Subs not used: Connelly, Lindsey, Harris, Dootson.

Though RMI suffered three heavy defeats in the closing week of the season, losing 6-1 at Yeovil Town, 4-0 at Doncaster Rovers and 4-1 at home to Stevenage Borough they recovered superbly to win their final three league games, including a double success over Morecambe.

Bolton Wanderers staged their reserve games at Hilton Park during the 2000-01 season and with rugby league as well the pitch was heavily used throughout the year.

In 2001-02 RMI survived comfortably at the increasingly competitive Conference level, finishing 16th with 53 points from 42 games. They won 15, drew eight and lost 19 and finished nine points clear of the relegation places. Boston United (84 points) and Dagenham & Redbridge (also 84) tied at the top of the table with the former earning the title on goal difference. For RMI fans the new twin striking partnership of Michael Twiss and Dino Maamria provided many highlights.

Twiss, a former Manchester United trainee had also played for Sheffield United and Port Vale scored 15 goals in 33 league games after making his RMI debut at Nuneaton Borough in September and the RMI faithful were saddened when he joined Chester City in May 2002. The Tunisia born former Doncaster Rovers and Southport forward Maamria scored 12 goals in 29 league appearances while Marcus Hallows, back with RMI after spells with Bolton Wanderers and Stockport County and having played in Ireland added nine in 37 games. In all games Maamria scored 19 goals, Twiss 18 and Hallows and the consistent Black ten apiece.

Neil Durkin was ever-present in league games alongside ex-Morecambe forward Ian Monk with Dave German making 36 appearances and goalkeeper Mark Westhead 33. Westhead, like Felgate, had started his career as a teenager with Bolton Wanderers and joined RMI from Wycombe Wanderers, moving on to Stevenage Borough after one season at Hilton Park. Felgate joined Hyde United on loan and went on to play into his forties for Bacup Borough before becoming a goalkeeping coach.

RMI opened the campaign with a 1-1 home draw against Hayes when their line-up read as follows: Felgate; Spooner (Scott), German; Durkin (Reynolds), Farrell, Swan; Monk, Fisher, Ridings, Maamria, Black (Hallows).

But manager Steve Waywell soon had to contend with a serious injury list with Jamie Udall, Iain Swan, Ged Kielty, Steve Thompson and Dave Ridings all long-term casualties.

Financial Realities Hit Hard

Recurring speculation over the costs of competing at this level of football and disappointing gates at Hilton Park surfaced during November 2001. Chairman Healey was forced announce a round of swingeing pay cuts, up to two-thirds in some cases but was then able to put the cost-saving measures on hold.

In a press release the club stated: 'To ensure continued payments of wages at their current level, the club has secured a £50,000 loan which was been guaranteed by members of the RMI committee. While the move safeguards the existing playing and coaching staff, RMI stress that the loan is a rescue package, not a solution to the cash crisis that has hit the Hilton Park club.'

Club secretary Alan Robinson said: 'Sadly we have joined the most fashionable club in football - those experiencing serious financial difficulties. For RMI to continue playing Nationwide Conference football, the full support of the people of the Leigh area, as spectators and sponsors, cannot be over-emphasised.

'The rescue package will take the strain off, but it clearly isn't a long-term solution. We need more people through the turnstiles on match days, need a major sponsor and need to make a bigger effort to attract smaller sponsors to the club.

'All this has been done with one thing in mind - keeping Leigh RMI in the Nationwide Conference. The management and players understand this and there is no doubt that they are making every effort to succeed on the field.'

Safety was secured with victory at Stevenage Borough with three games still to play, Hallows scoring the only goal of the game and after the trials and tribulations of the season both on and off the pitch their final position of 16th was impressive for a club with such small crowds and resources.

But as an indication of the difficulty of competing at this level RMI again finished bottom of the attendance chart, averaging just 498 in league games with a season's best gate of 788 for the visit of Boston United. All but six of the Conference sides averaged over one thousand with Yeovil Town topping the chart with an average of 2,872.

After beating Scarborough 2-1 in the first round of the LDV Vans Trophy RMI earned a trip to Boothferry Park to play Hull City. Then in League Two the Tigers won the tie 3-0 thanks to an excellent hat-trick from striker Gary Alexander, who converted an early penalty and added two further goals in the space of four second half minutes. But after being dumped out of the FA Cup by Worksop Town four days earlier and being condemned for a lack of effort by boss Waywell at least RMI had salvaged some pride with a battling performance.

The teams lined-up as follows: Hull City: Glennon; Edwards, Holt (Price); Whitmore (Lee), Mohan, Petty; Williams (Matthews), Johnsson, Alexander, Dudfield, Beresford. RMI: Westhead; Scott, Swan; Durkin, Farrell (Black), Heald; Fisher, Fitzpatrick, Kielty (Monk), Twiss, Maamria (Hallows). The referee was B Curson (Leicestershire) and the attendance was 5,226.

In the Lancashire Junior Cup RMI enjoyed a reunion with old foes Chorley, winning a first round tie 4-2 at Victory Park which included two goals from Maamria. The striker then scored a hat-trick in the second round victory over Rossendale United but RMI bowed out of the competition at the quarter-final stage after losing 2-1 at Accrington Stanley.

RMI earned another season at Conference level in 2002-03 but only just, finishing two points clear of the bottom three with 48 points from 42 games. RMI won 14, drew six and lost 22 games, scoring 44 goals- the second-lowest tally and conceding 71. Yeovil Town (95 points) were runaway champions, finishing 17 points ahead of runners-up Morecambe. Two teams were now to be promoted to the Football League and a play-off was introduced to determine the second, Doncaster Rovers defeating Dagenham & Redbridge at Stoke City's Britannia Stadium to regain their league status.

RMI had dispensation to the fourth qualifying round of the FA Cup, another reward of being in the Conference, but three years running failed to take advantage and lost 4-2 at home to Worksop Town in 2001, 2-1 at Moor Green in 2002 and 2-0 at Accrington Stanley in 2003. RMI fared little better in the FA Trophy though they did beat Wakefield & Emley in 2001 before losing 2-0 at Margate. In 2002 Vauxhall Motors won 2-1 at Hilton Park and the following year RMI suffered the indignity of being expelled from the competition for fielding an ineligible player in a third round tie against Stalybridge Celtic. RMI had fielded a goalkeeper (former Bury 'keeper Sebastian Rowe, who had spent the summer in the United States) without gaining international clearance after their two first-choice number ones (Gary Kelly and Lee Martin) had been injured and cup-tied respectively. It was an unusual case as prior to joining RMI Rowe had played 16 games for neighbours Atherton Collieries after returning from his stint abroad.

After seven successful years Steve Waywell left the club in December 2002 and was appointed manager at Hyde United. Criticism from the directors and supporters eventually forced Waywell out, and he was followed not too long afterwards by chairman and main benefactor Chris Healey.

Waywell left RMI soon after a 4-0 home defeat by Chester City with the club under an FA ban from signing new players. After the game, Waywell said: 'There is no competition for places and the players know it and some are not competing as much as I would like.'

Waywell's assistant, Mark Patterson was appointed to take over immediately. Patterson was a highly experienced Football League player with nearly 500 league appearances to his credit, the bulk of them with four Lancashire clubs, Blackburn Rovers, Bury, Preston North End and Bolton Wanderers. Though he had his critics who pointed to what they saw as a reliance on older players Patterson helped keep the club in the Conference while bringing silverware to the boardroom against a Kendal Town side playing in their first ever Lancashire Junior Cup Final. It was RMI's first success in the competition, now renamed the Lancashire FA Marsden Trophy since the days of Keetley, Mather and Co back in 1930.

Goals from Ian Monk and Ged Courtney gave Leigh RMI their victory in a final played at Accrington Stanley's Crown ground. Former Morecambe winger Monk headed RMI ahead after 15 minutes from Andy Heald's cross and Courtney fired home the second from 12 yards just before the hour-mark. Skipper Neil Durkin, a fine model of consistency throughout the season lifted the cup.

The sides lined-up as follows on 15 April 2003: Kendal Town: Ward; Pennington, Blamire (Shepherd); P Hodgson, R Close, Hayton (Simpson); Corcoran, Cliff, J Close, Walmsley (Jones), Prosser. Leigh RMI: Coburn; Durkin, Lancaster (Fitzhenry); Heald, Courtney, Pendlebury; Monk, Campbell, Salt (Maden), Heffernan, Dootson (Kielty). The referee was

Mr DG Commins (Preston) and attendance was 481.

Maamria top-scored with 12 goals in 25 league games and a further six cup goals but was transferred to Stevenage Borough for a five-figure fee in February 2003 after originally rejecting a move. The consistent Monk was second on the list with six goals. Former Altrincham goalkeeper Stuart Coburn was ever-present in the league and won the club's player-of-the-season award but was surprisingly released early in the following season and re-joined his former club. Durkin, who proved a shrewd signing from Darwen, missed only one game and Phil Salt (39 appearances), Neil Fitzhenry (37), Monk (37), Wayne Maden (35), Gerry Harrison (30) and Andy Heald (29) were other mainstays of the side.

In the LDV Vans Trophy RMI lost 4-3 on the golden goal rule after an exciting second round-tie against League Two side Wrexham at Hilton Park. Lee Jones with his second goal of the game won the tie in the second minute of extra-time. Lee Trundle and Carlos Edwards also scored for the visitors with Ged Kielty (2) and Maamria on the mark for RMI who led 2-0 and 3-2.

The line-ups were: Leigh RMI: Coburn; Maden, Durkin; Fitzhenry, Harrison, Salt; Kielty, Fisher, Williams, Maamria, Whittaker. Wrexham: Whitfield; Edwards, Bennett; Lawrence, Morgan (Carey), Edwards; Ferguson, Thomas, Barrett (Sam), Jones, Trundle. The referee was Eddie Jones (Greater Manchester) and the attendance was 703.

RMI again finished bottom of the Conference's attendance table, averaging 484 with a season's best gate of 864 for the visit of Doncaster Rovers. Yeovil Town averaged 4,741, Doncaster Rovers 3,540 and Chester City 2,406 and all but six of the Conference teams averaged four-figure gates.

The Decline Continues

The decline continued in 2003-04 as RMI finished second-from-bottom with 29 points from 42 games, six ahead of bottom-placed Northwich Victoria. They won seven games, drew eight and lost 27, scoring 46 goals and conceding 97, easily the worst defensive record in the league. Chester City (92 points) were champions and Shrewsbury Town won promotion from the play-offs. But RMI were reprieved from relegation after Telford United folded and Margate were demoted to the newly-formed Conference South division due to ground grading issues.

Patterson resigned as manager in October 2003 and Phil Starbuck, the ex-Huddersfield Town, Nottingham Forest and Sheffield United forward was appointed manager with Steve Redmond, the vastly experienced former Manchester City, Oldham Athletic and Bury defender assistant and player-manager. Starbuck had been player-manager at Hucknall Town prior to becoming Patterson's assistant.

Patterson revealed that off-field pressures prompted his resignation and not a dismal on-field return of two points from nine games.

'I have resigned from the job because of what has gone on behind the scenes,' Patterson told the local press. 'The politics have ground me down a bit. I am not prepared to carry on working for a football team that is not run to Conference standards.

'They deserve to be there because the football team have earned it, but the other part of it, which is probably just as important, has never come up to Conference standards and that is because they do not get the support, because they are playing in a rugby town, and are constantly bickering with the rugby people. They need someone to inject a substantial amount of money into the club and that has not happened recently.'

Patterson had also taken on the demanding role of commercial manager at the club. 'I have brought a few quid into the club on the commercial side and the managing side could possibly have suffered a little bit,' Patterson added. 'It is a thankless task when you are doing so many things on your own.

'Managing RMI is the most difficult job in the Conference because I had one of the smallest budgets and we share the ground with the rugby club, who have not paid their way over the years, which makes things even harder. I am not blaming anybody for that; I just know that is what I inherited.

'There is a team there that I believe is more than capable of staying in the Conference. The squad contains better players than eight months ago. I have said all along it will take time to turn things around. I kept them up last season and this season I have had two months to change things around. It will not happen overnight.

'I am not knocking the majority of people of Leigh associated with the football club. The club is a nice club run by, in the majority, nice people, but there are one or two there who did not want to know what I was trying to achieve. I have tried to fight as hard as I can to keep them as high as I can and have done it with my heart on my sleeve, sometimes upsetting people. It comes to a stage when you think to yourself: 'Why am I carrying on?'.'

Chairman Bill Taylor said: 'We have to thank Mark for the dedication he has shown us in the past 10 months and I have to say his resignation was accepted with great reluctance.

We do not have thousands of pounds to spend but most of the players he asked for he got.'

Starbuck was temporarily been installed as boss for the FA Cup fourth qualifying round tie at Accrington Stanley before being given the job on a permanent basis. RMI went out of the FA Cup at the Crown Ground and suffered a humiliating 4-1 defeat at Chorley, with Patterson now in charge of the Magpies in the Lancashire Junior Cup. With disqualification from the FA Trophy adding to the gloom around Hilton Park there was at least one shining light.

That was provided by the talented David McNiven, a July 2003 signing from Northwich Victoria, who enjoyed a fine first season at Hilton Park and virtually carried the team's striking responsibilities on his own shoulders. McNiven scored 25 goals in 41 league games, a remarkable feat in a struggling team and it was a measure of his dominance that next in the scoring list were defender Wayne Maden and the on-loan Stephen Brodie with four goals apiece.

McNiven also earned selection for the England non-league international squad, who played under the title of The National Game XI. He played as substitute in two games in the end-of-season Four Nations Tournament held in Scotland against Wales (at Keith FC on 20 May 2004; lost 2-0) and Scotland (at Deveronvale FC on 23 May 2004; won 3-1). He then made a starting appearance in the friendly with Iraq on 7 May 2004 when a crowd of 4,000 at Macclesfield Town's Moss Rose saw the visitors win 4-0. Finally, McNiven was a substitute as England drew 0-0 against the USA in Charleston on 9 June 2004.

The consistent Durkin (37 appearances) followed McNiven in the appearances chart with ex-Chester City defender Martyn Lancaster (33), Andy Roscoe (33), former Doncaster Rovers midfielder Warren Peyton (32) and former Scarborough forward Paul Shepherd (29) also regulars in the side. Maden and Harrison both made 27 appearances.

McNiven announced his arrival at Hilton Park with a two-goal salvo that saw RMI beat Dagenham & Redbridge 2-1 in the opening game of the season at Hilton Park and scored in each of his first four games. RMI's line-up for the first game was: Coburn; Harrison, Hill; Peyton, Lancaster, Durkin; Monk, Kielty, McNiven, Robinson, Heald. Subs: Courtney, Hallows, Pendlebury. When a Maden goal gave RMI a 1-0 win at Northwich Victoria they had begun the season promisingly with two wins and two draws from their opening five games.

But they won only five more times in league, at home to Morecambe, Margate and Morecambe and away at Hereford United and Dagenham & Redbridge. The Christmas-time derby games with Chester City were particularly disappointing with RMI going down 5-0 at the Deva Stadium on Boxing Day and 6-2 in the return at Hilton Park on New Year's Day.

Boosted by a gate of 2,002 for the Chester game and another of 1,219 for Shrewsbury's visit average attendances at Hilton Park rose to 565, even though they were again the Conference's worst-supported club.

RMI's five-season stint in the top echelon of the non-league game ended after the 2004-05 campaign. They won only four games drew six and lost 32 of their 42 league games, finishing 11 points adrift of Farnborough Town with a meagre tally of 18 points. They scored only 31 goals, the lowest in the league and with 98 conceded also had the worst defensive record. Barnet were promoted as champions and Carlisle United won promotion via the play-offs.

RMI began the season with a 2-1 home defeat at the hands of Crawley Town before an attendance of 401 when the following side was on duty: Martin; Lane, Miller; Holmes, Moran, Stoker; Gaunt, Meechan, Adams, Peyton, Mitchell. Subs: Rose, Roscoe. Former Hucknall player Craig Gaunt scored the RMI goal.

The first league win of the season did not arrive until the sixth game when goals by Chris Simm and Ian Fitzpatrick earned RMI a 2-0 victory over Forest Green Rovers. But RMI won only once more at Hilton Park in the league, when goals by Lee Mulvaney and Ben Jones earned a 2-1 win over Canvey Island in April, ironically on the day that results elsewhere confirmed the club's relegation. The only two away wins came in the space of five days in late February with single goal successes at Tamworth and Farnborough Town.

Though Altrincham ended RMI's hopes of FA Trophy success, some consolation was provided in the FA Cup and RMI again reached the first round stage after winning 2-0 at Accrington Stanley in the fourth qualifying round, Chris Simm and Karl Rose on target. But they disappointingly lost out on a potentially money-spinning run when bowing out at Conference South outfit Cambridge City in the first round. Simm gave RMI a 14th-minute lead but Dave Sadler equalised for City and substitute Jon Stevenson grabbed an injury-time winner.

The teams were: Cambridge City: Roberts; Pope, Chaffey (Summerscales); Scott, Langston, Fuff; Williams, Fiddes (Miller), Simpson, Sadler (Stevenson), Binns.
RMI: Crichton; Stoker, Lane; Connell (Shilton), Gaunt, Miller; Rose, Starbuck, Simm, Williams, Roscoe. The referee was Mr R Lee (Essex) and the attendance was 930.

RMI had three managers during the season with Phil Starbuck being replaced by Geoff Lutley and then Steve Bleasdale taking charge.

In retrospect the roots of the decline were traced back to the departure of David McNiven during the summer to Queen of the South. RMI never replaced their consistent marksman and despite wholesale changes could never field a settled team.

Starbuck left the club in November 2004 and was replaced by the 52-year-old Lutley, who had coaching experience amongst other clubs at Bradford City, Macclesfield Town and Bury. Soon after his appointment Lutley told BBC Sport: 'This is the most difficult job I've come across in football. We've got the lowest budget in the Conference. I'd challenge anybody to try and do the job I'm doing. But I've always been a fighter and though it looks very, very likely we will go down, I won't give up and nor will the players.'

But Lutley offered his resignation to chairman Bill Taylor after a 3-0 home defeat to York City at the end of January. Bleasdale, a former assistant manager at Chester City, Oxford United and Southport had little time or resources to change things before a disastrous season ebbed away. After battling against the odds for many years RMI seemed simply to have run out of luck. As a sign of that, RMI were winning 2-1 in their away game against Northwich Victoria on New Year's Day when the referee abandoned the game due to torrential rain and high winds. When the game was re-played Vics won 2-0.

RMI used 58 players in league games. The consistent Chris Lane missed only three league games and topped the appearances chart with 39, Warren Peyton making 34 and

Andy Roscoe 30. In all games Chris Simm, Gareth Stoker and Gary Williams each scored six goals. Chairman Bill Taylor and the town's MP Andy Burnham again appealed for more support with gave financial clouds hanging over RMI's continued existence. After Leigh Centurions earned what proved to be a short-lived promotion to the Super League after the 2004 summer season Mr Taylor said: 'We have a lot of ambition at the club and it gives us great heart, encouragement and excitement to see the achievements of the Leigh Centurions.'

At the end of the season RMI wrote to the Nationwide Conference, in an attempt to clarify if they would be saved from relegation due to problems at other clubs. The letter stated: 'There are reports that Margate, who have already enjoyed a two year dispensation, have astonishingly requested a further extension to ground share in order to maintain their Conference status. Telford amongst other matters are said not to have the necessary ground lease arrangements in place and Exeter still await the outcome of a number of issues. The Nationwide Conference must surely deal with these matters in an expeditious and most importantly correct manner as prescribed and clearly defined in league rules. Both Leigh RMI and Northwich Victoria should be able to plan properly now for next season and cannot do so until these matters are resolved. With Northwich Victoria and Leigh RMI either at, or moving to, new stadiums the future for both clubs looks exceedingly bright and therefore the Conference should surely take this into consideration in reaching its decisions. Leigh RMI have been informed that the final funding partner, the NW Development Agency has now approved their grant towards a new 10,000 seated stadium.' It was to no avail.

Average league gates at Hilton Park were 434 and that figure was boosted by the large travelling support from Carlisle United that contributed to a season's best gate of 1,540. But six home games each attracted less than 300 spectators.

In five seasons in the Conference RMI had played 105 home league games and averaged crowds of just 514 with only five four-figure attendances, the highest 2,002 for Chester City's visit in the 2003-04 season.

Another Reprieve

In 2005-06 Leigh RMI finished in the relegation places in Conference North with 39 points from 42 games, having had one point deducted. Hednesford Town (35 points) were bottom and RMI finished on the same number of points as Redditch United but with an inferior goal difference. They won nine, drew 13 and lost 20 games, scoring 45 goals against 79. Northwich Victoria, who had been demoted from the Conference National League due to issues with the lease on their ground were champions with Stafford Rangers also earning promotion via the play-offs. But RMI earned a reprieve from relegation for the second time in three seasons after Canvey Island resigned from the Conference and accepted a voluntary three-level demotion. The highest gate of the season was 639 for the visit of Northwich Victoria and RMI's average home league attendance was 233.

The season had got off to an interesting start when RMI hosted the newly-formed FC United of Manchester in a friendly at Hilton Park on 16 July 2005. Though the game ended scoreless the attendance was a remarkable 2,552, higher than any gate RMI attracted in five seasons of Conference National football. It was reported that RMI officials actually held exploratory talks with their FC United counterparts over a possible merger between the clubs but that these came to nothing.

Andy Nelson and Stuart Humphreys took over the managerial reins one month before the start of the 2005-06 season after leaving Atherton LR. The pair had previously been in charge of the RMI reserve team. Nelson resigned on health grounds after two matches of the 2006-07 season and Humphreys, four years his assistant, assumed the managerial job in his own right.

RMI bowed out of the FA Cup at Gainsborough Trinity in the third qualifying round in 2005 following a replay after a 3-1 win at Chester-le-Street Town. Stafford Rangers ended RMI's interest in the FA Trophy at the third qualifying round stage with a 4-1 win at Hilton Park.

The groundhopping website Footballgroundsinfocus.com carried the following 'Traveller's Tale' from the home game against Worksop Town which the visitors won 1-0 before a crowd of 205:

It's just over ten years since Horwich RMI left their much loved and idiosyncratic ground at Grundy Hill with its vast slope and views of Rivington Pike and moved several miles away to Leigh. The trustees of Grundy Hill sold the ground for housing, with the nature of the pitch having ruled out any hope of remaining in the pyramid for much longer had RMI stayed put.

With Leigh rugby league club in financial difficulties, Grundy Hill Estates bought their Hilton Park ground and moved lock, stock and barrel in a ground share arrangement that effectively saved the rugby club from going out of business and the ground being developed. Hilton Park named after late rugby club chairman Jim Hilton is one of rugby league's most atmospheric and loved grounds. Built in 1947 largely due to voluntary townspeople after the rugby club was forced to leave its Mather Lane home during the war, it was formerly the site of allotments. Two of the ground's former landmarks, Parsonage colliery and a large cotton mill have now disappeared and a town centre by-pass road now runs along the former site of the Manchester-Liverpool railway line behind the far goal, one of the first to be built in this country dating back to the 1830s.

A vast atmospheric ground that once held over 31,000 for a rugby league cup-tie against St Helens, Hilton Park staged Super League rugby in 2005. Leigh remains a rugby league dominated town and despite occasional flurries of interest, such as when Kevin Keegan's Fulham visited for an FA Cup-tie Leigh RMI appear to have made little impact on the town's sporting map, though they run a vast number of junior sides.

Named after the railway mechanics' institute in Horwich the roots of the club's history can be traced back to the 19th century but only a handful of the stalwarts that once lined the Grundy Hill terraces can now be seen at Hilton Park. Despite a spell in the Conference, ended by relegation last season, RMI struggle on poor gates and attracted only 205 for this Friday evening fixture despite the presence of several travellers and a number of Worksop supporters.

Despite heavy rain the pitch was in superb condition. Hilton Park has two open terraced ends and a small main stand, the framework of which dates back to the Mather Lane ground. For RMI games the crowd tends to gather on the supporters' club stand side, built in the 1950s and since named the Tommy Sale stand after the rugby club legend. With a terrace in front of neat rows of seats and further standing behind the facilities are excellent and give a great view of the play. The Mick Martyn bar underneath the stand is open to spectators and a tea bar, named Bellybusters, in the corner of the ground dispensed a good range of drinks and hot snacks.

Hilton Park still retains the feel and atmosphere of a rugby ground and it still seems strange for many people to see football played on the hallowed turf. RMI had no luck at all, striking the woodwork several times and having other goal attempts cleared off the line while a Worksop defender should clearly have been sent-off for a last man foul on a home striker in the first half, the referee doling out only a yellow card. Worksop's goal came from their only shot on target all evening- a long range strike from captain Paul Dempsey.

With plans for a new ground further down the by-pass gathering momentum as part of the Leigh Sporting Village Hilton Park's days are numbered and a visit to this historic ground is to be recommended.

Despite struggling in 2006-07 RMI finished in 17th position, four points clear of the relegation places, earning 49 points from 42 games with 13 wins and ten draws, scoring 47 goals against 61. Scarborough had ten points deducted and folded at the end of the season, while Lancaster City, who also had ten points deducted to leave them with just one point from a season of struggle were relegated two divisions due to financial problems. Droylsden won promotion as champions and Farsley Celtic joined them via the play-offs. Average home league attendances slipped further to just 184 with Worksop Town attracting the season's highest gate, 325.

RMI's safety was assured after a 2-1 home win over Worksop Town in the final game of the season when Dan Owen scored both his side's goals. RMI had remained unbeaten in their last seven league games, securing two wins and five draws as they clawed their way away from the relegation places. Chris Simm ended the season with 14 goals but to the dismay of many supporters left the club in the summer to join Hyde United. Former Notts County forward Kevin Rapley, who joined RMI on loan from Chester City, was a crucial figure in the late season revival scoring seven goals and creating several more.

Woodley Sports knocked-out RMI in the FA Cup with a 2-0 victory at Hilton Park in the second qualifying round. After wins over Cammell Laird and Harrogate Town in the FA Trophy, RMI went down 3-1 at Stevenage Borough in the second round.

RMI's good fortune ran out in 2007-08 when they finished bottom of Conference North with 26 points from 42 games, with just six wins and eight draws and 28 defeats. They scored only 36 goals, the lowest tally in the league and had the second-worst defensive record with 87 conceded. Kettering Town were champions and Barrow won the play-offs. Vauxhall Motors finished two points ahead of RMI and were reprieved from relegation due to Nuneaton Borough's liquidation and the Conference's decision to expel Boston United so RMI came desperately close to a third relegation reprieve in quick succession.

Bleasdale came back for a second spell as manager in October 2007 after Humphreys and his assistant Andy Roscoe left the club. Bleasdale had spells at Peterborough United and Bangor City in between and left again in November 2008 to re-join Mark Wright at Chester City.

RMI suffered a heavy FA Cup defeat, losing 4-1 at Harrogate Railway Athletic in 2007. They bowed out of the FA Trophy with a 3-1 home defeat at the hands of Workington in the first round.

Former Liverpool trainee Mark Smyth was top scorer with 11 goals with Kieran Lugsden netting seven. Andy Heald and Steve Settle topped the appearances chart with 35 apiece. Average attendances at Hilton Park were 209 with a season's best gate of 553 for Southport's visit.

A New Beginning

The downward spiral continued in 2008-09 despite a re-branding exercise that saw Leigh RMI re-named Leigh Genesis. A local business man, Dominic Speakman had become chairman in January 2008 and no sooner had the season ended than he revealed plans to bring in a Genesis brand, signifying a new beginning for the town's soccer club and effectively ending the final link with Horwich RMI.

It was intended that the club's new name and logo reflect an association with the town and the red and white striped jerseys were also ditched in favour of a smart new playing strip of a white and black shirt and black shorts and socks. Central to the plans was Genesis's intended move to the newly constructed Leigh Sports Village, but delays in the relocation added to the club's problems.

In a club press release Mr Speakman, 32, explained the thought process behind what was described as a 'radical move to give the club an all-embracing brand for the future.

'I became Chairman in January this year and apart from the possibility of a move to a brand new 12,000 seat stadium, the club was struggling and its future was stagnant,' Mr Speakman wrote. 'I could see that there was potential to build an appealing, prosperous and competitive club which would be capable of growing and climbing forcefully up the football ladder.

Logo

The club had adopted the generic Leigh town crest which did not give it any real identity; I believe the Club needed to develop its own personality and as part of this there needed to be a strong, individual emblem of association. Ideas of colour were professionally developed into a striking, versatile and contemporary logo which formed the core of the new brand.

Name

I began with the name; 'Leigh RMI' (Railway Mechanics' Institute) had followed the Club from its roots in Horwich where there actually was an R.M.I., Leigh on the other hand could not even boast a railway station! Research confirmed that there was little loyalty or attachment to the old name which would make the decision more welcoming than controversial.

Genesis fits perfectly with the club image on several levels; a meaning of 'New Beginning, Origin & Creation' being the most important, it has a contemporary edge and is unique in the world of football. It is miles away from the American 'animal' and doesn't join the usual 'Cities or Uniteds' which gives it a chance of making a real mark in non-league football.

Kit Colour

The Club is surrounded by 'reds' from both football and rugby; our red and white stripes simply merged with the crowd so a radical makeover was essential if we wanted to distinguish ourselves in the area. The alignment of football to fashion is pretty well recognised now, and in order to give the new Leigh Genesis FC an appealing, attractive image, the kit had to become less fussy and more modern. The result was a fresh, white shirt with black shorts and socks supplied by established sports brand Nike whose image complimented perfectly the effect we wanted to achieve.

Future

The new 2008-09 season will see Leigh Genesis playing in the Unibond Premier League which is a mere three jumps away from the football league. Genesis is aiming high and has ambitions 'to be the best that it can be.'

Already in place is a highly qualified coach, Steve Bleasdale who comes with his assistant Brett Harris, Coordinator James Standing and Physio Terry O'Brien. Running the club off the pitch are General Manager, Mary Croasdale and Commercial Manager Donna Middleton who come with experience from Premier Club Blackburn Rovers; the structure is designed for stability and growth.

Supporters

The club aims to appeal to all types of fans and has priced its tickets competitively to encourage families with children. Premiership football has become an incredibly expensive hobby; we can offer a family of four a day out at an impressive stadium at every home match of the season for just £18 per game. Now that's value! Replica shirts will be less than £30 which for a Nike brand is a fantastic deal; we want to be part of the community but more importantly we want the community to be part of us and keeping prices reasonable will definitely help.

Andy Burnham MP for Leigh and Secretary of State for Culture, Media and Sport said: 'We have sporting participation like never before at our magnificent Sports Village and we can now look forward with optimism to a professional football club providing the sort of entertainment on the pitch that supporters will want to see. I am absolutely delighted that Leigh Genesis will be flying the football flag for the town and am sure that this town will respond to the challenge and get behind them in their bid to climb swiftly up the football ladder.'

Genesis played eight pre-season friendlies, seven away from home and just one at Hilton Park against Woodley Sports. Their first league game under the name of Leigh Genesis was on Saturday 16 August 2008 when they lost 2-0 at Eastwood Town before a crowd of 364. The Genesis side was: Dickinson, Teague, Mortimer, Wilson (Watt), Marsh-Evans, Fitzgerald, Maylett, Holland, Mansaram (Booth), Berkeley, Chetcuti (Goulding). They then played their first two 'home' games of the league season at Victory Park, Chorley due to number of pitch problems before returning to Hilton Park for the game against Prescot Cables on Tuesday 2 September 2008.

Commenting on the pitch problems Mr Speakman said: 'Leigh Genesis don't have a lease as such at Hilton Park but have an agreement as part of the rugby club's lease that they will enable the football club to play its fixtures there. As part of that the rugby club are obliged to maintain the facilities in a condition such that the football club are able to play there.

'Over the summer the rugby club have used the pitch for matches, training and community activities to such an extent that the pitch is now in a dire condition. We were led to believe, before the end of last season, that we would be able to move to the new stadium for the new season. We still have no exact date we can move in, which makes planning near impossible.

'We're geared up – financially, administratively and on the pitch - for a move to the new stadium and the financial implications of not moving to the new stadium are significant. More disappointing has been the lack of support and assistance from those that have left the club in this situation. Both the LSV and the rugby club have a moral obligation to help the situation they've left us in.

'I've personally financed the club for the past six months to give the town a club to be proud of. After ploughing over £150,000 into the club, it is a kick in the teeth that I might now have to pay out to fix Hilton Park. I am disappointed for our supporters, who have been superb during my time at the club.' No-one from Leigh Centurions or Leigh Sports Village was available for comment.

Goodbye to Hilton Park

Though no-one knew it at the time the Prescot game proved to be the final football match to be played at Hilton Park. Despite missing several key players Genesis battled to a deserved 2-1 victory with Josh Wilson heading the winning goal twenty minutes from time. In the first-half Jordan Stepien's first goal for the club had been cancelled out by a Prescot equaliser by Steve Williams. The Genesis side was: Dickinson, Booth, Mortimer, Field (Kelly), Wilson (McHugh), Fitzgerald, Chetcuti (Goulding), Holland, Stepien, Berkeley, Smyth. The attendance was 215 and might have been more but for a torrential rain-storm that briefly threatened a postponement.

At this stage Genesis had won three and lost three of their opening six games but further pitch complications saw them switch their next 'home' game to Radcliffe Borough's Stainton Park where they beat Frickley Athletic 2-0. Leigh Centurions played their final game at Hilton Park the following Sunday and no sooner had that been staged than the ground began to suffer from serious problems with vandalism, ruling out any hope of a return for Genesis.

At the end of October chairman Dominic Speakman revealed that he was to withdraw his substantial financial support for the club and manager Steve Bleasdale had to hastily put together a makeshift side of reserve team players and unpaid first-team players for the FA Trophy second qualifying round tie against Cammell Laird at Victory Park on 1 November 2008. Not surprisingly Genesis went down to a 5-1 defeat before a crowd of 94. Mr Bleasdale then left the club and Lee Merricks, the reserve team manager took charge for the 'home' game against North Ferriby United which was staged at Ashton United's Hurst Cross ground.

Genesis, fielding an almost entirely new-look side then struggled in a competitive league and slumped down the table. At long last their first home game at Leigh Sports Village was finally staged on Tuesday 27 January 2009 against FC United of Manchester. Before an encouraging crowd of 1,302 the visitors ran out comfortable 2-0 winners with goals by Jerome Wright and Jamie Baguley. Genesis had now gone eight league games without a victory.

The following report appeared in the respected Groundtastic magazine:

Leigh Sports Village Stadium is an impressive addition to the non league football ranks and staged its first football match on Tuesday 27 January 2009 when Leigh Genesis were defeated 2-0 by FC United of Manchester before a crowd of 1,302.

The stadium is part of an £83million project that has revitalised the sports facilities in the town. Leigh was taken under the Wigan Metropolitan Borough wing during the government re-organisation of 1974 and the project is one of the biggest investments in the Wigan borough. The site encompasses sports, recreational and educational facilities as well as commercial developments, including a four-star hotel.

The 12,000 capacity stadium is also home to Leigh Centurions rugby league side, who staged the first match at LSV when they entertained Salford City Reds in a friendly game on 28 December 2008, attracting an all-ticket crowd of over 4,700.

Leigh East ARLFC are also based at the site and the Leigh Harriers athletic club, who sold their town centre ground to contribute to the project have a brand new athletics facility within the complex. Wigan and Leigh College has been relocated and there is also a sports and leisure centre with other land set aside for commercial development.

The stadium has 10,000 seats on three sides with the north stand set aside as a standing terrace for a further 2,000 spectators. The pitch has under soil heating, the floodlights are HD capacity and there are four changing rooms and 22 corporate hospitality boxes as well as the provision for high-level disabled seating for 75.

Leigh Genesis changed their name from Leigh RMI in an ambitious re-branding exercise by Chairman Dominic Speakman last summer. But the club soon hit difficulties after being unable to play at Hilton Park after staging their home game against Prescot Cables on 2 September 2008. Hilton Park was vandalised after the rugby league club's final game and the safety certificate was removed.

As a result Genesis had to stage 'home' games at a number of Unibond League clubs as far away as Clitheroe and Ashton. LSV was the seventh venue used by the team during a troubled 2008/09 season.

In October Speakman, who had employed a full-time manager and playing staff, resigned with Leigh homeless and no major source of revenue coming into the club. Delays over the move to the new stadium were one of the main reasons but the final straw for Speakman appears to have been the reported cost of the stewarding bill for the new ground. The council's health and safety committee decided the new ground required 45 stewards at a cost of £3,000 for games to proceed, compared to under £200 at Hilton Park.

The club released all its paid players and manager and soldiered on with their reserve team stepping up to the Unibond League under former reserve team manager Lee Merricks. The club slid down the table and the FC United defeat was their fifth league reverse in succession.

Leigh, an old mining and mill town, has always been famous for its rugby league side and senior football came late to the town. In 1995 the rugby club were in administration and the ground up for sale. Horwich RMI, faced with difficulties in bringing their Grundy Hill stadium with its famous sloping pitch up to league requirements sold the ground for housing and bought Hilton Park changing the club's name to Leigh RMI. The club enjoyed five seasons in the Conference between 2000 and 2005 but always struggled for support.

Leigh Sports Village was not often made available to Genesis and only four further home games were staged at the venue before the end of the season. After the initial enthusiasm many complaints were aired at what some supporters deemed to be heavy-handed stewarding and high prices of refreshments. Genesis lost 301 at home to Hednesford Town on 7 February (attendance: 344), beat Cammell Laird 2-1 at the end of March (348) and then lost 2-0 to Matlock Town (405) before defeating Bradford Park Avenue 2-1 (301).

There was some unexpected news for the long-suffering Leigh supporters though on 23 March 2009 when Bolton born Garry Flitcroft was confirmed as the new manager to replace Lee Merricks, who became first-team coach. The 36-year-old had enjoyed a successful playing career predominantly with Manchester City and Blackburn Rovers. Though he was unable to save the club from relegation Flitcroft, assisted by his former City team-mate Mike Quigley and with his brother Steve joining the playing ranks saw his new charges win four and draw two of his eight matches in charge.

Genesis closed the season with a 2-1 win at Hednesford Town with the following side on duty: Drench, Howarth (Sephton), King, Heald (Whitham), Smith, Page, Dorney, Settle (Stepien), Brown, Flitcroft, Ince. Jack Dorney scored both goals to at least end a traumatic season in some style. Not one of the players that started the season played in the final game. Genesis's first opponents, Eastwood Town were champions with 87 points. Genesis finished 21st with 11 wins, seven draws and 24 defeats, scoring 42 goals against 88. They were relegated alongside Witton Albion, Prescot Cables and Cammell Laird, the latter on ground grading issues.

All but six home games had been staged outside Leigh with Chorley, Ashton United, Radcliffe Borough, Clitheroe and Warrington Town all coming to the club's rescue and making their grounds available. Genesis suffered heavy 'home' defeats at the hands of Nantwich Town (lost 8-0 at Radcliffe Borough) and Buxton (lost 7-0 at Warrington Town).

Former Bury trainee Stepien finished top scorer with nine goals with Phil Marsh netting seven, including a hat-trick in perhaps Genesis's outstanding result of the season, a 4-2 win over FC United at Gigg Lane before a crowd of 1,850.

Ground Issues Resurface

Flitcroft's former Blackburn Rovers colleague Matt Jansen joined Genesis in a player-coaching role during the summer as the club again was plagued by ground issues. The Leigh Sports Village was not made available for all home games and the club had to again find alternative venues, often at short notice and relied upon the understanding of the league and its member clubs.

Genesis played the reserve sides of Bolton Wanderers and Blackburn Rovers at LSV in pre-season, attracting crowds of 1,105 and 403 respectively. Rovers had signed an agreement to stage their reserve games at the ground during the season and later would be given preference over Genesis fixtures.

Long-serving club officials Alan Leach and Gary Culshaw, both linked back to the Horwich RMI days were chairman and vice-chairman respectively while the popular Harold Taylor made a welcome return to the club in a match-day secretarial role.

Genesis began the season with a 3-1 victory at Rossendale United with Steve Flitcroft, Chris Baguley and Stepien all on target. The Leigh side was: Drench; Howarth, King; Page, Smith, Heald; Dorney (Whitham), Flitcroft (Dykes), Jansen (C Baguley), Stepien, Ince.

Despite bowing out of the FA Cup at the preliminary round stage at Warrington Town, Genesis's league form was commendably consistent despite the uncertainty surrounding the club and Flitcroft and his coaching staff earned praise for their innovative approach, thoroughness and attention to detail. With a predominantly young side many players stayed loyal to the club despite offers from elsewhere and the players were reported to have played in the second half of the season without pay.

Jansen scored his first goals for the club with a brace in a 3-2 win over Warrington at Chorley, just four days following the FA Cup exit and displayed the outstanding talent that almost earned him a place in England's World Cup squad in 2002. In the autumn Genesis played some sparkling football, earning five straight victories before suffering a 1-0 FA Trophy exit at the hands of Redditch United before a crowd of 283 at LSV.

One of the worst winters on record meant Genesis went a full month without playing a first-team game between 19 December and 19 January. They suffered the disappointment of a semi-final defeat in the Lancashire Co-Operative Challenge Trophy Semi-Final (the old Lancashire Junior Cup competition) when they lost 3-1 to Clitheroe at the neutral venue of the Lancashire FA County Ground in Leyland. Victory would have earned Genesis a potentially money-spinning final place against Southport at the Reebok Stadium.

But Flitcroft's young side soon clicked into gear and enjoyed a run of eleven games in the second half of February and March when they won seven, drew three and lost only once. On Wednesday 24 February 2010 Genesis were forced to play their 'home' game against Skelmersdale United at Chorley as Rovers reserves were playing Manchester United at LSV. While a crowd of 2,803 saw the reserve game Genesis went down 1-0 before gate of 106. One week earlier Jansen had scored a memorable hat-trick as Genesis came from behind to beat Rossendale United 4-3 at Chorley before a crowd of only 61. The highest home crowd of the season was 618 for the visit of FC Halifax Town.

The old rivalry with Chorley was renewed during February with the Magpies, managed by former RMI player and manager Steve Waywell (and with former RMI player and manager Ken Wright as chairman) winning 2-0 at LSV before a crowd of only 187. But three weeks later Genesis turned the tables in remarkable fashion, Stepien netting a hat-trick in a 5-1 win at Victory Park, a ground that the players knew very well indeed. Just 260 saw what could have been the last ever game between the clubs with Genesis's future beyond the end of the season in doubt.

On 4 February 2010 an open meeting between directors and fans had been held at Leigh East's clubhouse in an attempt to find a way forward for the club. Willingness was expressed by those present to find a way to continue the club beyond the end of the season. On Saturday 27 March a club statement on the official website revealed that there would not be an offer on the table to play at LSV in the 2010-2011 season. Without going into explanations finance and supporter numbers were presented as issues.

Talks took place with the League and the management at Atherton Laburnum Rovers with a view to Genesis moving to Crilly Park in a ground-sharing arrangement. Assessments made by the league and their recommendations for improvements to bring the ground up to minimum Unibond League standards were not considered excessive.

Genesis were in contention for a play-off place until the closing week of the season and finished a highly respectable sixth with 21 wins and eight draws from 42 games. Experienced players such as goalkeeper Steven Drench, defenders Karl Munroe and Lee Woodyatt and midfielders Andy Heald and Steve Flitcroft provided the backbone of the side. In his third spell at Leigh Heald completed 150 appearances for the club during the season. But the most pleasing aspect was the emergence of several highly talented younger players including defenders Kris King and Chris Page.

Stepien was top goal scorer with 21 despite suffering from a niggling injury towards the end of the season and Tom Ince and Jack Dorney emerged as goal-scoring midfield players. Ince, formerly with Bamber Bridge scored 15 goals and was voted Player-of-the-Year while the ex-Bury player Dorney scored nine goals. Chris Baguley (12), Chris Thompson (11) also reached double figures before leaving the club and with Jansen contributing 11 goals Flitcroft's side was not short of fire-power.

Of 53 games played during the season Dorney made 51 appearances, King and Ince 49 apiece, Drench 47, Page 42, Flitcroft 41, Stepien 40 and Heald 39. 18-year-old Dale Whitham made 37 appearances and also represented the England Schoolboys' Under-18s side on a tour of the United States.

In the final week of the season Genesis scored two late goals to beat Salford City 2-1 at Chorley and then defeated Wakefield 2-0 at LSV. Of their 21 'home' league games seven were staged away from LSV and Genesis recorded four wins and one draw. At LSV they won nine, drew two and lost three.

The final Genesis match of the season was at LSV on Saturday 24 April 2010 when they entertained Wakefield. Second half goals by Ince and Stepien wound up the campaign before a crowd of 136 and the line-up was as follows: Porter; Woodyatt, King, Ross, Munroe, Whitham (Chinthengah), Dorney, Flitcroft, Ince, Morariu (Stepien), Heald (Hill).

Epilogue

Immediately after the season was over manager Garry Flitcroft parted company with the club and gave his views on the season in an interview with the Bolton News.

'The situation with Leigh Sports Village has been horrendous,' Flitcroft was quoted. 'We have played eight of our home games at other grounds this season and that has been a total disadvantage. Apart from that we've had a great home record.'

The newspaper obtained a reply from the stadium company. A spokesman for LSV said: 'There was an agreement with Leigh Genesis made last summer that they could play the majority (but not all) of their home games at LSV stadium.

'When their financial backer withdrew at Christmas, Genesis were unable to honour their part of the agreement but LSVCo helped them to continue to play the agreed number of games at the stadium.

'With the crowds that Leigh Genesis were able to attract (a paying gate of less than 150 on average), even with the high profile management of Garry Flitcroft, it is not viable for Leigh Genesis to continue to play at LSV stadium.'

A spokesman for Leigh Genesis said: 'Garry has decided to leave because of a lack of finances. He couldn't put the team together that he wanted. We are sure that Garry will be successful having demonstrated natural leadership qualities and sound tactical and coaching skills.

'We wish Garry every success in his future career and thank him for the positive impact he has had on our club during the time he has been here.'

Leigh Genesis then completed a deal to play their home games at Crilly Park in a ground-share agreement with neighbours Atherton Laburnum Rovers after negotiations between the two clubs and Leigh Sports Village.

Genesis took up a one year tenancy at Crilly Park for the 2010-11 season (the league being renamed the Evo-Stick Division One North) with an option for a further two seasons.

Fears that the ground would not meet league standards were allayed after work was carried out to ensure it met the required level. A list of required jobs was provided to the Leigh Sports Village Stadium Company, who undertook a complete overhaul of the pitch, along with erecting a new block of toilets and a general tidying up of the ground. Supporters gave up their time to assist in a variety of tasks before the league inspection in early June.

Flitcroft subsequently joined Chorley as manager, replacing former RMI player and manager Steve Waywell. Mike Quigley and Matt Jansen joined him at Victory Park together with a host of former Genesis players including Jack Dorney, Tom Ince, Jordan Stepien, Lee Woodyatt, Mark Ross, Dale Whitham and Steve Flitcroft. The long-serving Harold Taylor also took over as secretary of the Magpies.

Meanwhile, Genesis completed their search for Flitcroft's replacement and appointed Mark Maddox as manager. Maddox, 37, spent two seasons at Hilton Park between 2006 and 2008 after a long playing career at Altrincham. He later played for Vauxhall Motors before taking the post of Centre of Excellence Manager at League Two side Accrington Stanley and later managing Formby.

Holder of the prestigious UEFA 'A' Coaching Licence Maddox said: 'I'm delighted to be here and to be given the opportunity at a higher level. I enjoyed my time with Formby, but this was too good a job to turn down. Leigh were always a well-run and friendly club when I was here as a player, so it made perfect sense to return as manager when the chance presented itself.

'Although we will be looking to consolidate our position in the league next season and take each game as it comes in what was a very tough league, I can certainly guarantee that I will be looking to build an honest, hard-working side that will do the club proud.'

Andy Heald was appointed player-coach as the new management team set about re-building the squad in preparation for the new season. Another challenging period in the club's long history was about to begin but this is where our story ends.

RMI in action on a former Football League ground—Borough Park, Workington. A mere 189 souls braved the rain to see RMI win 4-0 in April 1997.

Scenes from Leigh RMI's final game at Hilton Park against Prescot Cables

Scenes from Leigh RMI's final game at Hilton Park against Prescot Cables

Ground photos for the final game at LSV, Leigh Genesis v Wakefield

Leigh Genesis team for their final game at LSV. Back row (LtoR) Mark Ross, Karl Munroe, Kris King, Dale Whitham, Ilie Morariu, Andy Heald
Front row Steve Flitcroft (with mascot), Lee Woodyatt, Dean Porter, Tom Ince, Jack Dorney

Andy Heald challenges for a high ball against Wakefield at LSV

Scenes from the final Leigh Genesis game at LSV. (Above) Full Back Lee
Woodyatt and (Below) Tom Ince in action against Wakefield

Leigh Genesis forward Leroy Chinthengah in action in the final game at LSV against Wakefield

Above—Matt Jansen, Harold Taylor and Gary Flitcroft at the LSV.
Below—They are joined by club Chairman Alan Leach.

Leigh RMI / Genesis Statistical Section

Season by Season Results

Club Records

1995-96   Northern Premier League First Division

Date		H/A	Opponents	Comp	Res	F	A	Goalscorers	Att
Aug	19	a	Harrogate Town	League	W	2	1	Monk, Shaw	201
	26	h	Flixton	FACP	W	2	0	Briffa, Diamond	60
	28	a	Atherton LR	League	L	1	3	Birch	178
Sep	2	h	Whitley Bay	League	L	0	1		144
	5	a	Curzon Ashton	League	L	1	2	Schofield	101
	9	a	Guiseley	FAC1Q	L	0	3		484
	16	h	Alfreton Town	League	D	1	1	Shaw	176
	19	a	Worksop Town	League	D	1	1	McCarty	316
	23	h	Ashton United	League	L	1	4	Fahey	185
	27	h	Great Harwood Town	LC1	W	6	4	Monk 3, Shaw 2, Booth	145
	30	a	Gretna	League	L	1	3	Shaw	90
Oct	3	a	Lancaster City	League	L	2	5	Birch, C Walmsley	202
	7	h	Farsley Celtic	League	D	0	0		165
	11	h	Workington	League	W	4	2	Shaw 3, Birch	165
	14	a	Bridgnorth Town	FAT1Q	D	1	1	C Walmsley	90
	17	h	Bridgnorth Town	FAT1Q	W	7	0	Lewis 2, Arnold, McCarty, Shaw, Senior, C Walmsley	36
	21	h	Gretna	League	L	1	3	Schofield	132
	24	a	Witton Albion	LC2	D	2	2	Orrell, Shaw	305
	28	a	Netherfield	League	L	0	1		121
Nov	1	h	Witton Albion	LC2	L	0	3		72
	4	h	Matlock Town	FAT2Q	L	0	2		90
	11	a	Bradford Park Avenue	League	L	1	3	Shaw	163
	18	h	Congleton Town	League	D	1	1	Diamond	153
	22	h	Curzon Ashton	FDC1	L	0	1		36
	25	h	Lincoln United	League	W	2	0	Diamond, Briffa	137
	29	h	Atherton Collieries	LJC1	W	1	0	Birch	129
Dec	2	a	Fleetwood	League	W	4	0	Shaw 2, Kirkham, C Walmsley	85
	6	h	Warrington Town	League	D	2	2	Birch, Briffa	153
	9	a	Warrington Town	League	W	1	0	Shaw	109
	16	h	Curzon Ashton	League	W	1	0	S Walmsley	139
Jan	6	h	Bradford Park Avenue	League	W	1	0	Shaw	161
	13	a	Great Harwood Town	League	W	2	0	Edwards 2	102
	16	a	Morecambe	LJC2	L	0	2		266
	20	h	Netherfield	League	L	1	4	Wheeler	144
Feb	3	a	Whitley Bay	League	L	1	3	Birch	129
	10	a	Eastwood Town	League	L	0	1		94
	17	h	Worksop Town	League	D	1	1	Shaw	150
	21	h	Atherton LR	League	W	3	1	Schofield, Shaw, Briffa	202
	28	h	Fleetwood	League	W	2	0	Wheeler, Shaw	149
Mar	2	h	Harrogate Town	League	W	2	0	Shaw, Edwards	130
	9	a	Alfreton Town	League	L	0	1		140
	13	h	Lancaster City	League	L	0	1		151
	16	h	Eastwood Town	League	W	1	0	Wheeler	136
	23	a	Congleton Town	League	L	0	1		104
	30	a	Lincoln United	League	L	1	3	Opponent	174
Apr	3	h	Great Harwood Town	League	W	3	1	Shaw, Kirkham, Briffa	
	6	a	Radcliffe Borough	League	L	1	3	Charlton	
	8	a	Workington	League	W	3	0	Leishman, Wheeler, Briffa	208
	13	a	Ashton United	League	L	2	3	Leishman, Briffa	
	20	h	Radcliffe Borough	League	D	1	1	Leishman	
	27	a	Farsley Celtic	League	L	1	2	Briffa	
						72	77		

The Black & Whites - Season 95-96

OFFICIAL PROGRAMME

GRETNA F.C.
RAYDALE PARK, GRETNA

Gretna F.C.
extends a warm
Scottish Welcome
to all our Visitors

THE UniBond LEAGUE

60p

UNIBOND LEAGUE
LEIGH
30-9-95

Leigh RMI's rapid rise through the ranks is illustrated by these match programmes . . . In 1995-96 they were on the road to Gretna to play in front of 90 spectators; In 2002 RMI were playing host to the top names in Non-League football such as Telford United.

LEIGHRMI
FOOTBALL CLUB

TheRailwaymen

v Telford United
Nationwide Conference
Saturday, 30th November 2002
Match Sponsor: Body Image Fitness Centre
Official Programme: £2.00

LEIGH
Nationwide

1996-97 Northern Premier League First Division

Date		H/A	Opponents	Comp	Res	F	A	Goalscorers	Att	
Aug	24	h	Droylsden	League	L	1	3	Evans	205	
	26	a	Atherton LR	League	W	2	0	Evans 2	198	
	31	a	Belper Town	FACP	D	1	1	Wallace	256	
Sep	3	h	Belper Town	FACP	W	3	1	Ridings, Evans, McKenna	205	
	7	a	Whitley Bay	League	W	2	1	Ridings, Bermingham	138	
	10	h	Warrington Town	League	W	1	0	Ridings	146	
	14	h	Alfreton Town	FAC1Q	W	2	0	Shaw 2	165	
	21	h	Stocksbridge Park Steels	League	D	1	1	Shaw	164	
	24	a	Netherfield	League	W	3	0	Wallace, Bermingham, Evans	120	
	28	h	Billingham Synthonia	FAC2Q	D	1	1	Shaw	195	
Oct	2	a	Billingham Synthonia	FAC2Q	W	3	2	Shaw, Evans, Leishman	238	
	5	a	Worksop Town	League	D	2	2	Wheeler, Evans	309	
	8	a	Flixton	League	W	1	0	Evans	171	
	12	h	Marine	FAC3Q	W	2	0	Bermingham, Shaw	334	
	15	h	Radcliffe Borough	LC1	D	0	0		110	
	19	a	Droylsden	FAT1Q	D	1	1	Wallace	140	
	22	h	Droylsden	FAT1Q	L	1	3	Hill	112	
	25	h	Runcorn	FAC4Q	L	2	4	Ridings, Evans	820	
	29	a	Radcliffe Borough	LC1	L	1	3	Shaw	144	
Nov	2	a	Bradford Park Avenue	League	W	3	0	Shaw 3	304	
	4	h	Ashton United	League	W	2	0	Ridings, Evans	141	
	9	a	Gretna	League	W	2	1	Shaw, Bermingham	65	
	11	a	Ashton United	UC1	D	3	3	Fahey, Evans, Bermingham	130	
	16	h	Lincoln United	League	W	2	1	Shaw, McKenna	216	
	25	h	Bacup Borough	LJC1	W	4	0	Shaw 2, Wallace, Evans	83	
	30	h	Atherton LR	League	W	1	0	Ridings	230	
Dec	3	h	Curzon Ashton	League	W	2	0	Shaw, Evans	101	
	7	a	Stocksbridge Park Steels	League	D	0	0		165	
	10	h	Ashton United	UC1	D	1	1	Evans (AET, FT 0-0)	106	5-6 pens
	14	h	Matlock Town	League	D	1	1	Shaw	140	
Jan	14	a	Burscough	LJC2	L	0	1		115	
	18	h	Congleton Town	League	W	3	2	Shaw 2, Evans	135	
	25	a	Eastwood Town	League	D	0	0		127	
Feb	1	a	Matlock Town	League	L	1	2	Shaw	196	
	3	a	Ashton United	League	L	1	2	Shaughnessy	166	
	8	h	Whitley Bay	League	W	1	0	Wheeler	133	
	11	a	Warrington Town	League	D	1	1	Shaw	101	
	15	a	Droylsden	League	L	2	3	Schofield, Shaughnessy	128	
	18	h	Farsley Celtic	League	L	1	2	Evans	110	
	22	h	Worksop Town	League	L	0	1		143	
Mar	1	a	Congleton Town	League	W	1	0	Shaw	153	
	4	h	Harrogate Town	League	W	2	0	Booth, Ridings	104	
	8	h	Bradford Park Avenue	League	L	1	2	Schofield	162	
	11	h	Eastwood Town	League	W	2	0	Shaw, Evans	104	
	15	a	Lincoln United	League	W	2	1	Evans 2	210	
	22	a	Harrogate Town	League	W	2	0	Shaw, Opponent	154	
	25	h	Workington	League	W	2	1	James, Shaughnessy	132	
	29	h	Netherfield	League	W	3	1	Ridings, Shaw, Bermingham	128	
	31	a	Radcliffe Borough	League	W	1	0	Hill	529	

Season details continued on next page

1996-97 Northern Premier League First Division Ctd

Date		H/A	Opponents	Comp	Res	F	A	Goalscorers	Att
Apr	5	h	Flixton	League	W	4	1	Shaw 2, James, Ridings	130
	10	a	Farsley Celtic	League	D	0	0		147
	12	a	Curzon Ashton	League	W	1	0	Shaw	142
	19	h	Great Harwood Town	League	D	1	1	Evans	191
	22	a	Great Harwood Town	League	D	1	1	Schofield	130
	26	a	Workington	League	W	4	0	James, Ridings, Shaw, Bermingham	189
	29	h	Radcliffe Borough	League	D	2	2	James, Evans	830
May	3	h	Gretna	League	D	0	0		151
						90	54		

Steve Waywell—inspirational manager as RMI climbed from the Northern Premier League to the Conference

Dino Maamria

1997-98 Northern Premier League Premier Division

Date		H/A	Opponents	Comp	Res	F	A	Goalscorers	Att
Aug	23	h	Boston United	League	L	0	1		237
	25	a	Runcorn	League	D	2	2	Evans, Ridings	485
	30	a	Spennymoor United	League	W	3	0	Shaw, Evans 2	198
Sep	2	h	Radcliffe Borough	League	D	0	0		281
	9	a	Bamber Bridge	League	D	1	1	Evans	341
	13	h	Accrington Stanley	FAC1Q	W	1	0	Evans	343
	16	h	Barrow	League	L	0	1		246
	20	a	Blyth Spartans	League	W	1	0	Ridings	490
	23	h	Accrington Stanley	League	W	1	0	Schofield	243
	27	a	Halifax Town	FAC2Q	L	0	4		1103
	30	a	Workington	LC1	D	1	1	Ridings	86
Oct	4	h	Frickley Athletic	League	D	1	1	Cryer	201
	11	h	Workington	LC1	W	3	1	Evans, Shaw, Wallace	85
	18	a	Frickley Athletic	FAT1Q	D	1	1	Cryer	171
	21	h	Frickley Athletic	FAT1Q	W	2	1	Shaw, Evans	86
	25	a	Bishop Auckland	League	L	2	3	Evans, Schofield	174
	28	a	Radcliffe Borough	LC2	D	0	0		141
Nov	1	h	Marine	League	W	1	0	Schofield	201
	8	a	Radcliffe Borough	FAT2Q	D	1	1	Shaw	267
	11	h	Radcliffe Borough	FAT2Q	W	1	0	Brown	201
	15	h	Bamber Bridge	League	W	4	0	Shaw, Rostron 2, Cryer	236
	18	h	Marine	LJC1	L	1	4	Brown	90
	22	a	Hyde United	League	D	3	3	Cryer 2, Evans	522
	25	a	Altrincham	PC1	W	1	0	James	269
Dec	6	a	Barrow	League	W	1	0	Rostron	1012
	8	a	Bradford Park Avenue	FAT3Q	D	1	1	Rostron	127
	10	h	Bradford Park Avenue	FAT3Q	W	1	0	Cryer	120
	13	a	Lancaster City	League	W	1	0	Locke	176
	16	h	Radcliffe Borough	LC2	W	2	0	Ridings, Shaw	101
	20	h	Emley	League	W	2	1	Ridings, Shaw	267
Jan	6	a	Altrincham	League	D	2	2	Shaw, Hill	348
	10	a	Grantham	FAT1	D	1	1	Shaw	560
	17	h	Chorley	League	W	2	0	Evans, Shaw	367
	19	h	Grantham	FAT1	D	0	0		171
	21	a	Chorley	LC3	L	2	5	Evans, Shaw	210
	24	a	Colwyn Bay	League	W	3	2	Cryer 2, Opponent	323
	31	a	Marine	League	D	1	1	Rostron (pen)	322
Feb	3	a	Guiseley	PC2	D	0	0		137
	7	h	Bishop Auckland	League	L	1	3	Shaw	181
	10	h	Winsford United	League	W	2	0	Cryer, Evans	171
	14	a	Emley	League	D	2	2	Cryer, Williams	299
	17	h	Colwyn Bay	League	W	3	0	Brady, Cryer 2	228
	21	h	Blyth Spartans	League	D	1	1	Barker	208
	24	h	Guiseley	PC2	L	0	3		146
	28	a	Guiseley	League	L	1	2	James	227

Season details continued on next page

1997-98 Northern Premier League Premier Division Ctd

Date		H/A	Opponents	Comp	Res	F	A	Goalscorers	Att
Mar	3	a	Radcliffe Borough	League	W	1	0	Ridings	144
	7	h	Guiseley	League	D	0	0		201
	14	a	Accrington Stanley	League	W	3	1	Shaw 2, Rostron (pen)	1461
	17	h	Gainsborough Trinity	League	W	1	0	Rostron	133
	21	h	Altrincham	League	D	2	2	Rostron (pen), Cryer	449
	28	h	Runcorn	League	D	2	2	Evans 2	319
Apr	1	a	Winsford United	League	W	1	0	Ridings	153
	4	h	Hyde United	League	W	2	1	Ridings 2	251
	7	a	Chorley	League	W	1	0	Cryer	342
	11	a	Boston United	League	L	0	1		1145
	13	h	Lancaster City	League	W	2	0	Smythe, Evans	246
	15	a	Gainsborough Trinity	League	L	0	3		588
	18	a	Alfreton Town	League	L	2	3	McCrae, Hill	130
	21	h	Spennymoor United	League	W	4	2	Evans 2, Barker, Rostron	140
	25	a	Frickley Athletic	League	D	0	0		138
May	2	h	Alfreton Town	League	W	1	0	Evans	159
						82	64		

1998-99 Northern Premier League Premier Division

Date		H/A	Opponents	Comp	Res	F	A	Goalscorers	Att
Aug	22	a	Worksop Town	League	L	1	2	Matthews	476
	25	h	Stalybridge Celtic	League	W	3	0	Matthews. Evans, Monk	336
	29	a	Winsford United	League	L	0	2		195
	31	a	Spennymoor United	League	W	4	2	Evans, Matthews, Ridings, Smyth	225
Sep	5	h	Gainsborough Trinity	League	W	3	0	Evans, Matthews 2	201
	8	h	Colwyn Bay	League	W	3	2	Evans, Matthews, Rostron	245
	12	a	Whitby Town	League	W	2	0	Evans, Brady	742
	15	h	Accrington Stanley	League	L	1	2	Ridings	239
	19	a	Guiseley	League	L	0	2		366
	22	h	Ashton United	PC1	W	2	1	Monk, Matthews	156
	25	h	Lancaster City	League	L	0	2		328
	29	a	Marine	League	D	1	1	Evans	245
Oct	3	h	Winsford United	FAC2Q	W	1	0	Evans	336
	9	a	Runcorn	League	W	2	0	Turpin, Rostron	290
	17	a	Worksop Town	FAC3Q	W	2	1	Evans, Rostron	618
	20	h	Winsford United	League	D	2	2	Ridings, Evans	161
	27	a	Chorley	League	D	3	3	Cryer 2, Turpin	227
	31	a	Droylsden	FAC4Q	W	2	1	Matthews, Cryer	842
Nov	3	h	Burscough	LC2	L	0	1		133
	7	h	Emley	League	D	0	0		351
	15	a	Fulham	FAC1	D	1	1	Whealing	7965
	17	h	Skelmersdale United	LJC1	L	1	2	Evans	129
	21	h	Morecambe	FAT2	W	4	1	Monk 2, Evans, Ridings	435
	24	h	Fulham	FAC1	L	0	2		7125
	28	a	Blyth Spartans	League	L	1	4	Ridings	387
Dec	1	a	Bamber Bridge	League	D	1	1	Monk	430
	4	h	Hyde United	League	D	2	2	Ridings, Evans	287
	12	h	Bishop Auckland	League	D	1	1	Evans	183
	19	a	Emley	League	W	2	0	Keary, Cryer	244
	28	h	Spennymoor United	League	D	1	1	Rostron	278
Jan	2	h	Whitby Town	League	D	2	2	Evans, Hill	311
	9	a	Frickley Athletic	League	W	2	0	Matthews, Monk	174
	16	h	Southport	FAT3	L	0	1		864
	23	h	Worksop Town	League	D	1	1	Wallace	268
Feb	2	a	Altrincham	PCQF	D	1	1	Locke (pen)	366
	6	a	Stalybridge Celtic	League	D	4	4	Locke, Turpin, Opponents 2	419
	13	a	Gainsborough Trinity	League	L	0	2		378
	24	h	Altrincham	PCQF	W	2	1	Matthews 2	178
	27	h	Blyth Spartans	League	W	3	2	Matthews 2, Carr	191

Season details continued on next page

1998-99 Northern Premier League Premier Division Ctd

Date		H/A	Opponents	Comp	Res	F	A	Goalscorers	Att
Mar	9	h	Guiseley	League	W	3	2	Hill, Ridings, Opponent	151
	13	h	Altrincham	League	W	3	2	Black, Smyth, Monk	451
	16	h	Runcorn	PCSF	W	1	0	Black	171
	20	a	Bishop Auckland	League	D	0	0		204
	23	a	Runcorn	PCSF	D	1	1	Matthews	205
	27	h	Gateshead	League	D	2	2	Ridings, Opponent	192
	30	a	Colwyn Bay	League	W	1	0	Matthews	256
Apr	3	a	Accrington Stanley	League	W	2	1	Black, Tolson	429
	5	h	Marine	League	D	0	0		235
	7	a	Altrincham	League	L	0	1		518
	10	h	Frickley Athletic	League	L	0	1		161
	13	h	Bamber Bridge	League	L	0	1		151
	15	h	Droylsden	PCF	L	1	2	Black	355
	17	a	Lancaster City	League	W	2	1	Ridings, Tobin	248
	19	a	Hyde United	League	W	2	1	Tobin, Matthews	364
	22	h	Runcorn	League	D	0	0		185
	24	h	Chorley	League	L	0	1		292
May	1	a	Gateshead	League	W	3	1	Black, Ridings, Evans	226
						82	70		

1999-2000   Northern Premier League Premier Division

Date		H/A	Opponents	Comp	Res	F	A	Goalscorers	Att
Aug	14	a	Blyth Spartans	League	W	1	0	Matthews	401
	17	a	Lancaster City	League	W	3	1	Patterson, S Jones, Monk	260
	21	h	Gateshead	League	W	3	1	Butler, S Jones 2	215
	24	h	Bamber Bridge	League	W	3	0	Black, Matthews, S Jones	260
	28	a	Leek Town	League	L	0	2		325
	30	h	Guiseley	League	L	0	1		247
Sep	4	a	Emley	League	L	1	3	Black	316
	7	a	Frickley Athletic	League	W	4	2	Black 2, Matthews, S Jones	151
	11	h	Whitby Town	League	W	2	1	Black, Monk	202
	14	h	Ashton United	LCG4	W	2	1	Carr, S Jones	107
	18	h	Blyth Spartans	FAC2Q	W	5	3	Monk 3, Matthews 2	197
	25	h	Barrow	League	W	1	0	Black	331
	28	h	Marine	League	W	2	1	Locke (pen), Black	266
Oct	2	h	Crook Town	FAC3Q	D	1	1	Black	301
	6	a	Crook Town	FAC3Q	L	1	2	S Jones	445
	9	h	Boston United	FAT1	W	1	0	S Jones	377
	12	a	Radcliffe Borough	LCG4	W	2	0	Black 2	180
	16	a	Hucknall Town	League	W	2	1	Black, Ross	259
	26	a	Bamber Bridge	League	D	2	2	Ross 2	406
	30	h	Hucknall Town	League	W	1	0	Monk	209
Nov	2	h	Lancaster City	LCGA	D	2	2	Eatock, Locke (pen)	161
	6	h	Gainsborough Trinity	League	D	1	1	Wallace	201
	9	a	Droylsden	League	W	2	0	Ridings, S Jones	193
	13	h	Colwyn Bay	League	L	1	2	Ross	211
	16	a	Nelson	LJC1	W	2	1	Wallace, Ross	212
	23	a	Workington	LCGA	D	0	0		312
	27	h	Worksop Town	FAT2	D	1	1	Ridings	232
	30	a	Worksop Town	FAT2	L	1	3	Ridings	335
Dec	4	a	Winsford United	League	W	5	0	Black 3, Ridings, Ross	101
	14	h	Runcorn	League	W	2	0	Ridings, Harris	161
	27	a	Marine	League	D	1	1	S Jones	663
Jan	3	h	Emley	League	W	1	0	S Jones	419
	8	h	Hyde United	League	D	0	0		427
	11	a	Southport	LJC2	W	2	1	Ross, Wallace	294
	15	h	Leek Town	League	L	0	2		228
	18	a	Stalybridge Celtic	League	W	3	1	Ward (pen), Ross, Ridings	423
	22	h	Eastwood Town	PCQF	W	1	0	Quayle	120
	29	a	Gateshead	League	D	1	1	Ross	408
Feb	1	a	Accrington Stanley	LJCQF	W	2	1	Ridings, Matthews	303
	4	h	Winsford United	League	W	3	2	Black 2, S Jones	255
	12	a	Bishop Auckland	League	D	1	1	Black	226
	19	h	Frickley Athletic	League	W	5	0	Ridings, S Jones 2, Ross, Harris	241
	25	h	Lancaster City	League	W	2	1	Ross 2	401
	29	a	Barrow	League	D	2	2	Ross 2	900

Season details continued on next page

1999-2000 NPL Premier Division Continued

Date		H/A	Opponents	Comp	Res	F	A	Goalscorers	Att
Mar	4	h	Whitby Town	PCSF	L	1	3	S Jones	159
	7	h	Marine	LJCSF	L	2	4	Black, S Jones	179
	11	a	Whitby Town	League	L	0	2		489
	13	a	Hyde United	League	W	2	1	Black, Cumiskey	903
	18	h	Worksop Town	League	D	2	2	S Jones 2	275
	25	a	Guiseley	League	W	3	0	Ross, S Jones, Kielty	274
	28	h	Spennymoor United	League	W	4	0	Wallace, Ward (pen), Matthews 2	253
Apr	1	a	Gainsborough Trinity	League	L	3	4	Ward (pen), Ross, Matthews	341
	8	h	Droylsden	League	L	1	2	Ward (pen)	235
	11	h	Bishop Auckland	League	W	4	1	Black, Ridings, Ross, Ward (pen)	203
	18	a	Runcorn	League	W	2	0	Black, S Jones	254
	22	h	Stalybridge Celtic	League	W	2	0	Black, S Jones	304
	24	a	Colwyn Bay	League	W	5	3	Ross, Kielty, S Jones, Opponents 2	280
	29	a	Spennymoor United	League	W	3	1	Kielty, Ward (pen), S Jones	235
May	1	h	Blyth Spartans	League	W	2	0	Harris, Matthews	695
	6	a	Worksop Town	League	W	3	0	Matthews 2, Ridings	449
						117	68		

2000-01   National Conference

Date		H/A	Opponents	Comp	Res	F	A	Goalscorers	Att	
Aug	11	h	Lancaster City	NPL Shield	W	2	1	Mason, Opponent	251	
	19	h	Dagenham & Redbridge	League	L	1	2	Black	451	
	22	a	Southport	League	W	2	1	Black, Cumiskey	1589	
	26	a	Kettering Town	League	W	1	0	Black	1087	
	28	h	Scarborough	League	W	2	0	Ridings, Harris	836	
Sep	2	a	Stevenage Borough	League	L	0	3		1479	
	5	h	Hednesford Town	League	D	2	2	Jones 2	475	
	9	h	Boston United	League	D	2	2	Harris, Mason	1124	
	12	a	Telford United	League	L	1	2	Mason	281	
	16	a	Nuneaton Borough	League	L	1	2	Black	1145	
	23	h	Forest Green Rovers	League	D	1	1	Matthews	451	
	26	a	Hereford United	League	D	1	1	Matthews	1918	
	30	h	Dover Athletic	League	W	2	1	Black (pen), Jones	485	
Oct	3	h	Rushden & Diamonds	League	W	1	0	Jones	1405	
	7	a	Hayes	League	W	2	1	Ridings, Black	415	
	14	h	Telford United	League	D	1	1	Black (pen)	552	
	17	a	Northwich Victoria	LC1	D	3	3	Ridings, Kielty 2	309	
	21	a	Chester City	League	D	1	1	Black (pen)	1858	
	28	a	Scarborough	FAC4Q	W	4	3	Black 3, Jones	858	
Nov	4	h	Doncaster Rovers	League	L	0	1		811	
	11	a	Woking	League	D	1	1	Black (pen)	1421	
	19	a	Millwall	FAC1	L	0	3		6907	
Dec	2	a	Kingstonian	League	W	2	0	Jones, Black	929	
	16	h	Southport	League	D	2	2	Jones (pen), Ridings	835	
	26	a	Northwich Victoria	League	D	1	1	Jones	1208	
	30	a	Dagenham & Redbridge	League	L	1	2	Ridings	1231	
Jan	1	h	Northwich Victoria	League	W	3	0	Ridings 2, Kielty	501	
	6	a	Scarborough	League	D	1	1	Monk	1087	
	9	h	Rossendale United	LJC2	W	1	0	Jones		
	13	h	Hucknall Town	FAT3	W	1	0	Spooner	235	
	23	h	Northwich Victoria	LC1	W	1	0	Jones	169	
	27	a	Hednesford Town	League	W	2	1	Kielty, Jones	804	
	30	a	Lancaster City	LJCQF	D	2	2	Black, Murphy	155	aet; ft 1-1
Feb	3	a	Hereford United	FAT4	D	0	0		1491	
	10	a	Boston United	League	W	1	0	Opponent	1580	
	15	a	Morecambe	LC2	L	2	5	German, Black (pen)	395	
	19	h	Hereford United	FAT4	L	1	2	Black	441	
Mar	3	h	Nuneaton Borough	League	W	6	2	Monk, Kielty, Ridings, Jones 3	501	
	6	h	Lancaster City	LJCQF	L	0	3		131	
	10	h	Hayes	League	W	4	0	Jones 2, Swan, Kielty	414	
	17	a	Dover Athletic	League	W	2	1	Ridings, Jones	929	
	23	h	Hereford United	League	W	2	1	Monk, Ridings	503	
	28	a	Forest Green Rovers	League	L	1	3	Ridings	407	
	31	a	Rushden & Diamonds	League	D	1	1	Black	3882	
Apr	3	h	Kettering Town	League	W	1	0	Black	351	
	10	h	Stevenage Borough	League	L	1	4	Monk	403	
	14	a	Yeovil Town	League	L	1	6	Opponent	3401	
	16	h	Woking	League	W	2	0	Jones 2	455	
	18	h	Chester City	League	L	0	1		501	
	21	a	Doncaster Rovers	League	L	0	4		1532	
	24	h	Yeovil Town	League	L	2	3	Ridings, Jones	565	
	26	h	Morecambe	League	W	1	0	Kielty	467	
	28	h	Kingstonian	League	W	2	1	Hayder, Jones	402	
May	5	a	Morecambe	League	W	2	1	Ridings, Jones (pen)	1106	
						80	79			

2001-2002 National Conference

Date		H/A	Opponents	Comp	Res	F	A	Goalscorers	Att	
Aug	18	h	Hayes	League	D	1	1	Maamria	546	
	21	a	Doncaster Rovers	League	L	0	2		2433	
	25	a	Margate	League	W	2	1	Hayder, Maamria	815	
	27	h	Northwich Victoria	League	L	1	2	Monk	642	
Sep	1	a	Telford United	League	L	1	3	Maamria	737	
	4	h	Southport	League	L	1	2	Black	609	
	8	h	Stevenage Borough	League	L	1	2	Maamria	584	
	11	a	Nuneaton Borough	League	L	1	2	Monk	973	
	15	a	Dagenham & Redbridge	League	W	1	0	Hallows	1370	
	18	h	Chester City	League	W	3	0	Twiss 2, Hallows	547	
	22	h	Farnborough Town	League	W	3	0	Twiss 2, Monk	482	
	29	a	Yeovil Town	League	L	1	2	Hallows	2835	
Oct	2	a	Morecambe	League	W	3	1	Twiss, Hallows 2	1263	
	5	h	Hereford United	League	L	0	1		535	
	9	h	Forest Green Rovers	League	L	1	2	Black (pen)	405	
	13	a	Barnet	League	D	1	1	Fisher	1472	
	16	h	Scarborough	LDV1	W	2	1	Heald, Maamria	300	AET; ft 1-1
	20	h	Woking	League	W	3	1	Maamria, Twiss 2	425	
	27	h	Worksop Town	FAC4Q	L	2	4	Twiss, Opponent	674	
	30	a	Hull City	LDV2	L	0	3		5226	
Nov	3	a	Scarborough	League	W	5	2	Opponent, Maamria 2, Monk, Black	853	
	10	h	Dover Athletic	League	L	1	2	Fisher	325	
	13	a	Chorley	LJC1	W	4	2	Kielty, Maamria 2, Heald	158	
	24	a	Boston United	League	L	1	2	Twiss	1940	
Dec	1	a	Hayes	League	L	1	2	Maamria	507	
	8	h	Margate	League	D	2	2	Fisher, Ridings	439	
	15	h	Doncaster Rovers	League	L	1	4	Twiss	546	
Jan	5	a	Southport	League	L	0	5		1091	
	8	h	Rossendale United	LJC2	W	4	3	Maamria 3 (1pen), Black	122	AET; ft 2-2
	12	h	Wakefield & Emley	FAT3	D	2	2	Black, Twiss	301	
	14	a	Wakefield & Emley	FAT3	W	4	1	Twiss, Maamria, Black, Hallows	376	
	19	h	Telford United	League	W	3	1	Black, Ridings, Maamria	333	
	26	a	Northwich Victoria	League	W	3	0	Black, Maamria 2	769	
	30	a	Accrington Stanley	LJCQF	L	1	2	Black	285	
Feb	2	a	Margate	FAT4	L	0	2		608	
	9	a	Hereford United	League	W	1	0	Twiss	1443	
	16	h	Barnet	League	D	3	3	Maamria, Twiss, Black	458	
	26	a	Stalybridge Celtic	League	W	1	0	Twiss	404	
Mar	2	a	Chester City	League	D	1	1	Twiss	1572	
	5	h	Stalybridge Celtic	League	W	1	0	Kielty	404	
	9	h	Nuneaton Borough	League	L	0	1		410	
	12	h	Morecambe	League	L	0	1		451	
	16	a	Forest Green Rovers	League	W	2	1	Hallows, Heald	636	
	23	h	Dagenham & Redbridge	League	W	2	0	Twiss, Hallows	492	
	30	a	Woking	League	D	1	1	Hallows	1609	
Apr	1	h	Scarborough	League	D	1	1	Twiss	541	
	6	a	Dover Athletic	League	D	0	0		907	
	13	h	Boston United	League	L	1	2	Monk	788	
	15	a	Stevenage Borough	League	W	1	0	Hallows	1116	
	20	h	Yeovil Town	League	L	0	1		401	
	27	a	Farnborough Town	League	L	0	3		809	
						75	78			

2002-03 National Conference

Date	Date	H/A	Opponents	Comp	Res	F	A	Goalscorers	Att	
Aug	17	a	Dagenham & Redbridge	League	L	1	3	Black	1305	
	20	h	Doncaster Rovers	League	L	0	2		867	
	24	h	Burton Albion	League	W	4	2	Maamria 3, Kielty	503	
	26	a	Woking	League	L	0	3		2160	
	31	h	Margate	League	W	2	0	Monk, Maamria	327	
Sep	3	a	Southport	League	L	2	4	Harrison, Salt	1097	
	6	a	Chester City	League	L	1	2	Opponent	2273	
	14	h	Barnet	League	W	4	2	Maamria 3, Heald	405	
	17	h	Nuneaton Borough	League	D	1	1	Whittaker	401	
	21	a	Farnborough Town	League	L	0	1		595	
	24	a	Scarborough	League	L	0	2		950	
	28	h	Yeovil Town	League	L	2	4	Kielty, Whittaker	415	
Oct	5	a	Morecambe	League	L	1	2	Kielty	1258	
	8	h	Hereford United	League	L	0	2		425	
	12	h	Stevenage Borough	League	W	2	1	Kielty, C Ward	335	
	19	a	Gravesend & Northfleet	League	W	3	1	Maamria 2 (1pen), Monk	1246	
	22	a	Southport	LDV1	W	4	3	Kielty, Salt, Tolson, Opponent	481	
	26	a	Moor Green	FAC4Q	L	1	2	Maamria	680	
Nov	2	h	Kettering Town	League	D	2	2	Courtney, Tolson	402	
	9	a	Northwich Victoria	League	W	1	0	Maamria	608	
	12	h	Wrexham	LDV2	L	3	4	Kielty 2, Maamria	703	AET; ft 3-3
	16	a	Barnet	League	L	0	4		1021	
	19	h	Radcliffe Borough	LJC1	W	1	0	Tolson		
	23	h	Morecambe	League	W	1	0	Maamria	506	
	30	h	Telford United	League	L	0	3		406	
Dec	7	a	Forest Green Rovers	League	L	1	4	Heald (pen)	576	
	14	h	Chester City	League	L	0	4		851	
	26	h	Halifax Town	League	L	0	2		815	
	28	a	Doncaster Rovers	League	L	0	1		3719	
Jan	1	a	Halifax Town	League	L	0	1		2050	
	14	h	Vauxhall Motors	FAT3	L	1	2	Robertson	229	
	18	a	Burton Albion	League	W	1	0	Maamria	1393	
	25	h	Woking	League	W	1	0	Courtney	435	
	28	a	Flixton	LJC2	W	7	0	Maamria 3, Courtney 2, Blakeman, Opponent		
Feb	8	a	Margate	League	L	0	2		535	
	11	a	Rossendale United	LJCQF	W	4	2			
	15	h	Southport	League	D	1	1	Monk	565	
	18	h	Chorley	LJCSF	W	1	0	Courtney		
Mar	1	a	Nuneaton Borough	League	W	2	0	Heald 2	1187	
	4	h	Farnborough Town	League	W	3	2	Scott, Maden, Salt	305	
	8	h	Scarborough	League	L	0	2		525	
	11	a	Yeovil Town	League	L	1	3	Scott	5330	
	22	a	Telford United	League	D	1	1	Monk	802	
	29	h	Forest Green Rovers	League	W	1	0	Lancaster	445	
Apr	5	a	Stevenage Borough	League	L	1	3	Maden	2130	
	7	h	Dagenham & Redbridge	League	L	1	3	Monk	403	
	12	h	Gravesend & Northfleet	League	D	0	0		385	
	15	1	Kendal Town	LJCF	W	2	0	Monk, Courtney	481	
	19	a	Hereford United	League	W	1	0	Salt	1699	
	21	h	Northwich Victoria	League	D	1	1	Monk	439	
	26	a	Kettering Town	League	W	1	0	Scott	768	
						68	84			
		1	at Accrington Stanley FC							

359

2003-2004   National Conference

Date		H/A	Opponents	Comp	Res	F	A	Goalscorers	Att
Aug	9	h	Dagenham & Redbridge	League	W	2	1	McNiven 2	419
	13	a	Accrington Stanley	League	L	1	4	McNiven	2003
	16	a	Farnborough Town	League	D	1	1	McNiven	594
	23	h	Halifax Town	League	D	1	1	McNiven	849
	25	a	Northwich Victoria	League	W	1	0	Maden	582
	30	h	Woking	League	L	0	1		435
Sep	6	h	Forest Green Rovers	League	L	1	2	Robinson	415
	13	a	Gravesend & Northfleet	League	L	1	3	McNiven	723
	20	h	Tamworth	League	D	1	1	Redmond	427
	23	a	Morecambe	League	L	0	1		1393
	27	a	Stevenage Borough	League	L	0	4		1734
Oct	4	h	Aldershot Town	League	D	2	2	McNiven 2	545
	11	a	Margate	League	L	0	2		429
	18	h	Barnet	League	L	1	4	McNiven (pen)	348
	25	a	Accrington Stanley	FAC4Q	L	0	2		1361
Nov	1	a	Hereford United	League	W	1	0	Barrowclough	3231
	11	h	Scarborough	League	L	1	4	Maden	375
	15	a	Telford United	League	L	0	5		1377
	18	h	Shrewsbury Town	League	D	2	2	McNiven 2	1219
	22	h	Exeter City	League	D	1	1	Maden	630
	25	a	Burton Albion	League	L	2	3	McNiven, Maden	1327
	29	a	Forest Green Rovers	League	D	2	2	McNiven, Peyton	554
Dec	13	a	Dagenham & Redbridge	League	W	2	1	Shepherd, McNiven	1037
	20	h	Accrington Stanley	League	L	1	2	McNiven	612
	26	a	Chester City	League	L	0	5		3044
Jan	1	h	Chester City	League	L	2	6	Daniel, Peyton	2002
	3	a	Woking	League	L	0	2		2105
	6	a	Squires Gate	LJC1	W	3	1	McNiven, Whitehead, Kielty	
	10	h	Stalybridge Celtic	FAT3	D	1	1	McNiven	402
	17	h	Farnborough Town	League	L	0	2		295
	24	h	Morecambe	League	W	3	1	McNiven 3(1pen)	605
Feb	3	a	Chorley	LJCQF	L	1	4	Maden	
	7	a	Tamworth	League	L	3	4	McNiven, Roscoe, Barrowclough	905
	14	h	Stevenage Borough	League	L	1	3	McNiven	270
	21	a	Aldershot Town	League	L	0	2		2412
	28	h	Margate	League	W	4	2	Brodie 2, Daniel, McNiven (pen)	302
Mar	8	a	Shrewsbury Town	League	L	1	3	Brodie	3307
	13	a	Scarborough	League	L	1	4	Brodie	1093
	20	h	Telford United	League	D	1	1	Lancaster	315
	27	a	Exeter City	League	L	2	3	McNiven, Durkin	3635
	30	h	Gravesend & Northfleet	League	L	1	2	McNiven	304
Apr	3	h	Burton Albion	League	L	0	1		339
	9	a	Halifax Town	League	L	1	2	Daniel	1415
	12	h	Northwich Victoria	League	W	1	0	McNiven	339
	17	h	Hereford United	League	L	0	5		836
	24	a	Barnet	League	L	1	2	McNiven (pen)	2988
						51	105		

2004-05   National Conference

Date		H/A	Opponents	Comp	Res	F	A	Goalscorers	Att
Aug	14	h	Crawley Town	League	L	1	2	Gaunt	401
	17	a	Burton Albion	League	D	0	0		1305
	21	a	Woking	League	L	0	1		1499
	28	h	Halifax Town	League	L	0	3		575
	30	a	Morecambe	League	L	1	2	Meechan	1382
Sep	4	h	Forest Green Rovers	League	W	2	0	Simm, Fitzpatrick	305
	11	h	Aldershot Town	League	D	3	3	Byrne 2, Rose	464
	18	a	Accrington Stanley	League	L	1	2	Byrne	1507
	21	a	York City	League	D	1	1	Miller	1708
	25	h	Hereford United	League	L	3	4	Peyton, Stoker, S Smith	585
Oct	2	a	Gravesend & Northfleet	League	L	1	4	Williams	1340
	5	h	Carlisle United	League	L	1	6	Stoker	1540
	9	h	Stevenage Borough	League	L	1	2	Stoker	235
	16	a	Dagenham & Redbridge	League	L	0	2		1157
	23	a	Canvey Island	League	L	0	3		532
	30	a	Accrington Stanley	FAC4Q	W	2	0	Simm, Rose (pen)	1121
Nov	6	h	Tamworth	League	L	2	3	Connell, Williams	338
	13	a	Cambridge City	FAC1	L	1	2	Simm	930
	16	h	Marine	LJC1	W	5	1	Simm 2, Connell, Williams, Stoker	78
	20	a	Exeter City	League	L	1	5	Simm	3544
	27	h	Farnborough Town	League	L	1	2	Stoker	225
Dec	4	a	Barnet	League	L	2	3	Rose, Stoker	1961
	7	h	Scarborough	League	D	1	1	Williams	325
	11	h	Accrington Stanley	League	L	0	6		402
	18	a	Aldershot Town	League	L	0	2		2312
	28	a	Hereford United	League	L	0	3		3014
Jan	8	h	Gravesend & Northfleet	League	L	0	1		251
	11	h	Southport	LJC2	L	1	5	Tench	152
	15	h	Altrincham	FAT3	L	1	2	Reed	401
	18	a	Northwich Victoria	LC1	L	0	1		
	29	h	York City	League	L	0	3		701
Feb	5	a	Forest Green Rovers	League	D	1	1	Taylor	449
	15	h	Northwich Victoria	League	L	0	1		402
	19	h	Exeter City	League	L	0	1		451
	22	a	Tamworth	League	W	1	0	Peers	902
	26	a	Farnborough Town	League	W	1	0	Williams	501
Mar	5	h	Barnet	League	L	0	3		402
	8	a	Carlisle United	League	L	0	3		3047
	12	a	Scarborough	League	L	0	3		1219
	19	h	Burton Albion	League	L	1	4	Lane	325
	25	a	Crawley Town	League	D	2	2	Williams, Mulvaney	1831
	28	h	Morecambe	League	L	0	2		541
Apr	2	a	Halifax Town	League	L	1	5	Allen	1704
	5	h	Canvey Island	League	W	2	1	Mulvaney, Jones	201
	9	h	Woking	League	L	0	3		215
	12	a	Northwich Victoria	League	L	0	2		734
	19	h	Dagenham & Redbridge	League	L	0	1		245
	23	a	Stevenage Borough	League	L	0	2		3516
						41	109		

2005-2006　　Conference North

Date		H/A	Opponents	Comp	Res	F	A	Goalscorers	Att	
Aug	13	a	Redditch United	League	W	2	1	Simm 2	316	
	16	h	Droylsden	League	L	0	1		245	
	20	h	Stalybridge Celtic	League	W	2	1	Roscoe, Simm	301	
	27	a	Barrow	League	L	1	3	McDowell	1074	
	29	h	Hinckley United	League	W	1	0	Stoker	232	
Sep	3	a	Gainsborough Trinity	League	L	1	2	Roscoe	259	
	10	a	Vauxhall Motors	League	D	4	4	Shillito, Smith, Coyne, McDowell	155	
	17	h	Hednesford Town	League	D	0	0		301	
	24	a	Chester-le-Street Town	FAC2Q	W	3	1	Simm, Smith, Thompson	193	
Oct	1	h	Workington	League	L	0	1		185	
	8	h	Gainsborough Trinity	FAC3Q	D	1	1	Smith	165	
	11	a	Gainsborough Trinity	FAC3Q	L	1	2	Smith	361	
	15	a	Kettering Town	League	L	0	4		1211	
	18	a	Alfreton Town	League	D	1	1	Coyne	224	
	22	h	Stafford Rangers	League	L	1	3	Simm	301	
	29	a	Moor Green	League	L	1	4	Opponent	170	
Nov	4	h	Worksop Town	League	L	0	1		186	
	12	a	Hyde United	League	D	3	3	Simm 2, McDowell	436	
	15	h	Colne	LJC1	W	1	0	Smith		
Dec	3	h	Stafford Rangers	FAT3Q	L	1	4	Simm	165	
	6	h	Marine	LJC2	D	1	1	Stoker AET FT 0-0		1-4 pens
	10	a	Northwich Victoria	League	L	0	1		755	
	26	h	Harrogate Town	League	W	3	1	Simm 3 (2pens)	177	
	30	h	Hucknall Town	League	W	2	1	Willis 2	181	
Jan	2	a	Harrogate Town	League	L	0	3		428	
	7	h	Redditch United	League	W	2	1	Willis 2	178	
	10	h	Lancaster City	League	L	1	2	Simm	225	
	14	a	Droylsden	League	L	1	4	McDowell	285	
	21	a	Stalybridge Celtic	League	L	1	6	Willis	560	
	24	h	Nuneaton Borough	League	W	1	0	Willis	201	
	28	h	Barrow	League	D	1	1	Simm	301	
Feb	4	a	Workington	League	D	0	0		502	
	11	h	Kettering Town	League	L	0	2		225	
	13	a	Worcester City	League	L	0	2		818	
	18	a	Stafford Rangers	League	D	0	0		1035	
	21	h	Alfreton Town	League	D	0	0		148	
	24	h	Vauxhall Motors	League	D	1	1	Hay	185	
Mar	7	a	Lancaster City	League	L	0	2		246	
	11	h	Moor Green	League	L	1	3	Wilkinson	175	
	18	a	Worksop Town	League	D	3	3	Simm 2 (1pen), Williams	296	
	24	h	Hyde United	League	D	1	1	Roscoe	195	
Apr	1	a	Nuneaton Borough	League	L	1	3	Williams	1082	
	3	a	Hednesford Town	League	W	3	1	Willis, Smith, Roscoe	492	
	8	h	Worcester City	League	L	1	4	Smith	185	
	15	h	Gainsborough Trinity	League	D	0	0		125	
	17	a	Hinckley United	League	L	1	5	Williams	461	
	22	a	Hucknall Town	League	D	2	2	McGrath, Smith	304	
	29	h	Northwich Victoria	League	W	2	1	Willis, Simm	639	
						53	88			

2006-07 Conference North

Date		H/A	Opponents	Comp	Res	F	A	Goalscorers	Att
Aug	12	a	Vauxhall Motors	League	L	1	2	Simm	180
	15	h	Farsley Celtic	League	L	1	3	Simm	151
	19	h	Redditch United	League	D	0	0		155
	22	a	Nuneaton Borough	League	W	1	0	Simm	843
	26	a	Moor Green	League	D	0	0		217
	28	h	Gainsborough Trinity	League	W	2	0	Lee-Ellison, Willis	165
Sep	2	a	Blyth Spartans	League	L	0	1		573
	9	h	Kettering Town	League	L	1	2	Settle	251
	12	h	Lancaster City	League	L	0	1		156
	23	h	Alfreton Town	League	W	2	0	Settle, McAuley	157
	30	h	Woodley Sports	FAC2Q	L	0	2		130
Oct	7	a	Worksop Town	League	L	0	2		277
	21	h	Scarborough	League	D	1	1	Simm	215
	30	a	Hinckley United	League	L	1	3	Owen	564
Nov	4	a	Barrow	League	L	0	2		921
	11	h	Droylsden	League	D	2	2	Settle, Owen	209
	15	a	Nelson	LJC1	L	0	1		
	18	a	Harrogate Town	League	L	1	2	Hussin	383
	25	h	Cammell Laird	FAT3Q	W	1	0	Settle	130
Dec	1	h	Hyde United	League	W	2	0	Simm, Lugsden	151
	5	h	Hucknall Town	League	W	4	3	Jackson 3, Owen	140
	9	a	Worcester City	League	W	2	1	Lee-Ellison, Dillon	973
	16	a	Harrogate Town	FAT1	D	1	1	Settle	379
	19	h	Harrogate Town	FAT1	W	2	1	Porter, McAuley	101
	26	a	Workington	League	W	1	0	Porter	663
Jan	2	h	Workington	League	W	2	0	McAuley, Lugsden	207
	6	a	Kettering Town	League	L	0	4		1009
	13	a	Stevenage Borough	FAT2	L	1	3	McAuley	1184
	20	h	Stalybridge Celtic	League	L	1	3	Simm	216
	27	a	Alfreton Town	League	L	0	1		231
Feb	3	a	Droylsden	League	D	2	2	Jackson, Simm	431
	10	h	Harrogate Town	League	L	1	3	Owen	155
	16	a	Hyde United	League	L	0	2		334
	20	h	Hinckley United	League	L	2	3	Rapley, Simm	125
	24	h	Worcester City	League	W	2	1	Roberts, Rapley	175
Mar	3	a	Hucknall Town	League	W	3	1	Simm 2, Opponent	293
	6	a	Stalybridge Celtic	League	L	1	2	Rapley	397
	10	h	Barrow	League	L	0	3		251
	13	h	Blyth Spartans	League	W	3	1	Simm 3	145
	17	a	Redditch United	League	L	1	2	Rapley	443
	23	h	Vauxhall Motors	League	L	0	3		201
	31	a	Farsley Celtic	League	D	1	1	Simm	347
Apr	3	a	Lancaster City	League	D	0	0		198
	7	h	Moor Green	League	D	2	2	Rapley, Porter	131
	9	a	Gainsborough Trinity	League	D	0	0		361
	14	h	Nuneaton Borough	League	W	1	0	Rapley (pen)	191
	21	a	Scarborough	League	D	1	1	Rapley (pen)	1196
	28	h	Worksop Town	League	W	2	1	Owen 2	325
						52	69		

2007-08 Conference North

Date		H/A	Opponents	Comp	Res	F	A	Goalscorers	Att
Aug	11	h	Hinckley United	League	D	2	2	Owen, Rapley	175
	14	a	Barrow	League	W	2	1	Rapley (pen), Owen	803
	18	a	Redditch United	League	D	1	1	Willis	305
	25	h	Harrogate Town	League	L	0	2		155
	27	a	Stalybridge Celtic	League	L	1	3	Rapley (pen)	433
Sep	1	h	Kettering Town	League	L	1	4	Lugsden	255
	7	h	Southport	League	L	0	1		553
	15	a	Worcester City	League	L	1	3	Rapley	765
	18	h	Hucknall Town	League	W	2	0	Lugsden 2	101
	22	a	Nuneaton Borough	League	L	0	1		672
	29	a	Harrogate Railway Athletic	FAC2Q	L	1	4	Jackson	126
Oct	2	a	Barrow	LC1	L	0	4		346
	6	h	Solihull Moors	League	D	1	1	Heald	106
	20	a	Vauxhall Motors	League	D	2	2	Lugsden, Chetcuti	156
	27	a	Blyth Spartans	League	L	0	2		501
	30	h	Hyde United	League	L	1	5	Lugsden	231
Nov	3	h	Boston United	League	D	2	2	Roberts, Chetcuti	175
	10	a	Alfreton Town	League	L	0	1		269
	13	h	Clitheroe	LJC2	W	4	2	Smyth 2, Roberts, Settle	77
	17	h	Nuneaton Borough	League	L	1	3	Settle	177
	24	a	Burscough	FAT3Q	W	3	2	Settle 2, Heald	290
Dec	1	a	Tamworth	League	L	0	2		809
	11	a	Ashton Athletic	LJCSQF	W	3	1	Smyth 2, Fairhurst	
	15	h	Workington	FAT1	L	1	3	Smyth	101
	22	a	Kettering Town	League	L	0	3		896
	26	h	Workington	League	W	2	1	Smyth 2	103
	29	h	Stalybridge Celtic	League	L	1	3	Gibson	220
Jan	1	a	Workington	League	L	1	2	Lugsden	406
	5	a	Boston United	League	L	1	5	Gibson	1310
	12	h	Redditch United	League	L	0	1		125
	19	a	AFC Telford United	League	L	1	6	Lugsden	1784
	26	h	Vauxhall Motors	League	W	3	1	Smyth 2, Salmon	121
Feb	2	a	Solihull Moors	League	L	0	1		210
	5	h	AFC Telford United	League	L	0	3		345
	9	a	Hyde United	League	D	1	1	Smyth	404
	16	h	Gainsborough Trinity	League	L	1	3	Salmon	260
	26	a	Burscough	League	L	2	5	Gibson, Chetcuti	289
Mar	1	h	Barrow	League	L	1	2	Smyth	295
	4	a	Southport	LJCSF	L	0	4		178
	8	a	Hinckley United	League	L	1	3	Maylett	424
	15	h	Alfreton Town	League	W	1	0	Maylett	225
	22	a	Harrogate Town	League	D	0	0		445
	29	a	Hucknall Town	League	L	0	3		252
Apr	5	h	Tamworth	League	D	0	0		220
	8	h	Burscough	League	W	2	1	Marsh-Evans, Hanley	156
	12	a	Gainsborough Trinity	League	L	1	2	Chetcuti	372
	19	h	Worcester City	League	L	0	1		154
	22	a	Southport	League	L	0	2		861
	26	h	Blyth Spartans	League	L	0	2		238
						48	107		

2008-09   Northern Premier League Premier Division

Date		H/A	Opponents	Comp	Res	F	A	Goalscorers	Att	
Aug	16	a	Eastwood Town	League	L	0	2		364	
	19	h	Ashton United	League	W	3	0	Mansaram, Chetcuti, Maylett	140	at Chorley
	23	h	Ilkeston Town	League	L	1	2	Booth	101	at Chorley
	25	a	Ossett Town	League	W	2	0	Mansaram, Maylett	131	
	30	a	Worksop Town	League	L	1	2	Mansaram	155	
Sep	2	h	Prescot Cables	League	W	2	1	Stepien, Wilson	215	at Hilton Pk
	6	h	Frickley Athletic	League	W	2	0	Stepien (pen), Watt	165	at Radcliffe
	9	a	Nantwich Town	League	D	1	1	Stepien	547	
	13	a	Curzon Ashton	FAC1Q	L	0	1		158	
	20	h	Whitby Town	League	L	2	4	Holland, Field	151	at Chorley
	23	a	Marine	League	W	1	0	Teague	252	
Oct	4	a	Buxton	League	D	0	0		378	
	14	a	Cammell Laird	League	L	1	2	Smyth	145	
	18	a	Harrogate Railway Athletic	FAT1Q	W	1	0	Stepien	129	
	25	a	Witton Albion	League	W	3	1	Stepien, Maylett, Field	419	
	28	h	Marine	League	D	0	0		129	at Chorley
Nov	1	h	Cammell Laird	FAT2Q	L	1	5	Sefton	94	at Chorley
	8	h	North Ferriby United	League	L	0	3		70	at Ashton Utd
	15	a	Whitby Town	League	D	2	2	Parkinson, McCaughtrie	263	
Dec	15	a	Atherton Collieries	LJC1	W	2	0	Parkinson 2(1pen)	62	
	22	h	Radcliffe Borough	LJC2	L	2	3	Marsh, Clements	90	at Radcliffe
	26	h	Witton Albion	League	L	0	2		204	at Warrington
Jan	12	a	Ashton United	LC3	L	1	3	Marsh (pen)	125	AET, FT 1-1
	17	h	Eastwood Town	League	L	0	4		110	at Clitheroe
	20	a	Prescot Cables	League	L	0	2		196	
	24	a	Matlock Town	League	L	0	5		302	
	27	h	FC United of Manchester	League	L	0	2		1302	at LSV
	31	h	Worksop Town	League	L	1	2	Thompson	102	at Radcliffe
Feb	7	h	Hednesford Town	League	L	1	3	Marsh	344	at LSV
	14	a	FC United of Manchester	League	W	4	2	Marsh 3(2pens), Thompson	1850	
	17	h	Kendal Town	League	L	1	2	Thompson	120	at Ashton Utd
	21	a	Guiseley	League	L	1	3	Heald	292	
	24	h	Ossett Town	League	L	0	6		59	at Ashton Utd
	28	a	Ilkeston Town	League	L	1	3	Marsh	399	
Mar	3	h	Boston United	League	D	0	0		93	at Radcliffe
	7	a	Ashton United	League	L	0	2		162	
	10	a	Kendal Town	League	L	0	2		132	
	14	a	Bradford Park Avenue	League	L	1	2	Lambert	469	
	17	h	Nantwich Town	League	L	0	8		101	at Radcliffe
	21	h	Guiseley	League	L	2	4	Heald, OG	122	at Radcliffe
	24	a	Frickley Athletic	League	D	0	0		228	
	31	h	Cammell Laird	League	W	2	1	Stepien 2	348	at LSV
Apr	4	a	Boston United	League	D	1	1	Stepien (pen)	1212	
	10	a	North Ferriby United	League	W	2	1	Heald, Stepien	197	
	13	h	Buxton	League	L	0	7		257	at Warrington
	18	h	Matlock Town	League	L	0	2		405	at LSV
	21	h	Bradford Park Avenue	League	W	2	1	Brown, S Flitcroft	301	at LSV
	25	a	Hednesford Town	League	W	2	1	Dorney 2	467	
						49	100			

2009-10 Northern Premier League First Division North

Date		H/A	Opponents	Comp	Res	F	A	Goalscorers	Att	Notes
Aug	15	a	Rossendale United	League	W	3	1	S Flitcroft (pen), C Baguley, Stepien	136	
	17	a	Curzon Ashton	League	L	1	2	C Baguley	196	
	22	h	Garforth Town	League	W	2	1	Stepien, C Baguley	186	
	25	a	Lancaster City	League	L	0	2		252	
	28	a	Warrington Town	FACPR	L	0	1		167	
Sep	1	h	Warrington Town	League	W	3	2	Jansen 2, Dorney	101	at Chorley
	5	a	Ossett Albion	League	W	4	2	Heald, Opponent, Stepien, C Baguley	143	
	12	a	Mossley	League	D	1	1	Heald	163	
	15	a	Colwyn Bay	League	L	0	1		227	
	19	a	FC Halifax Town	League	L	1	3	Stepien (pen)	1292	
	23	h	Warrington Town	LC1	W	6	1	Thompson 4, C Baguley 2	138	
	26	h	Prescot Cables	League	W	6	0	Stepien 3 (2pens), J Baguley 2, C Baguley	378	
	29	h	Atherton LR	LJC1	D	4	4	C Baguley 4 AET, FT 3-3	101	4-3 pens at Atherton LR
Oct	3	a	AFC Fylde	League	L	1	2	Jansen	202	
	13	a	Woodley Sports	UPC1	L	1	2	J Baguley	72	
	17	a	Atherstone Town	FAT1Q	W	3	1	Ince 3	195	
	20	a	Clitheroe	League	W	2	1	Thompson 2 (2pens)	151	
	24	h	Mossley	League	D	1	1	Thompson	235	
	27	h	Mossley	LC2	L	0	4		131	at Mossley
	31	a	Skelmersdale United	FAT2Q	W	4	1	Stepien, Ince, J Baguley, Dorney	220	
Nov	7	h	Trafford	League	W	2	0	Thompson (pen), Whitham	151	
	10	a	Ashton Athletic	LJC2	W	3	0	Stepien (pen), Dorney, Jansen	58	
	14	a	Prescot Cables	League	W	4	0	J Baguley, Ince, Stepien (pen), Whitham	247	
	18	h	Harrogate Railway Athletic	League	W	5	1	J Baguley, Thompson, Dorney, Jansen, Ince	84	at Chorley
	21	h	Redditch United	FAT3Q	L	0	1		283	
	28	h	Colwyn Bay	League	W	3	1	Thompson, Whitham, Stepien (pen)	193	
Dec	1	a	Bamber Bridge	League	L	1	3	Smith	125	
	5	h	FC Halifax Town	League	D	1	1	Thompson	618	
	12	a	Radcliffe Borough	League	L	1	2	King	174	
	19	h	AFC Fylde	League	W	4	1	Stepien, Dorney, Page, C Baguley	174	
Jan	19	a	Colne	LJCQF	W	3	1	Stepien (pen), J Baguley, Ince	46	
	23	a	Harrogate Railway Athletic	League	L	1	2	Opponent	102	
	26	a	Warrington Town	League	D	0	0		111	
Feb	6	h	Chorley	League	L	0	2		187	
	10	h	Clitheroe	LJCSF	L	1	3	Heald	149	at Lancs FA, Leyland
	13	h	Clitheroe	League	W	2	0	Dorney, Ince	166	
	17	h	Rossendale United	League	W	4	3	Ratcliffe, Jansen 3	61	at Chorley
	20	a	Wakefield	League	D	2	2	Jansen, Heald	110	
	24	h	Skelmersdale United	League	L	0	1		106	at Chorley
	27	a	Chorley	League	W	5	1	Dorney, Stepien 3(1pen), Ince	260	
Mar	6	a	Trafford	League	W	2	0	Stepien 2(1pen)	124	
	13	h	Woodley Sports	League	W	2	0	Stepien 2(1pen)	185	
	20	h	Ossett Albion	League	W	1	0	Ince	196	
	24	h	Curzon Ashton	League	D	0	0		110	at Warrington Town
	27	a	Garforth Town	League	W	5	0	Ross, Heald, Jansen, Ince, J Dorney(pen)	190	
	30	a	Salford City	League	D	3	3	Heald, Ince 2	106	
Apr	2	h	Lancaster City	League	L	0	2		233	
	5	a	Skelmersdale United	League	W	2	0	Chinthengah 2	249	
	8	h	Radcliffe Borough	League	L	1	2	Ince	107	at Chorley
	10	h	Bamber Bridge	League	L	0	3		164	
	17	a	Woodley Sports	League	D	1	1	Jansen	82	
	21	h	Salford City	League	W	2	1	J Dorney(pen), Chinthengah	95	at Chorley
	24	h	Wakefield	League	W	2	0	Ince, Stepien	136	
						106	70			

366

Leigh RMI / Genesis Club Records 1995-2010

LEIGH RMI/ LEIGH GENESIS CLUB RECORDS 1995-2010

Changed name from Horwich RMI	1995
Changed name to Leigh Genesis	2008
Grounds:	
Hilton Park, Leigh	1995-2008
Leigh Sports Village	2009-2010

Honours:
League:

Northern Premier League	Champions (Premier League): 1999-2000
	Runners-up (Division One): 1996-97

Cup:

Northern Premier League President's Cup	
	Runners-up: 1998-99
Lancashire Junior Cup	Winners: 2002-03
FA Cup	First Round: 1998-99; 2000-01; 2004-05

HIGHEST SCORING WINS

Date	Venue	Comp	Opponents	Res	F	A
17/10/1995	h	FAT1Q	Bridgnorth Town	W	7	0
28/01/2003	a	LJC2	Flixton	W	7	0

Highest League win:

Date	Venue		Comp	Opponents	Res	F	A
26/09/2009	h		League	Prescot Cables	W	6	0

HEAVIEST DEFEATS

Date	Venue	Comp	Opponents	Res	F	A
17/03/2009	h1	League	Nantwich Town	L	0	8
13/04/2009	h2	League	Buxton	L	0	7

h1 home game staged at Radcliffe Borough
h2 home game staged at Warrington Town

LEADING SCORERS IN A SEASON (League and Cup):

Player	Season	Goals
Chris Shaw	1996-1997	28
David McNiven	2003-2004	27
Steve Jones	1999-2000	23

LEADING SCORERS IN A CAREER (League and Cup):

Player	Seasons	Goals
Tony Black	1998-2002	56
Keith Evans	1996-1998	54

MOST GOALS IN A MATCH

Chris Thompson	2009-2010	4 Warrington Town (LC1)
Chris Baguley	2009-2010	4 Atherton LR (LJC1)

Leigh RMI / Genesis League Record By Opponents

	Season First Played	Last Played	P	W	D	L	F	A
Accrington Stanley	1997	2004	8	3	0	5	10	18
AFC Fylde	2009	2009	2	1	0	1	5	3
AFC Telford United	2007	2007	2	0	0	2	1	9
Aldershot Town	2003	2004	4	0	2	2	5	9
Alfreton Town	1995	2007	10	3	3	4	8	8
Altrincham	1997	1998	4	1	2	1	7	7
Ashton United	1995	2008	6	2	0	4	9	11
Atherton LR	1995	1996	4	3	0	1	7	4
Bamber Bridge	1997	2009	8	2	3	3	12	11
Barnet	2001	2004	8	1	2	5	12	22
Barrow	1997	2007	10	3	2	5	9	15
Bishop Auckland	1997	1999	6	1	3	2	9	9
Blyth Spartans	1997	2001	10	5	1	4	12	13
Boston United	1997	2008	10	1	4	5	9	16
Bradford Park Avenue	1995	2008	6	3	0	3	9	8
Burscough	2007	2007	2	1	0	1	4	6
Burton Albion	2002	2004	6	2	1	3	8	10
Buxton	2008	2008	2	0	1	1	0	7
Cammell Laird	2008	2008	2	1	0	1	3	3
Canvey Island	2004	2004	2	1	0	1	2	4
Carlisle United	2004	2004	2	0	0	2	1	9
Chester City	2000	2003	8	1	2	5	8	20
Chorley	1997	2009	6	3	1	2	11	7
Clitheroe	2009	2009	2	2	0	0	4	1
Colwyn Bay	1997	2009	8	6	0	2	19	11
Congleton Town	1995	1996	4	2	1	1	5	4
Crawley Town	2004	2004	2	0	1	1	3	4
Curzon Ashton	1995	2009	6	3	1	2	6	4
Dagenham & Redbridge	2000	2004	10	4	0	6	11	15
Doncaster Rovers	2000	2002	6	0	0	6	1	14
Dover Athletic	2000	2001	4	2	1	1	5	4
Droylsden	1996	2006	8	1	2	5	11	17
Eastwood Town	1995	2008	6	2	1	3	3	7
Emley	1997	1999	6	3	2	1	8	6
Exeter City	2003	2004	4	0	1	3	4	10
Farnborough Town	2001	2004	8	3	1	4	9	11
Farsley Celtic	1995	2006	6	0	3	3	4	8
FC Halifax Town	2009	2009	2	0	1	1	2	4
FC United of Manchester	2008	2008	2	1	0	1	4	4
Fleetwood	1995	1995	2	2	0	0	6	0
Flixton	1996	1996	2	2	0	0	5	1
Forest Green Rovers	2000	2004	10	3	3	4	13	16
Frickley Athletic	1997	2008	8	4	3	1	14	4
Gainsborough Trinity	1997	2007	12	3	3	6	13	17
Garforth Town	2009	2009	2	2	0	0	7	1
Gateshead	1998	1999	4	2	2	0	9	5
Gravesend & Northfleet	2002	2004	6	1	1	4	6	11
Great Harwood Town	1995	1996	4	2	2	0	7	3
Gretna	1995	1996	4	1	1	2	4	7
Guiseley	1997	2008	8	2	1	5	10	14
Halifax Town	2002	2004	6	0	1	5	3	14
Harrogate Railway Athletic	2009	2009	2	1	0	1	6	3
Harrogate Town	1995	2007	10	5	1	4	13	12
Hayes	2000	2001	4	2	1	1	8	4
Hednesford Town	2000	2008	6	3	2	1	10	8
Hereford United	2000	2004	10	4	1	5	9	17

	Season First Played	Last Played	P	W	D	L	F	A
Hinckley United	2005	2007	6	1	1	4	8	16
Hucknall Town	1999	2007	8	6	1	1	16	11
Hyde United	1997	2007	12	4	6	2	19	20
Ilkeston Town	2008	2008	2	0	0	2	2	5
Kendal Town	2008	2008	2	0	0	2	1	4
Kettering Town	2000	2007	10	3	1	6	7	21
Kingstonian	2000	2000	2	2	0	0	4	1
Lancaster City	1995	2009	14	5	1	8	13	20
Leek Town	1999	1999	2	0	0	2	0	4
Lincoln United	1995	1996	4	3	0	1	7	5
Margate	2001	2003	6	3	1	2	10	9
Marine	1997	2008	8	3	5	0	7	4
Matlock Town	1996	2008	4	0	1	3	2	10
Moor Green	2005	2006	4	0	2	2	4	9
Morecambe	2000	2004	10	5	0	5	12	11
Mossley	2009	2009	2	0	2	0	2	2
Nantwich Town	2008	2008	2	0	1	1	1	9
Netherfield	1995	1996	4	2	0	2	7	6
North Ferriby United	2008	2008	2	1	0	1	2	4
Northwich Victoria	2000	2005	12	6	2	4	14	9
Nuneaton Borough	2000	2007	12	5	1	6	16	15
Ossett Albion	2008	2009	2	2	0	0	5	2
Ossett Town	2008	2008	2	1	0	1	2	6
Prescot Cables	2008	2009	4	3	0	1	12	3
Radcliffe Borough	1995	2009	8	2	3	3	8	10
Redditch United	2005	2007	6	2	2	2	6	6
Rossendale United	2009	2009	2	2	0	0	7	4
Runcorn	1997	1999	6	3	3	0	10	4
Rushden & Diamonds	2000	2000	2	1	1	0	2	1
Salford City	2009	2009	2	1	1	0	5	4
Scarborough	2000	2006	12	2	5	5	14	22
Shrewsbury Town	2003	2003	2	0	1	1	3	5
Slelmersdale United	2009	2009	2	1	0	1	2	1
Solihull Moors	2007	2007	2	0	1	1	1	2
Southport	2000	2007	8	1	2	5	8	18
Spennymoor United	1997	1999	6	5	1	0	19	6
Stafford Rangers	2005	2005	2	0	1	1	1	3
Stalybridge Celtic	1998	2007	12	6	1	5	21	23
Stevenage Borough	2000	2004	10	2	0	8	8	24
Stocksbridge Park Steels	1996	1996	2	0	2	0	1	1
Tamworth	2003	2007	6	1	2	3	7	10
Telford United	2000	2003	8	1	3	4	8	17
Trafford	2009	2009	2	2	0	0	4	0
Vauxhall Motors	2005	2007	6	1	3	2	11	13
Wakefield	2009	2009	1	0	1	0	2	2
Warrington Town	1995	2009	6	3	3	0	8	5
Whitby Town	1995	2008	6	2	2	2	10	11
Whitley Bay	1995	1996	4	2	0	2	4	5
Winsford United	1997	1999	6	4	1	1	13	6
Witton Albion	2008	2008	2	1	0	1	3	3
Woking	2000	2004	10	3	2	5	8	13
Woodley Sports	2009	2009	2	1	1	0	3	1
Worcester City	2005	2007	6	2	0	4	6	12
Workington	1995	2007	10	7	1	2	19	7
Worksop Town	1995	2008	14	2	6	6	18	21
Yeovil Town	2000	2002	6	0	0	6	7	19
York City	2004	2004	2	0	1	1	1	4

Leigh RMI / Genesis FA Cup Record By Opponents

	P	W	D	L	F	A
Accrington Stanley	3	2	0	1	3	2
Alfreton Town	1	1	0	0	2	0
Belper Town	2	1	1	0	4	2
Billingham Synthonia	2	1	1	0	4	3
Blyth Spartans	1	1	0	0	5	3
Cambridge City	1	0	0	1	1	2
Chester-Le-Street Town	1	1	0	0	3	1
Crook Town	2	0	1	1	2	3
Curzon Ashton	1	0	0	1	0	1
Droylsden	1	1	0	0	2	1
Flixton	1	1	0	0	2	0
Fulham	2	0	1	1	1	3
Gainsborough Trinity	2	0	1	1	2	3
Guiseley	1	0	0	1	0	3
Halifax Town	1	0	0	1	0	4
Harrogate Railway Athletic	1	0	0	1	1	4
Marine	1	1	0	0	2	0
Millwall	1	0	0	1	0	3
Moor Green	1	0	0	1	1	2
Runcorn	1	0	0	1	2	4
Scarborough	1	1	0	0	4	3
Warrington Town	1	0	0	1	0	1
Winsford United	1	1	0	0	1	0
Woodley Sports	1	0	0	1	0	2
Worksop Town	2	1	0	1	4	5

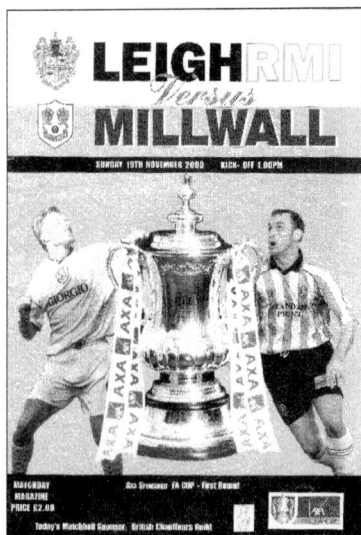

Postscript—from the Football Grounds In Focus Website

Travellers' Tales No.58   Michael Latham - Mon 30 Oct 2006: Conference North.
Hinckley United 3-1 Leigh RMI.
Attendance: 564; Admission: £9; 44pp programme: £2; FGIF Match Rating: 3*

I saw my friend Rachael's dad walking around Rivington on Monday morning and thought back to the days when he was a stalwart of the Scratchin' Shed at Grundy Hill, the lamented late home of Horwich RMI.

With his pals Rachael's dad liked nothing more than standing on the windswept slopes of Grundy Hill, the magnificent views across to Rivington Pike stretching into the distance watching opposing teams attempt to come to terms with the pitch that sloped not only downwards but from side to side.

Local folklore had it that Chris Bonnington used to practice for ascents on Everest trying to climb up to the far goal until he gave up the unequal struggle. Just like Everest Grundy Hill had its own micro-climate and sorted out the wheat from the chaff. And if the cold didn't get to you, Rachael's dad and his pals did. You had to be a good player to escape their mockery or wrath.

Horwich lost its football club 12 years ago now when Grundy Hill was sold for housing and the club acquired Hilton Park from the administrators acting for Leigh rugby league club. Moving a few miles away to a town where the oval ball dominates not only saved the Leigh rugby club from going out of business but enabled RMI, named after the Railway Mechanics' Institute in the old railway town, to stay within the pyramid system and, on the field, prosper as they attained the dizzy heights of a top-six place in the Conference despite pitiful gates. Rachael's dad and his mates did not follow them. They have never been to a soccer match since.

Monday evenings used to be Horwich RMI night and a chance to savour the best meat and potato hotpot in the football world, a far more consistent concoction than that served up on Grundy Hill's slopes. Now renamed Leigh RMI and, almost unbelievably, still surviving in the Conference North despite almost total apathy from their adopted town, a Monday night 12 years following RMI on meant travelling into Leicestershire to the new Marston's Stadium home of Hinckley United.

The excellent programme helped fill the time before kick-off and a two-page history of the visitors brought back happy memories of the day in 1988 when RMI defeated Weymouth 2-0 in the GMAC Cup Final and the £2,000 transfer fee that Bolton Wanderers paid RMI for their striker, Tony Caldwell.

Now Wanderers are the new team in Horwich which has become a football town again since the Reebok Stadium development in 1997 and million pound players from Greece and France fill the jerseys formerly worn with pride by Storer and Caldwell. What a pity that RMI couldn't hang on a few more years and develop maybe a second ground on the Middlebrook site that grew up from a vast area of wilderness known as Red Moss.

Caldwell became a Wanderers hero, scoring five goals in one of his first games, and one of his former team-mates was to be found in the home line-up. Stuart Storer, 40 next January, used to run up and down the wing at Burnden Park laying on crosses for Caldwell. Now he is a right-back with 267 Hinckley games under his belt and looking like he could play on for another ten years.

The tragic death of Matt Gadsby earlier in the season united the Hinckley club and the wider football world in grief and the programme has plenty of news over forthcoming events for the defender's dependants with a poignant picture on the front cover showing the Hinckley players taking part in a minute's applause before a game as a mark of respect.

The Marston's Stadium is everything that Grundy Hill was not - a neat well-manicured ground with an immaculate flat pitch and a feeling that you could be anywhere in the country. Witton Albion set the trend for sanitised characterless new stadiums when Wincham Park was developed in the early 1990s and Hinckley's new ground follows suit.

With a cantilevered main stand and shallow covered terracing on two sides with a flat standing area behind the other goal it is very similar to Northwich's new ground and countless more. Situated a couple of miles out of town on the Earl Shilton Road past a huge supermarket development, it has few memorable and defining characteristics.

It costs £1 to park on the spacious car park at the ground and the facilities are pretty impressive. Catering is above average and there is a neat club shop with a good array of programmes, souvenirs and second hand books for sale. The match programme, 'Knitters News' is a terrific effort packed full of information and statistics and with some interesting articles such as Simon Blyth's Away Days. His entertaining account of a recent trip to Hyde begins: "The week leading up to the Hyde game was quite physically draining. Demand for quarry products was very high and overtime was requested from myself and my co-workers." Terrific stuff.

Conference football, my friend Rupert says, is like kissing your sister. Often, he says, it is neither one thing nor the other. I thought of Rupert as the game unfolded. And then the thought struck me. I am sure he is an only one.

Hinckley won a decent enough game 3-1 in the end though Leigh RMI, an anonymous looking lot in a horrible yellow strip had two men sent off for second yellows from a fussy referee in the second half. It all seemed a long way away from Grundy Hill and its hotpot all those Monday nights ago.

Rupert had assured me that the A5 from J12 of the M6 motorway towards Hinckley was one of the finest roads in the kingdom. "Don't forget it is Watling Street, built by the Romans, straight as a die," he said. But the Romans did not have to contend with road works, contra-flows, speed cameras and the imposition of roundabouts that seem to try to tempt you on to the M6 toll motorway. It was a nightmare journey made worse by the car park attendant enquiring: 'Are you from Leigh?' as I proffered the one pound coin. My travelling companion chinked with laughter. Actually, I was born at the old Firs Maternity Home in Leigh but didn't realise it was that obvious. Maybe I should try and conceal that 'Made in Leigh' tattoo on my forehead.

We ignored Rupert on the way home and travelled via Burton-on-Trent towards Stoke and J15 of the M6. We both agreed that, despite the friendly enough welcome if all football grounds were like Hinckley's then the magic of ground-hopping would be lost forever. Do one and you've done 'em all. And you could never say that about Grundy Hill.

Out early morning with the dogs on Tuesday, I passed Rachael's father clocking up the miles, alone with his thoughts of Tony Caldwell, hotpot and stuffing Weymouth. He wouldn't have enjoyed the trip to Hinckley and, truth to tell, despite seeing Stuart Storer defying the ageing process and the excellent programme, neither did I.